the
Federalist
Papers

Masterworks in the Western Tradition

Nicholas Capaldi
General Editor

Stuart D. Warner
Associate Editor

Vol. 3

PETER LANG
New York • Washington, D.C./Baltimore • Boston • Bern
Frankfurt am Main • Berlin • Brussels • Vienna • Oxford

W. B. ALLEN
WITH KEVIN A. CLOONAN

the
Federalist
Papers

A COMMENTARY

"The Baton Rouge Lectures"

PETER LANG
New York • Washington, D.C./Baltimore • Boston • Bern
Frankfurt am Main • Berlin • Brussels • Vienna • Oxford

Library of Congress Cataloging-in-Publication Data

Allen, W. B. (William Barclay).
The federalist papers: a commentary: "the Baton Rouge lectures"/
W. B. Allen, with Kevin A. Cloonan.
p. cm. — (Masterworks in the Western tradition; vol. 3)
Includes bibliographical references.
1. Constitutional history—United States Sources.
I. Cloonan, Kevin A. II. Title. III. Series.
KF4515.A43   342.73'029—dc21   99-35641
ISBN 0-8204-3756-5
ISSN 1086-539X

Die Deutsche Bibliothek-CIP-Einheitsaufnahme

Allen, William B.:
The federalist papers: a commentary: "the Baton Rouge lectures"/
W. B. Allen, with Kevin A. Cloonan.
_New York; Washington, D.C./Baltimore; Boston; Bern;
Frankfurt am Main; Berlin; Brussels; Vienna; Oxford: Lang.
(Masterworks in the Western tradition; Vol. 3)
ISBN 0-8204-3756-5

Cover design by Nona Reuter

The paper in this book meets the guidelines for permanence and durability
of the Committee on Production Guidelines for Book Longevity
of the Council of Library Resources.

Printed in the United States of America

To Marc, for Dreams that Await

and

Marty, for Memories that Live

ACKNOWLEDGMENTS

I undertook this work with a single purpose in mind, to tell the story of *The Federalist Papers* as an accessible approach to the principles of the government of the United States. Whether I have succeeded will be gauged by minds well situated to judge, for they will have opened these pages with a cognate purpose in mind. What they will not see, however, is that I could not have reached them without the assistance of numerous persons whose support, judgments and efforts made its accomplishment a fact and not just a purpose.

My children then accepted my long absences from home in three successive summers while I worked through the lectures that enabled me to arrive at the final corpus. With funding by the U.S. Department of Education and the National Endowment for the Humanities, Professor John S. Baker of the Hebert Law Center at Louisiana State University conceived and organized the course in which these lectures became the core. Moreover, his intelligent reactions and extended conversations proved helpful in my working through the formulations. The students in those classes posed the questions that constitute the organizing foundations of this work, and assured that I would respond to the real concerns of persons who seriously undertook to teach *The Federalist Papers*.

In preparing the final manuscript I benefitted from the prodigious labors of Jeff Magnani, an undergraduate at Michigan State University's James Madison College. His research and editing skills are mature beyond his years. He is also an able interlocutor, whose insightful observations proved most beneficial. He worked under the guidance of my co-editor, Dr. Kevin Cloonan, whose contributions to this work are original and valuable. Historian Forrest McDonald generously shared his reactions to the manuscript and provided, as usual, a service beyond my merits. I am in his debt. I have also benefitted from the oversight and helpful suggestions of General Editor, Dr. Nicholas Capaldi.

The support of Michigan State University made completion of the project possible in the first place, and the support of editoral staff (especially Jacqueline Pavlovic) at Peter Lang, Inc. was essential to producing a work whose design was a challenge. Others, too, rendered important services. They remain unnamed but not unappreciated. Nor should they or those named be held responsible for the inevitable errors that I have introduced in this work.

I also wish to thank the publishers who have generously granted permission to reprint material from the following articles: "Federal Representation: The Design of the Thirty-fifth *Federalist Paper,*" *Publius: The Journal of Federalism* 6 (no. 3, Summer 1976): 61–71; "Justice and the General Good," in *Saving the Revolution,* ed.

Charles R. Kesler (New York: The Free Press, 1987); "The Constitutionalism of the *Federalist Papers," Political Science Reviewer* XIX (Spring 1990): 145–176; and the Epilogue is reprinted from "Radical Challenges to Liberal Democracy," in *The Political Order and Culture: Towards the Renewal of Civilization,* ed. Gary Quinlivan and William Boxx (Eerdmans, 1998).

CONTENTS

Part I: Overview

As the bicentennial of the U.S. Constitution approached in 1987, the state of Louisiana reawakened to a forty year old, neglected statute, requiring that high school students be taught the *Federalist Papers*. Seized with the obligations of patriotism, the legislature turned to the Paul M. Hebert Law School at Louisiana State University to prepare teachers to resume this important work. Responsive to their request, I prepared and mounted over three successive summers a *Federalist Papers* Institute for teachers, held on the campus at Baton Rouge. That is the origin of these lectures that have been redacted here into a sustained commentary, integrating the very helpful questions raised by the teachers.

It probably is apt to note at the outset why anyone should bother to read the *Federalist Papers*. It may seem to experts intuitive, but many people regarded as a doubtful proposition that anyone should read or teach the *Federalist Papers*. Some might argue that the *Federalist Papers* have two defects. The first is that they don't relate to American government today. They were propaganda for the era, and they don't say anything about how American government operates now. The second argument is that they aren't written in a manner that makes them very approachable. They're not accessible to ordinary intellects.

Each of those arguments betrays a certain ignorance. For in the first place, it's very unclear that one can expect to learn anything about the practices and principles of American government merely by asking what it is people do today. Note that when looking at the *Federalist Papers* or the documents of the Constitutional Convention, one deals with people who knew what they were doing. Perhaps they could not predict the future. Perhaps they could not know what we now know, but it is certain that they knew what they were doing. When we look at the operations of government today, it would be surprising if we could speak with equal confidence about the people who operate the institutions of the United States today. Thus, to start with someone who knows what he is doing gives us, at least, the hope of being able to understand what was intended and what was accomplished.

Moreover, it seems that there is no surer way to make clear to others the principles and practices of American government than by rehearsing the very arguments in the *Federalist Papers* and in the Constitutional Convention. Coming to understand people who had a clear aim and knew what they were doing gives us the ability to look reflectively upon what we do and what we think. We can, in fact, reconsider some of the assumptions we have held so easily about the practices of American political life. The role of democracy, for example, suddenly becomes more than just a notion of majority rule and a rather rich conception about the intricate pattern of relationships between public opinion and the offices of government within the United States.

The second objection, namely, that the *Federalist Papers* are overwritten, to put it kindly, reflects not so much the truth about the writing of the *Federalist Papers* but a certain impatience in our technological age that we probably ought to try to resist and ought to do something about. We must be willing to slow down long enough to take in a complete sentence that is composed of something more than a spare subject and predicate. Nor is the *Federalist Papers* overwritten beyond that. The essays consist in the main of declarative sentences; they speak the King's English with ordinary grace. Yes, certainly they are literate and in some respects accomplished but not overwhelming. Perhaps occasionally one has to resort to a dictionary to look up the meaning of an unfamiliar term or to appreciate a new turn given to an old term. But that is, of course, how we all read anyway. We read anything that way. Accordingly, I don't think the *Federalist Papers* is at any great disadvantage in that respect. And it has one singular advantage to boot. For nothing can so surely expand the range of our awareness and our grasp of the language and vocabulary as to be forced to discover new meanings in practices and principles that we care a lot about.

When I went to Baton Rouge, I made a calculated decision not to teach how to teach the *Federalist Papers* but just to teach the *Federalist Papers*. I thought that in the long run all would be happier with that approach and that indeed a greater sense of understanding of the *Federalist Papers* would take care of the teaching. So, I have always done it that way, and I have been pleased with the results. We found evidence that as people gain increasing command of them, they tend to lose some anxiety about sharing them with youngsters. So on the theory that that is the best way to make the papers accessible, I now teach the *Federalist Papers* in writing and leave to teachers to worry about *how* to teach the *Federalist Papers*.

Remember the circumstances in which the Constitution was framed in 1787—why the *Federalist Papers* came to be written in the first place. Also try to understand what it is that the authors thought that they had accomplished.

Correct that. I write "the authors of the *Federalist Papers*," because commonly we refer to them as Hamilton, Madison, and Jay. There were three writers who participated in the program; John Jay the least of all; Alexander Hamilton and James Madison splitting the balance of the essays between the two of them. But all the essays were signed "Publius" as they appeared in the press in New York City, first of all, and then around the country. No one knew who the authors were. After a short time people like Thomas Jefferson, receiving copies in Paris, began to guess the authorship. George Washington, in his correspondence with Hamilton, makes it clear that he understands who the authors are; but in general people were uncertain.

Not only did Publius write under a pen name in this era, but most of the Antifederalists, writing in opposition to Publius, wrote under pen names. Brutus, the Federal Farmer, and Cato, among many others, wrote frequently. It was, we might say, a fashion of the era. It was also important; for in writing under pen names one sought to distance oneself from one's own interest.

The whole point of assuming someone else's persona, someone else's name, was to invite the reader to think of the argument as standing on its own and not being supported by a particular party or class or interest. Now we can, of course, gauge the relative success of that attempt to invoke disinterestedness by what we know from the historical circumstances. We know there were two parties: one, the Federalist Party, was the source of the *Papers'* name, and the other was the Antifederalists. So it is clear that as one reads essays of the late 1780s, from one side or the other, one distinguishes the parties the essays spoke on behalf of.

Nevertheless I want us to try to give credit (and we'll see why in a few moments) to this attempt to be disinterested, to speak from a disinterested perspective. This is not something that is common in the late twentieth century. We ordinarily don't think that people can be disinterested; we tend to have acquired, whether through university or otherwise, the expectation that everything anyone does is somehow colored by his peculiar biases or interests.

And yet, when we are talking about a Constitution and establishing a way of life for a people that ordinarily is not going to change frequently, that is going to span several generations, there has to be a sense in which the impact of that work will extend beyond the immediate interests to carry it out. Whether drafters realize it or not, a Constitution will have an effect on people, wholly independent of its peculiar effect on the drafters. And that is perhaps the most important reason for people to attempt to think about these things from a disinterested perspective.

Nor need we be naive or simply idealistic about this Constitution. It was the work of a political party. And the party was not invented merely for the sake of defending the Constitution; it existed prior to the drafting of the Constitution. The party's efforts led to the drafting of the Constitution and its ultimate ratification. This party, which we call the Federalist Party for good reason, grew out of the weaknesses of the Articles of Confederation and the struggles of the United States, particularly between the Treaty of Paris (the peace treaty of 1783) and the calling of the Convention in 1787.

I would call this a party of nationalists, given this emphasis on continental policy—continent wide political structures. They were not provincial men. They were not interested in separating the differing parts of the United States but in pulling them together into a coherent, more perfect, nation. The language George Washington used in June of 1783 proclaims that we have a "national character" to establish. He made this claim in a circular address to the governors of the thirteen states as he was, in fact, resigning from the army. And in making that claim he seems to be saying it's not enough to have a United States with thirteen separate states, each understanding itself differently and independently. There ought to be a single character that defines Americans as a whole, as a people. And that work was left to be done. This nationalist party undertook that work—to define a national character—and that meant as well to define national institutions, national principles. The Articles of Confederation were taken to be insufficient for those purposes.

Accordingly, it was necessary to create a new Constitution that would place in proper relationships what we may refer to loosely, for the moment, as the parts and the whole, the states and the nation. What that relationship would be—that was the point of dispute. And at the origins of this dispute there are two categories of participants. On the one hand, we had the Federalists, or federal-minded men, as we see in the introduction to *The Essential Antifederalist*.[1] They were the ones who paid more attention to Congress, to the central government, and to the nation than to the states. Then we had, on the other hand, the unfederal men, who became ultimately the anti federal men, the Antifederalists. They are the ones who cared more about their state governments than about the Congress. They are the ones who wanted to defend the loose confederation, the loose association of states, the alliance of states instead of a powerful national government.

No. 84

No. 85

Initially then, let us rehearse the objections of the Antifederalists to a strong national government and indicate on behalf of the Federalists what they thought they were defending in defending the Constitution. The best way to do this is, of course, to begin at the end for as is well known, when we teach composition or theme writing, we always make clear that students are supposed to start out telling what they want to talk about, and then establishing their argument, talking about it, and coming to the end and telling us what they've told us. If we turn to the end of the *Federalist Papers* (assuming that this is a good composition) and look at what they tell us they've told us, that will serve as an effective outline for going through the essays from the beginning. And to do that I want to turn especially to that critical essay, the eighty-fourth essay. We have two final essays, of course, the eighty-fourth and the eighty-fifth.

Why do I call them two final essays rather than calling just essay eighty-five the final essay? Well, neither of these essays was included in the newspaper serialization of the *Federalist Papers*. The papers began to appear in October, 1787, less than a month after the Constitution had been signed in Philadelphia. They then continued to appear on a regular basis into the spring and summer of 1788. The first volume of collected essays was published as a book in May of 1788, and then finally later that summer all of them were pulled together in a volume. When that final volume was pulled together, these two essays—eighty-four and eighty-five—were added for publication in book form. They were not present when the essays were serialized.

Now at the beginning of the eighty-fourth essay pay attention to the language itself in the first paragraph:

In the course of the foregoing review of the Constitution, I have taken notice of, and endeavored to answer, most of the objections which have appeared against it. There however remain a few which either did not fall naturally under any particular head, or were forgotten in their proper places. These shall now be discussed; but as the subject has been drawn into great length, I shall so far consult brevity as to comprise all my observations on these miscellaneous points in a single paper.[2]

The eighty-fourth paper, then, is the final paper that summarizes all that remains to be said in defense of the Constitution. We are lucky that he wants to do so briefly, and indeed is able to do so briefly, because as it turns out all of the things that were supposedly left unsaid had, in fact, been accounted for in earlier discussions. That is what he goes on to say. One thing, however, was not accounted for, and that is the objection that the Constitution lacked a bill of rights.

We need to assume, right at the outset, that this is a critical question. What is the difference, what is the distinction, between a Constitution and a bill of rights? And why did this Constitution not have one? Why is it not until the eighty-fourth paper that Publius talks about the absence of a bill of rights? If this is a powerful objection—and I might say it is in fact one of the most important objections the Antifederalists laid against the Constitution—why then did they undertake to defend the Constitution without a bill of rights as opposed to simply adding it at the Convention?

George Mason of Virginia actually proposed a bill of rights on the floor of the Convention in August of 1787. This was almost a month before the Convention closed. George Mason and his proposition were both rejected by the Convention—this is another reason that George Mason did not sign the Constitution and went home to become an opponent of the document rather than a supporter.

Those who refused to write the bill of rights into the Constitution make one argument foremost. It is the argument that is in question in the eighty-fourth *Federalist Paper*: they are not proposing in this new Constitution to endanger the rights that are ordinarily protected in a bill of rights. They use the example of a monarch—they talk about Great Britain, they talk about the Magna Carta and all of the other great documents and statements of rights associated with the English tradition—and what characterizes those historically is nothing other than the fact that the king or monarch is held to make a promise to the people. The monarch has all power, and the people protect themselves only by extracting from the monarch a promise to use the power in a limited fashion. The same would be true if we were talking about despotic states as opposed to monarchical states, or aristocratic states. In all these states the ultimate power or sovereignty rests in the hands of one or a few; the notion of a bill of rights becomes sensible because it turns out that the many have no protection against this power, this sovereign authority, other than what they are able to extract in the form of promises or concessions.

The writers of the Constitution said that, in this government, there will not be power lodged in the hands of one or a few; sovereignty will rest with the people. We see this argument beginning already in the twenty-second *Federalist Papers* in which the author at that point, Hamilton (I will continue most of the time to say Publius), makes the assertion that the people are the true fountain of all authority. And in saying that Publius echoes the language that was first written or expressed by George Washington in 1775–76 when he was engaged in a dispute with the commander of the British forces over how he, Washington, was going to be addressed and whether the British commander was going to take heed of the fact that the American people were in fact in rebellion and were constituting themselves an independent people who deserved as much respect as the king's appointees deserved in the army of Great Britain. When Washington wrote that letter and referred back to his authority as commander of the American forces as resting on the true fountain of all authority, namely, the people, he struck a responsive chord throughout the people in the United States, and they spontaneously, in effect, ratified this constitutional doctrine. Ever after we find people using the same language to explain what they think the foundation of political power is in the United States.

No. 22

The answer, then, to the objection that there is no bill of rights, is to say, "How can the people protect themselves from themselves?" "If they have all the power, to whom are they supposed to make a promise not to use it badly?" Bills of rights, then, according to the argument of Publius and the drafters of the Constitution, are signs of defects in a Constitution. We need a bill of rights in proportion as our Constitution is not in fact fully and truly republican.

Pay attention to the use of the word *republican*. There are two important terms, the Constitution and the bill of rights, and we need to elaborate the distinction between them. The question is, what standard do we use to draw out that distinction? In the course of elaborating that distinction, we discover that the standard is republicanism. The question is, are these requirements of a republican system of government? They are not requirements of government in general—there are all kinds of governments one can have that have no constitutions and no bills of rights—but is republicanism essential to a constitution, properly understood, which expresses fully the sovereignty and the authority of the people? That is an argument, of course, that both Federalists and Antifederalists will agree about.

What we are really concerned about is the republicanism of the system, first and foremost. We later develop the meaning of that term, *republicanism*, but we want to note that this is where they began their dispute; this is what their argument is about at the outset. We might ask, for example, whether it's important—the distinction between a republic and a democracy—that is brought out in the tenth *Federalist Paper* and ever since has been much discussed in the United States—and where do the parties stand on that issue.

No. 10

At this stage, however, I want to emphasize that this distinction is not the foundation of their argument. It is a critical distinction after we've already accepted the necessity of republican government, or to speak generically, "free government." Antifederalists and Federalists agreed: they want to construct a free government. We will have frequent occasion to re-emphasize that, because much of the historical literature since this time has focused on the 1790s, when the Constitution and the government had been put in place, and the argument between the Federalists, as the party of Washington and Hamilton, and Republicans, under Jefferson and Madison, shows Republicans referring to the Federalists as "monarchists" or "monocrats." That is how they carried out their initial partisan dispute. And so people are likely to be confused. They may say, "Well, some of the founding fathers didn't believe in democracy," or, "Some of the founding fathers didn't believe in Republicanism." "Some of them thought the British system of government the most perfect in the world." That's been said of Alexander Hamilton—the very person who wrote the eighty-fourth *Federalist Paper* we now investigate.

Now, that is not an accurate representation of Hamilton's thought. Hamilton not only frequently connects himself to republicanism, just as the other founding fathers do, but Hamilton is the person who in 1777 invented the expression "representative democracy." Most people are not aware of that when they accuse him of being a monocrat. It was he who, describing a constitution for the state of New York in 1777, laid out the various principles that would make it a safe and sound government and referred to them as representative democracy. He was about twenty years old, by the way, at the time he invented that term that we have so often used since then. There are a number of such complicated historical details that interfere with the general narrative but that allow us to understand ultimately why these things are important. The point to bear in mind early on is that the general terms, having general meanings which all agree upon, form each side of the partisan dispute. We want to find out where they disagree; but we cannot do that without first paying due attention to the fact that they agreed.

No. 84

To return for a moment to the term *federalism*, we had Federalists and Antifederalists based on their differing attitudes toward the Confederation Congress, and the central government. In the eighty-fourth *Federalist Paper*, the argument concerns the lack of a bill of rights. Publius does not suggest at that point that the argument involves the fear that the Constitution is too national. It's very important to see that, at the end of the *Federalist Papers* Publius does not return to the objection that the system is too national, that it's too powerful. He thinks that he has completely responded to that argument in the earlier *Federalist Papers*. He no longer regards that as a difficulty to be assessed or addressed in dealing with the arguments of the Antifederalists.

A close look at his response to the bill of rights argument begins to show why that may be so. He acknowledged that the Convention's plan did not give a bill of rights but then mentions in the third and fourth paragraph of the eighty-fourth essay a series of clauses in the Constitution, each of which in fact might ordinarily be found in a bill of rights. Let's just look at a few of them. Article 1, section 3, clause 7: "Judgment in Cases of Impeachment shall not extend further than to removal from office . . . ." Or to take another, section 9 of the same article, clause 2: "The privilege of the Writ of Habeas Corpus shall not be suspended unless when in Cases of Rebellion or Invasion . . . ." Or further, clause 3: "No Bill of Attainder or ex post facto Law shall be passed." Those are all familiar; they sound very much like the provisions of bills of rights, which may therefore seem to suggest that his argument is disingenuous. If we can put some of these into a Constitution, why not put them all into a Constitution?

But let's go a bit further than that and read the concluding examples as well. Section 3 of Article 3: "Treason against the United States, shall consist only in levying War against them . . . ," a very narrow and concise definition of treason. And then clause 3: "The Congress shall have power to declare the Punishment of Treason, but no Attainder of Treason shall work Corruption of Blood, or Forfeiture. . . ." Thus the sins of the fathers are not descended to the sons. He then indicates three additional provisions: that which of course prohibits titles of nobility; the habeas corpus provision to which we have already referred; and the prohibition of ex post facto laws, which are essential to the defense of liberty. All provide security to liberty.

In what sense are these things essential here but not essential in a bill of rights? He goes on in the eighth paragraph of the eighty-fourth essay to begin the explanation: "It has been several times truly remarked, that bills of rights are in their origin, stipulations between kings and their subjects," the argument which I have already adduced.

Is that sufficient, or might we say that we want to protect ourselves against even a free government that evolves into something different from what it was initially? The argument in the tenth paragraph is meant to answer: "I go further, and affirm that bills of rights, in the sense and to the extent in which they are contended for, are not only unnecessary . . . but would even be dangerous."

Now why? Why would they be dangerous? Well one of the reasons he claimed they would be dangerous is because they would be, what he called in the last sentence of that tenth paragraph, handles for the doctrine of constructive powers. Now what would be this doctrine of constructive powers, particularly in light of the protections which are written into the Constitution? Let's take the protection against treason, and see how this might be applied. What the Constitution does is define treason very narrowly. We have applied a narrow definition of waging war against the United States or appealing to its enemies and have presumably made it next to impossible for anyone to invent any novel definition of treason. We have created, we might say, our own interpretation in the language of the Constitution itself, so there wouldn't be room for a court, perhaps, to give a broader interpretation. Most of the proscriptions written into the Constitution—no ex post facto law, no bill of attainder—are of that character. They rather narrow than broaden the scope of what government might be able to do in the area referred to.

It is of course true that one of the earliest constitutional decisions by the Supreme Court dealt with the ex post facto law. Notice that the Constitution did not make a distinction between civil and criminal cases, while the Court judged the case of *Calder v. Bull* on the basis of English practice, which was pretty much confined to criminal cases and did not apply in civil cases. So we see that there it was not quite so narrow as perhaps Publius took it to be in this eighty-fourth essay. But in general these are very narrow provisions that do not leave much room for construction. The point is not to open the door to construction, for construction would permit the substance of the Constitution to vary with the opinions of the office holders given the task of interpreting it. So the doctrine of constructive powers is a doctrine that would make the Constitution not a strict, stable, guiding source of authority for the government, but rather a vehicle for evolving standards and tastes, leaving quite up for grabs, really, what the Constitution could be taken to mean at any given point in time.

How then would we distinguish these provisions from other provisions? The other kinds of provisions we find in bills of rights tend to open questions of interpretation even more broadly. We can guarantee the freedom of the press, but it is very hard to do so in language that is narrow. Congress probably came as close as it is possible to come in the First

Amendment to the Constitution when it said, "Congress shall make no law . . ." The operative verb there, the predicate, deals with an activity not to be performed by Congress rather than with the substance to be aimed at through the activity. Hopefully if Congress makes no law, we will never have any question. But even that, as we know from history, proves not to be very narrow. And the same is true of most of the other elements, either in the Bill of Rights, as it was passed, or those that we see in most of the states.

Perhaps the best example of why bills of rights, in the eyes of Publius, lead to what he calls "the doctrine of constructive powers," has to do with the elements he finds the most offensive to the Constitution, but which we do not find in the Constitution. We find "checks and balances" essential, but we do not find checks and balances in the Constitution. "Separation of powers" we find essential, but we do not find separation of powers mentioned in the Constitution. And I could go on with, for example, that equal treatment for different classes is fundamental. We point out that these fundamental things are not there. Where do they come from then, if not from the Constitution?

I should point out at the outset that such provisions are not in the federal Constitution but are in virtually all the state Constitutions of the same era. So it is not as though we couldn't write them in, nor that there was some peculiar difficulty and folk wouldn't know how to express it. They were expressed in the constitutions of Pennsylvania, Massachusetts, Virginia, and elsewhere. We could start out with general statements such as that the three powers of government are always to be in separate hands. That affirms the necessity of separation of powers for liberty. But this Constitution didn't do that.

Now, Publius would say that he did not do it because that only leads to a dispute about what it is. It sets up the doctrine of constructive powers. And what he was trying to do was so to divide the constitutional agencies that would settle those disputes and settle them in such a way as not to leave it open to question that these principles were to be integral to the operation of American political institutions. And we will see when we read, for example, *Federalist* 47 to 51, how that was accomplished. That is, these things are to be integral without being mentioned. At this point they simply go hand in hand with lack of a bill of rights. Certain things do not have to be mentioned, because they invite people to exercise powers which it is not legitimate for them to exercise.

Nos.
47–51

We have received a Constitution that, oddly, tries to accomplish certain kinds of results which cannot be expressed in words. When we say a bill of rights is dangerous, what we mean is that we want to accomplish the results aimed at by a bill of rights, but we can't always express those results in words. We find in here a political dynamic, the end of which is to produce these results. And in fact the system works only if it does produce these results. But we cannot write them into the document and still expect to accomplish those results.

Next we have a long discussion on liberty of the press in the eleventh paragraph. Again, an example may demonstrate that the whole difficulty of specific freedoms comes with entrusting either representatives or the government itself to produce some of these protections as opposed to relying upon the people themselves to produce them. We will come back to that very critical argument later.

For now, let us jump ahead to the argument of the thirteenth paragraph:

> Another objection, which has been made, and which from the frequency of **No. 84**
> its repetition it is to be presumed is relied on, is of this nature:—It is improper
> (say the objectors) to confer such large powers, as are proposed, upon the
> national government; because the seat of that government must of necessity be
> too remote from many of the states to admit of a proper knowledge on the part
> of the constituent, of the conduct of the representative body.

This invokes the whole question of the relationship between citizens and the government, citizens and representatives. It almost concedes great power. It now says, "all right, you've got great power, but how do we know you're going to use it safely?"

Well, one device for guaranteeing its safety is to say that citizens can control their representatives. But how do they control their representatives if they don't even know who they are? How do they control them if they cannot communicate with them? How do they control them if they are at such great distance from them that the citizens will have no impact on them?

The response to that question, it seems to me, goes a long way to address contemporary as well as older questions.

This argument, if it proves any thing, proves that there ought to be no general government whatever. For the powers which it seems to be agreed on all hands, ought to be vested in the union, cannot be safely intrusted to a body which is not under every requisite control. But there are satisfactory reasons to shew that the objection is in reality not well founded. There is in most of the arguments which relate to distance a palpable illusion of the imagination. . . . They must therefore depend on the information of intelligent men, in whom they confide—and how must these men obtain their information? Evidently from the complection of public measures, from the public prints, from correspondences with their representatives, and with other persons who reside at the place of their deliberation.

In the rest of this essay Publius establishes this process. We call it the process of correcting and depending upon active, energetic, and intelligent representatives. But remember, the key here is the dynamic, the communication, the exchange between citizens and representatives. Ultimately, then, he means that it is the judgment of the citizen that is going to be relied upon. He makes this clear in the fourteenth paragraph when he says there, in the second sentence: "The executive and legislative bodies of each state will be so many centinels over the persons employed in every department of the national administration; . . . they can never be at a loss to know the behaviour of those who represent their constituents in the national councils. . . . Their disposition to apprise the community of whatever may prejudice its interests from another quarter, may be relied upon, if it were only from the rivalship of power."

So, we have a complicated system, office holders at all the levels and all of them taking an interest in what the others are doing, as they speak back and forth to one another. Then he says this of the citizens themselves: "It ought also to be remembered that the citizens who inhabit the country at or near the seat of government, will in all questions that affect the general liberty and prosperity, have the same interest with those who are at a distance; and that they will stand ready to sound the alarm when necessary. . . ."

Now, are we comfortable with that? Is it good enough to know that the people of Washington, D.C. are going to yell whenever anything goes wrong? Will the people of Baton Rouge feel that they have been protected? Does that satisfy us—the sort of representative liberty argument that is constructed here? Does that suggest that the dynamic reaches all the interests in the entire country? That's the problem, and he knows that's the problem. Finally, therefore, what he calls upon is the intelligence of his fellow citizens, these noble citizens who will have to judge not only their representatives but trust the ongoing conduct and structure of the government itself.

In making this argument we are reminded of certain things that go back to the beginning of the *Federalist Papers*. Relying upon the intelligence, the virtue, the nobility of its citizens, would properly seem entirely inconsistent unless we had some reason to expect citizens to be especially virtuous, intelligent, and watchful. But when people are comfortable, they are least likely to explore threats to liberty. So we have a paradox. We're supposed to produce stable and lasting government on a constitutional basis; it is feared that that we don't know how to keep that much power under control unless we are able to maintain some kind of vigilance on the part of the citizens. And so it remains to be told where that vigilance will come from.

No. 1 Now, interestingly, in the first *Federalist Paper*, the citizens themselves are called upon to make a decision. Naturally the decision they are asked to make is to approve the Constitution. And in the first essay, for the moment, because this is what is critical, he's already proposed that they approve it and says this about it:

This idea will add the inducements of philanthropy to those of patriotism to heighten the solicitude, which all considerate and good men must feel for the event. Happy will it be if our choice should be directed by a judicious estimate of our true interests, unperplexed and unbiased by considerations not connected with the public good.

Thus, not only statesmen but just plain folk will be disinterested, unbiased, and unperplexed.

So this is the thing "more ardently to be wished than seriously to be expected." Now remember this is the middle of a crisis: a Constitution has been proposed to the country, and there is little confidence in the existing constitution, called the Articles of Confederation. There recently had occurred in Massachusetts an armed rebellion within this political system. There was continuing economic difficulty. Reasonable people doubted, in fact, how far this country could go on the existing organizational basis. It was during a grave constitutional crisis, when folk should be most attentive and most concerned, that Publius avers it is more to be wished than expected that people will act judiciously, unperplexed, without biases, in deciding this question. This was a sober reflection indeed. He went on: "The plan offered to our deliberations, affects too many particular interests, innovates upon too many local institutions, not to involve in this discussion a variety of objects foreign to its merits, and of views, passions and prejudices little favourable to the discovery of truth."

At this critical moment when, folk must see most clearly, they are least likely to see clearly. That's how the *Federalist Papers* open. In other words, they've taken on the project of persuading the people (who are least subject to persuasion) in a disinterested fashion, to act for a projected future well beyond even their own immediate interest, to act on behalf of stable, sound, and free government, even though they can't be expected to do that. Nonetheless, in the eighty-fourth paper and even further in the Nos. eighty-fifth, Publius ends and thinks that he's accomplished through the 84, 85 presentation of the case precisely what is so hard to do: to get the people calmly to reason about their situation and to come to a decision as to how they shall proceed.

Publius thought he succeeded in that; the Antifederalists did not agree. We mustn't forget along the way that this is a debate. It's very hard in a monologue to convey the flavor of a debate without running awkwardly first to one side and then the other side. But it was a debate. There was not uniform opinion about what the Federalists needed to do. It's the Federalists we want to understand. We will try to understand them by forcing them to answer anew the charges that were made against them and their favorite system.

This is what we will look for next, the four powerful Antifederal objections: (1) the objection to strong central government; (2) the structure of the Constitution fosters what they call minority faction, aristocracy; (3) Congress has control over commerce, which the Antifederalists thought to be a threat to free enterprise; (4) representation is too small under the Constitution, and it was unrepresentative of the diverse interests of the society. As Publius responds to those charges, he should also then be responding to us, who wish to know how they accomplished this miracle of persuading people to do what they are least likely to do in a crisis, and then how they persuade us today that we can expect still to do it when we are comfortable.

The first *Federalist Paper* expresses some dubiety concerning the question of whether the people were in a position, whether they were able to be steady enough, to perform the task that had to be performed. Placing that doubt in the context of the Antifederalists' objections to the Constitution only radicalizes the question that we face. Before going on with the Federalists' response, let us review quickly what the results of the Antifederalists' objections are.

Turning to the *Essential Antifederalist*, the last paragraph of the introduction, I have summarized there the questions as they have come down to us. The Antifederalist perspective and recommendations are still alive in the American political tradition.

When we hear the argument that the Founding Fathers feared power, and thus separated government into three branches and tried to insure that no one branch would dominate, we are in fact hearing what the Antifederalists feared and desired. Their perspective did *not* prevail in 1787; nevertheless, the contemporary argument that the Founding Fathers created a "deadlocked" system is in fact assuming that the Founding Fathers were Antifederalists. And when we hear the argument that the Founding Fathers were wealthy and ambitious men who designed an undemocratic government in secret for their own benefit, we are in fact hearing a vulgarization of the Antifederalist critique of the leading proponents of change. Moreover, when we hear the claim that our representatives are drawn from a minority of the population; that they operate in a manner which is independent of the people; and that the Congress does not represent the broad cross-section of interest which it is supposed to represent, we are in fact repeating the Antifederalist critique of the scheme of representation found in the Constitution. When we hear the argument that the federal government is out of control, that it interferes too much with the life of American citizens, and that State and local officials understand the needs of the people far better than do representatives in Washington, we are in fact echoing the warnings of the Antifederalists. Finally, when Americans instinctively associate the Constitution and the meaning of democracy with the Bill of Rights, we are in fact honoring the essential contribution of the Antifederalists.[3]

Now, reminding ourselves that the Antifederalists set the tone for much, even, of our contemporary rhetoric about the Constitution, we can listen to

Publius's response, recognizing that he speaks as much to us as to his opponents in 1787 and 1788.

To emphasize how much we owe to the Antifederalists in terms of the Bill of Rights, let us pause on that last point. People often forget that when the Bill of Rights was added to the Constitution in 1791—it was proposed in 1789 and ratified from 1789 to 1790—what happened was that a promise to the Antifederalists was delivered. The Federalists finally got the Antifederalists to agree to vote for the Constitution by saying, "If you vote for it, we'll give you a Bill of Rights." It started that way in the Massachusetts Ratifying Convention, and then went through New York, Virginia and elsewhere. So James Madison introduced the Bill of Rights when he got to Congress in 1789 to fulfill that pledge. The Bill of Rights is part of the Constitution. And we owe them therefore to the Antifederalists.

When we pause today and ask, what do we know of the Constitution of the United States, we see that people often know little except the Bill of Rights. We see then how extraordinary is the Antifederalists' contribution. And it is true that some people do confuse the Bill of Rights with the whole Constitution. The ACLU did that some years ago when they were conducting a fund-raising campaign, and they wanted people to send in money, centered around the bicentennial of the Constitution. They sent nation-wide a fund-raising letter inviting folk to send money so that they could collect signatures and deliver them to the Justice Department, the White House, and the Supreme Court in defense of the Bill of Rights on the bicentennial of the Constitution. But the bicentennial of the Bill of Rights was still three years away! They weren't quite certain when the Constitution was adopted, but they were very sure that they wanted to defend the Bill of Rights. That illustrates the common perception of these events in our time. What we require to do is to recover somewhat that deeper, that richer tradition which is informed by the actual Constitution, as opposed to the Bill of Rights. But we do so knowing the Antifederalists carry for us an immense significance.

The first *Federalist Paper,* anticipating some of the concerns that we see developed through the eighty-fourth *Federalist Paper,* expresses some doubt about the people's ability to create or to judge well in the crisis they **No. 84** were confronted with. The doubt was expressed in the eighty-fourth *Federalist Paper*. Consider the footnote in the twelfth paragraph following this statement by Publius about liberty of the press, ". . . from this, I infer, that its security, whatever fine declarations may be inserted in any constitution respecting it, must altogether depend on public opinion, and on the general spirit of the people and of the government." The footnote to this reads: "It would be quite as significant to declare that government ought to be free, that taxes ought not to be excessive, &c., as that the liberty of the press ought not to be restrained." Thus, he doesn't have much confidence in these vague declarations of the way things ought to be in the world.

I take that passage to mean that there's no provision that can be written respecting free government that can make government free. Let me repeat that, and emphasize it. *There is no provision that can be written down concerning free government that can actually make government free.* Government, according to Publius, seems to be free only to the extent that it is a government whose citizens keep it free, whose citizens maintain it as free. And that, then, would explain why he refers in the footnote to "public opinion." That would explain the reliance on public opinion to defend liberty of the press. That means that what Publius is doing in terms of his—let me call it his constitutionalism—is providing an explanation about the organization of the polity.

In some respects it is a free people that make this a free government, and not the reverse. The condition of free government is that one have a free people. I am taking time to emphasize this, because we, I believe, are used to speaking of free governments making free peoples. I think that's the way we often think it works. And we see some of that reflected in China today, by the way, in conversations about what's happening over there. But Publius is saying the reverse, or seems to be saying the reverse, namely, free people make free governments. And so, the trick of these *Federalist Papers,* as a definitive interpretation of the Constitution, is to show how this is done. But where do we get the free people that are going to make the free government, if it doesn't take free government to make a free people? The discussions at the end of the *Federalist Papers* and at the beginning of the *Federalist Papers* establish this argument.

No. 85

But beyond the question of the Bill of Rights that we talked about in the eighty-fourth paper, we find a revealing set of questions in the eighty-fifth paper in which Publius in classical expository form returns to his thesis. He employs a final essay to survey his handiwork, and then talks about how that work was laid out in eighty-three previous papers. There were two things that he said had not been done, which I mentioned previously. One is the analogy of the proposed government to the state constitutions, because he had said at the outset that that's what he wanted to do. And, secondly, he noted, the additional security which the Constitution's adoption will afford to republican government, to liberty and to property—those three objectives. These topics are not discussed under a common heading in his outline, but they came up in the course of discussion, and so in the eighty-fifth essay Publius argues, "we've answered it."

Nevertheless, if we look at the third paragraph of the eighty-fifth essay, where he surveyed the additional securities to provide for republicanism, we will see that he concludes in the following words: "[They] consist chiefly in the restraints which the preservation of the union will impose on local factions and insurrections, and on the ambition of powerful individuals in single states who might . . . become the despots of the people; . . ." Now, this repeats an earlier statement, but there's quite a difference here. There are two promises, we might say, that he has stated in an uncharacteristically bold manner. First, he promises the Constitution will suppress local factions in the states. It's still courageous in 1787, even at the end of the *Federalist Papers*, to claim to do this, to declare outright that the new government will have power to control petty despots in the states. And then, secondly, he says this Constitution will prevent despotism.

That's not easy to do, and therefore one rightly asks, how? How is it accomplished, or how does the earlier discussion make clear that it is accomplished? There are several questions coming out of this that I think bear enormous importance. If the chief goal is to prevent despotism, how do we do it? How is it that powerful individuals in single states could acquire sufficient credit and influence that they might become despots of the people in the first place? Is it true in the 1780s that the state governments, which had been designed in the aftermath of the Declaration of Independence and under the influence of the exhilaration of liberty, we might say, were actual threats of despotism in the United States? Is this Federalist motivation for changing the Constitution justified? These questions, I think, show how ambitious the Federalists were.

The allegations against the States are not minor. The historian Merrill Jensen argued in defense of the State Constitutions that existed between 1776 and 1787. In his works we find an argument along roughly the following lines: The American revolution came and the ordinary citizens were inspired by the love of democracy. They shaped new State Constitutions to express their love of democracy. Participation exploded throughout all the States and the ordinary people were represented and involved in their State legislatures. We could see the extent of their involvement through such things as the various TENDER laws that they passed which expressed, of course, the interest of the debtor and the poor. They were in the driver's seat. And these democratic State governments, were working. That is to say, ordinary people had come into government and they were acquiring experience, governing themselves democratically. And while there might have been some exuberance here and there, there were not the excesses that the aristocrats complained about and who saw at Shays's Rebellion in Massachusetts an excuse to check these democratic forces.[4]

Thomas Jefferson even wrote a letter, in 1787, in which he feared that Shays's Rebellion will be used as an excuse to stifle democracy in the United States[5]. So this Jensen thesis has it that this is a new force in the world, a democratic force, and it rides on the strength of these state political institutions. These are the institutions that Publius said "threaten despotism" in the United States.

So the argument is the difference in night and day! Either these state governments were healthy, solid, democratic governments to be depended on in the future, or they were anarchical, threatening despotism, pitting class against class, and creating general instability. Here we talk about Publius; so we will make the case for "general instability." But we must notice along the way, that once Publius makes this claim, there's no turning back. If these states threaten despotism, then there's nothing to do, of course, but to change the form of government, to defend the people against that despotism. In that sense, I think we can place the Federalists in a somewhat different context than we're used to.

They're claiming that the original democratic Constitutions were fast descending into something akin to the Reign of Terror in France that eventuated in 1793 following the French Revolution. And that of course was followed by Bonapartism, the very despotism that we are now talking about. The Federalists worked before they had the example of France—and all the other revolutions in modern history since France's have ended the way the French Revolution ended, in despotism. For all the revolutions that we know, the modern revolutions, seem to have had a singular path and have led to immense bloodshed and persistent tyranny. Yet, the Federalists seem to claim that what they did puts the United States outside of that course of history. The Federalists proposed the Constitution to prevent that bloodshed and tyranny. That is their ambition. We see then why I call it a "very large ambition"—they want to set America outside of the course of history.

When we look at the essays on this broadest of foundations, we begin to see what measures to use to determine their accomplishments. Not only have the general terms been fully discussed, according to the thesis as it is set forth again in the eighty-fifth essay, but next Publius called upon the ordinary citizen to judge for himself whether it weren't done well. He says it is a "moral duty" which is imposed by all the obligations that form the bands of society. The essays were written precisely because the people must make a decision freighted with grave moral consequences. And remember that paragraph from the first essay, in which he claims that this is a difficult decision for them to make. And then read the fifth paragraph of the eighty-fifth essay in light of that. There he says, after talking about how the decision might be made, "No partial motive, no particular interest, no pride of opinion, no temporary passion or prejudice, will justify to himself, [that is to the citizen,] to his country, or to his posterity, an improper election of the part he is to act. Let him beware of an obstinate adherence to party. Let him reflect that the object upon which he is to decide is not a particular interest of the community, but the very existence of the nation." That's very different from the fear in the first essay: that people couldn't make this tough decision because they were too interested, they were too perplexed, they were not close enough to the decision to be

No. 85

No. 1

made. So somehow, between number one and number eighty-five, our citizens have been changed, or instructed, by the *Federalist Papers*.

I don't want to overdo the argument that this is an expression of great ambition, but we should take seriously the immensity of the distance between the first essay's claims and the final essay's claims. We should at least begin with an openness to the proposition that what Publius purports to accomplish, he has in fact accomplished. All we know on the surface is that these are the same people who wrote our Constitution or participated in writing it; they presented it to their countrymen; their countrymen had never seen it before, were not certain at first that they liked it; there was a debate about it; and these were the kinds of things they said in the debate. Then their countrymen voted, and they accepted the Constitution. That's all we know on the surface. So then the question becomes, "Why did they accept it?" And it becomes possible that they accepted it because of something that was done here, that an accomplishment which they claimed to have made, in fact had some effect on their fellows.

Resuming our discussion of the first essay, let's look at the fifth paragraph. There, we notice an interesting thing that is being done by Publius. Namely, he forswears any intention whatever to resolve the diverse perspectives about the Constitution into self-interested motives. He recognizes that people have interests, but he says, he will not just dismiss their arguments on the basis of their interests. In the third paragraph, he had argued that there may exist such a diversity of motives, including the ambition for self-aggrandizement, which we know of course to be perhaps the most serious. At length, however, he argued, "I don't want to dwell upon observations of this nature," and that for the sufficient reason that someone, somewhere, might judge dispassionately, even in situations that tempt human nature itself. So the possibility that a human being can, let us say, rise above human nature, is enough to justify Publius's reaching for that same disinterestedness, reaching for the highest things, or at least appealing to the highest in his fellow citizens. That is the reason the arguments of the opponents are treated seriously.

No. 1

A very interesting exercise to perform is to line up all the Antifederalist essays one can find (and there's a very nice seven-volume edition published by the University of Chicago Press called *The Complete Anti-Federalist*), and look at their dates. The chronology is what's critical. Then take out the *Federalist Papers*, one through eighty-five, by dates, and line them up alongside their critics. Notice the interesting yin and yang. They are talking to one another. We get these books, though originally the articles were in newspapers, and we read them off as if they just stood there by themselves, and we don't always see the conversation that's going on. What happened in fact is that an essay appeared in a newspaper here by an Antifederalist, and the response would appear over here from a Federalist. The Antifederalist would respond to the Federalist, and then the Federalist would respond in turn. And that's the way it goes—the perfect conversation. The best example of that conversation is in *Federalist Papers* number seventy-eight on judicial review, which is responding to the essays by Brutus (included in the *Essential Antifederalist*). The chronology is just about perfect in that regard. So we should remind ourselves, then, that when he says, "I will not resolve their arguments into interested motives," that what he is saying is, "I will take the arguments seriously, in their own terms, not in terms of the identity of the person making the argument." So he gives credit to the Antifederalists for having the greatest patriotism and disinterestedness.

Nor does Publius stop there in that first paper because he says that one has to assist human nature. One must bring aids to human nature. Look! Go back to the initial paragraph to see what it is we want to do. It is of considerable significance. Publius says, "It has been frequently remarked, that it seems to have been reserved to the people of this country, by their conduct and example, to decide the important question, whether societies of men are really capable or not, of establishing good government from reflection and choice, or whether they are forever destined to depend for their political constitutions, on accident and force." The people of this country are going to decide this question, not for themselves, but for humankind. That's what he says in that passage. It has been reserved to the people of this country to decide the important question whether societies of men, that means anyone, anywhere, whether they are capable of . . . what? in the end, of self-government. For to establish "good government from reflection and choice," contrasted with depending on "accident and force," means nothing less than bringing one's own responsibility for the life one lives to the fore, to make that the critical, the distinguishing factor in the political constitution. Now this is an interesting set of alternatives which we could explore at great length: reflection and choice versus accident and force.

Immediately though, some things are very clear. For example, war, that's force and accident, at a minimum, right? So what are we talking about? We're talking about people who sit down, with reason, rationally, to determine how they shall organize their political existence, and choose deliberately, not arbitrarily, "good government." It's not any choice that leads to success in this test reserved for the people of this country, it's the choice of good government by reflection and choice.

That seems to say something like the following: Human nature is aided by those things that we summarize in the expression, "reflection and choice." There may be temptations that will lead us in one direction; there may be misunderstandings that will lead us in another direction, and these are the things that have always characterized human society. Why do we say "always"? Because, this important question has been reserved to this people in this time to decide. It has never been decided before. All of human history, according to this claim, has been lived without this particular claim being justified, without knowledge of the possibility for human beings to order their societies in accord with rational principles. It is an extraordinary claim! Of thousands and thousands of years of human history, not one provides the suggestion that what they attempt to do at this moment is possible.

And let's be fair; it's possible that it can't be done. If we were in 1787 for the moment, all we would know is that the question has been posed; it hasn't been answered. At this stage, two hundred years hindsight is no help to us. We don't know that it can work, except something in the argument shows it to us. Remember, in the fourth paragraph of the first essay, Publius described the difficulty of expecting people to make these kinds of decisions. Then in the fifth paragraph of the eighty-fifth essay, he said that somehow, between essays one and eighty-five, he has provided for this magical transformation. They can do it; he can appeal to their nobility, their disinterestedness. And then in the first paragraph of the first essay we see what it was he has brought them to do, as he understands it: to choose good government based on reflection and choice. He goes on, speaking now of the opponents, "Candour will oblige us to admit, that even such men may be actuated by upright intentions; and it cannot be doubted that much of the opposition which has made its appearance, or may hereafter make its appearance, will spring from sources, blameless at least, if not respectable, the honest errors of minds led astray by preconceived jealousies and fears. So numerous indeed and so powerful are the causes which serve to give a false bias to the judgment, that we upon many occasions, see wise and good men on the wrong as well as on the right side of questions, of the first magnitude to society."

No. 85

Now I submit that there is no alternative but to explicate this passage in the first essay in light of the passage at the end of the *Federalist Papers*. To turn to citizens in the end and to request that they judge dispassionately, with the fate of posterity in mind, and without regard to their particular ambition, would beggar the imagination, if we didn't have other reasons to believe it. So perhaps it was anticipated at the outset that one of the accomplishments would be to prepare the reader to do what he has now called upon the reader to do. He must have removed the power of prejudice and bias, to lead to this decision. What in this work has eliminated bias, or at least the power of bias?

There is an essay that tells us how to eliminate the power of bias, by the way. It's number thirty-one. In the thirty-first essay, Publius actually discusses the effects of bias on the judgment, as obstacles to judgment and what must be done to remove them. And the context in which that work is undertaken is in a demonstration of exactly what this thing is that's called "self-evident truth." Now the importance of that, I hope, is readily apparent. Self-evident truths are important because of the principles that

No. 31

inform the Declaration of Independence. A self-evident truth must be something that can be rationally, intellectually established in order for men to take the Declaration seriously. The Declaration is still more fundamental than the Constitution. And there, where it is said that it is a "self-evident truth that all men are created equal," is the principle in light of which we are able to affirm, in the first paragraph of the first essay, that it has been reserved for the people of this country at this moment to decide the important question whether the societies of men are capable or not of self-government. So the thirty-first essay sets out this intellectual conception of self-evident principle, self-evident truth, in the process defending the Declaration of Independence as the moral foundation of the United States and also providing the reasons whereby we can understand how to combat prejudice and bias in making fundamental political decisions.

The self-evident truth of the Declaration, that all men are created equal, that they are endowed by their Creator with certain inalienable rights, that among these rights are life, liberty and the pursuit of happiness—it's like an axiom of geometry. The idea does not invoke the phenomenon of evident to every self. That's not what it means. It means that the proposition which leads us to conclude that the sum of the angles of a triangle will be 180 degrees cannot be demonstrated. We are able to demonstrate what the sum of the angles will be, because of the axiom, because of the truth underlying the axiom, and so too then, with the moral axiom that all men are created equal. Despite this clarity, we know that not every human being, not every self, sees the truth. Just as not every human being understands that the angles of a triangle sum to 180 degrees, or even what the axioms are that underlie that.

In addition to biases that affect understanding, or obstruct the view of the truth, there are additionally defects in the mind. That's what Publius called them. Or accidents that also occur and affect people. But very powerful prejudices, biases, interests are the most significant, and because of that he argues that, if there are indeed moral axioms as there are geometric axioms, then nothing is more important than that human beings should gain access to these moral axioms. Thus they will be able to construct their lives on the basis of true notions of human happiness. That's what he is talking about in that first essay then: choosing good government by reflection and choice. And this is the process: we must first develop in the minds of human beings the moral axiom that all men are created equal, and from there, lead them to accept the responsibility of self-government, to choose good government based on reflection and choice; and having done that, extending the axiom through such steps as are required, it becomes possible to produce the hope for the kind of decision that is discussed in the eighty-fifth *Federalist Paper*. Or let me state it more modestly: it at least becomes possible to hope that we have removed

No. 85

whatever obstructs the view of truth in human beings who go through that process.

How is it that these principles structure what has become a conversation between Publius and his fellow citizens? That's what's going on in all of this; this is not just a bit of soliloquizing à la Hamlet. I rather suspect Publius could cite the poet in this respect, had the poet lived by then who wrote, "I am not Hamlet, nor was meant to be, am an attendant Lord, one that will do to start a progress, swell a scene or two."[6] I think Publius could have been no less modest than the poet in that respect. And so we don't have to see this as just an academic exercise, an elegant soliloquy. I think we ought rather to see it as the conversation that he means it to be.

How then do his fellow citizens come to the conversation? They come, affected by powerful prejudices, biases, and interests. He told us that in the first essay. That's how they start. It's human nature. That's how we expect people to start. And so whatever it is that has been done in the course of these essays, it has been done taking that into account. Now, he does not separate them into their different interest groups. That's not how he handles it. He forswears such an approach. He says I am just not going to think about the question of what lies behind their opposition or their support of the Constitution, because people can end up on the right side of the question for the wrong reason, and on the wrong side of the question for the right reasons.

The ways for human imperfection to manifest itself are virtually infinite, and so Publius gives us a shortcut. He says, "Let's not look for all the imperfections, let's just look at the arguments themselves. Let's forget where they came from. Let's just ask the argument's questions and see how far they are right or wrong." Now there is much more going on here than the rhetorical device that Publius is too nice to stigmatize his opponents. We all understand the value of saying to the world, "I'm above mud slinging." In the political world, it is often important to be able to be above mud slinging. But there's more than just rhetoric going on here.

As the balance of the passage in the first essay makes clear, we are no less concerned to appreciate why people end up on the right side or the wrong side of questions of the first magnitude. We want to know why they got there because we want to know how to get consistently to the right side. And also he says it would furnish a lesson of moderation if we go through this process with people who are sure they know the truth. Publius draws the conclusion, which reveals to us clearly the rule of conduct by which he acts. It is not enough to want to defend liberty in order to defeat despotism; that is not sufficient. We saw that in Tiananmen Square, the "goddess of Liberty." Even the desire for liberty, by the way, can spawn despotisms, as we have often learned in the modern world. So he ends up warning his fellow citizens, not only against the opposition, but also against himself.

No. 1

That's strange conduct indeed: he warns them against himself. He says, "Yes, I confess I am not a source unfriendly to the new Constitution." But that's not very much of a confession, and these are the words he used: "I shall not however multiply professions on this head. My motives must remain in the depository of my own breast: My arguments will be open to all, and may be judged of by all." So this affectation of inscrutability serves admirably to disarm suspicion, at the same time as it invites the reader to aim at no less an achievement. I think that's the relationship in which this first essay stands to the eighty-fifth essay: every man has to try to accomplish the same degree of detachment. We offer up our argument, our judgment, to allow others to weigh it. We keep our motives to ourselves, and of course, by nature, we must keep our motives to ourselves, as it turns out.

It's a truism to say, "My motives must remain in the depository of my own breast," as Publius declares. It's a truism! Even if he had told me what his motives were, I still wouldn't know. I'd have no means to verify them. They'd still be within his own breast. I'm sure that Publius knew that. And so, I believe that what he is doing is in a very gentle way, to effect a formal political education, suggesting that it is indeed possible for us to arrive at the truth about politics, independently of the things that we cannot know. The things that we cannot know are the secrets of human life, of respective motivations and desires. We do not need to know all the darker recesses of the human soul in order to judge the fairest prospects of the human soul.

Now that is almost a gnostic claim. It's certainly an extraordinary claim. In the post-Freudian world, that's hard to sell because we think one doesn't know anything unless one knows the unconscious, right? The darker insides—we think that determines everything, and yet, Publius makes exactly the opposite claim. We can make these great earth shaking political decisions, without knowing that so-called unconscious. We don't have to get inside them. We can take the arguments. He starts off with the proposition that there is no unconscious, certainly not in the late eighteenth century. It wasn't invented until much later, so he's safe on that ground. There is no unconscious. So whatever private motives we may have, we keep them to ourselves. What we do is to hold men to the standard of stating publicly an argument for what they want to do. And we will just judge the argument, we won't judge the man.

Well, the Constitution is an argument. We see this laid out very clearly in the fortieth *Federalist Paper*, where Publius says, the Constitution is only a series of informal propositions. Propositions are arguments in logic. So it's only a series of informal propositions which have no standing whatever until authorized by the people. So when they come out of the convention, they are nothing—they are worthless. When they are ratified it becomes a way of life. Therefore that leaves us only to find out in the course of the survey of these many papers, what kind of way of life it was

No. 40

that was produced. To answer that question, what we'll do next is to inquire exactly what the way of life is that the *Federalist Papers* sought to elaborate.

NOTES

1. W. B. Allen and Gordon Lloyd, eds., *The Essential Antifederalist* (New York: University Press of America, 1985).

2. Alexander Hamilton, James Madison, and John Jay, *The Federalist,* ed. Jacob E. Cooke (Middletown, CT: Wesleyan University Press, 1961; Wesleyan Paperback, 1982), 575. Hereafter referenced by paper and paragraph number.

3. Allen and Lloyd, *Essential Antifederalist,* xiv.

4. Merrill Jensen, *The New Nation* (New York: Vintage, 1950). A precursor is Charles Beard, *An Economic Interpretation of the Constitution of the United States* (New York: The Free Press, 1935). Murray Dry notes that these are critiques of John Fiske's *The Critical Period of American History, 1783–1789* (Boston: Houghton Mifflin, 1888), in "Anti-Federalism in *The Federalist*: A Founding Dialogue of the Constitution, Republican Government, and Federalism," in Charles R. Kesler, ed., *Saving the Revolution: The Federalist Papers and The American Founding* (New York: The Free Press, 1987), 283 n. 6. Gary Nash, following Beard and Jensen in economic analysis, also sees the post-Revolutionary period as reactionary and argues that the "delegates at Philadelphia had been unwilling to advertise their abandonment of revolutionary principles." *Race and Revolution* (Madison, WI: Madison House, 1990), 78 and see 133f. To this argument that the lack of advertisement, the shame, of the founders' was later turned to good advantage, Thomas G. West responds in his *Vindicating the Founders: Race, Sex, Class, and Justice in the Origins of America* (New York: Rowman & Littlefield, 1997), 2–5.

5. In a letter to James Madison, Thomas Jefferson wrote on 20 December 1787, in the context of criticizing the Presidency of the Constitution, "I own I am not a friend to a very energetic government. It is always oppressive. The late rebellion in Massachusetts has given more alarm than I think it should have done. . . . No country should be so long without one. Nor will any degree of power in the hands of government prevent insurrections." In a postscript he adds, "The instability of our laws is really an immense evil." In the same context, his estimate on the frequency and effect of rebellions such as Shays's led him to write to William Stephens Smith, 13 November 1787, "Wonderful is the effect of impudent and persevering lying. The British ministry have so long hired their gazetteers to repeat and model into every form lies about our being in anarchy, that the world has at length believed them, . . . and what is more wonderful, we have believed them ourselves. . . . What signify a few lives lost in a century or two? The tree of liberty must be refreshed from time to time with the blood of patriots and tyrants. It is its natural manure. Our Convention has been too much impressed by the insurrection of Massachusetts: and in the spur of the moment are setting up a kite to keep the hen yard in order." *The Papers of Thomas Jefferson,* ed. Julian P. Boyd, Mina R. Bryan, and Fredrick Aandahl, vol. 12,

(Princeton, NJ: Princeton University Press, 1955), 355–57; 438–442. Jefferson also commented in his *The Anas,* "Mr. Adams had originally been a republican. The glare of royalty and nobility, during his mission to England, had made him believe their fascination a necessary ingredient in government; and Shays's rebellion, not sufficiently understood where he then was, seemed to prove that the absence of want and oppression, was not a sufficient guarantee of order." *The Writings of Thomas Jefferson,* ed. Andrew A. Lipscomb and Albert Ellery Bergh, vol. 1 (Washington, D.C.: The Thomas Jefferson Memorial Association, 1904), 279f.

6. T. S. Eliot's "The Love Song of J. Alfred Prufrock," in *The Complete Poems and Plays: 1909-1950* (San Diego: Harcourt Brace Jovanovich, 1971), lines 110–12, pp. 3–7.

Part II: The Constitutionalism of *The Federalist Papers*

The question left from *Federalist* number one and posed by its arguments, means that we are not done with that paper yet.

But before we go on to discuss the constitutionalism of the Federalists, let us make sure that we understand this broad question of the *Constitution*. I have been using the word in different ways. I understand it can lead to certain misunderstandings, so I want to clarify the term at the outset. What is this thing—a constitution? Some take a constitution to be a general plan of government, a structure, an outline of government.

That is of course what we ordinarily regard the constitution to be. I have been using the word in a slightly different sense, and that's why I need to clarify it. Though that meaning is correct, that is almost more a product of the inheritance we have had since the founding than it is the literal understanding of those Latin terms. We may elaborate the broader expression *constitutionalism* with the opposition *institutions* versus *forms* of government, which should not be intuitive. Ordinarily if one says forms of government, one would probably think "institutions, general outline or plan." But I'm using it rather differently. The term *institutions* invokes three branches of government that perform in accordance with certain provisions, etc. That is the Constitution, that is the plan of government, to use the expression that was introduced.

But this expression itself has a very intriguing history. It is, of course, Latin and means roughly something that has been set up or established. So that is certainly compatible with "form of government." But the Latin form also is related to the translation for the Greek word for constitution. The Greek word for constitution is a word which has come to us in this form, *polity*; the Greek form being *politeia*. We call it "polity."

Now *polity* has a different meaning than *constitution* does for us today. And the Latin word which translated the Greek "polity," or *politeia,* was "republic" or *respublica*. We begin to see a strange pattern of migration among those terms. *Politeia*, the Greek term, was translated or defined by Aristotle to mean "an arrangement of offices," which seems to get back to a plan of government. Except, in an arrangement of offices Aristotle doesn't mean the offices of government merely. He means to say that we have established in the city, the *polis*, a hierarchy, various rankings, positions for magistrates and others, and the way we arrange them in terms of the classes and characters of the citizens that defines the constitution.

So, for example, if the people in charge are selected according to their merits, their talents, say the few best are in charge, then the arrangement of offices is "aristocratic" and Aristotle would call that an "aristocracy." Or if we say the offices are set up such that in order to hold office one has to have wealth, the arrangement would be to place power in the hands of the few who are wealthy, and Aristotle would call that an "oligarchy." *Oligos* means few, and *archy* means rule. Continuing, democracy would be then for Aristotle rule of the many who are poor: *demos*, meaning the masses. So, by arrangement of offices, he is talking about the arrangement of types, characters, and status within the community. It is broader than just the plan of institutions that Aristotle is talking about.

When we speak about constitutionalism, in those broadest terms, we can substitute the expression, "way of life." And though we often hear it referred to, we don't often think of "the American Constitution" when people say "the American way of life." Yet, that expression, "the American way of life," would come closer to the ancient understanding of the meaning of constitution or *politeia* than even the expression "plan of government" would. For a way of life is a pattern that reveals the preferences of the citizens in a given community. The kinds of characteristics that they praise would be manifested in the people whom they advance into positions of prominence or authority. If they are all of a certain type we may say, "Well, in this society, this is the type that everyone wants to be, this is the type they praise most, etc. They identify that type with power and reputation and fame." So it is a way of life understood as a way of making choices, and expressing patterns of choice, that we ultimately mean by constitution.

This is especially significant if what we are talking about is Publius's concern to create a certain kind of decision making in the people at large, which is much more fundamental than simply the arrangement of offices. To be sure, we have legislative, executive, and judicial branches of government, and they are related and inter-related in ways that will be made clear, particularly in essays forty-six to fifty-one, and all that takes forethought. But the idea that the Founding Fathers are early versions of mechanical engineers doesn't do justice to their constitutional claims. They purport to be engaged in something far wider than simply designing the offices; they purport to be designing the lives that the people living under this constitution were meant to live.

So the distinction that was offered between the despotic tendencies of democracy in the states and the response under the new constitution is as much a distinction between ways of life as it is a distinction in forms of government. A country, a community, is more than a government. We ordinarily think our government is one thing and we are something else usually. Our lives are apart from our government; our government we pay taxes to; we vote occasionally; and we hope they leave us alone most of the

Nos.
46–51

time. That's how we think of our government. But in fact, we still live in a community (today it is often called civil society) even when we are not involved with our government. And the question is, do we live according to a pattern within this community? Do we have a way of life? And do the *Federalist Papers* purport to design a way of life? Well, I submit that they do indeed purport to design a way of life.

The essays that we have looked at to this point, essays 84, 85, and 1, state only in the most general terms what that way of life would be like, and then projects in those general terms what I consider a very ambitious goal. Then in essays 2 through 8, we begin to particularize some of the features of this way of life. Now in general, I would describe the *Federalist Papers* this way: papers 84, 85 and 1, and 2 through 10 lay out the broad description of the way of life to be associated with the new constitution. Essays 11 through 83 deal with the particulars; how it is in institutional terms we bring that way of life into being, organize it, and provide for people to govern themselves, to tax themselves, and to respond to calls of war or whatever else may be involved in the ordinary course of life for a people. But that would make the critical essays then to be not those central ones, laying out the patterns of organization, but those early ones, laying out the form of life, the way of life.

Now some people would criticize. They would say, "Now, wait a minute; this can't be true, because we all know that when it comes to *our* way, things materially important to that way of life are not controlled by our government, by our Constitution. We know that we have religious freedoms, and we can be any religion we want." This is how we tend to weigh that kind of question.

Notice, though, the difference between being told what one's religion will be and being told the question is open. It's not entirely clear that that is not a constitutional choice. It's one thing to say one is free to be a Baptist; it is another thing to be told one must be a Baptist. And each of those statements has a constitutional value. If one is told that one is free to be a Baptist, one is being told that he is not required to be a Presbyterian, and that's significant, because it means *vis-à-vis* Presbyterianism, or to take one of the established churches, let's say the Anglican Church, Episcopalianism, that it is no longer in fact consistent with the Constitution to require people to be Episcopalians. The Constitution is that far changed. Now what the substantive consequences of being told that one is free are, we will explore as we go along. But we must not think it means that it is simply open-ended, that there is no limit to what one can do.

One thing we know we can't do: we can't form a political party, the purpose of which is to establish in the State of Louisiana the Baptist religion, and to require everyone to be a member. We can't do that. We don't have the liberty to do that under the Constitution under which we live. And it's not just the Louisiana Constitution that prohibits it, because

Nos. 1, 84, 85

Nos. 2–10

Nos. 11–83

we know people change state constitutions about as easily as they change underwear, and might be able to change that. But we can't do it, even if we changed the State Constitution, because the United States Constitution is not going to permit it[1]. So therefore, even in the area of religion, there are certain consequences of this new way of life that is being defended by Publius that we need to begin to take into account.

We begin to take that into account by focusing on the manner in which is realized at the outset of the *Federalist Papers* the statement of this constitutionalism, the filling in of this outline with certain substantive conclusions. Now Publius begins the *Federalist Papers*, as I've noted before, with an outline. The first *Federalist Paper* provides an outline of the various subjects that will be discussed or the various objectives of analysis. And the first of these, that he called "interesting particulars," was in his words, "the utility of the union to your political prosperity." It's in paragraph seven of the first essay.

No. 1

We have, then, "the utility of the union to your political prosperity"—the union is an instrument, a tool. It's a means to some end. And that end is what is, for this moment, still undefined as political prosperity. It's very important to look at all the words when we read these documents. The words are not necessarily difficult. But we might want to ask questions about why these words are brought together in this fashion. What does it mean to speak of "the utility of the union to your political prosperity"? If the union is just a tool, and prosperity is the end, this term *political prosperity* will have a very special meaning for us.

Thus, the point last emphasized in the *Federalist Papers* turns out also to be the point first discussed, this notion of union. It's discussed through the first fourteen essays. Essays eleven through fourteen discuss union with respect to some of the consequences for the nation in terms of representation, commerce, etc. Essays one through ten discuss political union in the constitutional sense that I now invoke. After that, the next question that Publius raised is the insufficiency of the present confederation to preserve that union. He says that will be the subject he takes up, starting, in fact, in essay fifteen. And we can go through the *Federalist Papers* and check these off and see that he goes by the topics just the way he lists them. So he's made a distinction between the union and the political form appropriate to the union.

Nos. 1–14

We have first the necessity or utility of union to political prosperity. We have secondly, the insufficiency of the present confederation to preserve that union. The Confederation is a political form. It is insufficient, even while the union remains useful to the goal of political prosperity. So we can talk about our union independently of the political form that we have, and that is what Publius proceeds to do in this fashion.

Now, the confederation is not the union. If one regards the union as morally or logically prior, then the institutional form—constitution in the narrow sense—will not be sacrosanct. The Union is worth more than the Constitution if we put it in those terms. Only by taking constitution in the broader sense, as being the same as union, do we avoid that particular problem.

In the third place, Publius talks about the necessity of a government at least equally energetic with the one proposed to the attainment of this object. And what is this object? That is political prosperity. So we require a union, which will provide for political prosperity, and to do that we must have a political form invested with energy. There's going to be a general principle of *energy* in the government. These are all things that are revealed just by listing the topics to talk about without having elaborated them yet. Now energetic government I take to mean a government that is going to be able to do things, that is going to be able to get something done, even though at this point it is still unspecified what is to get done.

In the fourth place, we want to notice the conformity of the proposed constitution to the true principles of republican government. Publius must demonstrate that the new Constitution will be consistent with republican principles. Republican principles we don't adopt or invent. They exist independently of us. So this is a standard outside of ourselves that will be used to judge the accomplishments under the new constitution.

At that point, we have three principles, which stand out very clearly. We have union, which we know is not an end, for the end is political prosperity. And we now know as well that we want to judge the Union and political prosperity in light of standards of republicanism. And again, I repeat, we know all these at the outset just from the listing without having gone through any demonstration at this point. These are the three critical terms for the entire *Federalist Papers*. So, we have the idea of republicanism as governing principle, along with union, and union was the tool, the means. And these are all dedicated to the end of political prosperity.

Now, we have a special problem we are trying to deal with. The problem is we want to take these people, called citizens of the United States, and we want to turn them into something: not into monarchists; not into aristocrats; not into oligarchs; but into republicans. And we want to do so while at the same time assuring their political prosperity. So it turns out to be a moral puzzle. How do we turn three million people, at that time, into republicans and at the same time, assure their political prosperity? It's not intuitive. It's something that no one had done, so it's being, perhaps not attempted for the first time but, potentially accomplished for the first time. And unless the argument somehow reveals it, we can't be at all certain whether it's possible.

Publius listed two other interesting particulars or objectives in that seventh paragraph of the first essay. The first was the analogy to "your own state constitution," and the last was the "additional security" afforded to

No. 1

liberty and property. But as we know, those two interesting particulars were unveiled in the final essay as having been adequately unfolded during the discussion of the first four. So we don't need to go through them particularly; they somehow are included in what we provide for in looking to the question of union, republicanism, and prosperity.

It seems to me that we can show the character of the constitutionalism defended by Publius precisely by indicating how the initial terms of debate, these three principles, are defined in the opening essays. And that's why I set aside essays two through eight as of particular value in this respect.

No. 2

The language of new federalism is introduced to us in the second essay. The introduction comes in the form of a fundamental question, and that question is, "Is government necessary?" or more precisely, "How necessary is government?" The precise language that is used there is rather in the form of an affirmation: "Nothing is more certain than the indispensable necessity of government." We see that at the beginning of the second paragraph of the second essay. That kind of language is not meant to be in the form of a command, but it is to say that all rational minds have come to the conclusion that "nothing is more certain . . ." etc. So it's a principle that we can all agree to as it's used, as it's stated, and from which we therefore should be able to trace out the development of certain premises and conclusions.

But the statement is also a challenge. On the one hand, the necessity for government is logically necessary or a statement of a truism, but on the other hand, it's a challenge. We ask, "are we in fact safely beyond the need to reflect whether we can live without government, in some kind of spontaneous order, interacting freely with one another, without any common judge or superior above us?" Are we so sure that such a life would be impossible? Further, it's important to know whether all humanity is confirmed in this impression of things. We want to know whether the first essay's idea of reflection and choice might take on still greater force if one of the possible choices we might reflect upon is the choice to live without government. Given the moral certainty that government is necessary, the question of whether we can choose the government we wish becomes still more urgent.

Just weigh these things carefully. On the one hand, government is necessary. So we conclude that we must live under a government; on the other hand, the question is can we choose the government under which we live? Can we mitigate the effect of this necessity through prudent choice, prudent judgment? That is the question that is at stake. Organized society we would conclude, following Publius in number two, is the human way. I spoke above of the American way of life. Well, now we know there is also the human way, and the human way is organized society. That creates for us the limit, the horizon. So government is necessary—not a necessary evil, but necessary, morally compelling.

The conclusion that government is necessary is connected with the argument from natural rights. The argument from natural rights is at the foundation of the Declaration of Independence which I have discussed briefly. That argument also projects the notion that human beings, in order to defend the rights they have by nature, have to yield a part of those rights, they must cede a portion of them. Publius repeats this in the second paragraph of the second essay. Some portion of our rights are assigned to a common pool for society in order that people can then protect the rights which are dearest for them. The part that has to be assigned is at least the right to execute the judgments of nature. We deposit that authority in the hands of society (usually in the form of government), and therefore introduce a stability, a predictability which allows everybody to be secure in the rights they retain.

When we say "execute the laws of nature" or "execute the judgments of nature" we mean of course, the executive judgments of nature, those kinds of actions which usually take the form of recriminations for injuries done to us. It is where people who have no common judge between them find themselves in conflict that the execution of the judgments of nature becomes especially bloody. And that's the right that Publius is saying must be surrendered to the common pool in order to introduce stability and predictability.

The general purpose behind this move is to eliminate force and fraud in human dealings, what we call generally the rule of law. But long before it gets to be the rule of law as opposed to the rule of men, we find out that it is the elimination of force and fraud. The reason for this, by the way, is very straight forward: we can eliminate force and fraud without establishing the rule of law simply by conveying absolute power to one monarch or despot, who keeps everybody else in check. With respect to everyone else we may have perfect stability and predictability in our relationship, but we are all governed by just the whim of the despot rather than by law. So that, when we begin to seek the rule of law, over and above mere force or power, we are looking for additional advantages beyond simply protecting ourselves against the violence of our fellows.

Now the concept of rights is derived from, or introduced initially, in the context of the first question on the outline for the *Federalist Papers*, namely the utility of union. We affirm the necessity of government and talk about ceding a portion of our rights in relation to the question of the utility or usefulness of union, and therefore we see that the response takes this shape. Government is necessary in the first place, and in the second place, the work of government is precisely to make those tough judgment calls,which otherwise every individual would have to make on his own, dealing with his life, his property, and his liberty. So that's the precise and technical relationship, as it begins to sound somewhat like John Locke. It's perfectly natural. Locke is not the only one, of course, to have expressed these ideas, but it is certainly the case that John Locke gave them their prototypical expression in the seventeenth century.

Consequently, certain things become very clear, very plain, in the *Federalist Papers*. For one thing, the theory places a special focus on the United States, regarding which we may cite this passage from the second essay:

No. 2   It has until lately been a received and uncontradicted opinion that the prosperity of the people of America depended on their continuing firmly united, and the wishes, prayers, and efforts of our best and wisest citizens have been constantly directed to that object. But Politicians now appear who insist that this opinion is erroneous, and that instead of looking for safety and happiness in union, we ought to seek it in a division of the States into distinct confederacies or sovereignties.

This is a finely balanced argument. In effect we talk about the state of nature, natural law, the situation concerning all human beings, the necessity of government, the yielding of rights to protect life, liberty, and property. On the other hand, we talk about the question of whether in the United States we accomplish these objectives best through separate states, or smaller unions of states or through one large union. The immediate political question is always set by Publius in the context of the broader human question. It is never looked at merely as a political question.

Remember he said in the first *Federalist Paper* that we must look at the argument. The argument is what should settle the question for us, and Publius went out of his way to make the argument as universal as possible to defend this new constitution. The argument begins by looking at the idea of union, not any particular institutions. There are no legislative, executive, or judicial branches yet. There is no Bill of Rights, there is none of the stuff that we familiarly recognize as our Constitution involved in this process. The Constitution for Publius is obviously much more imminent than we would expect based on our traditional understanding of things. It is found in the very first decisions that are to be made, regarding whether this will be a union or whether it will be thirteen separate and independent states. He asks this question: Is it possible for thirteen independent states, however democratic, however prosperous, to accomplish the objectives that are meant to be served by government? That's the question he is raising, and his answer is that it is not possible.

But we need to see why it is not possible. We notice in the second essay that he continues in the paragraphs following the above quotation to take what is the theory such as we would discover it in John Locke and turns to opinion, to general opinion. He says there is a general opinion in the society, that union is necessary for prosperity. Now notice that these are the principles we are talking about from our first essay. He's not speaking about any old prosperity. It's the Americans who already believe union is necessary for prosperity; they already have a certain kind of constitutional expectation, a certain thought of what their life requires.

I don't know that I can say what people in general mean when they use the word prosperity. I suppose it brings a vast range of ideas and images into people's minds, but it is interesting to note, whatever may be said of the people, that they think prosperity (whatever they take prosperity to be) depends on their being with one another. That is an interesting observation; they don't image a prosperity for themselves apart from those around.

To my mind that means it has a constitutional status in much the same way as, say, something like Father's Day. It has a constitutional status or stature because we can't talk about a father without talking about someone in relation to whom the father is a father. To say father is to invoke three people. At a minimum, it's an interesting reflection. This argument about union and prosperity has that character, saying, "I can't be prosperous alone." It takes *us*, whatever the "us" is defined to be, to produce this prosperity.

We need to look at this term *prosperity,* because it recurs particularly in these early essays with great frequency. We cannot assume what it means but must struggle to try to find out what it means. That means to grasp the connection of prosperity with the argument for union. If union is a condition of political happiness then the people who counseled the vision of thirteen states represent an emerging heresy. If this general opinion that Publius referred to existed, then what threatens it is heresy. Publius thus gains a rhetorical advantage, because he becomes a conservative defending what people want in the established order against late comers who want to overturn everything.

This is a good place at which to take note of the fact that rhetorical advantage is not to be surrendered in argument that has a moral purpose. For those who have often taken the position that the *Federalist Papers* are mere rhetoric, the use of the adjective "mere" in the front of rhetoric, belies their failure to understand both what rhetoric is and its necessary relatedness to moral enterprises. Yes, of course, the *Federalist Papers* are rhetoric, even propaganda, if that's all one means by the term propaganda, but they aim to achieve specific objectives. The rhetoric subserves those objectives and therefore, in analyzing the argument, one is required to take note of the rhetoric even to understand fully what is being argued. So there is never any such thing as "*mere* rhetoric," unless it's the kind that takes place in our debating societies at schools, where we tell youngsters to get up and make a for or against argument on anything without being particularly for or against anything. That may be merely rhetoric, since they will reach into their grab bags and practice anything they can come up with, with little regard for what it might mean. But for people who are involved and actually making lives for themselves and carrying on genuine conversations, there is no such thing as mere rhetoric. So Publius gains rhetorical advantage by painting himself as a conservative and the others as heretics or radicals.

Next, he establishes himself within the court of public opinion, in the role of received and uncontradicted opinion he acknowledged at the outset of this second essay. So over and above serving to establish political legitimacy, public opinion sets the limits for all acceptable political opinions. Another way of putting this, as I like to say it, is that flesh sticks to the bones of political right only by means of public opinion. Public opinion is the vehicle for all political right, for every political argument, in the last analysis.

People have an awful difficult time dealing with that because they know the general arguments call for principles to be established by nature, and the minute we introduce public opinion, they think, "public opinion is a varying thing, it's not a fixed standard, therefore how can right be natural if it's dependent on public opinion? How can slavery be a matter of natural law, how can the wrongness of it be a matter of natural law if it depends on public opinion from one generation to the next?" But the question is not whether opinion determines the rightness or wrongness of an action, it is whether it admits the discussion of the rightness or wrongness of an action. It is whether the opinion admits the possibility of living by standards that are right or whether it requires adherence to wrong standards. Opinion has a power not based on its rightness but based on its being the essential means of human conduct, in the moral sphere to be sure, and in fact, in general.

We will discover this in the tenth *Federalist Paper,* where opinion will

No. 10   be specifically discussed as the necessary tool whereby human beings pursue even their interest. We say people are self-interested, and we seldom stop to explore what we mean by the term self-interested. We say they act in a self-interested way and number ten will make clear to us that what we mean is they act on the opinion that what they take to be their interests ought to be pursued. Opinion for human beings almost always must enter into the calculation, if human beings do anything. If they move, they move in accord with what they think. And public opinion is nothing other than that field of opinion that in any given community is established as the legitimate field within which human opinion should move. What stands beyond that is unacceptable. What stands beyond that is the radical. So Publius has set himself up early to move within what's taken to be acceptable political opinion. That way he makes it easier to establish his argument. After that, the discussion aims not merely to benefit from favorable public opinion but also to preserve salutary public opinion.

To accomplish that Publius writes in the second essay a brief overview

No. 2   of American history. He paints an idyllic picture of a land in which everything is readily accessible in this large, contiguous country, people more or less homogeneous, all speaking the same language, having wonderful rivers, and communicating easily with one another. He says the land was clearly designed by Providence for a happy and prosperous people.

What's interesting in this rather idyllic portrait of course is the claim of homogeneity: the claim, in effect, that there is a constitution, there is a people that share a common way of life. Others have denied this. "Agrippa," an Antifederalist, said the country is so heterogeneous it is too diverse to have one government. We couldn't possibly represent all the different interests. Agrippa thinks that the difference between the people of Massachusetts, his home, and those of Georgia is so vast, that only a tyranny could hold them together in a common union.

That is a vast separation in the opinions of Publius and Agrippa. What we will ultimately see, as I return to it later, is that Publius is somewhat disingenuous at this point. He makes the argument from homogeneity in order to be able to make the argument from public opinion—in order to be able to sustain the argument that there is a general opinion in favor of union, as a key to political prosperity. But he will go on, in subsequent essays, to show in fact that the homogeneity that he praises is rather more the work of the union than it is a received product from the past or from tradition.

So we begin to understand what the constitutionalism is. What the new constitution will do through building a union to provide for political prosperity is precisely to create a people who can be called properly a people, who are sufficiently homogeneous, sharing the same moral and political principles and therefore able to act on the world stage as a single people, rather than a heterogeneous collection of peoples with differing interests. We will see how that is developed in its foreign and its domestic aspects as we continue our discussion of the essays through number nine, and finally essay number ten.

To continue with the third essay, we want to explore the question of union, the question of prosperity, and Publius's reliance in the second essay on homogeneity in order to establish himself as the true exponent of American principles.

We still have, though, the question of the argument about opinion. The actual relationship to public opinion of the *Federalist Papers* is one question; the *Federalist Papers's* argument about public opinion is another question. That argument, as I said above, aimed to acquire for them the mantle of conservatism, to show that they were not the radicals, that they were not going to change everything. That leads to a number of questions, not the least being the question of how one is going to deal with the reality that in fact there was not homogeneity but rather heterogeneity of opinion in this country.

Publius presents in the essays starting from number three the sense in which union may be said to be better than disunion, having already raised   **No. 3** this question in number two. There he insisted first and foremost upon the matter of safety. It's a very elementary thing because people want to be safe. Why is government necessary? because it allows people to be safe from the violence of others. In the third essay he addresses the question of safety in a number of ways. And in the fourth paragraph of that essay he speaks of it as it respects security for the preservation of peace and tranquillity as well against dangers of foreign arms and influence as from dangers of the like kind arising from domestic causes.

The context is immediately clear. Which is better, the union or the states? That's what he's asking. Is it better for dealing with foreign enemies, on the one hand, and is it better for dealing with domestic violence, on the other hand? We could say "domestic enemies" also, because I'm reminded that when one takes the oath to the United States as an officer of the United States one is required to swear to uphold and defend the laws and the Constitution of the United States against "all enemies, foreign and domestic." So the oath admits the possibility of domestic enemies and that seems to be of course what Publius is talking about here.

There are two dangers, two threats to safety. One is foreign arms and influence, the other is domestic violence; and if we asked, what's the best protection against foreign arms and influence, I think most would say the union. If we asked, what's the best protection against domestic violence, what would most say? I think it's intuitive to say the states, exactly. I think that's what anyone in America would have said in 1787. One wouldn't think necessarily of the Union as protecting against domestic violence, because the natural instinct is to think that government on a scale to suit the threat near to home is appropriate. Publius however, is never simply intuitive and therefore gives a counter intuitive response to this question.

Nos. 3–9

In fact the entire strength of the argument for the new constitution depends on the force of this new argument. Publius dedicates the third essay and the fourth essay to dealing with the question concerning foreign arms and influence, and in essays five through nine he answers primarily the question about domestic violence with a climax saved for essay number ten. Now, I want to emphasize this way of looking at those essays because domestic violence is not characteristically the focus of discussion, especially at essay number ten.

No. 10

Characteristically we understand that essay number ten is about factions. But we think factions have to do with majority rule democracies and minorities. We don't think of it as primarily the question of domestic violence. But that is in fact the context in which the question is raised. We come ultimately to the distinction between a republic and a democracy in *Federalist Paper* number ten only because we're trying to show the counter intuitive response to the question about how to eliminate domestic violence in the society. So, essays three and four deal with the question of foreign arms and foreign influence. Essays five through ten deal with the question of domestic violence.

The utility of union, from the overall outline, gets rather large focus on a most elementary question, the question of dealing with the execution of the laws of nature. In the question of the self-preservation both of individuals and of nations the question of safety from violence comes first; it's the most important thing. If we can't be safe, we can't enjoy the good life or any life at all. But that still raises the question, what do we mean by first in this case? Is it first in importance, first in value, first in dignity or is it first only in time? If we find it a necessary condition but not a sufficient condition for further political reflection or effort, the implication is that it's not sufficient for prosperity. So if safety is a necessary condition for political deliberation but not a sufficient condition for creating wealth then it is not the condition of political prosperity. This first answer to the utility of union doesn't deal with the much larger question of political prosperity. We need union to get to political prosperity but union in itself is not what gets us there.

The reason for this has more to do with what I have called Publius's counter-intuitive response to the question about domestic violence than with the logical form of the argument. In order to see this we have to recognize that political prosperity calls for dealing with necessity or with the necessary conditions of political life in rather a special way. I want to get there though by contrasting it with what he does in the foreign arena, so let's go back to the third essay and investigate the causes of war.

There Publius seems to raise the question, not merely from curiosity but rather because it's important to be prepared to prevail in war and also to place oneself in the position to avoid war. The *Federalists Papers* seem for the moment to adopt this rather passive perspective in its approach to foreign policy, inquiring not how to adopt an active posture for engaging in war but rather how to make war as little likely as possible. It is a curious form of what, in today's language, we call deterrence theory. The argument is laid out by the end of the third essay and then stated outright in the fourth essay. There in the tenth paragraph he ascribes it to the American people in general. He says, "Wisely therefore do they consider Union and a good national Government as necessary to put and keep them in *such a situation* as instead of *inviting* war will tend to repress and discourage it." This deterrence theory is based on a number of factors deriving from human nature, and it therefore forces us to ask whether Publius generally understands the causes of war. Again, in the third essay we see a claim that the peace of America, we emphasize the peace of *America*, highly depends upon Americans' observance of the laws of nature towards all *foreign* powers, the thing which will be more perfectly accomplished in proportion as we have one national government rather than thirteen or some other

No. 3

No. 4

number. We expect therefore, to close with an argument from efficiency, less chance, greater consistency, greater stability in foreign relations.

The surprise is that Publius doesn't do that in the third essay. He instead states the following in the eighth paragraph: "When once an efficient national government is established, the best men in the country will not only consent to serve, but also will generally be appointed." He argues not from efficiency but from the character and talents of the officeholders. He claims that there are several reasons for increased efficiency, but the first reason for increased national security is clearly that one obtains the best statesmen.

Now, this is clear as a mere mathematical argument. In any group of human beings, some number X will have capacity sufficient to accomplish the work aimed at. The size of X increases when the total number of the human beings in the group increases. Divide this final number into thirteen parts and each part will have only a portion of X. So, we get more of the better minds, the better talents available to the nation than available to each of the thirteen states. This is not so much an argument of class or status or wealth but an argument about ability, and of the three sources of greater efficiency, the first is the presence of the best men. Secondly what one obtains is consistency in interpreting treaties, and that by itself is not enough. Therefore we want to assure quality, the quality of our statesmen. Intelligent statesmanship will somehow be consistent statesmanship and more so in proportion as the number of sovereignties is reduced to one rather than thirteen.

This is a very elementary discussion at this point, elemental I might even say, but it's important to understand the focus on these most elemental things. It's not the question of justice, it's not the question of natural rights; but it's the question of safety that calls for intelligence and consistency. Let us remember, we referred the question of natural rights, the question of justice, already to the people at large. Now this is strange. We're not asking for Socrates to judge what is right by nature, we're asking for Socrates to interpret a treaty, to judge when we need to go to war and when not to. The argument is that Socrates will make that judgment better than many and will avoid war. Publius says a knowledge of the causes of war is the surest means to avoid war and the surest means to a steady foreign policy of avoiding war.

In preference to a capacity for agility in war is a capacity to avoid war. Now, that's odd, to say the least, a form of early American pacifism, or at least something resembling it, found right here in the pages of the *Federalist Papers*. And I try to illuminate this somewhat by exploring it. The character of American isolationism, which has been very frequently condemned in our history since the time of the founding, has a constitutional foundation when properly understood and applied. And the condemnations I think are based on a misreading of this important dimension of American life. The policy really should not be called isolationist. It places first priority on avoiding war but not at all costs, and that's the reason they want intelligent people. The unintelligent will avoid war at all costs, and in the end they will always produce worse wars rather than avoid wars at all.

It is nevertheless wise to avoid war. Therefore Publius gives us an illustration, and in the eighth paragraph in the third essay, we find him using again the union and the state dichotomy. "Hence, it will result," says he, "that the administration, the political councils, and the judicial decisions of the national Government will be more wise, systematical, and judicious, than those of the individual States, and consequently more satisfactory with respect to other nations, as well as more *safe* with respect to us." The chief means to avoid war is good order at home, and it includes satisfying other nations. That is the first source of safety which is enjoyed strictly from the perspective of the people of the United States. It is isolationism therefore only in the sense that it accepts as its chief mission the safety of the United States. That in turn doesn't differ from maintaining the moral superiority of the union to the states taken separately.

No. 3

Publius gives a third reason for this foreign policy. In the eleventh paragraph of the third essay Publius states: "Because even if the governing party in a State should be disposed to resist such temptations [temporary loss or advantage], yet as such temptations may, and commonly do result from circumstances peculiar to the State, and may affect a great number of the inhabitants, the governing party may not always be able if willing to prevent the injustice meditated, or to punish the aggressors." The context in which this occurs is a discussion of the kinds of things people do whether intentionally or not that expose their nations to war, and one of the factors is this yielding to temptation. More such opportunities will confront thirteen states than one nation. More importantly still, such local circumstances will little impugn a national government. Thus, that government will possess the means to check others who could be seduced, while itself being proof against seduction. So I think the key to the argument is plainly what Publius expects to be the national government's detachment from local interest, from local concerns. The beginning of Publius's expectation is that the national government will be able to say no to local concerns. It will not yield to temptations that will expose the nation to danger.

Then as we skip one paragraph and look at the next we will see that Publius adds that one national government will equally avert the dangers deriving from those just causes of war proceeding from direct and unlawful violence. So even if we permit the claim that the United States will offer less offense under a single sovereignty than under thirteen, we still only get half of the argument. We must also argue that the United States will have less occasion to take offense under a single sovereignty, and that's the greatest test. It sounds strange that a change in our constitution could have an effect on nations not a part of our constitution, such that we would be less likely to have to be angry with them than otherwise. But that is precisely the argument he is making. One has to ask why would he make such an argument.

As I said before, most of Publius's argument is intuitive. If we just look at it and think about it, we see immediately and say, of course, this is what human nature provides for. But the position respecting domestic violence is not intuitive, and now I submit that the claim to have less occasion to take offense is equally counter-intuitive or if not so, at least very far from obvious. The further implications of this argument put our intuitions to an even greater test.

No. 4

The second paragraph of the fourth essay acknowledges the claim that the United States has to avoid putting itself in a position to invite hostilities, to invite insult. The third paragraph then shows how difficult this might be. "It is too true, however disgraceful it may be to human nature, that nations in general will make war whenever they have a prospect of getting anything by it, nay that absolute monarchs will often make war when their nations are to get nothing by it, but for purposes and objects merely personal, such as, a thirst for military glory, revenge for personal affronts; ambition or private compacts to aggrandize or support their particular families, or partizans. These and a variety of motives, which affect only the mind of the Sovereign, often lead him to engage in wars not sanctified by justice, or the voice and interests of his people." As we think about that I believe that we will see that many of the wars that arise will do so because people having the power to make or to avoid war yield to temptations that we find perfectly ordinary in human nature, nothing extraordinary about it. People see opportunities and try to take advantage of them, and the result is they're at war.

We can question the causes of war and the premise that if we knew the causes it would be easier to avoid war. In this point though, it seems that the very resource we relied upon in the beginning—namely, the people with the power to decide—is also one of the chief causes of war. We remember that we wanted to get the best men and they would avoid war. Well it turns out now that people in office who yield to temptation happen to be one of the chief causes of war, and Publius reminds us of this. We must never forget that.

After making clear that the ones who either possess or exercise sovereign authority yield to temptations that are common to human nature, Publius lets us see that what we're looking at is not some aberration. All we have to do is expect them to be human to expect these causes to operate. That is not the exclusive cause of war. Publius is clear about this; but it is the most difficult to deal with. And in that respect we ask once again, is the Union better at dealing with the causes of war? Will the Union make it less likely that national office holders yield to personal illusions to carry their nation into war? We recall that the significance of this is that with the national union our personal illusions come packed with a far greater punch. In spite of that, Publius says yes; in spite of the greater fire power, the greater temptations, the greater illusions, he says yes, and we must ask how.

Publius doesn't claim to alter human nature one bit at all. We have lots of questions: are the better sorts he talks about, these more intelligent who will take in hand this responsibility, less moved by the ordinary temptations familiar to human nature? He's raised the question, but he didn't answer it for us. He implies that we need to pay as close attention to the effect of the new government upon the governed as upon those who govern. So let's return to the statement of deterrence theory in the fourth essay.

The deterrence theory was put this way, "Wisely, therefore, do they consider union and a good national government as necessary to put and keep them in *such a situation* as, instead of *inviting* war, will tend to repress and discourage it." Now just after he'd introduced this deterrence theory, he repeated what he had said in the third essay. This is the eleventh paragraph of the fourth essay, but he's repeating the third essay:

> As the safety of the whole is the interest of the whole, and cannot be provided for without Government, either one or more or many, let us inquire whether one good Government is not, relative to the object in question, more competent than any other given number whatever.
>
> One Government can collect and avail itself of the talents and experience of the ablest men, in whatever part of the Union they may be found. It can move on uniform principles of policy.

No. 4

This is just a repetition of the argument to every appearance, only stressing our conclusion, but here he adds the following line: "It can harmonize, assimilate, and protect the several parts and members, and extend the benefit of its foresight and precautions to each." Now there is an entirely new argument—this notion of harmonizing interests and incentives for assimilating diverse factors. This government is going to possess an active power. The power, in fact, to create homogeneity where diversity existed previously. What does that mean?

It means that the early idyllic portrait in the second essay of American homogeneity was exaggerated. He's now taking it back. The geographical homogeneity was not accompanied by social and political homogeneity. This latter will be the product of the government itself. Part of the reason for the new constitution, then, is to operate on the souls and the characters of Americans so as to make them more homogeneous in their sentiments and in their interests.

No. 2

This is a very serious claim because it means of course that it's not merely for reasons of efficiency that we have the new Union. We are not going to take the people just as we have found them but we're going to change them. In the very end of the fourth essay Publius reveals what I consider a powerful inducement to this enterprise. He had insisted that foreign nations would accurately assess the American situation, whether united or disunited, and he uses the following words: "and they will act towards us accordingly. If they see that our national government is efficient and well administered—our trade prudently regulated—our militia properly organized and disciplined—our resources and finances discreetly managed—our credit re-established—our people free, contented, and united, they will be much more disposed to cultivate our friendship, than provoke our resentment."

Now, if we read in this passage only the happy results of prudent statesmanship, we will be very far wrong. For this passage is in fact strongly counter-intuitive, something we never ordinarily anticipate is really the burden of the argument. Here's what he's saying: If the people organize themselves well, if they become prosperous, successful, then they will have peace. The usual argument, unless I'm wrong, goes in the reverse direction. Usually we think peace brings prosperity.

That's not Publius's argument. I don't care how familiar it is. Publius maintains that success and prosperity will bring peace, and that is the foundation of his deterrence theory. He says that will much more dispose others to cultivate our friendship than to provoke our resentment. Success and prosperity will yield strength. It will yield opportunities for other nations to profit from peaceful associations with the new country, and this is the angle of events that makes it possible to avoid war.

A very curious thing has happened. Perhaps a digression can make this clear. We started out looking for safety and the means to assure safety. And why do we want to assure safety? because, we said, this is the first condition for carrying on the activities of life free from violence and threat, for having a little stability in our lives. We assumed that after we had safety and stability then we could go on to make rational choices for a decent way of life, to build prosperity. Now we are being told that what will actually make us safe is first to make ourselves prosperous. We can't take it step by step. We've got to make the choice that's outlined in the first *Federalist* paper for good government by reflection and choice, in such a way as to pull it all together, if we want to be safe, not just for the moment but for the long term. So when I say the argument is counter-intuitive, I mean that in very dramatic terms.

We have now a counter-intuitive argument not merely with respect to the domestic violence, we're going to come to that still, but even with respect to the foreign violence, the foreign threat of war. But we notice that in order to deal with the foreign threat of war, we have to change the character of our domestic institution and the status of our domestic life.

The United States for the past generation, no, for the twentieth century, has been the focus of the world largely with regard to a single question—whether Americans are not too materialistic. We've all heard it countlessly in our university classes, we've read it countlessly in news magazines and we've seen it on television. It's the favorite theme of every petty orator on the face of the earth, the materialism of the American way of life. Americans have for the past century consistently apologized for their materialism. They have apologized, even when they have not abandoned it, because they somehow have believed that there was something implicitly wrong with being wealthy and being concerned with wealth.

One of the reasons for that, I believe, is very straight forward. The older arguments, antedating the American Constitution and Revolution, still hold great influence in our minds. Namely the arguments that these material things are sources of temptations which, when people pay attention to them, go wrong; they live lives that are corrupt, that are given to vice, and that undermine ordinary decency. These are long-established principles and arguments, and they are true. Let us not be mistaken about that; they are true when applied properly to individual souls peculiarly subject to individual corruptions.

But there is a different argument now, a new argument that has been made in the *Federalist Papers* to which we have not paid systematic attention since that time; namely, there is a form of prosperity, which includes material prosperity, that is itself the condition of goodness; that indeed, wealth can become one of the defining characteristics of constitutionalism. This wealth is not a by-product of the success of our institutions, but the means to the success of our institutions, and therefore a thing to be taken into account precisely to the extent that we mean to preserve the institutions that have been defended by Publius.

Remember, Publius generally uses the term "political prosperity." He usually modifies "prosperity" with "political," and one could ask, well, does that necessarily mean material prosperity? Couldn't we have a politically happy society where we don't have this focus on wealth? And, of course, we know that is the precise vision that Karl Marx promised to the world, when he described the life of the socialist man after the withering away of the state: The socialist man, after the withering away of the state, of course, is one who will be able to get up in the morning and go fishing as he chooses, or make poetry as he chooses—whatever activity he chooses to engage in in the course of the day he'll be free to turn to because nothing will be absolutely required of him. He will be free from the material conditions determining his life. So it's liberation from material determinism that's the goal in the Marxist vision. Well, it is precisely that argument that Publius effectively denies by making prosperity (I don't think political and material prosperity are separable in his argument), the eventual success of political institutions.

Of course, Publius doesn't envision the withering away of the state. He began the second essay, remember, with the claim, government is necessary. He didn't say that government is a temporary delusion which we will eventually free ourselves from by eliminating class war. He said it is necessary. That means then, at least to all appearances, indefinitely necessary, eternally necessary. But its being necessary, we pointed out, didn't require our living merely by necessity. We can deal with this necessity, he argues, with reflection and choice. That is, we can do this necessary thing in such a way as to make it better rather than worse. And now the means of making it better, rather than worse, come to the surface as this peculiar combination of union and political prosperity.

Again, I must emphasize, not one word has been said about the forms of government. We've talked about the Bill of Rights here, only because I jumped to the end of the book. No congress, no executive, none of these things have been discussed, and yet, we have raised the most important questions about what this Constitution is supposed to accomplish. And I believe this is precisely Publius's intention at this phase of the work—to show what constitutionalism is about.

Again, Publius has taken arguments that are counter-intuitive and made them appear to us to be reasonable. There goes along with this understanding our recognition that these arguments are in defense of a way of life, which itself has been counter-intuitive throughout the history of the world. It's a defense of a Constitution which no intelligent person prior to the end of the eighteenth century ever would have defended. To that extent then, perhaps it takes such counter-intuitive arguments in order to defend such a Constitution.

In looking at the final phase of the argument over foreign war, we recognize that we've been concerned with the causes of war, thinking that if we knew the causes, we would be able to avoid a war. It turns out, of course, that it's not so clear that our knowledge of the causes will lead to that, since we have a constitutional argument that we rely on instead. When he gives us the further argument in terms of the Constitution, the broad argument that we are going to control the actions of others through our own situation, we begin then to see that there is a way to think about success and prosperity as conditions for peace that we had perhaps not realized.

People who are not prosperous, who do not succeed in establishing stable situations, are far more likely to have to live through war, according to Publius's argument. And, I think, by the way, that we would say, that historically it's hard to refute that. We know very well that we normally find the most miserable people, the most oppressed, continually undergoing new rounds of conflict. They are never free from war, misery, and conflict. The argument is counter-intuitive but it is not necessarily wrong or surprising.

It is perhaps what no one has ever thought and what anyone has hardly ever thought since that time, because we don't often go back to the *Federalist Papers* in this spirit. Nevertheless, this is the view at the foundation of the new and modern order. This is the view therefore which describes for us what is really meant by avoiding war. Avoidance of war is not a posture of submission, it is not a craven posture. Avoidance of war is the notion that individuals can persuade other individuals, and that not only individuals persuade other individuals but nations persuade other nations. The notion is that if nations strike the correct moral posture, along with appropriate incentives and inducements to friendly intercourse, wars can be avoided.

This sets up the final stage for us before getting to the institutions in terms of Federalist constitutionalism. We will look next at the argument, the counter-intuitive argument for domestic violence, and that will then propel us into the tenth *Federalist Paper*, which closes the cycle on the discussion of Federalist constitutionalism.

The *Federalist* itself sets forth the particular details of its constitutionalism, beginning in the ninth essay with what is there called the improved science of politics. But right now what we want to notice is what before I called the counter-intuitive solution to the problem of domestic violence, as that is expressed in the essays, number five through eight. And we want to do so in such a way as to show that the definition of constitutionalism in the *Federalist Papers* is a particular version of political prosperity, that we already developed with respect to foreign affairs. This really is the fundamental justification for the founding in the eyes, at least, of Publius.

Nos. 5–8

Going back to the second essay for just a moment, there we cited two areas of concern with respect to providing safety. The second area was that of domestic violence, but we didn't get to that topic until the fifth essay. Now the context in which the subject is introduced points to the previous question of the causes of war, or what appeared to be initially the foreign relations question. We can see in essay number five that it is unclear that the causes of war are differently affected by confederation than by a single national government, and I posed that test with respect to domestic violence: Which do we think would deal with it best, the nation or the state? The states indeed would be our intuitive response.

No. 5

One of the things we now must see, therefore, is that perhaps the causes of war are internalized and controlled in a union when a single national government prevails. And that was, as it turns out, the purpose of taking the ablest citizens from the various regions and concentrating them in one government, and also harmonizing and assimilating political diversity within the United States.

And the same causes of war are no less present in a confederation than among separate states, so that if the causes of war continue to operate internally, rather than just in terms of foreign powers or foreign enemies, then aggrandizing warfare will take place within the Union, no less than outside of the Union. This then, puts the whole question of domestic violence on a different plane it seems to me. Let me re-state what I am saying: If we find in human nature certain tendencies that lead foreign states to war, those aspects of human nature are no less present in human beings in separate states, within a confederation, than they are among separate and independent states.

So we can take Britain and the United States as the late-eighteenth century example, and say that if there are tensions, whether from commerce or otherwise between those two states that would lead to war, then those same tensions, insofar as they express human nature, ought to be present as between, let us say, Pennsylvania and Virginia. Then when we speak of having a confederation of independent states, what we are talking about doing, according to the analysis in the fifth *Federalist Paper*, is internalizing the causes of war, and raising the question of domestic violence, no longer as a petty question, but as a question that is every bit as large as the ordinary questions of international conflict.

In the fifth essay, then, and at this point precisely, we see a focus on Queen Anne and the union of England and Scotland. That union resolved a problem which would ordinarily be called "war." It would be called war, purely and simply, not domestic violence. What distinguishes England and Scotland from the United States, however, is the fact that England and Scotland were, in fact, separate sovereignties. For Americans, according to Publius in the second essay again, the union came first, morally and politically. So that Publius places the United States acting as one, at least from 1776 on, above the arguments some make, as we see in the Antifederalist, that the states were prior to the Union, that the states were first independent and separate. They did not enjoy, according to Publius, a proper political organization, but the people of the United States always intended to be Americans, they always intended to be one people. So, when their form of political organization exposes them to the prospect or danger of war between the states, then it becomes a family problem, a domestic problem, although operating on the scale of international conflict.

No. 5

So the language of domestic violence is a way of transforming the moral and political language of the relationships among the Americans. It is to say that we cannot admit, even from the beginning, the prospect that these are going to be separate peoples. This question of domestic violence to Publius is mainly a question of poor political organization, and the constitution is the way of addressing the question of poor political organization. Let me quote from the essay, starting at the fourth paragraph:

Should the people of America divide themselves into three or four nations, would not the same thing happen? Would not similar jealousies arise; and be in like manner cherished? . . . Hence, like most other *bordering* nations, they would always be either involved in disputes and war, or live in the constant apprehension of them.

Now we can see that the reason for this constant fear of war is only partially those aspects of human nature which he had previously identified as the causes of war. There are also matters of interest which conspire to produce warfare. He goes on in the seventh paragraph to describe some of these matters of interest:

> The North is generally the region of strength, and many local circumstances render it probable that the most Northern of the proposed confederacies would, at a period not very distant, be unquestionably more formidable than any of the others. No sooner would this become evident than the *Northern Hive* would excite the same Ideas and sensations in the more Southern parts of America, which it formerly did in the Southern parts of Europe.

There will be differences from region to region, differences in strength, and differences in interest, and we will end up mediating these differences ordinarily through warfare, unless we come up with a superior form of political organization to avoid that. In the next to last paragraph of this essay, he has the following clause or expression: "neighbouring nations, acting under the impulse of opposite interests and unfriendly passions, would frequently be found taking different sides." That seems to be the lesson that we learn from history as well as from human nature.

Take all these passages together and what do they describe, if not the disintegration of the union, the existence of pressures leading to disintegration in the union? Publius argues, in effect, that disintegration would be the necessary consequence of the existence of the union in the form of separate sovereignties or as a Confederation, and that this would come about inevitably. One of the reasons or causes for this is very clear, namely, rather than the people being assimilated, their differences will be heightened; their differences will be increased. Their living separately, however much friendly and allied defensively, will encourage heterogeneity, and as their differences increase, the causes and occasions of war increase.

We might want to place this whole conversation, at this point, in the language that is familiar to us in our time, and that is usually the language of pluralism or multi-culturalism. What Publius is saying is that any attempt to build a common life on the strength of differences rather than on the strength of similarities, in fact, will fall prey ultimately to warfare, that there is no middle ground on which we can preserve differences and still at the same time expect peace to prevail, in the long run. So Publius has taken on the project of eliminating differences through the power of a central government which is capable of assimilating, homogenizing the diverse interests and regions of the United States.

Union then is proposed with the firm intention to eliminate the strongest regional differences among Americans. It is a conscious effort to construct a nation, which will operate to shape citizens in a certain direction in terms of their habits, opinions, and characters, and above all, to ensure that, at least in North America, there will be no occasion for war. Taking seriously this desire to avoid war (and I take it very seriously by the way) leads to two interesting aspects: first, one avoids war with foreign powers, and secondly, one avoids war from state to state. This, as I said, becomes the problem of domestic violence, because the only remedy for war from state to state is to get rid of the distinction among the states. What that confirms then is that the supposed homogeneity that we read in the second essay was mythical or illusory. While the people spoke mainly the same language, and they had practically the same religion, to quote the second essay, they were not the same politically.

And so what is decisive in human affairs, according to Publius, is the political distinction, the political identity. That is what makes the real difference in human life. That settles the question, as I may put it, of what is "near and dear." That distinction is what lies at the root of warfare. It follows accordingly that one lessens the chance of war by setting things up so that people will all call the same things "near and dear." This means, of course, several important things. At a minimum it means this: When people seek to resolve their most important questions they will all expect the authoritative answer to come from the same source. They will all pray, so to speak, to the same Solomon.

Now, I am making the argument at this stage no more strongly than is required in order to demonstrate the constitutionalism of the *Federalist Papers*. That's a caution that I follow because of knowing that Publius makes no attempt whatever to try to envision a human landscape from which all war has been eliminated. He wants to talk about controlling war within the precise political environment of the United States as a means of constructing a political identity for these people who are to be called the Americans.

No. 6

In the sixth essay we will find that he even speaks explicitly against utopian speculation, and he tells us why. He says men are ambitious, vindictive, and rapacious. And why are they ambitious, vindictive, and rapacious? Precisely because they do have things that are near and dear to them, and they differ. And so one always reacts to those things which are not one's own more under the influence of those passions of ambition, vindictiveness, or rapaciousness than with respect to what is one's own. That's the way human beings are, according to Publius, and what we then are trying to do is to insulate this characteristic in human beings by teaching some set of human beings to hold the same things "near and dear."

We should also take note that the statement about human character in the sixth essay does not add the familiar language, "by nature." It is not required, apparently, to conclude that human nature is evil in order to see that certain evil is attached to human nature. And I must underline that, because so often it is taught that the Federalists thought human nature was evil, and therefore they constructed a constitution that would hem in the evil inclinations and temptations of human beings. This very negative portrait of constitutionalism makes it appear that the whole purpose of the constitution is to prevent human beings from doing all the evil they can to one another.

What we see in these first essays is exactly the opposite picture: It is admitted that evil is possible; it is admitted that government is necessary; it is admitted that people do violence; it is admitted that there are causes of war rooted in human nature; but there is still the positive endeavor, which is the real driving force of this founding effort, and that is the endeavor to build a nation of one people who call the same things near and dear. This is what Publius aims to do. It is not therefore a mere mechanical, negative, checking relationship that Publius wanted to establish.

Let's look at the third paragraph in the sixth essay again, in which he goes through the causes of hostilities:

> The causes of hostility among nations are innumerable. There are some which have a general and almost constant operation upon the collective bodies of society: Of this description are the love of power or the desire of pre-eminence and dominion—the jealousy of power, or the desire of equality and safety. There are others which have a more circumscribed, though an equally operative influence, within their spheres: Such are the rivalships and competitions of commerce between commercial nations. And there are others, not less numerous than either of the former, which take their origin intirely [sic] in private passions; in the attachments, enmities, interests, hopes, and fears of leading individuals in the communities of which they are members.

These separate categories that Publius has listed all relate to one another, but I would say the most important thing about them, on the surface, is that they are distinct, they are separate. The love of power, to take one example, is different than private passions. The rivalships and competitions of commerce are also different from private passions. So he has a list of things, each of which may be taken separately. In a manner of speaking, these factors may not be passions at all, they may be perfectly rational. If by passions, we mean what is not rational, then we cannot call all these things "passions." That would mean that the causes of war, therefore, are not necessarily irrational.

To imagine that wars come about only because of failures of reason is probably one of the greatest mistakes people make in the world. Some wars are thoroughly rational. Above all, in a case where people place themselves in a situation to invite war, and we must remember now what he said in essays three and four about foreign war; he said, "the nation must place itself in such a situation that it will not invite war." What it will do is invite friendly intercourse, not war. That's why prosperity is a precondition to peace among many of the other things set forth.

On the other hand, sometimes a people put themselves in such a position that they do invite war; it becomes in the interest of others to wage war against them. And in those cases, war is perfectly rational. Now we can state this another way. We can say that it may be irrational not to assail a people, speaking now from the perspective of a foreign state, who are ripe for plucking, when doing so would be of benefit to the assailant. And so what Publius is doing is trying to avoid war within and without, but being open-eyed about war, not by being rosy-eyed about it.

Having said that, and then having distinguished the private passions from other conceivable causes of war—we must note that the private passions are not less interesting because they are arational. At the very outset, we've noted the significance of this because they bear upon the question of public opinion. And, as we know, the preceding discussion turned almost entirely on the question of public opinion.

No. 6

Publius provides, in the seventh paragraph of the sixth essay, a particular statement of the problem. Having discussed the general causes and examples of wars, he now focuses on the United States. And then he remarks that great national events sometimes are produced by petty personal matters, and he describes Daniel Shays of Massachusetts as a desperate debtor. Then he says that it is much to be doubted whether there had been a rebellion had he not been a desperate debtor. Now this raises a straightforward question of causality. Publius is wondering whether the civil war was caused by the fact that a desperate person was carried away, or rather by the fact that a person of enormous capacity for leadership was desperate. There are two ways to look at that single question. The earlier reference to leading individuals becomes very important in this.

No. 2

In the second essay we were going to depend upon leading individuals as one of the guarantees of peace. It is perhaps worth reflecting that Shays's Rebellion was more than just Captain Daniel Shays. He had large numbers, indeed, thousands of debtors and farmers who were involved with him in that exercise, but the argument of Publius suggests that what one requires is the kind of catalyst that a Shays can be in order to mature, to ripen events such as Shays's Rebellion. Accordingly, private passions must be taken into account no less than rational opportunities. If Shays with his talent is not made desperate, he does not organize thousands of debtors and farmers. Many of Publius's historical examples speak from this perspective. Look at the way he treats Pericles of ancient Athens and we can see this very clearly; he is very hard on poor Pericles.

The fundamental questions go much deeper than the Shays's example suggests. In the next two paragraphs is set up a measure of the distance between what Publius calls visionary or designing men, on the one hand, and the hardheaded realists of political life on the other hand. The hardheaded realists don't expect a material improvement in human political practices, while the visionary designing men are looking for a new age. This is the language he uses in the eighth paragraph:

The genius of republics (say they) is pacific; the spirit of commerce has a tendency to soften the manners of men and to extinguish those inflammable humours which have so often kindled into wars. Commercial republics, like ours, will never be disposed to waste themselves in ruinous contentions with each other. They will be governed by mutual interest, and will cultivate a spirit of mutual amity and concord.

That's a very lovely, indeed a visionary, portrait of what the future will bring under the modern dispensation.

Notice how close it is to what we described before when we said prosperity is a precondition for peace. But the question is: "Is it the same?" Well, Publius now rejects this. He says it's not enough to be a republic; it's not enough to practice commerce. In fact, he answers both questions when he wonders whether "it is not the true interest," says he, "of all nations, whether republics or not, to cultivate the same benevolent and philosophic spirit." Well, of course. Monarchies, despotisms, everyone would profit from benevolence and peacefulness, presumably. So the most important thing then is to note that republics are not unlike other nations when it comes to causes of war. Commerce may well soften manners, but it equally well provides new occasions for jealousies, new occasions for conflict, new occasions for competition. In short, Publius rejects the new and modern principles, the principles of the enlightenment, that somehow greater human understanding will eliminate causes for war.

So now we've separated Publius's notion of a peaceful future for the United States from the general enlightenment notion that mankind is evolving towards a stage of human civilization where war becomes unthinkable because everyone thinks. That is not Publius's argument. His arguments are particular to the political organization of the United States. Commerce may indeed soften manners because it does create greater communications among peoples. There can be no doubt about that. To that extent, it also harmonizes and assimilates people, one of the objectives of Publius. Different peoples may actually adapt certain practices from one another, socially and politically, and we get the result of a blending effect. Does the blending affect the true interest of nations? Publius says it does not. It remains the case that they are still likely to go to war with one another. Thus men cannot rely on commerce, which is the modern principle, to protect them.

The earlier statement that prosperity could avoid war did not mean that prosperity changes human nature. It meant rather that prosperity operates to provide additional tools of influence than men could otherwise rely upon. Thus, Publius seems wildly optimistic, but at the same time, he is also coldly sober about what the future is likely to bring.

Let's remember that this whole discussion came up in the process of trying to settle the problem of domestic violence. Looking at commerce, for example, but not thinking of transatlantic commerce for the moment, we get the following reflection: "If there is no union, commerce among the states can be an occasion for war. And instead of softening manners, it would raise the stakes. And the higher the stakes, the greater the likelihood of conflict as people deal with one another." But union is not going to eliminate commerce. Further it is not intuitive that union as opposed to confederation will be more likely to make commerce peaceful, however certain it is that either would be superior to thirteen separate sovereignties. So there's no change that can be presumed to affect the individuals who engage in commerce simply because that commerce is regulated by a national government instead of a confederation.

There is however, a difference in practice, or in habitude. The various states (New York, New Jersey, Connecticut, whatever one would like as examples) would experience the same necessities, however they were organized, under a union as under a confederation. But under the union, they would all turn to the same source for help when problems arise. In that sense they would call the same thing near and dear, by turning to a single Solomon. This is how the argument goes, they would be less likely to resort to war to resolve differences—differences that are no less stark among them than among human beings anywhere else. So the mere act of identifying, agreeing upon a single Solomon, would make them more peaceful with one another, more like brothers than enemies. That's the thrust of Publius's argument.

No. 85

And it seems to be an argument which is based on experience as much as on theory. Publius said we have to depend on experience; that's the least fallible guide of human opinions. But I emphasize *human* opinions in that construction of his. This is the distinction that reminds us of what he says in the eighty-fifth *Federalist Paper*, when he quotes David Hume and says we should rely upon experience.

Publius has added some new wrinkles in the course of developing these arguments. The newest perhaps is that the Republic in a democratic spirit is no longer pursued on merely theoretical grounds. It is not an abstract statement that motivates Publius. Publius is, as I said before, often called a pessimist about human nature and politics by modern commentators. And maybe that is the way to reflect the distinctive realism, the cold soberness

I called it, that we see in him. We see, for example, at the end of the sixth essay, the third paragraph from the end says: "Is it not time to awake from the deceitful dream of a golden age, and to adopt as a practical maxim for the direction of our political conduct, that we, as well as the other inhabitants of the globe, are as yet remote from the happy empire of perfect wisdom and perfect virtue?" But we must remember always to place those sobering reflections in the context of the inspiring and ambitious project sketched in the first essay when we see it as reserved for the people of this country to decide that very important question, whether societies of men are capable or not of choosing good government from reflection and choice.

There is a new politics and Publius is aware that there is a new politics. It will not produce perfect wisdom and virtue, but that's the very difficulty. For how can one defend creating a government, a powerful government, capable of harmonizing and assimilating diverse peoples and interests, while denying at the same time that it can make these people virtuous and wise? How can one justify doing such a thing? Is there any guarantee at all of a government's goodness, apart from this prospect, apart from its people being virtuous and wise? The answers to all these questions it seems to me are conditioned on a single premise, namely that one refers to the consequences of the government and not its operations. And the chief of those consequences is peace where war would otherwise prevail. That's how Publius begins to answer. He says, first, I will give us peace; then we will talk about how people will conduct themselves within that peace.

Now it's true, that governments that are energetic—powerful governments—affect the characters of the people they govern. That is a necessary condition of energetic government, a fact of which the Federalists are not unaware, and which Publius makes clear. Let's admit two facts then, namely, that people will not be made virtuous and wise, and further, the government will be propelled by public opinion, as we have already said. We have created an urgent difficulty, for if the people should rule, but are neither virtuous and wise, nor able to make themselves so, doesn't it follow that the people who rule will do so foolishly and viciously?

It may be called by Publius an idle theory or utopian speculation to contemplate removing human weaknesses, but our question is not whether theories which transform human beings into angels are correct. It is rather the question of why should one confide all authority in society into the hands of imperfect human beings, ignoring all the other claims to rule that have existed in human history. There have been claims based on age; claims based on strength; claims based on reason, on wisdom. Why reject all those to place the entire society into the hands of what may be the foolish and the vicious, according to Publius's own argument?

From this perspective, even the principle of descent in monarchical Britain may seem more intelligent. We do get from time to time an occasional stupid bastard born to a king. But most of the time we get fairly decent people who are well bred, which may be well worth relying upon, if we don't have any better guarantees about order and stability in society. So, then, we would have, on the basis of descent, hope for stability, hope for good government.

The alternative seems to be to submit to people whom one admits are not going to be improved by the government that is being constructed. We would think they should not govern well. Publius does not answer this question. This is what he reserves for later essays when he discusses the operations of government. But as we see, he has built up an enormous test for himself to meet; he has to show to us that while the government will not itself make people virtuous and wise, it is nevertheless wise and virtuous to construct such a government. We can see that it is useful from the point of view of the ends aimed at: prosperity, peace, general stability, brotherhood we may say. But it is an entirely different question how those ends are to be accomplished, and whether there is anything within human reason to expect us to accomplish them.

No. 8

The eighth essay allows Publius to present his hypothetical case of a disunited United States, in order to demonstrate the propriety of this action. Even if it's not the case that we know yet how it's going to work and how it's going to turn out, he has a significant discussion there in which he talks once again about the influence of modern principles. In the eighth paragraph he says: "The industrious habits of the people of the present day, absorbed in the pursuits of gain, and devoted to the improvements of agriculture and commerce are incompatible with the condition of a nation of soldiers. . . ." From his further remarks we see that he says we will not have the old fashioned virtue, which was based on the martial spirit in small republics of ancient times. This is the modern era.

That only adds to our question, then, how Publius is going to deal with this problem of making the people suitable for rule in this new and modern context where we have no guarantee that the people, in fact, will be wise and virtuous. That summarizes the introductory notion of Publius's constitutionalism. The final answer to the question of domestic violence, comes in essays nine and ten, to which we next turn. Realizing that this is the question that we are responding to, we want to know how turning power over to the people is to produce the prosperity and peace Publius has promised without changing human nature.

NOTES

1. Arguably, the original Bill of Rights, as ratified, did not prevent religious establishment. It did, however, prevent religious tests for office and therefore obstructed the accomplishment of religious establishment by means of political organization.

PART III: HESITATIONS

There's a danger of getting carried away with the fullest and clearest expression of the Federalists' enterprise because it seems so ambitious and seems to speak so much to the history that we have experienced, that we forget that there were people at the time who were dragging, who were holding back, and who had serious doubts about the wisdom of this enterprise.

If we turn, for example, to the essay by Z in the *Essential Antifederalist*, we see in a very brief format the expression of some of these hesitations, some of these doubts[1]. To point out something that is true of almost every Antifederalist, Z begins by admitting that there are problems. The very opening paragraph says, "It seems to be generally felt and acknowledged, that the affairs of this country are in a ruinous situation." Thus, opponents do not pretend that everything is hunkydory. They say, yes, we know there are problems; the question is, what's the solution? This establishes their good will at the outset. They do not try to create false images of the situation of the country. Having accepted that there are problems that need to be dealt with, they nevertheless ask questions and those questions go to the very heart of the matter that Z writes about.

Z's essay, by the way, was written before the Constitution was drafted. The Convention, as we know, was called for May 14, 1787; and there were not enough delegates present to open the meeting until the twenty-fifth of May. Z knew the Convention was meeting and he wrote and published his essay on the 16th of May. Nothing had happened yet, not even the Randolph Plan; still this shot was fired across the bow of the Convention, letting them know what they should think about.

In the third paragraph, Z observes:

How the great object of their meeting is to be attained is a question which deserves to be seriously considered. Some men, there is reason to believe, have indulged the idea of reforming the United States by means of some refined and complicated schemes of organizing a future Congress in a different form. These schemes, like many others with which we have been amused in times past, will be found to be merely visionary, and produce no lasting benefit.

If it's "refined and complicated" we should already be suspicious, right? So, he warns us against trusting political scientists over politicians.

Now Z speaks, of course, in a context. The Convention met in Philadelphia, and it was in Philadelphia that the first issue of the *American Magazine* appeared in February, 1787, sponsored by Benjamin Franklin, and his Society for Political Inquiry with contributions from people like Franklin, James Wilson, and Benjamin Rush, among others. There, in fact, were exactly these rather abstract essays being published as if by political scientists, prescribing a future course for the United States and principles of reorganization. So Z lets it be known that he reads these things and is troubled.

He observed: "the error is not in the form of Congress." We have a ruinous situation, but what is the cause of it? The error is not in the form of the Confederation Congress. It is not in "the mode of election." It is not in the duration of the appointment of the members. "The source of all our misfortunes is evidently in the want of power in Congress." This is the beginning of that argument which looms so importantly throughout the entire Antifederalist corpus, namely, all we need to do is to change a little bit the grant of power to Congress. And we see this in the Convention, of course, in the New Jersey Plan that is introduced in June right after the Randolph Plan was brought back to the full Convention, ready for approval. What does the New Jersey Plan do, except to say, "Let us keep the Confederation as it is, but let us build more power into the Confederation Congress. Let us make their taxes mandatory, rather than simple requests." And Z initiated that way of looking at things. To be convinced of this, he argued, we need only recollect the vigor, the energy, the unanimity of this country a few years past, even in the midst of a bloody war, when Congress governed the continent.

That's an extremely important argument. The United States went through eight years of war, against the greatest military power on the face of the earth at that time. True, in the middle of that war, we may not have thought we were doing so terribly well. Troops had trouble getting supplies, and they walked through the snow with bloody feet, starving and dying of diseases. But, in retrospect, we were able to say, we did quite well! And the Congress that governed brought us through to the end with victory. What more may we ask for? Surely we can't complain about having a little trouble along the way, for all great things take some sacrifice, don't they? So, Z makes an argument which, certainly on its surface, has credibility. It is not simply an incredible argument.

At the beginning of the next paragraph, after introducing the problems that do affect the country, particularly those having to do with trade, he says: "To remedy these evils, some have weakly imagined that it is necessary to annihilate the several States, and vest Congress with the absolute direction and government of the continent, as one single republic."

Now, there's the rub. There is the central argument. There is every Antifederalist's fear spelled out. Usually that fear is expressed in the term, "consolidation." But this is what consolidation means—replacing the states with a single Congress directing the entire continent, and purporting to do so under republican forms. But "This," says Z, "would be impracticable and mischievous. In so extensive a country many local and internal regulations would be required, which Congress could not possibly attend to, and to which the States individually are fully competent; but those things which alike concern all the States, such as our foreign trade and foreign transactions, Congress should be fully authorized to regulate." So Z charts a compromise course for the moment, to resolve the urgent problems in the late 1780's without for all that surrendering the principle of Confederation and local control.

These are the terms of American political life continuing to this day, as we well know. So when we read them we must bear in mind, this is not simply an historical reference. What we see is how American political discourse was originally shaped and has persisted until this very day.

The whole question of whether local concerns are genuinely local, or shall I say merely local, or whether they extend with greater reach, that is of course the whole question of the Constitutional Convention and the *Federalist Papers*. How are we to distinguish the local from the national or the confederation? For Z, it seems very unproblematic. But, even Z, speaking as emphatically as he does, is nevertheless willing to say in the next to the last paragraph, let's try this for a few years and if it doesn't work, then we can do something different. So we have an additional aspect of the Antifederalist posture: What's the rush? What's the hurry? Why settle our fate for hundreds of years, perhaps in a way that will be irrecoverable, when we are now free to experiment with forms of government as we will? Let's add a little power to the Congress; if it doesn't work, later we can add a little more. Let's tinker; but let's not raze the foundations and start all over.

What he referred to, of course, was the newly acquired power in the aftermath of the Revolution for building constitutions in the first place; and wanting to keep government, we might say, near to the hands of the people, constantly within their reach, always able to be re-expressed, to be re-asserted. When we read the forty-ninth *Federalist Paper*, we look very No. 49 closely at the argument made by Thomas Jefferson, to which Publius responds. This is an argument that, in providing for the Virginia State Constitution, called for regular returns to the people, roughly every nineteen years or so with new constitutional conventions, to reappraise the Constitution, whether they wanted to keep it, whether they wanted to change it.

Thomas Jefferson had serious and frequently expressed hesitations about the ambition to make permanent constitutions. He suggested that there was something not quite right about one generation wanting so to establish its authority that subsequent generations would not be in a position easily to rescue themselves from the dead hand of the past. So he said, this is problematic, how can we do this? How can we make debts that aren't paid off in our own lifetime, that we impose on our own children? How could we do such a thing, Jefferson asked? As we see, this still speaks resonatingly to us.

But perhaps we do not see that a constitution is also a debt, as James Madison writing back to him responded. Jefferson had said the "earth belongs to the living," but that means of course that those who die can't leave behind their ownership, they can't continue to own it after they've gone; they must allow the next generation to do with it as they will. But Madison said, well, constitutions are debts in a way themselves, and not necessarily negative debts. Can we throw off the accumulated accomplishments of the past generation lightly? Can we keep the openness that Z wants to constant constitutional experimentation? Is it safe? is it sound? is it prudent to encourage people again and again to return to the fundamentals, to bring them up for full discussion and review?

No. 1

We noticed at the outset of the first *Federalist* essay that this important question has been reserved to the people of this country, to decide whether societies of men are capable or not of choosing good government. But is that a decision that is made once and for all? If we decide that societies of men are capable of choosing good government from reflection and choice, should that not suggest that they are always capable of it and even capable of doing it frequently? Or is there something unusual about constitution making, something that rather suggests once we've proven that it can be done, that we don't want to take the chance of doing it again? We will return to that whole discussion in the forty-ninth essay and with considerable emphasis on Publius's response to Jefferson.

But here, in the *Antifederalist*, it speaks to an attitude, the attitude that surfaced for example when Antifederalists said, well, this constitution isn't quite perfect so let's call another convention. We don't have to ratify this right away; let's propose some amendments to the draft constitution and hold a new convention, and let's keep doing that until we get it right. And the Federalists resisted this powerfully. They said, no, we can't do this; this is difficult, it's arduous; we run the risk of a new constitution; we will never get agreement; we will lose this opportunity to have a constitution at all.

The Federalists seem to take the position that what was taking place here was extraordinary—it was rare. Even in the circumstances, they seemed to understand that it was rare. The commentators of the era spoke about it that way. We didn't just learn from Lord Bryce and others who wrote about it later in the nineteenth and twentieth centuries and who would make such comments as, "the most wonderful work ever struck off by the brain of man."[2] Those kinds of comments that were made later didn't originate only in retrospect. People were saying such things in 1787 and 1788. People in Europe, like Lafayette, for example, were amazed at how all the wheels of government are brought to a halt in the society, while the people turn their eyes on their institutions and on themselves, and peacefully undertake to reshape their institutions, without it costing anyone a single drop of blood. They looked at that, and they said this is just simply imponderable, incredible, how could it occur? But it did. And the Federalists seem to have had that attitude from the beginning.

The Antifederalists did not think it a big deal. They said, of course we can revise our constitutions. What are constitutions for but for the people who make them to remake them as it seems fit to them? Doesn't the Declaration of Independence affirm that, indeed, all governments depend on the consent of the governed and that whenever, in the eyes of the governed, these governments, these institutions no longer seem to serve the purposes of their happiness, they have a right to alter or abolish them? Well, what is a right to alter or abolish, if it's too dangerous to make use of? So the Antifederalists posture is to say, no, there's no danger. We not only trust the people under the government that we have, we trust them implicitly even without government. That is the Antifederalists' posture.

In the recent past, people have called for constitutional conventions; and there's been nothing more common in this society than the expression of fear that they may get one. Everyone we hear, from political scientists to journalists, schoolteachers, all of us, everybody says, for heaven's sake, no! I've never seen anything quite like this. In this great republican society that we all celebrate, none of us seem to want to have a constitutional convention. We think it's an extraordinarily dangerous thing.

Now I must say that my own view on that matter has matured considerably. I'm less frightened about it than I used to be because I have reflected that if we called one, the prospects of our producing anything through that convention that could be agreed upon by Americans throughout all these States is next to impossible, and therefore it doesn't trouble me to have a convention. But, even that reflection is a far cry from this faith, this original faith. So let's look at the Antifederalists with this in mind, that if the new system is, as Z put it, too refined and complex, or as John Lansing observed, "too novel and complex," then what should the response be?[3]

Colonel Mason responded to Mr. Lansing in this debate at the Constitutional Convention, and in the process responds to Z, as well. Colonel Mason's contribution here is very important, because Colonel Mason early in the Convention supported the changes that were being developed in the Convention. It is only at the end of the Convention that his support disappeared, and he became an opponent. Thus, we have first remarks from when he was a supporter of what was going on, the Randolph Plan, for example, and then later remarks when he must oppose it. And they allow us to measure exactly what it is that is the cause of difficulty, at least for thoughtful Antifederalists, like Colonel Mason. He has this to say: "Is it to be thought that the people of America, so watchful over their interests, so jealous of their liberties, will give up their all, will surrender both the sword and the purse, to the same body, and that too not chosen immediately by themselves?"[4]

This is his argument against leaving Congress as a unicameral house, having greater powers. He says that we have notions of republicanism that are incompatible with this idea, so that even if we want a confederation we could not have a strong Confederation Congress that doesn't have bi-cameralism, that doesn't have checks and balances, that doesn't have separation of powers; so within the heart of the Antifederalist argument we already see creeping in some of the reservations that ultimately led the new constitution away from the Confederation.

When we look at the New Jersey Plan in the Convention we see the same thing happening. They strengthen the Confederation and they provide for calling out the militia to enforce requisitions on the States. And calling out the militia means, in effect, going to war in order to collect. As a way of avoiding that requirement we have bicameralism, checks and balances, the origination of money bills restricted to the popular house, etc. All of which are meant to be protections against excessive power in this single body, the Congress. Col. Mason went on to answer some of these concerns. In this case the people do not part with power, they only transfer it from one set of immediate representatives to another set. That is, the delegates in Congress are representatives, not directly of the people, but of the people's representatives in the states.

Col. Mason continued:

Much has been said of the unsettled state of the mind of the people. He believed the mind of the people of America, as elsewhere, was unsettled as to some points, but settled as to others. In two points he was sure it was well settled: first, in an attachment to republican government, and second, in an attachment to more than one branch in the legislature.[5]

This is Mason's statement of what he called the genius of the people. And we notice that if this is truly the genius of the people, it means certain things about how this Government will be constructed. In the first place, if the people must have republicanism and bicameralism, they will not be satisfied by the existing Confederation.

When we read Mason's "Objections to the Constitution of Government formed by the Convention," we see that he has found the genius of the people still to inform his reaction to the Constitution, in much the same way it informed his support of it earlier[6]. But he's found that the new Constitution, even with its bicameralism, has not given due heed to the people's attachment to republicanism. We get similar reflections from other Antifederalists, including Yates and Luther Martin in the pages following, but these concerns are stated still more emphatically and more generally.

Consider an essay by A Georgian[7]. The importance of the Georgian essay can be stated in three words, "Declaration of Independence." In sum, the Georgian essay says simply, let us not accept any Government that isn't founded on and compatible with the Declaration of Independence. Well the Georgian seems to me then to elaborate what George Mason calls "the genius of the people." Again, like Z, he admits to problems that require to be resolved. But these problems should not expose us to building excessive power in a national government. And particularly a power that might be construed as what he called an "aristocratic government." And what the Georgian sees happening is the evolution of distinctions between those who govern and those who are governed. In proportion as we build a powerful union, a powerful national government, we give the advantage to those aristocratic forces and effectively build distinctions between citizens and rulers that are incompatible with the republican genius.

This is the argument which animates the spirit of Winthrop of Massachusetts who wrote the Agrippa essays that followed the Georgian's.[8] They are important because they go to the heart of Publius's early claim that what we are trying to do is to harmonize and assimilate the diverse interests of the people of the United States.

Before we look particularly at Agrippa's argument, let us be clear that what we have brought out of Publius's first essay thus far is brought out through analysis and interpretation. I've shown, for example, in the second essay the claim of homogeneity and how, by the sixth through eighth essays it's replaced by a portrait of heterogeneity. We can discern in relating these claims, and the arguments made for them, that Publius wants an active government, an energetic government, actively harmonizing the people. Those are clear, and yet one must also confess that it is not so palpable, not so explicit on the surface of the text of the *Federalist Papers* at this point, that we could expect Publius in effect to challenge Agrippa with a direct contradiction of Agrippa's arguments in these terms. In that sense Agrippa's argument is even more emphatic, and we should pay attention to it.

Agrippa asserts: "Experience has since shown, that, instead of trying to lessen an evil by altering the present course of things, every endeavor should have been applied to facilitate the course of law, and thus to encourage a mutual confidence among the citizens, which increases the resources of them all." Why do we want to do that? "Pennsylvania, with one port and a large territory, is less favorably situated for trade than Massachusetts, which has an extensive coast in proportion to its limits of jurisdiction. Accordingly a much larger proportion of our people are engaged in maritime affairs. We ought therefore to be particularly attentive

Nos.
2, 6–8

to securing so great an interest." He goes on and on. What is he saying? He's saying that we differ. We have differing interests, and we have to govern ourselves with an eye to those different interests. We cannot take it to be the case that one government can serve all those interests well; therefore we must construct only such a government as leaves to each interest the independent right to defend itself. "The perfection of government depends on the equality of its operation, as far as human affairs will admit, upon all parts of the empire, and upon all the citizens. Some inequalities indeed will necessarily take place. One man will be obliged to travel a few miles further than another man to procure justice. But when he has travelled, the poor man ought to have the same measure of justice as the rich one. Small inequalities may be easily compensated. There ought, however, to be no inequality in the law itself, and the government ought to have the same authority in one place as in another."[9]

What does that then produce by way of conclusion? He directly says, "Be careful then to give only a limited revenue and the limited power of managing foreign concerns. Once surrender the rights of internal legislation and taxation, and instead of being respected abroad, foreigners will laugh at us, and posterity will lament our folly." What is he complaining about? He's complaining about the power to harmonize and assimilate the differing interests. What he means by local internal legislation and taxation is the organization of power along the lines of distinction, character, culture, etc. So that power should indeed track the lines of distinction throughout the society as a whole, in much the way rivers cut their paths through mountains and forests. Any other arrangement would be unworkable in Agrippa's eyes. He continues: "to attempt to reduce all to one standard is absurd in itself, and cannot be done but upon the principle of power." And by principle of power he means force; only force can reduce all to a single standard.[10]

What is the "all" he's talking about that can have a common standard only by force? He makes it quite clear. What is the object of government? "To render the people happy, by securing their persons and possessions from wrong." That's unexceptionable. "To this end, it is necessary there should be local laws and institutions." Why? because people inhabiting various climates will unavoidably have local habits and different modes of life and these must be consulted.

He goes on to describe these local habits and different modes of life in particular. He says, "The idle and dissolute inhabitants of the south require a different regimen from the sober and active people of the north. Hence, among other reasons, is derived the necessity of local governments, who may enact, repeal, or alter regulations as circumstances of each part of the empire may require." As you see, Agrippa's sense of the difference is extraordinary. It's not a difference that's going to be effaced by the operations of government because even climate imposes those differences;

unless people no longer live in either the South or the North they cannot all be the same. What is this powerful government that's going to harmonize and assimilate us to solve the problem of the impact of climate? Agrippa says it's impossible without a resort to force; they have to become in fact despotic in order to achieve that harmony.

Agrippa doesn't leave it as merely a question of climate. Agrippa looks at the United States as an extremely diverse society culturally, in terms of religious differences, and educational principles, and thinks, therefore, that there is no way for the United States to be governed by a single law that is equal law. The only way to have equal laws throughout the entire continent so to speak, is to allow each to make laws for themselves in their respective locales.

Agrippa's argument is the strongest Antifederalist argument for the principle of heterogeneity. The principle of Confederation or states' rights is the principle of heterogeneity. The argument for states' rights is the argument against the active power of a central state harmonizing and assimilating the people of the United States. The foundation of the argument is as much what Mason calls the genius of the people , what Z calls the love of liberty, or what the Georgian calls the principles of the Declaration of Independence. Their understanding of these principles is that they require to be defended in precisely this manner, if indeed liberty is to prevail.

Agrippa gives the concise expression of this:

In a republic, we ought to guard, as much as possible, against the predominance of any particular interest. It is the object of government to protect them all. When commerce is left to take its own course, the advantages of every class will be nearly equal. But when exclusive privileges are given to any class, it will operate to the weakening of some other class connected with them.[11]

So the Antifederalists defend what we can call loosely here "free enterprise," and they are reading Adam Smith's *Wealth of Nations,* which appeared in 1776, but are not necessarily doctrinaire in replicating its terms. Nevertheless they defend "free enterprise" as part and parcel of the defense of distinct and local interests.

The assumption is that power should follow defining characteristics. That's a principle which is not easy to apply in the contemporary context, but it is one I would invite us to think about if we want to organize power along the lines of identifiable characteristics or defining interests. It certainly creates an entirely different principle of organization than that enunciated in the *Federalist Papers.* Let's just take the most obvious distinction at this point from the sixth *Federalist Paper.*

No. 6

Power assigned in accord with definable characteristics accentuates what the *Federalist* has identified as one of the most serious causes of conflict. The differences of interests, they say, will inevitably lead to war to the extent that the interests have independent power to defend themselves. In proportion as they can exist independently, to the same degree will they defend themselves against all comers. And that will inevitably lead to hostility, to conflict, in the argument of the *Federalist*.

The Antifederalists do not think that is the case. They think that rather than leading to war the differences of interests lead to people's abilities to defend themselves, to protect themselves. We may say these are just opposite sides of a single coin. Why do we have to protect ourselves if we are not going to go to war? That's a reasonable question to ask, but I think the Antifederalists would respond to us, "why shouldn't you defend yourself if you are going to go to war?" Are these not in fact aspects of human nature? Do we fully intend to try to repeal laws of human nature? and is anyone so foolish as to think we can succeed? So that their response to the Federalists is not to say that the Federalists misread human nature but to say that the Federalists are imprudent in responding to it. That is, the prudent individual always responds first on the side of safety.

I offer the example of Centinel: "I would ask how is the proposed government to shower down those treasures upon every class of citizens as is so industriously inculcated and so fondly believed?" These treasures, I believe, are summed up in the language of political prosperity which I have already explained. He continues to ask how this is done:

Is it by the addition of numerous and expensive establishments? Is it by doubling our judiciaries, instituting federal courts in every county of every state? Is it by a superb presidential court? Is it by a large standing army? In short, is it by putting it in the power of the future government to levy money at pleasure, and placing this government so independent of the people as to enable the administration to gratify every corrupt passion of the mind, to riot on your spoils, without check or control?[12]

Obviously Centinel spoke in the context of specific institutions. This is much beyond the mere general argument made on behalf of political prosperity at the outset of Publius's argument. As I said, though, we would not have finished Publius's argument until we have figured out how in fact power can be accorded to the people to assure their prosperity without that power being subject to abuse.

Agrippa does not think it's possible after reviewing the proposal. The office of the president looks to be a grand office of state. There is provision for a standing army. He saw threats to liberty in the general power of taxation through the whole society and no way in which we can in fact account for these promises of prosperity apart from the supposed new government offices.

And by the way it seems to me there is something to this argument. If we have state government still under the new constitution and they purportedly have all the offices they have already, it is the case that a new and stronger federal government simply adds more offices on top of the offices that existed. And so that gives a reasonable pretext for asking the question, how necessary are these offices. Can't we do this job? Is this what they mean by political prosperity, that they invent new jobs for people all over the place and therefore tax us to pay them, and they therefore become rich at our expense? That's essentially what Agrippa means at this point of the argument.

The balance of the Antifederalist critique is seen through a number of sources, especially the Federal Farmer (whom we generally take to be Richard Henry Lee). He goes much more directly to the point at issue. Agrippa tends to have far more polemical ability, but the Federal Farmer provides a more refined analyst of these questions and raises the question of how we can control this government. Like Brutus he's concerned with the question of representation. Whether it will be equal. Agrippa argues that the laws must be equal. How will we guarantee the equality of laws? Well we can't create some Heavenly court to pass on them all, which can be free of interests. And Brutus, the Federal Farmer, Cato and others take the position of saying, there is no way to be sure of it, except to have adequate representation. Adequate representation will assure the equality of the laws. But we can't have adequate representation in a large republic, and therefore we now are faced with the thing that Agrippa himself asserts, namely, a small aristocratic representation. This, in fact, makes impossible all expectation of equal laws.

The Federal Farmer says, "But it is asked how shall we remedy the evil, so as to complete and perpetuate the temple of equal laws and equal liberty? Perhaps we never can do it. Possibly we never may be able to do it in this immense country under any one system of laws however modified; nevertheless, at present, I think the experiment worth a making."[13] And the experiment, of course, will then be confederation, strengthening of the Confederacy.

As with Z, we still have an open mindedness in the Federal Farmer. The Federal Farmer makes the case that we have these twin evils; one, we have to do something to correct our ruinous situation in the country, but, two, we must do so in a way that doesn't threaten liberty. We mustn't so build power as to build it at the expense of liberty. He doesn't know that we can find a solution to this question. He doesn't know that this notion of founding per se accommodates a prospect for republican safety in founding. His challenge to Publius is to prove it, prove that the experiment is worth the making, prove in this extensive country that we can have equal laws and liberty at the same time. And the response to that central Antifederalist challenge to the Federalist is primarily what we'll be concerned with, particularly in looking at the improved science of politics that Publius offers and which we look at next.

NOTES

1. Z (Philadelphia) Freeman's Journal 16 May 1787 in Allen and Lloyd, *Essential Antifederalist,* 4–6.

2. James Bryce, *American Commonwealth,* New ed. (New York: Macmillan, 1910).

3. John Lansing, George Mason and Luther Martin (from Madison's records of the Federal Convention) 20 June 1787 in Allen and Lloyd, *Essential Antifederalist,* 8.

4. Lansing, et al., in Allen and Lloyd, *Essential Antifederalist,* 9.

5. Lansing, et al., in Allen and Lloyd, *Essential Antifederalist,* 9.

6. George Mason, "Objections to the Constitution of Government formed by the Convention," 1787, in Allen and Lloyd, *Essential Antifederalist,* 11–13.

7. A Georgian, excerpts, in Allen and Lloyd, *Essential Antifederalist,* 226–28.

8. Agrippa, Essays VII, IX, XII, XIV (Boston) *Massachusetts Gazette* 18 and 28 December 1787, 11, 14, and 18 January 1788, in Allen and Lloyd, *Essential Antifederalist,* 282–42.

9. Agrippa, in Allen and Lloyd, *Essential Antifederalist,* 229.

10. Agrippa, in Allen and Lloyd, *Essential Antifederalist,* 232f.

11. Agrippa, in Allen and Lloyd, *Essential Antifederalist,* 240.

12. Centinel, Letters III, IV, VII, and VIII (Philadelphia) *Independent Gazette* 8 and 30 November, 27 and 29 December 1787 in Allen and Lloyd, *Essential Antifederalist,* 247.

13. Federal Farmer, Letters VII, VIII, IX (Poughkeepsie) *Country Journal,* 31 December 1787, 3 and 4 January 1788 in Allen and Lloyd, *Essential Antifederalist,* 268.

PART IV: NEW SCIENCE

Please notice the opening sentence of essay nine. I hope after all I've said it will no longer seem so strange as it ought otherwise to seem. "A firm Union will be of the utmost moment to the peace and liberty of the States as a barrier against domestic faction and insurrection." Now that we've talked about domestic violence and talked about the transition from warfare and foreign relations to domestic relations, suddenly the idea of a firm union as a barrier to domestic violence, to domestic faction and insurrection, is no longer unexpected even if it remains counter-intuitive.

No. 9

Characteristically in talking about domestic faction we turn to the tenth *Federalist Paper*. Everyone does it. We immediately go to the tenth *Federalist Paper* because we say that's the essay on faction. It takes a good deal of hard-headed attention and slowing ourselves down and insisting on looking at all the essays, even the ones we're not used to reading, to recognize that the tenth essay is not the first statement on the question of faction, far from the beginning, and that these all work together.

No. 10

This is a good point also for me to re-emphasize why I speak of Publius rather than Hamilton, Madison and Jay. Some people say there are three arguments: Hamilton's arguments, Madison's arguments, and Jay's arguments. But I say that if we look at the order of these papers and the relationships of these arguments, it's very clear that one argument exists here and that's why it's proper to call it Publius's argument. The ninth *Federalist Paper,* written by Hamilton, leads naturally to the tenth *Federalist Paper,* written by James Madison. The arguments in essays five through eight build naturally to the essay in number nine and lead to the necessity of the conclusion stated in number ten. They're not separate arguments. They are one argument with separate steps and, therefore, we might as well treat them as if they had all come from the mind of a single writer, Publius, the name that they chose.

Again, the opening sentence of number nine speaks of "a firm Union," not mere union. We can go back to the second essay and see the claim that public opinion is attached to union and to republicanism. But the intervening essays have elaborated the necessity that the Union be firm, mere confederation will not do. Further, we want to see the Union as conducing to the peace and liberty of the states, invoking the discussion of prosperity that we've had, as well as resisting domestic faction and insurrection.

It's still less clear why it should, in fact, discourage domestic faction and insurrection. Drawing a fence around a rebellious crowd does not necessarily make it less rebellious. And so far the Union only looks like a fence around potentially rebellious citizens. Notice what the conversation is like in the ninth essay at the outset. It is not particular to the United States, as it had been made in the end of the eighth essay. It is now the question of the petty republics of Greece and Italy. It's a general argument. It's a historical argument. What does the historical argument purport to teach us? It teaches us in fact that we must look for new solutions to age old problems. The age-old problem is that these republics—he didn't say monarchies or aristocracies, he said petty republics—of Greece and Italy are disgusting. They incite sensations of horror and disgust. They were continually agitated by distractions. They had a rapid succession of revolutions. They were kept in the state of perpetual vibration between the extremes of anarchy and tyranny.

These remarks are being said of republics. They are not by nature peaceful. They were not organized so as to avoid distraction, faction, and insurrection. So that the question of how we're going to avoid that in the United States becomes all the more urgent if republicanism in itself isn't sufficient to do it. What is it about a firm union that does so? The petty republics of Greece and Italy, as individual republics, were certainly firmly established. One cannot say that Athens for example, was not firmly established. Athens was so firmly established as an independent state that during the war with the Persians they were able to abandon the city altogether. That is what indeed Themistocles had them do. He put them on ships and took them out to sea. They left their homes, their buildings empty, to continue to resist the invading Persians; and they did so successfully. But the point of course, is that for Themistocles, the city existed in the minds of the Athenians, not in the buildings and the grounds. They left Athens, but in fact Athens went with them. Athens was wherever they were. They were united, firmly so. And this is how Publius describes even Athens, which had a succession of revolutions, constant distractions, movements back and forth between tyranny and anarchy.

No. 9

Publius concludes the first paragraph: "If momentary rays of glory break forth from the gloom, while they dazzle us with a transient and fleeting brilliancy, they at the same time admonish us to lament that the vices of government should pervert the direction and tarnish the luster of those bright talents and exalted endowments for which the favoured soils, that produced them, have so justly been celebrated." So, even when we're looking at the best that comes out of ancient Greek or Latin or Italian democracy, we still have to regret the fact that it has been produced in circumstances that are otherwise unworthy. This is an important argument because it again steers us to the human scale, the scale that we use at the opening of the *Federalist Papers*.

We may not judge what happens in the United States merely on the basis of what people wish or do not wish in 1787 in the context of the

United States. We're going to judge it on the human scale. We're going to judge it the way the Americans asked the world to judge them in the Declaration of Independence, when they appealed to a candid world and they announced their principles, meaning that they were willing to submit their principles to judgment and were confident that they would be found strong and justifiable. We're going to place the United States on the scale of world history; and the claim, of course, is to make it a success beyond that.

In the next paragraph we learn how we must judge that success. "From the disorders that disfigure the annals of those republics," he argues, "the advocates of despotism have drawn arguments, not only against the forms of republican government, but against the very principles of civil liberty." The historical scale, the human scale, says that republicanism is stupid, insane; that no one ought to try it; that liberty is a failure, because liberty always leads to license and to abuse. If we looked at this as, let us say, an eighteenth century SAT test, for example, the point might be of course, that the answer sheet doesn't leave room for a correct answer that marks republic or liberty. So on any important question, the answer sheet always shows those as wrong answers. That's what he's saying, that they have undertaken a project in the face of existing standards of judgment that condemn what they are about to do.

So naturally the defense that Publius offers in that one text has a double burden: "They have decried all free government, as inconsistent with the order of society, and have indulged themselves in malicious exultation over its friends and partizans." Some people at least know what it's like to be in a circumstance of needing to speak up on behalf of a principle, idea, or person whom everyone else looked upon with scorn. And that's what he's describing. Anyone who has been in that situation knows how hard it is to do. It's hard to speak against what generally accepted opinion calls for, and yet he's saying that the generally accepted opinion of the ages is incorrect. "Happily for mankind, stupendous fabrics reared on the basis of liberty, which have flourished for ages, have in a few glorious instances refuted their gloomy sophisms." Just enough, so that the friends of liberty may stand attached to it and use the example.

But what will they look like, these examples, that the friends of liberty must recur to? What will they learn from them? The third paragraph answers: "it is not to be denied that the portraits, they have sketched of republican government, were too just copies of the originals from which they were taken." So to begin with, not much. The critics are right. They criticize these republican governments, and the fact is they are right about them. **No. 9**

The eighth book in Thucydides' history of the Peloponnesian war discusses the constitutional changes in Athens that came about when Alcibiades was exiled and then returned after Athens is threatened with defeat, and finally exiled again[1]. The people of Athens finally established a constitution there in which they set up a smaller group of people in charge of the government. This government was mixed; some of the well-to-do, some of the not well-to-do, and some of the merely free born mixed in the constitution, rather than having just the assembly with everyone or just the wealthy alone to govern. And Thucydides said that this was the first time in his knowledge that Athens had ever been well governed, which is an extraordinary statement at that point in the war, long after Pericles had since died and long after Themistocles, and so long after all the other great Athenian legislators and statesmen—"the first time it had been well governed."[2] And of course we also know that shortly after that, that government passed out of existence. This is what Publius means when he says that there are fleeting moments when hope breaks through the gloom.

Ordinarily, these governments have been miserable and the critics are right in attacking them. "If it had been found impracticable, to have devised models of a more perfect structure"—We should weigh every word here: "impracticable." If we had not been able to do this—what?—"to have devised models of a more perfect structure"—more perfect than what? More perfect than anything history has shown us. If it had been impracticable to do so, "the enlightened friends to liberty would have been obliged to abandon the cause of that species of government as indefensible."

So now we begin the positive construction. We say, if it were impossible, we wouldn't be doing this. If it were impracticable, we wouldn't be doing this. But happily, the enlightened friends to liberty did not find it impossible. Why not? Because "the science of politics, however, like most other sciences has received great improvement." There is an improved science of politics. It's an improved science which, like the other sciences, has benefitted from enlightenment. "The efficacy of various principles is now well understood," he says, "which were either not known at all, or imperfectly known to the ancients."

For us, this doesn't sound as striking as it ought to, because we have all been reared, educated, to put faith in progress. We think progress is the most natural thing in the world, and it just comes to human beings. All we have to do is to be born in order to become wiser than those who've lived before. That's what we think. We don't think that our fathers were half as wise as we are, and we're certain that our great-great-grandfathers were abysmally ignorant compared to all that we know and are exposed to.

That's certainly the idea of progress that has colored the world in which we live and grow and in which technology has come to be the symbol of our greater power and understanding. But that wasn't the world of the eighteenth century. While it's true that basic philosophical notions of progress were being laid at that point, in general the world still lived in the eighteenth century on the basis of the principle that the best things, the wisest things, were the old things. That's how humanity had always lived.

We talk about golden ages—the golden age is always in the dim and distant past. Why is it that demi-gods always lived long ago? That's always the way human beings have looked at things. The modern world has reversed that, turned the world upside down. We think we are wiser.

I do not believe that Publius is merely doing what we have since done in the contemporary world. Our fairly-simple minded notions of progress are totally indefensible. Yes, of course, we can call it technological progress to move about in an automobile instead of a horse-drawn carriage, but whether that produces moral or political progress, well, it's quite clear that it does not necessarily do so. It's quite clear when we look at the totalitarianisms of the twentieth century, moreover, how backward politically and morally, the contemporary world can be, despite access to great technology. Therefore, we need to place this claim, not in the context of our expectation of general progress in the world, but rather in the context of the dependence on science that Publius is talking about, what he called the "efficacy of various principles."

A principle that is efficacious, that can work, that can produce the product we aim at is one thing; that we will use it for what it's good for is another. The progress Publius is talking about is that we now know that the principles can work. There's an open question, whether we will rely on those principles, whether we will have moral progress to go along with our scientific progress, that's an open question. But for the scientific progress, he says it's there.

There are new discoveries in politics that the ancients didn't know about. And what are they?—"the regular distribution of power into distinct **No. 9** departments." This is as close as we come at this early point to admitting how central are these notions of separation of powers, checks and balances, etc., to the first argument over constitutionalism in this work. Even though they are not going to be mentioned in the constitution itself, these are principles that work, which makes it all the more important to understand how they come to be there. The "institution of courts composed of judges, holding their offices during good behaviour—the representation of the people in the legislature by deputies of their own election—these are wholly new discoveries or have made their principal progress towards perfection in modern times." So that they are either new or newly improved. That's the argument. It's not exactly the same as new, improved Cheer, but it has some of that rhetoric attaching to it. These are means. They are "powerful means by which the excellencies of republican government may be retained and its imperfections lessened or avoided."

That's a powerful qualification, isn't it? What are they means to? They're not means to more efficient government in general. They are means to increasing "the excellencies of republican government." These modern discoveries and scientific principles don't apply to just any old government. They apply only to republican government. And that is not all.

He says, "To this catalog of circumstances that tend to the amelioration of popular systems of civil government, I shall venture, however novel it may appear to some, to add one more, on a principle which has been made the foundation of an objection to the new constitution."

Again, I'd like to emphasize the words. What were the things the Antifederalists criticized? They criticized refinement and complexity, novelty and complexity. What do we see first in the list of the improved science of politics, these new improvements. We see complexity, separation of powers in distinct departments, checks and balances, judges independent, holding their offices during good behavior. We see the system being made ever more complex and now we're told there's yet a new principle which they have specifically objected to, which is novel. I remind you of what happened in the second essay where Publius makes clear that he's conservative. He said "look, the American people have always been attached to Union and republicanism and we're defending that. We're not on the side of the radicals, we're on the side of the conservatives." And now suddenly in the ninth essay, with science in his hands, he becomes heretical. He defends something novel even though people object to it.

What that means of course is that Publius, while he has to persuade citizens to vote for the constitution and therefore has to employ rhetoric, is not going to employ mere rhetoric. He's willing to be candid also. He knows that novelty is always the weakest argument in politics. Historically, that's certainly the case. You understand why that's the case? I'll be very straight forward. In any existing political situation, change must always be change for the better or for the worse. That's what change means. And given the sense in which the existing situation is at all tolerable, generally speaking, fear of change for the worse will always prevail over the hope of change for the better. And so novelty is always a threat in any situation. When somebody proposes to do something differently, the reaction is going to be, wait a minute, we'll be worse off than we were. But Publius says, I'm going to propose a novelty to you. One that I know is objected to, one that I know inspires fear of being worse off. And I'm going to propose to you that what this novelty does is to solve a problem that otherwise cannot be solved and has not been solved in human history. That's the scope of the argument at this point.

And what is this novelty? "I mean the ENLARGEMENT of the ORBIT within which such systems are to revolve either in respect to the dimensions of a single State, or to the consolidation of several smaller States into one great Confederacy." Of course the latter is our subject of discussion. He's going to examine the principle itself. So we're going to enlarge the orbit of what? The orbit is not of the Union; firm Union says nothing about size. He makes it very clear that what he's talking about is the defense of republican government. The "enlightened friends" of liberty have defended and discovered these new means towards the excellences of republican government and now we're going to have republican government in an enlarged sphere. This is counter-intuitive.

Why is it counter-intuitive? In simplest terms, because we expect government by the people, of the people and for the people to depend on the people knowing one another. It's as simple as that. That's a perfectly reasonable expectation. Aristotle lays out the curves of that expectation in his *Politics*. It's clear that in order for people to take responsibility for their common life, each in proportionate measure, they ought to be able to have familiarity with one another. By definition, that means the size of the city has to be small because human beings can know only so many other human beings. There's a natural limit to the reach of our acquaintance. So, when he says we can have republican government and we can enlarge the sphere, he's challenging fundamental principles, fundamental expectations, on the grounds of a new improved science of politics.

What does he have to do then to make this argument stick? The first thing he has to do is to respond to the objections, because he said at the outset that we see people have objected to this form of proceeding. The objections are taken from Montesquieu. The opponents to the Constitution have cited Montesquieu's dictum that republics are only suitable for small territories; we cannot have large republics.

One might ask, who in the world is Montesquieu and why should we care? Well, Montesquieu was an eighteenth century philosopher in France who wrote the book, *The Spirit of the Laws*. In *The Spirit of the Laws*, Montesquieu developed several principles, not the least important of which were the principles of the separation of authorities, and checks and balances. So we already see that he stands at a critical point in relationship to this improved science of politics that we're depending upon to build the new republic. One way to put the argument is this way: part of the reason we have an improved science of politics is because of philosophers like Montesquieu.

Naturally then this leads to the question, if we're going to depend on these philosophers to change our constitution oughtn't we to follow everything that they say? And if they tell us we can't have a republic in a large territory, aren't we then acting inconsistently with what they teach? We find this in the Antifederalists. The Antifederalists quote Montesquieu constantly throughout. Agrippa even plagiarizes from him without citing him. They rely on him implicitly and his argument that republics are good for small territories; monarchies are good for moderately sized states; despotisms are required for large states. It's an absolute rule. At the beginning of his *Spirit of the Laws* he gives a typology of various regimes in which it becomes very clear that, in fact, there are these three, and only these three, and this is the way they must be organized. So, Publius has the problem of trying to show that there's no objection to what he wants to do with Montesquieu. He can't reject Montesquieu's authority because that would mean rejecting the improved science of politics.

So we have the authority; how do we deal with the dictum? Well, we see that Publius's argument quotes from Montesquieu at length. He says that so far as Montesquieu's suggestions oppose a general union of the states, in fact, they oppose even the republics in some of the existing states. That is, what he called a large republic wasn't simply something the size of the thirteen states taken together. Almost any one of the states, leaving aside Rhode Island perhaps, was already too large for what Montesquieu had called a republic in *The Spirit of the Laws.* So there's the first argument, a good debater's point, we might say, though it certainly doesn't dispose of the objection to the constitution, which means Publius has to go beyond that.

He does this by proffering from Montesquieu the reason for Montesquieu's defense of the confederal republic, and secondly, reassessing what he means by the confederal republic. In the eighth and ninth paragraphs of this ninth essay we have the quotations that extend through the thirteenth paragraph. The critical one comes in the ninth paragraph: "This form of government is a convention by which several smaller *States* agree to become members of a larger *one*. It is a kind of assemblage of societies that constitute a new one, capable of encreasing by means of new associations, till they arrive to such a degree of power as to be able to provide for the security of the united body."

What we see in that passage, according to Publius, is something that the critics of the Constitution neglect in Montesquieu. He said earlier that the critics in fact had cited one part of Montesquieu while ignoring another part. At the fourth paragraph he says: "The opponents of the PLAN proposed have with great assiduity cited and circulated the observations of Montesquieu on the necessity of a contracted territory for a republican government. But they seem not to have been apprised of the sentiments of that great man expressed in another part of his work." There are two sentiments in that other part of the work that Publius is concerned with.

The first has to do with this definition of the confederal republic. How did Montesquieu get to that idea? Very simply this: He pointed out that a small republic could not defend itself and therefore would not survive. This is in his ninth book of *The Spirit of the Laws.* He says, there are small republics and they're all very nice and they're based on virtue but the problem is, they can't defend themselves. So how do we deal with that problem? Take several of them into a confederal republic. Then they will have the internal strength of a republic and the external force of a monarchy, able to defend themselves, according to Montesquieu. But, what is a confederal republic? Is it a mere confederation or is it a new nation? Montesquieu himself was somewhat ambiguous about that but the passage in which he says, "it is a kind of assemblage of societies that constitute a

No. 9

new one," is critical for Publius. Publius sees that as the formation of a new society, rather than simply an association of previously existing societies.[3]

The scholarship has fought over this passage for many years and one of my teachers many years ago made the argument that at this point in the language what Publius is doing is misusing Montesquieu to try to avoid this criticism. The French, he said, doesn't read that way. What Montesquieu says in French, in fact, is "*une société des sociétés.*" So, "one society of societies." My teacher said that this shows that Publius despite, the French, used a misleading English translation. Publius abuses Montesquieu to take advantage of the opposition. Well, I read it slightly differently, because it seems to me that the French does say an assemblage of societies rather than a society of which states are members. It says, "*une société,*" one society of societies, which I think is properly translated by an assemblage of societies, and which therefore would mean that Publius is right in finding that Montesquieu speaks differently in another place than the opponents to the constitution thought he spoke elsewhere.

Publius also cites Montesquieu at the end of this ninth essay as showing which confederacy he liked best. And I draw our attention to it closely, **No. 9** because Montesquieu does indeed cite the Lycian confederacy. He does make the statement, ". . . were I to give a model of an excellent confederate republic it would be that of Lycia." And Lycia is a confederate republic which does not retain the two critical principles of confederations. What are those two critical principles? One, equality of the states, each state has one vote in the confederation. Complete equality means no proportional scale of representation in the confederation, because the states are represented as independent states and not in terms of their populations. And the second critical principle in a confederation is the ability of the individual state to veto the rule of the confederation or to express it differently, the rule of unanimity for action in a confederation. Both of those principles are violated in the example of Lycia, where a common council has proportional representation, and the ability for rules to be enforced above the vetoes, the choices, of the independent cities. In short, it looks more like a single nation than a confederation.

Something more needs to be said about Montesquieu's invocation of the confederal republic and why Publius thinks it defends the large republic in an extended sphere. In the sixth chapter of the eleventh book of *The Spirit of the Laws*, Montesquieu not only describes separation of authorities, checks and balances, and those principles he says are found in the English constitution that make it possible to envision republican liberty being defended in a new way, but he sets it forth in a context that makes clear that this is a large state, not a small state. And when he comes to the twenty-seventh chapter of the nineteenth book of *The Spirit of the Laws,* he says he's going to take the principles he developed in the eleventh book, sixth chapter, and elaborate them to show what kind of life it is these people will live. In that twenty-seventh chapter he paints a picture of this new republican mode of life based on commerce in a large state. It is not based on face to face dealings where everyone knows everyone, but based instead on institutional arrangements that are meant to guarantee, as he said, in the eleventh book, liberty. This in fact makes liberty, as he argued in the fifth chapter of the eleventh book, the direct object of the constitution. Clearly, what Montesquieu provided is a transition from the ancient view, in which virtue was the object of the constitution of the republic, to the view in which liberty becomes the object of the constitution. He claims that making that shift carries with it the kinds of institutional protections he has otherwise designed, and which can apply in a large territory. To have extensive commerce, by the way, a state must have a large territory. That's one of the things that goes with it. A very small territory can participate in commerce, but not to a very large extent. It's limited in natural resources, limited in its manufacturing capabilities and many other respects. So the greater the commerce we intend to sustain, the greater must be the extent of the state. This is what Montesquieu calls for in the new and modern republic. And therefore Publius seems to be justified in applying the improved science of politics to the enlargement of the orbit within which the republic is expected to operate.

No. 9

Publius himself, I repeat, begins the ninth essay by saying that we have provided for curing domestic faction and insurrection. We are therefore rightly advised to ask, how does an enlargement of the orbit cure domestic faction and insurrection? I ask this in all honesty. How can anyone imagine such a thing to occur? In the first place we've got more people, we've got more places for them to hide and run, and we've got more interests at stake. How is that going to reduce rather than to multiply faction and insurrection? It sounds almost as if we're applying a microscope or a magnifying glass to those elements of human nature which would otherwise lead to the difficulties we expect in the form of domestic faction and insurrection. So that when he sets it forth as a boast, as a proud claim, of a new discovery, he's defying all of common sense entirely. And he defends it by citing some philosopher from France—and here he is in the middle of the United States and these people have now been making constitutions for eleven years and they are indeed attached to liberty, the genius of the people is the love of liberty. It is not the case in that context, that we ought to let him get away with this claim easily.

He had made a slight suggestion of the kind of liberty he wanted to take when discussing the problem of Montesquieu at the beginning of the fifth essay. Notice, he refers to the opponents' citing observations on Montesquieu. The word "observations" is what I'm looking at there. But then he says, "they seem not to have been apprised of the sentiments of that great man." There was a difference between observations and sentiments. Observations are explicit, and he was explicit—republics are in small territories. This notion of sentiments, on the other hand, required the kind of argument I have given and in which we relate one part of the book to another part of the book and draw out the implications from what is said. In short, we might make the argument that the notion that Montesquieu had certain sentiments or feelings about things is only a cover for what Publius wants to say. Publius wants somehow to invest Montesquieu with a meaning which otherwise cannot be found there.

Well, look at the fourteenth paragraph of essay nine in which he tries to reveal what he's up to:

> I have thought it proper to quote at length these interesting passages, because they contain a luminous abridgment of the principal arguments in favour of the Union, and must effectually remove the false impressions, which a misapplication of other parts of the work was calculated to produce. They have at the same time an intimate connection with the more immediate design of this Paper; which is to illustrate the tendency of the Union to repress domestic faction and insurrection.

No. 9

He's introduced a new word, hasn't he? It not only solves the problem, but we now know how it solves the problem. It represses domestic faction and insurrection. The application of the magnifying glass to the extent of the republic will in fact repress those tendencies in human nature which otherwise would lead to faction and insurrection.

The counterintuitive solution to the problem of domestic violence requires us only to ask one final question, how does it repress faction? This sets up the following *Federalist Paper* that we will look at next, because that is in fact where the question is answered.

Federalist Paper ten resolves all the tensions that have been built up through *Federalist Papers* one through nine. The very last sentence in the ninth *Federalist Paper* says: "Thus we perceive that the distinctions insisted upon were not within the contemplation of this enlightened civilian [Montesquieu], and we shall be led to conclude that they are the novel refinements of an erroneous theory." I point to that because of its standing in stark contrast with what Publius means to do.

He speaks of the novel refinements of an erroneous theory, sort of old errors in new clothes, as I would put it. But of course, he himself is going to do something quite novel, as he led us to see. So there are two kinds of novelty, there's the old error which wears new clothes and therefore is a novelty not worth the name, we might say. The old error being that democracies or republics can only be established in small territories. And then there is his novelty, the one which *Federalist Paper* ten introduces us to, therefore, with the greatest emphasis.

Look at the beginning of the tenth essay: "Among the numerous advantages promised by a well constructed Union, none deserves to be

No. 10

more accurately developed than its tendency to break and control the violence of faction." This is what remains to be developed. We have shown through the ninth essay that it does so, but we haven't shown how. This essay, then, takes on the purpose of showing how, and it's a purpose unfolded not by a mere theoretician. It's unfolded by what he calls a friend of popular governments. This friend of popular governments "never finds himself so much alarmed" as when he contemplates their propensity to the dangerous vice of faction, the violence of faction.

Now, popular government, democracy, republic, these are all synonyms. We must constantly remind ourselves that we saw this set forth at the opening of the ninth essay, when we talked about the petty republics of Greece and Italy. There are arguments against popular government, but there are also friends of popular government. Sometimes friends can be deceived by their love into thinking the things they love are good even when they're not. So the question for us is, are these friends of popular government deceived by the appearances of popular government or is there a persuasive argument for it? Well, they themselves have said to us, our argument will persuade you only if we succeed in persuading you that popular government belongs in a large territory. That's the test they must pass, but therefore we too must pass, in order for this government to be finally defended.

The violence of faction now exclusively concerns us. We pay attention to nothing else. We don't care if popular government can wage war against the outside; we don't care how effective it is at levying taxes; we don't care how it conducts negotiations. We care about only one thing: Does it in fact break and control the violence of faction?

Notice the language. In the ninth essay, the language was "repress domestic faction." Now it's said to be "break and control the violence of faction." Perhaps there's no distinction there, but let's be sure that we are attentive to any distinction that will emerge in the course of our reading. Then, finally, he says we must cure the violence of faction without violating the principle to which we are attached. So there's an enormous task built up. Let's consult an outline of the argument. It carries with it some basic principles and also the outline of the argument. If any of the arguments of the *Federalist Papers* speaks to us in a manner that is strictly logical, *Federalist Paper* ten does. It goes through an argument stiletto fashion, without wasting any time, and simply getting the premises and conclusions lined up. It goes from syllogism to syllogism. It does so with certain basic principles in mind.

No. 9

FEDERALIST PAPER No. 10

Republic—a state in which the supreme power rests in the body of citizens entitled to vote and is exercised by representatives chosen directly or indirectly by them.

Faction—"a number of citizens, whether amounting to a majority or minority of the whole, who are united and actuated by some common impulse of passion, or of interest, adverse to the rights of other citizens, or the permanent and aggregate interests of the community."

I. How violence occurs
   A.   Clashing factions give rise to instability.
   B.   Instability can provoke violent incidents.
II.   Cures for factional violence: prevention and control
   A.   Prevention or removal of causes involves:
      1. *Destruction of liberty,* upon which faction thrives; unwise, is worse than the disease.
      2. *Communalizing passions, interests, and opinions* (state controls all to make them uniform) is impracticable, unwise since man's reason can be flawed, resulting in errors and differing opinions.
        a. Varying abilities exist in people. All interests cannot be the same. Varying interests form the basis of the right to acquire property; inequality results.
        b. Government's first task is to protect diverse faculties—liberty. This necessarily involves protection of different degrees and kinds of property.
   B.   Control or regulation of factions
      1. *Ordering of different interests in a republic*
        a. Factions arise for many reasons, but the most common cause is the various and unequal distribution of property. Classes have always existed in society.
          • the rich who are generally few
          • the poor who are generally the majority
        b. Differing classes are divided by conflicting interests.
      2. Modern Legislation
        a. Its principal task is to regulate conflicting interests.
        b. Legislation aims to avoid factional violence.
   C.   Factions cannot be eliminated—effects can be controlled
      1. A faction that has less than majority power can be controlled in a republic.
      2. A faction with majority power might find itself able to dominate unless the Constitution makes it difficult for this faction to discover and act on its strength.
      3. Cure is an extended republic using single district representation

    a. Voters in an area send one representative to legislate and act for them.
    b. Representatives are limited in number by area and population.
    c. Representatives speak for a vast number of interests within their geographical area or population.

The main theme of the essay, as we see on the outline, is that factional violence is one of the greatest challenges to a republic. That's where they begin. It is not the external enemy, but the internal enemy that's the greatest challenge. What is a republic, therefore, is a question. The republic is a state in which the supreme power rests in the body of citizens entitled to vote and is exercised by representatives, chosen directly or indirectly by them. That is the definition of the republic.

A republic is not, as we see, in the course of the essay, a mere democracy; but a republic is cognate to democracy—it is a friend or brother of democracy; it grows out of democracy. Both republics and democracies may be called popular government. I have never received so much difficulty as on those occasions, when traveling about this country, and speaking about the Constitution or institutions, I make the slip of referring, in certain audiences, to the United States as a democracy. And there's almost always someone there who very angrily checks me, and says, "Wait a minute! We're not a democracy! We're a republic!" And I say, "Well, yes, you're absolutely right, and obviously well read, and there is a distinction between the two..." However, the distinction does not cut so deeply as some people seem to think it does. For the point of our being a republic is not to check the democracy. The point of being a republic is, as is said here in *Federalist Paper* ten, to cure the ills of democracy with democratic means. So that when we call the United States a democracy today, we are in fact being true to the purposes of Publius in this tenth essay.

After "republic," we define "faction." He tells us a faction is "a number of citizens, whether amounting to a majority or minority of the whole, who are united and actuated by some common impulse of passion, or of interest, adverse to the rights of other citizens, or to the permanent and aggregate interests of the community." This is a compound definition, and every part of it is required in order to define a faction. There is no one part of it that does so; hence, it is not correct to say a faction is an interest; or a faction is a special interest group, or any of those kinds of expressions. One must make the whole statement in order to define a faction: a number of citizens, whether a majority or a minority, who are united and who are motivated by a common impulse of passion or of interest—we must have all of that and on top of all that—they must act adversely to the rights of other citizens or to the common good. If you get a group of people who organize, who are

No. 10

united, who act on a common impulse of passion, but who act consistently with the rights of others, they are not a faction. It is not by being separate that one becomes a faction; it is the thing on the basis of which, and for which, one acts that makes one a faction or not a faction.

We see, in the forty-ninth *Federalist Paper*, a reference to political party, which is akin to this reference to faction, in the tenth *Federalist Paper*. In the general thought of 1787–89 parties were, of course, things that were not looked upon with approval. Parties were thought to be ordinarily destructive of social order and stability. Parties were thought to express, almost by definition, the interest of a part against the interest of a whole, and therefore, an internally destructive principle in a society; a subversive principle. Well, party, in that sense, is close to what is meant by faction here. No. 49

We, of course, ultimately evolved a very differing notion of the political party in the United States, including ultimately the sense that parties were themselves an expression of human nature. We find this even in George Washington's "Farewell Address," where he advises his countrymen against the dangers of parties, because they build up loyalties to a faction as opposed to loyalty to the nation as a whole. He says this is a dangerous thing. But in the same process, he acknowledges that they exist by nature; there are elements of human nature that lead ineluctably to the development of political parties. Faction and party are condemned at this point in 1787, because they have not been understood to make a contribution to the common life of the society. They are defined as acting adversely to the interest of other citizens or the aggregate interest of the community.

What we want to do in the name of the republic is to eliminate or "to break and control," not faction, but the "violence of faction." If we compare the language of the ninth essay with the language of the tenth, we begin to see clearly where we're headed. The ninth essay says we want to repress domestic faction. It does not say "eliminate," it says repress domestic faction. The tenth essay says we want "to break and control the violence of faction." No. 9

In each case it's clear that we aim at the consequences of faction rather than the faction itself. The essay makes it clear why we require to do that. We can never hope to remove faction. In the first paragraph of the essay it is said that "instability, injustice, and confusion" are mortal diseases that have caused the death of popular government and that are still fruitful topics for declamation. We further see a reiteration of the argument that there have been valuable improvements made by the American constitutions on popular models, whether ancient or modern, and moreover, that we should do something more to eliminate the danger of the violence of faction. Then he gives examples of that violence and how it operates within the society. Notice in the example that what faction does is to render **No. 10** ever more tenuous the effort of government to harmonize and assimilate diverse interests within the society.

Perhaps I should make very clear at this point that when I speak of harmonizing and assimilating, or homogenizing, I do not mean what we find in Plato's *Republic,* where the utopian ideal of the republic requires everyone essentially to be the same, to think the same thought, to be elevated in the same way, factually to be the same; when one feels a toothache, all the rest must feel it too. That's not what I'm speaking about when I speak of harmonizing and assimilating. I mean that we take the diverse interests that people have and allow them all to be subjected to the same referee, the same Solomon, so that each expects his interest to be protected by the same Solomon, and each therefore, will call the same things near and dear. This is not to make the people the same, it is only to make them depend in the same way for their protections, for their defense.

This is what faction threatens. Faction elevates a competing Solomon within the breast of the community. Therefore, Publius says this about factions in opening the essay:

No. 10   However anxiously we may wish that these complaints had no foundation, the evidence of known facts will not permit us to deny that they are in some degree true. It will be found indeed, on a candid review of our situation, that some of the distresses under which we labor have been erroneously charged on the operation of our governments; but it will be found, at the same time, that other causes will not alone account for many of our heaviest misfortunes; and, particularly, for that prevailing and increasing distrust of public engagements, and alarm for private rights, which are echoed from one end of the continent to the other. These must be chiefly, if not wholly, effects of the unsteadiness and injustice with which a factious spirit has tainted our public administration.

Closing that introduction leads him, of course, to the definition of faction and the whole question of how to cure and remove faction. The arguments proceed very directly. I want to emphasize that he rejects the notion of preventing faction because that would be inconsistent with the principles to which the friend of popular government is attached. He essentially makes clear what the work of harmonizing and assimilating will come to. We can't remove the cause of faction because it means destroying liberty. That he makes clear. Nor can we communize passions, interests, and opinions. And that leads to certain conclusions that are important for us in thinking about the whole question.

We know, for example, that if people are going to be protected in their native abilities, certain inequalities are going to result. People have different abilities and therefore, all interests cannot be the same because they will pursue those differing abilities leading to differing results with differing property and other forms of relationship. These varying interests will form the basis of the right to acquire property. So when we protect the different abilities, we will also end up protecting inequalities and the unequal holding of property in the society generally will follow. This is what he means when he says "the latent causes of faction are thus sown in the nature of man." You cannot remove them without violating that nature, without violating human liberty. And yet, the argument is made that there is one source of faction which stands out over and above this common human picture, which is what he calls the most common, the most durable cause of faction, and that is the unequal distribution of property.

Why would anybody in his right mind raise the question of the difference between the rich and the poor in this way? That's the question of the tenth *Federalist Paper*. When everything is said and done, we can boil it down simply to the tensions between the rich and the poor and we ask, did we start off in the second *Federalist Paper* raising questions about safety and foreign and domestic violence just to come to this, the struggle between the rich and the poor? And if so, why? Isn't it intuitive to everyone that inequalities of property produce social tensions, that they're difficult to deal with, and that we need to make special provisions for those kinds of things? Doesn't Aristotle teach that in the third book of the *Politics*? What's special about the way in which the argument is derived here?

I think two things are very special in the way in which he derives his argument. First is the fact that the inequality of property is rather a residual consequence of a more important inequality. He applies it even to people's different ideas about religion and prominence. With different individuals in society all kinds of things dispose people to vex and oppress one another. These different abilities lead to different opinions and lead to people acting in different ways. This is the more fundamental question than the inequality of property.

The inequality of property is the most common and durable source of faction. The inequality of property, however, does not explain to us how we control faction in its own terms. Simply to say, for example, that we can equalize property will not do so. Why? Because it turns out that the other inequalities are what produced the inequality in property. We cannot equalize property because that simply starts a new round and we'll produce new inequalities in the next round. We might think that if the inequality in property had resulted by accident, it would be a simple matter to handle this through legislation. To be sure, this is the principal task of modern legislation, to regulate these various and interfering interests. There is something else that came before the principal task of modern legislation, however, and that was, of course, the first object of government, to protect the interests, the differing abilities, the differing faculties of people, which includes their faculties of acquiring property.

Look at the sixth paragraph in the essay: "The diversity in the faculties of men from which the rights of property originate, is not less an insuperable obstacle"—to what? to a "uniformity of interests." Now, we're going to harmonize and assimilate the diverse interests. We need an energetic, active government to do that, but we're told that in fact nothing can create a uniformity of interests. So the question is, how do you harmonize and assimilate diverse interests without being able to create uniformity of interests? That is precisely the question. He goes on in that passage to say, "The protection of these faculties is the first object of Government." The safety talked about in the second essay is now made particular to each individual. Why would we interpret our safety this way, rather than in terms of the executive power of nature as we discussed before? Why would we say it's more important to say that our diverse faculties are protected than to say that we are held free from the violence of others?

Well, it turns out that the only reason to be free from the violence of others, from the restraints of others, is in fact, to be free to do the things we're capable of doing and that we can carry out in safety to others. So this is a more direct expression of the object of government than is the notion of safety. It focuses on the reason that human beings require the freedom to move and to act in the first place.

From the protection of different and unequal facilities of acquiring property, the possession of different degrees and kinds of property immediately results. That is, it's a several-step process that brings us out in the end with differing degrees of property. The different degrees of property then suddenly have a magnified effect in the society at large. Why? Because property has an impact on peoples' passions, interests, and opinions. As people either long for property or long to protect the property they have, they will do things that will lead them to be placed in opposition to others. The paragraph referring to the latent causes of faction shows this in the broader context of zeal for different opinions concerning religion, concerning government, etc. These are no less important than differences in property holdings. And it is no less important that the resolution of the one problem and source of faction also contribute to resolving the other. So that what we do, for example, to mitigate or minimize the influence of an inequality in property must act equally well to minimize the influence of various opinions concerning religion, government, and other points of speculation as well as of practice.

In looking at these two aspects of the argument dealing with the prevention of faction, which he said we could not accomplish, and then turning to the question of the control or regulation of faction, something becomes apparent. Somehow or other, the constitution has to produce an order or arrangement or pattern of relationships for all the interests in the

society that is inclined to break and control or diminish faction, rather than
to exaggerate it. So we're talking about a constitution in that sense of
ordering or arranging various characters, various interests within the
society. While doing that we have to pay particular attention to the danger
that is derived from differences in property. More precisely, as I said
before, the dangers centered on the difference between the rich and the
poor.

Let me just say for a moment something about the rich and the poor that
we learn already in Aristotle and that remained true in 1789. The rich are
generally few. The poor are generally many. I hate to state obvious truisms
like that but it's important because we live in a time when we no longer
recognize that. Everything's changed. It's changed because of this essay,
because of the founding. But, at this time, in 1787, it was still true. The rich
were the few and the poor were the many. Think again about the definition
of the faction. Look at it. A faction is any number of citizens, whether
amounting to a majority or a minority and so on from there, right? Well,
that's like saying either the many or the few.

We begin to see why we say the most common and durable source of
faction is the inequality of property and why it creates a special problem in
the context of democracy. What is the fundamental principle of
democracy? It's the principle of decision by majority. So, what we're
talking about whenever we speak of democracy is exposing the few to the
power of the many. That's the first and most obvious difficulty, one that
even Aristotle had already noticed.

It is argued here that the society is going to be popular government and
will cure the ills of democracy with democratic means. We must so order
the interests in this society, we must so order the rich and poor, that even
as the power of one to despoil the other is confirmed it will not be
exercised that way. That's what's being asked for. Give the many the
power to expropriate, to despoil the rich, and design it in such a way that
they won't do that. This is what's called for in writing a constitution to
break and control the violence of faction.

Remember, the violence of faction never ends with the poor despoiling
the rich. That produces a cycle of events, a cycle of regimes if you will.
One day we will have a democracy, which Aristotle defines as rule by the
many who are poor, and we'll have an oligarchy tomorrow, when the
oligarchs get even and take their turn. So we're also talking about breaking
the cycle of regimes, that cycle in which we oscillate from one constitution
to the other, depending on who has the upper hand. All this is involved in
the discussion of breaking and controlling the violence of faction. The rich
and the poor must, in terms of their impact on the unity of the society, be
neutralized, which is another way of saying harmonized and assimilated.

Since we have to control, because we cannot eliminate, factions, we
must control their effects. In a republic Publius argues, if the faction is a

minority, the effect is controlled first of all by the principle of majority rule. So the rich are harmless, initially, in popular government, because they can be outvoted. That's what that means. But what do we do with a majority faction? It will have the power to dominate, unless our constitution makes it difficult for it to discover and act on its strength. What is the cure?

The cure is nothing less than the novel idea presented in the ninth *Federalist Paper,* namely, an extended republic. As we analyze the argument for this extended republic, remember that he makes an argument against pure democracy in the process, and we will come back to that at a later time because it's important in the context of *Federalist Paper* fifty-one. As he makes the argument for the extended republic, it is not merely the extension of the sphere that he talks about. He says, large republics are more favorable, indeed, not just to electing a proper representation but also because, as I would put it, stifling the voice of faction.

Nos.
9, 51

Here's how it works. Factions require a common impulse of passion or of interest. That's part of the definition, remember. People must be motivated by the same passion or interest. One of the ways we undermine common motivation of passion or of interest is, in fact, to make it more difficult for people to discover who are those of like passions and interests. One of the ways we make it more difficult is to make it harder for them to know one another. It becomes harder for them to know one another as there are more of them to know, and as they come from a greater distance. All the things we previously relied upon to affirm the intuition that democracy should be small become in fact inverted.

We discovered that we don't want people to know one another so well that they can act on common impulses of passion or interest. We want them to have cross-cutting loyalties, cross-cutting interests so that someone in this county may have more in common, but not realize it, with someone removed two states than with someone living next door. As we introduce that degree of complexity, we must remember the Antifederalist complaint about refinement and complexity. If we can create a multiplicity of interests, the language of the fifty-first *Federalist Paper,* then the consequence of extending the sphere of the government will be that we make it less likely that factions will rule. We do not take away majority rule. We only make it more difficult for those of a factious temperament to discover that they are the majority. That is the argument in favor of the extended sphere in the tenth *Federalist Paper.* Later we shall reconsider some of these arguments in greater detail, particularly the tales that lead to single district representation and that explain why that is necessary for the system to work, why winner-take-all elections are necessary for the system to work, why we must have representatives who are limited in number by area and population and why they must speak for a large number of interests within their geographical area rather than for a single interest.

These are all yet to be developed and we'll come back to them as we deal with the further question of how modern principles allowed republican government to be safely mounted in the late eighteenth century.

Now, regional factions? That is a great question. We remember what Agrippa said about the "northern hive," which certainly echoes very well to us who know the history. The writer of the tenth *Federalist Paper* is James Madison, of course, and Madison, in the Constitutional Convention is the very person who broke apart the small state—large state controversy by introducing the question of north-south differences in slavery[4]. He pointed out that this is the most serious problem in the small state—large state view. So he is aware of the difference in interests. The fact that in the tenth essay he abstracts from it is rather a different question. I would submit that he hopes this whole project of harmonizing and assimilating the diverse interests will not only deal with factions in the narrow sense of the term but also in that broad regional sense. It aims to take an issue like slavery and in the end illuminate it, neutralize it rather than making it a threat to the republic. Now, we know that that did not happen. We know that it was not only a threat to the republic but that only war in the end could resolve the difficulty. So, we could ask the question, how successfully the project is defended in the tenth essay if it couldn't deal with the question of slavery, the real north-south difference. We will come back to that, because it's very important when we read the fifty-fourth essay which talks about slavery.

No. 54

Let's return to the general outline of the argument about faction and be emphatic about particular aspects of it. To begin, notice the extent to which the discussion of faction plays a central role in the *Federalist Papers* as a whole. Everyone knows, of course, that the tenth *Federalist Paper* is the primary citation for the discussion of faction. And we've already seen in discussing essays six, eight, and nine that they prepare for the tenth *Federalist Paper* with references either to suppressing faction, as in number eight, or making, directing barriers against faction, or repressing domestic faction, as in number nine.

No. 10

There are also numerous references subsequent to number ten. Number fourteen, of course, fulfills the argument in number ten where Publius speaks of the proper antidote for the disease of faction as the extended republic in the presence of the principle of representation. In essay number fifteen Publius invokes the spirit of faction, which is apt to mingle in the ordinary operations of government, and goes on therefore to explain why it is we need a strong central government with an overriding authority in order to deal with the spirit of faction. The sixteenth essay, again, refers to faction and the intrigues of faction.

Nos. 14–16

When we look at the term as it appears frequently throughout the essays we see that it operates in some degree as an organizing principle. So this whole question of constructing the government so as to deal with the problem of domestic violence, which has now come to be called domestic faction, is somehow at the core. It is the core principle of the argument for the constitution that Publius makes in the *Federalist Papers*.

I mentioned before that *faction* is in some way, in the negative sense at least, a synonym for *party* and that's why in the tenth essay the expression Publius was able to use was the "spirit of party and faction" when he described it as being sown in the nature of man. He speaks of the "spirit of party and faction," linking the two terms, not seeing, therefore, the term *party* in the manner in which we regard it as a legitimate function of a democratic system. This use of *faction* or *party*, as the primary difficulty to be resolved in constructing a popular government, forces us to pay attention to the whole question of popular government in the original sense or meaning of the term because factions arise in the ordinary course of the expression of human interests and human opinions. What we're asking throughout this discussion, therefore, is how to provide for stable government on a popular foundation without unleashing those tendencies in human nature that would otherwise and ordinarily be expected to create disorder when having their full influence.

Several contemporary theories about the Federalists make the argument, roughly speaking, that they were anti-democratic, that the Federalists were anti-majoritarian. We saw before how one might arrive at that idea. If a faction is a minority, it gets voted down by the majority. And so the real problem turns out to be majority faction. Well, that leads people then to deduce that Publius is afraid of the democratic majority, and that the whole constitution has been constructed as a series of obstacles to the expression of majority opinion because Publius is unfriendly to democracy, unfriendly to majority rule.

It is for that reason that we require therefore to look even more deeply into the argument of the tenth *Federalist Paper* as well as succeeding arguments in order to put Publius to the test. Are you or are you not a "friend of popular government"? As you know, that was the expression he used at the opening of the essay. At the end of the essay you will recall Publius indicates the character of the solution that he came up with as a republican solution to the peculiar problems that he's dealing with. It's in the last paragraph where he says: "In the extent and proper structure of the Union, therefore, we behold a Republican remedy for the diseases most incident to Republican Government."

This is of course the passage I was referring to earlier when I spoke of curing the ills of democracy with more democracy. And an ordinary physician, of course, would be skeptical of the proposition that you cure a disease with more of a disease, but that is the claim. We have found a republican remedy for ills that are natural in popular governments, natural in republican societies. If Publius can respond to this accusation that he's anti-democratic, then his answer must be in the form of making clear to us why we can expect these republican adaptations of the popular system to further the end of popular control in the society. Robert Dahl is a scholar who indirectly makes the argument that the Federalists were anti-democratic people. He makes the claim that the Federalists were aristocratic and that their whole effort was to restrain, to check, the democratic impulse in the society.

We see a version of this argument in the very important history textbook by Gordon Wood[5]. Wood is much more informed about what actually happened than either Dahl or Burns has been, but he still makes the argument that the Federalists use the rhetoric of democracy in order to establish undemocratic institutions, to establish a constitution that is ultimately unfriendly to popular government. So, that argument requires a precise response, and the outline of the argument in the tenth *Federalist Paper* isn't sufficient for that purpose because it's merely a logical structure. It only shows how we move from one stage in the discussion to the next stage. It only shows why it seems logical to think we might extend the sphere of the republic, but it doesn't enter into the discussion of doing so for the sake of making the system more democratic.

The seventh paragraph discusses the principal task of modern legislation, which is the regulation of various and interfering interests. It says:

No. 10

But the most common and durable source of factions, has been the various and unequal distribution of property. Those who hold, and those who are without property, have ever formed distinct interests in society. Those who are creditors, and those who are debtors, fall under a like discrimination.

We get at the outset two of the sources of opposition, creditors and debtors, in society. Further, a "landed interest, a manufacturing interest, a mercantile interest, a monied interest, with many lesser interests, grow up of necessity in civilized nations, and divide them into different classes, actuated by different sentiments and views."

Remember, he'd said earlier that it is in fact the uneven distribution of property that is the most common and durable source of faction. That leads us to concentrate on two classes, the rich and the poor. Also we see there differing classes that are keyed to differences in interest; creditors or debtors need not correspond automatically with the rich and the poor, with the rich always being creditors and the poor always being debtors. For example, people like James Wilson, one of the founding fathers who was present at the Constitutional Convention and was one of the original associate justices of the Supreme Court, ended his life miserably and in debt and threatened with debtor prison. Very rich people, in fact, are often much more dramatic debtors than very poor people for certain obvious reasons. So this particular distinction in interests cuts against the grain of the mere distinction between the rich and the poor. So too with the landed interest and the manufacturing interest. They can be opposed without opposing the rich and the poor. It is in fact highly likely that we will have rich and poor in each of those interests. And the question, of course, is whether the rich and the poor who are landed will have more common interest as between themselves than either will have with either the rich or the poor of a manufacturing class.

Well, he says, all of these differing interests produce differing classes and what is of critical interest to us is the argument that these differentiations in the society grow up of necessity in proportion as nations become more civilized. The kinds of activities and interests that people participate in become more complex in proportion as nations become more civilized.

This is one of the key factors he counts on in this argument about factions in the tenth *Federalist Paper,* and that is what we want to look at now as we introduce the argument in the eighth paragraph, because it is the claim that government will focus exclusively on regulating these interests that produces the key problem we're concerned with. He says that this introduces "the spirit of party and faction in the necessary and ordinary operations of Government." We really oughtn't to be surprised. Do we not see hearings that take place all the time in American government about one form or the other of some improper influence or the role of lobbying, the role of money in the development of policy?

We realize that that's not necessarily a thing that we ought to be surprised about, however much we might want to control it, because it is the regulation of these various and interfering interests, according to Publius, which is the principal task the government ought to be trying to accomplish. Therefore, we can expect the people subject to it to try to influence that process to a significant degree. This is what he says about why we're going to structure it the way we do:

No. 10

No man is allowed to be a judge in his own cause, because his interest would certainly bias his judgment, and, not improbably, corrupt his integrity. With equal, nay with greater reason, a body of men, are unfit to be both judges and parties at the same time; yet what are many of the most important acts of legislation, but so many judicial determinations, not indeed concerning the rights of single persons, but concerning the rights of large bodies of citizens?

Do we see the argument here? The acts of legislation are a form of judgment, a form of judicial determination. Why? because they end up affecting people's holdings, particularly their property holdings, and of course other rights as well. It doesn't take them one by one. It takes them as whole classes and either leaves them better off or worse off, which means it's just like going into court and winning or losing. That's why the language has taken the form it has at this point.

We establish courts of law, of course, because we believe that people are incapable of judging in their own causes without bias. We call it the rule of law. We say we want to live under the rule of laws and not the rules of men. We want neutral parties to decide these tough and sensitive issues, but what is more tough, what is more sensitive than the question of whether we're going to pay taxes or not? This legislative question is just as much a judicial decision as, to give an example, a decision in a court of law as to how much alimony one would have to pay. And these are the questions that have to be fought over, not simply debated but fought over, in the political system, according to Publius. So what we're proposing to do is to come up with a mechanism, a means for fighting over these questions, which in itself will contribute to minimize the violence of faction in the society.

Publius goes on to say:

Justice ought to hold the balance between them. Yet the parties are and must be themselves, the judges; and the most numerous party, or in other words, the most powerful faction, must be expected to prevail. Shall domestic manufactures be encouraged, and in what degree, by restrictions on foreign manufactures? are questions which would be differently decided by the landed and the manufacturing classes; and probably by neither, with a sole regard to justice and the public good.

This is not the policy question we would call in the contemporary era industrial policy; in fact, it is a question of who gets to decide who is going to benefit. And we say, well, obviously the people who are involved must make this decision, so how do we structure their decision making in order to make it safe for the rest of us?

He gives the example of taxes and says these things are open invitations for people to trample on the rights of others. If we give them the power to levy taxes, to take from their pocket or our pocket and put it into their pocket, we automatically invite abuse. And so how do we control this?

In the twentieth century we've talked a lot about the principle of redistribution. We've talked about social policy that aims to redistribute the so-called resources of the society. We've even developed an entire way of talking about the question that belies the truth of what is actually going on. We say we have a gross national product, for example. We talk about the wealth of the country as if the wealth somehow originated in a common pot to which all had a putative equal share or interest, and therefore it was up to the society to decide how to divide it up and parcel it out.

Of course, we know that's not the way wealth originates. We only have to go back to the earlier passage in which he describes the origin of factions and the differing abilities to see why that is the case. He tells us in

No. 10

the sixth paragraph of this essay that what we have, of course, is a "diversity in the faculties of men from which the rights of property originate." And that is an insuperable obstacle to a uniformity of interest, so that this gross national product is in fact, not a national product at all.

It is a collection of all the products of individual efforts which we named gross national product for purposes of analysis so we can treat it statistically as if it were a single thing, but it's not a single thing. It's a thing that's subject to infinite divisions and every single division is a cause for dispute, a cause for conflict; people fight over it. They say, mine, not yours. And then when we try to redistribute it through taxing or other forms of policy then, of course, people become upset. The people say, "you can't take what's mine and give it to someone else simply by calling it by a name that makes it seem common."

This is what Publius is talking about. He says, how are we going to control that kind of policy making which touches on the issues people are willing to fight about. Well, he goes on in the argument to indicate that the control is not so easy as we might think. Recall, we found out in the first series of essays dealing with the problems of foreign violence and domestic violence, that our chief reliance would be on bringing the best men into office. The argument was made explicitly that if we have this large Union, this nation, there will be more of the best men available to make these policy decisions than would be the case if we had it in thirteen separate states, just by a factor of mathematics.

What does he tell us now? "It is in vain to say, that enlightened statesmen will be able to adjust these clashing interests, and render them all subservient to the public good." "It is in vain to say" that this will happen. Now perhaps it's not in vain to say that enlightened statesmen can navigate successfully the waters of foreign negotiations and foreign dangers. But when it comes to domestic dangers, no. That's not sufficient. We can't depend on the wisdom and virtue of our rulers.

Enlightened statesmen will not always be at the helm: Nor, in many cases, can such an adjustment be made at all, without taking into view indirect and remote considerations, which will rarely prevail over the immediate interest which one party may find in disregarding the rights of another, or the good of the whole.

So, these are very powerful human motivations that are at stake and it will take considerably more than the disinterested wisdom of an enlightened statesman to overcome those powerful human motivations. Therefore, Publius concludes that what we must do is to control the effects of faction *because* we cannot deal with the causes.

No. 10   We can't remove the causes. The causes are part of our liberty, part of our nature. How will we control the effects? We must then talk about the question of majority rule and this is opened up in the eleventh paragraph.

"If a faction consists of less than a majority, relief is supplied by the republican principle." So, the ground, the bottom line is still there. We are republicans. We know how to deal with minority faction. We deal with it by voting. The whole process and institution of the vote is the first step in reducing the threat of domestic violence. It turns out not to be the last step for some very interesting reasons which we are now going to develop; but it is the first step and we must remember that.

In our time, it's very difficult to use the language in the manner that Publius is using it, because we've taken the terms *minority* and *majority* and turned them into racial epithets. We can't even remember any longer, most of the time, that these terms refer to the processes of republicanism and not to races and not to the curious politics of the twentieth century United States that has altered our language in the process. For Publius, minority is not a racial category. It's simply the acknowledgment of a relationship that exists at a given moment in a republican society. And that relationship is some number of persons on one side of a question, less than the majority, and the majority standing on the opposite side. That's what minority and majority are.

It's important to recognize in that framework that minorities and majorities are calculated issue by issue. We only know what the minority is and what the majority is in any given case when we see how people's opinions or interests shake out, how they line up. There's no such thing in that sense as a permanent majority or a permanent minority. If we don't have republican principles at the foundation of a society, then we might envision some vague permanently established order of the society which we can call more or less a majority but without any significance attaching to the term. When these are the decision makers, however, when the majority actually governs, then it's a much more touchy question, how to calculate who is in and who is out of the majority, and what the will of the majority actually speaks to. We will see in the fifty-first *Federalist Paper* how extraordinarily sensitive that question can be.

No. 51

Publius, for the moment, however, goes on in the eleventh paragraph to tell us what our problem is. Consider for a moment, "When a majority is included in a faction, the form of popular government on the other hand enables it to sacrifice to its ruling passion or interest, both the public good and the rights of other citizens." Now, notice the parallel here to the argument in the sixth through the eighth essays. There the question was raised, are republican governments inherently pacific? Do republican governments in the context of modern commerce inevitably lead to world peace? Are they not threats to other nations because, somehow, democratic people simply don't wage wars? Well, the parallel of course is on the domestic side. Is it the case that people who govern themselves democratically do not govern themselves the way tyrants govern people? The answer is no. We can have a majority which will "sacrifice to its ruling

No. 10

Nos. 6–8

passion or interest, both the public good and the rights of other citizens." It can be no less despotic than the coldest tyrant. So here's the problem. We have conveyed authority and power into the hands of a majority which now has the opportunity to be precisely that despotic, that tyrannical.

Publius continues: "To secure the public good and private rights against the danger of such a faction, and at the same time to preserve the spirit and form of popular government, is then the great object." Majority faction, this is the language which leads commentators to say he's anti-majoritarian; they don't attend to the next clause. He wants to do both, restrain the majority but preserve the spirit and form of popular government. This is "the great object to which our enquiries are directed," and it is also, he says, "the great desideratum by which alone this form of government can be rescued from the opprobrium under which it has so long labored." So, this is the deciding issue, this very question, that will judge once and for all whether republican government is in fact government which suits human beings, whether we can trust to societies of men the question of establishing good government on the basis of reflection and choice.

The whole project outlined in the first essay is summed up at this point in this one challenge. Thus, his next question is a very important question. "By what means is this object obtainable?" He answers:

Evidently by one of two only. Either the existence of the same passion or interest in a majority at the same time must be prevented or the majority, having such co-existent passion or interest, must be rendered, by their number and local situation, unable to concert and carry into effect schemes of oppression.

So, either we do not have such a common sentiment in the majority or the majority does not become aware of the existence of that common sentiment. Reason: "If the impulse and the opportunity be suffered to coincide, we well know that neither moral nor religious motives can be relied on as an adequate control." Why? because those things hardly restrain individuals and they are much less powerful in proportion as people act in groups rather than individuals.

This is strong language. Neither moral nor religious motives restrain people from invading the rights of others. Given that we will not be able to restrain a majority that has a common impulse of passion or interest to invade the rights of others, we can only, therefore, avoid the evil by avoiding the existence of the common motive, the common impulse of passion or of interest. So the deduction is very straightforward. The problem is, can anyone imagine a way that we can avoid people discovering that they have a common interest? That is what seems the most incredible in the argument in the tenth *Federalist Paper*. That is precisely the argument he then goes on to make, but he pauses to explain something to us so that we understand precisely what is going on.

Publius tells us we cannot solve this problem in a pure democracy. As he tells us, "a pure democracy, by which I mean, a Society, consisting of a small number of citizens, who assemble and administer the Government in person, can admit of no cure for the mischiefs of faction." Democracy in the pure form, in the form of direct democracy, is radically defective for the reasons set forth in this argument. There's no way to impose a barrier to the operation of a majority passion that leads to despotism, to tyranny. He says in this situation, "a common passion or interest will, in almost every case, be felt by a majority of the whole."

If we want to understand what he's talking about, I submit that what we ought to do is to place the argument in the context of life in small towns. We often, of course, praise that life in contrast with the life of the urban town where people are alienated from one another and don't know one another. In the urban town people often suffer in obscurity, sometimes under the very eyes of their neighbors who could care less about their sufferings. We say in small towns that won't happen. People look out for one another in small towns, they take care of one another, and if we are involved in some crisis they come to our aid. On the other hand, people in small towns know us sometimes too well. They mix in our business. They form opinions about us very easily. They share those opinions with others around town. If we happen to fall on the wrong side of an important question, we're easily ostracized, we're stigmatized. This is what he's talking about.

In a pure democracy where we have a small number of citizens who can assemble and administer the government in person, we in fact place those who will be dissenters under an intolerable burden. We also increase the pressure on those who are likely to submit when submission is demanded of them by the majority. Now we who have lived in small towns understand exactly how that process works and therefore we can see intuitively where this argument is leading. **No. 10**

A small, purely democratic government cannot be made safe through institutional means. We cannot use checks and balances. We cannot use separation of powers. Why? Well, we will see when we get to the forty-seventh *Federalist Paper* that in fact any attempt to do that will be defeated by the very notion that whenever we get the whole town together to act, they can change the constitution at whim. They don't have to act as a legislature, leaving the judges alone. Whenever we get the whole society together, they can act with the whole power of the society no matter how we try to set it up along institutional lines. So, the majority is always in the driver's seat in a pure democracy and those who happen to be on the other side simply lose. They have no appeal that they can make. Thus, as he puts it: No. 47

[T]here is nothing to check the inducements to sacrifice the weaker party, or an obnoxious individual. Hence it is, that such Democracies have ever been spectacles of turbulence and contention; have ever been found incompatible with personal security, or the rights of property; and have in general been as short in their lives, as they have been violent in their deaths.

This leads him to a rather important reflection. Publius refers to some politicians as "theoretic politicians." He speaks disparagingly of these politicians who spin "Utopian speculations" and theories in their closets. He may even be thinking of his good friend, Thomas Jefferson, at this point. "Theoretic politicians," who have patronized this pure democracy have made the mistake of imagining that "by reducing mankind to a perfect equality in their political rights, they would at the same time be perfectly equalized and assimilated in their possessions, their opinions and their passions."

There's the problem. Equal rights we can guarantee, but are equal political rights to be also equality of property, equality of opinions, equality of passions? No. The foregoing argument makes clear that it is human nature itself, the diverse faculties of human beings, which make that latter equality impossible; but without having that equality of passions, opinions, and property, we will, in fact, be open to the disease of faction. And so the equality of political rights in itself will not eliminate the problem of faction.

Political equality in the United States has always been the central, organizing, moral principle of American life since the Declaration of Independence. It is the principle of American society. But that political equality has often been misunderstood as involving notions and relationships of equality apart from what is called here the equality of rights. This equality here and in the Declaration of Independence takes expression primarily in the form of the consent of the governed. An equality which goes beyond the recognition that no human being can be governed by another without his consent is simply impossible. We cannot produce a greater equality by exaggerating the powers of majorities in small democracies because the more power we give, in fact, the more radically will we create inequalities. So we're going to use the republic; we're not going to use the pure democracy.

What is the republic? Well, one way to say it is, a republic is a democracy which has been purged of the evils of democracy. And that's what he's giving us. His definition is: "a Government in which the scheme of representation takes place." A republic, representation, "opens a different prospect, and promises the cure for which we are seeking." It differs in several points from democracy, not just one. And it's because it differs in two important points that it's secure. We see this immediately.

First, we could have representation in a small democracy, as in a large republic. Take pure democracy and convert it into a representative model so we can then have separation of powers and all the rest. Will that save that democracy? No, because it's still too small; people are still too close to one another. The majority can still take over any time it wishes. It can alter the form of government and, therefore, the majority can behave with all the violence of an oppressor, to quote Montesquieu.

The second great point of difference between a democracy and a republic, therefore, is the greater number of citizens and greater sphere of country over which the latter may be extended. And it's only in proportion as we extend the reach of the government that the representative principle facilitates an impact on the violence of faction, according to Publius's argument. The two great points of difference between a democracy and a republic for Publius are, not only the delegation of the government in the republic, which is important, but more so, the extent of which a republic is capable.

These provisions lead us of course, to ask questions about the quality of representatives. Who are they? Why is it they will act differently than the majority would act on its own? Won't they simply represent the interest of the people who send them? And if so, how is it a protection? These are the questions that Publius goes on to answer in the balance of the tenth *Federalist Paper*.

As a result of representation, he says we "refine and enlarge the public views, by passing them through the medium of a chosen body of citizens." **No. 10** Now, what does this mean, "refining and enlarging"? At the minimum, it must mean that the opinions, the interests, the views of the citizens are expressed with greater coherence; they're refined. It is not now just a babble of voices but it is an organized expression; and that's refinement.

He also says we will enlarge these views. How do we enlarge them? Well, in the ordinary sense, of course, we enlarge a person's view by extending it beyond that person's private sphere. We take other things, other persons, and other interests into account in forming our view. Somehow representation is supposed to accomplish this. The representative will not simply reflect the views of those who have sent him but rather will reflect those views in relationship to all the other views that are important in shaping the society. This is one of the things he expects.

Remember we said at the outset, however, that we can't depend on enlightened statesmen to solve the problem of faction. They will not always be at the helm. So, although ordinarily we expect to refine and enlarge public views through representation, that can't be the decisive remedy for the problem that we're dealing with. We must go beyond that then, and ask whether this voice of the representatives is, as he says, more consistent with the public good than the voice of the people themselves expressed directly. We must ask whether there's something else that takes place along with increasing the pool from which to draw statesmen.

We begin to see that in the essay starting at paragraph sixteen: "On the other hand, the effect may be inverted. Men of factious tempers, of local prejudices, or of sinister designs, may by intrigue, by corruption or by other means, first obtain the suffrages, and then betray the interests of the people." That is, we can have representatives who refine and enlarge their views or we can have representatives who are corrupt. That's the problem. It won't work entirely. We want to know then if there's something about the large republic itself that solves this problem.

In the seventeenth paragraph, he says:

It is to be remarked that however small the Republic may be, the Representatives must be raised to a certain number, in order to guard against the cabals of a few; and that however large it may be, they must be limited to a certain number, in order to guard against the confusion of a multitude. Hence, the number of the Representatives in the two cases, not being in proportion to that of the Constituents, and being proportionally greatest in the small Republic, it follows that if the proportion of fit characters, be not less, in the large than in the small Republic, the former will present a greater option, and consequently a greater probability of a fit choice.

No. 2

This argument goes back to the second essay. We will get more of the good people if we take in more territory and more people; and we will structure the system of choosing them in such a way as to bring the better people to the fore. We'll see whether that works or not.

Publius goes on, then, to address the question, how are we going to protect ourselves from unworthy candidates? "As each Representative will be chosen by a greater number of citizens in the large than in the small Republic, it will be more difficult for unworthy candidates to practice with success the vicious arts, by which elections are too often carried." Now what does that mean, particularly for us who are always rather unhappy with our elections and the vicious arts by which they are often carried, to all appearances?

Well, it must mean at the minimum, this: demagoguery is much less likely to succeed where it has to appeal to diverse interests, such that the demagogic appeal to one interest has an automatically offsetting effect on another interest. It must mean, at a minimum, that we require the representative in campaigning to present himself before such a variety of interested views that he can't get away with a simply demagogic appeal. For what he seeks to appeal to one with will in fact alienate another.

Furthermore, he says that we will find that "the suffrages of the people being more free, will be more likely to centre on men who possess the most attractive merit, and the most diffusive and established characters." Why?

Attractive merit we can leave aside momentarily, but what does "diffusive and established character" mean'? Today, I suppose, it would be called by our campaign experts, name ID. (We tend to trivialize everything and say everything in small letters rather than the capitals of honorable discourse that they used in those days. So, it's name identification now.) It used to be "diffusive and established characters." It means people who are known generally, who are more, or well known; they are not known just to a narrow constituency, or a narrow corner of a district.

Why would it be important for people to be known generally in order to prevail in an election? It could only be in the situation that they have to be elected by a plurality, at a minimum, of the entire district.

Now, there are various election schemes, such as proportional representation. We could say, we're going to elect representatives on the basis of the principle that whatever share of the vote a person's party gets in the election, they get that share of representation for that district. And so we could have a congressional district with 500,000 people in it and we could put twenty-five candidates in an election and send all twenty-five of them up, if they had room to go, to vote their one twenty-fifth share, or whatever proportion, of that district's vote in Congress. There are systems on this earth that do that, in effect. They have cutoffs, they don't allow it to be carried to the extreme in my example, but they do say, if we participate in the election, and we get, say, five percent of the vote, then we have that share of representation in the national legislature. But, that would not then surface diffusive and established characters, because we could get a small share of the vote in a large district just from the people we know. Obviously what Publius means to say is, we're going to operate on the basis of winner take all, not proportional representation, in a large district with single district representation. This means that one candidate will represent all the people involved in the district.

This has very interesting, dynamic effects on the conduct of elections and on the conduct of representatives. For in the first place, the representative will probably go into office having won narrowly. At least originally that was certainly true, and it fits the conception, whatever has happened since that time. We will win narrowly, which means that we always have the question of the people who were against us. How are we going to deal with them next time we're running for re-election? Can we ignore them because we had a majority once? How did we put the majority together? In all probability, if the district is large enough and diverse enough, we had to build a coalition. Well, there are elements of that coalition which, by definition, are going to be unstable because they had to give up something in order to become a part of it. They're not getting everything they wanted, and they may jump to the other side next time. So, we're constantly trying to buy-off this kind of movement, if we are incumbent representatives. This inclines us then to try to build consensus, to try to appeal broadly, to try to bring the diverse interests together.

The effect operating on the different parties is the recognition that being a minor party is of no value whatever, when we have winner-take-all elections. We don't need an absolute majority to win, we only need a plurality. That pushes us towards what ultimately will become a two-person contest or a two-party system. It pushes us that way because the significance of our possibility of winning increases only as we diminish the number of contestants for the office.

Therefore, what he's describing are the dynamics of campaigning, of holding office, of the relationship between office holders and constituents which operate in such a way as to mute the most extreme claims. For this coalition-building process couldn't take place if everyone was always insisting on the most extreme version of his own interest. We're not going to get others to join us unless we're going to entertain, to some degree, their interest. This means giving up a little bit of our interest.

The process Publius describes will begin to fashion what we might call a political culture. And in this political culture we will begin to eliminate the possibility of the faction with a single identifiable interest forging to the forefront and taking control. We need, then, single-district representation. We need winner-take-all, not proportional, representation. We need a large-enough district such that the parties, the persons, the citizens, the constituents will be pulled in crosscutting ways, in different directions.

If we have every citizen having only one strongly identifiable interest, that would be a problem. But remember he said that a variety of interests "grow up of necessity in civilized nations." The complexity of relationships increases in proportion as we increase the civilization. The likelihood is that, if we increase the size of the society, and the size of the districts therefore, we will have people who will be not only, say, labor union members, but also teachers, farmers, or a whole list of possible associations of interests. Sometimes the interests don't in fact sit so neatly together. Sometimes our interest as a deacon in the Methodist church may be inconsistent with our role as a shop steward in the union. And then we have to make choices. Publius is saying he wants people to have to make as many of those kinds of choices as possible because that will prevent their being insistent on their own interest on every occasion. They won't have that clearly articulated interest to defend.

Now, the new constitution, he says in the nineteenth paragraph, offers **No. 10** us a nice combination where we get what he calls "the great and aggregate interests being referred to the national" government, and local interests being referred to the state legislatures. Therefore, we will have resolved the inconveniences associated with democratic representation because larger districts allow national representatives a distance from the people immediately affected to pursue national objects, while leaving local representatives closer and more intimately acquainted with local interests.

"The other point of difference," he says, "is the greater number of citizens and extent of territory which may be brought within the compass of Republican, than of Democratic Government; and it is this circumstance principally which renders factious combinations less to be dreaded in the former, than in the latter." And of course we know the familiar argument about size which follows.

Now, I think, when we go through this argument in this fashion, we have to come to the conclusion that what Publius has done is not merely to make a counter-intuitive argument, but in fact Publius has challenged us, and indeed challenged the Antifederalists. The Federal Farmer says expressly that we can not accomplish republican government in a large society for the very reason that we can not harmonize and assimilate the interests of the citizens.[6]

We have seen harmonizing and assimilating defined in rather a differing way because Publius acknowledges that we can't give people the same opinions, passions, and interests. That is not the way harmonizing and assimilating works. Thus, the new version of harmonizing and assimilating is one in which the people agree, they concur in removing the power over certain questions to a great distance from themselves. They concur in pursuing their immediate personal interests in this indirect way through the procedures and institutions of republicanism and therefore make themselves, though not consciously perhaps, less likely to go to war over their interests because they have adopted this fairly indirect method of prosecuting it. This form of harmonizing and assimilating comes close to what I called earlier, teaching them all to appeal to the same Solomon. And so far as we have more and more interests, all of which expect to achieve their advantage, not through their direct exertion, but from the intercession of a single Solomon we will make them in fact brothers where they began, perhaps, as enemies.

I'm now disposed to admit that Publius is a nationalist and he's building a nation, a strong central government in a context in which people obviously had expressed preferences for something weaker, of a more confederal nature. The argument against factions, and in favor of the extended republic, is meant to convey the sense in which the defense of a strong national government is consistent with republicanism.

It's easy enough, when we have begun this argument to get swept along with the progress of the argument and to forget there were the foot draggers, constantly reminding that this is not exactly what we bargained for. It certainly was not what many of the states, at least, sent delegates to the Constitutional Convention for in 1787. So I want always to keep the Antifederalists there as a little conscience for us, to remind us of these things. I would particularly direct our attention to the Maryland Farmer essay, and Letter IV by Agrippa that follows in the *Essential Antifederalist*[7]. Both are very brief, but very direct.

The Maryland Farmer, for example, says, there are just two ways of organizing society, one is a national government, the other is essentially a confederation of states, or a league. He says, we don't want a national government. He even objects to the fact that the Federalists call themselves "Federalists." He says, look, these people are nationalists. They are stealing this name Federalists—it's an imposition, about which we ought to be irritated, and we should reject them, and call them what they are truly, national men.

I explained previously how the names originated, and so, we can no longer say that it was some kind of imposition or counterfeit or thievery, that led to the Federalists being called Federalists. Some have argued that the Federalists were very clever devils, and they knew that the Americans liked federalism, so they called themselves Federalists, although they were defending a national constitution. And that's a very nice story. It's charming. But the truth is, they were called Federalists because they espoused the cause of the Federal Congress. So they came by their name honestly.

It is nevertheless true, as the Maryland Farmer objects, that they are not defending federalism in any traditional sense of the term. I would remind us that the Latin root for federalism is *foedus*, faith. A federal structure and a confederal structure are really synonyms in the dictionary of the era. They are not differing words. Therefore, it means only a loose alliance, held together by faith, nothing more. It's a pledge of loyalty, nothing stronger than that when we have a federation or a confederation.

We of course speak today of our federal government, which is the legacy of the Constitution that was defended by Publius, and drafted by the convention. And so we're using the language differently than it was used at the end of the eighteenth century. We're using it the way we use it because of what happens in the thirty-ninth *Federalist Paper*. The argument is made in very explicit terms about the kinds of compromises between nationalism and federalism that took shape in the Constitution of the United States.

No. 39

The Maryland Farmer is not willing to be imposed upon. He says, in fact, not only that these people are nationalists but that we don't need a national government. It will turn into a military oligarchy or something worse. He doubts that it's needed "to keep us at peace among ourselves."[8] One of the most important claims Publius makes for this is that we will in fact repress domestic violence. But the Maryland Farmer says, no, we don't need that to keep peace among ourselves; we're perfectly capable of doing that within our states. And we don't need the glory that comes from "cutting a figure in history." Therefore there's nothing to recommend the national government at all.

Further, a national government has certain dangers. If we look at the last paragraph, the Maryland Farmer claims that the large nation, especially where we introduce notions of majority will, has a greater facility of corruption.[9] He says, "The facility of corruption is increased in proportion as power tends by representation or delegation, to a concentration in the *hands of a few*."

As we noticed in the tenth *Federalist Paper*, the argument was made that there is only a certain range within which representation is effective, whatever the size of the society. However small it is, we must have enough representatives in order "to guard against the cabals of a few" and to be able to carry on reasonable discussions; and however large it is, we must keep the number small enough so as to avoid the babble of a mob. So that beyond a certain point, we can keep increasing the size of the nation and it would not be profitable, it would not be worthwhile, to increase the size of the representation.

No. 10

We don't know what that absolute size is, by any stretch of imagination. At the end of the eighteenth century, the House of Commons in Britain held seven hundred members, and Britain of course was not a very much larger society than the United States at that time, and certainly, very much smaller than the United States in the twentieth century, where we have come to a House of Representatives of 435 members. We still don't have seven hundred members, and of course in 1787, they provided only for sixty-five members. So there's obviously some scope to talk about the optimal size of a legislative assembly. But even when we admit the scope, everyone must still recognize that certain numbers are simply imponderable. An assembly of ten thousand members makes no sense because they couldn't work together; we'd have to divide them up into different assemblies to represent one another in order to get anything done. So clearly, something far short of ten thousand is a maximum number for representatives, no matter how large a society is.

Well, this is what the Maryland Farmer means when he says that this representation will involve concentrating power in the hands of a few. These representatives, to whom we delegate the authority, will in the end be a few, in relation to everyone else. We're giving them power, and they're going to abuse it. We're going to tempt them and encourage corruption among them.

I'm not sure that corruption is less to be anticipated in smaller direct governments than in large indirect governments; but, perhaps it's so. Perhaps there's some foundation for the argument. Where people can see more directly what those in charge are up to, and have, in addition, the powerful influence of community sentiment and moral judgment on their side, perhaps corruption is far less to be expected. But then the question would be, are there off-setting advantages? So that's the kind of argument that Publius and the Maryland Farmer have.

The Maryland Farmer goes on to deny even that we get the off-setting advantages. He says: "The same government pervading a vast extent of territory terrifies the minds of individuals into meanness and submission."[10] Now that's an extremely important argument. Because if it turns out that the character of the citizens will be decisively and negatively affected by the size of the government, then the extended sphere will not have been a net gain. We say we are curing the ills of democracy with more democracy—which is what republicanism means. Well, that's all very well, if in fact we come out of it with republican citizens still. But what if it's true, that this powerful government at a great distance from the ordinary citizen turns the ordinary citizen into rather a servile character, a mean, submissive spirit instead of the independent yeoman.

The old agrarians used to speak of this spirit of "independent yeomanry," citizens who were people of pride and substance. They looked out for themselves and provided for their own lives and depended on no one else. Like Cincinnatus or some of the other old Romans, they could at a moment's notice take up their swords, go off and defend the country, and return to their farms afterwards, without being moved by any aggrandizing ambitions. They were just good solid, salt-of-the-earth people. Well, if we're going to lose that kind of people by extending the sphere of the country, we're going to have a problem. John Taylor of Caroline, a Virginian, spent a brief term in the Senate in the 1790s and published a book after the turn of the century, roughly about 1816, called *An Inquiry into the Principles of the Government of the United States*. He makes precisely this argument. Now Taylor of Caroline is an heir of the Antifederalists. He is one of the old republicans from the Virginia aristocracy who very much resented the growing influence of commerce, manufacturing, the change of manners in the society; he celebrated the agrarian virtues. Now, the Maryland Farmer doesn't call himself the "Maryland Farmer" for nothing. Of these supposed agrarian virtues, he thinks the Federalists have put them at risk under this new order.

We didn't speak about this yet, and we will speak more about it later, but we must recognize how extraordinarily important it is that commerce be a part of this extended republic. It's almost implicit of course, because we don't get the complex interests Publius described without commerce: creditors and debtors; manufacturing; money and other lesser interests. The specific cause of the multiplicity of interests in the extended republic is commerce. We're going to encourage and pursue the spirit of modern

No. 11   commerce. This is made very clear in the eleventh essay. There, Publius in fact even projects a vast empire of the North American continent, which the United States is going to become.

One of the most interesting things in reading through works of the founding is the continual recurrence of the forethought of the founding fathers. We so often hear the argument made that we can't take what the founding fathers did as serious, beyond a certain point, because they could not possibly have foreseen all that would come in the United States. But I find it always far more remarkable how much they did foresee and how much they did explicitly ponder about the growth and development of this society. The eleventh essay is a very good example. We find other examples. Another shows how complex their thought was at the same time as they were open to doing things that produced some of the dangers they feared. James Madison, at the Constitutional Convention on August 7, 1787, participated in the debate on the question of the suffrage: to whom should we extend the right to vote? And there were propositions made that we should find some way to limit the suffrage to those who held some definable amount of property. There were objections to that, which necessarily led to the question of whether we would have universal suffrage. Most people said, well, no, that makes no sense of course, because the importance of suffrage is that it's an expression of one's commitment to the community. One should somehow have a stake, have set down roots and made a life here. That really is the fundamental basis of suffrage as it was understood in that day and age.

In the debate Madison looked at the question from the perspective of what was going to become of the United States. He accepted that we might use a modest property requirement in the context of 1787, because it would exclude virtually no one. The character of the society was such that property holding was so diffuse that virtually no one would be affected by a modest property requirement. But he asked, what will happen when we have a much more complex society, with much larger cities, with vaster numbers of people who hold no property themselves and who make their living by laboring for others, by living off of wages? As the debate developed, of course, they ultimately resolved the question of suffrage in the Constitution by not writing a rule, but piggybacking on the rules that existed in the various states, and leaving suffrage fundamentally open, or at least implicitly open, with the expectation of eventual universal suffrage.

But Madison, in addition to his contribution to the debate, wrote a footnote in his notes on the Convention, in which he turned this question around, again and again, in his mind, and tried to project it still further. He said, well, look, the problem here is that we can't have large numbers of people in a society who are not represented, because what we want to protect is not just property, but persons. And yet, if you turn over power to what may become a majority of persons who have no property, we may expose property to being abused by that majority. It's the very kind of problem we're talking about in the tenth *Federalist Paper*. At some point No. 10 in the future, he's saying, the diversity of interests will cease to operate because these other conditions, in what looks like a large industrial society, will come into play. He concluded that footnote leaving it as an unsettled issue but one that perhaps will be resolved eventually.

In roughly 1821, reviewing his notes on the Convention (they hadn't been released to the public yet), he looked at that, and he sat down and wrote out another discussion of it. He revised the footnote. (We still have the original, he didn't change that a speck.) But almost thirty-five years later, he sits down and he's thinking through the debates of August 7, 1787, and restating his argument. He didn't publish it, he just wrote it out in his own notes. And it became all the more complicated; he projected a still more complicated society and complicated future for the United States. And finally, he came to the conclusion that we can not sacrifice rights of persons to rights of property. We have to have a rule that protects both. He went through several hypothetical possibilities considering how to maintain the republican complexion of the system. It becomes clear that it is necessary to take the risk that the wage earner, the propertyless wage earner, will become a majority, and will in fact destroy the Constitution. There's no way in principle to avoid taking that risk, he argued.

What I find so intriguing about that is the ability to foresee the future. Precisely to foresee it, to foresee the complex industrial society emerging, before there had been, for practical purposes, an industrial revolution. It had begun, but we could hardly expect anyone to see it, in 1787, and still it was not necessarily easy to see in 1821. And this was characteristic of the thought of the framers. They did project far into the future. Indeed, if we look about ourselves, we find they projected far into our own time.

No. 14 This is also reflected in what Publius did in the fourteenth essay, where he in effect responds to the Maryland Farmer's claim that the same government pervading a vast extent of territory terrifies the mind, and Agrippa's argument that no extensive empire can be governed upon republican principles because such a government will degenerate into a despotism. Publius responds by re-emphasizing the conclusions of the tenth essay, and those preceding it. At the outset he says:

We have seen the necessity of the union as our bulwark against foreign danger, as the conservator of peace among ourselves, as the guardian of our commerce and other common interests, as the only substitute for those military establishments which have subverted the liberties of the old world; and as the proper antidote for the diseases of faction, which have proved fatal to other popular governments, and of which alarming symptoms have been betrayed by our own. All that remains, within this branch of our enquiries is to take notice of an objection, that may be drawn from the great extent of the country which the union embraces.

He claims to have demonstrated the necessity of the Union as the conservator of peace among ourselves, which is the very thing that the Maryland Farmer denies. And the "alarming symptoms," of course, are primarily Shays's Rebellion.

Publius has argued in the tenth essay, that we needed a union in an extended sphere to break and control the violence of faction. But there is still an argument against the great extent of the Union that hasn't been responded to; so he says we will give a few observations on this subject in order to show that there are some, what he calls, "imaginary difficulties," some errors of reasoning, or largely, as he presents them here, historical errors that are yet to be refuted. So we go once again into the question of the difference between a democracy and a republic:

The error which limits Republican Government to a narrow district has been unfolded and refuted in preceding papers. I remark here only, that it seems to owe its rise and prevalence, chiefly to the confounding of a republic with a democracy: And applying to the former reasonings drawn from the nature of the latter. The true distinction between these forms was also adverted to on a former occasion. It is, that in a democracy, the people meet and exercise the government in person; in a republic they assemble and administer it by their representatives and agents. A democracy consequently, must be confined to a small spot. A republic may be extended over a large region.

It's become pretty much a mechanical feature, hasn't it? A democracy is small, because of the limitations of face-to-face meetings; republics can be larger because representatives can travel.

That means then we shouldn't apply some of the observations that apply to democracies to a republic; we need particularly to look at the effect on the character of the republic that a large territory makes possible. In the fourteenth essay, he comes to what is very revealing in this context—the Founders see themselves in the overall context of European and Enlightenment thought:

Such a fallacy may have been the less perceived as most of the governments of antiquity were of the democratic species; and even in modern Europe, to which we owe the great principle of representation, no example is seen of a government wholly popular and founded, at the same time, wholly on that principle. If Europe has the merit of discovering this great mechanical power in government, by the simple agency of which the will of the largest political body may be concentred and its force directed to any object which the public good requires; America can claim the merit of making the discovery the basis of unmixed and extensive republics.

What does he mean by "unmixed and extensive republics"? Well, those words, of course, are code words. They are signals for good Whigs in the eighteenth century. We know that the theory of the mixed republic, the mixed regime, was largely celebrated in the works of writers like Harrington, Sidney, and indeed, even present in the works of the American John Adams in his *Defence of the Constitutions of the United States*. This is a theory which has a history descending all the way from Aristotle and Polybius. It applied to the British Constitution. It held that the mixed republic is the republic that has solved the problem of social contradiction, of social tensions, by taking each of the principal classes and representing them distinctly in the government of the society. In Rome, for example, plebeians and patricians mix. What that means of course, in generic terms, is the rich and the poor. These are the great classes. All political history has been distinguished by a discussion of how to bring the rich and the poor together in a single society. They can't live without one another, but in history, they never lived well with one another. So we came up with the notion of the mixed regime. In Whig theory the British Constitution has three parts: a Senate where we put the rich; a House of Commons or Assembly or whatever we want to call it, where we represent the poor; and a third part, which represents no one in particular, comes ultimately to be identified with the monarch in whose person the interest of the whole society is supposed to be represented. And that produces a mixed constitution. The decisive characteristic of the mixed regime is that we distinguish the classes by giving them separate places in the constitution. They are to defend themselves through the institutional power that they hold.

In the fourteenth essay Publius argues that America has discovered the merit of making the mechanical principle of representation the basis of unmixed and extensive republics. This is not only an extended republic, but it's a republic in which we don't have to make a special place for the rich and the poor. We will not reserve one house for the rich, another house for the poor. We will not create these formal classes in government. We will make a government that doesn't depend on the class distinction.

No. 10

One of the things that we didn't point out in talking about the tenth essay is the necessary consequence of the operation of these principles in the extended sphere. Commerce we know is there. Single district representation we know is there. We understand the multiplicity of interests. Do we understand as well, that as the interests multiply, they have to affect more people? Do we understand what the consequence of that is on the distinction between the rich and the poor? Do we not see that the only way we can multiply the kinds of interests described in the tenth essay is to reduce the number of poor? The logic and dynamic of this extended commercial republic is precisely to squeeze rich and poor towards the middle.

The real impact of this constitutional design is to get rid of the struggle between the rich and the poor by getting rid of the extremely rich and extremely poor. In other words what we today talk about as the great American middle class is of course an extraordinary historical oddity. It is true of the whole modern world of course, in the aftermath of the Industrial Revolution, in the company of principles of modern republicanism. All across the face of the Western World, the middle class grew—but it grew first in the United States, most decisively here, and now we can see it was intended. This growing middle class, grows at the expense of the other two classes, and was the ultimate consequence of making it unnecessary to be particularly concerned about the other two classes in organizing one's constitution.

An unmixed constitution is a constitution which is founded on the middle class, but where the middle class becomes virtually the only class. That's the important consideration. Aristotle too described a healthy polity which is based on the middle class. But his middle class was still small. The largest class was still expected to be the poor; and what Aristotle was trying to do was to bring as many interests together in this first form of the mixed regime such that all would consider the stability of the regime to be in their interest. But he still had to bring them as separate classes. Publius, however, is trying to get rid of the distinction in classes.

One of the most extraordinary things about the argument in the tenth essay, which is reflected as well in the fourteenth essay, is that it anticipates the nineteenth century form of the debate about class and political life. Class has always been part of the discussion of politics. Always. Universally. But with the emergence of socialism and Marxism in the nineteenth century, it takes on a decisively differing tone, and direction. It comes to be allied with notions of history and evolution and the expectation that one of the competing classes would eventually prevail, and, therefore, change history itself. Well, the tenth *Federalist Paper,* in effect, has responded to the arguments of the nineteenth century by anticipating Marx and saying, no we won't have the rich overcome the poor; we won't have the poor overcome the rich; what we will have is a social, economic, and political dynamic at work through which in fact they disappear.

Nos. 10, 14

And I submit that, materially, they have disappeared. It is no accident that if we go out and poll Americans about the class they belong to, we will most often find that they will say that they are middle class, no matter how rich or how poor they are. Americans identify themselves as middle class, either because it's vague, what it is, or because that is everyone's aspiration.

Granted, we can still find what are called the super-rich today, and we can still find the tabloid sheets that celebrate the super-rich, but we're not talking about the rich as a class when we're talking about the super-rich in that form. That's why they can be just about anyone, from extraordinarily rich athletes to people of very old money and very old families. They are isolated, they are individuals. They are not a class in this society any longer. In fact, the only thing that distinguishes them today is their money. They otherwise, in fact, seem just like everybody else, and sometimes less. So it is important to see that this has not happened by accident; it happened

by design. The purpose of the constitutional design is to see to it that the
Constitution is supported on the strength of a very large middle class.

No. 14 This claim, then, in the fourth paragraph of the fourteenth essay, that we
have an unmixed and extensive republic, goes to the very heart of the
challenges from Agrippa and the Maryland Farmer. That leads Publius to
ask some serious questions in the paragraphs following: What are the limits
of a democracy? and How are we supposed to calculate this? The questions
must be asked because we all know that these general arguments must in
principle be subject to some limit. Could we assume that there are no limits
whatever so long as we have a principle of representation? Well, that
would not make sense, particularly if we take seriously the notion of
harmonizing and assimilating differences. We must at least want to keep
the differences at such a level that they are subject to being harmonized and
assimilated, and if they become so extraordinarily distinct then we
wouldn't be able to do that.

He gives us a calculation in the fifth paragraph and those following.
The calculation is interesting because of what it says, both about 1787 and
the future. Note what he says of a democracy, "the natural limit of
democracy is that distance from the central point, which will just permit the
most remote citizens to assemble as often as their public functions
demand." The natural limit is the distance determined by public
function—that's the point. That's the general principle here. Ask how
should the system operate, and how can human beings make it operate that
way, to yield a calculation of the natural limits for democracy?

The natural limit of a republic is that distance from the center, which will barely
allow the representatives of the people to meet as often as may be necessary for
the administration of public affairs. Can it be said the limits of the United States
exceed this distance? It will not be said by those who recollect that the Atlantic
coast is the longest side of the Union, that during the term of thirteen years, the
representatives of the States have been almost continually assembled.

So they've been going to the Confederation Congress, backward and
forward.

Saying they were continually assembled is a little bit disingenuous,
because one of the complaints about the Confederation Congress is the
notoriously poor attendance of delegates to the Confederation Congress.
Some did come, of course, from as far away as Georgia on the South, and
what became Vermont, on the North.

Publius continues by saying, "that we may form a juster estimate with
regard to this interesting subject, let us resort to the actual dimensions of
the Union." He gives a very meticulous account of the geography of the
United States, and this leads to the following: "On a comparison of this
extent, with that of several countries in Europe, the practicability of

rendering our system commensurate to it, appears to be demonstrable. It is not a great deal larger than Germany," etc. This then leads to his ultimate conclusion, and a rule for determining how to look at these things. If we can project, within a certain time period, reaching the capital, where the business has to be conducted, from any point within our geographical limits, then we can say that sets the size of the system.

We notice that that's not a fixed definition, that's an expanding definition. It will change as conditions of travel change. Here, of course, the period of time he selects is two weeks. If the representatives can reach the capitol in two weeks, that will suffice, for being certain that the business can be done so that the country may be as large as is compatible with two weeks travel time to the capital. Well, in 2000 that produces one figure; in 1900, that produced yet another figure; and in 1787, as you know, it produced quite another figure. And so the question then becomes, does that mean that there are no natural limits for this extended republic? Could it be "earth-wide," so to speak? Has his argument gone that far, or are there other principles to be taken into account?

In this essay, we not only get the mechanical argument that leads to the two week measure, we also get the defense of what he called the novel principle of the extended republic. And he returns in the twelfth paragraph, to the question of whether we should run the risk of disunion and the related question of how large the system should be:

No. 14

I submit to you my fellow citizens, these considerations, in full confidence that the good sense which has so often marked your decisions, will allow them their due weight and effect; and that you will never suffer difficulties, however formidable in appearance or however fashionable the error on which they may be founded, to drive you into the gloomy and perilous scene into which the advocates for disunion would conduct you. Hearken not to the unnatural voice which tells you that the people of America, knit together as they are by so many chords of affection, can no longer live together as members of the same family; can no longer continue the mutual guardians of their mutual happiness; can no longer be fellow-citizens of one great respectable and flourishing empire.

In other words, he reminds us, we started with a Union. We did not start with a theory, on the strength of which we generated a Union. We start with a Union. The theory tells us that the Union is not too big for its britches; but it doesn't tell us that we can extend it indefinitely. The condition for extending the Union is the continual existence of the Union.

The continual existence of the Union, then, would depend upon people accepting the principles, first and foremost of course, expressed in the Declaration of Independence. Those principles are the ones that will define the Americans as a Union. So that we have two things operating at the same time. We have first, the notion of the mechanical theory, the mechanical distance limits, and the moral limits, the moral distance. In proportion as we accomplish Union on the scale of the moral distance, it becomes possible by the mechanical theory, to justify extending the reach of the Union.

Finally, in the fourteenth essay, there is this assertion we saw at the beginning that the principle of representation was taken from Europe and improved upon by the United States. The United States made the decisive improvement because it gave us the "unmixed and extensive republic." There is also the question of whether this is a novelty, and we see in the twelfth paragraph that he suggests that even if it is novel, it ought to be accepted. Novelties, he said, are not necessarily to be shunned, and there would, in fact, be no wilder novelty than taking the risk of destroying the Union. It is this curious defense of novelty (remember we introduced that question in the ninth essay when we talked about the improved science of politics) that leads us constantly to weave back and forth between Publius reaching for tradition—a very recent tradition, mind you, of the Declaration of Independence—and on the other hand, reaching forward, to objective principles of inquiry, and objective principles of explanation.

It reminds us, in a way, of the relationship between the Declaration of Independence, as it generated a new national holiday, Independence Day, the Fourth of July, and that previous holiday that existed until the time of Independence Day. The previous holiday was December twenty-second each year, primarily in New England, but it was for all intents and purposes a national holiday; they celebrated "Forefathers Day." When Independence Day became the national holiday, Forefathers Day disappeared. The disappearance of Forefathers' Day, in relation to this revolutionary principle, Independence Day, gives us a very poignant picture of the relationship between novelty and tradition. When we celebrate our Forefathers, of course, tradition lives most among human beings. When we celebrate revolutions, presumably we are then least attached to traditions.

This interplay, for Publius, is at the heart of his discussion in the fourteenth essay because the form of union, the form of nationhood Publius envisions, is one in fact that exposes the society to risk. He makes an enormous statement when, in the last paragraph, he says of the Americans that "they accomplished a revolution which has no parallel in the annals of human society." He is therefore emboldening them, giving them courage to continue to act in that brave way that they acted in the Revolution. By the same token, he is suggesting that it is somehow the magnitude of the work itself—its inherent dignity and importance—which becomes ultimately a way of re-invoking tradition.

NOTES

1. Thucydides, *Peloponnesian War,* ed. T. E. Wick, Crawley translation (New York: Modern Library, 1982), Bk. viii, 47–56, 81–86, 97.

2. Thucydides, *The Peloponnesian War,* Bk. 8, 97.

3. William B. Allen, "Theory and Practice in the Founding of the Republic," *Interpretation* IV (no. 2, Winter 1974): 79–97.

4. William B. Allen, *Let the Advice Be Good: A Defense of Madison's Democratic Nationalism* (Lanham, MD: University Press of America, 1993), 14–16.

5. Gordon Wood, *The Creation of the American Republic* (University of North Carolina Press, 1969; reprinted New York: W. W. Norton & Co., 1972).

6. Maryland Farmer, Essays III (part II) and VII (Baltimore) *Maryland Gazette,* 18 March, 4 April 1788 in Allen and Lloyd, *Essential Antifederalist,* 254–69; see also Federal Farmer, Letters VII, VIII, IX (Poughkeepsie) *Country Journal,* 31 December 1787, 3 and 4 January 1788 in Allen and Lloyd, *Essential Antifederalist,* 261–69.

7. Maryland Farmer, Essay III (part I), (Baltimore) *Maryland Gazette,* 7 March 1788 in Allen and Lloyd, *Essential Antifederalist,* 117–21; Agrippa, Letter IV (Boston) *Massachusetts Gazette,* 3 December 1787, in Allen and Lloyd, *Essential Antifederalist,* 121–23.

8. Maryland Farmer, in Allen and Lloyd, *Essential Antifederalist,* 118.

9. Maryland Farmer, in Allen and Lloyd, *Essential Antifederalist,* 120.

10. Maryland Farmer, in Allen and Lloyd, *Essential Antifederalist,* 122.

PART V: UNION

Exactly what will be the shaping character of this Union? We see the kind of citizens that Publius desired to create, but we need to know how the Union is going to do this.

The chief question, of course, is whether this is a federal or a unitary structure. Does it have the built-in protections for localities and states that we expect from a federal structure, or is it completely exposed to the power of the central government? Looking at essays fifteen through seventeen is essential for answering those questions, and the answers are in some respect surprising—surprising, that is, in their candor. Nos. 15–17

The fifteenth essay deals with the problem of why the Articles of Confederation need to be replaced. In doing so it repeats the earlier argument that the articles are insufficient to the preservation of the Union. No. 15 This is, of course, one of the subjects on the outline. We begin now with the second topic on the outline from the first *Federalist Paper*. But, in this fifteenth essay, the insufficiency of the Articles to preserve the Union does not answer the whole question. Publius makes a rather strong argument to the effect that the true defect of the Confederation is the fact that it wasn't a government at all. He says, taking the term literally, it was no government and it was unable to provide for government. The third paragraph begins the construction of his argument by completing the destruction, if you will, of the Articles of Confederation: "We may indeed with propriety be said to have reached almost the last stage of national humiliation."

The word *nation* was used in the eleventh essay in a somewhat subtle, not particularly obvious way. This is much clearer. The concern with No. 11 national humiliation is very important, for it means that for Publius the work here is not simply to improve the Articles. Recall that when the Constitutional Convention was summoned, it was summoned to amend the Articles of Confederation. Publius cares about national character; he cares about avoiding national humiliation. Publius says that the worst thing about the Articles is that they make us look bad in the eyes of the world.

There is scarcely any thing that can wound the pride, or degrade the character of an independent nation, which we do not experience. Are there engagements to the No. 15 performance of which we are held by every tie respectable among men? These are the subjects of constant and unblushing violation.

He means here, for example, the treaty of peace, the Treaty of Paris with Great Britain. The United States had not been able to remove the British from the western posts or to recover property taken during the war largely because of American violations of that very treaty. So these things somehow impugn the credit of the nation.

He already regards it as a nation. The question isn't whether to make it a nation, the question is whether to make the nation effective; whether to organize it so that it can be a respectable nation. So, in the fifth paragraph he asks that Americans take their stand on behalf not merely of safety but also of reputation.

Starting in the fifth paragraph and going through the ninth paragraph, he explains what's wrong with the other systems. "It is true, as has been before observed, that facts too stubborn to be resisted have produced a species of general assent to the abstract proposition that there exist material defects in our national system." I've said before, the Antifederalists always admitted things were wrong. He now says, well, they admit that but purely abstractly; when it comes to cases they don't want to deal with the problem. "The usefulness of the concession, on the part of the old adversaries of fœderal measures, is destroyed by a strenuous opposition to a remedy, upon the only principles, that can give it a chance of success."

He calls them "the old adversaries of federal measures." That's how they got the name "Antifederalists." While they admit that the government of the United States is destitute of energy, they contend against conferring upon it those powers requisite to supply that energy. And what are those powers? That's what we're building towards. "They seem still to aim at things repugnant and irreconcilable." We can't have an augmentation of federal authority without diminution of state authority. We've got to give up one to get the other. They want sovereignty in the Union, but they want complete independence in the members. "They still in fine seem to cherish with blind devotion the political monster of an *imperium in imperio*," the Latin to mean, then, "a kingdom within a kingdom." "This renders a full display of the principal defects of the confederation necessary." What is the major defect? "The great and radical vice in the construction of the existing Confederation is the principle of LEGISLATION for STATES or GOVERNMENTS, in their CORPORATE or COLLECTIVE CAPACITIES." Confederation is based on the notion that the Confederation Congress governs not the citizens of the United States but the states of the United States. "Though this principle does not run through all the powers delegated to the Union; yet it pervades and governs those, on which the efficacy of the rest depends."

This is a form of constitutional construction. The whole debate is a form of constitutional interpretation, not unlike what we would do today in discussing Supreme Court opinions. The Confederation was a constitution. So, he's analyzing the constitution and how it works, and he says that we discover at its heart, in its principles, that in fact it is no government at all. He brings this out in the seventh paragraph. It is, in fact, "incompatible with the idea of GOVERNMENT." It is a principle, this legislation for states instead of citizens, which in the end, can only be supported through warfare, not through the ordinary administration of laws. That's the end of the seventh paragraph. It is basically only a compact then, or a treaty.

The radical vice of the Confederation was that it couldn't reach the citizens directly by the laws of the central government; Publius and the new Constitution aim to correct that. The signal aspect of the new Constitution is the fact that any citizen, anywhere in the United States, can now be held liable to pay taxes without going through a state government, or they can be held liable for offenses committed that violate federal statutes rather than just state statutes. We can send federal marshals out rather than asking the state sheriff to go and see them. That is the change; that is the transition that's absolutely critical.

This change goes along with and parallels the other very important transition that's taking place in this constitutional exercise. For the people themselves, as I have said before, became the guardians of the constitution, of their national constitution. They will not be people who have state constitutions and whose state governments, state legislatures, enact a national constitution. They will, themselves, enact the national constitution. Otherwise, that constitution's authority over the individuals in the society wouldn't be legitimate. So he's talking about transforming the basic political relationship between the citizens and the Union, or nation. And as I said at the outset, this is candid; he admits it. Yes, the government will be unitary in the decisive respect that the central government can deal directly with its citizens, wherever they are, without requiring the intermediation of the state governments.

In the ninth paragraph, we see some of the consequences. "If the particular States in this country are disposed to stand in a similar relation to each other, and to drop the project of a general DISCRETIONARY SUPERINTENDENCE, the scheme would indeed be pernicious." If they wanted to have a compact or a treaty, instead of a unitary government, then that would be dangerous. That would mean, of course, destruction of the Union. It would mean, as he says at the end of that paragraph, "mutual jealousies and rivalships," fed by foreign intrigues. No, instead what we must do is to incorporate the principles that would give to the national government "a superintending power under the direction of a common Council; we must resolve to incorporate into our plan those ingredients which may be considered as forming the characteristic difference between a league and a government; we must extend the authority of the union to the persons of the citizens,—the only proper objects of government."

I want to emphasize this distinction between the objects of government and the objects of force or warfare. Legislation for states, which only can be enforced through war, only by force, is not government, according to Publius. We know, of course, many governments or institutions that go by the name of government which rely exclusively on force in order to make good their will. So that Publius's argument here is, in fact, a standard of judgment; it is a condemnation of all such institutions. He is saying that the only thing that deserves the name government is what we would call the "rule of law," and the rule of law must be directly over individual citizens, over persons, and not over other corporate bodies or states.

Government is not without coercion as the eleventh paragraph will make very clear.

Government implies the power of making laws. It is essential to the idea of a law, that it be attended with a sanction; or, in other words, a penalty of punishment for disobedience. If there be no penalty annexed to disobedience, the resolutions or commands which pretend to be laws will in fact amount to nothing more than advice or recommendation. This penalty, whatever it may be, can only be inflicted in two ways; by the agency of Courts and Ministers of Justice, or by military force; by the COERTION of the magistracy, or by the COERTION of arms.

I think that's a peculiarly happy formulation, by the way. To speak of the coercion of the magistracy or the coercion of arms allows us to distinguish very clearly what we mean by the "rule of law" and the "rule of force," or the "right makes might" argument and the "might makes right" argument. The coercion of the magistracy is the rule of law but it's still coercion. It still recognizes the necessity that citizens, persons, be held to account for their conduct, but it's done through due procedure with attention to the rights of individuals, and to the safeguards of constitutional order. That is what Publius means now to exercise. That's why he goes on to say that we shouldn't call a military dictatorship a government. To do so confuses the issue and gives government a bad name.

This leads us to reflect on the coercion of the magistracy in the federal government, why is it necessary? And that takes us back to the question we opened in the second essay, "Is government necessary?" Publius is saying that the Confederation Congress is not a government and therefore that's a defect. The implication is, it should be a government. The question, then, is why should it be a government; is government necessary? Looking at paragraphs eleven and twelve we begin to see the answer. He says in paragraph twelve, "Why has government been instituted at all? Because the passions of men will not conform to the dictates of reason and justice, without constraint. Has it been found that bodies of men act with more rectitude or greater disinterestedness than individuals?" The argument about passions and reason recurs.

No. 2

No. 15

Here the argument is not serving the same role it served in the tenth *Federalist Paper,* although those terms are present. At the end of this paragraph we see the spirit of faction once again introduced, and we are told, therefore, we need government to control the spirit of faction. But here it serves the additional purpose of justifying the specific form of government argued for at the federal level or the national level. He says that in politics, where government occurs, there goes along with it certain things, such as the love of power. The love of power will, of course, encourage those who have access to it always to exaggerate it, to increase it and to do so at the expense of liberty.

No. 10

Now, that of course applies to the United States. It applies to the central government to which we are going to give real power instead of pretend power. That raises the whole question of how it is this new and general authority can avoid that ambition which would, otherwise, destroy liberty and overturn freedom in the society at large. He argues that we can't trust those persons who administer the affairs of the particular members of the confederacy to be ready to defend national power. Therefore, we want to have a defense of central power at the central level. The Confederacy has the inefficiency of divided responsibilities. The national government presumably will be efficient.

No. 15

Publius goes on to say, finally, that the states will have a role in this government. They will, in fact, be subordinate agents of the federal government. And this argument is continued in the next essay to make clear exactly how that subordination will take place. Then in the seventeenth essay, Publius develops what I call, following a colleague, "the principle of propinquity" to show how we will, in fact, distinguish concerns of the state.

No. 17

Propinquare is Latin for "to come near," "to draw near." So, the things that are within propinquity are things close to us, near to us. And the seventeenth essay is the essay that says the affairs of the state shall be primarily, those things within the scope and competence of people in their local communities. Of course, those are the kinds of things no one who cares about real power at the federal government would be interested in anyway. And so, the principle of propinquity will mean that we keep the states alive to deal with the petty local interest and, by the same token, people who care about the things nearest to them will resist the intervention of national authority to take over, if there were by chance, someone at the national level who would wish to do so. The reason this discussion has to take place is because now we have admitted that we are going to subordinate the states to the central government, and that raises the urgent question, how can the states believe themselves to be guaranteed once we tell them they are subordinate?

When I lived in France some thirty years ago, I discovered for the first time, what it meant to live under a truly unitary or centralized system of government. One weekend there was a dance in a municipal hall and there was a fire in the hall. There was quite a considerable loss of life and great national discussion over the whole issue. The next morning, a Sunday morning, the President of the Republic called the mayor of the town and fired him because of the fire. And to an American, it's just inconceivable that the President of the Republic could call a mayor in a town and fire him. France, however, is a thoroughly centralized republic, and every office is dependent in a hierarchical chain. The President can do that. One works for the President of the Republic in effect, just the way they used to work for the King in France.

No. 9

Now, that question is raised by the claim that states are subordinate. Does their subordination mean that they must answer to this new hierarchy at the central level? Could the new President designed in the Constitution call up a local mayor and fire him? We know the answer to that question is no, today, but it wasn't obvious immediately. In the ninth essay, Publius has said that the states will exist by a constitutional necessity, but that expression *constitutional necessity* had not yet been interpreted. We were left with needing to ask the question, does constitutional necessity guarantee the rights of local people to choose local offices without being answerable to persons at higher levels?

A system in which local officeholders are immune to the interventions of persons at higher levels in the federal system will certainly be unique and unusual. This was the characteristic of the United States that the Frenchman, DeTocqueville, noticed when he traveled here in the 1830's and described American government as a whole founded on two related functions. The related functions were, what he called, "centralized government" and "decentralized administration." That is how he tried to make sense of it. We had centralized government in the fundamental sense that the Constitution, the organizing principle of power, was centralized. But the responsibility for actually conducting the lives of people throughout the society was based on a decentralization of authority, so that people could actually make decisions in their own lives without having to be answerable to someone who was a thousand, two thousand, or three thousand miles removed. Well, those kinds of results and considerations are brought forth and made necessary by the admissions in the fifteenth essay, the sixteenth essay, and the seventeenth essay.

Nos. 15–17

Many of the questions responded to by Publius are questions of efficiency, and that leads to one set of responses. Others are questions of what we call "necessity." For example, he suggests that this nation, which he claims already exists, stands in peril if ever faced with a foreign enemy. The triumph in the War of the Revolution ought not to be taken, according to Publius, as indicating the nation's capabilities.

No. 16

The nation requires better organization in order to provide for its defense. For example, in the fourth and fifth paragraphs of the sixteenth essay, we see him setting forth the argument that we have to prepare in advance for such things as wars with good organization, because when the war comes there's no time left to organize[1]. That certainly was reflected, by the way, during the War of the Revolution. The war began in 1775, the Declaration of Independence came in 1776, the Articles of Confederation were finally drafted and were under consideration from 1776 through the final drafting in November of 1777. They were not finally approved until 1781, and of course, the war ended two years later. The United States went through most of the war with only an *ad hoc* government. So, this is the point that Publius wants to make: if we're not ready before the crisis, our ability to act during the time of crisis is probably going to be greatly impeded. Moreover we also are not likely to act on the basis of moderate opinions given that war generates much in the way of passion and pride.

Now, that leads to the further argument that we should change from the confederation principle to a principle that allows for such things as the maintenance of a standing army. Turn to the eighth paragraph of the sixteenth essay:

To this reasoning it may perhaps be objected, that if any State should be disaffected to the authority of the Union, it could at any time obstruct the execution of its laws, and bring the matter to the same issue of force, with the necessity of which the opposite scheme is reproached.
The plausibility of this objection will vanish the moment we advert to the essential difference between a mere NON COMPLIANCE and a DIRECT and ACTIVE RESISTANCE. If the interposition of the State-Legislatures be necessary to give effect to a measure of the Union, they have only NOT TO ACT, or TO ACT EVASIVELY, and the measure is defeated.

In other words, if the federal government imposes a tax on the state, the state simply can refuse to pay it and the federal government can enforce it only through war. If the federal government imposes a tax on an individual within the state, there is nothing the state can do by just refusing to act to prevent the collection of the tax; the state would have to resist actively in order to bring it to a halt.

This neglect of duty may be disguised under affected but unsubstantial provisions, so as not to appear, and of course not to excite any alarm in the people for the safety of the constitution. The State leaders may even make a merit of their surreptitious invasions of it, on the ground of some temporary convenience, exemption, or advantage.
But if the execution of the laws of the national government, should not require the intervention of the State Legislatures; if they were to pass into immediate operation upon the citizens themselves, the particular governments could not interrupt their progress without an open and violent exertion of an unconstitutional power. No omissions, nor evasions would answer the end. They

would be obliged to act, and in such a manner, as would leave no doubt that they had encroached on the national rights.

Then comes the centerpiece of this whole argument: "If the people were not tainted with the spirit of their State representatives, they, as the natural guardians of the constitution, would throw their weight into the national scale." In short, if we can govern the people directly, we could also involve the people directly with loyalty to the central government. A state seeking to interfere with the operation of the federal system, could be defeated by its own citizens, who might be more attached to the national government than to their state government.

This leads him into a dilemma. If the people might, in fact, be disposed to be more loyal to the federal government than to the state governments, what is there in that proposition to recommend this Constitution to the states? Will they, in fact, be likely to adopt it if they think that it might be possible that the affections of the people may be displaced from the states to the federal government? That's the question he takes up in the seventeenth essay.

No. 17   Having made it necessary by his response to the other questions in essays fifteen and sixteen, he says in the first paragraph:

An objection of a nature different from that which has been stated and answered, in my last address, may perhaps be likewise urged against the principle of legislation for the individual citizens of America. It may be said, that it would tend to render the government of the Union too powerful, and to enable it to absorb those residuary authorities, which it might be judged proper to leave with the States for local purposes. Allowing the utmost latitude to the love of power, which any reasonable man can require, I confess I am at a loss to discover what temptation the persons entrusted with the administration of the general government could ever feel to divest the States of the authorities of that description.

We have to take that language seriously. See, he can't conceive of any ambitious man wanting to run some state sewage program. It doesn't make sense to him. So, naturally they'll keep that power, because it's not a power anyone would want. But that's, in fact, precisely what has been provided here. Look further down the first paragraph: "Commerce, finance, negociation, and war seem to comprehend all the objects, which have charms for minds governed by that passion [for power]; and all the powers necessary to these objects ought in the first instance to be lodged in the national depository." So, the people who are ambitious, who love power, will be drawn to the national government. That's where they will find offices.

Those who are more concerned with local interests will presumably be drawn to state offices. That will not be great power, but it will be great opportunity to pursue private interests and to deal with the administration of private justice between citizens within the single state, or as he says, "the supervision of agriculture and of other concerns of a similar nature." He tosses these things off very lightly, which for us, of course, must seem somewhat humorous when we look at the list of federal departments that exist in the late twentieth century.

Very many of these concerns, including our sewage and garbage are matters of federal policy and regulation today. We have an Environmental Protection Agency, among many, many others that have taken up precisely these questions. Well, that may be only a reflection, not of any fundamental error in the argument, but of the inevitability of certain kinds of issues being federalized because that's where power has been concentrated in the society. And that, of course, is the Antifederalist concern, that where we put the power is where the action is going to be.

One may say that people ambitious for power only care about commerce, finance, negotiation and war, but the people who need people of power are going to insist that they also think about the other issues that concern them and drive them forward. Publius, however, is not troubled by that. For the federal councils to regulate agriculture would be a bother:

But let it be admitted for argument sake, that mere wantonness and lust of domination would be sufficient to beget that disposition, still it may be safely affirmed, that the sense of the constituent body of the national representatives, or, in other words the people of the several States, would controul the indulgence of so extravagant an appetite.

How would the sense of constituents from the states control the federal government's appetite to exercise power over agriculture and garbage and other such things? Well, he says, in fact, what will happen is the people will be more attached to their states than to the federal government. They will be more attached to what's close to them than to what's far away from them. They will be more interested in having their states take away federal powers than having the federal government take away state powers. In the second paragraph Publius says:

The proof of this proposition turns upon the greater degree of influence, which the State governments, if they administer their affairs with uprightness and prudence, will generally possess over the people; a circumstance which at the same time teaches us that there is an inherent and intrinsic weakness in all Fœderal Constitutions; and that too much pains cannot be taken in their organization, to give them all the force which is compatible with the principles of liberty. **No. 17**

So, the central government is going to be weak by definition, because people want to do things at home. They're going to love their states and they are going to prefer them.

In the forty-sixth essay we return to this question, who will enjoy the greater affection of the people: state governments or the federal government. And the argument in the forty-sixth essay is put in the following terms: we expect people to prefer what is close to them unless they perceive evidence of a so far superior administration of the one that they come to prefer it to the other. In other words, number forty-six admits that if the federal or central government is superior in administering its affairs, in managing its business, then the people may come to prefer it to their state governments.

No. 46

A preference for the federal government would mean, of course, that they would begin transferring concerns from the states to the federal government. So, Publius, while being candid, and remaining candid in a sense, speaks in a very complex way about this question. He leaves us to try to discern exactly what is his response to the Antifederalist fear. It seems to me that Publius says the people will have a stronger attachment to their local government initially. Naturally, we might say, in the sense that we always like best what we know. Publius, however, thinks that eventually they're going to come to know the federal government. They may not know it immediately. It will be new. It will take some special efforts for it to make itself visible to them in a part of their lives. But eventually, they will come to know it.

Nos. 2, 10, 17

Clearly, Publius thinks the national government will have certain advantages over the state government. Perhaps the most important advantage derives from taking the best persons from the state and placing them in the national representation. The best have the most diffusive, the most established characters. They can refine and enlarge public views. Their minds will be charmed by the great national objects of commerce, finance, negotiation, and war. In short, the national government will have the advantage of a certain class, not in the social class sense, but in the sense of abilities.

When we then ask the question, "which government is likely to be better administered?" the answer becomes almost intuitive. That government will be best administered which is administered by the best men. Thus, it would stand to reason to say that Publius ultimately expects that the federal government will supplant the states in the affections of the people and that would not be a surprise.

No. 9

This is a problem, but less of a problem to the degree that the eventuality can emerge slowly, rather than all at once. It can be put off. Further, it is less of a problem to the extent that the states have, as he said in the ninth essay, a constitutional existence. They exist "by a constitutional necessity"; there's nothing that can be done in the Constitution to eliminate the states. Remember, there are very few terms in the Constitution that cannot be amended, but two of those terms are the number of senators for a state and the limits of a state, its geographical, institutional existence. Because they are beyond the reach of amendment, he is able to affirm that the states exist by a constitutional necessity. So, Publius seems to be relying on the fact that once the new order is installed, a new pattern of relationships will develop.

The states will undertake their duties as if they were subordinate parts of a decentralized system. The distinctive character of them will be their coming into office without being selected by the central power. That will be a great and significant distinction. It will probably introduce a lot of diversity and local color into the United States, but it is one well worth preserving if one can do so without exposing the national government to serious injury at the hands of provincials, if I may affect the mood and language of Publius himself.

This addresses the question of the insufficiency of the Confederation to the preservation of the Union. Clearly, one doesn't want merely to preserve the Union. One also wants to structure it. It has been pointed in a direction which we know from the point of view of the objective. We now can perceive that that objective requires certain particular characteristics. It requires a certain emphasis on the representation. It requires a certain understanding of how the national government will act; how it will be administered.

We have, at least until recent times, unless I make a mistake about this, a general expectation that the federal government is more efficient, trustworthy, and better administered, than our local governments. I think that's generally the rule, and the question would be for us, why do we have that? Do we have it because of the design? Because it was meant to work that way? Or do we have it because it went wrong? That's an important question. Very often people suggest, things went wrong, they didn't work the way they were designed, and that shouldn't have happened. Is that following Publius's analysis? Rather, that's exactly the way it should have happened. We should make light of county sheriffs, and celebrate FBI agents the way we do, because country sheriffs deal with petty things and FBI agents deal with great national objects. And the human mind, of course, naturally celebrates great national objects, matters of dignity, nobility, and refinement.

Now, the reason for this seems to be that Publius wants this government to have the capability or the flexibility to deal with the kinds of urgencies that, otherwise, would bring a nation to heel, if not destroy it completely. He thinks the central government must have this capability. The states will be insulated against that necessity. The truly great questions will not have to be dealt with by the states according to this reasoning. Consequently, it is appropriate that one could make a distinction between the kinds of persons who will hold office in the states and those who will hold office in the federal government.

Publius, I think, wants to found and build a nation. If one wants to build a nation, to be a founder, then it's very important that one sets one's sights by objects of ambition, because they're worthy of that kind of effort. It's not enough to tinker, if we really mean to found a lasting institution. What these essays show us, I believe, is precisely the character of Publius's determination to found a way of life and institutions appropriate to that way of life. When we turn to the next series of essays, we will see that he is very candid still, in setting forth the specific powers appropriate to it.

No. 15

No. 14

Before making that turn, let's summarize again the argument from the fifteenth *Federalist Paper,* that is central to this development. Now, however, let's put it in a contemporary context, discussion of a possible global government, in which even the nation could become a subordinate state. By measure of the allowable travel time needed to secure effective representations at a single capital, it is clear that the whole earth could now support a single government—a blessing of technology. Could it also do so on the basis of the fundamental principles intrinsic to the founding of the United States?

No. 1

What commentators frequently refer to as the "global community" constitutes by definition what Alexander Hamilton called in the first *Federalist Paper* a realm of "accident and force." Matters stand thus for the sufficient reason that the alternative to constructing political institutions by accident and force is to adopt them by "reflection and choice," where deliberate reflection and choice expressly invoke the role played by natural individuals in instituting the political order. In short, where the architecture of the global community cannot be referred to the collective agency of "citizens of the world," that architecture must be imposed by accident and force (which includes conventions among states) rather than chosen by popular will.

I do not concentrate on the obvious bias of democratic or majority rule in order to render the claims of democracy problematic. I do so rather to demonstrate that the most interesting questions regarding global community must sooner or later encounter the same questions of legitimacy which bedevil democracy. In that sense, of course, one uses the United Nations as a proxy for the "global community," not in the form of a straw man but as a reasonable approximation to institutional standards which serve to surface the most crucial issues.

For example, a typical conceptual error is the idea that economic development and political development operate largely as independent if interactive variables. This leads analysts to speak erroneously of market economies, planned economies, capitalist economies, etc. On any accurate account, there is only one economy, namely the market economy, which operates under more or less exiguous constraints dependent on political forms and practices. Accordingly, the variations in politics are much more decisive in the determination of human prospects, whether in the form of a separate state I call the state-nation or in some conceivable form of global community.

This matter of technical definition poses a practical problem for the advocates of global order. The problem is illustrated by the persistent discussion of democracy, or rather the absence of democracy, within the United Nations. As it happens even the staunchest advocates of international democracy mean by it nothing more than weight proportioned by respective member populations in international councils, with no design whatever to institute that representation by popular election. Where states, sovereign states, remain the units of membership, even when exercising differential weights of decision based on population, it remains true that what is reflected in the architecture must be the relations of states and not the relations of peoples. The practical problem, therefore, is to know what are the prospects of a global people (where the term global has the same cognitive value as the term national) in whom one would found a global community.

We may further survey the context of the question. Recently I wrote that the terms of modern sovereignty have elevated the state above the nation as the fundamental unit of social organization and draw upon raw humanity as the exclusive source of authorizing political principle. In this account particularity and membership exclusivity persist, but rather as practical conditions for realizing the goals of political community. Thus citizenship has come to mean foremost the extracting of certain humans from lives subjected wholly to the whims of accident and force. Yet, the transition from state-organized community to global community would require such a change of conditions as would make protections for "human rights" redundant. This occurs because the terms of modern sovereignty require that one addresses the needs of the individuals in order to generate collective order.

The arguments presented in *The Federalist Papers* constitute a comprehensive account of the prospects for a global state, even if further elaboration is required in order to apply it to discussions of a global community as opposed to the consolidation of the original thirteen United States. Moreover, I urge that the presumption that such an analysis is either deliberately or necessarily unfavorable to the prospects of global community strongly misreads the sources of opposition in Publius's argument. For the reality is that an argument which proposed a transcendent union as the specific means required to eliminate differences of interest and power among separate states is precisely what prevailed on Publius's terms. Since the notion of a global community is spurred by a similar or identical motivation, even if its adherents aim at a qualitatively different result, it follows that the constraints which operated in the prior case likely operate in the present case.

Unless the state-nation constitutes the ultimate form of political organization, Publius's option of a transcending union may apply on a global basis. At a minimum, there will remain scope for the emergence of fewer—and larger—state-nations (which I regard as likely). The remaining question with respect to a global state or community is whether such a development would entail a withering of citizenship. This may happen not only because lesser sovereignties (or civil societies) disappear but also because exclusivity may no longer derive from universal principles. The notion of citizenship declines with declining significance of rights guarantees. While the governed remain the consenting individuals from whose rights the need for political guarantees arises, as governed they would no longer require a form of emotional identification with the state. Indeed, one would think government in this case to be completely subject to the governed. Whatever might be the basis of rights guarantees in such a global state, it could not be citizenship.

In arguing for the superiority of national union over a confederation of sovereign states in the fifteenth *Federalist Paper,* Publius opened with "the dark catalogue of our public misfortunes." These bear the significance of suggesting utilitarian or expedient measures of political sufficiency, leading to the implication that a regime choice might be founded in the response to uncontroversial questions regarding public happiness rather than in what we are wont to call "ideology" in our day. Consider the list of items which express "the last stage of national humiliation":

No. 15

1. Routine violation of sworn engagements
2. Non-payment of debts honestly and beneficially incurred
3. Foreign occupation of national territory with impunity
4. Lack of treasury, troops, government
5. Lack of right to appeal for justice on account of our own injustices
6. Denial of recourse to natural resources by superior powers
7. Lack of public credit
8. Lack of commerce
9. Lack of respect in the eyes of other nations
10. Depreciated value of properties
11. Lack of private credit due to failure to secure guarantees of repayment.

Publius traced these specific evils not to any intrinsic incapacities among the Americans but to "defects" in their political organization, chief among which was the prejudice against a transcending political community to unite the energies of all in common purpose. The "evils we experience do not proceed from minute or partial imperfections, but from fundamental errors in the structure . . . which cannot be amended otherwise than by an alteration in the first principles and main pillars."

Publius argued that the very idea of the system of thirteen sovereign states seeking to act in coordination to resolve these problems was flawed:

The great and radical vice in the construction of the existing Confederation is in the principle of LEGISLATION for STATES or GOVERNMENTS, in their CORPORATE or COLLECTIVE CAPACITIES and as contradistinguished from the INDIVIDUALS of whom they consist.

That this vice inheres in the principle undergirding the Confederation and not its circumstances, Publius demonstrates by showing next that powers fully adequate to the circumstances have been conveyed to the Confederation but remain ineffective. They remain ineffective because it is not possible for the Confederation to bind the member sovereigns to performance of their obligations. The very idea of legislating for states instead of individuals, he insists, is "incompatible with the idea of GOVERNMENT."

Publius's critique does not aim to invalidate every form of alliance among states. He insists only that such leagues can pursue but limited purposes and can rely on nothing for enforcement of their terms but the interests of the contractors or the "sanguinary agency of the sword." The natural conclusion from such arrangements is that allies exist alternately as friends and enemies as their circumstances dictate. It is only in the case where men aim to eliminate the swings of fortune in such relations that they must adopt "those ingredients which may be considered as forming the characteristic difference between a league and a government; we must extend the authority of the union to the persons of the citizens,—the only proper objects of government."

To this point the argument is clear: to create government means to erect over individuals "the mild influence of the Magistracy," which is achievable only through the creation of citizenship on the same plane as the magistracy. At the same time one must note that the presence of consent alone makes possible the creation of citizenship on the same plane as the magistracy. "Reflection and choice" generate the moral authority which makes mild magistracies.

The last portion of *Federalist Paper* number fifteen explains the reasons for this conclusion, namely, that "government implies the power of making laws," laws require "sanctions," and of sanctions there are but two, "the COERTION of the magistracy, or the COERTION of arms." Because armed coercion applies properly to collective bodies, states, arrangements which entail enforcement against sovereign states necessarily imply war as the means to ensure compliance. Over individuals, realists would insist, the sword is also the ultimate recourse. Publius's response is decisive, however: Not only may men be nurtured in their obedience through means which have no influence over states (men blush; states do not; and men care about their reputations as individuals in ways to which they pay no heed as members of a collective body), but individual citizens are little likely to feel and less likely to manifest those centrifugal tendencies which commonly spin states out of the orbit of common effort. While the "love of power" animates the individual soul, it requires for its indulgence the soil of collective effort. Thus, ambitious souls holding authority in corollary or subordinate bodies will contend with the lawful requisitions of a central power. Such is the decree "of human nature."

Publius, then, argues that the only rational design for a transcending political authority is one that diminishes opportunities for organized challenges to that authority. While every political society must avail itself of subordinate bodies and mediating institutions, the idea that a political society can be erected on a framework of sovereign members constitutes a "solecism" in politics in theory and in practice.

No. 20

The application of Publius's analysis to a discussion of state sovereignty and global community will seem immediately obvious. Pessimism regarding any robust form of global community incorporating continuing state sovereignty would be warranted. A distinction requires to be noted at this stage, however. As I have written, the state-nation appears to be the ultimate form of political organization. If that is true, then the option of a transcending union is foreclosed on a global basis. While there will remain scope for the emergence of fewer—and larger—state-nations, there will not emerge a global state for the sufficient reason that such a state would entail a withering of citizenship. This happens not only because lesser sovereignties disappear and exclusivity may no longer derive from universal principles. The notion of citizenship loses significance when it ceases to be the vital occasion of rights guarantees. The governed would remain the consenting individuals from whose rights the need for political guarantees arises, but as governed they would command their government without a need to love it or defend it. On these terms, indeed, one would think of government as completely in subjection to the governed. Whatever might be the basis of rights guarantees in such a global state, it could not be citizenship.

No. 10

Nos. 8, 9, 14–16

Organizing the institutions of the central government to break the violence of faction is not only the argument of the tenth *Federalist Paper*. We find throughout the *Federalist Papers* that this argument plays a crucial role, the central role, in organizing the defense of the Constitution. It is true, the term faction, or some version of the term, occurs twenty-one times in the tenth *Federalist Paper* and no more than thrice in any of the other *Federalist Papers*. But, we've already seen that it also occurs in the eighth and ninth *Federalist Papers* where we anticipate the argument of the tenth *Federalist Paper*, and the term appears in the fourteenth, fifteenth, and sixteenth *Federalist Papers*, and many of the others. The interesting fact about this is precisely that these papers are equally the papers written by Hamilton and by James Madison.

For a long time, people have looked upon the tenth *Federalist Paper*, in some respects, as the *Federalists Papers* altogether. In focusing on the analysis of interest, or what has come to be called pluralism in latter-day political science and history, they are following the work of Charles Beard early in the century. Much of the rest of the *Federalist Papers* has been ignored. It is crucial for us to recognize, though, that the terms of analysis of the tenth *Federalist Paper* go well beyond the mere question of interest groups. They go to the very heart of the distinction between republics and democracies and to the project as it's set forth in the first *Federalist Paper*.

Repeating in greater detail what I said earlier, the problem of factions permeates the other essays. In the eighth essay Publius speaks of suppressing faction. In the ninth essay he speaks as well of building a barrier against domestic faction and insurrection and also of the power of the Union "to repress domestic faction and insurrection." Later in the *Federalist Papers*, as late as in the eighty-first *Federalist Paper*, he speaks about the "pestilential breath of faction"; considering it as a poison in the body politic. Publius speaks in the seventy-third essay about the spirit of faction in much the same way as in the fourteenth *Federalist Paper*. In the fifty-first *Federalist Paper*, of course, the argument about the stronger faction readily uniting and oppressing the weaker faction, is the centerpiece of the defense of the entire system of checks and balances and separation of powers in the United States. It is also the centerpiece of the argument made by Publius in the fifty-first essay for what we shall later discuss as the just majority. The argument in the fifty-first *Federalist Paper* demonstrates that the discussion of faction in the tenth *Federalist Paper* is not a discussion against majorities, though it certainly is a caution about the way in which majority rule is to be organized.

Nos. 8, 9, 51, 73, 81

Nos. 10, 51

When we seek, therefore, to provide an antidote to what the fourteenth *Federalist Paper* calls the effects of faction or the diseases of faction, we are in essence talking about the entire founding project from the perspective of Publius. A project which aims, not only to structure terms of participation within the society at large, but also which aims to fashion a nation or a Union that can be seen as one. That can take the expression, as George Washington might have put it, of a single national character. The argument about faction is really an argument towards that harmonizing and assimilation of characters and opinions which is set forth at the outset of the *Federalist Papers* and which, therefore, makes it important for us to focus very carefully our attention on the argument in the tenth *Federalist*, much as has been done historically.

Nos.
4–10

I always like to caution, it is important to look beyond the tenth *Federalist* and not to take that as the whole of the *Federalist Papers*. It is not an isolated essay, which is independent of the rest of the *Federalist Papers*. Just as *Federalist* four, five, six, seven, eight, and nine lead up to *Federalist* ten, all the essays which come afterwards are no less significant in setting forth the arguments in the tenth *Federalist Paper*. Throughout these essays the question of faction becomes the question of how to turn the government at the national level effectively into an umpire and an arbitrator. And the point is, of course, that we will not be able to eliminate faction, but rather that we will have to organize factions such that they become positive rather than negative influences within the society. We will look more closely at that argument presently.

Nos. 6,
8–10,
14–16,
18, 21,
22, 27,
29, 37,
43, 45,
51, 59,
60–62,
65, 66,
70, 71,
73, 81,
85

If we just take a count, as I said at the outset, of the various occurrences of the term *faction* through the *Federalist Papers*; we can then appreciate the central organizing power of the use of the term *faction* in the document as a whole. I've mentioned essays eight, nine, ten, and fourteen and we find it in essays fifteen and sixteen. We speak about the intrigues of faction in essays eighteen, twenty-one, and twenty-two. Again faction appears in essays twenty-seven and twenty-nine; fifty-one, of course was mentioned; and we also find it in fifty-nine, sixty-one, sixty-five, seventy, seventy-one, seventy-three, and eighty-one. Moreover, variants of the word, either in its plural form or in the adjective "factious," are in essays six, where we looked at the problem in light of the experience of the Union of England and Scotland, thirty-seven, forty-three, forty-five, sixty, sixty-two, sixty-five, sixty-six, seventy, and eighty-five. So, it appears almost consistently throughout the work. *Faction* represents a single expression in which all the authors of the *Federalist Papers* concur in expressing their ambition to produce a government. Their discussion goes beyond the rather simple-minded question of how to arrange interest groups. Instead the broader question is how to produce, if not homogeneous, at least harmonious social interaction.

Nos.
15–17,
18–20

After completing the attack on the Articles of Confederation in essays fifteen through seventeen, we have in essays eighteen through twenty a series of essays that intend to introduce us to a history lesson. Go back momentarily to essay nine so that we can remember how we get this far and what it is we are attempting to do. In the sixteenth paragraph of the ninth essay, we remember that Publius offers the definition of a *confederate republic*. It is important that we emphasize the words at this stage, because the question becomes ultimately, whose definition is it? In defining the confederate republic, he says:

No. 9

The extent, modifications and objects of the Fœderal authority are mere matters of discretion. So long as the separate organisation of the members be not abolished, so long as it exists by a constitutional necessity for local purposes;

though it should be in perfect subordination to the general authority of the Union, it would still be, in fact and in theory, an association of States, or a confederacy. The proposed Constitution, so far from implying an abolition of the State Governments, makes them constituent parts of the national sovereignty by allowing them a direct representation in the Senate, and leaves in their possession certain exclusive and very important portions of sovereign power.

Of course, this raises a question. Where does this definition come from and why would he say, "the extent, modification, and objects of the Fœderal authority are mere matters of discretion"? We know, in fact, that traditionally, if we speak of a confederation as a league or an association of states, there are certain fundamental requisites. The equality of the independent states is fundamental. Each has a vote. We also know that it is traditionally regarded as fundamental that the confederacy acts by a rule of unanimity. It decides questions by unanimous decision. Hence, the *liberum* veto in the Polish Constitution allowed any one individual to suspend the operation of the government. These have always been insisted upon as necessities, not mere matters of discretion by the exponents of federal theory and certainly by the Antifederalists. The Maryland Farmer complained that the Federalist shouldn't be called Federalist because they don't know what federalism is, and certainly Publius's definition seems to confirm at least a basis for Antifederalist suspicions.

When, therefore, in essays fifteen through seventeen the focus shifts and Publius begins to talk about real government and real law as his true aim, we begin to understand why he generated that rather novel definition of the confederation. He doesn't want a national Union which is subject to the veto of the local units or the states. It is to be truly a national government and not merely a federal government. The government takes on a different structure because built into the Constitution are certain local concerns, which is a matter of significance, but not a matter which is ultimately determinative.

Nos. 15–17

The principal argument of the seventeenth essay is, as we pointed out previously, that the people will have a stronger bias towards their local governments than towards their national or central government because people care most about the things that are close to them. In other words, the principle of propinquity. Yet, at the end of that essay, there is also what amounts to an introduction to the history of "federal constitutions." This is a very important though brief introduction. Publius closes with the history of what he called the "ancient feudal systems." The history of federal constitutions continues through essay twenty.

Nos. 17–20

On the surface the feudal history Publius gives at the end of essay seventeen is an analogy to confederacy, as he is now defining confederacy. He describes the rule of the monarch or emperor as having several barons or lords who have their own independent domains. And within those independent domains they have dependents themselves, serfs and others. The barons or lords maintained armies. They were subject to be called upon by the king for the defense of the realm. Just as often, however, they themselves, in fact, resisted the king and occasionally even organized against the king.

No. 15   This example of how the feudal system operated permits Publius to give a very concrete example of the centrifugal tendency that he explained in the fifteenth essay. He said the problem with the confederation is the tendency
No. 10   for the subordinate bodies which orbit around the solar system to want to fly away from the center. That's the problem we're trying to overcome. We're going to overcome that by a policy of legislating for individuals rather than legislating for states. But we need more than just the formal constitutional arrangements of identifying the objects of legislation. We also need what we might call, centripetal tendencies. Now we explained the centripetal tendencies, the principles that will operate in such a way as to force people to move towards the center, when we looked at the tenth
No. 10   *Federalist Paper*. That's the whole point of the argument of the large, extended, republic. We can create a dynamic where the centripetal tendencies will come to play and will bring people towards the center and permit that assimilation that we've been talking about from the very beginning. Yet, the centrifugal tendencies are real. They have a practical, concrete existence and so we need to say more than that we have extended the sphere. We also have to describe what the particular relationships of all the parts will be in this whole, if indeed, it is to be a whole.

In the history of feudal times Publius, at least, finds a foundation of confederacies which differs markedly from the foundation of many Antifederalists and many other participants in the American Revolution. Indeed, it differs from what is commonly seen today as our foundation. When we read contemporary scholarship, scholarship that has been fostered by the work of historians such as Bernard Bailyn, Gordon Wood, or Michael Kammen and other distinguished historians, we notice it focuses almost exclusively on something called Whig theory. Whigs we know, of course, from the English revolutionary tradition. They were the forebearers, the antecedents, to the American revolutionaries by and large. Whig history played an important role in the writings of the people who created *Cato's Letters*, Trenchard and Gordon, and was reflected even in the work of a philosopher like Montesquieu. That Whig history basically found the origins of English liberty far in the past, before the emergence of a monarchical order and before the emergence of the feudal order.

The traditional Whig history account of the origins of the modern world is an argument that says that people were basically free peoples associated loosely in tribes or clans in the German and Frankish forest. These peoples had no king or ruler over them. They operated on the basis of principles of equality. This was not democracy in the formal sense of being organized, but they operated democratically in the sense that each man was responsible for himself and answerable to himself. And in that context they ultimately came to experience the competitions that led to the construction of larger societies, such as the struggles between the strong and the weak. Out of such competition came the feudal order that produced barons who came together as free spokesmen for their particular areas and elected from among themselves a king. So, we have this rather organic picture of the evolution of monarchical society as being produced by the freedom that people originally enjoyed in the German forest. That's called Whig History and it's used in England and used in the United States in order to show from time immemorial a sense of the privileges and rights of Englishmen and the privileges and rights of Americans.

When we look at Publius's analogy of feudal history to confederacies, the one thing that becomes most evident is his rejection of Whig History. He instead follows the line of the British philosopher-historian, David Hume. Publius uses what we might call Tory history rather than Whig history. If we look at the fourth paragraph in the twenty-sixth essay, we have it stated succinctly, the same argument from the end of the seventeenth essay. Here in essay twenty-six he says:

No. 26

In England for a long time after the Norman conquest the authority of a monarch was almost unlimited. Inroads were gradually made upon the prerogative, in favor of liberty, first by the Barons and afterwards by the people, 'till the greatest part of its most formidable pretensions became extinct.

This is not Whig theory. For Publius, liberty emerges as a limitation on the power and prerogative of the monarch. The monarch comes first, the liberty comes second. That's Hume's version of the history. Liberty is nothing more than concessions extorted from the monarch by powerful barons. The monarch was not created by the exercise of liberty that the people already enjoyed.

For Publius, English liberty was recent rather than ancient. Continuing in the fourth paragraph, he says: "But it was not 'till the revolution in 1688, which elevated the Prince of Orange to the throne of Great Britain, that English liberty was completely triumphant." Of course, in Whig theory the highest state of liberty was in the golden age back in the time that no one can really remember.

Hume's and Publius's version is that there isn't full liberty until the revolution itself in 1688.

As incident to the undefined power of making war, an acknowledged prerogative of the crown, Charles IId. had by his own authority kept on foot in time of peace a body of 5,000 regular troops. And this number James IId. increased to 30,000; which were paid out of his civil list. At the revolution, to abolish the exercise of so dangerous an authority, it became an article of the bill of rights then framed, that "the raising or keeping a standing army within the kingdom in time of peace, *unless with the consent of Parliament*, was against the law."

Of course the twenty-sixth essay is concerned with the problem of standing armies, which is not immediately germane to us. Nonetheless, it is clear that the traditional notion of English liberty, that Hume defended in opposition to the Whigs, was a positive construction resulting out of the political struggles between the Crown and commons, and originally between the Crown and barons—the barons being succeeded by what became the House of Commons.

Nos. 17–20
In the twelfth paragraph of the seventeenth essay, Publius says Scotland is an example of baronial triumph. This suggests we're going to have three essays, eighteen through twenty, which deal with the history of confederacies so as to place the history of the Articles of Confederation in proper perspective. This history will be a history that is not a Whig history. We expect to look at the positive accomplishments of previous states and to measure the accomplishments of present states against those in order to assess the possibilities of liberty in the context of the United States. Liberty is not just an inheritance. That's the point that Publius is trying to make.

No. 22
Liberty is not merely positive. At the end of the twenty-second essay, for example, is a reference to the principles of the Declaration of Independence which founded liberty, of course, on a law of nature. The principles continue to animate Publius. But the point is that that law of nature has not had an inevitable historical development. It is something that has to be affirmatively, consciously, acted upon in a moment of history. It cannot simply be recaptured from an immemorial past. And that then is the role of this series of histories of confederacies, which start with the ancient world in the eighteenth essay and go on to the modern world in the nineteenth essay. The suggestion is that there is something to be learned from the contrast and comparison with previous peoples; and this is not merely evolutionary development.

No. 18
It is quite clear in essay eighteen that there is a general line of interpretation present here concerning the original Enlightenment theories that led ultimately to such documents and doctrines as the Declaration of Independence. We remember the state of nature, which was introduced by Thomas Hobbes back in the seventeenth century and followed, of course, by John Locke. The notion of a state of nature in the modern theory was of a state that Hobbes defined most succinctly as short. It's a life of war, of all against all, where the principle that prevails is, of course, the principle of force. And the social contract that brings an end to the state of nature is, in the Hobbesian sense, a rational device to escape the violence of nature. Well, much of this history that we now read has that appearance. These are organized societies already but also systems of ever shifting and changing

alliances in which strength and weakness seem to determine everything. This begins with that portrait of the feudal past in the seventeenth essay and the principle of force continues to be revealed, particularly with the discussion of the Amphyctionic and Achæan leagues.

One of the things that's perhaps most revealing of Publius's attitude comes at the end of the eighth paragraph in the eighteenth essay. Citing the Abbé Milot, Publius rehearsed the history of the relationships between Athens and Sparta and concluded with the observation that "their mutual jealousies, fears, hatreds, and injuries ended in the celebrated Peloponnesian war; which itself ended in the ruin and slavery of the Athenians, who had begun it."

What's interesting about the observation that the Athenians began the war is, of course, that that was a disputed point. It was a disputed point between Athens and Sparta. In fact, at one point after roughly ten years of war, during the first period of peace in the Peloponnesian War, the Spartans, in fact confessed that they had begun the war and they went through an elaborate series of religious exercises to expiate their guilt. They thought that their suffering in the war had been a direct reflection of the gods' unhappiness with them for beginning the war.

Now the start of the Peloponnesian War is interesting. It began when Sparta's allies, those who constituted the Peloponnesian League, came to Sparta and insisted that Athens was getting to be too strong. They said, "you've got to stop this. If they continue to become so strong, they will become a threat to all of us. And they will act on the strength that they have."

At that stage, at least to follow the account of Thucydides and not Plutarch or some others, the impression is that Athens did nothing overtly to challenge the Peloponnesian League. Athens had done nothing towards Sparta, Corinth, nor any of their lesser allies, but Corinth and Sparta were exercised with the fear that Athens would do something. Thucydides, of course, tells us that "the truest pretext of the war" was the fact of Athens's increasing strength. He therefore indicates that it may have been rational for Sparta to act at a moment when they might still be able to arrest the development of Athens, rather than allowing it to go unchecked.

If that's the case, that's at least a very interesting reflection. Under the doctrine of preemptive war a state does not wait until it's struck. It is said that Queen Elizabeth once had it whispered into her ears regarding such a situation, "strike before you are struck." It certainly could be an effective policy. But whether it is also a policy that can be brought within the principles of just war is another question. Publius says Athens began the war, and seems to accept the argument for preemptive war.

If Publius accepts that argument, I suggest that Publius probably does so only in the sense of accepting something like the state of nature in which self-preservation is rational and it is folly and irrational not to secure one's life. That is why, then, his language is a language of strong governments and weak governments. It is the same thing as speaking about strong persons and weak persons. Publius uses the same language later in the fifty-first *Federalist* when he says a weak government, even when not at war, is ever agitated by internal dissension; and internal agitations never fail to bring on fresh calamities from abroad. Their very weakness invites attack.

No. 11

We see also from Thucydides that if Athens began the war, so does strength invite attack of a certain order. Yet, we remember from the beginning, essays two and three in particular, and four as well, that we expected there was a certain kind of strength that would ward off attack.

Nos.
2–4

In those essays, however, it wasn't mere strength, it was political prosperity as we recall, that wards off attack. Political prosperity was more than just force; it was that situation that would invite others into friendly association. The ancient world clearly lacked the sense of inviting others into friendly association and friendly relations with the state, whether the state was weak or strong. A strong confederation, he argued in the eleventh essay, could perhaps have protected Greece.

This reminds us of the Spartan king and general, Agesilaus. Sparta won the Peloponnesian War, the Athenian empire fell, and Agesilaus was the new king. And he's a different king for Sparta because he was a bastard child and wasn't raised as a king. He was raised among the folk. But finally, he's elevated to the kingship and yet has the attitude and character of the folk, which makes him much beloved. He went to Persia to defend his country and did so with considerable success, but eventually was called home. On the way home he hears of a battle in Greece involving several of the Greek city states, and his Spartan forces ultimately prevailed. But he, rather than celebrating, was saddened by it. He thought what a terrible thing it is to see so many Greeks fall in this way, when they could have been a united army defending Greece.

That was an extremely unusual perspective, and not just for a Spartan but for any Greek to think of Greece as a whole and Greeks as brothers. There was no such thing in Greece. None of these various leagues we are reading about, including the Amphyctionic league and the Achæan league, covered the whole of Greece. They were usually competing leagues, alliances, or confederations of independent states. The Greek city-states regarded themselves in the same way we regard nations in the contemporary world. Athens and Sparta were utterly and completely different. They had nothing in common, other than the land they perhaps shared, to speak loosely, on this peninsula. Apart from that, they had nothing in common. They were different in constitutions, societies, and gods. They differed in everything.

Nonetheless Publius speaks about Greece failing to take advantage of some of its opportunities because it didn't have a strict enough confederation. To organize Greece that way would have meant overcoming differences. It would have meant Athenians no longer being Athenians, and Spartans no longer being Spartans. And that's what's interesting about Agesilaus' reflection. It is as if this king of Sparta was not quite so Spartan as he would have been expected to be.

Is that a just criticism of the ancient confederation? If the weakness of the ancient confederations stems from the facts that these were differing peoples, who worshipped different gods, is it a just criticism that they didn't overcome their differences merely for the sake of being stronger militarily? What is the point of social organization? Why would we want to sacrifice the distinctive quality of our society? Why sacrifice the reason for our enjoying to live in our society or the reason for seeking to accomplish the goals, the ends, of that society? If we must sacrifice these merely for the sake of prowess in war, what do we gain by that? That is precisely the character of the criticism here, if we can take lightly these things that otherwise define human life.

Now, I repeat that Publius says we are going to harmonize and assimilate the Americans. That means, of course, that we are going to overcome whatever differences there may have been. If there were differences as great between Georgia and Massachusetts as Agrippa described, and he makes it sound like differences between Athens and Sparta, then Publius must face those differences. Is Publius going to create a new American nationality in the process? Is that what he's doing? Is he facing that difference in the interest of a superior difference, if I may use the word in that way. If there is only self-preservation to be gained by union, union seems far less compelling than the case where there is a superior difference and one forgoes one's Spartanness for something greater than Spartanness. Clearly Publius's history of confederations raises these questions in a way that makes them questions about Publius's intentions and not just about his application of the historical lesson.

To give a historical lesson for a moment, James Madison, before he went to the Constitutional Convention of 1787, sat in his study and pulled all of his books off the shelf and wrote out a memorandum on the histories of the ancient confederacies. He went into the Convention preparing himself by studying through the very materials we see presented here in *The Federalist Papers*. He didn't do that for the purpose of writing essays or for trying to persuade someone else that this is like our situation and we can react that way because they reacted this way and it worked or didn't work, etc. It was just a way of informing himself, we might say, of the range of human possibilities based on the things that are known to us. We can speculate about the infinities of time, but we know we have a certain human record, and so he pulled it out.

It is a very serious question of how far the study of ancient and modern No. 9 confederacies could be instructive in the American context. That's one of the problems we are dealing with. Remember in the ninth essay we are given a definition of the confederate republic, which is not the standard definition. If all we learned from these histories of ancient confederacies is not to do things this way, we would still have the very powerful question, what is the way to do things? It has been observed from the earliest moments of recorded thought that error is irrelevant, because there are an infinite number of ways to do things wrong but only one way to hit the mark. So, to proceed by learning the things we shouldn't do could turn into quite an endless task. There is in principle no end to it.

No. 19

The question, therefore, is where did that answer concerning what should be done come from? How was the question finally resolved in a positive spirit if these histories that we see in eighteenth, nineteenth, and twentieth essays will not do that? Well, when he gets through the eighteenth essay and comes to the nineteenth, it changes at least a little bit and I want to be emphatic about this. The opening of the nineteenth essay is explicit. It says we've looked at the examples of ancient confederacies, now let's look at modern institutions. So Publius draws a sharp distinction between the examples of ancient confederacies and the modern examples. Why?

In the second paragraph, Publius says:

In the early ages of Christianity Germany was occupied by seven distinct nations, who had no common chief. The Franks, one of the number, having conquered the Gauls, established the kingdom which has taken its name from them. In the ninth century Charlemagne, its warlike monarch, carried his victorious arms in every direction; and Germany became a part of his vast dominions. On the dismemberment, which took place under his sons, this part was erected into a separate and independent empire. Charlemagne and his immediate descendants possessed the reality, as well as the ensigns and dignity of imperial power. But the principal vassals, whose fiefs had become hereditary, and who composed the national Diets which Charlemagne had not abolished, gradually threw off the yoke, and advanced to sovereign jurisdiction and independence.

Whenever we hear the word Christianity, we know we're in the modern context, while a discussion of pagan Greeks is ancient. We have yet to discern what is the political characteristic of a Christian age. And the reference to the Franks having no common chief is as close as Publius comes to the Whig theory, by the way. It is not exactly compatible with the end of the seventeenth essay if you go back and look at it. It is not Whig theory because the kingdoms were established by conquest. They were not established by mutual agreement among these independent chiefs.

Again the history of feudalism is given to us, but an interesting contrast between it and the ancient Greek history ought to detain our attention for a moment. Unlike the history of the Amphyctionic or the Achæan leagues, this is a history of individuals such as Charlemagne, the great Charles. It is a history of individuals with individual intentions, or individual nations with individual purposes, setting forth to accomplish designs. This feudal history is not portrayed as a parallel to that Greece. The parallel case would be Europe. At no point will Publius refer to the interest of Europe or how Europe might have conducted itself. These are separate intentions of separate peoples or persons and it's natural then to talk about imperial power.

"The imperial authority, unable to maintain the public order, declined by degrees, till it was almost extinct in the anarchy, which agitated the long interval between the death of the last Emperor of the Suabian, and the accession of the first Emperor of the Austrian lines." Does the whole problem of succession characterize the modern world differently than the way that succession was a subordinate question in the ancient world? The ancient world was disturbed by constant revolutions in their constitutions. Similarly, there is constant struggle in the modern world. The struggle, however, is all over succession, as if the rest of the political order were beyond question. **No. 19**

Consider the history of the German confederacy, which he presents starting at paragraph seven in the nineteenth essay. He says in the middle of the eighth paragraph, "Controversies and wars among the members themselves have been so common that the German annals are crowded with the bloody pages which describe them." Their life is based on the series of alternate oppressions between the strong and the weak. That's the modern story. It's very much the kind of story the philosopher Hobbes told according to Publius.

Unlike the Greek leagues, the modern confederacies persisted despite their constant warfare and despite the weakness of their organization. Publius raises this question in the thirteenth paragraph, why didn't they just fall apart? What is the explanation for this? He doesn't give a full explanation but he does suggest something that is of immediate interest. In the middle of that thirteenth paragraph he says that there are certain things that "support a feeble and precarious union." There are circumstances, there are accidents that keep it from falling apart. No one emerges who is strong enough simply to overwhelm it and therefore they continue to exist in the struggle of warfare. But then he goes on to say, "whilst the repellent quality, incident to the nature of sovereignty, and which time continually strengthens, prevents any reform whatever, founded on a proper consolidation."

Publius's response to this almost state-of-nature existence is a *proper consolidation*. These independent parts of Germany, all of which manifest this centrifugal tendency described in the fifteenth essay, are in the position of needing to be organized in some coherent unity, in a proper consolidation. This is, of course, precisely what is being attempted under the Constitution in the context of the United States. It is not so much an **No. 15** overturning of the democracy of 1776 as it is a structuring of that democracy into "a proper consolidation."

The seventeenth paragraph repeats the idea in a different context. The Swiss Cantons "are kept together by the peculiarity of their topographical position, by their individual weakness and insignificancy; by the fear of powerful neighbours, to one of which they were formerly subject; by the few sources of contention among a people of such simple and homogeneous manners; . . . ." There we have a people who enjoy the benefit of proper consolidation almost by nature. Their homogeneity helps to provide for it. But where we cannot either through natural circumstances or political circumstances or simple homogeneity create such union, then we must create it politically.

The examples of ancient and modern confederacies seem to reveal Publius's intention of raising the value of conscious political choice in structuring societies. He focuses our attention on how significant it is that someone somewhere sits down and undertakes the express task of organizing a society along political lines in order to achieve certain kinds of objectives. The twentieth essay then, accentuates that argument.

No. 20

No. 10

The twentieth essay uses the examples of the Netherlands confederacy. The argument here is stronger still because this is a confederacy which comes very close to doing what Publius provides for. The weakness of the confederacy provides invitations to excess power through a defective constitution. At the very end of this twentieth essay in the twenty-third and twenty-fourth paragraphs, he makes a couple of observations which help show the significance of this: "The first wish prompted by humanity is, that this severe trial may issue in such a revolution of their government, as will establish their Union and render it the parent of tranquility, freedom, and happiness." In the context of constant revolutions, they should have a humane revolution that will establish their union and make it the parent of tranquility, freedom, and happiness. These people are always undergoing, what is called in the ancient world, *stasis*. The word *stasis* in Greek is what we ultimately call faction, and when we talk about factions in the tenth *Federalist* we are talking about that process of constant sedition and revolution. This is what they are experiencing in the Netherlands, and he says they should have a revolution.

At the end, in the last paragraph he observes:

The important truth, which it unequivocally pronounces in the present case, is, that a sovereignty over sovereigns, a government over governments, a legislation for communities, as contradistinguished from individuals; as it is a solecism in theory; so in practice it is subversive of the order and ends of civil polity, by substituting *violence* in place of *law*, or the destructive *coertion* of the *sword*, in place of the mild and salutary *coertion* of the *magistracy*.

Here Publius re-invokes the argument of the fifteenth *Federalist Paper* in which he says we must supplant the coercion of force with the coercion of the magistracy. The expression, "coercion of the magistracy," has now been repeated in the *Federalist Papers*. How is it established? This question has to do with the provisions we make for reining in egocentric, powerful, centrifugal forces in a society.

In the twentieth essay we saw that discretionary power in the Netherlands confederacy was one way to answer or to deal with centrifugal forces. In the Netherlands they created an office called the Stadtholder. The Stadtholder was a chief executive officer whose power was almost unlimited; it was almost arbitrary because it took almost unlimited power in order to rein in all of the otherwise petty despots who would make life intolerable.

The question is how to establish an authority that would rein in the varying, self-seeking power centers of a society but without conveying arbitrary and unlimited power into the hands of any individual or individuals. That's what the question of the coercion of the magistracy is about.

Patrick Henry's speeches that are reproduced in the *Essential Antifederalist* show his concern about arbitrary power. He goes so far as to say, if we have to purchase prosperity at the price of liberty, better give me poverty. As we can see this is an echo of the original statement that made him famous, "give me liberty or give me death." He doesn't want prosperity at the price of liberty. Nor does he want to take the risk of extraordinary power placed in the hands of someone capable of organizing the rest of the society towards that end. So when Publius introduces this notion of the coercion of the magistracy, he's speaking to the central question of the entire founding. If we cannot produce an orderly method of exercising great political power without entrusting power into the hands of individuals, then Publius's argument fails.

Further, entrusting power is part and parcel of the argument that Henry introduces to us. He raises the question, who are the fundamental constituents, the units of this Constitution, this new nation? Remember that he starts with the preamble to the Constitution, "*We, the People*." He objects to the first three words. This seems perfectly innocent on its face, so much so that we teach youngsters to recite it. He asks, what do you mean "*We, the People*"? How dare they to speak in the name of "*We, the people*"? Already he sees an assertion of power that is unjustified. Who sent them there? Was it the People or was it the States? This is a question to be debated. They could have said "We, the States" but they said "We, the People." Does that not tell us what their intentions are?

Henry is very unhappy with the results, with the product of the Constitution. But unhappy, I submit, largely because this one factor, this notion of the coercion of the magistracy does not, certainly at first glance, come through clearly to him. What he sees is an enormous risk that has been taken. A risk that might be no different in Henry's mind than what happens in the Netherlands when the Stadtholder is created to preserve order there.

No. 23

The twenty-third essay takes up this question of power and does it in a very interesting way by separating the question of the government's power from the power holder. To separate the government's power from the power holder is not easy because when human beings ordinarily contemplate power they are sufficiently impressed with the urgency of power to turn to the person who exercises it as the source of power. People even come to imagine that power somehow descends rather from the person exercising power than from an independent foundation or justification. So Publius is at pains to show that there is an independent foundation, there is an independent justification, which we can deal with as an abstract rational principle before raising the question of who will exercise that power.

We don't use the term *magistracy* much, and when we do we generally don't use it correctly. The term *magistracy* is replaced in the modern world largely by terms such as *delegate* or *representative* or *assemblymen*, *executive*, etc. In the ancient world men could talk about magistrates because there were no "powers." There was no recognized division of powers of government in ancient constitutions. I'm speaking now of our familiar pattern of executive, legislative, and judicial powers.

No. 10

The ancient republics had these functions, judges, generals, treasurers, and of course, in most of them, the whole community assembled to legislate. So all of these things were done, but there were no legislative, executive, and judicial powers, or, as I would prefer to translate the French from which we derived this idea, authorities. The magistrates were seen in the ancient context as carrying out delegated tasks all derived from the central authority of the legislative assembly. So that, everything depended on the power, sovereignty, authority in the society, and everything was clearly delineated right down to the generals who were elected. For example, before the Athenians sailed off to Syracuse in the Peloponnesian War, they debated before their assembly. They brought in Nicias, an older general, and Alcibiades, a younger general, and debated whether to go on the expedition or not, and who should be the generals. In this there is no room for talk of a separation of powers. This is really what is meant in the tenth *Federalist Paper* when the argument is made that it is impossible to make pure democracy safe. It's impossible because all power is concentrated there by definition.

In the era of the separation of powers, or more precisely a separation of authorities or offices, we define the activities and practices of government along the lines that we recognize as distinct offices. Not any one of the executive, legislative, judicial functions depend on any of the others for the legitimacy of its function, and therefore for the power that it exercises. They may be related to one another and they can't work if they don't cooperate. The whole system comes to a halt if they are not coordinated but neither depends on any one of the others.

How did that come to be? The change means that we no longer have magistrates in the classical sense, we have representatives. What do the representatives represent? Publius begins to respond to the question of what the coercion of the magistracy is. It is not the coercion of the office holder, of the representative. It is the coercion of the arrangement of offices and the laws that they will sponsor as a result.

Portions of the twenty-second essay are important in understanding the argument that is made in the twenty-third essay about power. If we start with the seventh paragraph in the twenty-second essay, we see a suggestion made by Publius that there is a "fundamental maxim of republican government, which requires that the sense of the majority should prevail." The principle of legitimacy is that the sense of the majority must prevail. This of course originates the question of how to collect that sense of the majority. As a theoretical question, that comes first, but in the twenty-second essay we see, as a practical question, that is not the first thing. As a practical matter, the first question is how to protect the sense of the majority against the power and influence of a minority. **No. 22**

This is exactly the inverse of the problem in the tenth *Federalist Paper*. In the tenth *Federalist Paper* we observed that we defeat a minority by a straight majority vote, so there is no problem, no further question. But some things incline people to ask for super majority votes, or to build in other kinds of procedural protections. The twenty-second essay observes that those procedural protections, to the precise degree that they protect, convey power into the hands of minorities. What does a two-thirds vote requirement mean in practice? It means that one third plus one can decide every question. That becomes a problem if the sense of the majority is to prevail. How then is the majority to prevail in such a way as still to provide protections to the minority? He uses the example of Rhode Island, Delaware, etc. to show that we may, if we try to treat the states as equal sovereignties, create impossible circumstances. Then in the ninth paragraph, he elaborates the whole problem in terms of the minority prevailing. No. 10

This problem has its origins in the related discussion about the principle of unanimity. Unanimity is of course at the origin of free societies, and everything after the origin of the free society is based on the question of how far away from the principle of unanimity must we descend? Must we descend so far as to enable offices or subordinate corporations to determine the direction of society in the absence of society being able to act as a unified whole? Publius argues "no." We see this above all when we're adopting a constitution.

We want the broadest possible support for a constitution. This is critical, because this is a fundamental, organizing document. Not for ordinary law do we want unanimity, but are we going to permit one-sixtieth, one-twentieth of the people to prevent the balance from organizing into a constitution? What did Patrick Henry ask? Patrick Henry said look what they've done, they've made it possible for nine states to form a constitution. Can they do that to us, he asks. What happens to the other four states? Is it fair? Is it right? Well, Publius asked in return, why can't nine of us form a constitution? Why should we allow the four of you to veto that? Of course this was allowed under the Articles of Confederation.

In the tenth and eleventh paragraphs, we see that there are some practical problems that concern Publius. They are problems of warfare, as well as of domestic violence. He wants to place the government of the society in a condition to react to these. But, once we have conceded his principle that we can no longer leave the Constitution in the hands of a tiny minority and make it impossible for rule to take place, we then have to ask the question, how are we going to exercise this power that we have liberated? This is liberating the power of the majority. The majority, however, is not being liberated to act directly. How will all this be done?

No. 15   In the fifteenth essay, he suggested that the greatest defect of the Confederation is the want of a judiciary power. He says laws are a dead letter without courts to expound and define their true meaning and operation. Notice he's already talking in terms of separate offices. He's talking about a judiciary power and not the judges; he names no particular judge. The judicial function must be clearly elaborated so as to bring support to the orderly procedures and laws and to allow the government to function. How are we going to get there? According to Publius, only by remembering where we start, and that's the closing paragraph of the twenty-second essay. Publius says:

No. 22   It has not a little contributed to the infirmities of the existing fœderal system, that it never had a ratification by the PEOPLE. Resting on no better foundation than the consent of the several Legislatures; it has been exposed to frequent and intricate questions concerning the validity of its powers, and has in some instances given birth to the enormous doctrine of a right of legislative repeal [or a doctrine of nullification]. Owing its ratification to the law of a State, it has been contended, that the same authority might repeal the law by which it was ratified. However gross a heresy it may be to maintain that *a party* to *a compact* has a right to revoke that *compact*, the doctrine itself has had respectable advocates. The possibility of a question of this nature, proves the necessity of laying the foundations of our national government deeper than in the mere sanction of delegated authority. The fabric of American Empire ought to rest on the solid basis of THE CONSENT OF THE PEOPLE. The streams of national power ought to flow immediately from that pure original fountain of all legitimate authority.

Note, we must lay the foundation "deeper than in the mere sanction of delegated authority" so that the delegated authority, the executive, legislative and judicial offices, have to stand on something to operate in such a way as to provide this coercion of the magistracy. Also note, the fabric of the empire and the streams of national power "ought to flow immediately from that pure, original fountain of all legitimate authority."

There is a connection between the foundations and the power. Why is he going to go on in the twenty-third essay to talk about power without talking about power holders? Because the decisive power holder is what he calls his true fountain of all legitimate authority. If we know where the power is coming from, then we can know as well where it's going in terms of its intent, the end, or the use to which it must be put. All those questions may be answered independently of the question of who exercises the power.

No. 23

Why belabor that point? Because no one ever raises the question of a particular political power or legal relationship without taking into account the so-called interests, the people who are going to be using this power and what they are going to get out of it. That's the way we habitually talk about those things. We've learned to be cautious and we're not going to accept anybody's abstract characterization of anything. We assume there is always something which lies behind the abstract characterization which is what really counts. That's what answers the question, who gets what, when and how.

Seventy years ago political scientists Harold D. Lasswell and Harold J. Laski taught that any political scientist who couldn't answer the question who gets what, when, and how, couldn't tell us anything about politics[2]. I must respectfully dissent from that approach to things this far, to acknowledge with Publius, that there is an understanding of principles and practices which is prior to raising the question of interests. And if we are not able to formulate and express that understanding, we shall never be able fully to comprehend the role that interest plays in politics. We will never move beyond the merely defensive posture of looking out for our own. And of course, that would be a fatal concession with respect to the question of the common good.

This is the subject of the twenty-third essay. Remember we had opened our discussion with the outline from the first *Federalist Paper* of the topics that we want to discuss. We discussed the first of these topics, the utility of Union in the essays one through fourteen. So we disposed of "the utility of Union to your political prosperity." Then we had a second topic, the insufficiency of the present confederation to preserve that Union. That, it turns out, was fully discussed in essays fifteen to twenty-two; and the central idea in that discussion again was that the present confederation does not provide for the coercion of the magistracy. Then, thirdly we have the topic which is now introduced at the head of the twenty-third essay, "the necessity of a Constitution, at least equally energetic with the one proposed, to the preservation of the Union, is the point of the examination at which we are now arrived."

This word, *energetic*, and all of its various forms, recurs repeatedly in the *Federalist Papers* and in the debates of the founding. We see it already discussed in the earlier essays. Publius wants a government that is energetic. The question for us, of course, is what do we mean by it and are we sure we want a government that is energetic? How do we distinguish a government that is energetic in this context from the Stadtholder in the Netherlands? This is just another way of posing the question about the

No. 2   coercion of the magistracy. From the second essay, we saw that we want a government that can do something; we want one that can harmonize and assimilate diverse interests, a government that shapes and pursues policy.

We also know that we want to do it in safety; but safety comes after energy. We make certain that what is done is done safely after we provide for doing it. That is the order of Publius's discussion. He says therefore that this inquiry will naturally divide itself into three branches, the objects to be provided for by the federal government, the quantity of power necessary to the accomplishment of those objects, and then the persons upon whom that power ought to operate.

As a rule of thumb, unless people can speak to us about political proposals in this manner, in which they come to the persons upon whom the power ought to operate or who ought to exercise it, at the end of the discussion, then we ought to be suspicious that they do not have sufficient concern for the common good. The ability to articulate their argument in the broadest principles and practices is a test of how well they really care about the common good. That's what Publius intends to do.

He starts out in the third paragraph with a restatement. Let's see if it's

No. 23   a full restatement. "The principal purposes to be answered by Union are these—the common defence of the members—the preservation of the public peace as well against internal convulsions as external attacks—the regulation of commerce with other nations and between the States—the superintendence of our intercourse, political and commercial, with foreign countries." These are the purposes of the Union.

Does that completely restate what we have discussed through the first several papers? Is it a broader or a narrower interpretation? That is an argument or a question that should stay with us through the balance of these readings because we want to make certain that Publius doesn't pull a fast one over on us. We know, for example, that we did start out talking about the foreign danger, which seems to give credence to his referring to the common defense of the members. And we know that we've talked about political prosperity. The preservation of public peace seems perhaps a somewhat less expansive expression than political prosperity, so we're not entirely certain that he means the same thing by that as was meant at the beginning of these papers. When people alter language, sometimes they do so only because they seek to avoid being clichéd. Other times they do so because they seek to convey different meanings and it is up to us to figure out which is which.

Publius is straightforward in this essay. I said the tenth essay was the one essay that proceded with the most inexorable logic in the *Federalist Papers*. I would submit that the twenty-third essay is the second in order on that score. It too precedes with an inexorable logic. The argument is very straightforward. We have certain things we want the government to do. That calls for certain powers. The powers cannot be less complete than the purpose. That's the argument. If we convey the purpose, we convey with it the power to accomplish the purpose. He says in the fourth paragraph, "these powers ought to exist without limitation: *Because it is impossible to foresee or define the extent and variety of national exigencies, or the correspondent extent & variety of the means which may be necessary to satisfy them.*"

The United States has what we call limited government. We are told at the outset of this essay that with respect to common defense, the first in these series of purposes, the powers ought to be unlimited. The question is obvious and imminent. How can we have limited government with unlimited powers? How is it possible? How do we entertain such a notion? I say the logic here is inexorable.

Let's just read the fifth paragraph to get that logic firmly in our minds:

This is one of those truths, which to correct and unprejudiced mind, carries its own evidence along with it; and may be obscured, but cannot be made plainer by argument or reasoning. It rests upon axioms as simple as they are universal. The *means* ought to be proportioned to the *end*; the persons, from whose agency the attainment of any *end* is expected, ought to possess the *means* by which it is to be attained.

Now that's the logic. If we want the job done, give up the means to do the job. So I again raise the question, how then, can we have limited government where we must have unlimited powers to accomplish the ends of government?

In the ninth paragraph, Publius begins to explain to us how this is. Note what he now calls the United States: he takes two terms, *compound* and *confederal* and treats them as synonyms at this point. Publius begins by saying that we distinguish government's powers by distinguishing the objects of government. Why do we call this a limited government? Not because its powers are limited, but because its objects are specified and limited. We do not institute the government for every conceivable purpose or object, but only for certain objects; that means it's limited. In those areas to which its powers and authority should not extend, it has no power whatever. So that the familiar way of looking at this limited government as a government that somehow puts a cruise control on power is wrong. It's not what is intended. It is to say rather that we convey only certain powers and not others, and that we can select among the powers. How do we go about doing that? by selecting among the objects we would choose to have the government pursue.

Significantly, this argument responds to people like Patrick Henry who say they are fearful of this power. It responds by saying, don't fear the power, look to the objects. We won't ask this government to do anything that isn't necessary for government to do. This goes back to that first question that's raised in the second essay, how necessary is government? And it adds, necessary for what? And only as we say what the powers are for, do we then elaborate the activities of government; and the powers to pursue those activities will be, in Publius's terms at least, unlimited.

No. 23

He says in the eleventh paragraph, "a government, the Constitution of which renders it unfit to be trusted with all of the powers, which a free people *ought to delegate to any government*, would be an unsafe and improper depository of the NATIONAL INTERESTS." The Constitution must make it possible, then, to convey these unlimited powers in the areas that are sought for the federal administration, distinguishing of course from the state and local administrations. It's no accident, therefore, that American history has turned largely on disputes over the question of which sphere of government ought to exercise what power. It's built into the design. Sometimes we are vexed, frustrated by those arguments. We want to get something done and rather than having someone tell us how to do it; they start talking about who should do it and whether they can and cannot do it; and we think, isn't that a bother? But then there is a very fundamental respect in which that is the essential condition for preserving limited government in the United States. It's fighting the whole question of who should do it, and only insofar as we resolve that question wisely are we then in the position of claiming to vindicate the constitution of free government in the manner suggested here.

Nos. 24–29

No. 41

Following essay twenty-three, in essays twenty-four through twenty-nine, we see the application of this principle with respect to certain specifics mainly having to do with the power to raise armies and such things. The first, most evident and I think most powerful, application of the principle of essay twenty-three comes in response to the accusation that we provided for a standing army that is going to threaten our liberties. He's put to the test because his first example was common defense. Publius said that we cannot limit the power if we mean to accomplish the end. Publius asks in the forty-first *Federalist Paper*, how can we limit the means for defense if we can't limit the means for offense? Of course the means for offense are in the hands of people not under our control. So now he has to demonstrate how this works.

Publius points out two things. First, the prohibition against standing armies was never meant to be a prohibition against the power of the legislature. In fact, even in the Bill of Rights of the Glorious Revolution it is said that the prohibition against standing armies is a prohibition against the Crown maintaining a standing army without the consent of Parliament. That concedes then, that Parliament could maintain a standing army if it wished and, of course, that is what makes logical sense. Secondly, he points out that what has happened in the Constitution is more effective than an outright prohibition, which any executive would then have to find ways to circumvent.

This is an argument which will recur throughout the *Federalist Papers*: we must never in a constitution write in language that we will be forced to evade; for then we undermine the authority of the constitution. We confront that in contemporary times in the form of people who insist upon balanced budget amendments to the Constitution. They never seem to quite grasp that we don't have control enough over circumstances to guarantee that it remains within the power of individuals to live within such a constitutional provision. So if we write it into our Constitution, we're condemning our Constitution. We make it cheap; we make it easy for people under pressure to ignore it, and therefore to depreciate all of the other provisions which they could in fact live up to if they chose to. Well, that's what he says here.

Publius says we have limited appropriations for the army to two years, so that the only way that we could have a standing army is that our entire legislative body reaffirms its commitment to it every two years. This is more effective than an outright prohibition, which people would then find ways to evade. An example is the case of Philadelphia during most of the eighteenth century which, true to its Quaker heritage, disparaged the maintaining of any military forces, and therefore forced people to go about organizing military forces covertly. And so the question is, well what's better for the Constitution, the covert, the underhanded, or the open discussion of the necessities of the nation? That's how he answers the question of the standing army in the twenty-fourth essay.

Along the way he suggests there are a number of principles that we learn. For example, we learn the necessity of leaving the matter to the discretion and prudence of a legislature because of its impact. And then in the thirteenth paragraph of the same essay, he enlarges the purpose. I said at the outset when he restates purposes in the twenty-third essay we need to ask, is it the same statement?

We begin to see the enlargement of the purpose at work in the last paragraph of essay twenty-four. He begins the paragraph, "If we mean to be a commercial people." He hadn't said that explicitly before, but we derived it by interpretation. From the tenth *Federalist,* and some of the earlier essays, it was clear that we meant to be a commercial people. That is to say, the founders meant for us to become a commercial people. Now he speaks explicitly:

If we mean to be a commercial people or even to be secure on our Atlantic side, we must endeavour as soon as possible to have a navy. To this purpose there must be dock-yards and arsenals, and, for the defence of these, fortifications and probably garrisons.

And we could obviously carry on that enumeration. There are natural consequences to the choices we make. Publius is among those making certain choices in 1787. These constitutional provisions are meant to reflect those choices. Likewise we must, with open eyes, accept the consequences. That's the character of his argument.

No. 25   He continues then, in the twenty-fifth essay, talking primarily about the militia as well as separate standing forces. These essays ought to be read by us as largely applying specifically the terms of analysis offered in the twenty-third essay. It is no accident therefore that in these essays Publius does not talk about the chief executive, how the chief executive will command the forces, or whether the chief executive will be responsible to the society at large. Only in discussing the legislature does Publius point to office holders as key to the operation of these institutions and principles.

Nos.   We've mentioned, of course, that we have to have a judiciary in order
22–29   to have a coercion of the magistracy. We saw that at the end of *Federalist* twenty-two; but in twenty-three through twenty-nine the legislature is the only branch of government that is fundamental because that's where the options will be raised. That's where the choices must be decisively made. It's important to emphasize that, because it means that we are not depending upon the mere interplay of politicians to accomplish these results. We are depending on the essential structure and character of the society itself.

Publius is always sober. This is another reason for putting off a specific concern with individuals and office holders. Sober people know that no matter how much confidence we place in any given office holder, we still will have to deal with the fact that most people, most often will be confronted with the ordinary temptations of humanity. One wants to be safe not just in good weather but in bad weather. And so the provision is for institutions and practices which incline to safety even when the inclination must lean against the tendencies of those who are making the decisions.

The provision for institutions comes out sharply in essay twenty-six.
No. 26   The argument there is of course for energy in government and why we need it. There's something else here that is more directly related to the historical question. We know, for example, that Alexander Hamilton was suspect. He was regarded as a monarchist. I've talked about that earlier. He made a speech in the constitutional convention on the 18th of June, 1787 in which

he praises the British government as the freest government on the Earth. Because he praised the British government, it has been said ever since that he's a monarchist. Thomas Jefferson recorded it for posterity in a little memorandum he wrote called his *Anas* and it's been repeated by historians. We do know, whether he were a monarchist or not, that he favored what came to be called high-toned government.

Very often this expression, energetic government, or energy in government, is taken to be a synonym for the expression high-toned. High-toned is a very difficult term to deal with. I'm not quite sure how to convey fully all that is implied in it, but it means at least, of course, not only government that can do something, that's active, energetic, but it also means the kind of government that has regard for reputation. That it establishes prestige among nations. From essays such as eleven and fifteen, Nos. it's been clear that Publius thinks prestige is something important. National 11, 15 image is not a small matter. So we see in this twenty-sixth essay that it is important in a slightly differing way.

He says expressly that the Antifederalists, the opponents, are ready to take risks that we shouldn't take. "As if the tone of government had been found too high, or too rigid, the doctrines they teach are calculated to induce us to depress, or to relax it, by expedients which upon other occasions have been condemned or forborn." He responds then on the grounds of prudence to those who think that this effort to produce high-toned government is somehow to be resisted. He says that we have acquired principles from our jealousy of monarchs which we mustn't apply with too great zeal when we deal with our own legislatures.

The turn from the monarchy in Britain to the legislature in the United States is for Publius then one of the decisive victories of the revolution. The victory is subject to many difficulties, including the spirit of party and faction being involved in the very processes of government. The promise of these essays is that those are the things we precisely provide for and once we've provided for them, then we will begin to talk about the people who can exercise these powers safely. What will follow this, of course, will be further consideration of the specific powers, and ultimately of the people themselves whom we must depend upon to exercise those powers.

NOTES

1. See also *Federalist* twenty-five.
2. Harold D. Lasswell, *Politics: Who Gets What, When, How* (New York: McGraw-Hill, 1936), Harold J. Laski, *A Grammar of Politics* (London: G. Allen & Unwin, 1925; reprinted 1967).

PART VI: STRONG GOVERNMENT

As Publius takes up the specific powers in the Constitution, it will probably come as no surprise that for a revolution that took place under the age-old formulation *non tallagio, non concedendo,* no taxation without representation, taxation is the first of those powers considered. Taxation remained the single most important power of the state, but not necessarily the organizing principle.

Recall that the Articles of Confederation shipwrecked especially on the question of taxation. The Confederation Congress repeatedly attempted through the early to mid eighties to get the states to approve a five percent impost so the nation could meet its obligations and carry out its activities. The repeated failures finally exasperated people like George Washington and James Madison and Alexander Hamilton among others, and ultimately led to the Constitutional Convention. One expects taxation then to play a very prominent role in most of the essays. Beginning with essay thirty-one, in fact, the essays numbered in the thirties conform to that expectation.

These essays, however, have a relationship to the foregoing essays which ought to be borne in mind before we look at them in detail. The No. 31 whole question of no taxation without representation ties together the two principles which we discussed in reference to the essays from twenty-three Nos. 23–29 through twenty-nine, namely, how power is limited by objects rather than by quantity, and the centrality of the legislature in relation to that. To re-phrase that, the existence of the legislature founded on the people themselves, "that pure, original fountain of all legitimate authority," makes it possible to define limited government in terms of powers specified by objects rather than in terms of quantity.

Along with reliance upon the legislature goes an expectation of a continual reaffirmation of support for the legislature by the people. The doctrine of consent applies first and foremost in the constitutional framework, but it's not exhausted by constitution making. Consent is, of course, an ongoing phenomenon.

There are no specific opportunities or mechanisms for the expression of consent between elections or outside of critical moments, but it remains no less a continuing factor in assessing the adequacy of political institutions. To understand the struggles that developed in the 1790s, once the government had been put in place, is to see the debate between the Jeffersonians and the Hamiltonians as largely a debate over differing understandings of how to make public opinions manifest under the Constitution and therefore in the operations of government.

The Hamiltonians take the position that once the government is fully constituted, once the representatives are in place, having been duly elected, those representatives are themselves the expression of public opinion. Everything they do gives voice to public opinion until such time as another election is held and the public expresses its opinion again, and the system goes on through that cycle. So that anyone attempting to speak on behalf of public opinion outside of the government, from a Hamiltonian perspective, is at war with public opinion and is in fact a subversive and revolutionary influence.

The Jeffersonians, on the other hand, took the position that the people do not exhaust their opinion merely by participating in an election. Their opinions can change momentarily, even day by day, and the government which is established through election has a responsibility to see, to comprehend those opinions. The government certainly has a responsibility not to act decisively at odds with a broad and deeply rooted public opinion. This is what led the Jeffersonians ultimately to construct the political party as the vehicle for the constant expression of public opinion. Before political parties there was no institutional way to make good on this argument.

Nos.
17, 27

This whole question of the ongoing role of public opinion mediates our attempt to understand the relationship between the legislature as central and the specified powers of the federal government. The early form of that discussion is in the twenty-seventh essay with its implications for what was discussed in the seventeenth essay. The discussion in the seventeenth essay was a discussion of the people's predilection for their local or state governments as a counterweight to possible affection for the national or federal government. Publius reassured the states that they were in no particular danger of being usurped in the people's affections or in their functions by the federal government. Responding to objections, Publius said in the twenty-seventh essay that we would not see a particularly usurping military force or national state emerging because there will be no reason to expect the people to resist federal authority to the extent that the federal authority would have to rely upon force rather than the coercion of the magistracy.

In explaining why reliance on force is not necessary, Publius states in the very first paragraph:

No. 27

. . . let us inquire what ground there is to presuppose that disinclination in the people? Unless we presume, at the same time that the powers of the General Government will be worse administered than those of the State governments, there seems to be no room for the presumption of ill-will, disaffection or opposition in the people. I believe it may be laid down as a general rule, that their confidence in and obedience to a government, will commonly be proportioned to the goodness or badness of its administration.

That is an extraordinary argument in light of what we learned previously. We expected the people to have a predilection for the state government, not to be deciding merely on the basis of good or bad administration.

Publius goes on to argue in the next paragraph that there's a different way of looking at this. He says:

Various reasons have been suggested in the course of these papers, to induce a probability that the General Government will be better administered than particular governments: The principal of which reasons are that the extension of the spheres of election will present a greater option, or latitude of choice to the people, that through the medium of the State Legislatures, which are select bodies of men and which are to appoint members of the national Senate, there is reason to expect that this branch will generally be composed with peculiar care and judgment: That these circumstances promise greater knowledge and more extensive information in the national councils: And that they will be less apt to be tainted by the spirit of faction, and more out of the reach of those occasional ill humors or temporary prejudices and propensities, which in smaller societies frequently contaminate the public councils, beget injustice and oppression of a part of the community. . . .

He's saying, if we pay attention, that this is going to give us better government, better administration than we have had from the states. The question is, of course, whether this elaboration of the earlier argument that spoke about getting the best office holders, the best participants from a larger pool, actually speaks to the question that is being raised. Does this speak to whether the people will obey peacefully the national government or whether simple force will be required to establish the national government's authority?

In the fourth paragraph he risks an observation:

. . . the more the operations of the national authority are intermingled with the ordinary exercise of government; the more the citizens are accustomed to meet with it in the common occurrences of their political life; the more it is familiarized to their sight and to their feelings; the further it enters into those objects which touch the most sensible cords and put in motion the most active springs of the human heart; the greater will be the probability that it will conciliate the respect and attachment of the community.

Many factors involved in this passage require close attention.

To "intermingle the national authority and the ordinary exercise of government" means that it obviously must reach beyond the limits that affect foreign commerce, for example, or foreign negotiations. The limited

Nos. 15, 23

powers which we specified in the twenty-third essay may be limited with respect to the objects but not with respect to the reach. The whole notion in the fifteenth essay of legislation over individuals, over citizens rather than over states, presupposes then that "marblecake" formulation popularized by Morton Grodzins[1]. This federal government, whether the power is in the military realm or in the taxing realm or elsewhere, will affect citizens at every level of their lives once we have delegated the power. The power will not be segmented in such a way as to leave people unaffected by the national government in their ordinary activities. Why is this important? It is important, he says, because "man is very much a creature of habit."

No. 17

"Man is very much a creature of habit." Habit, of course, is another word for familiarity. That principle of propinquity that we spoke of in the seventeenth essay is a principle of familiarity. It is important that the people be in a position to become as familiar with their national government as they are with their local government, if it is to work on the basis of the coercion of the magistracy rather than the coercion of force.

We're beginning to see certain principles of this analysis that diverge. On the one hand we reassure people initially that this is no threat to the way of life in the existing states. On the other hand, it's very clear that the government is not going to work unless it creeps into the affections of the community; and to the extent it creeps into the affections of the community it will, of course, displace rival affections. That is human nature. It is inescapable. Publius therefore is led to an inference in the fourth paragraph:

No. 27

. . . the authority of the Union, and the affections of the citizens towards it, will be strengthened rather than weakened by its extension to what are called matters of internal concern; and will have less occasion to recur to force in proportion to the familiarity and comprehensiveness of its agency.

This argument—and remember the Constitution is the supreme law of the land—takes on peculiar force in light of the Antifederalist fears. Publius says in the fourth paragraph of the twenty-seventh essay that these things will operate to the extent that the constitutional authority reaches. He gives that qualification, leaving us to wonder, therefore, if ultimately it represents a qualification of those powers.

No. 31

The significance of this argument for the discussion of taxation which opens in the thirty-first *Federalist Paper* is readily apparent. The thirty-first *Federalist Paper* is concerned with the question of bias, prejudice, and interest to the extent that they impede fair and just judgment of political truths. Before even talking about the specific problem of taxation, Publius speaks at some length about how human beings proceed in marshaling and evaluating the evidence of moral and political truths. Why is this important? Because if we are going to make the success of the nation to depend upon the habits of human beings, the principles of association, familiarity, then we're going to have to accomplish it by moving in the medium of prejudice, bias, and interests. We shall have to make the prejudices of the community, in fact, stand on the side of the new order that we're going to establish. This is said expressly in the forty-ninth *Federalist Paper,* where Publius makes the argument that however much rational principles may defend the life we seek to live, there is no foregoing those "habits of the heart," to quote the contemporary sociologist, Robert Bellah, quoting Alexis de Tocqueville.

No. 49

We can't forgo those habits of the heart which, in fact, make a real community. So, this nation isn't simply going to be a collection of thinkers who promulgate abstract policy formulations and expect people to conform to them. It's rather going to be a dynamic process seeking slowly to win the hearts as well as the minds of American citizens. This would enable us, incidentally, to understand why it's possible to speak of the founders often as looking to a future when some of the more intractable realities of late eighteenth century life might not be dealt with. They are looking to a point at which this slow process of acculturation will have reached its maturity and will then permit the nation, as nation, to act on some of these intractabilities in the way that they had hoped.

Of course, the most obvious of these intractabilities was slavery in the late eighteenth century. When they say they look for it to wither away, they don't mean to say they look for it to disappear without anyone ever having to lift a finger. What they meant was, they look for the point at which public opinion had quickened sufficiently, had reached sufficient maturity, that it would then turn upon the institution itself and it would perform, what would in that context become a relatively painless excision[2]. Well, that process is a process which is sponsored by the very institutions that they have designed and which they expect to work.

To shape prejudices, interests, and expectations is to make it possible to achieve that acculturation, while in the thirty-first essay we find out that's not easy to do. That's difficult, because moral maxims are not like the axioms of geometry. They have the same intellectual status, roughly speaking, according to Publius, but people have no trouble understanding axioms of geometry because they don't compete with their biases, their prejudices or their interests.

In some respect, Publius is under the spell of the Enlightenment in making even that statement, because sometimes human beings are blinded to the first principles of mathematical axioms by prejudice—that is at least the implication of the familiar story of a tribe in South America. Its warriors would paddle their canoes up to the bay and park them; they would count canoes. The tribe had numbers; counting seems to be natural in human beings. Were the canoes of other tribes present, they could count those canoes, and they could count their own canoes; but they couldn't count all of the canoes. They could count up to some point and then they would have to stop; and in order to count the rest of the canoes they would have to start over, because they couldn't count their canoes and the enemy's canoes in one series of numbers.

No. 31   That means, of course, that yes, prejudice can get in the way of understanding even mathematics. Still, the essential point that Publius wants to make is very clear in the thirty-first essay. He says, these first principles, these primary truths "contain internal evidence which, antecedent to all reflection or combination, commands the assent of the mind." That language says that independent of demonstration there are certain propositions which, when presented to the intellect of a functioning human being, automatically conveys their own truth through their own terms. It "commands the assent of the mind." We can not help but agree with those kinds of propositions. And where this doesn't happen, according to Publius, it is because there's some defect or disorder in the organs of perception or the influence of some strong interest or passion or prejudice.

So, then, we have axioms in geometry such as, that the whole is greater than its parts. That is the sort of thing that, once said to a normally functioning human being, must be perceived as true. It has no choice about it, and there's not a demonstration of it from outside. In other words, stating this is to say that the truth of the proposition itself is internal to the proposition. We aren't going to get help from somewhere else to understand it. Two straight lines cannot enclose a space. The truth is contained within the very terms that we're using. If we know what straight lines are, we don't need a demonstration that two straight lines cannot enclose a space. Things equal to the same are equal to one another—the same kind of principle. There is no demonstration of that. It is an axiom. That's what it means to be an axiom.

Why belabor this point? because we know of course, as Abraham Lincoln so often repeated, that the self-evident truth of the Declaration of Independence, that all human beings are created equal, is meant to be self-evident in precisely the sense that's discussed here in the thirty-first

No. 31   *Federalist Paper.* It is axiomatically true. It's not self-evident in the sense that every self knows it because some selves have either disordered organs or strong passions, prejudices, or interests that interfere with seeing it. But, every normally functioning human mind has to see the truth of that proposition.

"Of the same nature are these other maxims in ethics and politics, that

No. 23   there cannot be an effect without a cause." That's to start at the most basic level in morals, no effect without a cause. Everyone has to understand that. We don't demonstrate it. He continues with other maxims, the first of which we saw in the twenty-third *Federalist Paper*:

. . . that the means ought to be proportioned to the end; that every power ought to be commensurate with its object; that there ought to be no limitation of a power destined to effect the purpose, which is itself incapable of limitation. And there are other truths in the two latter sciences [the moral and the political], which if they can not pretend to rank in the class of axioms, are yet such direct inferences from them, and so obvious in themselves, and so agreeable to the natural and unsophisticated dictates of common sense, that they challenge the assent of a sound and unbiassed mind, with a degree of force and conviction almost equally irresistible.

Publius then points out the differences. "The objects of geometrical inquiry are so intirely abstracted from those pursuits which stir up and put in motion the unruly passions of the human heart." The axioms of geometry don't threaten the things that are near and dear.

I never forget, though, the time I was teaching a mathematics tutorial. We were doing Euclid first and then modern geometry, Lobachevsky and Wolf. We went through Lobachevsky who, of course, is one of several but the one who most decisively challenges the fifth axiom in Euclid about parallel lines. Lobachevsky shows that parallel lines aren't necessarily parallel. The idea of asymptosis is derived from this, the idea of lines that never meet but always approach. That becomes a new definition of parallelism in the modern world. There was one student present from a rural background who reported having tried to explain this to her father. After hearing this, and thinking of parallel lines, geometry and property on the farm, the father said, leave it up to a Russian to find a new way to cheat a man out of his land! So, sometimes even geometry can have moral and practical applications apparently. But, the thrust of what Publius has to say, I think, must be clear.

Interestingly, the geometrical axioms are clear but not always simple. They do not lack for complexity, and we're able to accept them even when they're most complex. We accept the idea of infinity. We accept it easily. We never resist it, even though it's an extraordinary concept which we only get by coming up with the notion of infinite divisibility—the endless division of a finite thing, of a thing which has an end. How is it possible?

We accept that without any difficulty, but when it comes to morals and politics we're not so willing to go along with whatever presents itself as the truth. He argues:

To a certain degree it is right and useful, that this should be the case. Caution and investigation are a necessary armour against error and imposition. But this untractableness may be carried too far, and may degenerate into obstinacy, perverseness or disingenuity. Though it cannot be pretended that the principles of moral and political knowledge have in general the same degree of certainty with those of the mathematics; yet they have much better claims in this respect, than to judge from the conduct of men in particular situations, we should be disposed to allow them. The obscurity is much oftener in the passions and prejudices of the reasoner than in the subject.

This is an extraordinary discussion to put at the head of a treatise on taxation, to say the least. But it is explained by the expectation that this government which is going to tax people is going to do something that they are very alert to. It's going to have to win their affections. It's going to have to enlist the prejudices of the community on the side of the taxes. And so, this shows the difficulty of the task that is to be performed. He says immediately in the fifth paragraph, "A government ought to contain in itself every power requisite to the full accomplishment of the objects committed to its care, and to the complete execution of the trust for which it is responsible, free from every other control but a regard to the public good and to the sense of the people." Nothing is to control this government but the "public good" and "the sense of the people."

That expression, "the sense of the people," tells us why it's so critical that we understand that we have to deal with people's passions, prejudices, and interests. That sense is going to have to be collected from these very murky materials. We have to give the power because that's what government means. In other words, we have to accept the force of the axiom. It's truth. We can't resist it simply because we recognize that human beings are otherwise murky and may not do what we expect them to do on the basis of the axiom. The government has to have every power to accomplish the objects we want from it. Then we have to recognize it's going to take special efforts to work our way through this murky ocean of human opinions.

He gives us, by the way, these four axioms as a way of showing how to do that. First, "a government ought to contain in itself every power." Second, "as the duties of superintending the national defence and of securing the public peace against foreign or domestic violence, involve a provision for casualties and dangers, to which no possible limits can be assigned, the power of making that provision ought to know no other bounds," etc. Third, "as revenue is the essential engine by which the means of answering the national exigencies must be procured, the power of procuring that article [revenue] in its full extent, must necessarily be comprehended in that of providing for those exigencies." And fourth, "as theory and practice conspire to prove that the power of procuring revenue is unavailing, when exercised over the States in their collective capacities, the Fœderal government must of necessity be invested with an unqualified power of taxation in the ordinary modes." That means it must be able to reach into our homes to get its revenue. It must be able to reach into our pockets to get what it needs. So, he projects these as axioms. They're no longer political proposals. They are truths invested with all the dignities and the principles of geometry.

This leads him to a conclusion that is of value to us at the end of the eleventh paragraph. "I repeat here what I have observed in substance in another place that all observations founded upon the danger of usurpation, ought to be referred to the composition and structure of the government, not to the nature or extent of its powers." So, if we are jealous, if we are cautious, if we're afraid, fine. Let's talk about the composition and structure of the government. Let's talk about the people and the offices; but let's not talk about the nature or extent of its powers.

The original jealousy of the revolution had led to a logical confusion according to Publius. The original jealousy not only dispensed with kings, with monarchy, but dispensed with necessarily useful social power. So Publius was trying to rebuild. He says look, it is true that we need to be done with kings. We need to be done with arbitrary power and authority. We need to be done with despotic office holders. But it is not true that we need to be done with power. Power is the first line of defense in civilization. Bear in mind what he had said in the second and third essays, as he continues:

Nos. 2, 3

The State governments, by their original constitutions, are invested with complete sovereignty. In what does our security consist against usurpations from that quarter? Doubtless in the manner of their formation, and in a due dependence of those who are to administer them upon the people. If the proposed construction of the Fœderal Government, be found upon an impartial examination of it, to be such as to afford, to a proper extent, the same species of security [dependence on the people most of all], all apprehensions on the score of usurpation ought to be discarded.

No. 31

From the earlier essays, we recall that the states were thought to be sources of impending despotism. They were thought, in fact, not to be sufficiently well organized; they were not sufficiently dependent on the people. At least, they were not sufficiently protected in their dependence on the people against certain despotic tendencies. So the true claim here is that the federal government, the national government, which would be dependent on the people and ought to have this full power of taxation and otherwise, will even be sounder than the state governments. The national government's dependence on the people leads to happier results than one would otherwise have wished or expected.

The whole question of the people's prejudices is brought about by the necessity of the government to be dependent on the people. I raised this question earlier in the context of whether people who are not wise and virtuous can be entrusted with power. I suggested that one might think it were foolish to establish government on the strength of the authority of people who were foolish and vicious. Assuming, of course, that the one considering the question is wise enough to see the distinction and prudent enough to defend himself against that kind of mistake. Well, effectively, Publius is doing the same thing. Publius acknowledges the dangers, but at the same time promises the salvation. How does this salvation come about?

There are several theories about how to make government by the people safe without first making the people wise and virtuous. One theory we get from the Antifederalist. This government would be safe only if the people can directly protect their own interest. We said three things were present to obscure a view of the truth in the thirty-first *Federalist Paper*. They were prejudices, interests, and passions. The central of these is interests and this is the one we talked about in essay ten. It now plays a very different role because the Antifederalists claim that people,s ability to defend their interests is the key condition of liberty. In the legislature, their interest must be represented or they cannot be defended.

No. 10

The anticipation is very clear. There is a certain kind of self-interested-ness in human things, which generally takes precedence over the public good. What did Publius say in essay thirty-one with our very first axiom? He says there are only two things which will limit this power that must be afforded to the government. Namely, a concern for the public good and the sense of the people.

This concern for the public good is at stake in the thirty-fifth essay; for the Antifederalists say no, we do not depend on a concern for the public good in representatives. We depend rather on the direct representation of people's interests. Publius responds, but if we appeal to people's interests we will obstruct their understanding the truth of moral axioms. They will see everything through the lens of their interests. They will not see beyond that. If we structure the relationships, so as to depend on those interests, they will never raise their sights beyond their own navels. That's Publius response in *Federalist Paper* thirty-five. So he says, no, Antifederalists, that will never work. That will not give us the government, the society, we want.

No. 35

Today, as originally, the principal difficulty that confronts students of the American regime is the necessity of discovering solutions to the problems of a diverse citizenry, solutions which will simultaneously reaffirm the attachment of the citizen to the principles of popular government. The great difficulty resides in the fact that the readiest solutions of interested struggles always tend towards the absolutization of majority rule, or the conversion of a transient majority into a permanent ruling class. Hence, to the agrarian who wins by numbers today it will always seem prudent to provide for the preservation of his way of life tomorrow. But that process creates permanent minorities as well. And it is precisely the arrival of such permanent distinctions of class that spell the end of popular government.

The issue is seen most clearly in the question of representation, because all questions of rule must return at some point to the matter of who rules.

The clearest formulation of the notion of republican representation is found in the *Federalist Papers,* though one need not travel so far to discover the sources of their reflections. The most dramatic evidence of the continuing importance of that question is the structure of the Democratic National Convention since the reforms of 1972. The problems of the Democratic Party fully mirror the American regime—an advantage of the extra-constitutional nature of the American party—but need not necessarily involve the fate of the nation. Since the expression of majority sentiment in the Democratic Party is tied to recognition of distinct groups or interests as the basis of representation, it may result that the emergence of a party-wide majority in a single group must compel either the rewriting of the rules of representation or the abandonment of the principle of majority rule. But the party can endure such a crisis without compromising the status of the nation as such. Problems of representation in the constitutional organs of the nation—both as to constituency and as to operation—are of a different nature.

The founding fathers thought the question of representation could be satisfactorily answered only in relation to alternatives of sufficient moment to decisively determine the form of the regime. Their argument envisions the continued existence of major interests or "parties," the settlement of conflicts between which would constitute the acid tests of republican representation. But those parties must be susceptible of being comprehended within a single form of rule and, hence, of such a nature as to be capable of agreement. When, therefore, Publius in *Federalist* thirty-five identifies commerce and agriculture as the great interests—as opposed, let us say, to slaveholding and non-slaveholding—it is clear that the horizon is not unlimited. Some forms of opposition cannot be reconciled. On the other hand, in the broad categories of commerce and agriculture we **No. 35** may still discern many lesser oppositions.

In turning to the founding to consider the question of representation, ever present is the question of how far America is yet ruled by that model. What makes the question significant is the current view that the opposition between commerce and agriculture has been superseded. By what has it been superseded? No one has offered a convincing suggestion, and yet the relevance of the founding to the present would seem partially to rely on our ability to do so. An attempt at a new characterization was Charles Reich's "New Property."[3] But Professor Reich did not proceed so far as either to demonstrate the paramount interest of those holding the new property or even to suggest the nature of an equally broad contending interest. To understand the "New Property," we must assume a decisive resolution of the original division between commerce and agriculture as to kinds of property. That is to say, the two have been homogeneously reduced to a single kind of property. Call it capital if you wish. Then might be raised the question: what distinction as to sources of property is yet possible to characterize modes of life? That is, from capital, what sources of income are possible, and do they still permit distinctions as fundamental as the original distinctions? Professor Reich's response is that the sources are fundamentally public and private (though modes of life are essentially homogeneous and unquestioned in his analysis). Income may be generated either by private exploitation of the growth capacity of capital; or it may be derived from the taxation of property. Joining John C. Calhoun, he divides the essential classes into the tax producers and the tax consumers. The "New Property" is the property held by the tax consumers, whether these last receive direct tax property or receive private property by virtue of some tax-related mechanism, such as licensing. Thus, the sphere of the public need not be defined simply as the totality of policy-making mechanisms. It may be understood as comprehending all those interests essentially, rather than incidentally, dependent on public policy for the opportunity to generate income. In those terms, there could exist two great classes: the public and the private.

To determine whether the germ of a new characterization is in Professor Reich's article—or whether some other candidates fulfill that role—the student of American institutions must develop at least the rudiments of a characterization of major parties. It is clear that they must be comprehensive, for example. They must also fundamentally embody some choice as to the form of the regime in their very operation. And their principles or interests must be susceptible of indirect rather than direct representation. These broad requirements emerge from a consideration of *Federalist* thirty-five. They—and more particular requirements—are the result of the founders' consideration of the requirements of representation in the context of a new federal Constitution. The explanatory power of their defense depends upon the accuracy of their portrait of the original parties. To judge of that accuracy, it is first necessary to form their argument as a point of departure for a new inquiry.

America's founding fathers were conscious of the newness of their enterprise. This consciousness serves to confirm not only their ambition but their faith in new-found tools of political construction. The design of representation presented the chief obstacle to be overcome. Though the initial view of the newness of Publius's approach to representation is

No. 63   corrected in *Federalist* sixty-three, he maintains early in essays nine and fourteen (if we understand the extended territory discussed there in terms of coincidence with the confederate *republic*) that it is through the modern form of representation that a decisive break is made with the ancient world. But the distinctions between ancient and modern political life go deeper than that. It is a radically different form of republican life that necessitates a principle of republican rule unknown to the ancients. It was decided once and for all that might cannot make right. In its extreme form, that means that no virtue is inherent in strength nor in the things required for strength.

Virtue becomes, indeed, antithetical to strength. In this manner, the standard of right was wholly dissociated from those endeavors necessary to ensure the continued existence of right. Hence, men's attentions could be wholly turned towards the virtues of peace, as an ultimate goal to be immediately possessed. Once it was understood that the virtue of the warrior cannot be the end of political life, that ancient example of virtue had to be abandoned[4]. The new republic replaced the citizen's virtue with the citizen's interest as a safeguard for decent politics. But the nurturing of interests in the public required, above all, commerce. Yet, alone, that was thought insufficient. There had been commercial republics before, but they were still among those "petty republics" which could not defend themselves. The modern republic, then, was formed to exceed the ancient republic with respect both to internal "happiness" and external power. The fulfillment of these conditions forms the basis of the problem of federal representation. The one condition requires extensive commerce, while the second requires extensive force and territory. The *Federalist Papers* is largely devoted to a discussion of the advantages and disadvantages involved in combining and distinguishing these problems of extent.[5]

As the combination of an extensive commerce with an extensive territory limits the possibility of republican tyranny, it raises the question of the nature of that representation which must be peculiar to decent republican government. The thirty-fifth *Federalist Paper* provides a midway answer which permits us to connect the circumstances seen in essays nine and ten and which make the representation necessary with the form that it must take as discussed in essays sixty to sixty-three. **No. 35**

Nos. 9, 10, 60–63

Publius begins with the understanding that a republic must be firmly founded. The republic is defined in the third paragraph of essay thirty-nine as that "government which derives all its powers directly or indirectly from the great body of the people"; that is, from the whole society as nearly as possible. Genuine founding of republican government is rooted in consent, and consent is rooted in an equality of rights. But this does not establish a basis for the direct or plebiscitary action of citizens, one or some, upon others. Representation is secondary; it is the artifice, created in the act of founding, which establishes the *form* of governmental action. Those who so govern must be "persons holding their office during pleasure for a limited period, or during good behavior." In essay thirty-eight we see the limitation of republican representation derives from the nature of republican liberty, which requires not only that power come from the people, "but that those entrusted with it should be kept in dependence on the people by a short duration of their appointments; . . ." (In the same moment, as we see from essay thirty-seven, stability seeks to assure "that the hands in which power is lodged should continue for a length of time the same.") Dependence protects the indivisibility of sovereignty in spite of the fact that we see in essays fifteen and sixty-three that citizens alienate their

No. 39

No. 38

Nos. 15, 37, 63

collective legislative capacity—an absolute necessity for the establishment of federal representation.

No. 22

The principle of representation broadly based is but the mirror of the founding. That is, it is the power *in* the people that flows *from* the people. In the first instance, the people *exercise* its power in founding the system; in the second instance, the very exercise of power *delegates* the people's power to representatives. Hence, the nature of representation is such that all power must flow from the people as directly as feasible. As Publius said in *Federalist* twenty-two, the "streams of national power *ought* to flow immediately from that pure, original fountain of all legitimate authority."

No. 35

This basis of republican representation is, among a range of possibilities, the necessary *mean* in an expressly republican government intended to provide for more than the common defense. Publius judged it a consequent principle that the great legislative branch, the House of Representatives, was to be chosen for short terms and kept strongly dependent on the people. When, therefore, the House was attacked as the nursery of oligarchs, *Federalist* thirty-five confronted the dual task of defending the republican character of its composition and the necessity of its mode of operation. In defending representation in the House in essay fifty-seven, Publius says in the second paragraph that though the objection "is levelled against a pretended oligarchy, the principle of it strikes at the very root of republican government." That is, the Antifederalist preference for direct representation of interests as interests was anti-republican. Their objection, then—tied to the other that the House was insufficiently numerous to represent all the different classes of citizens—appeared both "impracticable" and "unnecessary." In fact, there can be *no* alternative

No. 10

resolutions to the problem of republican representation if *Federalist* thirty-five is accurate. Representation must be so constructed as not only to be faithful to the notion of popular government but also to facilitate on the basis of republican principles the safest solutions to the greatest questions. Beyond the argument that a free vote makes automatic representation of particular interests impossible, Publius suggests that the principles of *Federalist* ten must be understood in terms of the Great Struggle between the Great Interests: commerce and agriculture. The struggle is decided, in the final analysis, only by the growth of a class of men who "truly form no distinct interest in society." Publius says in the seventh paragraph that these are the men of the "learned professions." They arbitrate the differences between, and in fact determine whether the Constitution will pursue, the goals of the one and/or the other.

Nos.10, 60–63

The justification of this interpretation is in the organization and implications of *Federalist Paper* thirty-five. Here Publius deals with the charge that only the well-to-do will be represented in Congress and that the interests of the yeomanry will be neglected. Of course, in *Federalist* ten, he has preemptively dealt with the charge as well. Yet, Publius returns to the theme once again in his "more particular examination" of Congress in essays sixty to sixty-three, and in a manner which suggests that essay thirty-five strikes the balance of the divergent chords in their analysis. In *Federalist* sixty, he both summarizes and reflects the cogency of the argument in *Federalist* ten. However, he adds, "But the circumstances which will be likely to have the greatest influence in the matter will be the dissimilar modes of constituting the several component parts of the government."

This emphasis on the benefits to be derived from contrasting modes of selection of representatives is at once an affirmation of the importance of bestowing still more particular attention on the character of representation than was possible at *Federalist* ten. It is the coupling of an extensive territory with a certain kind of representation that achieves the end of *Federalist Paper* ten. Similarly, Publius argues in the sixty-second and sixty-third essay the necessity of understanding the Senate as compounded on the basis of like considerations. He says in the eighth paragraph of essay sixty-three:

No.62

It may be suggested that a people spread over an extensive region, cannot like the crouded inhabitants of a small district, be subject to the infection of violent passions; or to the danger of combining in pursuit of unjust measures. I am far from denying that this is a distinction of peculiar importance. I have on the contrary endeavoured in a former paper, to shew that it is one of the principal recommendations of a confederated republic. At the same time this advantage ought not to be considered as superseding the use of auxiliary precautions. It may even be remarked that *the same extended situation* which will exempt the people of America from some of the dangers incident to lesser republics, *will expose them to* the inconveniency of *remaining for a longer time,* under the influence of those misrepresentations which the combined industry of interested men *may succeed* in distributing among them. [emphasis supplied]

Publius speaks with clarity as to the necessity of employing "auxiliary precautions" to preserve the benefits of an extensive territory. Yet, the precautions are *only* "auxiliary" in essays sixty to sixty-three. In *Federalist* thirty-five, the emphasis on the form of representation prevails.

Only a less than superficial admission in essay sixty-three suggests the resolution of the dichotomy between the advantages of extent and the advantages of republican representation. The admission of the possible evils of an extended territory is coupled with the most frank depiction of the nature of representation. In the sixty-third *Federalist,* Publius forcefully presents the view implicit in *Federalist* fifteen and sixteen. In the fourteenth paragraph representation is the "*exclusion of the people in their collective capacity*" from governing. Coupled with this admission is the further admission that representation was not unknown to the ancients. The latter was the more painful admission, for it unsays *Federalist* fourteen,

Nos.15, 16, 63

No. 14

where it was claimed that "America can claim the merit" of making representation the basis of unmixed and extensive republics, "if" *modern* Europe must be said to have discovered it. The former may be true—indeed, radically true—even while the latter is false.[6] The ancient and modern world differ only with respect to the uses they make of representation and the ways of life consequent to those uses.[7]

No. 35   The superiority of the modern regime rests, therefore, on the avoidance of ancient or genuine representation: that which involves the people as

No. 9   people or regime in the task of governing. Citizenship is distinguished from participation in the *polis*. The modern form of representation—responsible for this "most advantageous superiority"—is of greatest consequence in determining the character of modern political life. It is appropriate,

Nos.10,   therefore, that *Federalist* thirty-five should rely more heavily on
60–63   representation than on the extent of territory as a weapon for undermining the effect of faction. There is no quarrel with the benefit to be derived from extent of territory (as the ninth *Federalist* shows abundantly); there is only a reassessment—to speak tactically—of the relative value of the two phenomena. In being more extreme in its reliance on the form and character of representation than essays sixty to sixty-three appear to be, while not less aware than essay ten of the advantage to be derived from an extensive territory, essay thirty-five stands as a mean between the two. It stands at precisely that distance from each that permits it to commute its terms into those of the other. But to understand its own terms, we must join hands and walk through.

In *Federalist* thirty-five, after implicitly denying that interests or factions will determine policy, Publius expands the offering of *Federalist* ten and adds a new wrinkle. The true gloss on the apparent denial of the effect of faction is that of essay sixty-three, where one discovers that it is

Nos.   not greatness of size that confers superiority to modern republics. Direct
10, 63   access to power will indeed be impeded by an extensive territory. But it will be denied by republican representation. Republican representation does not come immediately to light in essay thirty-five, for Publius begins with a discursus on taxation. The discursus is referred to as a "general remark" on the necessary biases that result from revenue limitations. Publius says in the first paragraph that he wants to make this general remark before proceeding to "any other objections to an indefinite power of taxation." But this general remark extends and is developed through two and one-half pages. Only then does he say at the end of the fourth paragraph, "Let us now return to an examination of objections." One such objection was the charge that the House of Representatives was too small to permit entry to all classes "in order to combine the interests and feelings of every part of the community." The objective sought in this argument, Publius holds, was both "impracticable" and "unnecessary." But, he adds, the specific complaint that the House is insufficiently numerous will be

discussed elsewhere. Hence, the immediate subject matter of essay thirty-five is whether the *"actual representation of all classes of people by persons of each class"* is necessary (emphasis supplied).

In this seven-page essay, only the last four and one-half pages deal directly with the announced subject. The first two of these last pages present a description of the commercial classes, the learned professions, and the agricultural classes, in that order and in terms of their relative positions in the political system. Each category—only the first and last are "classes"—serves as the specific vehicle for the political choices of lesser classes or interests. Publius says, therefore, that the merchant will ever represent the mechanic and manufacturer as well as other allied interests; and, the "middling farmer" will ever represent the poor and the rich landholder. In both cases, however, these choices can be presumed only to the extent that citizens vote explicitly in terms of their class identification (the notion that all men vote "in their interests" does not necessitate that all men be represented by "like interested" men) and that majority rule governs.

But this prospect is attenuated by the central factor, the learned professions who "truly form no distinct interest in society." These, it is held, will be "indiscriminately" chosen by themselves and "other parts of the community." The representatives chosen from the two Great Classes will protect their respective classes. We see in the ninth paragraph that the man of the learned profession, however, "will feel a neutrality to the rivalships between the different branches of industry." And will he not, therefore, "be likely to prove an impartial arbiter between them, ready to promote either, so far as it shall appear to him conducive to the general interests of the society"?

The decision as to whether society be commercial or agricultural lies to a significant extent in the hands of men of the *learned* professions. It is proper, therefore, that the last mention of the learned professions appears last in the last mention of the three groups. Further, it is reasonable to surmise that these representatives, because disinterested, are more likely those who need, as we are told in the last paragraph, "in order to a judicious exercise of the power of taxation . . . be acquainted with the general genius, habits and modes of thinking of the people at large and with the resources of the country. And this is all that can reasonably be meant by a knowledge of the interests and feelings of the people."

Publius had made the argument completely in essay ten after all. But he speaks there in guarded fashion. We had need of essays thirty-five and sixty-three to see it plainly, and, thus, return to the resolution of the struggle between the haves and the have-nots on different ground. After distinguishing between democratic and republican government, he crucially speaks of *substituting* the representative for the direct power of the citizen.

Nos.
10, 63

Now we can read the twenty-first paragraph of *Federalist* ten understanding "substitution" emphatically rather than merely rhetorically:

No. 10   Hence it clearly appears, that the same advantage, which a Republic has over a Democracy, in controling the effects of faction, is enjoyed by a large over a small Republic. . . . Does this advantage consist in the *substitution* of Representatives whose enlightened views and virtuous sentiments render them superior to local prejudices, and to schemes of injustice? It will not be denied, that the Representation of the Union will be most likely to possess these requisite endowments. [emphasis added]

The conclusion, therefore, is that the struggle between commerce and agriculture will essentially replace (or mute) that between the haves and have-nots, and that the effects of that struggle—an interested struggle—will be mitigated by non-interested intervention. This is not to suggest that the interested struggle is impermanent. It is permanently recurring. This is assured by the fact that the representative body, where votes are free, will ever be composed of landholders and merchants or their *semblables,* and men of the learned professions. The struggle is permanent, and so is the provision for compromise.

No. 35   *Federalist Paper* thirty-five defends republican representation both as to objective and to results. Its fundamental basis is the free vote, and the
No. 57   results of a free vote are the elements of interested conflict. The objective of republican representation, however, is the general welfare. Indeed, as Publius tells us in defending against the charge of oligarchy in essay fifty-seven, "every political constitution" should seek to obtain those most endowed with the "wisdom to discern, and . . . virtue to pursue the common good of the society." An extended republic will moderate the struggle of interests, but—left untended—it can result in the most pressing and enduring reign of a single interest or opinion. *Federalist* thirty-five shows that the tending of the extended republic is the work of a federal representation based on a free vote. Publius tells us in the fifth paragraph of essay fifty-seven that federal representatives are to be chosen by the "great body of the people." He then says in the following paragraph, "Who are to be the objects of popular choice? Every citizen whose merit may recommend him to the esteem and confidence of his country."

It is proper to suggest that the esteem and confidence of a vote freely cast is an insufficient barrier to usurpations. But, neglecting other safeguards in the pages of the *Federalist Papers,* is it possible that human prudence can guard against every inconvenience? When citizens of merit fail to recommend themselves to their countrymen, there remains that maximum of securities that can be effected short of refusing all delegation of authority, and there lies beyond only the genius of the people to safeguard its liberty. A prudent statesman seeks to nurture that genius, but it remains only the genius of the people. Yet, Federalists thought that those securities that do exist were extensive. Publius says in the fourteenth paragraph of *Federalist* fifty-seven that representatives were chained by "duty, gratitude, interest, and ambition itself." These must and do constitute both their dependence upon and responsibility to the people. And, finally, as Publius tells us in essay forty-nine, the ground of that dependence is the genius or opinion of the public which must be ever fortified by examples *"antient* as well as *numerous"* if federal representation is to reach its end. That genius is best expressed in the "pleasure and pride we feel in being republicans," and—to paraphrase the tenth essay—the degree to which we feel so ought to be reflected in our zeal in cherishing the spirit and supporting the character of federal representation.

No. 49

No. 10

To bring this series of reflections through the first several essays to some kind of culmination, I want to change my approach just slightly. I want to use a straightforward examination of the text for the thirty-seventh *Federalist Paper*. I want us to look at this argument in very close detail and go through the essay itself, for it is the linchpin essay for tying together all the things that we've been talking about. It is the linchpin for demonstrating how it is that this rather active and energetic project of Publius can best be understood in light of shaping the characters of not only the institutions but also of the people in the republic.

No. 37

At the beginning of the thirty-seventh essay he tells us we have been through a survey of the defects of the present confederation and that they cannot be supplied in any form offering less energy than is proposed. This is, of course, the third element in the outline taken from the first *Federalist Paper*. But there are several important principles involved in this that we need continuingly to consult. What is the ultimate object of the essays? It is "to determine clearly and fully the merits of this Constitution." Never forget that. We have a practical job; we want to persuade people to adopt the Constitution. But "our plan cannot be completed without taking a more critical and thorough survey of the work of the convention."

Suddenly the Convention comes to light. And this is one of the reasons for analyzing this essay so closely. Heretofore, we've looked at Publius as speaking in his own name, not in the name of the Convention. Publius is just an essay writer in a newspaper saying to his fellows, "you should adopt the Constitution." All of a sudden he adds to that posture the authority of the Convention.

I might say parenthetically again that few knew who Publius was. There was of course speculation, often correct speculation about Publius's identity. And that speculation always included the question of whether Publius was part of the convention or not. Was Publius speaking with the authority of the Convention? This becomes increasingly more urgent as Publius's candor becomes increasingly more evident. So now in the thirty-seventh essay it comes out that Publius can talk about the Convention almost as if he were there.

Publius says in the first paragraph, "this remaining task may be executed under the impressions conducive to a just and fair result, some reflections must in this place be indulged, which candor previously suggests." So he wants to let us on the inside.

In the thirty-first *Federalist Paper* there were problems in dealing with the public at large because ordinary humanity operates, we might say, in second gear. It doesn't often get to fourth gear. All these prejudices, passions, and interests produce men operating in second gear. Well, but is it true only of general humanity? What about the rest of us so to speak? Where do we operate?

No. 31

Necessity will raise the question about American prejudices, passions, and interests. Publius continues, "It is a misfortune, inseparable from human affairs, that public measures are rarely investigated with that spirit of moderation which is essential to a just estimate of their real tendency to advance or obstruct the public good." Remember we said we want two things to control the national government, concern with the public good, and the sense of the people. This is all too rare, even on the part of those who should be capable of acting this way. "This spirit is more apt to be diminished than promoted by those occasions which require an unusual exercise of it." So the more we need candor, disinterestedness, and goodwill the less we are likely to get it.

Publius continues:

No. 37

To those who have been led by experience to attend to this consideration, it could not appear surprising, that the act of the Convention, which recommends so many important changes and innovations, which may be viewed in so many lights and relations, and which touches the springs of so many passions and interests, should find or excite dispositions unfriendly both on one side, and on the other, to a fair discussion and accurate judgment of its merits.

Another way of stating this is to say, if we think it's hard to formulate ordinary policy in such a way as to speak through people's passions, prejudices and interests, just imagine how hard it would be to formulate extraordinary policy. A constitution speaks through those. We multiply the difficulties many times once we raise the stakes in that fashion.

"In some, it has been too evident from their own publications that they have scanned the proposed Constitution, not only with a predisposition to censure; but with a predetermination to condemn." Now recall what I said at the outset, looking at the first *Federalist* or rather what Publius said. Publius said that we don't care about people's motives; we want to see the arguments. Why do we not care about people's motives? because we have no way to know them. They can declare them, but we can't verify them. So why bother talking about their motives, their prejudices, their passions, and their interests? Let's hear the arguments.

No. 1

With the thirty-first essay, of course, there comes a new reason for
taking prejudices, and passions and interests into account. It's not because No. 31
we can judge people in light of their prejudices, passions, and interests, but
because we must judge our own work with sensitivity to their prejudices,
passions, or interests. To paraphrase, perhaps it's true that I don't know
what the motivation of another is in proposing a specific policy. But I had
better well know what *would* move him if I want to do something. I may
not be able, therefore, to assess his motivation, however he declares it. But
I ought to be able to make a shrewd guess about that motivation when my
concern now is not what he wants, but getting what I want done. That's
what Publius is saying in thirty-one and here in thirty-seven. If we are
going to go through this exercise of trying to establish the Constitution in
the hearts and minds of a society, then we have got to take into account
who those people are and how it is that we need to move them. We need to
know how to move them, because we *are* trying to move them.

"In placing however, these different characters on a level, with respect
to the weight of their opinions, I wish not to insinuate that there may not
be a material difference in the purity of their intentions. It is but just to
remark in favor of the latter description, that as our situation is universally
admitted to be peculiarly critical, and to require indispensably, that
something should be done for our relief, the predetermined patron of what
has been actually done, may have taken his bias from the weight of these
considerations, as well as from considerations of a sinister nature." So we
return to the first *Federalist*. We can be right for the wrong reasons. We
can also be wrong for the right reasons and the obverse of both of those.

There is at least one situation that is unforgivable, the predetermined
adversary. "The predetermined adversary on the other hand, can have been
governed by no venial motive whatever. The intentions of the first [the
predetermined patron] may be upright, as they may on the contrary be
culpable. The views of the last cannot be upright, and must be culpable."
Whatever reasons, the one who is wrong because he intends to be wrong
cannot be admitted into civilized conversation. "But the truth is, that these
papers are not addressed to persons falling under either of these characters.
They solicit the attention of those only, who add to a sincere zeal for the
happiness of their country, a temper favorable to a just estimate of the
means of promoting it."

Turn to the very end of *Federalist* ten, so that we place this in its proper
prospective. The very last two sentences say, "In the extent and proper No. 10
structure of the Union, therefore, we behold a Republican remedy for the
diseases most incident to Republican Government. And according to the
degree of pleasure and pride, we feel in being Republicans, ought to be our
zeal in cherishing the spirit, and supporting the character of Federalists."
Now we have taken a square aim at certain categories of opinion. And
that's what this thirty-seventh essay is about. We want those who have a

sincere zeal for the happiness of their country. They are the same ones who take pride and pleasure in being republicans and whom we address in *Federalist* ten. We are not now saying that we dispose of the arguments by virtue of their motives; we're saying we only care about those who are motivated by the love of republicanism because we can move towards the Constitution on the strength of their activity. That's the point that's being made.

No. 37

"Persons of this character will proceed to an examination of the plan submitted by the Convention, not only without a disposition to find or to magnify faults; but will see the propriety of reflecting that a faultless plan was not to be expected." Once we have good will on our side, then we have lots of scope for humility. We can admit the possibility of error once we know we're dealing with people who don't mean us ill. "Nor will they barely make allowances for the errors which may be chargeable on the fallibility to which the Convention, as a body of men, were liable; but will keep in mind that they themselves also are but men, and ought not to assume an infallibility in rejudging the fallible opinions of others." That is to say, not only the general mass of the population operates in second gear, but perhaps the rest of us do too. So we have to be especially solicitous when we are challenging ourselves to move beyond second gear.

No. 63

"With equal readiness will it be perceived, that besides these inducements to candor, many allowances ought to be made for the difficulties inherent in the very nature of the undertaking referred to the Convention." On one side we have the difficulties of the fallibilities of human beings themselves. Human beings are imperfect. On the other side, is the difficulty of the subject matter. There is something about constitution making which is not easy, and therefore we oughtn't expect it to be done unproblematically. We must still deal with the appearance that it gives of novelty. *Novelty* constantly recurs throughout the *Federalist Papers* and finally we see it disposed of in the sixty-third *Federalist Paper* when we admit that in the decisive respect what has been done is not novel.

And here we say, "the novelty of the undertaking immediately strikes us. It has been shown in the course of these papers that the existing Confederation is founded on principles which are fallacious; that we must consequently change this first foundation, and with it the superstructure resting upon it." So, we admit the Antifederalists are correct. We are changing the whole thing; ambition drives us.

It is political necessity. "It has been shewn that the other confederacies which could be consulted as precedents, have been vitiated by the same erroneous principles, and can therefore furnish no other light than that of beacons, which give warning of the course to be shunned, without pointing out that which ought to be pursued. The most that the Convention could do in such a situation, was to avoid the errors suggested by the past."

Although we want to know how to hit the target not just how to miss it, these examples have not hurt us.

"Among the difficulties encountered by the Convention, a very important one must have lain, in combining the requisite stability and energy in Government, with the inviolable attention due to liberty, and to the Republican form." This looks like a formula; and these formulas have a grace and easy accessibility about them. Since we have the requisite stability and energy with attention to liberty and republicanism, that explains the Constitution. In a way it does. But, of course these formulas also are just a way of introducing us to the subject matter. When we come across an easy formula like this, be reminded that Publius said there is something inherently difficult about this. The easy formula belies the difficulty in the undertaking. So we become cautious.

Continuing in the sixth paragraph he says:

Without substantially accomplishing this part of the undertaking [combining stability and energy with liberty and republicanism], they would have very imperfectly fulfilled the object of their appointment, or the expectation of the public: Yet that it could not be easily accomplished, will be denied by no one, who is unwilling to betray his ignorance of the subject. Energy in Government is essential to that security against external and internal danger, and to that prompt and salutary execution of the laws, which enter into the very definition of good Government.

We need energy in government in order for it to do anything and to do it well.

"Stability in government, is essential to national character, and to the advantages annexed to it." National character requires stability. That means people must settle into a course of life which is identifiable by others and do so for a period of time long enough to give the appearance of permanence. That is stability in government. It is essential as well "to that repose and confidence in the minds of the people, which are among the chief blessings of civil society." So repose and confidence are the blessings of civil society. Peace. We remember that we do not begin with peace, but we end with it. So, this difficult process that's meant to leave peace, and that he outlines, is one that we have to master both in terms of its conditions, as well as in terms of the specific performance of the government.

Some of these are intuitive principles. Everybody would agree that laws that are constantly changing are harmful because people aren't able to predict their relations with others. And when people cannot predict their relations with others, what they can expect from others, they tend to fall back on the native impulse simply to act on the basis of self interest and with precautionary protection of one's own interest. That returns us, of course, to something that looks like the state of nature. There is more, however, than simply avoiding "irregular and mutable legislation."

As Publius puts it here, "it may be pronounced with assurance, that the people of this country, enlightened as they are, with regard to the nature, and interested, as the great body of them are, in the effects of good Government, will never be satisfied, till some remedy be applied to the vicissitudes and uncertainties which characterize the State administrations." So, the American people are those who have the zeal for republicanism. He seems to have narrowed his audience here. They have an idea of good government by which they are moved, and presumably appealing to that idea is a first condition for moving them further in the direction of constitutional change.

What is this genius of republican liberty, if that's how we're going to move them? "The genius of Republican liberty, seems to demand on one side, not only that all power should be derived from the people; but, that those entrusted with it should be kept in dependence on the people, by a short duration of their appointments." The genius of republican liberty is that power comes from the people, "the pure, original fountain of all legitimate authority." The genius also is that those who exercise the power remain dependent on the people through a short duration of the appointment. So, we don't come to questions like the term of office as if through some lottery process.

No. 22

The point is that there are necessary relationships we aim at, and if we settle on a certain term of office it's because it's meant to reflect these kinds of principles. It is not just a counting of heads, asking how long do we think it should be, and then spiking an average. It's much more precise than that. It's got to fit the necessities and principles in order to do the job.

"Stability, on the contrary, requires that the hands, in which power is lodged, should continue for a length of time, the same." So the genius of republican liberty calls for dependence, and it calls for stability. Dependence leads in one direction, stability in another. We must weigh, assess, and balance.

"Energy in the government requires not only a certain duration of power, but the execution of it by a single hand." Again, it's one of those mathematical formulas. The greater the deliberation to consider, the less energy. Energy means not force. Energy means what I would call celerity, the ability to act surely, swiftly, decisively. We can act more decisively in proportion as we can act by a single will and that's why he says, then, that energy would depend on placing power in a single hand.

We don't place legislative power in a single hand because there are other things besides energy that we seek to accomplish. If we wanted only energy, then we would place all legislative power in a single hand. It's an intricate balancing operation and what we're asking of course, is how could anyone have succeeded in doing all of this balancing so as now to be able to present it to the public persuasively? That's what he asks in the fifth paragraph, "how far the convention may have succeeded in this part of their work will better appear on a more accurate view of it. From the cursory view here taken, it must clearly appear to have been an arduous part."

Now, he goes to the second question, one "not less arduous," and that is the proper line dividing the authority between the federal government and the state governments. How could that have been done? He says in the sixth paragraph:

Every man will be sensible of this difficulty, in proportion, as he has been accustomed to contemplate and discriminate objects, extensive and complicated in their nature. The faculties of the mind itself have never yet been distinguished and defined, with satisfactory precision, by all of the efforts of the most acute and metaphysical Philosophers. Sense, perception, judgment, desire, volition, memory, imagination, are found to be separated by such delicate shades, and minute gradations, that their boundaries have eluded the most subtle investigations.

Pay attention to the language. How do we go from the question of the dividing line between states and federal governments to acute metaphysical philosophers? How is that possible?

Well, we remind ourselves of the histories of the confederations he used. There, he says at the outset, they point out the course to be shunned but not the mark to be hit, not the choice to be made. So Publius argues that the federalism question is in fact not intuitive. People have taken it to be   No. 9
intuitive for years and years. We see that in the arguments of the Antifederalist presented in the ninth essay; but the reason we come up with a definition in the ninth essay that is not traditional is precisely because it is not intuitive. Everyone thought they knew what the dividing line was. Publius says we don't know that. Why don't we know the dividing line?

We don't know the dividing line between national and state authority because there are problems of the human mind. There are problems of sense perception and so many other things that we don't know.

The boundaries between the great kingdoms of nature, and still more, between the various provinces, and lesser portions, into which they are subdivided, afford another illustration of the same important truth. The most sagacious and laborious naturalists have never yet succeeded, in tracing with certainty, the line which separates the district of vegetable life from the neighboring region of unorganized matter.

He assimilates this political condition called federalism to the whole order of the universe, i.e. all of the things that we think we know and see clearly.

In fact, we do see and know some things clearly. When we make the claim "all men are created equal," we're saying we know how to distinguish man from other living beings because we can't know the equality of the species without knowing the species. To be able to say that all men are created equal means to say I know a man when I see one. That's a distinction we can make, that's a moral axiom.

Federalism is not a moral axiom. Federalism is a political truth that labor must discover, that must be deduced just as the boundaries of nature separating organized nature from unorganized nature or separating the different provinces of the animal kingdom. The line that separates man from all of the other animals is clear. What happens with the other animals we may be in doubt about. Some things are axiomatic, others are subject to demonstration. Federalism requires a demonstration.

The Antifederalists took the notion of federalism as if it were axiomatic. Publius is saying, "No, it's not axiomatic, you must demonstrate it." And guess what? it hasn't been demonstrated yet. Publius presents the founders' claim that they're going to do it for the first time. With all of the other claims to fame that they have, they're going to have this one too. Note the important thing here in the sixth paragraph; nature is precise, but we cannot see or comprehend it:

When we pass from the works of nature, in which all of the delineations are perfectly accurate, and appear to be otherwise only from the imperfection of the eye which surveys them, to the institutions of man, in which the obscurity arises as well from the object itself, as from the organ by which it is contemplated; we must perceive the necessity of moderating still farther our expectations and hopes from the efforts of human sagacity. Experience has instructed us that no skill in the science of Government has yet been able to discriminate and define, with sufficient certainty, its three great provinces, the Legislative, Executive and Judiciary.

So we go from saying we can't tell the difference between state and federal governments, to saying within the federal government we can't tell the difference between the legislative, executive, and judiciary.

Certain terms don't appear in the Constitution. Separation of powers is among them. We see why. It's not there because we can't discriminate precisely. We know that the functions can be discriminated conceptually but in practice it turns out to be a far more difficult question. These functions shade into one another. The offices, as we will see in the forty-seventh *Federalist Paper,* must rather share responsibilities than exercise clearly *distinguished* responsibilities. Political science deals with certain kinds of obscurities. These obscurities at the institutional level parallel the murkiness and the obscurity of the individual human mind. And the human mind is obstructed in its view of these things by certain passions, prejudices, and interests. It becomes increasingly interesting to know, then, how it is Publius has worked his way through these difficulties.

At the end of the paragraph he summarizes:

Here, then, are three sources of vague and incorrect definitions; indistinctness of the object, imperfection of the organ of conception, inadequateness of the vehicle of ideas [the words themselves]. Any one of these must produce a certain degree of obscurity. The Convention, in delineating the boundary between the Federal and State jurisdictions, must have experienced the full effect of them all.
No. 37

The Convention was a deliberative assembly of fifty-five persons, although usually there were no more than thirty-seven present at a time. That's also the number of this essay. Thirty-seven people participated in the deliberative assembly, being subject to all of the fallibilities described here, attempting to settle the question which is by definition obscure. That's what Publius is talking about. He's asking, should we expect them to have succeeded in such a way as to make it demonstrable to us? The answer is, "No." In what dimension would they have failed? It could have been any one of the three. It could be because the object is indistinct, because the organ of perception is imperfect, or because the vehicle of expression is inadequate.

We saw already in the ninth *Federalist Paper* that there might be a problem with the vehicle of expression, for the word federation or confederation doesn't say all that needs to be said in order to project the notion of a compound government such as they have elaborated. Publius had to make a choice, he suggests, when he was in the Convention: "Am I going to stick on established means, or am I going to scout, am I going to try to arrive at a structure which accomplishes the end we've laid out conceptually and allow the means to conform to the work, rather than conforming the work to the means?" Republicanism, we see at the outset of this essay, provides a standard to which all must conform. Is the implication of this essay, then, that everything else must rather be conformed? Must federalism conform to the republicanism rather than standing as an independent standard? Every other consideration such as the separation of powers must conform to the demands of republicanism rather than standing as an independent standard. Every consideration must conform, because the political science is subject to the kinds of difficulties Publius has addressed in this thirty-seventh essay.
No. 9

We are able then to see that Publius, perhaps the Convention as a whole, has made a deliberate choice about constructing this Constitution. A choice which says we'll only hold one principle sacrosanct. And that's the genius of republican liberty. Why? That goes back to the question in the thirty-first essay of what it is that must be the standard for the exercise of this power, the public good and the sense of the people. That expression,
No. 31

"sense of the people," is sometimes expressed in the language, "genius of the people." The genius of the people is the genius of republican liberty.

What Publius is trying to tell us, in what may seem fairly obtuse language, is that he has accepted for himself the task of delivering to the people the promise of republican liberty because they desire it. They desire it even if they do not understand what it entails. And his task is to deliver that product even though delivering it may mean presenting it in ways that seem counter-intuitive and in ways that don't always accommodate themselves to other passions or prejudices that the people may happen to have. This comes in a passing reflection at the eighth paragraph of the thirty-seventh essay after talking about the differing interests among the citizens in the states and the problem of organizing and harmonizing these things.

Publius then says, "although this variety of interests, for reasons sufficiently explained in a former paper, may have a salutary influence on the administration of the government when formed, yet everyone must be sensible of the contrary influence which must have been experienced in the task of forming it." That passing concession says just about everything.

No. 10   He's speaking of course about the tenth *Federalist Paper* and factions. He described there how we would construct a government which would turn those passions and interests and opinions to the service of the Union. He talked about a government which would multiply those interests and which in the end would be able to harmonize and assimilate them in a coherent pursuit of a public good. To the extent that the design and ordinary operation of the government that's expected and described in *Federalist* ten is novel and extraordinary, to that extent the founding must have been difficult, both in the convention and outside.

Nos.   When I compared the claim of homogeneity in the second essay to the
2, 4   claim ultimately that we are going to harmonize and assimilate these diverse interests in the fourth essay, I said that obviously what Publius had done was to draw a line of distinction between geographical homogeneity
Nos.   and political and social homogeneity. The first invocation of homogeneity
10, 24   was really only geographical. He used it as if it were more than that in order to score a point, but then eventually conceded that we do not yet have the social and political homogeneity we aimed at. We saw in *Federalist* ten how that social and political homogeneity would be created within the regime as a whole once it was operating and doing all the things intended by the language of the twenty-fourth essay, "if we mean to be a commercial people."

No. 37   In the thirty-seventh essay, all the reflection on the future of this regime is only an inverted portrait of the immense task of creating it without any of those protective institutions and practices. That's what this essay is about. That's why its language becomes so complex, so academic, so conceptual. While maintaining that character of good will, that appearance of positiveness, of optimism, Publius is trying to convey the sense that this is a creative work. He is trying to convey the sense that we are shaping something difficult here and we are going to persist in this effort; but we need to understand that it takes effort. It's not automatic. The work is not just a choice to line up the interest groups and take a vote and then say *this* interest wins. That world of interests does not contain within itself the seeds of political progress. We are going to produce political progress. That's what the thirty-seventh essay is saying to us. That's what Publius's project is all about.

Publius celebrates the Convention's freedom from animosities and divisions. I've always thought that this was a curious part of the essay because even James Madison himself, September eighteenth, the day after the Convention closed in 1787, was rather doubtful about whether this would succeed and very unhappy about the outcome of the Convention. James Madison, Wilson, Hamilton and one or two others were among the most dogged people in the Convention. They were the ones who didn't accept the great compromise. We teach the Convention now and we talk about the great compromises that saved the Convention—the slavery compromise and the origination of money bills in the House of Representatives. We think these were great moments in the course of that three and one-half months that pulled together the Constitution.

These are the very things that they hated. The man who is known as the Father of the Constitution thought the origination of money bills in the House of Representatives was no compromise at all. Even George Washington didn't understand what Benjamin Franklin and the others were doing. Franklin and the others came in and they said, "look, you want proportional representation in both houses, you want to have a real nation and have it based on population only. Here's what we're going to do for you. We're going to give you one of the Houses and we take the other for an equality of representation. In exchange, we're going to let you originate money bills in the House of Representatives."

Madison and the nationalists looked back at them and said, "wait a minute, we don't care about originating money bills in the House of Representatives, what kind of compromise is this?" And of course, it proved in the end to be no compromise at all because they would bring it up and it would get voted down. They did accept the first stage proposal, the Senate's equality of representation and proportional representation in the House. That was done around the end of July, but throughout that period they kept bringing up this origination of money bills and the nationalists said "no," because the House may be in the hands of people that obstruct us and we want to be able to bring it in from the Senate if that's the case. Why would we want to originate money bills in the House?

When the compromise was imposed on them, they amended it so that the Senate had liberty to amend money bills. This was just as good as being able to originate them, so it eviscerated the whole provision in any case. But the only reason it was finally voted in around August fifteenth, is because George Washington and the Virginia Delegation which had been consistently voting it down, finally said to James Madison, presumably, "I don't know why these people keep insisting on this thing and forcing the vote on it. It seems useless to me, but on the other hand if it matters that much to them that we have this compromise, let's take it. Let's take it so we can go on." And at that point when Washington changed his vote, the whole thing turned around, they accepted the money bill and the small state faction said thank you, now we've compromised.[8]

I still, to this day, have not figured out where the compromise is in the great compromise. What actually happened is the Nationalists lost, period. They didn't get what they wanted and the proportional representation in the House of Representatives was not such a great gain for them because the small states were largely willing to concede that in any case. The only way the Nationalists would have resisted it is if they had persisted in demanding a unicameral legislature instead of a bicameral legislature and also would have insisted on equality. They were perfectly happy with the arrangement on bicameralism.

Also James Madison wanted a council of revision. He fought to get a council of revision in which Supreme Court justices and cabinet types would sit with the President to review laws *before* they would go into effect and to say whether they were constitutional and were wise policy. He didn't get it and he thought it was going to be disastrous for the Constitution if we didn't have that. A long list of such tensions marked the Convention along these lines and show why Madison said at the end that this is not a Constitution that's worth much.

No. 37   The whole description of a Convention getting along harmoniously that is presented in the thirty-seventh essay raises a question about Publius. I believe what actually occurs then is that Publius has in a way transcended the merely political level of this work. He has raised it to another level in which the relationship with the people, to whom after all he is writing, is no longer merely political but it has the character of exhortation, even in some degree of piety. And so what he's invoking is a purpose greater than himself and greater than others when he contrasts the Convention with other efforts of like character. He says in the last paragraph:

The history of almost all the great councils and consultations, held among mankind for reconciling their discordant opinions, assuaging their mutual jealousies, and adjusting their respective interests, is a history of factions, contentions, and disappointments; and may be classed among the most dark and degrading pictures which display the infirmities and depravities of the human character. If, in a few scattered instances, a brighter aspect is presented, they serve only as exceptions to admonish us of the general truth; and by their luster to darken the gloom of the adverse prospect to which they are contrasted.

In this light the Convention does take on higher recommendation and a more imposing stature and I believe that that is the intention of the thirty-seventh essay. Now that we have reviewed the general question of power under the new government, it is an urgent question to see who it is that recommends this extensive, unlimited power to the American people. Then it becomes urgent to show that it is a Convention of their friends and fellow patriots.

The thirty-seventh *Federalist Paper* establishes certain fundamentals of republicanism that were clear and distinct and essential for a judgment of the accomplishment of the Constitutional Convention. Basically those boiled down to four things. On the one hand, responsibility and dependence in the government itself and then stability and energy.

The meaning of those terms of course, is subject to continuing elaboration. They are set forth initially in the context of an argument that says of two things you wish to accomplish in the founding experience, you want to guarantee republicanism and ultimately you want to establish federalism. But in the thirty-seventh essay it is made clear that while republicanism is clear and distinct, federalism is murky and obscure. The boundary lines that separate the great departments of government, the three branches, as well as of the different levels of government, according to Publius, are uncertain.

In the context of an argument that says it's uncertain how to establish separation of powers and uncertain how to establish federalism, but certain that we require to establish republicanism, it should be very clear what the primary emphases are. And those emphases are on the kinds of choices reflected in the Declaration of Independence and which I discussed in the first several *Federalist Papers* starting with number one.

Going through papers one to fourteen, we saw, of course, the emphasis on the utility of the Union, the first subject in our outline. This was really an emphasis on what the Federalists called political prosperity. At the end of this line we find that political prosperity is, in fact, almost a synonym for republicanism. At least, we take republicanism to be the essential condition of political prosperity. Along the way we found that one of the chief obstacles to establishing this political prosperity was, as set forth in papers fifteen to seventeen, initially, the relationship between the general government and the state governments. The claim that we could separate these and there would be a war between them for the affections of the people, therefore, looms as the largest practical difficulty we confront. When we come to essay thirty-seven and we are told, "we don't know exactly how to separate these," we might wonder whether in fact it is possible politically, practically, to achieve the result aimed at in the *Federalist Papers*.

In the thirty-ninth *Federalist Paper* Publius discussed exactly what was accomplished in the distinctions made between a national and a federal

Nos. 1–14

Nos. 15–17

No. 39

state. Then Publius's succeeding essays talk about the Constitutional Convention, powers given to the government, and the authority exercised by the Convention, whether they had abused their authority or whether, in fact, it had been appropriate for them to conduct themselves in the manner that they did. The argument in the thirty-ninth *Federalist Paper* is a peculiar argument. On the surface it begins with what's set forth in the thirty-seventh *Federalist Paper*. It takes republicanism as what the essay calls essential or necessary. Then the argument takes up the arrangement of power in the government, which has to do with federalism, separation of powers, and many other things, as the sufficient conditions for the establishment of this republican government.

We begin by getting a new definition of the republic at the outset of the thirty-ninth essay. It occurs in the third paragraph and it reads as follows: "We may define a republic to be, or at least may bestow that name on, a government which derives all its powers directly or indirectly from the great body of the people; and is administered by persons holding their offices during pleasure, for a limited period, or during good behaviour."

This is a very elaborate application of the argument I noted from the end of *Federalist Paper* twenty-two. There the people were referred to as the "fountain of all legitimate authority." It's also a further development of the definition of republic that we saw in *Federalist Paper* ten, in which we distinguished the republic from the democracy by the principle of representation. In the present definition, it is not the principle of representation, strictly speaking, but rather the mode of both acquiring and exercising the powers of government that is essential and is fundamental in defining the republic.

What is the first and most important thing? The government derives its powers directly or indirectly from the great body of the people. That is to say, it is fundamentally a popular government. We reinforce the argument from *Federalist Paper* ten that by republics we do not mean governments which turn against the people or derive their authority from sources external to the people. It is a government that is administered by persons holding office during pleasure for a limited period or during good behavior. That is, it is representative government but the representative government is limited by conceptions of either terms of office or of responsibility.

No. 37

The expression, "terms of office," synonym for the notion of dependence, was developed in the thirty-seventh *Federalist Paper*. The representative is more dependent to the precise extent that the representative is subject to be appraised, evaluated, removed, or renewed in office by the people. The more frequently the occasion for such evaluation, the greater the dependence. It is nevertheless a representative principle. The people will convey or surrender their authority to their representatives. Their grant of authority is made directly or indirectly. The limited period could refer, of course, to periodic elections. It doesn't necessarily have to do so. We'll see later why that is the case.

In order to judge that a government is a republic there are certain conditions that have to be met. Those conditions are said to be, first, "that it be derived from the great body of society, not from an inconsiderable proportion." No small number of people will suffice for creating a republic. This raises the familiar question, who were the people who approved the constitution? Who drafted it, who ratified it, were they a majority of the society? Can we really call them the people or were they just a small class? Well, at least in their own minds, in the arguments they make to themselves, it has to be the great body of the society, "not an inconsiderable proportion, or a favored class of it." The alternative to republicanism that's always kept in mind by Publius is tyranny, despotism, monarchy or aristocracy. That is, the one legitimate government against the whole array of possible illegitimate governments.

The fundamental point is not that the people in this country have chosen this form of government but that they have chosen it for a reason. This is the argument that Publius wants us to understand. The choice is not arbitrary. It's not a matter of taste, it's not a matter of culture or tradition. There is a reason for choosing republican government. Republican government is legitimate government and all of the other forms are regarded as illegitimate. Why consider it legitimate? Where does this argument come from? We have seen much of that elaborated already through the first essays and I'm going to turn to the subject again in the fortieth. For the moment, let us take it as an indication of the argument yet to come. The argument has to do with some appraisal of the rights of man and human nature itself. This argument speaks not to this or that people here or there but to human beings everywhere.

Nos. 1, 40

The second condition for establishing republicanism is a sufficient condition. The *essential* condition is that which makes a thing, such as it is, fundamental, whereas a sufficient condition is that without which it cannot be. It is necessary for its existence though it is not what makes it be the kind of thing it is. He says it is a *sufficient* condition that the government of this character be administered by persons who are appointed directly or indirectly by the people. This places the whole subject of elections in a somewhat less prominent position in the argument than we would otherwise expect it to have. Often we take elections to be fundamental to the notion of republicanism. We say if there are no elections, it's not a republican system. Well, the elections are not the essential condition of republicanism according to Publius, they are a sufficient condition. We require some such means, some such tool or agency, in order to establish the system but there is no independent value to the election. It is simply the result that we have in mind.

Incidentally, we might want to bear in mind at this stage where the term *election* comes from. It ultimately derives by way of Latin from the Greek verb meaning to choose, the Latin translation being *elire*. The whole notion of election, to choose, is of course the exercising of a choice with respect to some standard. The Greek word, *aristos*, of course forms half of the combined word, aristocracy. The standard of choice when we choose is always the best and aristocracy means precisely rule by the best. So characteristically we would expect to have elections in an aristocracy, because elections are about choosing the best. We wouldn't find elections in democracy characteristically. That is why Publius is able to say this is a sufficient condition but not an essential condition for republicanism. As Aristotle said of democrats, if we really meant that any free born person is capable and has title to rule, then our principle of selection would be entirely by lot. We would not use elections, we would simply place all of the names of the citizens in a pot, draw them out by lot and those chosen would, for that space of time, be the rulers. That is the democratic way to establish rule, to establish representation. So if we use elections we are using non-democratic means.

Publius therefore says that having the government administered by persons appointed directly or indirectly is a sufficient condition. Even though elections are a non-democratic means, they can still further democratic or republican purposes, and that's what is done in this context. So, the people appoint representatives either directly or indirectly, and they hold their appointments by some such limited tenure as those we've outlined.

Otherwise, according to Publius, we lose the ability to preserve the republican character of the government. In this respect, he compares the proposed constitution to the states. And as is well known, the comparison of offices that are subject to election and length of terms throughout the States raises a very important question as to whether there is any formula. Publius is suggesting that these things are really little more than questions of prudence, of practical decision in given circumstances. In one case one method works, in another case another method works; each is recommended for differing reasons. All of this conduces in the context of this essay to sustain the argument that everything possible that needs to be done to reinforce the goal of republicanism is the requirement of a new constitution. And the new Constitution is to be assessed in light of its capacity to reinforce its republicanism, which is defined fundamentally as having all of the various instruments of government resting largely on the people.

Nos. 2, 17, 41   Governments, of course, have to be workable. They have to work in the sense that we must have stability in societies to build government. In order to attain that stability we must do certain things. We must have energy, such that the government accomplishes the purposes it sets forth for itself.

We see in the forty-first *Federalist Paper* the repetition of the same argument made in the second and seventeenth *Federalist Papers* about the purposes of government. Throughout the *Federalist Papers*, in fact, we always start with war or national defense whenever Publius lists the objects of government. Then we go through two or three stages descending from that first immediate object. Well, it takes a certain energy in government in order to prevail in war. It is essentially known that any government of any society succeeds only in proportion as it is capable of prevailing in war. A government that cannot prevail in war cannot defend itself; it cannot defend the society that has been entrusted to it.

Whether that government is a government that seeks war, whether that government is a government that fosters war, that sponsors war, that loves war, are different questions than whether a government can prevail in war. We know, of course, from our survey of the first six papers that, in fact, the posture of Publius is very different from that. Publius's posture, as we pointed out, was to indicate how important it was to foster peace, almost to guarantee peace, by first accomplishing a certain kind of political prosperity. Nevertheless, even in that state for which peace is of primary importance, it is still the case that it must be capable of prevailing in war in order to justify the particular existence of the government. Nos. 1–6

The government is not the society. This is a digression but I think it's important for us to remember. One of the consequences of modern political philosophy is the separation of the public and the private realms or the separation of the state and society. We talk in a familiar way about these things today and do not often recognize that these are relatively new conceptions, only 200 years old, 300 years old at the very most. They begin with the architects of modern political philosophy, Hobbes, Locke, Montesquieu, Rousseau, Comte, Hegel, and on into our time. Prior to that no one would have conceived of thinking that there was a private sphere of life that was somehow apart from and privileged over against the public sphere. In ancient Greece, the very word for the individual, for the private thing, is the word, *idiotes*. That word, *idiotes* is the direct ancestor of our word, idiot. And it is no accident that it is the direct descendant, because they would have thought anyone who pursued private things in the ancient world to be an idiot. One's whole life was somehow captured in one's participation in a public realm and in the public expression of the objectives of human life.

We, on the other hand, have discovered rights, we've discovered a sphere in which individuals live and that we don't expect the society to enter. We no longer entrust to the state the care of our religion. We're not even certain that we want to address education to it, though, certainly in the twentieth century we come more and more to repeat familiar shibboleths about the importance of public education. We're not certain even now that that's something that we want to put into the hands of the state. We imagine somehow that there are moral, religious, personal concerns which grow only to the extent that they are not under the prevailing influence and authority of the state.

As I say, this is a product of the line of thought developed through modern political philosophy. This thought emphasizes above all, the primary role of what we would call today, I suppose, managing conflict. I mentioned before the state of nature. Hobbes conceived of that world as a war of all against all. Human beings form a social contract, not because society has any independent value or benefit but because it's a way of minimizing the violence to which they would otherwise be subject in the absence of the protections of society. Beyond eliminating the violence, however, there is no positive virtue associated with the state.

In this thought, the state is largely a negative influence. This is implied in the expressions that have been associated with Thomas Jefferson, Thoreau, and others. Namely, that government is best which governs least. We've the notion of government as a concession. It's a minimal notion. It's a concession to necessity; it's a concession to the irregularity of human passions and the conflicts that result therefrom. There must be in this new conception then, a private realm—a realm apart where the things we treasure most are kept, and where we don't permit the state to interfere.

In that sense, when we say the first object of the state is to defend the society, we are in a way also acknowledging the very limited role of the state in human life altogether. So that it is not a contradiction in terms for Publius at one point to say, we want to limit government and foster peace, and on the other hand to observe that the chief characteristic, the first test the government must pass is to be able to defend itself.

No. 39   In looking at the question of the choice of representatives whether directly or indirectly by the people, the thirty-ninth essay suggests there are two factors to consider. This is brought out in the third paragraph. The first is the mode of appointment. Whether the representatives are appointed directly by the people or indirectly by the people is the measure that one wishes to invoke. We find this throughout the founding era, by the way. For example, in one of a series of letters to John Taylor in 1816, Thomas Jefferson goes through a fairly straightforward analysis of the democratic character of the government. He simply assesses each office by considering whether the officials are appointed directly by the people, or indirectly, and if indirectly at how great a remove the representatives are from the direct influence of the people. Jefferson works his way from the House of Representatives all the way through the electoral college of the President through the judges. He finds ultimately, of course, the judges to be the farthest removed from the people.

At each step in this process, when we look at the distance representatives are removed from the people, we have to look also at countervailing necessities; some principles recommend greater distance from the direct involvement of the people. If indeed we want judges to act impartially as arbiters and be independent of those who appointed them, so that they may exercise due judgment even over those who appoint them, then we appoint them for good behavior. If we are going to appoint them for good behavior, which means effectively for life, then we try to devise means of appointment so as to highlight, to give due emphasis to, talent and judgment and learning in the process of selection. Consequently, we don't hold a national election to appoint Supreme Court justices; we ask the political branches to go through an elaborate process in which they sift through the qualifications of a candidate.

When we look at the electoral colleges, Jefferson says in this letter to Taylor of Caroline, that the people would choose their electors. The electors could have been appointed by the state legislatures but in fact, as a matter of practice by 1816, they turned to elections of electors. And the people would choose electors only in theory. As Jefferson explained it, Elector "A" would vote for Candidate "A," Elector "B" would vote for Candidate "B." So that the people, in effect, were expressing their choices among the presidential candidates. While this did not amount to direct election of the President, it was very close to it according to Jefferson's argument. Therefore the electoral college shows a sound degree of democracy in the system.

So, to look at the mode of election is to consider the extent of the people's influence on the choice. If they do not make the choice themselves, to what extent do they influence it? As we said, the healthy government must be dependent upon the people and must derive its authority directly or indirectly from the great body of the people.

The second element to keep in mind is the duration of the appointment, because duration is a subject which is independent of the mode of selection to the extent that differing offices are subject to differing requirements. In the determination of the duration of the office one perceives most readily the reason for differences by looking at the specific characteristics of the offices. One could ask, why should the House be in office for two years while the Senate is in office six years? What's the difference in these bodies? Do these numbers reflect a judgment, a rational principle operating that allows one to observe why we should have differing terms? Why aren't all the officers of government in office for the same term and coterminously? That's an option. We could elect representatives, senators, presidents, and judges and they could all have four-year terms. They could all come in together and go out together. Why do we not do that?

One of the first things we notice in looking at duration in office is the emphasis on stability. Concern for stability warns against the attempt to produce coordinated policy through equal election cycles because that exposes society to rapid changes in policy in any given election year. Turning over all the officers could turn over all the policy and make it very difficult for others to deal with the government of the country in a predictable manner. It's very easy to elaborate the kinds of conditions that suggest an error in having all the officers of state begin and end coterminously.

Moreover, once we've said we need to stagger their terms, why don't we still give them all four-year terms? Why not have this group start one year, this group start the next, this group start the next? That way they overlap, and that solves the problem. No, because some we want in office for a longer time, some we want in office for a shorter time. Terms vary because some more directly reflect the opinions of the people and that involves two things.

First, we want the representatives that are going to directly reflect the opinions of the people to change frequently. We want them to return to the people often enough to be sure they are reflecting the opinions of the people. If we have a popular branch, its popularity is reflected in the fact that it has been recently endorsed by the people, and that's the stronger argument for keeping representatives on a relatively short tenure of office. There are people who have said we should keep members of the House in office for four years because they spend all their time campaigning in a two-year term. Well they are absolutely correct in that respect. If we find the cost of campaigning and this constant seeking for the public pulse an inconvenience, we should lengthen their term. But then we have to ask the question on the other side, don't we want them constantly to be taking the pulse of the great body of the people if we want to have at least one branch of government which directly reflects as closely as possible public opinion? These are the kinds of consideration that are being invoked when we raise the question of duration of office. Both the mode of selection and the duration of office feed back into the fundamental question of the republican character of the regime.

Consider that we say that what republicanism entails is distinct. There are no imperfections of the organs of perception, no prejudices, no biases that obscure our view of the importance of republicanism. This is very different from the situation with federalism. Whereas in number thirty-seven we saw all kinds of things get in the way, we're seeing republicanism clearly. Publius argued in number thirty-seven that political science has not yet delineated with sufficient clarity the boundary lines between the levels of government and the departments of power. So, when we operate in that realm, we have to operate with a greater trust than we do in the realm of republicanism.

No. 37

We can be demanding and insistent about republicanism, because there is no doubt that if we're human beings there is no superior way of life or better form of government than the republican form. No doubt whatever. We know with a moral certainty that government based on the proposition that all men are created equal and government established on the strength of the consent of the governed is required for human nature to flourish. We know that to a moral certainty. We do not know to a moral or scientific certainty what are the expressions of federalism that will allow us to accomplish the results of republicanism.

Notice what is happening. A subtle shift took place in the thirty-seventh essay and we're now going to see the fruit of that shift borne out in the thirty-ninth essay and the essays following. The Antifederalist question of whether due regard ought to have been paid to federalism is now being put on a new ground. Publius is saying, federalism is important but dependent on republicanism. We want federalism only to the extent that it furthers republicanism. We will abandon federalism if federalism gets in the way of republicanism. We cannot make the mistake of thinking there is a checklist of important principles all equally valued. There is one principle, republicanism, which controls all the rest. This is the argument in essay thirty-seven. This is the argument in essay thirty-nine.

After having introduced the question of federalism in the sixth paragraph he says in the eighth paragraph:

First. In order to ascertain the real character of the government it may be considered in relation to the foundation on which it is to be established; to the sources from which its ordinary powers are to be drawn; to the operation of those powers; to the extent of them; and to the authority by which future changes in the government are to be introduced.

No. 39

All of these questions are to be answered with recourse to the standard of republicanism. When we ask what are the foundations on which it is established, we're asking the republican question not the federal question. We accept federalism insofar as it enhances the claims of republicanism.

In the seventh paragraph he laid out a series of differing questions that make this very clear. "Without inquiring into the accuracy of the distinction on which the objection is founded," namely, that we consolidated the states when we should have kept them federal, "it will be necessary to a just estimate of its force, first to ascertain the real character of the government in question." That is to say, is it republican? Secondly, "to inquire how far the Convention were authorized to propose such a government; and thirdly, how far the duty they owed to their country could supply any defect of regular authority."

We have three questions. We have the question of the character of the government. That's the question of republicanism. The form of this essay will suggest that that really has to do with the federalism. Secondly, we have the question about the authority of the Convention. Could they in fact, propose such a government? And thirdly, did they have a duty that went beyond any legal authority they might have had?

These are critical questions at this point in the series of essays because Publius now, as I suggested when we discussed the thirty-seventh essay, is

No. 37

speaking for the Convention. Up through essay thirty-seven, Publius spoke for Publius, as a concerned citizen. From essays thirty-seven on, Publius speaks as a member of the Convention. It was a tough job but somebody had to do it. That's Publius's orientation. He asks, why was it a tough job? Perhaps, because what had to be done couldn't be done within the strict confines of legal authority. And so he had to take the responsibility for speaking to his countrymen, and speaking the truth, speaking with candor about what was needed. So the whole question, "what is the real character of the government in question?" is connected with the question of, "is the real character consistent with the authority exercised by the Constitutional Convention, and defended by Publius?"

Now, before I go through the balance of the thirty-ninth essay, which deals with the question of whether its character is federal or national, I must point out something important from the fortieth essay. The fortieth essay begins with the statement, "the *second* point to be examined is whether the convention were authorized to frame and propose the mixed constitution." This is a repeat of the statement from that seventh paragraph of number thirty-nine which has the three questions. So, presumably, the balance of the thirty-ninth essay still answers the first question about the government's real character.

No. 40

The opening of the fortieth essay takes up the second question, how far the Convention were authorized to propose such a constitution. In the discussion of the authorization of the convention, certain things appear which are interesting to say the least. We notice the second paragraph where Publius says, let's look at the charters we were given and let's first take the charter that we got from the Annapolis convention or better yet let's take the one from the act of Congress of February of 1787 and what does it say? It says that we are, in fact, to revise the Articles of Confederation, but for what purpose? The very last clause of the fourth paragraph says, "such convention appearing to be the most probable means of establishing in these States *a firm national government*." So he answers a question already. The question to be discussed in the thirty-ninth essay, is it national or is it federal? is partly answered by seeing that Congress wanted to establish a firm national government. So he says in the seventh paragraph, "they were to frame a *national government,* adequate to the *exigencies of government* and *of the Union*." That was their authority. So people who say they were to preserve a federation are mistaken, according to this existential analysis of the text of the charters received from the Annapolis convention and from the Congress of the United States. But the argument doesn't end there.

Publius suggests that if it were in fact the case that the Convention exceeded its authority, might there not have been a reason to do so? The reason has to do with the question of whether in fact the Convention were going to allow a rule of unanimity under the Articles of Confederation to overrule the interest of the people in the Union. The thirteenth paragraph of the fortieth essay makes this clear. There he admits that "the Convention have departed from the tenor of their commissions. Instead of reporting a plan requiring the confirmation *of the legislatures of all the States,* they have reported a plan which is to be confirmed by the people and may be carried into effect by *nine States only.*" The plan was to be confirmed by the great body of the people.

Publius continues and points out that, "the forbearance can only have preceded from an irresistible conviction of the absurdity of subjecting the fate of 12 States, to the . . . opposition given by *a majority* of 1–60th of the people of America." Notice the mathematics there? We have "the example of inflexible opposition given by *a majority* of 1–60th of the people," although he'd spoken about subjecting the creed of twelve states to the corruption of the thirteenth. Why didn't he say one-thirteenth of the people? Why did he say one-sixtieth as opposed to one-thirteenth? Of thirteen states, if one state holds out, isn't that one-thirteenth of the people? Well, no; because states are of different sizes. But if we're going to count them by their population rather than their sovereign and independent status, we're not counting them as states, as equals and sovereigns. If we say one-sixtieth of the people, talking about Rhode Island of course, then we're treating the people of Rhode Island, along with the other fifty-nine-sixtieths as one national mass. It's the only way we can count them as one-sixtieth of the people.

Publius makes very clear in this essay that it is the people as a whole that he means when he talks about the public good and the public interest. He is not talking about the people in their states or the people representing their states. Therefore the ultimate question of whether the exigencies of the Union have been confronted by creating a firm national government is a question of whether the nation doesn't come first for Publius. This fortieth essay suggests that it does. That the justification for the Convention is the preservation of the Union as a nation, as a mass of people, means that everything else is just a way of accomplishing this end. It is a means to the end. No. 40

We must return to the thirty-ninth essay to assay the different elements of the constitution in terms of their federalism or their nationalism but we must recognize that the conclusion of the fortieth essay really comes before the thirty-ninth essay. It is really the case that we're working with a nation and every qualification of that national principle is done merely for reasons of prudence, not to say expedience. **No. 39**

The fortieth *Federalist Paper* logically anticipates the thirty-ninth *Federalist Paper*.

The *Federalist Papers* mentions Rhode Island for a second time. Recall that the argument about the size of the state of Rhode Island was already invoked in the twenty-second *Federalist Paper*. The argument had been No. 22

that we don't want to subject public decisions to a veto of a small proportion of the country. In paragraph seven of the twenty-second *Federalist*, Publius says, "It may happen that this majority of States is a small minority of the people of America; and two thirds of the people of America, could not long be persuaded," etc.

This means, then, that we can count two differing ways. We can count the people as a whole which leads to one set of results, and we can count them by states which leads to a different set. It was possible to come up with a majority of states that had less than half the people in the country. So then we ask the question, would it be just to allow them to rule?

No. 37   Wouldn't that be allowing a minority to rule the majority, and on what ground could we defend that? Well, one of the grounds certainly could not be the republicanism of the thirty-seventh and thirty-ninth essays. That would be inconsistent with that republicanism. So if we insist on republicanism in the nation as a whole, we must sacrifice federalism to the degree that it's required to accomplish republicanism.

When essay forty introduces the objective of a firm nation, we realize

No. 40   a moral commitment to this nation, and to nationalism. I like to call it *democratic nationalism*. There is a moral commitment to nationalism on the part of Publius and the founders. The Antifederalists, therefore, are correct in their criticism of them for building a nation in place of a confederation.

We've given new meaning to the term federalism, or at least to the expression Federal Government, because Publius won. We define the beast; we've built a new structure in the world. This nation has constitutionally imposed differentiations that resemble federal structures but are not premised on federal principles. There is no principle of the states that's sovereign. Even a principle of state equality is not invoked in this new arrangement. In the forty-fifth essay when the expression, "the federal Government," is used by Publius, already it has a new meaning. The

No. 45   meaning has changed on the weight of the argument that we're making a decision for the people as a whole. Let's go back to essay thirty-nine then and review with Publius the five questions that were raised in the seventh paragraph about the real character of the government.

He takes us through a series of discussions. In the ninth paragraph he says:

No. 39   On examining the first relation, it appears, on one hand that the Constitution is to be founded on the assent and ratification of the people of America, given by deputies elected for the special purpose; but, on the other, that this assent and ratification is to be given by the people, not as individuals composing one entire nation; but as composing the distinct and independent States to which they respectively belong. It is to be the assent and ratification of the several States, derived from the supreme authority in each State, the authority of the people themselves. The act therefore establishing the Constitution, will not be a *national* but a *federal* act.

I hope we can follow the legerdemain, the sleight of hand that is at work in that passage. Why does Publius conclude that the ratification of the Constitution is a federal and not a national act? With the people divided up into conventions in each of the states, they commit themselves state by state and federalism means acting state by state. But, we lost the question, in the name of what do they commit themselves? They commit themselves in the name of the American people. So that while they are building a nation, the means used to build a nation are federal. Publius uses this as a defense of the Convention. Of the process Publius says, what do the Antifederalists have to complain about? This is a federal act and not a national act.

Publius has a series of such observations. Before we go through them, take a brief look at James Monroe, among the Antifederalist writings[9]. He addresses the same question. He discusses in a very interesting way whether in fact the states are going to be preserved.

It will readily occur to you that this plan of government is not submitted for your decision in an ordinary way, not to one branch of the government in its legislative character and confined under the constitution to the sphere it has assigned it, but to the people to whom it belongs and from whom all power originates, in convention assembled.

He is saying that if the Constitutional Convention had regard for the independent, sovereign existence of the states, they had no right to speak to the people. The people had already formed state constitutions, and they have legitimate legislatures, governors, and judges. These are the folk we should deal with. He's pointing out that this Convention doesn't do that, it doesn't ask for the legislatures to approve the Constitution. The Convention asks for the people themselves to elect conventions to approve it while ignoring the existence of the present state government, even if operating within the present state boundaries.

Monroe takes the people assembled in convention as the origin of all power and he goes on to say, "In this situation your present state constitution was or should have been formed, and in this situation you are of course, able to alter or change it at pleasure." The key thought here is that the people are always able to call a convention to change their state constitutions. That is their native right and power; but, once they have acted, they have a constitution. They had in 1787 existing constitutions. They had not intimated any desire to change those state constitutions. Yet someone from outside called them to a state convention. Monroe then warns, "You are therefore to observe that whatever act you now enter into," and this becomes critical, "will be paramount to all others either of law or constitution, and that in adopting this [the proposed Constitution,] it becomes in reality the constitution of the state and binding on you as such."

Monroe's argument is absolutely correct. It is in fact, deeply incisive, brilliant I would say. The people live under a constitution which they have previously approved or at least should have done so. That forms governments, legislatures, executives, judges. Now, as a society, how do they live? They conduct themselves through these representatives as a society. Now they could assemble, of course, to change that. All the people could come together and say we're tired of it. Let's have a new government. They could do that. But they haven't done that, so they have existing spokespeople, we might say, who come before them or go before the world and obligate the state. They are able to go into debt, they're able to spend money, they tax. They do all of the things that governments do. Then along comes this Constitutional Convention and sends a note to whom? Not to the state legislatures, in effect, but to the people themselves summoning them to a convention to consider a new constitution.

What is this new constitution? It is the new Constitution for the nation. The call for the people to convene doesn't say a thing about those state constitutions, even though there are provisions in the new Constitution that affect the states. The Constitution says what the states can do and cannot do. They cannot emit bills of credit. They cannot coin money. They cannot print paper money. They cannot pass bills of attainder or *ex post facto* laws. There are all kinds of things this Constitution says a state can't do. The people of the states are called in convention to act on this new Constitution and the state governments have nothing to say about it. Well, it's not strictly speaking true, because the state governments sent delegates to the Convention. We can't leave that out. But nevertheless, when it comes back, it doesn't come back through the state legislatures that sent the delegates. It comes back directly to the people who are asked to sit down and vote on this Constitution.

Monroe asked, doesn't that mean that if we adopt this Constitution, that wherever it happens to contradict our previous state constitution, it must prevail because it is the most recent expression of our will? And of course that's true. The act of adopting the federal Constitution turns out to have been simultaneously a re-establishment of state constitutions. That's Monroe's argument. Everybody who says the state constitutions are older than the federal constitution and concludes that states' rights are based on something that was prior to the original Constitution are wrong. Every state that ratified the new Constitution gave itself a new state constitution even if it didn't change a word in the state constitution. It gave itself a new state constitution because now the states are creatures of the federal Constitution. That's what Monroe is arguing. The states are not independent. They've become creatures of the federal Constitution.

When Publius says, therefore, that this method of ratifying is federal and not national, we must smile. Well sure it's federal if, by federal we mean that the new Constitution has states underneath it and we allow the states to play their role. But it's not federal if we mean the states remain independent and sovereign. The states are being done away with and brought into being in a new form by the new Constitution.

Publius goes through a series of similar remarks in talking about the ratification by people in the tenth paragraph. The argument is that somehow it is a majority of the state not a majority of the people that provides for ratification. Again, the argument is fairly subtle on Publius's part. Not wrong, mind you, but certainly subtle and certainly important. If you collect the majority in each ratifying state, that is not necessarily a majority of the people. Publius says that the Constitution "is to result neither from the decision of a *majority* of the people of the Union, nor from that of a *majority* of the States." The states that become members have to agree unanimously and that makes it look like a true federal system. In signing a treaty, everybody has to agree. But of course, it is being collected in a way that was prescribed not by the independent states but by the Convention.

Ordinarily in treaty negotiations independent states decide for themselves how they ratify treaties. They don't allow someone from outside to decide what procedures to follow to ratify a treaty. So this collection of a majority of the people in the majority of the states will not change the fact that this means or procedure, that looks federal, is in fact in service of an end which is entirely national.

Next, where do the powers of the government come from? He goes through the branches. He speaks of the House of Representatives. The Representatives are directly elected by the people. So he says the government is in this respect national, not federal. The Senate is chosen by the state legislature and there is a principle of equality. He says in this respect it is federal, not national. (He will tell us later in the seventy-fifth essay that the federal character of the Senate is qualified in the manner of its operation, however. The Senators do not vote by states, they vote as individuals, which makes a very big difference. We'll come back to that at a later time.) Then we go through the election of the other officers and come to the conclusion that we have as many federal as national features, he says, in putting together this government.

In the twelfth paragraph Publius says:

The difference between a federal and national government, as it relates to the *operation of the government* is supposed to consist in this, that in the former, the **No. 39** powers operate on the political bodies composing the Confederacy in their political capacities: In the latter, on the individual citizens, composing the nation, in their individual capacities. On trying the Constitution by this criterion, it falls under the *national,* not the *federal* character.

We may be more emphatic because we saw in the fifteenth and sixteenth essays that the very definition of government is to be able to pass laws that operate on individuals and not on political bodies. So yes indeed that makes it national.

In the thirteenth paragraph he continues:

But if the Government be national with regard to the *operation* of its powers, it changes its aspect again when we contemplate it in relation to the *extent* of its powers. The idea of a national Government involves in it, not only an authority over the individual citizens; but an indefinite supremacy over all persons and things, so far as they are objects of lawful Government. . . . Among communities united for particular purposes, it is vested partly in the general, and partly in the municipal Legislatures. In the former case, [not necessarily the consolidated case,] all local authorities are subordinate to the supreme; and may be controuled, directed, or abolished by it at pleasure. In the latter the local or municipal authorities form distinct and independent portions of the supremacy, no more subject within their respective spheres to the general authority than the general authority is subject to them, within its own sphere.

So in this case he says we can't call it a national constitution but rather a federal one because we have independent local authorities. Whether the national government can appoint or remove local officials is an indication of whether the system may be national or federal, or we might say, whether centralized or decentralized.

In the following paragraph he says,

If we try the Constitution by its last relation to the authority by which amendments are to be made, we find it neither wholly *national,* nor wholly *federal.* Were it wholly national, the supreme and ultimate authority would reside in the *majority* of the people of the Union.

This is the question at which we began. If we only count the people one by one, it doesn't matter where they are in states. We just want fifty percent plus one to determine a majority of the whole. So the national foundation of republicanism is to count the people at large. In this, authority would be competent at all times like that of a majority of every national society to alter or abolish its established government.

Now, we know of course, that the amendment procedure does not operate that way as he goes on to show us here. We ask for more than a majority of citizens to approve of amendments. We ask them to be approved in three-fourths of the states, in fact. And in the votes to be taken in state legislatures, we ask for the Congress to propose them by votes of two-thirds and we also allow for the states to generate amendments by appealing for a Constitutional convention. We still debate this today. The Constitution says states may summon, in effect, the constitutional convention through petition to Congress. It's not clear, by the way, whether Congress is bound to comply with that request. But I think it is clear from this, and comments made at the time of the founding, that the founders thought Congress was bound whether they said so in the Constitution or not. He says then, by taking these differing aspects of the amending process, those which are based on the nation acting, those which are based on the states acting, and the need for a super majority, we've come to the conclusion that it is partly national and partly federal.

This is an interesting argument. We know as a matter of fact, that we cannot establish a constitution on the basis of a fair majority. It is a matter of principle as well as fact, that in the formation of a society and the establishment of a constitution for a society, one requires if not unanimity, at least a super majority in order to give a constitution a chance to work at all. The original process for ratifying the Constitution emphasizes this, which is a unanimity of the states in the ratifying process and a majority of the people in each state. Even then, if we only look at the people, we have more than a mere majority of the people because it relies on a majority in each state. The majority cannot be localized.

In the political philosophy of the era, it is always recognized that it took some such scale as a super majority to establish the moral authority for the foundation of a government to make it workable. Government that rests on consent always has this tremendous obligation to invoke consent, not only in its founding but in its continuing operation. The surest ground for its ability to invoke that continuing consent is that it begins at least with the expectation from the great number of people involved that it is in fact standing on a footing of which they approve. That is essential at the outset. A federal aspect of the system is in fact necessary to make a soundly established nation. In State of Nature theory this is stated more emphatically. The social contract requires unanimity because there is no way to take a given individual, who has not agreed to be subject to the authority of the community, and to subject that individual without his consent. It can't be done, legitimately. If we do it, it's merely by force. It's a violation of the individual's rights. So the social contract is in principle based on unanimity.

After we form the social contract according to law, and standard republican theory, we next enable the majority to act on behalf of the whole. So the social contract produces a society and gives itself a constitution by which it will govern itself. The constitution gives the power to act on the basis of the majority but we have to agree unanimously that the majority is going to have that power. So that majority rule only comes to the fore after unanimous agreement produces a society in which majority rule will prevail. That is why, in forming constitutions, one speaks of the need for a super majority to make certain that those who are involved are involved willingly and not under coercion.

Looking at the summary of these characterizations, we are led to the conclusion that the system is "partly federal and partly national." This expression "partly federal and partly national" was first invoked by Oliver Ellsworth of Connecticut in the Constitutional Convention itself. It is a formula which came to define or at least characterize the new meaning of federalism altogether that the United States has given to the world. Many political scientists today talk about federalism as a theory, as a principle of social organization or of governmental practice, and it all stems from this particular arrangement as it's defined by Publius in this context.

I have indicated that as a response to Monroe and the Antifederalists this notion of the government being partly federal and partly national is slightly disingenuous. In fact, the whole operation serves the end of creating a firm national government. Building into the constitutional structure these kinds of federal elements, now using federal in the modern sense, works better than simply establishing the overall power and authority of a central government. These federal structures are the ones, in fact, that have a chance to survive in the world for certain reasons which we can explore later.

No. 40

If we come back to the fortieth essay then, recognizing that the fortieth essay is in some respects logically prior to the thirty-ninth essay, we can see a new reason for taking the defense of the Constitutional Convention seriously. Rather than go through the whole essay, I will just jump to the heart of the matter. The thirteenth paragraph we have seen already invoked the question of the people as a whole. We object to having one-sixtieth of the people determine the happiness really of the whole society. That then leads to the question in the fourteenth paragraph, "how far considerations of duty arising out of the case itself, could have supplied any defect of regular authority."

The reason for that question is the admission earlier that the Convention itself did not accomplish a Constitution. What they accomplished was a proposal. Let's look at the fifteenth paragraph to see how the argument is made.

It is time now to recollect, that the powers were merely advisory and recommendatory; that they were so meant by the States, and so understood by the Convention; and that the latter have accordingly planned and proposed a Constitution, which is to be of no more consequence than the paper on which it is written, unless it be stamped with the approbation of those to whom it is addressed [We the People]. This reflection places the subject in a point of view altogether different, and will enable us to judge with propriety of the course taken by the Convention.

So, this Constitution is merely advisory; it's a draft constitution. It's recommended to the people, but it doesn't become law. It doesn't have force until the people themselves, in fact, agree that it will have force.

He says in the sixteenth paragraph:

. . . it is impossible for the people spontaneously and universally, to move in concert towards their object; and it is therefore essential, that such changes be instituted by some *informal and unauthorized propositions*, made by some patriotic and respectable citizen or number of citizens.

The draft constitution consists of informal and unauthorized propositions. They get their weight from approval by the people and not from the drafters.

Preceding the above quotation, he explains what the process rests upon. The people "must have reflected that in all great changes of established governments, forms ought to give way to substance." Now we know what he's referring to. The form is federalism and the substance is republicanism. Forms ought to give way to substance. The federalism has to give way to the republicanism. He continues, "that a rigid adherence in such cases to the former [federalism], would render nominal and nugatory, the transcendent and precious right of the people to 'abolish or alter their governments as to them shall seem most likely to effect their safety and happiness.'" It is a direct quotation from the Declaration of Independence.

Republicanism, therefore, is associated with the Declaration of Independence. The Constitutional Convention and the people's ratifying it is likened to an act of revolution. It is a peaceful revolution. It is deliberative revolution. It is calm and rational revolution. It is, however, the same native right of revolution that was expressed in the Declaration of Independence that they rely upon to establish the legitimacy of the Constitution. So, when people argue that they were sent to the Convention to revise the articles and they didn't have authority to come back with a whole new constitution, Publius's response is to say, we had a moral obligation. We could see that a mere revision of the articles would not suffice to provide for the happiness of the nation. Accordingly we had a moral obligation to propose such means as would produce that happiness. We couldn't impose them and we didn't impose them. They were informal and unauthorized propositions. They became legally and morally compelling only when the people ratified them. So that the traditional argument about the authority of the Convention, from Publius's point of view, is simply misplaced. The question is not whether the Convention have a right to propose a new government. We should be asking the question, did the people have a right to change their government? Standing on the Declaration of Independence, Publius confirms that they had exactly this right.

Publius says in the eighteenth paragraph:

But that the objectors may be disarmed of every pretext, it shall be granted for the moment, the Convention were neither authorized by their commission, nor **No. 40** justified by circumstances in proposing a Constitution for their country: Does it follow that the Constitution ought for that reason alone to be rejected? If according to the noble precept it be lawful to accept good advice even from an enemy, shall we set the ignoble example of refusing such advice even when it is offered by our friends? The prudent inquiry in all cases, ought surely to be not so much *from whom* the advice comes, as whether the advice be *good*.

And it is the peoples' judgment whether the advice be good and whether to approve the Constitution.

With that argument completed and the authority of the Convention resting on a moral duty and the people's right of approval, Publius is open to begin the heart of the *Federalist Papers*. The remaining *Federalist Papers* have an exclusive concern with the powers of the government because there are two fears for the Antifederalists. The first fear was the abandonment of federalism. The second fear is that we can't abandon federalism without giving excess power to this government.

Publius has discussed in the first part of the *Federalist Papers* the axiomatic bases of the Constitution. So we saw in the twenty-third essay No. 23 the logical structure which supports the assignment of power to the government. We see there unlimited power in the areas where the government has power. That was axiomatic. There is still the question of what are the specific powers.

Thus the forty-first essay opens by suggesting that the Constitution has **No. 41** to be examined, not only in terms of the sum or quantity of power, but also in terms of the particular structure of the government and the distribution of this power among its several branches. We have two things that remain. We want to look at the sum or quantity of power; it's hard to talk about a quantity of power. It's a metaphor. Power doesn't come in drams or pounds or rods or feet. So, it's a metaphor. But it's a metaphor that human beings usually can readily comprehend because we experience power usually as more or less burdensome. That is the traditional view and experience of power. And so we speak of the quantity or the sum of power. We think we can abide a little power, but a lot of power becomes troublesome.

Then Publius says he wants to examine two questions with regard to the quantity of power. First, he examines whether any part is unnecessary or improper, and second, whether the entire mass is dangerous to the portion of jurisdiction left in the several states. The reasons for the powers assigned start in the forty-first essay. Going from this through the forty-fourth essay is a series of discussions of particular powers in the Constitu- Nos. tion. We can line the Constitution up and read it clause by clause, as he 41–44 goes through these summaries and asks why this power, why that power, why another power is there. In the fifth paragraph of this forty-first essay, he outlines the method of proceeding for the next several essays:

That we may form a correct judgment on this subject, it will be proper to review the several powers . . . ; and that this may be the more conveniently done, they may be reduced into different classes as they relate to the following different objects;–1. security against foreign danger–2. regulation of the intercourse with foreign nations–3. maintenance of harmony and proper intercourse among the states–4. certain miscellaneous objects of general utility–5. restraint of the States from certain injurious acts–6. provisions for giving due efficacy to all these powers.

Each of these six functions has to be conceded. The one about which we may have doubt is the one that is vaguest, namely, number four, "certain miscellaneous objects of general utility." What does that mean? Well, we'll have to read that as it appears in the forty-third essay before we can understand what it means. But each of them ought to be investigated one by one in order to appreciate the responses.

To highlight some in passing, war is the first question. The forty-first essay deals with war and is a parallel to the discussion in the essays twenty-four through twenty-nine where we talk about a standing army and the militia. So we can put it in the context of the particular and the general. Nos. 24–29

Look at the beginning of the forty-second essay where Publius says, "The *second* class of powers lodged in the general government consist of those which regulate intercourse with foreign nations." From the beginning we want to defend the powers given for making treaties, sending ambassadors, counsels, etc., "including a power to prohibit, after the year 1808, the importation of slaves, and to lay an intermediate duty of ten dollars per head, as a discouragement to such importations." **No. 42**

This whole list of powers goes obviously to the question of the government's ability to conduct its business in the world and he defends it in just that way. We cannot protect ourselves against excessive power by hamstringing government. This is the first lesson that Publius sought to inculcate. That the impulse to obstruct government as a means of defending oneself against power is a mistake. That we rather have to find other means of defending ourselves. We see in the provision dealing with the importation of slaves that Publius takes it to be a concession, and that the placing of a tax on the importation of slaves is meant to be not a revenue enhancing device, but "a discouragement to such importations."

This is odd in the context because it's not the same kind of power as the others. It's rather the kind of power that expresses something abut the character of the regime and not about the efficiency of the regime. The other powers have to do with efficiency. We want the government to do something. We don't want the government hindered or obstructed. We have this problem with the language about slavery precisely because there has been an obstacle placed in the face of the operation of the government as a whole with respect to its moral consequences. Its moral consequences would be to discourage the importation of slavery. Efficiency and morality are two different kinds of questions.

This leads in the sixth paragraph to an observation:

It were doubtless to be wished that the power of prohibiting the importation of slaves, had not been postponed until the year 1808, or rather that it had been suffered to have immediate operation. But it is not difficult to account either for this restriction on the general government, or for the manner in which the whole clause is expressed. It ought to be considered as a great point gained in favor of humanity, that a period of twenty years may terminate forever within these States, a traffic which has so long and so loudly upbraided the barbarism of modern policy; that within that period, it will receive a considerable discouragement from the fœderal Government, and may be totally abolished, by a concurrence of the few States which continue the unnatural traffic, in the prohibitory example which has been given by so great a majority of the Union. Happy would it be for the unfortunate Africans, if an equal prospect lay before them, of being redeemed from the oppressions of their European brethren!

There is a problem in shaping the substance of the regime. It wishes to move in a certain direction. But it cannot move completely in that direction, because it has not carried all of public opinion with it to this point. The clause is clearly an obstruction. By the way, notice that he freely uses the word slave here in each of these passages, whereas the Constitution does not. It uses the term person. And that's what he's partly referring to when he says "the manner in which the whole clause is expressed." They didn't want to stain the document with the word slave.

No. 38

Go back very briefly to the thirty-eighth essay to see something of relevance. In the second paragraph, Publius talks still about the Articles and the dangers they've undergone and why we need to change. He speaks there of the situation in New Jersey. He says, "if we except the observations which New-Jersey was led to make rather by her local situation than by her peculiar foresight, it may be questioned whether a single suggestion was of sufficient moment to justify a revision of the system." That is, people raised lots of questions about the Articles, none of them sufficient to justify a revision of the system, except New Jersey's. This is related to the passage we're looking at in the forty-second essay because it involves the question of slavery.

New Jersey objected to the martial law under the Articles of Confederation on the grounds that the articles have provided for summoning militia in proportion to the number of male white inhabitants in each of the states. New Jersey thought this was unfair because states like New Jersey which had almost no slaves would end up sending a very large proportion of their entire population of their white males, while people in the slave states would send very few and keep most of their inhabitants at home working their farms or whatever. New Jersey pointed to the Declaration of Independence and suggested that the notion that all men are created equal should not permit this kind of apportionment of responsibility. It said, however, that New Jersey did not wish to interfere with the peculiar institutions of other states. Although believing that they shouldn't have slavery, if they are going to have it, there should be a fair balance. At least the slave states ought to be forced to make the decision whether they are going to send all of their white males to war or whether they are going to liberate some of their slaves to send them. That was an observation sufficient to lead to a revision of the system, according to Madison, because it spoke to the principle at the foundation of the system.[10]

The same kind of observation applies to the forty-second essay meaning, of course, that it has been accepted in the Constitution as a compromise, a concession, but inconsistent with the moral influence the Constitution is expected to exercise throughout its presumed existence. That argument is in fact also closely related to the defense of that fourth class of powers which seemed rather vague, the following miscellaneous powers of general utility that he discusses in the forty-third essay.

Continuing our discussion of the question posed by Publius as to whether any of the powers granted to the federal government are unneces- **No. 43** sary or improper in his consideration of the general sum or quantity of power, let's turn particularly to the forty-third essay which deals with the fourth class comprising miscellaneous powers. The first of the powers he lists is, of course, the "power to promote the progress of science and useful arts by securing, for a limited time, to authors and inventors the exclusive right to their respective writings and discoveries." The defense of that power is straightforward. It relies upon the habit established already in Britain of securing copyrights to authors and extends it in the American context to what are called useful inventions.

We often neglect the sense in which provisions such as this play a role not simply because they are tradition but because they are part and parcel of an overall design. We mentioned earlier the need to organize this society as a commercial republic. We saw the significance of organizing it as a commercial republic to perform the work assigned in the tenth *Federalist*. There, we recall, the principal task of modern legislation is said to be "the regulation of these various and interfering interests." We also know that we **No. 10** have to multiply these interests. It is not enough to have a few clamant interests in order to create the pattern of stability which is otherwise desired from the extended republic. Part of the work of multiplying these interests is to foster the kinds of activities which in fact generate interests and diversify them. That is the kind of activity which is associated particularly with inventions. So securing patents is part and parcel of giving a spur to that industrial development which ultimately comes to be called the industrial revolution. The point is not that the founders are choosing the industrial revolution, but they are choosing the way of life, the pattern, which ultimately results in the industrial revolution.

In the fourth paragraph, he introduces the miscellaneous power "to exercise exclusive legislation in all cases whatsoever, over such district . . . as may by cession of particular States and the acceptance of Congress, become the seat of the Government of the United States." Remember, this was defined as the category of miscellaneous powers that may be necessary for general utility. These don't belong in this or that branch of government. They are the kinds of necessary things that go along with having a government rather like including closets in building a home. We must have a capital, and it turns out it needs to be an area that is not subject to the authority of any other jurisdiction but that of the federal government in order that people throughout the nation will have appropriate confidence in the government.

In this discussion is the expectation that naturally the people of this area will have their rights protected. They will have the power and authority of local administration according to Publius. But this is an argument, and it will be necessary for the state ceding the territory to obtain their consent in the process. In going through this argument, he just ticks off matter-of-factly republican checkpoints.

Some might wonder as, of course, many of the Antifederalists did, why we required an independent seat of government. But I think in the aftermath of reading the strong argument in *Federalist* forty, that is not likely to seem an enormous consideration to us. Clearly this is meant to be not merely an independent government, but a strong government of considerable dignity and the point of having an independent capital is of course to enhance that dignity.

We have similar reasonings that apply to the erection of forts and

No. 43 magazines and ports and other needful buildings. These may be in fact the property of the general government which are instanced in the sixth paragraph. Then next we talk about the power "to declare the punishment of treason, but no attainder of treason shall work corruption of blood, or forfeiture, except during the life of the person attainted."

Publius is sensitive on this discussion of treason. He indicates that the differing definitions of treason (artificial treasons as he has called them) have been historically the devices employed by violent factions to attack one another. He also calls these violent factions at this point "the natural offspring of free government." We have been witnessing throughout these discussions the implicit argument for foresight on the part of statesmen. We might overlook this if we don't take the time to call it forward.

Publius thinks even violent factions to be the natural offspring of free government, even as Publius seeks to establish free government. The

No. 10 argument was laid out in the tenth *Federalist Paper*. There it was quite clear that there were certain things we could do to reduce the violence of faction. But to reduce the violence of a natural offspring as opposed to an unnatural offspring places this in a somewhat different perspective. We know that these are risks that we choose to run for what must be very great benefits. That is the point.

In this context we know exactly what he means by violent factions. He's not talking about people who wage commercial wars over their products and call one another names. He's talking about people who commit treason in order to carry on their battles; they usually wage their wars by killing one another. And that's why the charge of treason is one of the more plastic tools that are used by illegitimate government in order to defend its power in the course of its existence. So, what we've done is to define treason in a very narrow way and then to limit the punishment to the precise offender rather than to relatives or others associated with them. We are as concerned to prevent treason being accessible to violent opinion as we are to protect the society from treason itself.

There is a very nice republican balance there that we often forget as we debate various policies in our own time. The same kind of balancing ultimately will show up of course in things like the first amendment to the Constitution and discussion of freedom of speech. In this balance, the liberty being defended is not being defended at the cost of the ability to sustain society itself.

Publius next speaks of admitting new states into the Union, ". . . but no new State shall be formed or erected within the jurisdiction of any other State, nor any State be formed by the junction of two or more States," etc. Again, this is a matter of general utility, but a matter of significance because it speaks to the expectation of what shall happen under the Constitution. To admit new states into the Union presupposes several factors of normal significance. And notice that he begins at the outset by excepting the open door for Canada as had been done in the Articles of Confederation. Anytime Canada decides it wants to join the cause of North America, it can become part of the United States. I believe, by the way, that invitation is still open to the Canadians, just to keep the record clear in that regard. As a matter of politics this can be seen as a way of increasing pressure on the enemy, Britain. But the new Constitution goes beyond what may have been regarded as a matter of politics.

We anticipate the establishment of states and territories not even organized as yet. We are anticipating that people will be moving into them, in addition to the natural growth of the United States. Presumably this is anticipating immigration. There are hosts of expectations that tell us what Publius thinks the character of the society is going to be. Where do we think these new states are going to come from? They're not new states in the form of tinker toy sets. They are new states of vast numbers of human beings whose lives are being transformed in much the way the lives of the people who first sailed to North America were transformed by their decision. And that has become a consistent part of the expectation of the founding itself.

We said republicanism is the substance of a nation. We are committed to building a nation. And now we see that this nation is not a proposition that is fixed by a defined limit, but in fact is open ended. So we have an open-ended republican nation. The reason we use a mathematical formula in *Federalist* fourteen to determine representation is precisely because of this kind of open endedness. We don't know what the physical, the natural, the geographic limits are. We know what the moral limits are. That's how Publius approaches this question and, therefore, it is extremely revealing of their foresight. They project the future beyond the lives that they themselves were living. That is what was critical.

We wish to make it possible to dispose and make all needful rules and regulations respecting the territory and other property of the United States, etc. He says this is a power of very great importance. This power, perhaps as much as any, will reveal to us the meaning of that expression "general utility." Clearly, we have to be able to do something with our garbage. That's one way of putting it. It's a matter of general utility. And as we discovered in the twentieth century it's not always intuitive what to do with it. Sometimes we can't just dump it because we create other problems. We've got to think through things; we've got to see beyond the immediate preference what it is that we ought to prefer.

The next power is in fact that portion of the Constitution which has been the least interpreted. Indeed the Supreme Court never interpreted it. In many respects this power has been most problematic. This power is "to guarantee to every State in the Union a republican form of government; to protect each of them against invasion; and on application of the legislature, or of the executive (when the legislature cannot be convened), against domestic violence." This is the republican guarantee clause. This is the one clause which even in the aftermath of the War of the American Union, no one has quite known what to do with. There has been language added in the postwar amendments, of course, that suggests the possibility of States being disciplined for their failure to ensure republicanism. But the republican guarantee clause itself has never had an application.

What's odd about is that this clause is included by Publius in a list of those powers that have general utility. We might say it is a minor or miscellaneous power. However, Publius doesn't seem to have the least hesitation to tell us at great length what it means. He gives an elaborate discussion, even an enormous discussion compared to all the other objects we've come through to this point. He tells us that this is a necessary power and not just a matter of general utility. Given a society built with certain relatively independent federal elements, it is enormously important to guard against monarchical or aristocratic pretensions in the members. The elements can't be permitted to go off and adopt non- or anti-republican forms.

There used to be a favorite exercise in civics classes called "Capitalism and Democracy in the United States" in the 1950s and 1960s. For the exercise, students would be asked whether it were possible for a people freely to adopt totalitarian forms by their own consent, given the expectation that totalitarianism denied the legitimacy of the principle of consent. And so people would argue back and forth. I don't think there's a classroom in the country that ever brought that debate to a conclusion, but it was a staple. Had in fact the guarantee clause ever been woven into the texture of our life, and not just into the language of the Constitution, there wouldn't have been room for such debates. This is very clear.

Let's see what the guarantee clause is, such that people aren't permitted to adopt anti-republican forms by means of an expression of consent. It is the nation's power to protect itself against such pretenses, even if we had unanimous sentiment in a given state, to alter the form of regime to some anti-republican form. The guarantee clause would purportedly prevent that. So it would veto that express will unanimously expressed by the people in the given state. That raises very interesting questions.

We say it is a nation, so we see immediately that the nation considered as a whole places people living unanimously in a given state at a certain disadvantage. They are a part of a larger union to which they have conceded a right to the majority to make certain decisions. So it is not so easy for them to opt out.

We can deal with the whole framework and perspective of secession. The country's history has shown sufficiently we can deal with that problem of secession. But it doesn't make it so very clear what has become of the right of consent in this case, assuming a state acting unanimously. The question has to do with whether their obligations to the rest of us are of such a character as to qualify the things to which they may give consent. One practical form of this was involved of course in the 1860s. We have talked about that war from a number of perspectives. The one that we least of all recur to is the perspective of what the rest of the Union owed, not to the seceding states qua states, but to the minorities in the seceding states.

We've often asked whether people, a majority in the seceding state, didn't have a right to secede to establish their own form of government. But that wasn't the question from the point of view of Abraham Lincoln. The question was whether the people who constitute a minority in the seceding states and who continue to affirm their allegiance to the Union are not owed certain protections by the Union in which they have always been members. Do they not, when combined with the balance of the Union, constitute a majority in the nation at large? That's the real struggle in the war which we rarely find adequately represented in our textbooks on the subject. It is not that the majority in South Carolina wanted to secede; it's that the minority in South Carolina were part and parcel of a national majority which had a constitution and which obligated the government to defend them. And that's the argument that is being raised in the context of this guarantee clause.

In the middle of the fourteenth paragraph, Publius says:

These questions admit of ready answers. If the interposition of the general government should not be needed, the provision for such an event will be a harmless superfluity only in the Constitution. But who can say what experiments may be produced by the caprice of particular states, by the ambition of enterprising leaders, or by the intrigues and influence of foreign powers? To the second question it may be answered that if the general government should interpose by virtue of this constitutional authority, it will be of course bound to pursue the authority. But the authority extends no farther than to a guaranty of a republican form of government.

There is not a right to guarantee arbitrarily the interest of any old thing whatever, but only republicanism. This presupposes a pre-existing government of the form which is to be guaranteed. It is not a power to institute republican forms of government. It's a guarantee of republican forms of government.

We know there is a collateral power that institutes such forms that was expressed through the *Northwest Ordinance.* The first act of the new government under the new Constitution was of course to re-enact the Northwest Ordinance which had been enacted originally by the Confederation Congress. The Northwest Ordinance does include a social compact that deserves attention. There is the ordinance as a whole, but within the ordinance there is actually something called the social compact that the United States enters into with the people who will live in these territories. And that social compact in the Northwest Ordinance expresses, as coherently and succinctly as I think we will ever find, the republican expectations of the Americans of the founding era. In the Northwest Ordinance, therefore, they seek to prescribe republicanism by making it a basis for admission into the Union.

In the Constitution, republicanism is guaranteed. We have the assumption of a pre-existing form and we say that the federal Constitution has a legal and moral obligation to those pre-existing forms. The only restriction imposed on the states is that they shall not exchange republican for anti-republican constitutions. This is our substance and it is not subject to change.

Also in this language is the agreement to protect states against invasion and to protect them against domestic violence. This leads to a question in the seventeenth paragraph which goes to the heart of what we now discuss.

At first view it might seem not to square with the republican theory, to suppose either that a majority have not the right, or that a minority will have the force to subvert a government; and consequently that the fœderal interposition can never be required but when it would be improper. But theoretic reasoning in this, as in most other cases, must be qualified by the lessons of practice. Why may not illicit combinations, for purposes of violence be formed as well by a majority of a State, especially a small State, as by a majority of a county or district of the same State?

What then does the federal government owe to the minority? Publius's answer is all the more interesting because it involves what he calls republican theory.

Republican theory serves to suppose that right and might will always be on the side of the majority, any majority, apparently. But then that's a problem. That's a paradox. It creates enormous political and moral difficulties which he begins to elaborate in the eighteenth paragraph.

Is it true that force and right are necessarily on the same side in republican governments? May not the minor party possess such a superiority of pecuniary resources of money, of military talents and experience, or of secret succors from foreign powers, as will render it superior also in an appeal to the sword?

No. 43

Publius begins at the outset by distinguishing force and right. He says that we don't have to have the greatest number to have the greatest bite. So, with foreign help, with super weapons or whatever, suddenly they're in control. They may even only have a strategic or tactical advantage, such as a compact and advantageous position and therefore they may defeat superior numbers. It simply will not do to count the numbers and assume that they are going to prevail. What we'll have to do is to build the argument in defense of right more soundly.

Publius continues and makes an important distinction. He says:

Nothing can be more chimerical than to imagine that in a trial of actual force, victory may be calculated by the rules which prevail in a census of the inhabitants, or which determine the event of an election! May it not happen, in fine, that the minority of CITIZENS may become a majority of PERSONS by the accession of alien residents, of a casual concourse of adventurers, or of those whom the Constitution of the State has not admitted to the rights of suffrage?

Look at the distinction between citizens and persons. Where does the strength of the majority derive from? It derives from our expectations of the rights of persons, not citizens. We do not say in the Declaration of Independence that all citizens are created equal; we say that all men are created equal. (And by men they do indeed mean human beings, by the way.) But persons possess the rights of nature and not the rights of citizens. Persons possess those natural rights and therefore are able to make themselves citizens. Our problem then arises from this. The minority of citizens may become a majority of persons by the accession of alien residents. That is we can take X number of citizens and Y number of non-citizens and put them together and we may get a majority of human beings.

Now what do we do? If we've got citizens, that means we have a constitution, and a government with obligations. Its first obligation is defense and war. Foremost in this is defense against domestic violence, and defense against invasion is next. But now this government is confronted with the majority of persons. Is it going to do its job to fight them all? And on which side will right be found? It may not sound terribly difficult, but look at what he next notices. This makes it very difficult indeed.

I take no notice of an unhappy species of population abounding in some of the States, who during the calm of regular government, are sunk below the level of men; but who in the tempestuous scenes of civil violence may emerge into the human character, and give a superiority of strength to any party with which they may associate themselves.

We know of whom he speaks—the slaves. The slaves are not citizens. They are very much persons. What if the slaves united with the minority of citizens to create a majority of persons in North America? On what side then would right lie? As you see, it is a very complicated question. The principle of the right of the majority, the right of a people to form themselves into a society which acts upon the basis of the right of the majority always exposes any organized society to the eruption or intervention of newly formed majorities of persons.

Publius recognizes this. The guarantee clause is meant to ensure that the organized society continues to operate consistently with this notion of the rights of a majority of persons. The guarantee clause is meant for an environment in which it is not always clear what the practical consequences might mean. Let us distinguish if we will, the political majority and what I will now call the natural majority.

Publius is asking this question: Does the political majority ever have the right to say no to the natural majority? Or is it only by force that it does so? That is the question Publius is asking. He responds in the nineteenth paragraph:

In cases where it may be doubtful on which side justice lies, what better umpires could be desired by two violent factions, flying to arms and tearing a State to pieces, than the representatives of confederate States not heated by the local flame? To the impartiality of Judges they would unite the affection of friends. Happy would it be if such a remedy for its infirmities, could be enjoyed by all free governments; if a project equally effectual could be established for the universal peace of mankind!

The first difficulty, the first problem is easily resolved. Where violent factions remain a minority, the intervention of the nation is a Godsend, a saving grace, if you will.

He then says in the next paragraph:

Should it be asked what is to be the redress for an insurrection pervading all the States, and comprizing a superiority of the entire force, though not a constitutional right; the answer must be, that such a case, as it would be without the compass of human remedies, so it is fortunately not within the compass of human probability; and it is a sufficient recommendation of the Fœderal Constitution, that it diminishes the risk of a calamity, for which no possible constitution can provide a cure.

Remember that a constitutional right is only a political right as expressed in the organized society by the majority which rules that society, which is not simply the natural majority. So the natural majority, should it occur could not be resisted by the political majority as a matter of right. That is Publius's conclusion. What is the significance of this conclusion?

Publius isn't calling for a slave insurrection. He's not calling to abandon the proposed Constitution in favor of some, as yet unspoken ideal constitution. Publius thinks that the principle, what he calls republican theory, has to command our every choice in this context. It can do so only if we begin by being open-eyed about what it commands. And what republican theory commands is our recognition that the natural majority has right on its side. And the fact that it's not probable that such a majority will emerge, reassures us in the practical world in which we live that we have nothing to fear. That's what this complicated language means. But were it to emerge, we would have to concede that it had every right to prevail.

I noticed previously James Madison's struggles over the question of suffrage beginning with the Convention in August of 1787 and continuing into 1820s as he rewrote his notes. This is the same question. He consistently came out on the side of recognizing that we must bow to republican theory whatever we take to be the immediate practical implications of that theory.

This discussion of the natural majority has a very important role in the work as a whole. It shows on the one hand the extent to which he's willing to carry his principles and on the other it shows us the kinds of dangers to which the system will be exposed. He rests in this essay, every much as in number forty, on the Declaration of Independence. He invokes it after introducing a few other miscellaneous powers and then we turn to the fundamental question.

The fundamental question is, again, are right and might on the side of the majority under the republican theory? This leads to the observation in the thirtieth paragraph:

No. 43

The first question is answered at once by recurring to the absolute necessity of the case; to the great principle of self-preservation; to the transcendent law of nature and of nature's God, which declares that the safety and happiness of society are the objects at which all political institutions aim, and to which all such institutions must be sacrificed.

We recognize that language coming from the Declaration. It is again the language which justifies the revolution. It is the language which implies potential surprise based on the historical and political character of the natural majority. It tells us that we have to live with that kind of surprise.

After addressing the republican guarantee, he continues to deal with the seventh, eighth, and ninth powers. He easily disposes of questions regarding the power to deal with debts contracted and engagements entered into before adoption of the Constitution. It is a matter of moral obligation that those debts be repaid. He briefly covers the eighth power to provide for amendments to be ratified by three-fourths of the states including only the exceptions to protect the states and to protect the 1808 provision regarding slavery. The ninth power, the power of nine states to establish the Constitution, he says, speaks for itself. The express authority of the people alone could give due validity to the Constitution; to have required the thirteen states to act unanimously would have subjected the essential interest of the whole to the caprice or corruption of a single member, "would have marked a want of foresight in the convention."

Publius not only practices, but demands foresight in statesmanship. This argument recurs to the argument as to whether we consider the member who would veto the Constitution a thirteenth part or a sixtieth part of the nation. It is foresight that has permitted him now to return to the simple federal formulation, one of thirteen. But we know what he means by that. He makes clear what he means in a slightly different way, however, in the twenty-ninth and thirtieth paragraphs:

Two questions of a very delicate nature present themselves on this occasion. 1. On what principle the Confederation, which stands in the solemn form of a compact among the States, can be supereded without the unanimous consent of the parties to it? 2. What relation is to subsist between the nine or more States ratifying the Constitution, and the remaining few who do not become parties to it?

The first question arose because the confederation had a rule that we could change it only by unanimous consent. The question is, can we successfully break the contract unilaterally? Ordinarily, one says no because contracts with mutual obligations are binding and enforceable. We can't sign a contract today and walk away from it tomorrow. Well, if we have a contract providing that the thirteen states must agree unanimously to change it, and we find it is not conducive to our happiness, can we affect a change without waiting for unanimous consent? The answer is that we change it based on reasonings of necessity, on the one hand, and republican theory, on the other hand.

Publius says in paragraph thirty that the answer to this first question "is answered at once by recurring" to the right of self-preservation, "to the transcendent law of nature, of nature's God." Whatever the contract calls for, when it becomes hurtful, we can indeed get out of it.

He says in the thirty-first paragraph:

The second question is not less delicate; and the flattering prospect of its being merely hypothetical, forbids an over curious discussion of it. It is one of those cases which must be left to provide for itself. In general it may be observed, that although no political relation can subsist between the assenting and dissenting States, yet the moral relations will remain uncancelled. The claims of justice, both on one side and the other, will be in force, and must be fulfilled; the rights of humanity must in all cases be duly and mutually respected.

He's calling the possible lack of unanimity hypothetical, although it is entirely a real possibility that Rhode Island will not ratify the Constitution. What then will be our relationship with Rhode Island?

He says, there will be moral relations that remain uncanceled. What are those moral relations? How will the claims of justice be enforced if they remain uncanceled? His answer is to say, "the rights of humanity must in all cases be duly and mutually respected; whilst considerations of a common interest, and above all the remembrance of the endearing scenes which are past, and the anticipation of a speedy triumph over the obstacles to re-union, will, it is hoped, not urge in vain MODERATION on one side, and PRUDENCE on the other." That answer means, of course, that we recur to necessity and force if need be; but we pray that need will not be and that Rhode Island will not be permitted to remain outside. We pray that a sixtieth part of the people will not be permitted to give the tone to fifty-nine-sixtieths.

There is a real politics, a sense of dealing candidly with historical and political events, that permeates the essays at this point. We have the theory to be sure and it is clear and it guarantees certain rights and certain structure and certain tone. But we also have the necessities that must be confronted and dealt with. In the best of worlds the theory will prevail to shape the necessities to the object that we aim for. And that's what Publius is concerned with. The forty-fourth essay, therefore continues, going on to the fifth class of provisions and those involve a number of questions that we will skip over.

In the second part of this forty-fourth essay, he turns to what is called the sixth and last class of powers which is the necessary and proper clause **No. 44** of the Constitution. We will not develop this at length, but I point to the twelfth paragraph in which he says there are four other possible methods that could have been taken to deal with this so-called *elastic* clause. He ends up rejecting the four alternatives because they all have certain negative consequences. He overlooks a sixth possibility, the one that I call the negative general. Whereas the Constitution states that all powers necessary and proper may be executed, it could have said that powers not necessary and proper may not be executed. That's the negative general without the enumerations and all the problems.

The negative general would, however, have had a consequence of concern that he makes clear in these passages. The negative general would have given far more emphatic rise to the doctrine of construction, as the prominent mode for the determination of powers and the struggle over politics. If we say we may not exercise powers that are not necessary and proper, we then say we must have a formal finding in every case of where the powers are necessary and proper. Stating it as it has been stated leaves it open to challenge whether powers are necessary and proper, but does not impose a formal investigation at each step of the political process.

This then is the conclusion Publius is reaching. If we're going to deal with problems of construction, we want to aim those problems of construction in a certain direction. That direction in the end is going to be one that focuses on the offices of government and their relations rather than on the powers of government. We want to make the powers as much accepted and expected as possible, leaving only the question as to who administers those powers to be the subject of construction and of political debate. That is a question which will become very clear to us as we look at the subject of the separation of powers and checks and balances or what I call, government by the just majority.

No. 41

Government under the Constitution as defended by Publius is divided into two principal questions. Recall the beginning of essay forty-one. He lays out the questions: "The FIRST relates to the sum or quantity of power which it vests in the government. . . . The SECOND, to the particular structure of the government and the distribution of this power among its several branches." Dividing the question that way leads naturally into the emphasis which we find going through to essay forty-four. Publius avoids having battles over the sum or quantity of power and focuses the attention on the particular structure and the division of powers between the branches. He creates a great advantage for the national government. People who divide over how to distribute the powers have to begin by accepting the powers they want to distribute. So Publius's division of the question into these two areas is meant to facilitate that accomplishment. That accom-

Nos. 45–46

plishment is reflected in essays forty-five and forty-six. The reflection of the accomplishment may appear in rather minor ways, but they appear less minor in proportion as they invite us to remember comments that have been made in the *Federalist Papers*.

In the second paragraph of the forty-fifth essay, for example, Publius makes the argument:

. . . if, in a word, the Union be essential to the happiness of the people of America, is it not preposterous, to urge as an objection to a government without which the objects of the Union cannot be attained, that such a Government may derogate from the importance of the Governments of the individual States?

We've inverted the old question whether the Union will replace and subordinate the states. We have said the Union is essential to the happiness of the people of America. We have made the judgment that republicanism is the essential, the substantial thing.

We see the argument from the second *Federalist Paper* return in full force with the conclusion that government by the states is useful, conducive to the happiness of the people; but not essential to it. It is a secondary but not a primary condition. Then he goes on in that paragraph to argue that particular municipal establishments must be sacrificed to the public good and this must be the last word on the distribution of power under the Constitution.   No. 2

Now in the fifth paragraph, the observation on feudalism confirms the argument that was given to us at the end of the seventeenth essay, where the history of feudalism was presented as an analog to federalism. This leads him to consider then in the sixth paragraph what the relationship between the federal government and the particular state and municipal governments will be.   No. 17

The State Governments will have the advantage of the federal Government, whether we compare them in respect to the immediate dependence of the one on the other; to the weight of personal influence which each side will possess; to the powers respectively vested in them; to the predilection and probable support of the people; to the disposition and faculty of resisting and frustrating the measures of each other.   **No. 45**

The whole argument from propinquity now resurfaces and there's added to it more direct reflection on interest. Publius goes through a series discussions about why the state governments will retain the favor of the people. The state will employ more people, will spend more money, will pass more laws, and will more directly affect the lives of people. The federal government will be limited to the very same powers or concerns that were expressed in the seventeenth essay, and this comes out in the ninth paragraph. He lists the federal powers as "war, peace, negociation, and foreign commerce." In the seventeenth essay it was simply commerce; the adjective *foreign* had not been placed in front of it.   No. 17

He concludes this forty-fifth essay with an observation about why the Confederation failed:

Had the states complied punctually with the articles of confederation, or could their compliance have been enforced by as peaceable means as may be used with success towards single persons, our past experience is very far from countenancing an opinion that the State Governments would have lost their constitutional powers, and have gradually undergone an entire consolidation.

That is, had the states done their jobs well and been responsive and responsible, they would likely still be the primary sources of political authority within the Union. But, of course, they did not do their jobs well.

No. 46

No. 27

That leads to the forty-sixth essay which opens a very interesting question. Will the federal government or the state governments have the advantage with regard to the predilection and support of the people? We saw that same question raised in a somewhat different context in the twenty-seventh essay and the results were inconclusive. The question there was whether the better administration of the federal government would install it in the people's affections over the state governments. It was an open question. Publius concluded in the twenty-seventh essay that while we will conciliate the respect, the attachment of the community, through a good administration of the federal government, the state governments will always be a match to it. By the fourth paragraph, we see that it's fairly well set out in the twenty-seventh essay. We recur to the question now in a different context.

Having pointed to the failures of the states under the Articles of Confederation, Publius in the forty-sixth essay asks the question whether it will be the one or the other that will ultimately prevail in the people's affections. He says in the first paragraph, "The federal and State governments are in fact but different agents and trustees of the people, constituted with different powers designed for different purposes." Now we have the full constitutional argument. We no longer have separate sovereignties and separate governments. We have different agents and different trustees designed for different purposes assigned different powers under one constitution. That is the perspective in which we are going to answer this question. The adversaries to the Constitution, according to Publius, must be reminded that ultimate authority is in the people taken as a whole and not in their respective states.

Nos. 17–27

Then the forty-sixth essay gives us the general argument that resembles essays seventeen and twenty-seven. State governments are near to the people. It would be most natural for the people to be attached to them. They will affect more of the people's interests. The people will defend assaults on their power, etc. In the fourth paragraph he begins the turn:

If therefore, as has been elsewhere remarked, the people should in future become more partial to the fœderal than to the State governments, the change can only result, from such manifest and irresistible proofs of a better administration, as will overcome all their antecedent propensities. And in that case, the people ought not surely to be precluded from giving most of their confidence where they may discover it to be most due: But even in that case, the State governments could have little to apprehend, because it is only within a certain sphere, that the fœderal power can, in the nature of things, be advantageously administered.

The argument has changed. The federal government is going to be better. It is going to be more efficient. People are going to like it better. They are going to care more about it. It's going to have more dignity attached to it and more responsibility attached to it. However, the states still will have to do those things that are not assigned to the federal government. People will still have an interest in their states, in spite of the fact that state legislatures are prone to commit errors, as the sixth paragraph so indelicately reminds us. In the federal government people will decide issues with detachment, with disinterest, with foresight, and with a view to the public interest. Whereas, at the state level they will decide narrowly at the expense of those who are for the moment unpopular and who do not have the immediate ear of the decision makers. He says towards the end of the sixth paragraph:

I mean not by these reflections to insinuate, that the new Fœderal Government will not embrace a more enlarged plan of policy than the existing government **No. 46** may have pursued, much less that its views will be as confined as those of the State Legislatures; but only that it will partake sufficiently of the spirit of both, to be disinclined to invade the rights of the individual States.

Meaning that all of the bad habits of the states will have their impact on the federal government, and these detached, disinterested federal representatives will pay just enough attention to these parochial interests to assure the states that their powers will not be threatened; I might say their petty powers will not be threatened.

The conclusion we seem to have come to is that Publius expects an incomparably superior administration of the federal government to the state governments. He seems to expect over time the people to reward that incomparable superiority with a deeper affection for their federal institutions than for their state institutions. He presumably desires this result as a condition to accomplish the objective noted in the forty-sixth essay of assuring the people's happiness through Union. This has now become prior to any advantage or virtue to be gained from their existence in the respective States.

This leads us very directly to the particular structure of the government. He says, at the beginning of the forty-seventh essay, "Having reviewed the **No. 47** general form of the proposed government, and the general mass of power allotted to it: I proceed to examine the particular structure of this government, and the distribution of this mass of power among its constituent parts." In other words, let's now put behind us this whole question of power. We have examined it from several perspectives, and most prominently from the perspective of the effect of federal power on state power. We have candidly concluded that federal power will be exercised so carefully and so responsibly that people will prefer it to state power, but that there will be lots of room left for states to operate in.

There remains only to ask how we organize the particular powers. The power itself we concede to be safe because it's necessary for the happiness of the people; but is it safely organized?

Publius is building a case. Monroe, for example, says it is impossible to put together a government with that much power. He says in his letter to his constituents:

This government, it is manifest, can never be an efficient one. Strong necessity and imminent danger may make it so occasionally, but whenever this cause ceases to operate, its repellent principles will prevail. . . . The stronger the problems of the government are, the more repellent will its qualities be, and the sooner its dissolution; at least certain it is that the conflict between the general and state governments will be proportionally more violent, and its or their ruin be sooner accomplished.[11]

He goes on in that vein questioning the tone of the federal government. Finally he recommends to his constituents that they really shouldn't approve this government and that they should simply modify the Confederation. He says, by the way, that he would very much like to think that this government could work, that the whole idea of it is intriguing, that it inspires an ambitious soul, and he would love to have the opportunity to operate such instruments. But he thinks it can't work. It will become despotic and we don't want to expose the country to that danger. That's his bottom line.

One more passage puts this in context. Remember, he is the only Antifederalist who understood exactly what was happening between the nation and the states, and this is another example of that understanding. He says, "To organize a general government that shall contain within it a particular one for each state or, in other words, to form a constitution for each state which shall acknowledge that of the union, is no easy thing, for there has never been an example of the kind before."[12] Here are lots of strong, powerfully phrased Antifederalist reservations. Publius, in turning to the particular structures, in effect is saying, I've answered that, it's all over with.

Now, Monroe writes in June of 1788 and Publius writes the essays that we've been looking at in the period from January to February of 1788, so there's not a direct correspondence between these two. There would be more correspondence to the arguments from John Dewitt, December of 1787, and George Clinton, the Cato letters in November and January of 1788. Those are more directly being responded to by Publius than Monroe. But the point, of course, is that the arguments are laid out by Monroe and Publius.

No. 47 With the arguments having been laid out, Publius takes it as given in the forty-seventh essay that the only remaining objections to the Constitution relate to what I would call the engineering. The philosophical opinion has been rendered and it finds everything well established. Now the question is whether he's a good engineer, is it properly designed? Publius has the answer to that question, because everyone knows there are certain basic engineering principles that have to be respected in order to preserve liberty.

This is part of what they call the genius of the people. They could recite these things from memory partly because they showed up in every newspaper almost every day, and partly because they were written down in every state constitution or organizing charter that they knew. The separation of powers, the checks and balances among the offices, and the rotation in office were extremely important. The limitation of terms, and other structural principles go on and on and were taken by the people to be absolutely necessary to freedom. They didn't admit any room to qualify these requirements, or to shade these meanings at all. And therefore the Constitution was founded in an environment that is especially unforgiving on these scores.

In that context, Publius has a particularly difficult job to do because the federal Constitution doesn't rise to most of the standards that were accepted as they were generally phrased in that era. The federal Constitution doesn't even mention the separation of powers, let alone guarantee it in the way that it was usually phrased in that era.

The forty-seventh essay begins meeting the burden in its third paragraph:

No political truth is certainly of greater intrinsic value or is stamped with the authority of more enlightened patrons of liberty than that on which the objection is founded. The accumulation of all powers legislative, executive and judiciary in the same hands whether of one, a few or many, and whether hereditary, self appointed, or elective, may justly be pronounced the very definition of tyranny. Were the federal constitution therefore really chargeable with this accumulation of power or with a mixture of powers having a dangerous tendency to such an accumulation, no further arguments would be necessary to inspire a universal reprobation of the system. I persuade myself however, that it will be made apparent to every one, that the charge cannot be supported, that the maxim on which it relies, has been totally misconceived and misapplied.

It's a different challenge than the challenge of federalism. How did he meet the challenge with regard to federalism? Ultimately, he subordinated it to republicanism. That's to make a long story short. We could start with number nine and go through all the complex and clever arguments but the bottom line is that federalism is important but not most important, whereas the Antifederalists simply said federalism is important. Publius said federalism is important, but republicanism is worth more. And he succeeds, he persuades the people. They accept it.

What does he do on this question? Will he handle this question in the same way and say separation of powers is important but not most important? Well, as it turns out, he doesn't, although it looks like he's going to do that. He starts at first by telling us we're not sure how to define the

No. 37

separation of powers. This recalls the thirty-seventh essay which told us our science had not yet succeeded in delineating clearly these three branches of power. That reflects on what everybody believes.

Everybody holds a common opinion about something; it doesn't matter what it is. Imagine then that someone comes along and says that science proves that we don't know exactly where this comes from. Then suddenly we wonder about our opinions. Maybe it's not true. After all, we believe in scientists, don't we? So in number thirty-seven he says, science has not yet clearly delineated the three branches of power. And if science has not delineated them, how can all of these state constitutions talk about absolute separation? So already we've got a problem, and that's what he sets out to show in the fourth paragraph.

Publius says in the fourth paragraph:

The oracle who is always consulted and cited on this subject, is the celebrated Montesquieu. If he be not the author of this invaluable precept in the science of politics, he has the merit at least of displaying, and recommending it most effectually to the attention of mankind. Let us endeavour in the first place to ascertain his meaning on this point.

How shall we ascertain his meaning? Shall we read Montesquieu? No. Publius continues, "The British constitution was to Montesquieu, what Homer has been to the didactic writers on epic poetry. . . . [T]his great political critic appears to have viewed the constitution of England, as the standard, or to use his own expression, as the mirrour of political liberty." So why go back to the copy? Let's take the real thing. Publius says put Montesquieu aside and let's look at the English Constitution itself. So we won't mistake his meaning, let us recur to the source from which the maxim was drawn.

Now, in order to show that, he goes through the British Constitution. He says, "On the slightest view of the British Constitution, we must perceive that the legislative, executive, and judiciary departments are by no means totally separate and distinct from each other." He doesn't say Montesquieu wasn't smart enough to see that on the slightest view. He assumes that Montesquieu saw that and meant something else, and that we obviously don't understand Montesquieu. The point is, the example does not show complete separation. This is a more complicated story than we thought it was. We see that the executive gets mixed in with the legislative authority and the legislative gets mixed in with the executive and mixed in with the judicial. It's all complicated and interlacing and involved. Therefore, we need to return to the basic argument.

In the seventh paragraph Publius says:

No. 47   From these facts by which Montesquieu was guided it may clearly be inferred, that in saying "there can be no liberty where the legislative and executive powers are united in the same person, or body of magistrates," or, "if the power of judging be not separated from the legislative and executive powers," he did not mean that these departments ought to have no *partial agency* in, or no *controul* over the acts of each other. His meaning, as his own words import, and still more conclusively as illustrated by the example in his eye, can amount to no more than this, that where the *whole* power of one department is exercised by the same hands which possess the *whole* power of another department, the fundamental principles of a free constitution, are subverted.

We don't have to separate powers, we only have to make sure that the whole power doesn't stand in the hands of one person or one body of persons. This argument has to go a bit deeper before it can become meaningful to us and the eighth paragraph does that.

Publius begins the restatement:

The reasons on which Montesquieu grounds his maxim are a further demonstration of his meaning. "When the legislative and executive powers are united in the same person or body" says he, "there can be no liberty, because apprehensions may arise lest *the same* monarch or senate should *enact* tyrannical laws to *execute* them in a tyrannical manner."

The emphasis is not on the power but the power holder. This is very important.

Publius is saying separate power holders, not powers. It is a tough question how we actually separate power. It's a tough question how we can even identify a power in many very important respects. We can define legislative powers conceptually. That's making general laws. The executive power is enforcing general laws in particular cases. The judicial power is interpreting the application of laws subject to enforcement, making them ready for enforcement. Conceptually, we can define them. But, how do we put our hands on it? Where is it exactly? It's easier to put our hands on the power holders. So Publius already has made a transition.

It's never entirely clear, when the founders cite Montesquieu, where they derive their understanding. Most of them apparently derived it from reading the English translation. The English translation is often misleading, as we saw in the ninth *Federalist Paper*. It's misleading in this case as well. Some of them we know could read the French, and did. We know that Hamilton, Madison, and Jay could read and speak French. We don't know whether Jay read Montesquieu in the French, but we rather suspect that it's probable, and certainly Madison and Hamilton did.

In the French, Montesquieu uses two expressions. He speaks of *pouvoirs* which we could literally translate separation of powers and a *separation des puissances,* which is also translated separation of powers but which might in fact better be translated separation of authorities. And there is a passage in the *Spirit of the Laws* in which Montesquieu defines

puissances. What would the difference be if we translated it as separation
of authorities instead of separation of powers? In most of the examples we
see in the text here, the word Montesquieu is using is *puissances* not
pouvoirs. If that means authority, it means power holder rather than the
power. And if we want to make distinctions based on power holders, it's
somewhat easier to accomplish. We can distinguish legislators, executives,
and judges far more clearly than we can distinguish the powers of
legislation, of execution, of judgment. When is a judge interpreting and not
legislating? That's tough. It's easy to say when is a judge a judge and not
a legislator.

No. 51

If we look at it as a separation of authorities rather than a separation of
powers, truly what's involved is creating a political dynamic in which
differing people are given independent bases of action within the political
arena. From these independent bases they are able to influence the actions
of others and therefore able to set off countervailing tendencies within the
political system. We will see in the fifty-first *Federalist Paper* that the
theory of balances and checks is a subordinate part of the theory of
separation of powers, or separation of authorities. The balances and checks
are the means of getting the authorities to relate to one another in such a
fashion that they get their jobs done.

This interpretation of Montesquieu leads in a certain direction that is
rather critical for our understanding how Publius responds to the
Antifederalist criticism. Let me just complete the passage in the eighth
paragraph before going on with that.

"Were the power of judging joined with the legislative, the life and liberty of the
subject would be exposed to arbitrary controul, for *the judge* would then be *the
legislator*. Were it joined to the executive power, *the judge* might behave with all
the violence of *an oppressor*." Some of these reasons are more fully explained
in other passages; but briefly stated as they are here, they sufficiently establish the
meaning which we have put on this celebrated maxim of this celebrated author.

The emphasis is on the power holders.

Publius then goes through the state constitutions. And we find that in
Madison's analysis the state constitutions do not do what they declare at
the outset. They declare complete separation, but they in fact have all kinds
of intermixture. They sometimes have governors appointed by legislatures.
How can that be if we want them completely separate? We make the
governor dependent on the legislature by doing that. And they have
legislatures that elect or appoint the judges or can override the decisions of
judges, etc. So he points out that it's impossible as a practical rule to
maintain this absolute separation that they have talked about when they
focus on a separation of powers. Separation of authorities is easier to do
and permits Publius to talk about the Constitution without admitting that
it violates the separation of powers, because there's no question it has

distinct legislators, distinct executive, distinct judges, however much they may exercise one another's powers.

This separation of authorities no longer sounds like the statement in the third paragraph of the forty-seventh essay. Recall the third paragraph: "The accumulation of all powers legislative, executive and judiciary, in the same hands, whether of one, a few or many, and whether hereditary, self appointed, or elective, may justly be pronounced the very definition of tyranny." Publius's version of the definition is very close to the definitions we see quoted from Montesquieu. It has a few differences I want to draw attention to that ultimately form the foundation of this argument.

"The accumulation of all powers," speaks to the powers and not the power holders. "In the same hands" speaks to the power holders. It may be that we can not clearly delineate the lines of separation between the powers, but we can delineate the lines between and among the power holders. And who are they? Publius says, "whether hereditary, self appointed, or elective, whether one, few or many." That's an interesting way of specifying the power holders. We have two scales, call them X and Y. X is a scale of numbers, one, few, or many; Y is hereditary, self-appointed, or elected. This sounds very much like the traditional political philosophy of Aristotle or Montesquieu or Locke or a number of others who would in fact define the different constitutions, the different regimes. The accumulation of all the powers into the hands of one that is hereditary sounds like a monarch. The accumulation of all the powers of one in the hands of the self-appointed sounds like a tyrant or a dictator. Accumulate powers into the hands of one that is elective, and we have elective monarchy or something equivalent. Then we can go through the rest in that way. We're actually talking about constitutions in Publius's definition of the separation of powers.

Remember, the problem is not stated as the definition of the separation of powers but what he calls the very definition of tyranny. So, the accumulation of all the powers of government in the hands of the one, the few, or the many whether, hereditary, self-appointed, or elective is the very definition of tyranny. Tyranny is by definition government by the many that is elective. Does that come out right? Yes, in fact it does. Just take out the options of one or the few, and get rid of self-appointed and hereditary. It turns out that this definition works most against what was defined in *Federalist* ten as pure democracy because we can not separate authorities in a pure democracy. In a monarchy we can do it if we can contemplate the monarch holding executive powers and not holding legislative or judicial powers. We can set up such a constitution and still call it a monarchy. We can do that with an aristocracy or even with an oligarchy as far as that goes. But we can't do it where all power is invested in the community.

We could see how we would try to do it. We would say that we're a democracy, say the Athenian Assembly. The people exercise all the powers

No. 10

of government, but we don't think that's safe, so we're going to make a series of courts and appoint judges that have the judicial power, and we're going to name a chief magistrate and call him the archon, who has all the executive power and then we'll meet in assembly with the legislative power ourselves. That way we'll have separation of authorities. But what's wrong? Why does that model break down? It breaks down for the simple reason that every time the assembly meets it's more than just a legislative assembly. It is what we call a constituent assembly.

Remember the constituent assembly from the French Revolution, which was not the whole people. A constituent assembly at any moment remakes its constitution. So what if it set up judges? It can take the power back any time it wants. So what if it set up an executive? It could take the power back any time it wants. That is, any attempt to divide authorities where pure democracy rules, where the direct operation of the elective principle rules, is impossible. It is by definition tyranny. All the other forms of government we can make safe in some degree. We can avoid this accumulation of all the powers of government in them, but not in a pure democracy.

No. 22   So now we begin to understand why the representative principle and the separation of authorities is the key to safety. It is not the separation of conceptual powers but the separation of power holders. It turns out that the power in the republican society, the republican constitution, defended by Publius, indeed originates, as number twenty-two says, from the people, but it is never exercised by them. This republican power is exercised by certain authorities. We can separate these authorities and tell them how much of the power they get to hold or what kinds of operations they get to perform. But in fact, the real power is in the community.

No. 63   The language Publius uses in essay sixty-three to define this is the language of alienation. Publius says that the people alienate their power, their sovereign authority to rule. They place it into the hands of designated representatives. They no longer have direct control. That's the only way that people can govern themselves democratically without being tyrannical, according to Publius. So his response to the Antifederalists' objection about the separation of powers is that he thinks separation of authorities is a good thing, that can't be implemented in a pure democracy. Nor can we do it in a representative government that is so close to the people that in fact they can at any moment override the will of their representatives; and that's why the extended republic becomes necessary. A representative democracy in a small territory has the same problem as a direct democracy. Any time the people wish, on a whim, they can get rid of representatives and rule directly. And where we facilitate that prospect according to Publius, tyranny will inevitably result.

No. 47   The forty-seventh *Federalist Paper* opens our discussion of the particular distribution of powers under the Constitution. We want people to debate who has what power. They won't debate who has what power if it is possible to separate powers clearly and leave no disputed territory. The key to the separation of powers for Publius, therefore, is the disputed territory, which will make one power holder decisional over the exercise of another power holder's power. This will engage them in the mutual operation of checking and restraining one another. We will have our constitutional battles over the question of who gets to do what, not over the question of what gets to be done.

Now, that sounds ideal. We know enough American History to know we have fought over questions of what gets to be done. One of the earliest is whether we can have a national bank and there have been several such questions. If we return to the history, however, we will find in fact that the questions of what gets to be done have been few compared to questions of who gets to do what. And this is precisely the kind of political struggle Publius has sought to set off. He thinks there's a special safety involved in doing it that way, and we will discover it when we look at government by the just majority in the fifty-first *Federalist Paper*.

No. 51

NOTES

1. Morton Grodzins, "Centralization and Decentralization in the American Federal System," in *A Nation of States: Essays on the American Federal System,* 2nd ed., ed. Robert A. Goldwin (Chicago: Rand McNally, 1963; reprinted 1974), 1–24.

2. See James Madison speech in the House of Representatives on 13 May 1789, in *Works of Fisher Ames*, ed. and intro. William B. Allen (Indianapolis: Liberty Press, 1983), 573f.

3. Charles Reich, "The New Property," *The Yale Law Journal,* 73, no.5 (April 1964), 733–87.

4. Cf. Aristotle, *Politics,* 1255a–1255b4; with Hobbes, *Leviathan,* end of ch. 15, chs. 22 and 26, and ch. 29, pp.174 and 10–20.

5. See William B. Allen, "Theory and Practice in the Founding of the Republic," *Interpretation,* 4, no. 2 (1974): 79–97.

6. Martin Diamond, "The Federalist," in *History of Political Philosophy,* eds. Strauss and Cropsey (Chicago: Rand-McNally and Co., 1972), 640.

7. This is an evaluation not only of the new Constitution but of the trend of modern constitutions—a trend which is merely perfected in the new Constitution.

8. Allen, "Washington and Franklin," in *The Political Science Reviewer* XVII (Fall, 1987): 109–138.

9. James Monroe, "Observations on the Constitution," June, 1788 in the *Essential Antifederalist,* 139–152.

10. For a fuller discussion see W. B. Allen, "A New Birth of Freedom: Fulfillment or Derailment?" in *Slavery and its Consequences: The Constitution, Equality, and Race,* ed. Robert A. Goldwin (Lanham, MD: American Enterprise Institute [with University Press of America], 1988, 64-92).

11. Monroe, "Observations," in *Essential Antifederalist*, 141.

12. Monroe, "Observations," in *Essential Antifederalist*, 146.

PART VII: THE MECHANICS OF LIBERTY

In number forty-seven the separation of powers does not create an absolute separation of the offices of government, but rather an intermingling of their respective operations and authorities. The final paragraph in that essay is instructive in that regard. It reads:

No. 47

> In citing these cases in which the legislative, executive, and judiciary departments, have not been kept totally separate and distinct, I wish not to be regarded as an advocate for the particular organizations of the several state governments. I am fully aware that among the many excellent principles which they exemplify, they carry strong marks of the haste, and still stronger of the inexperience, under which they were framed. It is but too obvious that in some instances, the fundamental principle under consideration has been violated by too great a mixture, and even an actual consolidation of the different powers; and that in no instance has a competent provision been made for maintaining in practice the separation delineated on paper.

The argument reminds us of the one that led in *Federalist* thirty-seven to the criticism of federalism. There Publius says that natural "delineations are perfectly accurate" but not those in "the institutions of man." He says, "no skill in the science of Government has yet been able to discriminate and define, with sufficient certainty, its three great provinces—the Legislative, Executive, and Judiciary." We associate that argument with the state constitutions and state government because it is clear that the most evident failure in that respect is in the constitutions previously established by the states. Thus, defense of the Constitution is meant to represent an advance beyond the stage that political science has accomplished to that point. He puts it in these words:

No. 37

What I have wished to evince is, that the charge brought against the proposed constitution, of violating a sacred maxim of free government, is warranted neither by the real meaning annexed to that maxim by its author nor by the sense in which it has hitherto been understood in America.

No. 47

With that conclusion we cannot charge the Constitution with an impermissible mixture of the powers of government and then can go on to the forty-eighth essay to outline a system of mixture.

The argument from the forty-eighth essay is made in terms of the relationship of checks and balances to the separation of powers. We need

No. 48

to mix the powers sufficiently to enable each branch to become an agent in screening the other branches of government. That is a very practical task. It carries with it certain implications which we need to explore not in the context of the forty-eighth essay itself but ultimately in the fifty-first essay.

No. 49

Along the way in essay forty-nine, Publius considers whether the Constitution as established will be enduring and if not, what provision will be made for eliminating any defect that might surface in it. Now that argument in the forty-ninth essay should be read in light of the criticisms that have been made about the state of political science to this point. We are given to expect that, whatever it is that is accomplished in the federal Constitution, it, no less than the state constitutions, will be in some measure imperfect. It will be imperfect because political science is not yet as advanced as one would hope it might be. Naturally, that leads to the question of making arrangements for perfecting it ultimately. It is not sufficient to point to the amendment process because we also have to identify the sources or the resources that we rely upon to obtain those amendments that speak directly to the imperfection that ultimately will surface.

This question had been addressed in a draft constitution for Virginia by Thomas Jefferson in 1783. There the draft constitution called for periodic return to the people in their constituent role as the opportunity for reappraising the constitution and particularly for resolving any disputes that might have emerged in the course of time among the several branches precisely as between parties in the system. As seen in the forty-ninth essay, the chief question is whether all political disputes don't boil down ultimately to parties. If so, will we not in fact bring these parties into our periodic constitutional conventions meant to resolve the difficulties between the contending parties? Won't this produce a decisively partisan result rather than a result that will in fact enhance the constitution as comprehensive, organic, organizing principle for the society? So Publius takes up Thomas Jefferson's draft of the Constitution for the State of Virginia and criticizes it, with the understanding that the whole point of a founding is decisively to establish the rule of a single, fundamental party.

It is important to understand the role of this criticism. Of course, Thomas Jefferson and James Madison are two friends in the founding era. So the criticism isn't meant to be petulant. It is not ill tempered or petty. It is serious criticism. It is indeed very close to the criticism that Madison offers to Jefferson two years later. Jefferson wrote to Madison from Paris a year later a letter in which Jefferson says in fact that the earth belongs to the living and we should neither try to establish governments that reach beyond the appointed tenure of a given generation nor incur debts that reach beyond the appointed tenure of a given generation. We should recognize that each generation comes on to the stage with full and proper authority to bind itself, to make its own decisions unbound by past generations. Madison wrote back a lengthy letter in which he rejected Jefferson's theory, although Madison agreed that each generation must bind itself. His rejection boiled down to the claim that generations inherit not only debts from the past; they also inherit assets. They inherit treasures for which they owe some obligation. The most obvious of these treasures, of course, would be in the form of the sacrifices of blood and treasure made by the Americans and the founding generation in the revolutionary war. He asked Thomas Jefferson whether he would completely eliminate in the next generation any moral obligations to those who in fact gave the inheritance of liberty to their offspring by taking great risks of their own personal fortunes and lives as well as the broader social risks? So his argument is that people do in fact have ties that bind across the generations.

Moral obligations extend across the generations. People should be able to reach back to recover those strengths of a given society which in fact have given them in the first place the resources they rely upon in order to have a fuller expression and appreciation of their opportunities. That is meant to reject the claim that the earth belongs to the living. The earth is, in its useful sense according to James Madison, a product of the dead. The dead presented it to the living as a free gift. That free gift should not be used in a cavalier manner, and one should of course show a proper gratitude to those who offer such gifts.

In the draft constitution for the state of Virginia, we have a cognate argument to the argument in Jefferson's letter that the earth belongs to the living. The proposition in the second paragraph of the forty-ninth essay is from the draft; it says: "that whenever any two of the three branches of government shall concur in opinion, each by the voices of two thirds of their whole number, that a convention is necessary for altering the constitution, or *correcting breaches of it*, a convention shall be called for the purpose." **No. 49**

Publius recognizes, of course, that a convention of people is consistent with the republican theory. The "people are the only legitimate fountain of power." We have seen that thought repeated throughout these papers and it will be repeated again. Yet, there is a problem that is best illustrated by recurring momentarily to the argument of the forty-seventh *Federalist Paper*. In that argument we discern that the definition of tyranny operates most forcefully against the people as a constituent assembly. Tyranny is most likely to occur where the people are permanently assembled and can exercise at its will all the powers of government. No. 47

Reliance on constituent assemblies to settle disputes among the branches implies a frequent recurrence to the people in their constituent role. Clearly then, this frequent recurrence to the people in their constituent role is evocative of the danger of tyranny through inviting the majority to ride roughshod over minorities. The argument then insists in the third paragraph:

It seems strictly consonant to the republican theory, to recur to the same original authority, not only whenever it may be necessary to enlarge, diminish, or new-model the powers of government; but also whenever any one of the departments may commit encroachments on the chartered authorities of the others. The several departments being perfectly co-ordinate by the terms of their common commission, neither of them, it is evident, can pretend to an exclusive or superior right of settling the boundaries between their respective powers.

Remember the question of construction. What we want to do is to make the government fight over who gets to do what, not over what gets to be done. The question is, how will we carry on this fight? We carry it on in the form of periodic constitutional crises or we can stage the debate over interpretation of powers and who will exercise them in a regular part of government. That is what he is now describing:

How are the encroachments of the stronger [branches] to be prevented, or the wrongs of the weaker to be redressed, without an appeal to the people themselves; who, as the grantors of the commission, can alone declare its true meaning and enforce its observance?

So he is caught on the horns of a dilemma. On the one side we don't want to foster an over great reliance on the people and their constituent role because that produces instability. On the other hand we want to foster some debate about who should do what. The problem is, who will arbitrate the debate? How will we settle their battles once they have begun without having these frequent constitutional conventions?

Publius admits in the fourth paragraph:

There is certainly great force in this reasoning [in support of recurrence to the people], and it must be allowed to prove, that a constitutional road to the decision of the people, ought to be marked out, and kept open, for certain great and extraordinary occasions. But there appear to be insuperable objections against the proposed recurrence to the people, as a provision in all cases for keeping the several departments of power within their constitutional limits.

Publius draws a distinction between the great and extraordinary crises and the ordinary occasions of political dispute.

How can we resolve ordinary political disputes without making them a constitutional crisis? It is rather like asking the question about flag burning in the contemporary United States and wondering if this really is the kind of question one wants to have a constitutional crisis about? Or is it the kind of question one rather displays for the ordinary dispensations of public opinion and political institutions? Does one want to raise it to the level of great constitutional interpretations? If one follows Publius one would suggest "no." So, what are the procedures to be established to permit us in fact to reduce such questions to ordinary proportions and then deal with them within the confines of these ordinary proportions.

Publius says in the fifth paragraph:

In the first place, the provision does not reach the case of a combination of two of the departments against the third. If the legislative authority, which possesses so many means of operating on the motives of the other departments, should be able to gain to its interest either of the others, or even one-third of its members, the remaining department could derive no advantage from this remedial provision. I do not dwell however on this objection, because it may be thought to lie rather against the modification of the principle, than against the principle itself.

So he wants to argue this very idea of forcing things back to the people and not the inconveniences that in one particular arrangement leave one righteous branch exposed to the more powerful.

We see eventually, by the way, why it is the legislative department has always been regarded as most powerful. This is an essential element of republican theory from Publius's perspective. It is the reason that we define pure democracy as tyranny and it ultimately defines for us the expedience that is appropriate to make government itself safe under the United States Constitution.

In the sixth paragraph he proceeds with the argument.

In the next place, it may be considered as an objection inherent in the principle, that as every appeal to the people would carry an implication of some defect in the government, frequent appeals would in a great measure deprive the government of that veneration, which time bestows on every thing, and without which perhaps the wisest and freest governments would not possess the requisite stability.

This is a nicely poised analysis. Pay attention to its separate parts. The frequent appeals would suggest, to the precise extent they are more frequent, far more inherent defects of the constitutional order.

Constantly to suggest a defect in the Constitution is of course constantly to erode the confidence of the people in the Constitution as a whole. It is to suggest to people that they are governed by institutions of civil life which lack that essential dignity derived from long endurance. Publius is of the opinion that government should not be deprived, certainly not lightly, of the veneration that time instills.

By time, of course, Publius means habit. People get in the habit of giving obedience to the laws. Habits take time to establish. They are precious and it is very important to enlist a habit of obedience on the side of sound institutions. Sound institutions do not within themselves have the power of habitual obedience. It is not the simple fact that they are right or rational that makes civil institutions effective. They, no less than defective institutions, must depend to a large degree on those principles identified in the thirty-first and thirty-seventh essays. Involved are passions and prejudices and interests and, indeed, habits that people build up in their ways of looking at things. Public opinion generally sustains a certain thrust or direction in social life wholly apart from the intrinsic merit of the institutions themselves.

Good institutions no less than bad institutions rely upon habits in order to achieve preservation. That is the argument Publius wants to make and therefore he makes it starting in the sixth paragraph. He says, "If it be true that all governments rest on opinion, it is no less true that the strength of opinion in each individual, and its practical influence on his conduct, depend much on the number which he supposes to have entertained the same opinion." Individuals taken alone regard themselves as peculiar. Opinions are held perhaps strongly but in some contexts weakly. They gain in strength in proportion as others reflect similar opinions. They are more willing to stand up and express themselves when they can expect such suggestions will in fact meet in the return the approving nods of their fellows. This is the argument of Tocqueville in *Democracy in America,* written in the 1830's; nothing is so powerful as majority opinion. No one wants to step outside this stream of majority opinion. No one wants to impose upon himself the stigma of difference, so that our opinions are enlarged in proportion as we find others who reflect them back to us. Governments survive on this very natural human habit to seek the security and comfort of common opinion.

Publius continues and says:

The reason of man, like man himself is timid and cautious, when left alone; and acquires firmness and confidence, in proportion to the number with which it is associated. When the examples, which fortify opinion are *antient* as well as *numerous*, they are known to have a double effect.

So the older this opinion is in addition to its contemporaneous reflection the more surely we find it incontrovertible. We take it to be a truth if it has been there for a long time and never refuted; and all our fellows agree that this is how we should view the world. Well, we require precisely to bring such a moral weight to the defense of Publius's arguments.

This discussion of opinions is an extraordinary argument because we've often taken the perspective that somehow free institution shouldn't need to depend on myth or illusion, and shouldn't need to depend on the prejudices or thoughts by which we often think we perceive one another. Yet Publius is as conversant with propaganda as any, and it is still true that the best of governments must depend no less on these subtle aspects of humanity.

The argument, by the way, that all governments depend on opinions perhaps is seen most clearly in the works of David Hume. There is no such thing as an absolute dictatorship or absolute monarchy. We may have such a monarch or despot who disposes of absolute power, but that power in its exercise depends no less on public opinion than power in the most direct democracy because it operates through the souls of subjects. They and their wills make good the monarch's command. If their opinion, therefore, does not sustain the least of the monarch's commands as legitimate, or what ought to be obeyed, then the monarch ceases to command. That is what Publius meant when he said that all governments depend on opinion.

Some governments, of course, are better than others. For some governments, opinion is made integral to the functions of the institutions and powers of the state. There are others in which the opinion is there as a limiting condition but not integral. That distinguishes the legitimate from the illegitimate governments.

The opinion of persons that government is the necessary medium for the accomplishment of the will of the sovereign is no less true of the relationship between a master and a slave. The master commands and the slave obeys, but the slave's will must intervene between the command and the obedience. If the slave does not will to move himself in accord with the command of the master, the command is frustrated. Opinion is, of course, the specific engine of movement in any given person. We are self-moved beings; but that self-motion receives strength from the fuel that is provided by opinion.

In a nation of philosophers, this consideration ought to be disregarded. A reverence for the laws, would be sufficiently inculcated by the voice of an enlightened reason. But a nation of philosophers is as little to be expected as the philosophical race of kings wished for by Plato. And in every other nation, the most rational government will not find it a superfluous advantage, to have the prejudices of the community on its side.

So there is no utopia. From the first essay passions and prejudices are present; and we find a parallel reference to the nation of philosophers in *Federalist* fifty-five. "Had every Athenian citizen been a Socrates; every Athenian assembly would still have been a mob." Nos. 1, 55

That is an extremely important perception. There is no particular kind of human soul that we seek or encourage in order to make our society safe and our government free and decent. Rather, we must construct the institutions of civil life to fit the human soul, whatever that soul may be, whether philosophers or non-philosophers. There's something about human beings living in a community that disposes them to operate on the basis of principles. And it is necessary to fortify the rational principles of society with moral inducements and with the passions and prejudices of the community on the side of the institutions. A reverence for the laws is necessary to a condition of obedience to the laws. It is not enough that the laws be good; we can't all simply look at the law as a Socrates and say this is rational and obey. According to this argument, our obedience to the law must come before our judgment of the law as rational. We must expect by habit the laws to be good, if the laws are to achieve their proper objective.

To some people this can be a very disturbing argument. I understand that. We are an individualist society; we like to think that we judge every single thing ourselves and if we don't put our own stamp of approval on it, we have at least suspended judgment. We may not disapprove but we at least suspend judgment. Publius has challenged precisely that contention. It is just as important for individuals to consent, or to yield their will to the proposition of another. Consent for the Declaration of Independence defines where our institutions and liberty come from, but the fact of the matter is that we are moral agents and moral agents act on the strength of their opinions. Our opinions are not generated by independent selection. Most of us most of the time live on the strength of opinions which we inherit, which we in a sense breathe in the atmosphere. And so the task is to construct such an atmosphere as to inspire us, and I mean that literally, with opinions that are sound and healthy.

Orthodoxy, remember, which has become an epithet in our time, means originally right opinion. It needn't be an epithet. Orthodox, in its original Greek, simply refers to those opinions which we all hold to be true. They can't be demonstrated as true; that's why they are opinion rather than knowledge. But right opinions are still true. Publius is saying that all civil right depends on the establishment of orthodoxy. And that is not an insult to our intelligence.

No. 49
On the strength of that argument, Publius proceeds through the forty-ninth essay to show what's wrong with his friend Jefferson's proposal, which is rather more theoretical than it needs to be according to Publius. One of the reasons for its being erroneous, he says in the eighth paragraph, is that Jefferson forgets the tendency of a legislative branch of government to aggrandize. This is the greatest threat to government; this is the greatest threat to liberty.

But the greatest objection of all is, that the decisions which would probably result from such appeals, would not answer the purpose of maintaining the constitutional equilibrium of the government. We have seen that the tendency of republican governments is to an aggrandizement of the legislative, at the expence of the other departments. The appeals to the people, therefore, would usually be made by the executive and judiciary departments. But whether made by one side or the other, would each side enjoy equal advantages on the trial?

Now we needn't follow him through this analysis in detail. I think what it amounts to in the end is the strongest part of this argument: the final recognition that legislatures are by nature divided into dramatically defined parties. Political party at this stage doesn't mean an organized party or competition to elect candidates into office as we know it. What we know are what we call tamed or civilized parties. But ad hoc parties that grow up in every legislature can take any number of forms. They will tend to divide every legislature, according to his argument, in proportion as the legislature has any serious work to perform. Serious issues will be fought over.

In this context the major party in the legislature would start out every constitutional crisis with an advantage. The legislature reflects more directly than either of the branches of government the will of the people. The legislators are closer to the people. They are the more directly elected. They are from smaller districts and are closer to their constituents. The major party in the legislature is very likely then to reflect a major party in the community at large. So that if in fact we bring on such a constitutional crisis through partisan dispute, according to Publius, the constitutional convention called to resolve the crisis will replicate the same parties. People of the legislature could go out and appeal for the election of their party to the convention's delegates. They will sit in the convention and then they will write their will into the constitution where they had previously been limited to writing ordinary law.

Publius would rather see these things reduced to ordinary law. In the tenth paragraph he tells us, "The *passions* therefore not the *reason,* of the public would sit in judgment. But it is the reason of the public alone that ought to controul and regulate the government. The passions ought to be controuled and regulated by the government." Now we really need to parse those two sentences. If we go through this process and the party takes over the crisis generated by and dissolved by party, he says the passions not the reason would control. What does this mean, "the reason of the public," and "the passions of the public"? We understand the passions of individuals and we understand the reason of the individual; but is there such a thing as collective passion or collective reasoning? And if so how do we create this opposite situation in which the reasonable role of the public orders the control and regulation of the government? Government provides what could be called public reasoning as distinguished from public faction. Is this idealism again, or is there really something called the reason of the public, with which we can become conversant?

Key to understanding what he means is the following sentence, "The passions ought to be controuled and regulated by the government." So we see that it is not just a choice to rule by reason instead of passion. What he's doing is choosing to submit the law of passion to the rule of reason. If passion is regulated by the government, what got us here? Well, we have a clue in the tenth essay. The tenth essay says that the principal task of   No. 10 modern legislation is the regulation of these various and interfering interests. Remember that. That was the return of thought. This government engages principally in the task of regulating the various and interfering interests in the society. These interests are the expression of the passions. Interest and passion are synonymous in the tenth essay. That's how Publius sees it. Expressions of the passions can become public faction when we find a group actuated by a common impulse. A common impulse of passion or interest is part of the definition of faction.

The common impulse is only part of the definition. We could have according to the definition of a faction, a group actuated by a common impulse of a passion or interest that is not adverse to the rights of the community or a part of the community. That is to say, we can have a group actuated by a common impulse of passion or of interest that is not a faction. Government by such a group is not adverse to the rights of the community, but is never-the-less rule by passion or interest. Well, this is what we want to regulate now in the forty-ninth essay. We want to regulate these various and interfering interests not only when they become faction, but when they are healthy and are consistent with the aims of the polity. We want to regulate these interests when they do nothing more than their own interest and mean no harm, but have a primary or chief concern with their own interest.

No. 10

We said it twice. Remember, the first object of government that was detailed in the tenth *Federalist Paper* is the protection of the diverse and unequal faculties of human beings, including the unequal faculties of acquiring property. The protection of property was deduced from the general proposition that we will protect the diverse and unequal faculties of human beings. People who are free to pursue their talents in the direction that they think best suited will equally be free to raise the claim of their factions or interests and seek public attention. Vanity becomes crucial. Well, on what standard will the factions and interests be regulated? The standard in the forty-ninth essay is the reason of the public.

The reason of the public stands over against the passions of the public. We have a general sense of what the passions of the public are. It is the expressed pursuit of some specific faction or interest. We may even go so far as to limit it, at least for illustrative purposes, to the pursuit of material advantage, say interests in the narrow sense of self-interest or an economic sense of the word. It doesn't matter for our purposes. We can see part of the objective. We want to see that the claims pressed on the basis of passion or interest are settled on some other basis. The basis is expressed here as the reason of the public.

Based on the general discussion, we know that the reason of the public will at least then not be passion or interest. Even if we can't know what the reason of the public is, it is not passions or interests. It is presumably some assimilating standard. And therefore, it must entail some process in which we take the particular passion or interests and elevate them to the level at which the tenth *Federalist Paper,* of course, was to refine and enlarge the public sentiments. So, we want to take these claims of each that are proffered on the basis of the pursuit of passions or interests and make them more comprehensive of the interests of the whole society. We want to address the common good.

The reason of the public is, then, this specific medium by which we articulate and enable the pursuit of the common good and this must be accomplished by institutional means. Ultimately, of course, there are no such things as institutional judgments. We know that we are in the habit of thinking that there are institutional judgments. The Supreme Court decided. Congress decided. No. Only human beings make judgments. Of that we can be certain, whether Publius says so or not. Take it on my authority. Human beings have the ability to make judgments and defend them. But here the judgment must be made through certain processes, through certain institutional forms. From the argument we are sure that these judgments will stand on what Publius is now identifying as the reason of the public.

The final paragraph indicates the directions that we will take for this definition of the public reason: "We found in the last paper that mere declarations in the written constitution, are not sufficient to restrain the several departments within their legal rights." Again, the last paper, essay forty-eight, was the elaboration of essay forty-seven. These dealt with the separation of powers. Just writing down on a piece of paper that we shall have separation of powers and checks and balances means nothing. It's useless. Publius despairingly speaks of it as a "parchment barrier." It will not restrain the departments within their legal rights, so we must go beyond that. It appears here in essay forty-nine that occasional appeals to the people are dangerous and insufficient for that purpose. So, we can't check the branches by writing it in our constitution, and we can't check the branches by going back to the people periodically.

No. 49

Nos. 47, 48

Finally, then what must we look for? He says, "How far the provisions of a different nature contained in the plan above quoted, might be adequate, I do not examine. Some of them are unquestionably founded on sound political principle, and all of them are framed with singular ingenuity and precision." So, what has it left us with? We have nowhere to turn.

We know that separation of powers and checks and balances are not just written into the Constitution. We said at the outset we can't find those words in the Constitution. We see now a principled argument for their not being in the Constitution. The mere literary declaration of the existence of those essential legal and moral purposes doesn't suffice. On the other hand, we can't accomplish it by saying that we are going to have a permanent board of monarchists in the form of a Constitutional Convention of the people. To what then must we turn? That will be the burden of our analysis of the fiftieth and fifty-first essays.

Essay fifty opens, "It may be contended perhaps, that instead of *occasional* appeals to the people, which are liable to the objections urged against them, *periodical* appeals are the proper and adequate means of

No. 50

preventing and correcting infractions of the Constitution." Publius will go on to say that appeals, whether occasional or periodical, will not do and therefore leave us with a challenge of asking, how are we going to make this government work and properly check the departments; and making it work, make it so that the reason as just opinion of the public will prevail over its passions. How will the founding make Solomon's party of liberty the permanent ruling party?

No. 51   In *Federalist* fifty-one we have the solution to the problem of trying to establish the reason of the public in command under the Constitution. This is the solution to a problem differently expressed as well, namely, how it will be possible to make the branches of this government contest, one with another, over their rightful powers, their rightful authorities, and to make out of that contest a healthful principle for the body politic. This question is answered in the climactic essay, number fifty-one, in the *Federalist Papers*.

No. 10   We have for a long time been misled in focusing on *Federalist Paper* ten as the heart and soul of the *Federalist Papers*. That process began late last century and early this century in the work of Charles Beard, who rediscovered the *Federalist Papers* and promoted *Federalist* ten as the most important of the *Federalist Papers*. Ever since Charles Beard scholars have focused on that essay in either trying to prove Beard's thesis or trying to refute Beard's thesis. *Federalist* ten is an important essay. It is the culminating essay of the answer to the first question on the outline of the *Federalist Papers;* but of course there are five other questions on that outline.

Federalist Paper fifty-one accomplishes what *Federalist Paper* ten does not accomplish. It demonstrates precisely how it is that the government is going to work and why it is going to accomplish the ends of just policy. *Federalist* ten lays out the theoretical foundation to this argument. *Federalist* fifty-one shows the moral operation of the argument. *Federalist* fifty-one is the demonstration of the operation of the just majority. Throughout these papers it has been made clear that the *sine qua non* for this Constitution in Publius's eyes is that it be popular and wholly popular; and yet we have consistently found along the way the expression of reservations about government operating merely on the basis of popular principles. So how can a government be wholly popular and not be merely popular? That is our conundrum.

Essay fifty-one tells us how to accomplish the objective. It opens appropriately with the very question:

To what expedient then shall we finally resort, for maintaining in practice the necessary partition of power among the several departments, as laid down in the constitution? The only answer that can be given is, that as all these exterior provisions are found to be inadequate, the defect must be supplied, by so contriving the interior structure of the government, as that its several constituent parts may, by their mutual relations, be the means of keeping each other in their proper places. Without presuming to undertake a full development of this important idea, I will hazard a few general observations, which may perhaps place it in a clearer light, and enable us to form a more correct judgment of the principles and structure of the government planned by the convention.

Publius has a practical answer. Note the word *expedient*. The word *expedient* means we are looking for a tool or means to accomplish our purpose. The end is no longer in question. The only thing that is in question is how to accomplish the end. The word *finally* indicates that we have weighed a number of possibilities and dismissed them as either insufficient or ineffective. The mere separation of powers written on paper is insufficient; periodic recurrence to constitutional conventions is ineffective and destabilizing. All along the way, all of the other expedients have been ruled out. We've come to the bottom line. Somehow the Constitution, as it's written, must foster political *practices* which will accomplish the end aimed at in our earlier theoretical discussions. So at the first level we have the design problem of "contriving the interior structure." It is a matter of engineering; if we set it up just so, and the widgets react to one another just so, then there will be an equilibrium established. They will keep one another in their proper places. We turn our attention away from moral declarations to the hard work of legislation—legislation in the sense of founding—namely, how we design institutions which of their own weight accomplish our moral goals. Publius argues that we needn't develop this fully. We will see in a moment why, because this is only the introduction to a far more important question. But we at least want to be able to form what he calls a correct judgment of the principles and structure.

We said before that we wanted to set up construction as the chief instrument for assuring the effectiveness of these institutions. This construction determines who has the power to do what, rather than what power the government as a whole has. This is now what we shall discuss:

In order to lay a due foundation for that separate and distinct exercise of the different powers of government, which to a certain extent, is admitted on all hands to be essential to the preservation of liberty, it is evident that each department should have a will of its own; and consequently should be so constituted, that the members of each should have as little agency as possible in the appointment of the members of the others. Were this principle rigorously adhered to, it would require that all the appointments for the supreme executive, legislative, and judiciary magistracies should be drawn from the same fountain of authority, the people, through channels, having no communication whatever with one another.

There's that question again: "will." We've had public passion, public reason, and now "departmental will." So now our first principle and level of separation is appointment through independent sources. They do not appoint one another, or at least they play as small a role as possible in one another's appointments This gives them independent will; they act independently of one another because they stand on independent authorities. So we understand this.

We have now returned to the world of *Federalist* thirty-seven to thirty-nine. We have defined "republicanism" and "representation." We want responsibility. We want dependence. That means to tie them as strictly as possible to the people. But this has been qualified to some extent, for reasons that become evident.

Perhaps such a plan of constructing the several departments would be less difficult in practice than it may in contemplation appear. Some difficulties however, and some additional expence, would attend the execution of it. Some deviations therefore, from the principle must be admitted. In the constitution of the judiciary department in particular, it might be inexpedient to insist rigorously on the principle; first, because peculiar qualifications being essential in the members, the primary consideration ought to be to select that mode of choice, which best secures these qualifications; secondly, because the permanent tenure by which the appointments are held in that department must soon destroy all sense of dependence on the authority conferring them.

So we change in the case of the judiciary because, though they are appointed by the other two branches, they are left in office long enough not to feel a sensible dependence upon them; they still have an independent will. At the same time, having them appointed in that way assures that we gain the special qualifications required for the office. We compromise the principle but only in such a way as indirectly still to achieve the end aimed at, namely, independence of will.

This independence of will is extremely important. It is an independence of each other. It is not an independence absolutely, but each must be able to make decisions and act without being accountable to the other branches.

It is equally evident that members of each department should be as little dependent as possible on those of the others for the emoluments annexed to their offices. Were the executive magistrate, or the judges, not independent of the legislature in this particular, their independence in every other would be merely nominal.

The Constitution does not permit Congress to lower the pay of these other offices for the people who are in the offices. Once the pay is set, constitutionally it is guaranteed to those office holders. The constitutional convention, at the outset, showed a due regard for structuring the relations between the branches.

These provisions in the Constitution are not there because they are boiler plate legal language. Remember, if we compare this Constitution to the state constitutions, we will find it departs markedly from the state constitutions. It is not like going into a bookstore and getting a book of wills or real estate contracts off the shelf, and coming home and just filling in the particular facts with boiler plate language. They weren't doing that; they were thinking at each step of the process what they would include. They departed so far from the only models they knew, the state constitutions, that it is clear their departure represents conscious reflection and choice. So when they write into this Constitution that Congress cannot reduce the pay of judges who are sitting in the Supreme Court, it is in fact a new reflection partly generated by experience. They had seen what happened in the states. They had seen legislatures try to get even with judges, when judges made decisions that legislatures didn't like, by cutting their pay or removing them from office, or reversing their decisions.

Again, we are doing this because we can't establish the branches so purely and independently of one another that each can see to itself. If we gave the judges the right to establish their own pay, we'd run into a different set of abuses, and so we have to build this carefully calibrated mechanism. It's a design question.

But the great security against a gradual concentration of the several powers in the same department, consists in giving to those who administer each department, the necessary constitutional means, and personal motives, to resist encroachments of the others. The provision for defence must in this, as in all other cases, be made commensurate to the danger of attack.

After we have looked at the design considerations, after we've seen the conscious choices, there is still yet an entirely different level, a step above, in the whole conversation. Why do we echo the original definition of tyranny, from *Federalist* forty-seven, by speaking of "the great security against a gradual concentration of the several powers in the same department"? *No. 47*

"But the great security against a gradual concentration of the several powers of government in the same department," or the real guarantee of the separation of powers we might want to read it, is giving to "those who administer each department, the necessary constitutional means, and personal motives, to resist encroachments of the others." So we must make each the sentinel over the rights of the community against the other branches of government. How will we do that? "Ambition must be made to counteract ambition." We are going to look, not at the offices, but at the office holders. We are going to depend, not on written provisions in the Constitution, but on the eternal elements of the human soul. We're going to depend on the very ambitions that were described in *Federalist* seventeen that will attract office holders into the Federal Government in **No. 51**

No. 17

the first place. We're going to depend on these ambitious souls being sufficiently ambitious, that in seeking to advance themselves, they will do so following the only road open to them, namely, resisting those in the other branches. These are what are called in the foregoing paragraph the "necessary constitutional means and personal motives."

We must bring together the opportunity to check the other branches with the incentive to do so, because of the encouragement to one's own ambition.

The interest of the man must be connected with the constitutional rights of the place. It may be a reflection on human nature, that such devices should be necessary to controul the abuses of government. But what is government itself but the greatest of all reflections on human nature? If men were angels, no government would be necessary. If angels were to govern men, neither external nor internal controuls on government would be necessary. In framing a government which is to be administered by men over men, the great difficulty lies in this: You must first enable the government to controul the governed; and in the next place, oblige it to controul itself.

No. 49

Again, parse the sentence carefully. Notice how finely balanced it is. We said, in the forty-ninth essay that we want the government to regulate the public passions. That's what he means when he says we will enable the government to control the governed. And see, that's to regulate the public passions. Next, we want the reason of the public to prevail. We don't want the passion of the office holder to prevail; we don't even want the reason of the office holder to prevail; we want the reason of the public to prevail. And therefore, we must oblige the government to control itself. Government controlling itself and controlling the governed is the condition for establishing the reason of the public to prevail.

We begin to flip-flop as Publius continues: "A dependence on the people is no doubt the primary controul on the government; but experience has taught mankind the necessity of auxiliary precautions." The people show up in their two roles: they are the governed, who are being controlled by the government; and, they are the sovereign who control the government. They hold both functions. Institutionally we are trying to give the advantage to the people through both of these channels.

A dependence on the people is the primary control, but what is an "auxiliary precaution"? It is over and above primary control; it is additional safeguards. Publius will soon call them, "inventions of prudence." They are ways to make the institution stronger, not central to the institutions, not the fundamental principle, but add-ons. "This policy of supplying by opposite and rival interests, the defects of better motives, might be traced through the whole system of human affairs, private as well as public." We are going

No. 10

to adopt a policy of supplying "by opposite and rival interests, the defects of better motives." That is to say, we can't rely upon good will, or better motives. Better motives will be wanting; or as we put it in *Federalist* ten, "enlightened statesmen will not always be at the helm." So, not being able to count on better motives, we will use a policy of supplying opposite and rival interests.

What is the "defect of better motives"? Whose motives are defective? Is it not clear that he is talking about the office holders? Ambition counteracting ambition, here, applies to the office holders. This is a critical moment in the *Federalist Papers*, because very often people take this to mean that he is talking about the same argument he made in *Federalist Paper* ten; they assume he is talking about factions, and people in society at large. He is not. Note, he said, "the primary controul is dependence on the people." The people should control the government, but we need a secondary control on the government. The secondary control on the government is to supply, "by opposite and rival interests, the defect of better motives." It is not a defect in the people. It is a defect in the office holders which is being supplied in this way. In the fifth paragraph he says:

We see it particularly displayed in all the subordinate distributions of power; where the constant aim is to divide and arrange the several offices in such a **No. 51** manner as that each may be a check on the other; that the private interest of every individual, may be a sentinel over the public rights. These inventions of prudence cannot be less requisite in the distribution of the supreme powers of the state.

The private interests of every individual office holder may be a sentinel over the public rights. Recall that we are going to separate the power holders, not the powers. That is the key to making separation of powers work.

An invention of prudence is precisely not a natural occurrence. It is an artifice. It is produced by design, by conscious decisions. True, it depends on natural elements of the human soul: ambition, being the one most clearly invoked at this stage. But once we invoke this ambition, and put these ambitious people in the certain circumstances, we are, in fact, inclining them to act in ways that they would not otherwise act but for the circumstance we've put them in. That's what makes it an invention of prudence. Remember, prudence is the deliberate judgment that aims for the right end through the appropriate means.

These inventions of prudence, as opposed to the counsels of nature, he says then, "will be no less requisite to distribute the supreme powers of the state." This is what's going to make separation of powers work. But now the question begins to change.

But it is not possible to give each department an equal power of self-defence. In republican government the legislative authority, necessarily, predominates. The remedy for this inconveniency is, to divide the legislature into different branches; and to render them by different modes of election, and different principles of action, as little connected with each other, as the nature of their common functions, and their common dependence on the society, will admit.

That is, we have bicameralism, differing tenures of office, and different modes of election because otherwise the legislature will ride roughshod over the community. It's a way of slowing it down. Think of it this way: suppose one were schizophrenic, what would that mean? It would mean being divided in one's will. At one moment he'd want one thing; at another moment, another. And being divided in his will would mean that he would move less surely towards anything, because of the division. Bicameralism is meant to divide the legislature in its will, to make it a little bit schizophrenic, thus to slow it down. Slowing it down protects the people's liberty. That's the defense for the different modes of appointment, and the different tenures of office.

This is an entirely different orientation for us today. Publius expects the executive to be weak, exposed, and a prey to the powerful legislature:

It may be even necessary to guard against dangerous encroachments by still further precautions. As the weight of the legislative authority requires that it should be thus divided, the weakness of the executive may require, on the other hand, that it should be fortified.

So let's strengthen the executive, and there are a number of devices that have been added for this purpose, including giving the executive a mode of appointment, independent of the legislature.

Now it is true, in discussing the electoral college, there was some expectation that, in fact, the President would be, more often than not, elected by the Congress. But the original mode, the first step in the process, is not election by the Congress and is meant to give the President additional strength in dealing with the Congress which would be lessened in the case where a tie vote in the Electoral College forced a vote in the House of Representatives. It is also the case that the presidential veto is an indication of that strength. He says:

An absolute negative, on the legislature, appears at first view to be the natural defence. . . . But perhaps it would be neither altogether safe, nor alone sufficient. On ordinary occasions it might not be exerted with the requisite firmness; and on extraordinary occasions it might be perfidiously abused. May not this defect of an absolute negative be supplied, by some qualified connection between this weaker department, and the weaker branch of the stronger department . . . ?

Hamilton in the Convention wished for an absolute veto at the outset. Now here we see an example, I think, of where Publius's views had matured from the time of the Constitutional Convention to the writing of these essays. He had actually come to persuade himself that a qualified veto was more powerful than an absolute veto, for an absolute veto has the difficulty that it can be used rarely. Whereas a qualified veto allows the executive to make a point with frequency and to get even more use out of it.

This discussion of the relationship between the executive, the legislature, and the judiciary is meant to show how the internal principles operate, and to bring the branches together. Bicameralism at first brings the two branches of the legislature together. The executive branch, the veto and similar principles show, that we have to involve the executive in the legislative branch, both to fortify the executive, but also further to divide the will of the legislature. The fact that the executive exercises one-sixth of the legislative power (and we will show later how that comes out), means that we've not only divided the legislature twice, but three times. To the extent that the executive is a part of the legislature, it is a third and independent branch of the legislature; it's actually tri-cameralism.

All of these interconnections and intermixtures are the prescription for making the government more deliberate. Giving them an independent will protects them against one another. But this is a will as against one another, and not a will as against the community. So how do we keep that independent will from becoming a will as against the community? We so design the offices as to force them to be more deliberate, so they cannot act on mere will, and in being more deliberate, they then will presumably reflect more surely public opinion.

If the principles on which these observations are founded be just, as I persuade myself they are, and they be applied as a criterion, to the several state constitutions, and to the federal constitution, it will be found, that if the latter does not perfectly correspond with them, the former are infinitely less able to bear such a test.

There are moreover two considerations particularly applicable to the federal system of America, which place that system in a very interesting point of view.

So, once we've improved over the state constitutions, we now make a virtue of federalism. Federalism is good because it also plays a role in the separation of powers in permitting such a design of the institutions of government and their interactions as thereby to produce safety. (Remember the definition of federalism given by James Monroe, in his address to his constituents. It's still the best definition of the federalism created by the Constitution that we have available to us.)

First. In a single republic, all the power surrendered by the people, is submitted to the administration of a single government; and the usurpations are guarded against by division of the government into distinct and separate departments. In the compound republic of America, the power surrendered by the people is first divided between two distinct governments, and then the portion allotted to each, subdivided among distinct and separate departments.

The beginning sounds very much like the Monroe argument But what is he talking about? Not only do we have a horizontal separation of powers, but we also have a vertical separation of powers. At each stage along the vertical, we have a horizontal separation of powers. So it's an extraordinarily complex system in which we build in additional safeguards for liberty. He says, "a double security arises to the rights of the people." That is, the coordinated branches are separated at each level of government (horizontal) and the governments at different levels exercise mutually interacting powers (vertical). The different governments will control each other, just as the different branches will control each other.

No. 10

In the tenth paragraph, Publius gives us the second point in favor of federalism. He says, "It is of great importance in a republic, not only to guard the society against the oppression of its rulers, but to guard one part of the society against the injustice of the other part." Remember, we had the people as the governed, then we had the people as the authority of the government, i.e. those who were the sovereigns, and now they come up in the form of society. And this is a transition in the argument that gives us pause. Publius says, there are two considerations that especially apply to the federal system of America. The first was a system of vertical and horizontal separation of powers; the second is to guard one part of the society against the other. What does guarding one part against the other have to do with the discussion of separation of powers and checks and balances? That sounds like the discussion of faction in Federalist ten.

We have shown that the inventions of prudence, the auxiliary precautions, do not apply against the people, but against the office holders. So why, all of sudden, in the middle of this essay, have we left the question of how the government is controlled and thrown up into the air again the question of how the people are controlled, now that they have sovereign power? Publius says:

No. 51

Different interests necessarily exist in different classes of citizens. If a majority be united by a common interest, the rights of the minority will be insecure. There are but two methods of providing against this evil: The one by creating a will in the community independent of the majority, that is, of the society itself.

No. 10

The "different interests" tell us that we're restating *Federalist* ten; but now Publius is softening it because he is talking about interests and not factions, although some interests could become factions. He is not saying that the majority is hostile to the minority, he is just saying that as a general principle, there will be insecurity for the rights of the minority. A "will in the community independent of the majority, that is, of the society itself," is such a will as we would know in a non-republican system—a monarchy or an aristocracy, where someone has absolute authority, or power to command without any intervening authorization. But, we reject that.

Publius says, "the other, by comprehending in the society so many separate descriptions of citizens, as will render an unjust combination of a majority of the whole, very improbable, if not impracticable." We have two methods here to guard one part against the other, as we had two methods to control the effects of faction in *Federalist* ten. Remember we could either give everybody the same opinion, or failing that, make it impossible for people having the same opinion to discover one another and act on their opinions. Here, we institute a will independent of the society, or we separate people so they don't know they all have the same opinion. We have "so many separate descriptions of citizens, as will render an unjust combination" extremely unlikely.

The first example, again, is unrepublican and therefore a will independent of the society is not to be admitted. This means that none of the branches of government can have a will independent of the society. They are independent of each other but they must still depend upon the society. We had said earlier that the primary control in a republican government is dependence on the people. So, neither the courts, nor the executive, nor the legislature can have a will independent of the society. That's a great challenge for contemporary Americans who often think, for example, of the Supreme Court as being entirely independent of the society and requiring its will to be obeyed, no matter what.[1] Abraham Lincoln, doubtlessly better than anyone in our history, has given the answer to that perspective, in the manner in which he challenged the *Dred Scott* decision in 1857. We can summarize here. It's clear from Publius's point of view that not even the Court has a will independent of the society. It ultimately too must depend upon the society, and the society can of course disabuse itself of any errors by the Court if it chooses to do so.

The first method prevails in all governments possessing an hereditary or selfappointed authority. This at best is but a precarious security; because a power independent of the society may as well espouse the unjust views of the major, as the rightful interests, of the minor party, and may possibly be turned against both parties.

The terms here, separation of powers, hereditary, and self-appointed, all go back to the forty-seventh essay. At the opening of the forty-seventh essay Publius defined tyranny as the concentration of all powers of government in the same hands. Now we say, the first method, the will independent of the society, occurs wherever we have hereditary or self-appointed

No. 47

authority. So, we are dismissing two of those elements of our definition of a tyranny. That is clear.

Now consider the elective option. Suppose we nominate a czar and say to this czar, "your job is to protect minorities." What's to stop the czar from abusing minorities? What's to stop the czar from abusing minorities and majorities? What would make anyone think just because someone has been given license to protect minorities, that minorities will therefore be protected? There is no protection, according to Publius, apart from the society itself or a "due dependence on the people."

This by the way is a real question for us, not an imaginary question. For we have established in this country, since 1938, in a very important Supreme Court case footnote (*U.S. v. Carolene Products,* 304 U. S. 144, 153, note 4) where the Supreme Court said, vis-à-vis what it called "discrete and insular minorities," that they could not be protected by ordinary political processes. Therefore the Court would make it its special burden to protect the interests of minorities. And most of what we have experienced in the United States, in Supreme Court litigation and questions dealing with minorities since 1938, is based on that footnote.

Publius asks, who's the court? Why should anyone depend on the Court to do that? If the Court could protect minorities, the Court could abuse them; if the Court could protect minorities from majorities, it could abuse both minorities and majorities. Therefore we do not establish a will independent of the society for those purposes. We're going to reject that.

The argument continues: "This at best is but a precarious security." So we use what? The extended republic.

The second method will be exemplified in the federal republic of the United States. Whilst all authority in it will be derived from and dependent on the society, the society itself will be broken into so many parts, interests and classes of citizens, that the rights of individuals or of the minority, will be in little danger from interested combinations of the majority.

In the extended republic, the federal republic of the United States, we will never see a majority come together in opposition to the rights of the minority. That's the argument.

He didn't say we will never see a majority come together. He said, we will never see a majority come together in opposition to the rights of the minority. The rights of the minority "will be in little danger from interested combinations of the majority." What other kinds of combinations of the majority are there? Well, there are disinterested combinations of the majority and there are just majorities. Remember, the primary control is dependence on the people. He has not abandoned that argument. He argues that we cannot have a will independent of the society to defend minorities. What then is the deduction? It's very clear. Majorities will still rule, but the system has been so elaborated as, one, to make the policy process deliberate among the institutions of government and, two, to make the possibility of majorities combining on the basis of interests next to impossible. Together they produce the result that the deliberative process will reflect just majority rule. This is Publius's answer to the really tough question of how to make good on the separation of powers and checks and balances.

Publius gives an example as he continues:

In a free government, the security for civil rights must be the same as for religious rights. It consists in the one case in the multiplicity of interests, and in the other, in the multiplicity of sects. The degree of security in both cases will depend on the number of interests and sects; and this may be presumed to depend on the extent of country and number of people comprehended under the same government.

That's a most felicitous analogy, because we all can recognize immediately that the multiplicity of sects does, in fact, conduce to avoid the establishment of one overriding religious principle which also then comes to dominate the government and to impose itself on other parties. It may not be equally intuitive that the same thing happens with interests, but Publius makes the argument to persuade us that that is exactly what happens. It is further the case that Publius wants us to know that there is an additional principle at work, namely, what I would call, the energizing principle of the government.

This energizing principle makes the government move. In the following sentences of the fifty-first essay, he gives us his sense of that, first by introducing the question of justice. He says, this view recommends itself to friends of republican government because it allows us to avoid oppressive combinations of majorities, etc. "The best security under the republican form, for the rights of every class of citizens, will be diminished; and consequently, the stability and independence of some member of the government, the only other security, must be proportionally increased." That is, if we take the wrong way out, we have to undermine republican government.

No. 51

The alternative is to recognize that "Justice is the end of government. It is the end of civil society. It ever has been, and ever will be pursued, until it be obtained, or until liberty be lost in the pursuit." From the balance of this passage it seems clear that Publius means that people move the government through their own demands. We described passion from essay forty-nine to mean the claims people make in their own interests. These claims are what ultimately must set the government in motion. So we've not outlawed interests and we've not outlawed passions. These things have a role in initiating the policy process. "The regulation of these various and

No. 49

No. 10

interfering interests forms the principal task of modern Legislation." This is what initiates the policy process, but the society is so structured and the government is so structured as to defang, if I may put it so, these interests as they pass through the process. There is a winnowing that takes place so that the unjust majorities that might emerge in the absence of these obstacles are slowly bleached out of the system; what remains is the claim now associated only with the equally important claim for justice.

In all societies, according to Publius, we will have the struggle of the strong against the weak, and this society must seek to organize that struggle in such a way as to produce a concatenation, a harmony, of interests between the strong and the weak. It can't be done by getting people to abandon their interests; it can be done by getting them to submit their interests to a single way of resolving these questions. What is that way of resolving questions? It is the republican way. By getting them all to expect the republican system to produce the results they aim for, Publius aims to get them to reinforce all of the safety providing measures that have been built into the system as articulated in the fifty-first essay.

The foregoing summary does not suffice for a full and accurate account of *Federalist* fifty-one. I will restate the argument in technical detail. First, though, let's place it in a broader contemporaneous context. Do the civil rights Publius invokes here apply to what we call "human rights" today or is that something that we've invented in the mid-twentieth century?

In some respects "human rights" is an invention in the twentieth century. We do find the use of the term human rights occasionally in the eighteenth century. For example, Patrick Henry used the expression in a passage cited above. The terms were brought together in the late eighteenth century, although it was far more common to hear the expression, rights of man, and the expression, natural rights. Publius's notion, however, of the rights of man, is that their rights universally are possessed by human beings, and in that sense they are human rights. The very idea of equality that's expressed in the Declaration invokes a very simple formulation. Namely, that there is no one human being who is established by nature the ruler of any other human being; that the only just rule is rule based on consent. That's what equality means. Now, it is on the strength of that recognition that rights then come also to be clear, because if all rule not founded on consent is unjust, then one has a right to all of those agencies that would permit one, not only to govern himself, but to defend himself against unjust government. That's how we begin the enumeration of the rights that human beings possess. In that sense, then, I would say human rights is not invented in the twentieth century. It is at the very core of the modern principle that leads to the founding of the United States.

The difference we experienced in the twentieth century has to do with a rather differing expectation of right than the one I have just defined built around the notion that all human beings are equal. The best statement of this I have seen is the one that was issued by President Carter in December of 1977, if I remember correctly, end of his first year in office when he spoke on the theme of human rights, which was a major effort of his administration.[2] And President Carter defined human rights there in terms of an evolutionary principle, a principle of certain levels of life to be obtained by human beings. And he went so far as to say that the recognition of human rights, our recognition that human rights were safely established in the world was in fact, imprisoned in an historical way, by the rate at which other people came into the full possession of these rights, defined not as a liberty from unjust rule but as the attainment of certain levels of living, or standards of living. Along the way President Carter made the reflection that our own Declaration of Independence and Bill of Rights were incomplete because they were uttered at a time in which the security of the rights of all human beings had not been established, that the U.N. Declaration on Human Rights was a fuller statement, though not yet complete, and that there couldn't be a complete understanding of human rights until, in fact, this positive operation of the principle had worked to affect the lives of all human beings. So what we've seen in our time is the emergence of a theory that right can only be positively established and one can only speak to rights to the degree that one actually sees them enjoyed by people; if we have a right to be free from hunger or a right to work or a right to any of these things, any one of those rights is a full human right only in proportion as all human beings enjoy it and live it fully. And that gives an entirely different orientation. It's no longer the liberty to do something but rather the freedom from certain wants that comes to be defined as rights. So, today's human rights are indeed new, but human rights are not new.

Remember that the *Federalist Papers* speaks in two voices. It speaks in the voice of the theory of republicanism in which we have set forth a coherent and highly developed argument which elaborates not only the character of this specific Constitution but also of the political principles underlying republican government in general. On the other hand it speaks in the midst of a political debate, a practical struggle, over the future of the country and therefore speaks to the immediate interests and concerns of people that are to be addressed in the course of such a debate.

There is no mutual exclusion or incompatibility between those two voices as people sometimes imagine. They assume that whoever undertakes a political campaign for the season of that campaign places his intellect on vacation and certainly puts his truth-telling faculty out to pasture. Certainly there's no requirement that we understand political life thus. Marshaling not merely the strongest but also the truest arguments to that end of political victory is entirely consistent, in fact, with a genuine attempt to persuade others.

Aristotle's *Rhetoric* presents a rather elaborate discussion of the forms of political reasoning and the most important part to that discussion is his introduction of what he calls the *enthymeme*. The *enthymeme* is a very important concept precisely because it is the practical syllogism, as Aristotle calls it, the practical counterpart of the logical syllogism. What one does in an *enthymeme* is try to persuade the hearer, the auditor, to a true view by means of those steps in the argument that are best calculated to bring the auditor to a true view. That means, of course, that it's not a strictly syllogistic argument, but in fact, its elements are subject to rules known as stricter than the rules that govern the formation of syllogisms. The practical, or deliberative argument, carries the burden of fidelity to truth no less surely than does the merely logical argument but it takes account of the hearer. That's the difference. The logical argument has no regard to the hearer. Its regard is for the argument itself, for the truth of the thing being recounted, whereas the *enthymeme,* the practical syllogism, is structured based on the hearer. So the same truth may be presented through differing arguments as one in fact speaks to different audiences. In speaking to differing audiences one has differing hearers and seeks to enlist in aid of the process of reflection the peculiar experiences or prejudices of the hearers themselves.

It seems to me that the two voices of Publius merged as they addressed differing audiences. We can see this in contrasting the arguments of the Federal Farmer, Richard Henry Lee, with the arguments of Publius with respect to the republican system, and particularly the system of just majority rule. Consult the letter by Lee on the eighth of October in 1787 just after the draft Constitution had been adopted; he's read it very quickly. It's only been a couple of weeks, and he indicates at the outset of this letter that he had been writing, and anticipating the Constitution before the Convention had released it. His thoughts are fairly well formed. And he makes very clear what he thinks has transpired: "I am pretty clear the result of the convention would not have had that strong tendency to aristocracy now discernible in every part of the plan." That is to say, had certain people been present who weren't present, then it would have been purged of aristocracy. "There would not have been so great an accumulation of powers, especially as to the internal police of the country, in a few hands, as the constitution reported proposes to vest in them." Then he says, "the young visionary men" (that's how he characterized them) "and the consolidating aristocracy would have been more restrained than they have been."[3] He thinks these young fellows (Hamilton, about thirty, and Madison roughly the same age, and Wilson, somewhat older, the younger Pinckney, and a few others) are the young visionary men who have not been restrained by the elder hand and guidance of a Patrick Henry and a few other souls whom Lee would have named, perhaps including himself.

But he goes on, having said this, to give us a hint of why he thinks the plan tends to aristocracy and accumulates powers in a few hands.

This view from the Federal Farmer is simply an inverted view of the picture given by Publius in essays forty-seven through fifty-one. Where he sees a tendency to aristocracy, Publius has shown us in fact rather elaborate design criteria which have the express purpose of making good on the separation of powers rather than simply promising them. But one, I think, can readily see why that might appear to be aristocratic in its focus. It focuses so much attention on the office holders and on the appeal to their ambition, and does seem to give them so much opportunity for freedom of action that one thinks perhaps they may become independent of the society. Federal Farmer responds, "The plan proposed appears to be partly federal, but principally however, calculated ultimately to make the states one consolidated government."[4] We have the traditional Antifederalist perspective at that point. If it's a consolidated government, there are certain criteria which flow from that that cannot be avoided. It has to be aristocratic; it has to have immense power because we otherwise cannot govern a vast and complicated society.

Nos. 47–51

The late Cecelia Kenyon, when she published her version of the Antifederalist essays, wrote an introduction to it which she gave the title, "Men of Little Faith." She meant to convey in that title that the Antifederalists never quite understood the novel arguments that were being made by the Federalists. The argument for an extended republic simply passed them by so that they continued to react from a perspective that doesn't include the newer arguments that the Federalists have offered to show that the more complicated society, the extended sphere of the republic itself, is an element to be calculated on to provide republican safety.[5]

When the Federal Farmer says it's a consolidated government, one should fairly conclude that, yes, from his perspective it has exactly that look. And so the next thing to do is to deduce the consequences that flow from establishing a consolidated government. He goes on to say, "there are three different forms of free government under which the United States may exist as one nation." He accepts the notion of nationhood, or at least appears to. The first is "distinct republics connected under a federal head." "In this case the respective state governments must be the principal guardians of the people's rights, and exclusively regulate their internal police; in them must rest the balance of government." So, we leave it up to the states to do the main work of governing under the confederation theory. "The congress of the states, or federal head, must consist of delegates amenable to, and removable by the respective states." That's the other side. States do most of the governing. States control the delegations to the congress, to the central government. Then we leave congress only to direct the powers "to make treaties, peace and war, to direct the operations of armies, etc." and little else.

He then comments, "under this federal modification of government, the powers of congress would be rather advisory or recommendatory than coercive." This is, of course, what *Federalist* fifteen said was the defect of the Articles of Confederation. Lee agrees with this. He says this is one way we can do it, but he agrees in the end that it's utterly unworkable in the United States.

The second form would "do away the several state governments, and form or consolidate all the states into one entire government, with one executive, one judiciary, and one legislature."

Under the third form, he says:

> We may consolidate the states as to certain national objects, and leave them severally distinct independent republics, as to internal police generally. Let the general government consist of an executive, a judiciary, and balanced legislature, and its powers extend exclusively to all foreign concerns, causes arising on the seas, to commerce, imports, armies, navies, Indian affairs, peace and war and to a few internal concerns of the community. . . .

As we go through this list it begins to look very like the Constitution.

The Federal Farmer, Monroe, Cato, and a number of the Antifederalists eventually came to understand the new definition of federalism emerging even out of the Constitution itself, and they are relatively friendly to it. So, the problems with the Constitution seem more and more to center on the fact that it has what they call this consolidating aspect, which goes beyond what they would call for.

Federal Farmer says:

> The third plan, or partial consolidation is, in my opinion, the only one that can secure the freedom and happiness of this people. I once had some general ideas that the second plan was practicable, but from long attention, and the proceedings of the convention, I am fully satisfied that this third plan is the only one we can with safety and propriety proceed upon. . . . The convention appears to have proposed the partial consolidation evidently with a view to collect all powers ultimately in the United States into one entire government; and from its views in this respect, and from the tenacity of the small states to have an equal vote in the senate, probably originated the greatest defects in the proposed plan.[6]

So, he thinks the Constitution looks like the consolidation he would prefer, a minor consolidation with central powers, states otherwise independent, but that it has a tendency, what Patrick Henry at the Virginia Convention called, "a squinting towards monarchy."

I submit that this squinting that Henry sees, the tendency that the Federal Farmer, Richard Henry Lee, sees, is nothing other than the characteristic of the government, which is, according to Publius, a result of the two-fold operation of the internal design to make separation of powers and the extended republic work.

At the end of the fifty-first essay, we can see what begins to distinguish the Antifederalists from the Federalists. The Antifederalists, remember, placed an entire dependence on the people, and so such things as rotation in office and the ability to recall office holders are critical from their point of view. These are the kinds of innovations in state constitutions we experienced in the United States during the Progressive era. The Antifederalists put their confidence in these things. They wanted real constitutional avenues to protect society against the abuses of governors. They didn't want elaborate dynamic processes to put faith in. They wanted solid provisions in the charter of government enacted to assure that anytime the people wished, they could use them. This is the context in which *Federalist* fifty-one reveals why Publius turned away from that route.

No. 51

Publius held that the attempt to rely on popular redress by the Antifederalists is a flirtation with the great principle of instability that derives from the struggles between the strong and the weak. The Antifederalists would expose the society in every crisis to a demand that some strong figure come forward and rule tyrannically in order to settle disputes. That's what Publius does not want for the society. Rather, he defends minority rights by incorporating them within every legitimate expression of majority power rather than by bracketing them and setting them aside for special privileges or special protections. This is what Cecelia Kenyon says the Antifederalists could not understand. When they saw the large consolidating government, they predicted monarchy, aristocracy, and despotism, because they didn't see the extended republic enhancing the opportunity for self-government.

Let's pause to take up this very common expression among the founding fathers, this notion of self-government. We do not often enough ask the question what is meant by *self-government*. We, therefore, sometimes make the mistake of assuming that it is just another synonym for democracy or majority rule or any of the other principles which ordinarily characterize the system. The observations made by Publius on the character of democracy, pure democracy, popular rule, the kinds of qualifications, and the need to govern the passions of the public with the reason of the public should lead us to think that nowhere is self-government ever meant to say simply the process of deciding things by majority rule. Good government is more complicated than majority rule. The term self-government originally never meant the process of government in itself.

Self-government speaks of the government of a self. A self is at least an individual, and not a society. A society is a differing thing. We can speak of a society itself; grammatically that's not a contradiction in terms. But the expression self-government was applied originally to the capacity

of a human being to govern himself. When we describe the equality of
human beings, we say that there is no one made by nature the ruler of
another. There's no one fitted out by nature with greater intelligence,
greater beauty, greater strength, greater age, or anything else in the name
of which that individual becomes the ruler of all the others. We affirm
every human being to be capable of *self-government*. So that the objective
to establish self-government is part and parcel of the recognition of the
fundamental equality of human beings. When in the founding era they seek
to make self-government secure, they do not seek to secure processes, such
as majority rule, but they seek to secure this affirmation about the character
of humanity itself.

The idea that one can build a society on the affirmation that mankind
in general is capable of self-government is an extraordinary and striking
idea in the late eighteenth century. Some people would say it's a very
foolish idea. We saw, of course, in the first eight *Federalist Papers* the
emergence of this theory to turn power over to people whom we did not
know to be virtuous and wise, and we asked the question, is that a wise
thing to do? Why, we asked ourselves, would we put great power in the
hands of the foolish and the vicious?

Nos.
1–8

We can now modify that observation to say, yes, indeed, people can be
foolish and vicious, there's no denying it, but that does not answer the
fundamental question about the capacities of mankind for self-government.
George Washington, as he was about to retire from the army in 1783, wrote
what he called his political legacy to the country. His Circular Address was
sent to the governors of the thirteen states and through the governors to the
people of the thirteen states. That address was the opening gun in the battle
for the Union which launched the whole process that eventuated in the
Constitutional Convention. In the Circular Washington severely criticized
the government under the Confederation[7]. At stake is a theory, a principle,
an affirmation, namely that we're capable of self-government. We have the
chance for the first time in human history to demonstrate that mankind is
capable of self-government; but to do that, we've got to take our affairs
into our own hands, we've got to set right the political institutions by which
we live so as to vindicate this claim that the revolution was fought for a
moral cause. Then, he says, if we fail to take advantage of this opportunity
we will have none to blame but ourselves.

The unhappiness of the American people with the Articles of Confederation is perhaps to be attributed to the powerful influence of George
Washington, not just to the 1783 address but repeatedly through the period
of the war. Antifederalists, for example, defended the Confederation
against the charge that the Confederation is just "a rope of sand." The
inventor of that expression was George Washington. That's what he called
the Confederation Congress while he was trying to lead American troops
through the Revolutionary War. No one had greater moral influence than

George Washington in the United States during that critical period. So, if he called the government a rope of sand we might imagine that his countrymen would be somewhat less attached to it, and would be themselves not indisposed to speak critically of it and think ill of it. Some of the Antifederalists blamed him for that. They say that important, persuasive, and powerful people undermined the social consensus needed to build a society. But by the same token it is that same influence that presents to people the ideal, the goal, of self-government that makes this objective a persistent part of the political landscape of the United States in the late eighteenth century.

These elaborate attempts to devise institutions aim to accomplish the rule of self-government. They sought to devise institutions through which they will be able to understand themselves as primarily governing themselves, not through social policy or laws, but as individuals. Laws structure social relations. Social relations sustain the work of self-government, but the fundamental moral objective is self-governing. Every self needs a government, at a minimum, but every self is also capable of governing itself.

This notion, self-government, is a moral proposition. It is an inheritance from the ancient world, from classical philosophy. In classical philosophy the expression that was used as a synonym for self-government was moderation. Moderation meant self-government. The objective was ever to place the passions, the appetites as they were called in Plato and Aristotle's discussions, under the influence of reason. In their tripartite view of the soul there were the appetitive, the rational, and the spirited parts; the important thing was to align them in a proper hierarchy with reason overseeing the totality. The soul that had its parts in the proper working order was a moderate soul, or a self-governing soul. Classical philosophy presented this notion of self-government as the pinnacle of the achievement of human goodness. If we ask what is the end for a human being, the end is self-government, or moderation. Of course there were other ends offered having to do with contemplation and philosophic insight, but the decisively human end, as opposed to the human activity which verges on divinity, was self-control, moderation, or self-government.

Classical thought argued that very few human beings were capable of achieving this self-control or possessed the intellectual power that was necessary to the attainment of self-government. They, therefore, arrived at the conclusion that in all societies and all times some few human beings would be self-governing and would accordingly have to take responsibility to govern communities, for most other human beings would be incapable of achieving self-government. This was the view that prevailed throughout human history, and even Machiavelli accepts the distinction between the few and the many.

In the *Prince* Machiavelli does not reject the ancient distinction between the few and the many but approaches it differently. Whereas the ancients said that, because of this difference between the few and the many, the few have an obligation to rule, Machiavelli says that we don't have an obligation to rule just because we're better than they are. In his view the only thing we have an obligation to do is to keep them out of our way; so, we need to rule. It's prudent. It's expedient that we rule, but we want to rule so that we can keep them quiet like cattle and we can pursue the things of immediate concern to us, which for the greatest minds, of course, are scientific questions. The only way to accomplish that is to take political power away from the unlearned, take it out of the church, and take it out of the established institutions where prejudices prevail and stifle science. Liberate science. That becomes the political goal of Machiavelli and political science.[8]

Americans affirmed that all are capable of self-government. This is truly extraordinary. In the whole history of human reflection on this question and for the first time a people says, we think that all mankind is capable of self-government, not just a few. There are none who are made, by nature, rulers of others. We're willing to wager everything on that proposition. We're willing to structure a government so as to realize the demonstration of that proposition. So this notion of self-government is a moral conception. It is a principle that stands at the root of all that has transpired in the founding and all that has transpired in this country since.

To give an example in contemporary terms, when we debate policies having to do with the social and economic welfare, it is a matter of grave urgency how we understand that work. It has been common to talk about a "permanent underclass," and we could ask the question, what do we accomplish when we put the word "permanent" in front of the word "underclass"? What do we accomplish except, in fact, to appear and, in fact, to reject the affirmation of the founders that all human beings are capable of self-government? To say there is such a thing as an underclass that is permanent means they will never be capable of self-government. They are *permanently* incapable of seeing to their own necessities or providing for themselves, of governing themselves. That in turn rejects the founding insight of the constitutional design.

Publius, by generating the institutions and practices of republicanism and by seeking to build an attachment to republicanism, intended thereby to validate the judgment that human beings are capable of self-government. This attachment to republicanism is not just intellectual but is emotional and moral as essay forty-nine makes clear. There we saw that we must have habit to support it. Publius thinks self-government is achieved most effectively in an extended republic with the kinds of provisions that have been outlined particularly in this series of essays on the question of the

No. 49

separation of powers. Just majority rule constitutes the ultimate defense of the founding, making *Federalist* fifty-one the pivotal essay.

Publius said it in the last paragraph of *Federalist* fifty-one:

No. 51

In the extended republic of the United States, and among the great variety of interests, parties and sects which it embraces, a coalition of a majority of the whole society could seldom take place on any other principles than those of justice and the general good.

In *Federalist* 63, Publius made clear that the rare occasion on which some other kind of coalition could take place would be the end of the extended republic of the United States. Accordingly, we must regard it as Publius's rule that, so long as the extended republic of the United States endures, it operates on the basis of the formation of majority coalitions grounded in principles of justice and the general good. Further, we must note that the condition for its so enduring is that restraints upon the majority do not reach so far as to transfer power to any minority—which the requirement of a super-quorum in the legislature would do. Publius says at the end of essay fifty-eight:

No. 63

In all cases where justice or the general good might require new laws to be passed, or active measures to be pursued, the fundamental principle of free government would be reversed. It would be no longer the majority that would rule; the power would be transferred to the minority.

No. 58

His definition of the general good therefore implies this: a form of social life wherein the weaker party may forcefully maintain its claims of right within the very structure and processes of the government. Under these conditions, political and social contradictions (e.g., class conflict) are eliminated. The majority confirms and protects the rights of the weaker party because the stronger party can exercise its powers only on behalf of the public good. Accordingly, there is "no pretext" for defending minority rights (qua *minority* rights) in a well-constituted republic.

More impoverished versions of Madisonianism—typically presented as the doctrine of a multiplicity of interests within an extended republic—fail systematically to express the correct foundations of Publius's founding principle because they fail to take seriously *Federalist* fifty-one's invocation of justice. The operative analogy throughout is that justice inheres as fully in the arguments of *The Federalist* as piety inheres in the *Torah,* although neither is frequently mentioned in either.[9]

James Madison most fully reveals his idea of a decent regime in *The Federalist.* But Madison's draft of a "farewell address" for President Washington in 1792 merits consideration alongside *The Federalist* as a kind of commentary on the implications of its republican nationalism. In that address Madison spoke in unrestrained terms of America's providential advantages and achievements. He found the "theatre of our fortunes" well adapted to every important national consideration.

> All its essential interests are the same: while its diversities arising from climate, from soil, and from other local & lesser peculiarities, will naturally form a mutual relation of the parts, that may give to the whole a more entire independence than has perhaps fallen to the lot of any other nation.[10]

His efforts to construct a democratic nationalism had since 1780 been bent precisely to the search for this "entire independence." To that end, nothing was so essential as the elaboration of a national interest or identity even if, finally, it was constructed on the foundation of mutually interlocking particular interests.

Madison identified the popular establishment of a "common government, . . . free in its principles" and "intended as the guardian of our *common right* and the patron of our *common interests*" as the decisive event in the achievement of the goal he sought. This work, the provision for amendment being admitted, "must approach as near to perfection as any human work can aspire. . . ."[11] Madison, we can see, did not underrate the achievements of the founding. What is less apparent is that this express claim—made at the very height of his efforts on behalf of the Republican party press in 1792—leaves no doubt that Madison imagined a common good to be framed in the new regime.

We may render this last conclusion even more convincing, however. And in the process we shall demonstrate that *Federalist* fifty-one stands at the very center of the Madisonian project, as much in 1792 as in 1787[12]. The purpose in demonstrating this is to insist upon the political relevance of an interpretation of Madison's "Publius" contributions, and to indicate the range of interpretation to which *Federalist* fifty-one must be subjected before we can speak definitively of the Federalists' project.

No. 51

At some point, probably in 1792, Madison seems to have envisioned writing a regular treatise on the foundations of government. His notes exhibit a plan to set forth the fundamental principles at stake in the party contests of that era; the editors of the *Madison Papers* have entitled these fragments, "Notes for the National Gazette Essays," and dated them between December 19, 1791, and March 3, 1792[13]. The foundation of their educated guess on both scores seems to have been that the notes contain direct passages and the obvious first drafts of other passages that appear in six of Madison's *National Gazette* essays, which were published contemporaneously.

Madison, however, published seventeen *National Gazette* essays, extending from November 19, 1791, through December 22, 1792. Further, of the eleven essays not reflected in these notes, three fell within the period assigned for the notes composition. Those three are the essays on "Charters," "Universal Peace," and the "Spirit of Governments." If Madison's notes were merely first drafts of the essays composed during this period, it would be difficult to conceive why these three important essays were not included, especially since the notes do not correspond exactly with the essays. That is to say, some notes under one heading, "Public Opinion" for example, do not appear in the essay of that title but in another, namely "British Government." Consequently, the organization of the notes departs significantly from the organization of the essays.

The three omitted essays are distinguished by the fact that they discuss principles or theories at the heart of the development of European political philosophy. "Charters" opens with the words, "In Europe," and proceeds to distinguish the notions of contract prevalent east and west of the Atlantic. "Universal Peace" tempers the spirit of Rousseau, and "Spirit of Governments" broadens the understanding received from Montesquieu. The main work of these essays, therefore, seems to be to correct mistakes that might be made if Enlightenment thought were simply applied to the American scene with main force. I submit, accordingly, that the notes reflect only the essays that they do ("Public Opinion," "Government," "Parties," "British Government," "Government of the United States," and "Republican Distribution of Citizens") precisely because Madison had set about organizing a separate and independent work, a principled response to the questions at issue between Federalists and Republicans—questions about the necessary relations of the parts of American government, rather than about philosophical antecedents.

What Madison's outline for a treatise on the foundations of government contributes to the present discussion is a solid indication of how *Federalist* fifty-one should be read. Madison's notes deserve a full exegesis in their own right; here, however, I limit myself to a summary in order to come to the main point—namely, the centrality of *Federalist* fifty-one[14]. Because my discussion must be limited, I will reproduce Madison's outline (without annotation, and indicating his pagination) so that the reader may more easily see the comprehensive scope of his work.

[Part A]
I. Influence of the size of a nation on Government.
   Page 1
II. Influence of external danger on Government. Page 10
III. Influence of the stage of society on Government.
   Page 16
IV. Influence of Public opinion on Government. Page 22
V. Influence of Education on Government. Page 30
VI. Influence of Religion on Government. Page 35
VII. Influence of Domestic slavery on Government.

Before turning to Madison's discussion of these matters, I hasten to forestall the easy assumption that Madison, metamorphosing from Federalist to Republican, had set out to redo *The Federalist.* For in the course of his inquiry he not only invokes "Federalists No. X et alia," but he also cites explicitly *Federalist* seven, thirty, fifty-one, as well as volume one's discussion of federal governments. Furthermore, he tacitly relies on *Federalist* forty-three at the very heart of this outline (in chapter VII), making explicit what he had cautiously discussed in 1788 as the "natural majority."[15] The only portion of *The Federalist* he seems directly to call into question was written under a professed veil in any case, and that is number forty-seven, in which Madison aimed to express the meaning of Montesquieu and then only by describing Montesquieu's British model. Accordingly, he now promises to reveal the *"true* reasons for keeping great departments of power separate." I confine the implications of this statement to *Federalist* forty-seven—and absolve *Federalist* fifty-one—because under the section on the "Government of the United States" Madison refers the reader to the entire *Federalist,* but "particularly No. 51." The division Madison himself makes tells us that number fifty-one in its true bearings is less a discussion of separation of powers than of the governing of the United States.

Madison goes beyond *Federalist* fifty-one in making his conclusion explicit. "Partitions and internal checks of power" deserve high praise but not the highest praise. For "the chief palladium of constitutional liberty" is its "authors" and "guardians," the people. They are called upon to signal, judge, and "repel aggressions on the authority of their constitutions."[16] Madison later provides the reason why this is so, as the character "Republican" responds to "Anti-Republican," debating the question, "Who Are the Best Keepers of the People's Liberties?"

The people themselves. . . . The centrifugal tendency then is in the people, not in the government, and *the secret art lies in restraining the tendency, by augmenting*

Nos. 7, 10, 30, 43, 51

No. 47

the attractive principle of the government with all the weight that can be added to it.[17]

This is in Madison's eyes the real subject of *Federalist* fifty-one. Through it he aims to explain how the essence of a representative republic" is to *"chuse* the wisdom, of which hereditary aristocracy has the *chance,"* while avoiding the oppression incident to the latter.[18]

To achieve this goal, the government must be brought more fully under the power of "public opinion," which means in the first place under the power of the natural majority to the extent possible.

In proportion as slavery prevails in a state, the government, however democratic in name, must be aristocratic in fact. The power lies in a part instead of the whole; in the hands of property, not of numbers. . . . In Virginia . . . the slaves and non-freeholders amount to nearly ¾ of the State. The power is therefore in about ¼. Were the slaves freed and the right of suffrage extended to all, the operation of the government might be very different.[19]

While "property and "numbers" contend for political power in every state, and thereby influence it either towards aristocracy or towards democracy, Madison does not reduce the question of the character of the representative republic to the mere question of interests. Public opinion and not cash is the nexus, and the question is, in what "proportion" the government is influenced by public opinion in the true sense—the opinion of the whole instead of a part.[20]

Here Madison relies on Aristotle to authorize his conclusion. He reads the discussion of the cycle of regimes in *Politics,* Book V, to suggest that the cycle is not an iron law and is alterable by changes in opinion. Aristotle had arrayed three good forms of regime against their respective opposites: monarchy versus tyranny, aristocracy versus oligarchy, and polity versus democracy. The order represented an order of descent in terms of relative excellence. The forms were defined primarily by the number of persons participating in office and secondarily by the objective of their rule—that is to say, rule in the private interest of the ruler or rulers, or rule in the interest of the common good. He indicated, however, that two bad regimes, democracy and oligarchy, each presented a partial view of justice, insisting on the one hand that the free-born should rule and on the other hand that only the well-to-do should rule. Madison's reading yields an untraditional emphasis. Above all, by regarding the defenders of oligarchy as lovers of justice (they do not think it just that those who contribute unequally should share equally) instead of as lovers of money, Madison teaches that by replacing a partial view of justice with a whole view, one can provide the motive force for a change of regime which is not a corruption but an improvement.

Government is instituted to protect property of every sort; as well that which lies in the various rights of individuals, as that which the term particularly expresses. This being the end of government, that alone is a *just* government, which *impartially* secures to every man, whatever is his *own*.[21]

No. 51

This, then, is the subject of *Federalist* fifty-one and the heart of the Madisonian project. Simply by making Virginia a part of a true federal republic, and thereby reducing the effect of the number of slaves as a part of the whole, one may effect a change in the regime contrary to the iron cycle. Enhancing the republican character of the whole is necessary to perpetuate that salutary motion. And the question, how the system may operate so as to preserve and enhance its republicanism, is the burden not only of Madison's career as a partisan but of Publius's analysis in *Federalist* fifty-one. In undertaking an exegesis of that paper, we are assured only of one thing, that it "is a perversion of the natural order of things, to make *power* the primary and central object of the social system, and *liberty* but its satellite."[22]

No. 60

Nos. 28, 56

No. 51

Auxiliary precautions once provided, the benefits of an extended territory may be placed in proper perspective. Publius says in the third paragraph of *Federalist* sixty that the great diversity in the "state of property, in the genius, manners, and habits of the people" from the various parts of the country will reproduce itself in the government through the "diversity of disposition in their representatives." The prevailing interest in each part will be reflected in the government, and there will be a sufficient variety to avoid the predominance of any single interest. Secondly, the states can expect very material increases in population and diversification of interests, which will necessitate, as Publius says in the next to last paragraph of essay fifty-six, a yet "fuller representation." Next, as we know from *Federalist* twenty-eight, the effect that an extensive territory has in thwarting foreign attacks will similarly thwart the designs of ambitious officeholders. Finally, we see from the last paragraph of *Federalist* fifty-one that no greater protection can be afforded minorities than the extended republic, without which they would be all too easily threatened by clear and intractable majorities. Evidently, to the degree one compresses the size of the territory, one augments the probability of injustice, therefore demanding for justice's sake a corresponding increase in the "stability and independence" of governing institutions. Hence discussions of the relative worth of liberty and justice are constrained by the necessity to take into account circumstances, as well as human passions and character. The "extended republic" of America renders it highly improbable that a viable majority could ever occur except on principles of "justice and the general good."

In this way we arrive at the central conclusion of Publius, even in the standard interpretation: a full determination of the worth and fitness of a government can be made on but one principle, "the public good, the real welfare of the great body of the people." No government is worthy except insofar as it is adapted to that end. As we saw in *Federalist* forty-three, to that end "all such institutions must be sacrificed." We threaten to lose sight of the fact, however, that the means to this end are not at all entirely clear at this point. Let us agree, then, that there are two requirements for a good government: faithfulness to the happiness of the people, and sufficient wisdom to attain that object. Concede that there has rarely existed a government that fulfilled the first requirement, and that many acknowledge neither. The key for us is the claim under the third point of essay sixty-two that until now, in American governments "too little attention has been paid to the last." Thus the new Constitution provides not only for the public happiness, but for, as we see from *Federalist* fifty-seven, the "most wisdom to discern" it. That wisdom is a wisdom as to means; and if the claim of Publius is to be vindicated, our exegesis must reveal not only the structures and general principles of the regime, but the peculiar means that will produce this excellent result. Let us therefore re-examine *Federalist* fifty-one in an attempt to discern how the standard interpretation of it omits something that may deepen significantly our understanding of the founding. Nos. 43, 45 Nos. 57, 62

The fifty-first *Federalist* follows the forty-fourth as logically as the fortieth could well precede the thirty-ninth.[23] When Publius closed the forty-fourth *Federalist* with the claim that only the propriety of a regime such as the proposed one remained to be discussed, he was partly right, partly wrong. Although it is true that the "mass of power" delegated had been discussed—and its particular arrangements remained to be discussed—it was not true that he had completely demonstrated that this government invested with energy and stability could act with safety. The fifty-first *Federalist* responds precisely to that question—the *safety* of the regime as a whole, once set in motion and without respect to the operation of one branch vis-à-vis another. In this sense the paper logically follows the general conclusion of *Federalist* forty to forty-four, and the whole is the prelude to any particular consideration of the branches or offices of government. This is in keeping with the outline that opens the forty-first *Federalist*.[24] Nos. 39–44 **No. 51**

The great desideratum that results from the emphatic defense of a regime of character and power sufficient to secure the public good is the necessity to account for its being *confined* to pursue the public good or "justice."[25] The strictly formal argument from the separation of powers seems to provide the account sought, which is why the papers detailing the separation of powers intervene between forty-four and fifty-one. But the formal account itself poses a problem. As *Federalist* forty-one to fifty reveal, the separation of powers raises a pretext for constitutional adjudication of the powers—and abuses of power—of government. But the Nos. 41–50 deeper question beneath the doubt as to who properly must do what is the question, what remains to give a regime thus impeded the impulse to do anything? The question of the safety of the regime is really a question of its safety in operation, safety in motion when all the parts move together. (It is correct to say "regime" rather than "government" here, for when the whole moves together its deeds are presumably determined by its character as a regime.) The regime might be envisioned as some unchained behemoth, in keeping with that modern appreciation of politics, which denies that the essential judgment of political life is founded on a judgment of the character of human beings as distinguished from beasts. No one would voluntarily unchain the behemoth without reassuring himself at least of the possibility of keeping it on a path of safety. In this manner the fifty-first essay continues the defense of the regime.

Nos.
40–44

    Federalist fifty-one specifically repeats key themes from essays forty to forty-four at least five times. Beginning with an invocation of that "fountain of authority, the people," which recalls essays forty, forty-two, and forty-three, and passing by way of a remark echoing essay forty-four to the effect that the states are to be created anew by the Constitution,[26] the paper concludes with an emphatic rejection of the mere rule of the stronger, which possibility was raised in number forty-three[27]. The fifty-first paper serves to disprove that the regime of *Federalist* forty to forty-four will be victim to any of the common illnesses of regimes. Its purpose is far wider than the opening claim would indicate.

No. 51

To what expedient then shall we finally resort for maintaining in practice the necessary partition of power among the several departments, as laid down in the constitution?[28]

Publius himself licenses the view that he will not pursue this narrow question when he immediately adds that he will only "hazard a few general observations"—rather than undertake a "full development" of this theme—sufficient *both* to make it "clearer" and to "enable us to form a more correct judgment *of the principles and structure*" of the regime as a whole.

    The actual "general observations" on the "mutual relations" of the separate departments of government are preceded by the recognition that the purest separation would surely arise from distinct popular appointment of each branch. Each would accordingly have "a will of its own"—that is, each would exercise the will of the people on the basis of a distinct authorization. This purity is attained only to some degree, however, because of practical difficulties. It is more nearly a question of the character of the branches than of the representatives themselves; but the succeeding question involves the character of the men as such, and introduces in paragraph four one of those "auxiliary precautions" that necessarily supplement the "primary control," dependence on the people.

Publius drew the distinction here so finely that to fail to recognize it is to fail utterly to comprehend the essay. In the fourth paragraph, we see that the regime must invoke the character of the representatives in order to supplement a separation (which cannot be absolute) of the branches of government. This is not a discussion of interests or factions in the society itself (except perhaps indirectly). This is an invocation of that "ruling passion," fame, and perhaps, though surely to a lesser extent, of avarice.

In the next paragraph we see that the passions or interests that will make each representatives in this government into a "centinel of public rights" are not the same passions or interests that will set the regime in motion. While the latter "enable the government to controul the governed," the former oblige it to controul itself." The people are rendered amenable to government by means of those very private passions and interests that incline them to seek to win the influence of power to their causes, whereas representatives, driven by ambition, are charged with mastering those diverse private passions and interests as the price of maintaining their public standing. The representative must then at one and the same time satisfy the clamant interests of his constituents as far as possible, while fighting off the clamant interests of the constituents of fellow representatives as far as possible. In doing so, his regard is less for the interests at risk than for the office or station he holds. Accordingly, though it "might be" possible to trace this policy of supplying, by opposite and rival interests, the defect of better motives . . . through the whole system of human affairs, it is not necessary to trace "these *inventions of prudence*" beyond the "distributions of power."

The discussion of the "mutual relations" of the branches of government occupies but the first half of the paper through paragraph seven. The second half examines the safety to be derived from the "federal system of America." Here Publius offers "two considerations." The first repeats the argument that the "compound" relationship of the general government and the states will operate to the same effect as the separation of powers among the branches of government, thus offering "a double security" to the people's rights. The entire discussion takes only four sentences. The remainder of the paper discusses the further question: after a society is guarded "against the oppression of its rulers," how is "one part of society" to be guarded against the injustice of "the other part"?

This argument is of peculiar interest not only because of its restatement (not merely a repetition) of *Federalist* ten. It is of peculiar interest because No. 10 number fifty-one had opened by invoking that "fountain of authority," society, as the primary ruler in republican government. Insofar as the people do indeed rule, the protection of one part of the people from the other is still a protection against the oppression of rulers—the critical problem of majority faction, which we find in *Federalist* ten and think the only problem to be solved, inasmuch as minority faction would be handled by the "republican principle." But now, equally important, we see that once the people's *direct* authority has been qualified, it becomes important to protect one part of the people, namely, the ruling majority, against the violence or injustice of another part—namely, the minority or the few, since Publius writes explicitly of only two parts, "one part" and "the other part." But this, it seems, is identical to *our* original question: Once the regime has been made safe—impeded in its movement—how can it again be made to move, to attain the end sought from the government, the public safety? Publius seems to say that this is something more than the familiar "deadlock" conundrum hackneyed in contemporary analysis[29]. For representatives as such, even with the defect of better motives supplied, seem insufficient to the task.

No. 10

What sets the regime in motion—what will make the representatives *do something*—will be the clamant interests of the "different classes of citizens." But what will make this motion safe? Auxiliary precautions would be no barrier to a majority that rules. And *the point* of this essay is that the people will rule! We are working with a distinction between the "opposite and rival interests" that must be *supplied* to the representatives and the interests that *exist of necessity* in "different classes of citizens." These more fundamental interests—*Federalist* 10 interests—may have to be worked with (or regulated), perhaps even manipulated; but they do not have to be created.

Precisely because the people do rule, "if a majority be united by a common interest, the rights of the minority will be insecure." The danger in this regime is in fact identical to the danger the natural majority[30] poses to every republic. It is inconsistent with republican principles to erect a "will in the community independent of the majority, that is, of the society itself." This means the minority is left exposed to the violence of the majority, which *appeared* to be the problem we were handed. So here Publius reaffirms the *Federalist* ten solution, though it is still unclear how "one part" of the society is protected against "the other part." The reaffirmation does no more than assure that no minority "will" or veto is permissible. And the minority cannot otherwise be expressly defended without arresting the motion of the regime.

Hence, the minority must be left theoretically exposed. Majority rule must govern, but in such fashion that the minority no longer requires protection. The remedy in this regime, as under natural circumstances, is to render the majority unfit for concerted action in pursuit of unjust ends. Because the defect of better motives cannot be supplied, the only recourse will be to a diversity or confusion of motives. Suspicious self-interest must limit the seeking after extra advantages to the degree that minorities will benefit. This method "will be exemplified" in the new regime.

Whilst all authority in *it* will he derived from and dependent on the society, the society itself will be broken into so many parts, interests and classes of citizens, that the rights of individuals or of the minority, will be in little danger.

The question, however, had been, given this hobbling of the majority, how could it then protect itself from minority violence? Publius's obtuse return to the question of preventing majority violence begins to be vexing, until, that is, this reiterated theme takes on another voice. The "multiplicity of interests" is a natural occurrence that is artificially encouraged in a "proper federal republic." The point is to avoid government under the majority's "unjust views." *That alone is at stake.* Not the majority's power, but its injustice is curtailed; hence it remains able to defend itself against minority violence.

The republican operation of the regime itself defends against minority-inspired injustice: ". . . justice is the end of government. It is the end of civil society. It ever has been, and ever will be pursued, until it be obtained, or until liberty be lost in the pursuit." The interest of justice is served by distinguishing right and might. Where "the stronger faction can readily unite and oppress the weaker, anarchy may as truly be said to reign, as in a state of nature." The rule of the stronger faction, even a majority, is implicitly distinguished here from majority tyranny. The definition of tyranny applies most forcefully in democracy, where the actual separation of powers is not possible. The rule of the stronger faction, likened to the anarchy of the state of nature, is however not founded in the abuse of power as such. It is grounded in the denial that anything beyond force legitimizes the claim of right. It is a denial of a genuine public good, wherein the weaker maintain a claim of right as forcefully as the stronger.

While essentially democratic tyranny affirms the bonds of citizenship, essentially undemocratic anarchy denies the bonds of citizenship. Anarchy, the rule of the stronger faction, is rule by a will independent of the society. It has more in common with "governments possessing an hereditary or self-appointed authority" than it has with either democracy or tyranny[31]. The provision for republican safety, the method for avoiding the evil of a majority united by a common factional interest, is to confine the formation of majority views to principles of "justice and the general good." This unexpected result comes from one source only: namely, the necessity for republicanism, *a conscious attachment on the part of the citizens to republican principles and processes,* in order to impart motion to the regime. This result is unexpected precisely because it had appeared that the regime would be set in motion by the diverse interests forcefully asserting their respective claims. Upon reflection, however, it would seem that no self-interested endeavor could be confined to channels so pure as those Publius described—"justice and the general good"—unless the self-interested agent was at the same time of the opinion that some principle either of right or necessity *obliged* him to have recourse to the prescribed channels. Majority rule, in short, is not just the republican mode; it is the mode for making republicans. Majorities there must be, at least formally. Accordingly, one cannot speak of rendering majorities as such powerless or impossible.

Another element of Publius's solution is to confine majority sentiment to salutary principles.

No. 51   In the extended republic of the United States, and among the great variety of interests, parties and sects which it embraces, a coalition of a majority of the whole society could seldom take place on any other principles than those of justice and the general good.

It is a further refinement, once concession is made to the "fountain of all authority," to pose "justice and the general good" as the necessary *means* of action. Through this device, the *majority* is confined as nearly as possible to pursuit of the public good. The pursuit of self-interest is not incompatible with this result, so long as the road to profit runs through a "coalition" of do-gooders.

But how is the public good defined? Publius offers a negative characterization in the tenth paragraph: It is that condition in which the weaker part of society may forcefully maintain its claims of right within the very structures and processes of government. Insofar as that condition obtains, political and social contradictions are eliminated. The majority confirms and protects the rights of the weaker party when and only when the majority party can exercise its power in behalf of the public good[32]. Accordingly, there is "no pretext" for separately defending minority rights in a well-constructed republic. And the absence of these special precautions is itself evidence of a public good that animates the regime. What Publius calls self-government is then government by the majority for the sake of the public good without recourse to "a will independent of society." This he regarded as "the *republican cause*" which is made possible, made realizable by "judicious modification and mixture of the *federal principle.*" This is, in other words, democratic nationalism—the regime quality—the character of public opinion—necessary for the protection and consecration of natural right in republican government.

We are within our rights to wonder exactly how far Madison embraced Publius's scheme. His 1792 outline suggests that he would carry it quite far indeed. We may take a more direct measure, however. For Madison himself returned to this subject—in some ways the most consistent theme of his lifework—at a time when he was confident that he would never hold office again, and in a manner that reveals lingering doubts about his solution.

More than thirty years later, Madison resurrected the argument he had raised in the 1787 Philadelphia Convention and wrestled with it anew. On August 7, 1787, the Convention had debated the report from the committee of detail, scrutinizing the fourth article's provision to leave in the hands of the states the rule of suffrage for choosing the national legislature. The leading alternative was a freehold or property qualification—and Madison was tempted by it, given the circumstances of the country. "The freeholders of the country would be the safest depositories of Republican liberty."[33] Above all, such a provision would guard against the abuses of power by a propertyless majority. Somewhere around 1821, however, Madison rethought his contribution to the debate of August 7[34]. On his own testimony, his speech had been too much colored "by the influence of Virginia" on his mind. That is to say, the problem he had originally set forth, presumably including the original note he appended to it in his records of the Convention debate, had not taken sufficient account of the distinctively American solution to this problem.

In the original formulation, a property qualification had been a safe-guard against a *future* propertyless majority. But even then Madison had hastened to note that "this does not satisfy the fundamental principle that men cannot be justly bound by laws in the making of which they have no part."[35] The true solution, he had maintained, would assure security both for persons and for property. Nevertheless, this rule had been breached only in principle and not in fact, and therefore Madison had been willing to suffer the violation in a society in which "conflicting feelings of the class with, and the class without property" were not yet mature. Originally he had been content to rely on enlarging "the sphere of power without departing from the elective basis of it" as a sufficient safeguard, as the best mode of forestalling the anticipated breach.

Thirty years later Madison thought it wise to advance beyond that expressly provisional formulation. His re-evaluation of his earlier discussion begins by admitting the problem:

These observations [see Debates in the Convention of 1787, August 7th] do not convey the speaker's more full and matured view of the subject, which is subjoined.[36]

In his note Madison restates the problem, this time with clarity: "The right of suffrage is a fundamental article in republican constitutions." From here he proceeds to describe the "peculiar delicacy" touching this right, namely, that to secure the right with recourse to persons could leave property exposed, and vice versa. In the nature of civil life, property requires as much to be safeguarded as every other essential right. Accordingly, a "just and free government" accomplishes both of these fundamental objectives.

But how? Universal suffrage leads to severe problems; but then so does suffrage tied to a property qualification.

The correct solution depends on comprehending the nature of the problem in its details. Madison distinguishes the *degree* of exposure to danger in the two cases, namely, when property alone is represented and when personhood alone is represented. He notes that property holders participate in common with others in the rights of persons; but nevertheless a suffrage confined to freeholders creates tendencies that make it imperative that "the poor should have a defence." Similarly, because groups of men feel the sting of interest no less than individuals—and are "less controlled by the dread of reproach"—property needs protection.

Who would rely on a fair decision from three individuals if two had an interest in the case opposed to the rights of the third? Make the number as great as you please, the impartiality will not be increased, nor any further security against injustice be obtained, than what may result from the greater difficulty of uniting the wills of a greater number.[37]

To avoid the dangers either on the side of majority rule or on the side of a will "independent of the society," Madison turns to an examination of "the characteristic excellence" of the American system—its particular arrangement of powers—which secures "the dependence of the Government on the will of the nation" and at the same time provides protection against majority factions.

In addition, the United States enjoyed in 1821 the advantage that "the actual distribution of property" and "the universal hope of acquiring property" produced a situation in which perhaps a majority of the nation are even freeholders, or the heirs or aspirants to freeholds." That advantage, however, would not continue forever and therefore is cause for special concern in a regime "intended to last for ages."[38] Hence, the fateful question, "what is to secure the rights of property against the danger from an equality and universality of suffrage, vesting complete power over property in hands without a share in it," when the moment of reckoning shall come? Madison is particularly worried by the dependence of more and more propertyless persons on the wealth of a few.

In the U. S. the occurrence must happen from the last source; from the connection between the great Capitalists in Manufactures & Commerce and the members employed by them. Nor will accumulations of Capital for a certain time be precluded by our laws of descent & of distribution; such being the enterprize inspired by free Institutions, that great wealth in the hands of individuals and associations, may not be unfrequent. But it may be observed, that the opportunities, may be diminished, and the permanency defeated by the equalizing tendency of our laws.[39]

Against the equalizing tendency of the laws, there was the permanent and natural tendency of mankind to form into parties, above all along the line between those who own and those who do not own property.

Madison tests five possible "modifications" that might offer some security to the propertied minority. The first four seem to approximate progressively the final modification, out-and-out "universal suffrage and very short periods of elections."[40] At last, then, Madison embraces the feared prospect:

The security for the holders of property when the minority, can only be derived from the ordinary influence possessed by property, & the superior information incident to its holders; from the popular sense of justice enlightened & enlarged by a diffusive education; and from the difficulty of combining & effectuating unjust purposes throughout an extensive country.[41]

Madison, in the end, is thus willing to confront the future, not quite sanguinely, but with a determination to rely upon the principles of *Federalist* fifty-one. "If the only alternative be between an equal & universal right of suffrage . . . and a confinement of the *entire* right to a part of the Citizens, it is better that those having the greater interest at stake, namely that of property & persons both, should be deprived of half their share in the Government; than, that those having the lesser interest, that of personal rights only, should be deprived of the whole."

Yet eight years later Madison seems to have qualified even this conclusion. He produced yet another statement on the subject, this time during the Virginia Convention called to amend the state constitution. One must pay close attention to the context, however. Again Madison opens with an affirmation that "the right of suffrage [is] of vital importance, and he proceeds from there to deal with the immediate question, namely, the extension of that right to "housekeepers and heads of families." In other words, in Virginia Madison is now defending a broadening of the suffrage! No longer under the influence of the "situation in Virginia"—slave-holding Virginia—as he had been at the 1787 Constitutional Convention, he undertakes the task of bringing the state into line with the broadened basis of republicanism that he had done so much to create in the nation at large. He reassures the Virginians, however, that even if "an unlimited" extension of the suffrage were attempted in the "present circumstances," it would "vary little the character of our public councils."[42]

Accordingly, Madison encourages efforts to widen the franchise as the surest means to regulate the changes sure to follow. In effect, in 1829 Madison seeks to produce what he had promised in 1792, namely, that Virginia's inclusion in the larger republic would ameliorate the dangerous situation in which Virginia then found itself, concentrating the franchise in the hands of one-quarter of the people subject to its laws.

What is to be done with this unfavored class [the other three-quarters] of the community? If it be, on one hand, unsafe to admit them to a full share of political power, it must be recollected, on the other, that it cannot be expedient to rest a Republican Government on a portion of society having a numerical & physical force excluded from, and liable to be turned against it; and which would lead to a standing military force, dangerous to all parties & to liberty itself.[43]

No. 43

Accordingly, Madison silently invokes the problem of the "natural majority," first set forth clearly in *Federalist* forty-three, and demonstrates the true nature of the solution Publius had envisioned in the beginning. The genius of the people is to be cultivated to the point where it can embrace as citizens all of the people subject to the laws. Thus, the images of disfranchised and unpropertied masses, constantly increasing in population, serve not to foreclose extension of the suffrage but to defend a prudent extension of it. The result is to "embrace in the partnership of power every description of citizens having a sufficient stake in the public order, and the stable administration of the laws." Joining them to the "owners" of the country would serve to increase the numbers of those who would benefit from "the political and moral influence emanating from the actual possession of authority, and a just and beneficial exercise of it."

No. 51

Many practical considerations may affect and qualify the instant application of this principle, but it *is* the unqualified tendency of the laws encouraged by Publius. His project—the heart of *Federalist* fifty-one—is to generate that attachment to republicanism that alone can safeguard the regime. To that end he recommended such changes as would foster in the motion of the regime a further motion towards its ultimate salvation. Madison's words alone can describe the desired result: "To the effect of these changes, intellectual, moral, and social, the institutions and laws of the country must be adapted, and it will require for the task all the wisdom of the wisest patriots."[44]

There remains, therefore, only for us to consult the question of the actual structure in operation of the branches of government. We see how we've organized these particular structures. We wish now to inquire how they actually operate in order to understand this political system. And that's why starting in the fifty-second essay we turn to the House of Representatives and go straight through to the end branch by branch.

NOTES

1. William B. Allen, "The Constitution, Not Just a Law: A Dissent from Misspelled Original Intent," in E. B. McLean, *Derailing the Constitution* (Bryn Mawr, PA: Intercollegiate Studies Institute, 1995).

2. See Bill of Rights Day, Human Rights Day and Week, 9 December 1977, *Public Papers of the Presidents of the United States, 1977*, 2086.

3. Federal Farmer, Letters I and XVII, *Country Journal* (Poughkeepsie), 8 October 1787, 23 January, 1788, in *Essential Antifederalist*, 80.

4. Federal Farmer, Letters I and XVII, in *Essential Antifederalist*, 81.

5. Cecelia Kenyon, *The Antifederalists* (Indianapolis: Bobbs-Merrill, 1966).

6. Federal Farmer, Letters I and XVII, in *Essential Antifederalist*, 82.

7. See George Washington, *George Washington: A Collection,* ed. William B. Allen (Indianapolis: Liberty Press, 1988), 239–49,

8. Niccolò Machiavelli, *The Prince,* trans. and ed. Angelo M. Codevilla (New Haven: Yale University Press, 1997), ch. 22, 85f.

9. This section is indebted to Colleen Sheehan, who brought James Madison's 1792 "Notes on the foundations of government" to my attention, and to David F. Epstein's *The Political Theory of the Federalist* (Chicago: University of Chicago Press, 1984). Epstein's work is not cited in the text only because it is largely an exegesis of *Federalist* ten, the centrality of which I mean to call into   No. 10
question here.

The following analysis assumes an orientation towards the founding that is not made explicit herein. The question of the character of the American regime, given its foundation in modern principles, constitutes an important point of difference among many profound interpreters of our past. I refer above all to the exchanges that have taken place for more than twenty years now among Harry V. Jaffa, Martin Diamond, Paul Eidelberg, Irving Kristol, and others. This analysis reflects my understanding of those exchanges, as I expressed it even twenty years ago. The central question in those exchanges has been the role of equality in the founding; that the discussion of *Federalist* fifty-one has been possible without a special consideration of equality does not imply its insignificance.   No. 51

As I understand Jaffa, the differences stem precisely from the necessity of discovering philosophy in an understanding of this regime. The thought of studying philosophy *instead* of American government, in Jaffa's terms, is a non sequitur. His chief criticism—or mine read into his intentions—is that a studied indifference to kinds of regimes and a pretense of a universal standard of judgment that transcends modern regimes in particular is no more than an uninformed parroting of a regnant morality. They who assume such a posture are intellectuals. Only by coming to terms with the quasi-philosophic demands of this regime can one fully judge of the requirements of philosophy. This runs the risk of nihilism.

Harry Neumann's essays on *Madame Bovary* and *Salambo* describe the necessity of a cosmopolitan horizon to judge both prephilosophic piety and cosmopolitan humanitarianism. But that transcendent cosmopolitanism shows both the impossibility of prephilosophic piety and the evil of *all* cosmopolitan horizons. Hence its nihilism. Only prudent intellectuals escape this nihilism, because, in fact, their cosmopolitanism, their philosophy, is nothing more than the ascetic application of a regnant morality. They judge of pre-philosophic men as examples of mankind; they judge of universalistic moralities as examples of mankind: they maintain that there exist irreconcilable differences; and yet they say that we must examine—nay, insist on the existence of—diverse forms of regime as a counter to the modern project. Yet, what is their entire study but *the* manifestation of the intent of the modern project? Studied indifference is not, itself, indifferent.

The other alternative is to resist—i.e., refute—both studied indifference and an eros for philosophy independent of the love of justice. That is, one may immerse—not lose—himself even in this regime. The key: to know and perhaps love it not for its quasi-philosophic demands but for itself. And what do we find behind the door? A particular regime which dedicates itself to the relief of man's estate. But is there no difference between a particular regime so dedicated and the *idea* of such a project? According to Aristotle there must be. Hence, it is not the idea—the modern project—that compels Jaffa's attention. That is but an intellectual pretense. It is rather the fact of the regime and those things required for its health.

Diamond and Kristol argue in effect that the moderns deny that (1) moral virtue is the proper purpose of a well-constructed regime, and (2) that it is even—whether laudable or not—necessary for it. If this is so, then the regime is essentially hostile to virtue, which means that those who are not must take their bearings from non-American sources. I would caution us, however, not to take our bearings from a form of speculative positivism: "As the moderns say, so shall it be." Giving due allowance for the weight of a regnant morality, once created, it remains the task of philosophy to consider the human end not as man decrees it but as nature decrees it—or to put an end once for all to the notion of nature. This latter alternative we recognize from the "second wave" of modernity, and therefore we can more fully appreciate the distinction between ancients and moderns in the context of the American regime by grasping this impulsive "transcendence" on the part of modernity itself. The real thrust of the "second wave"—the antirational modernity—is to reject the possibility of utopia and thereby to consider the modern project in its rational bearings as superseded. This is the manner in which the intelligible question, "Is man essentially hostile to virtue?" comes to be replaced by the unintelligible question, "Is modernity essentially hostile to virtue?"

To question what bearing we should take in this context is a problem indeed. We take "non-American" to mean non-modern, in the context. Thus, it would follow that we cannot become conversant with the demands of virtue save through our acknowledgment of the demands of ancient, particularistic piety. Nevertheless, the only access we have to ancient, particularistic piety in the nature of things is through the radical attack on that particularity. To rephrase: If we can discover virtue's demands only by means either of birth in an ancient regime or the universalizing inquiry that destroys the basis of that virtue, we are forever barred from appreciating virtue. There can be none of us who is not hostile to virtue! It is at this point that we seem forced to recall that the battle of the ancients and the moderns is a *Battle of the Books,* not a battle of cities and nations. And because we enter this battle of philosophers from the protective precincts of a nation, we are enabled to discover the ways of cities. Still, to forget the necessary condition of our discovery and seek bearings we cannot have is to foreclose prematurely the prospect of reaching an end.

That possibility remains open to us when we confront the fundamental demands of the American regime, which collapse into an argument about equality and speak in a manner wholly intelligible to ancient souls. That no one can decide (Locke says "judge") for another the means necessary to preservation does *not* suggest that no one can *know* better than another the means necessary to the other's preservation. Consequently, the question is still whether the wisdom (natural superiority) of the few confers upon the few a title to rule. The insistence on consent is the formal means of denying this. Thus, men never consent to be ruled by their superior as such; they consent rather to be ruled in accord with their own judgment of the necessities of preservation (however they arrive at that judgment). Within that horizon the rule of the naturally superior as such will always be an accident. The enlightenment that legitimizes consent is this radical understanding of a necessary equality—an equality that abstracts from the unequal faculties of men.

10. Victor Hugo Paltsits, *Washington's Farewell Address* (New York: New York Public Library, 1935), 162f.

11. Letter Enclosure [draft farewell address], To George Washington, Orange June 20th. 1792 in *The Papers of James Madison,* ed. Robert A. Rutland *et al.* (Charlottesville: University Press of Virginia, 1983), 323f.

12. On the consistency of the Madisonian project see William B. Allen, *Let the Advice Be Good: A Defense of Madison's Democratic Nationalism* (New York: University Press of America, 1993).

13. "Notes for the National Gazette Essays," in Robert A. Rutland et al., eds., *The Papers of James Madison,* (Charlottesville: University of Virginia Press, 1983), vol.14, pp.157–169.

14. But see Colleen Sheehan, "The Politics of Public Opinion: James Madison's 'Notes on Government'," *The William and Mary Quarterly,* 3rd series, XLIX (no. 4, October 1992): 609–27.

15. "Notes," in *Madison Papers,* vol. 14, pp. 160f.

16. "Government of the United States," for the *National Gazette,* February 4, 1792, in *Madison Papers,* vol.14, pp. 217f.

17. December 20 [1792], in *Madison Papers,* vol .14, pp. 426f, emphasis added.

18. "Government," for the *National Gazette,* December31, [1791], in *Madison Papers,* vol.14, pp. 178f.

19. "Notes for the National Gazette Essays," pp. 163f.

20. "Charters," in *Madison Papers,* vol.14, pp. 191f.

21. "Of Property," for the *National Gazette,* March 27, 1791, in *Madison Papers,* vol.13, pp. 266f.

22. "Who Are the Best Keepers of the People's Liberties?" for the *National Gazette,* December 20, [1792], in *Madison Papers,* vol.14, pp. 426f.

23. Remember, an uncomfortable hiatus intervenes between *Federalist* thirty-nine and *Federalist* forty. Number thirty-nine poses several questions about constitutional authority and the performance of the Constitutional Convention. That essay answers only one of those questions. Number forty turns immediately to the "second point." Where is the hiatus? Number forty establishes the purpose of the Convention after a summary of enabling documents and political necessity. The provisional form of its conclusion is that the convention was to frame a *"national government . . . adequate to the exigencies of government and the preservation of the Union. . . ."* Number thirty-nine, however, had already *proved* that the Constitution was neither federal nor national! Apparently, number forty proves, in light of number thirty-nine, that the Convention failed to achieve its goal. This only apparent paradox stems from the fact that the "second point" was in fact the original question, hence the first point in number thirty-nine. Insofar as the latter does prove the government to be neither national nor federal, the Convention's task, as conceived in numbers forty to forty-four, remained unfulfilled. Insofar as that is not the case, number forty stands in the place of, rather than follows, number thirty-nine.

I therefore dissent from Martin Diamond's judgment that *Federalist* thirty-nine "is in a sense the central essay." See his essay "The Federalist," in Leo Strauss and Joseph Cropsey, eds., *History of Political Philosophy* (Chicago: Rand McNally, 1972), 651, n. 5. For the best account of the results of number thirty-nine, consult Diamond's "What the Framers Meant by Federalism," in Robert A. Goldwin, ed., *A Nation of States* (Chicago: Rand McNally, 1962).

Publius's sleight of hand in numbers thirty-nine to forty sets the stage for all the following essays, which purport to prove that the advice given by the Constitutional Convention is good—that is, for the public good. Not accidentally, Publius returns to strict Declaration of Independence language in order to answer his own questions. And not surprisingly, he dedicates papers forty-one to forty-four to a detailed discussion of the institutions of government with the intention of vindicating their faithfulness to the Declaration. Accordingly, the argument of number thirty-nine, there said to be secondary to the question of the Convention's authority, *logically* follows rather than precedes the argument developed in numbers forty to forty-four. The national-federal dispute, in logical terms, is a mere side-light to the question of the architectonic scope of the vision of the public good which animated the fathers. That, in turn, leads ineluctably to number fifty-one.

24. Publius offers a sixfold consideration of those capacities essential to realizing the public good of America. They are the following: (1) the capacity to secure the nation against foreign dangers; (2) the capacity to regulate relations with foreign nations; (3) the capacity to maintain "harmony and proper" relations among the states; (4) the capacity to provide "certain miscellaneous objects of general utility"; (5) the capacity to restrain "the states from certain injurious acts"; and (6) to provide that all these "powers" are efficacious. Number forty-one discusses the first capacity, number forty-two the second and third. Number forty-three treats the fourth, and number forty-four discusses the fifth and sixth.

Publius announces the "necessary and proper" clause as the last hurdle in this discussion. His analysis makes clear that there is no "pretext" for "drawing into

Nos. 39, 40

Nos. 39–44

No. 51

Nos. 41–44

Nos. 39, 40, 44, 51

question the essential powers of the Union." We note that what is actually accomplished in his discussion is to display the devices employed to avoid debilitating constitutional adjudications of the powers of government. This enabled the founders to focus on strict construction of the public good as opposed to strict construction of the Constitution. According to Publius, the "necessary and proper" clause restricts not the government but those factions that form the base of free government. That conclusion alone explains how a provision can be defended as a restriction on government after being introduced as an instrument "by which efficacy is given to all the rest" of the powers of government. The question of possible abuses of public authority is not allowed to undermine authority itself. Publius turns to the people, via the states, to reform officers of government who would corruptly wield these extensive powers. *Federalist* fifty-one explains how the people fulfill their assignment. Accordingly, number fifty-one logically follows number forty-four, as part of the scheme which is revealed in the analysis of the relation between numbers thirty-nine and forty.

25. Consult Edward Erler, "The Problem of the Public Good in *The Federalist*," *Polity* 13, no. 4 (Summer 1981): 649–667.

26. Publius describes the relation between the states and the nation thus in number fifty-one: "In the compound republic of America, the power surrendered   No. 51 by the people is *first* divided between two distinct governments, and then the portion allotted to each, subdivided among distinct and separate departments" (emphasis added). By placing the line of division between the states and the nation on the same grounds as that among the departments of the government, Publius implies that both divisions are created in the same instant by the same authority. Accordingly, one may say the states are created anew in 1787–1788.

27. In number forty-three Publius had reflected that reality may contradict theory and place right on the opposite side of might even in republican   No. 43 governments. Accordingly, it was necessary to investigate the question of the legitimacy of the republican form in those cases in which the majority of citizens did not amount to the majority of persons. Far from vindicating an idea of the right of the stronger, however, this consideration led Publius to emphasize more strongly the inherent tendency of republicanism. In the middle of the tenth paragraph of number fifty-one, therefore, he is able to make still clearer the inadequacy of might as a standard of legitimacy: "where the weaker individual   No. 51 is not secured against the violence of the stronger: And as in the latter state even the stronger individuals are prompted by the uncertainty of their condition, to submit to a government which may protect the weak as well as themselves: So in the former state, will the more powerful factions or parties be gradually induced by a like motive, to wish for a government which will protect all parties, the weaker as well as the more powerful." In short, the popular form of government—and rights therefore—is secure only insofar as it is distanced from the idea of the right of the stronger.

28. Note that Publius implies by these words a continuation of the discussion   Nos. in papers forty-six to forty-nine.   46–49

29. James McGregor Burns, *The Deadlock of Democracy: Four-Party Politics in America* (Englewood Cliffs, NJ: Prentice-Hall, 1963), is the celebrated progenitor of this view, which Gordon Lloyd has described as reading "the

history of American democracy and the history of democracy backwards." Akin to Burns's theory that Madison's fear of majority faction produced a veto-ridden, ineffective political system is the work of Burns's spiritual ally, Robert Dahl, *A Preface to Democratic Theory* (Chicago: University of Chicago Press, 1966). Lloyd reviewed this theory for the Western Political Science Association at its annual meeting in Sacramento, California, in 1984. His essay is titled, "The Burns Thesis Twenty Years Later: Has the Deadlock Interpretation Stood the Test of Time?"

30. Consider Thomas Hobbes's *Leviathan,* in which in chapter thirteen Hobbes argues that the strong cannot be ever watchful in the state of nature and thus cannot escape fear of the weak.

31. Publius likened rule by the stronger party to the anarchy "in a state of nature." By this he seems to mean that it is less a form of rule than a condition of individual oppressions, "where the weaker individual is not secured against the violence of the stronger." When "a will independent of the society rules," individuals may yet be governed if only tyrannically. This is the way of "hereditary or self-appointed authority." In this discussion in number fifty-one Publius drops the terms "elective" and "many," as they applied in an apparently similar case in number forty-seven: "The accumulation of all powers . . . whether of one, a few, or many, and whether hereditary, self-appointed, or elective, may justly be pronounced the very definition of tyranny." When the passages from these two essays are compared a singular meaning emerges: not only is nontyrannical pure democracy impossible by definition (for how could the powers be separated at all in that situation?), but insofar as tyranny is rule by a will independent of the society, rule by a majority faction is better understood as anarchy—no rule—than any form of rule whether legitimate or illegitimate. The reason seems to be that although the majority faction may appear to express the will of the many or the society, it is in fact only a concurrence of individual wills. In this situation, every man is for himself. In other words, if there were the direct, nonfactious rule by the many, it would be tyrannical, while factious rule by the many would be anarchical. The only way for a majority to rule dependent on the will of society, then, is indirectly—the Hamiltonian argument. Hamilton's coining the term "representative democracy" in 1777 set the tone for these conclusions. We can see then that where, in the interest of republicanism, Publius elevates our notion of the conceptions of oligarchs, he also depreciates our expectations of democrats.

Nos.
47, 51

32. See PART VI above where such qualification as this principle admits is discussed in terms of *Federalist* sixty-three. Also, see Harry V. Jaffa's analysis of the causes of political parties, the second and central of which is "the partisanship of those animated by a knowledge of human nature, who would set up a regime of liberty and so dispose the competing interests of an emancipated human nature that they are permitted or compelled to co-operate for the common good." Jaffa, "The Nature and Origin of the American Party System," in his *Equality and Liberty* (New York: Oxford University Press, 1965), 20.

No. 63

33. Max Farrand, ed., *The Records of the Federal Convention of 1787,* 4 vols., (New Haven: Yale University Press, 1966), vol.2, p. 203; the debate of August 7.

34. See "Property and Suffrage: Second Thoughts on the Constitutional Convention," in Meyers, *The Mind of the Founder,* 501–509.

35. Farrand, *Federal Convention,* note 17, p. 204.

36. Meyers, "Property and Suffrage," 502.

37. Meyers, "Property and Suffrage," 504.

38. Farrand, *Federal Convention,* vol. 1, June 26 debate, p. 422.

39. Meyers, "Property and Suffrage," 505.

40. After reviewing the possibilities, Madison says that "three modifications present themselves." He went on to list five, however. The first was to confine "the right of suffrage to freeholders." The "objection to this regulation is obvious," namely, it "violates the vital principle of free Government" relative to non-freeholders. Secondly, he speaks of confining "the right of suffrage for one Branch to holders of property," while leaving the other to the propertyless. This would *seem* fair, for "the rights to be defended would be unequal, being on one side those of property as well as persons, and on the other those of persons only." Nevertheless, the frank class division would create Roman-like tensions. Thirdly, one could confine "the right of electing one Branch to freeholders" and admit all others in common with freeholders to elections for the other. The theory of this system is that non-freeholders would ultimately gain a majority and thus ultimate defensive power. "Experience alone can decide how far the practice in this case would correspond with the theory." Nor, it must be said, is it clear how in the eventuality foreseen, it would not simply become a special case of the second option. Madison says nothing further, but that is perhaps the reason he goes on to a fourth modification: namely, to grant "an equal and universal suffrage for each branch." In this case, however, we may protect the propertied by "an enlargement of the Election Districts for one Branch of the Legislature, and an extension of its period of service." Madison offers no objection to this back-door approximation of the remedy achieved by the Constitutional Convention, but he does propose a fifth modification. He offers it in case the fourth modification should "be deemed inadmissible, and universal suffrage and very short periods of elections within contracted spheres be required. . . ." In that case, the security for property holders must be "derived from the ordinary influence possessed by property, & the superior information incident to its holders; from the popular sense of justice enlightened and enlarged by a diffusive education; and from the difficulty of combining & effectuating unjust purposes throughout an extensive country." Meyers, "Property and Suffrage," 506–508.

41. Meyers, "Property and Suffrage," 508.

42. See "Partnership of Power: The Virginia Convention of 1828–1830," in Meyers, *The Mind of the Founder,* 516.

43. Meyers, "Partnership of Power," 517.

Nos.
39–44,
51

44. Meyers, "Partnership of Power," 519. For a further discussion of Madison's view of republicanism, the public good and *Federalist* essays thirty-nine to forty-four, and fifty-one see William B. Allen, *Let the Advice Be Good: A Defense of Madison's Democratic Nationalism* (New York: University Press of America, 1993). On slavery and Madison's republicanism see W. B. Allen, "A New Birth of Freedom: Fulfillment or Derailment?" in *Slavery and its Consequences: The Constitution, Equality, and Race,* ed. Robert A. Goldwin (Lanham, MD: American Enterprise Institute, 1988).

PART VIII: GOVERNING A NEW PEOPLE

Article One sets the tone for the entire Constitution, and for the entire society. We have the testimony of the framers themselves that this is indeed where we need to begin and where we ought to discern the essential tendency of the Constitution.

What follows is the particular discussion of the manner in which we constitute the popular legislative branch. Why do we elect them for two years rather than one year or three years? These are questions ultimately of prudent judgment. In the first place one has to bargain to get what one can in the context of a convention. In the second place, we seek always to enhance certain advantages of the Constitution. We seek to increase, for example, the stability and energy of the system, without sacrificing the responsibility and dependence of the system. Those terms that were introduced in *Federalist Paper* thirty-seven now ought to be applied in the analysis of these institutions.

We have drawn out the term for the popular house past the usual one year to two years on the theory that it gives us greater stability. But we keep it not more than two years because we still want responsibility and dependence. I should reflect that these are terms of art in the late eighteenth century. They're not the colloquial terms that we use. The term "responsibility" comes into use as a technical term in political discourse only at this period. Responsibility means precisely the accountability to the appointing authority. That's what it literally means. From the Latin, to be responsible is to have to answer back to someone. The representative answers back, or responds, to the constituent. Dependence is, of course, his sensitivity to the constituent's response when the constituent evaluates him.

Elections must have, as is pointed out here, certain frequency to enhance the dependence and also to provide for the effective expression of public opinion. We can talk about the tone of society and the base of these institutions, but, of course, the final step has to be taken. Public opinion must be integrated as a controlling element. Why is the constitutional design constrained to influence the development of society in a certain direction rather than just to command it? For example, why are not the states simply ordered to change the rule of suffrage? Why do we take this subtle approach of influencing suffrage through the drafting of the Constitution, which is broader and more liberal in suffrage than state constitutions? The reason is simple. Command without public opinion to sustain it is illegitimate in a republican government. A certain frequency of elections helps to integrate public opinion into the processes of government and to make it deliberate.

We want to establish the principles and processes of self-government. That means we want to govern by and through the people's opinions. We've said earlier that all government depends on opinions. There's a difference, though, between recognizing that even the most tyrannical government must depend on opinion and asserting that we're going to form a government whose very existence hinges on courting of opinion. In the former case we recognize the mere necessity and in the latter we recognize a virtue. In that sense we enlarge the opinion. We give it its dual and proper role and its fit dignity. So, we do not command the states to enlarge the suffrage, but we do seek so to fashion, shape, or form public opinion that it eventually becomes the natural thing to enlarge the suffrage.

All of the particular considerations are subordinated to the role of opinion in the government. The intent is to give it voice without leaving it to run rampant. In the ninth paragraph the argument is made respecting power:

No. 52

It is a received and well founded maxim, that, where no other circumstances affect the case, the greater the power is, the shorter ought to be its duration; and, conversely, the smaller the power, the more safely may its duration be protracted. In the second place, it has, on another occasion, been shown that the Fœderal Legislature will not only be restrained by its dependence on the people as other legislative bodies are; but that it will be moreover watched and controuled by the several collateral legislatures, which other legislative bodies are not. And in the third place, no comparison can be made between the means that will be possessed by the more permanent branches of the Fœderal Government for seducing, if they should be disposed to seduce, the House of Representatives from their duty to the people; and the means of influence over the popular branch, possessed by the other branches of the government above cited. With less power, therefore to abuse, the Fœderal Representatives, can be less tempted on one side, and will be doubly watched on the other.

No. 78

So, we can judge by the shortness of the duration of office of the House of Representatives that it has the greatest power, and by the length of the duration of the Supreme Court's offices that they have the smallest power, or can we? Well, that's a question of course we must yet consult. But the formula we have, and I believe that it actually produces precisely the result, however humorous or ironic it now seems. The Supreme Court has been called *The Least Dangerous Branch*, and that is the title of a famous book by the scholar Alexander Bickel. That title is taken from *Federalist Paper* seventy-eight. We will find grammatical defects when we parse that argument, but it is nevertheless the case that the structure of these papers and the principles of this argument do lead to the conclusion that the

Supreme Court is the weakest branch. It possesses less will than any of the other branches of government.

There's an interesting distinction made between dependence and responsibility in Publius's second observation. The legislature as a whole can be dependent. The legislator, as an individual, must be responsible. The legislature as a whole answers to nobody. It's the legislator that must answer to constituents.

In his third observation, we consult the rule of republican safety in constructing these institutions and we construct the rule of power. That is to say, we measure the requirements of safety in proportion to the power that is present in order to deal with the construction of the branches of government. We will notice in the fifty-third essay, where we speak particularly about the question of annual elections versus biannual elections, that Publius, as usual, turns familiar apothegms around and finds defects in what had been a warm, cuddly blanket for people theretofore. Where they could easily point to annual elections as an established truth, Publius stands up and suggests there might be problems with this that we want to reconsider. No. 53

One of the difficulties that arose from the argument in the twenty-third *Federalist Paper* is reflected in the fifty-third *Federalist Paper* in the middle of the second paragraph, which reads as follows: No. 23

The most simple and familiar portion of time, applicable to the subject, was that of a year; and hence the doctrine has been inculcated by a laudable zeal to erect some barrier against the gradual innovations of an unlimited government, that the advance towards tyranny was to be calculated by the distance of departure from the fixed point of annual elections. But what necessity can there be of applying this expedient to a government, limited as the federal government will be, by the authority of a paramount constitution? **No. 53**

Publius finds the discovery of this one-year principle in the British experience with unlimited government. But there is a new principle adduced in the *Federalist Papers,* namely, a constitution above the government.

This new principle of a paramount constitution changes so many of the theories that people have otherwise depended upon. They had not previously either understood or enjoyed a constitution above the government. They had only had constitutions which were themselves in the hands of the government. Benjamin Rush, in 1787 after the Constitutional Convention, and James Wilson, in the Pennsylvania ratifying convention discussions of November and December 1787, pointed out that the distinctive American contribution to republican theory is the idea of a constitution above the government that is not left to the ordinary care of legislators, executives, or judges and that reposes in the hands of the people. These branches of government, then, are an expression of the existence of the Constitution above the government and are to be judged accordingly.

We judge arguments respecting them in terms of the degree to which the independent branches remain restrained and controlled by those who ultimately control the Constitution itself. For Publius to establish that simple clarity, though, he must first dispose of the objections of the opponents to the Constitution.

Nos.
52–59
In the series of essays, fifty-two through fifty-nine, Publius must respond to the objections from the Antifederalists concerning the character and expected operation of the House of Representatives. It is helpful, though, to understand how we come to look at the branches of government. We've discussed previously the role of the organization of the *Federalist Papers*, placing the discussion of the particular branches of government at the end of the work rather than at the beginning of the work. Ordinarily we think of constitutions as starting with a list of institutions, and that's itself probably a result of the existing Constitution. Our Constitution opens with Article One devoted to the legislature, Article Two devoted to the executive, Article Three to the judiciary and the balance of the articles dealing with miscellaneous items such as amendments, limitations on states and other provisions ultimately including the Bill of Rights.

Prior to the adoption of the Constitution of 1787, the pattern was reversed in the constitutions of the states. We read the state constitutions and discover that they all begin with fairly lengthy statements, not only of a bill of rights but narrative statements about the natural rights background of their constitution-making powers themselves. The first several pages are usually hortatory in character. They set forth the claim that all men are created equal, and all of the associated claims in the name of which those who wrote the constitutions went about exercising that authority. So that, in 1787 a traditional constitution would not have opened with a focus on the branches of government. That would come later. *The Federalist Papers* then does not mirror the Constitution drafted in 1787, but it does mirror the tradition of constitution-drafting in the era by having placed in front of the discussion of the branches of government, the discussions of the general principles upon which government is founded.

Realizing that the state constitutions were organized that way helps us to understand some of the Antifederalists' fears and some of their objections to the new Constitution. Conceive what it's like to sit in a particular state and receive from the Constitutional Convention a draft instrument that looks so radically unlike the known constitutions. During eleven traumatic years much had been invested both in the way of thought and sentiment in the forms of constitutions under the state governments. So the new federal Constitution was shocking in its appearance, starting off so boldly as it does with apportioning power in the branches of government.

The Federalist Papers makes clear the reason for putting off the discussion of the branches until the end. We must first establish the end of the government. We must establish the constitutional purpose itself before descending to speak about the constitutional means. The constitutional purposes and constitutional means go together ultimately to make a constitutional whole. The constitutional means are not defensible until there is consensus on the constitutional purposes. In the constitutional convention there was such consensus. The consensus was expressed almost immediately upon the introduction of the Randolph plan before the end of the first week of the convention. The Randolph plan sets forth a radical departure from the Articles of Confederation. It proposed a national government and it found very ready concurrence among the delegates who were assembled. That degree of agreement doubtless contributed to the fact that in the Constitutional Convention of 1787, it was not thought necessary to write into the document the kinds of prefatory comments that had characterized the state constitutions. The Preamble to the Constitution sets forth far more pithily the ends of government for the federal Constitution than was ever the case in dealing with the state constitutions.

It is only in the face of Antifederalist objections that we now must canvas anew the purposes of this Constitution so as to be certain that there is that same consensus in the society at large, to be certain that what Publius so often refers to as the genius of the people fully expresses the ends and aims that these institutions presuppose. Thus when we come to the defense of the branches of government, what we look for is how these means fit precisely into the purposes that have been set forth through the first fifty-one essays of the *Federalist Papers,* and most significantly, of course, the fifty-first. The fifty-first essay introduced us to the conception [No. 51] that in the society that is being organized by this Constitution, two things will occur. First, majority rule will determine the course of policy in this society. And secondly, majorities will never form, except on principles of justice. This is the objective of the Constitutionalism of the *Federalist Papers.*

Now, we can ask the question, what do the Federalists mean by majority rule? Do they mean majority rule within the branches of government? Do they mean majority rule in the society at large? One of the most familiar teachings of contemporary social science is that, in the United States, majorities do not rule. Instead, we have a system of elites, and elites rule, and there are many elites. There is a plurality of elites. They circulate. [No. 51] We find them in differing lines of endeavor and differing ranks and statuses in society, but basically it's always a few people who make the decisions and vast numbers of passive people. There are even forms of contemporary social science which argue that it's a good thing that most people are passive and allow the few who make the real decisions the space within which to operate and to build the kind of social consensus that will support their decision making. Well, that argument, of course, is a direct challenge to the argument Publius is making. Publius does not mean majority rule in the legislature when in the fifty-first essay he says that the majorities will govern in this society. He means to say the society itself will determine the course of policy and determine that course by the rule of a majority, by majority opinion.

One may ask contemporaneously then how, if the majority rules, it rules in the United States. The answer would have to be found in Publius's terms, in our trying to reassemble the opinion of the majority in such a way as to determine whether it in fact sponsors and in fact is responsible for the decisions that do take place or whether those decisions have been made against the will of the majority.

I have often reflected upon how little we seem to understand the limits of decision making in the United States today. In fact, few office holders are what we can call free actors. They are not free to decide and do things without regard to that very ambiguous creature called public opinion. Public opinion is somehow at the center of this defense of the Constitution that Publius makes. Take, for example, the 1954 Supreme Court decision in the case, *Brown v. Board of Education*, 347 U.S. 483 (1955). Many people will make the argument that there we have the Supreme Court interfering in the ordinary course of social and political development against the tide of majority sentiment, against the tide of majority opinion, in order to do what was right rather than waiting to be led by a majority that was consistently and pervasively wrong. If one revisits the era, the late 1940s and early 1950s, one will have a hard time making that argument stand up. It seems to be not so much a courageous Court that has arrested perverse opinion in the country at large, but it is quite evident that opinion in the country itself had already undergone massive, if silent, changes over the course of decades and coming particularly to a head in the forties and the fifties. This began, of course, with the war in Europe and the changes that were imposed ultimately in the American military as a consequence of that war. This included reflections on how that war was being conducted with regard to the relations of Blacks and Whites in the American military service. The administration of President Truman greatly accelerated that process. By the end of the 1940s and beginning of the 1950s, we saw such anomalies as coins being published in the United States bearing the likeness of people such as George Washington Carver and others and bearing mottoes testifying to the importance of brotherhood in the United States. All this was in advance of *Brown v. Board of Education*, which would suggest that we undersell the weight of public opinion and the direction of public opinion when our interpretation of these events is such that we think that institutions set rather than follow the pace.

Supreme Court decisions are extremely tenuous except in proportion as they are found acceptable by public opinion—witness the pro-abortion decision *Roe v. Wade,* 410 U.S. 113 (1973). They do not shape opinion so much as they run the risk of offending opinion, which is the reason that justices have to be so very careful in the expression of their sentiments. Today we have the same thing happening, when some accuse the Justices of turning back the clock in the area of "affirmative action," and they say that they are inconsistent with the moral consensus we have developed in this country. Nothing is more clear than that what the Justices are doing reflects very well the state of opinion in the country on certain questions, such as quotas, preferences, and others. That so-called moral consensus in favor of preferences, in fact, does not exist. Majority opinion is fairly easy to demonstrate through polls, or whatever else we want to choose, and is leading precisely in the direction the Court is now following rather than setting. So that what *Federalist* fifty-one hopes we will understand is that majority opinion will in fact set the tone for policy in the society.

The critical question from the political science perspective is how that majority opinion becomes translated into policy, not whether it exists at all, but what is the translation mechanism that operates? And when we have concluded the argument at that point, then we are ready to inspect the branches of government, because that is where the translation must take place.

The House of Representatives is first in that canvass for the simple and sufficient reason that it is the most democratic branch of the government. It is the branch that is in principle most powerful and the branch that also will most directly carry out the task of translating public opinion into established policy. The House translates public opinion by the ordinary means most evident to us, but also Publius wants to show us that even the most minute details of the structure of the office play their role in shaping the ability of representatives to perform this function. The whole question of who the representatives will be, i.e. what is their character, is part and parcel of shaping the institution to perform this function of translating public opinion into established policy in the nation. So we began in the fifty-second *Federalist Paper.*

No. 52

The most important questions deal with the office holders, namely how do we elect them, and who can be elected. These are the most important questions throughout all of political philosophy. Recognize that the character of a constitution is determined by the question of who gets the suffrage and who may be chosen. That tells us what is praiseworthy and what is blameworthy in the society. And if we express it in those terms, it becomes much more intuitive that we are trying to establish through the Constitution a standard of appraisal of those human characteristics to which one would look to establish principles of priority in society. Whatever brings a given people together into a single regime and whatever constitutes a standard of appraisal for certain kinds of things is what's most obviously required. Who will be those we would expect most to lead? Who are the chosen ones to hold office? Where do we turn for moral guidance? Where do we turn for the statesmanly vision? That is not a random process; it's done in accord with certain principles.

There are some societies, for example, in which people think only those who have displayed courage in battle are genuinely praiseworthy and should consistently occupy the foremost offices in the state. In those societies we find those who have displayed courage in battle, military officers, rule across the board, because there is an established standard, a way of looking at these things. They praise military prowess; and because they praise military prowess, they then choose military heroes as their leaders. The things they blame will be the things that they consistently avoid to choose, just as the things they praise will be the things that they consistently choose. So, what has been established under this Constitution, as the principles of praise and blame in terms of the human characteristics that will prevail in the House of Representatives initially?

It is clear that nothing could be more open at the outset than those standards of praise and blame in looking at the qualifications for membership in the House of Representatives. It is extraordinary how widely open it is. The Federal Farmer complains about federal representation and the broad basis on which it has been established. There he says:

This is fixing the federal representation, as to the elected, on a very broad basis. It can be no objection to the elected that they are Christians, Pagans, Mahometans, or Jews; that they are of any color, rich or poor, convict, or not. Hence, many men may be elected who cannot be electors. Gentlemen who have commented so largely upon the wisdom of the constitution, for excluding from being elected young men under a certain age, would have done well to have recollected that it positively makes pagans, convicts, etc. eligible.[1]

The Federal Farmer is really wroth with the drafters of this instrument for their oversight in this respect. It's a broad field of qualifications that apply to membership in the House at the outset. But is that all? Do we expect because the field is wide open, that the choices will fall indiscriminately and randomly on those who are citizens in order to bring them into this body, to invest them with this high authority? Well before answering that question, of course, Publius passes by certain related though apparently distinct questions, namely the tenure in office and biannual elections versus annual elections. And further the question of re-eligibility for office.

We begin to notice there is a connection among those issues with the question of character. One of the things, for example, that Publius accomplishes in defending the biannual election, is to argue that we need to be able to keep them in office just long enough so as not to lose

No. 53

dependence on the people, but sufficiently long such as to acquire a knowledge that we cannot otherwise expect representatives to have. He begins his argument in the fifty-third essay. He expects them to acquire a knowledge of federal concerns. They come prepared with a sufficient knowledge of their parochial concerns. It is only when they are entrusted with this larger task, that they too begin to be shaped by the very task of governing the nation. We want them there sufficiently long to gain knowledge about certain federal questions, about a common interest, but not so long that they lose their dependence.

In the seventh paragraph of the fifty-third essay, we see one aspect of this set forth fairly clearly.

A branch of knowledge which belongs to the acquirements of a federal representative and which has not been mentioned is that of foreign affairs. In regulating our own commerce he ought to be not only acquainted with the treaties between the United States and other nations, but also with the commercial policy and laws of other nations. He ought not to be altogether ignorant of the law of nations, for that, as far as it is a proper object of municipal legislation, is submitted to the federal government. And although the house of representatives is not immediately to participate in foreign negotiations and arrangements, yet from the necessary connection between the several branches of public affairs, those particular branches will frequently deserve attention in the ordinary course of legislation and will sometimes demand particular legislative sanction and cooperation.

Notice that this is calling for a fairly highly developed knowledge on the part of our representatives. He explains here, why, for instance, we can't pass a bill dealing with migratory bird patterns, unless we're also aware of some foreign implications. We've got to raise our sights above the hunting season in our local counties if we want to deal with that kind of legislation.

He goes on in the same paragraph and says:

Some portion of this knowledge may no doubt be acquired in a man's closet; but some of it also can only be derived from public sources of information; and all of it will be acquired to best effect by a practical attention to the subject during the period of actual service in the legislature.

So here is an extraordinary claim, that one is going to prepare one's representative by putting one's representative in office. They will not come to office already shaped to the task they are asked to perform. One will put them in office, and having put them there, develop in them the knowledge which is suitable to the task. Now, obviously, one of the praiseworthy characteristics is a certain breadth of knowledge of fairly recondite subject areas. One has to become indeed a representative to acquire the knowledge.

But it raises a question, why do we not select people who have this knowledge, whether from study or otherwise, in advance? Why do we select them and expect them to gain the knowledge after they're selected? Let us look at the practical side of the question. Consider the representatives' environment with all this power, with all the people at their command to do their bidding, with their ability to influence the law and the interests of millions of other people. Isn't it likely that they are the least likely to learn? that they are going to be too preoccupied in dealing with the temptations and the ambitions? Of course we count on their ambition to make the system of separation of powers work, but are they the least likely to pay attention to these broader questions? If they have not been shaped before they've gotten there, are they likely to get anything done at all? Are they likely to have time to read a book? Are they likely to use these sources of public information in this statesmanlike way that Publius envisions? Has Publius constructed a system that in fact can operate only with the kinds of people we never expect to see in office? That's the question that's raised by this, because he says they will gain the knowledge from being in office and we're going to expose them to federal questions.

Let's say this in defense of it on the other side. We have structured the business in such a way that when we elect members of the House of Representatives, we in effect lift them out of that world of parochial or petty temptations. If they're going to pursue their ambitions in this new world with any degree of success, they will have to have knowledge sufficient to deal with the broad federal questions. If it's true that there are differing kinds of questions and they impose different demands on people who deal with them, then in fact learning is in their self-interest. They will be compelled to learn in order to survive in that environment. So we have two sides of the issue. The bottom line remains the same. We praise a certain kind of knowledge, but we expect to get it by experience rather than by prior training.

No. 54

Having raised that question, Publius goes on to talk about a question which is no less significant in the fifty-fourth essay. The question he raises is a digression, and therefore, we have to ask what it's doing here. Remember, what we try to do is figure out what are the praiseworthy and blameworthy things. We see the Federal Farmer has just launched a broad side against the Constitution on the principle that these people have written a Constitution that will allow anybody, no matter what color, no matter what religion, whether pagan or Muslim or Jew, a convict, or anybody, to be a representative. And therefore, we say that there is a strange kind of openness in this Constitution that we don't expect to see. And then full in the middle of trying to answer that question, what are the praiseworthy things, we see this discussion of apportionment of representatives in relation to the questions of taxation and representation. And we see this discussion of the rule of apportionment that raises the three-fifths question—the question of slavery.

Does Publius directly address praiseworthy characteristics? Why are slaves included in the form of three-fifths of all slaves to be counted as a whole number for purposes of representation and taxation? Why does Publius at this point become strangely reticent? Why does Publius put the entire discussion in quotation marks and not in his own voice, as Publius himself says at the end of the third paragraph: "This is the objection, as I understand it, stated in its full force. I shall be equally candid in stating the reasoning which may be offered on the opposite side." And then he starts with quoting a hypothetical Southerner: "We subscribe to the doctrine, might one of our Southern brethren observe." And for the rest of the sentence, and until the very end of the essay he writes in this fictional name. He won't even take responsibility for the argument himself.

Again, I ask, what has this got to do with the praiseworthy things and the blameworthy things? Well it's clear that one of the problems of the original Constitution is the existence of slavery. It has often been argued that the Constitution condones slavery. Publius has said to us in the forty-second and forty-third essays that he does not condone slavery and he thinks the aim of the Constitution is to discourage it. That dealt with the provision covering the importation of slaves and bringing an end to the slave trade by 1808. What about the three-fifths clause, and the fugitive slave clause? They also are there. Do they not give an official stamp of approval to the existence of slavery? Nos. 42–43

Publius thinks the question about slavery must be answered, however embarrassing the question is. And how embarrassing is the question? Well, let me put it in the words of Charles Pinckney from South Carolina. He was in the Constitutional Convention. He fought to get this provision included in the Constitution. He went home to South Carolina. He was in the South Carolina ratifying convention and he stood up on the floor when called by his fellow delegates to account for the absence of a bill of rights. He said that such bills of right always open by acknowledging that all men are created equal and "your representatives in Philadelphia thought that, considering the certain species of property we hold in this state, we would make such a claim with decidedly ill-grace." So they avoided a bill of rights?

It turns out that Pinckney knew that the substance and the intention of the direction of the Bill of Rights spoke with full thrust against the institution of slavery. Many people have said that he didn't know this. They didn't use that language with slaves in mind. They understood completely. That's why Publius is embarrassed. And he has to address this question. He says, "Yes, it is there. No, we don't exactly mean to say we sanction slavery, but we have a political reality, a practical reality. We have to deal with it. We think ultimately the Union is of such value, even in the anti-slavery cause, that it is worthwhile to make the compromise with slavery now." But, it is also the case that we can't bring ourselves fully to put this argument in our own words and in our own lips.

We should digress ourselves before even taking up the Southern argument, which I think is certainly on the surface understandable and we don't need to belabor it. But, we should remind ourselves that the three-fifths clause originates in the Confederation Congress in the debates of March and April, 1783. Those debates do not deal with the question of representation. They deal exclusively with the question of taxation. The Confederation Congress, as we know, foundered on the inability of the Confederation Congress to produce a general impost, a five percent impost or any other tax that would allow the government to work, to pay its bills, and to handle the Western territory. That's why we have the Convention of 1787. In 1783, they were still trying to find a way around this logjam. And one of the things they realized they had to do if they were going to impose any taxes whatever, was to generate a rule of apportionment. This rule of apportionment would have to be fair to each state. And as they talked about this, they began first by looking at using the value of land. A state's share of the whole value of property in the United States would be its share of taxes. But they discovered that that's nearly impossible in the crude conditions of those times. They couldn't yet depend upon surveys, and didn't know how much land people had, let alone what it was worth. So, someone suggested numbers of people as a substitute for land and for wealth. That ought to correspond loosely to the relative wealth of the several states. So, they tried setting up a rule for counting people, but then of course, they noted precisely what we noted in New Jersey. Earlier on, New Jersey objected to the militia rule. When we start counting people, we run into a problem counting the difference between slaves and non-slaves. Are we going to exempt the slaves from the count? Well, if we do that, that means we allow people with enormous wealth to get away with virtually no contribution to the common pool and to the common crisis of war. So we count the men. What consequence does that have?

It turns out, if we count the men and count the men altogether, we end up imposing from their perspective a much greater burden on people who own slaves in great numbers in proportion to their participation in the common councils of the nation. But they were not counting slaves for that purpose in 1783. The question of representation does not come up, because there was one vote per state in effect. Each state sends its representatives, and only those people who participate in the political life of the state then participate in the political life of the nation. They debate this, they argue over it, and finally come to the three-fifths clause as a compromise on the question of taxation exclusively. And what does the three-fifths clause say in 1783? It's worded slightly differently than the one we have in 1787. The three-fifths clause in 1783 reads, and this is a paraphrase but almost a literal quotation, that taxes shall be apportioned among the several states on the basis of the whole number of free white inhabitants of every age, sex, and condition, and other free persons, excluding Indians not taxed and including also those bound to a term of service, and including three-fifths of all other persons. That's the original three-fifths clause.

We see in the language of that clause certain implications that tell the direction and meaning of the clause itself. Take the first phrase: The whole number of free white inhabitants of every age, sex, and condition. That means that we're counting men, women, children, old folk; nobody is neglected. The language is not meant to be exclusive. It's inclusive. That is followed by the second phrase: "And other free inhabitants." Who are "other free inhabitants" who are not free white inhabitants of every age, sex, and condition"? There were no Asians yet in the United States. It's clear, of course, the other free inhabitants are Black people. They are virtually the only other ones except for a handful of Indians. The only category here with significant numbers were in fact Black people. And then the rest of the clause is the language in which we except the Indians and the indentured servants, and include three-fifths of all other persons. In that context, all other persons doesn't mean all of the Black people; it means all slaves. The defined category are those held in slavery. So, there is a distinction held between Blacks who are slaves and Blacks who are free, in the original language in 1783.

When the three-fifths clause was written in the Constitution of 1787, it was changed. Now, we have two things together, not just taxes, but representatives and taxes, "according to their respective Numbers, which shall be determined by adding to the whole Number of free Persons, including those bound to Service for a Terms of Years, and excluding Indians not taxed, three fifths of all other Persons." What's happened to it? Nothing except that the language has been edited to eliminate redundancy. Why do we have to say, "whole number of free white inhabitants and other free inhabitants," when the "whole number of free persons" says the same thing? Why do we have to say, "all free persons of every age, sex, and condition," when all free persons says the same thing? In short, they listen to a good English professor in 1787. They made the language more economical, more direct, and entirely inclusive. It is not exclusive of women, children, Blacks, or anybody. So that the language does not convey an attitude towards a given race. That's the first and most important thing we have to notice in order to free ourselves to understand this argument in the *Federalist Papers*. The language was never meant to convey an attitude towards a race. It was meant rather to convey a practical attempt to resolve a difficult political problem by speaking in terms of the political and legal distinctions that were current in the age. It was as simple as that.

If we look at the defense given by the Southerner in quotation marks, we see that it boils down to a very simple question. The South is not willing to give up slavery, nor willing to join a Union without having its distinct interests taken into account. Those interests tend to move in opposite directions. On the representation scale it moves one way; it encourages them to wish to count slaves as much as possible. On the taxation scale, it moves the other way and they wish not to count slaves any more than they have to. In the end they come to a compromise. Why is the compromise the same language that we have in the 1783 three-fifths provision? Because after arguing and arguing over this in the Constitutional Convention, threatening to break the Constitution up over it, people like Gouverneur Morris declare that he just will have no part of this. He thinks slavery is an abomination. Human beings should not be treated as property. They decide we can't do any better than the Confederation Congress did in 1783. And thus we have a compromise where there is virtually no room for compromise in this most vexed business.

No. 54
This then gives us a rule of representation that counts three-fifths of the whole number of slaves for purposes of representation. It doesn't treat a human being as three-fifths of a person. Those who have for years said this have abused both the ordinary sense of the language and the intentions of the framers. Not even the Southerner would go that far, for the Southerners are aware, as this Southerner is, that slaves, while treated as cattle, as property, are certainly very much human beings, and therefore, as they always were, amenable to the indications of responsibility that we find in criminal laws and other forms of penalties for bad behavior. People don't give trials to their cattle, but only to human beings.

The defense of the three-fifths clause has nothing to do apparently with the questions of what's praiseworthy or blameworthy in a representative. Except it shows that in struggling with the question of slavery, Publius understands that question, too, to involve the question of what kind of society we expect this to be and who are the people to be comprehended within it. We will see when we talk about further aspects of this argument, especially the question of the virtue and the wisdom of representatives in the essays following, what the implications of that might be.

Let us continue our discussion of the House of Representatives and the search for those praiseworthy characteristics which will identify members, and prospective members, of that body. In passing on beyond the question of slavery, which I think contributes to this in the negative sense, in that it reveals an area of the founding in which the founders could not do all that they wished, we can still raise the question of what representatives ought to look like with respect to the more technical questions raised in the fifty-fifth *Federalist Paper*.

No. 55
The opening of essay fifty-five announces itself as concerned with charges against the Constitution. There are four of them:

The charges exhibited against it are, first, that so small a number of representatives will be an unsafe depository of the public interests; secondly, that they will not possess a proper knowledge of the local circumstances of their numerous constituents; thirdly, that they will be taken from that class of citizens which will sympathize least with the feelings of the mass of the people and be most likely to aim at a permanent elevation of the few on the depression of the many; fourthly, that defective as the number will be in the first instance, it will be more and more disproportionate, by the increase of the people, and the obstacles which will prevent a correspondent increase of the representatives.

So, sixty-five people in the first house is not enough to run the government in accord with the public interests. And generally this series of charges boils down to the charge that the House will be insufficiently democratic. That is the Antifederalist perspective on the Constitution. We see some of this in the Federal Farmer when he says that we will not have in this representation a mirror of the people in the society.

And also he adds a fillip, which I'd like to emphasize at this point, but after first reading the Federal Farmer's definition of fair representation.

A full and equal representation is that which possesses the same interests, feelings, opinions, and views the people themselves would were they all assembled. Fair representation, therefore, should be so regulated that every order of men in the community, according to the common course of elections, can have a share in it.[2]

So we have two things. We directly reflect the sentiments of the community and we directly reflect the classes of the community. That's called full representation and fair representation.

The Federal Farmer indicates some limitations on this:

The people of this country in one sense may all be democratic; but if we make the proper distinction between the few men of wealth and abilities and consider them, as we ought, as the natural aristocracy of the country, and the great body of the people, the middle and lower classes, as the democracy, this federal representative branch will have but very little democracy in it.[3]

There are going to be too few representatives and those few will be the better sort who can't represent the country because they will neither speak to the interests of the people nor come from the interests of the majority of the people.

It's to be noted that this demand for representatives, who have the same interest, feelings, and opinions as the people themselves have, contradicts the earlier assertion by Publius that the representatives will be fit for their jobs by being placed in their jobs and gaining new knowledge. If we place intention to gain knowledge from a broader exposure, a broader experience and new study, over against what we bring from home, the feelings, the opinions, the views of our constituents, then we realize that we're raising a fundamental question. What is the representative's task? Is it to speak from a superior vantage point to the interest of the community or is it to speak the voice of the community? Publius, of course, takes the former as his course and now he defends this. There's no hiding in Publius's terms from the implications of his argument.

Federal Farmer, with many other Antifederalists, draws the distinction between the so-called natural aristocracy and the natural democracy. They think there are some people, the better sort, and they're not better by birth, necessarily. The natural aristocracy are better by natural endowments, and when those natural endowments are favored with a well cultured soil, they of course sprout and flourish and that gives them the opportunity to prevail over their less fortunate brothers and sisters. The natural democracy, however, still requires representation. The natural aristocrats are acknowledged to have great talents but they're not acknowledged to be the natural exponents of the interests of the natural democracy. This is the argument that Publius is trying to knock down, and particularly in this fifty-fifth *Federalist Paper.*

Publius therefore argues at the outset of the fifty-fifth *Federalist Paper,* having listed before the charges, that this question of the number of representatives is not easy. Do we want to settle this question by looking at how many people we need to represent the interests, the diverse interests in the society, or wouldn't we rather take as our rule the question of the efficiency of the body? What would it take to make it work, to accomplish its purposes?

No. 35   Now I remind us of the thirty-fifth *Federalist Paper,* in which Publius has already rejected the idea of directly representing the interests of the people. There he said we have two great classes, the manufacturing, commercial class, on the one hand, the agricultural, landed class on the other hand; and then we have the learned professions who will arbitrate between them. So Publius is not naive. Publius knows there will be class tensions. Publius knows there will be interests; and he knows there will be labor unions, for example. And he's got to take them into account, but the question is, do we represent them directly, and his answer there was no. We don't directly represent them because we have a combination of things working together. At work above all are the free votes in the people at large who are exercising their choice in election with respect to the standard of the best, because that's what we do in elections. On the other hand, we have the operation of what we can call the principle of statesmanship.

No. 27   We have invited people to take an extended view. We had noted back in the twenty-seventh essay that there's a question of how high-toned this government might be and it's clear that Publius wants a higher-toned

government than is called for by the standard of the Federal Farmer.
Federal Farmer wants a government which directly represents the interests,
which is merely the mouthpiece of the masses, let us say. That is a
government, from Publius's perspective, which is not high-toned and does
not take an extended and enlarged view. Therefore that government is not
capable of seeing to the true interests of the society.

In the third paragraph of the fifty-fifth essay he reasons:

Nothing can be more fallacious than to found our political calculations on
arithmetical principles. Sixty or seventy men, may be more properly trusted with **No. 55**
a given degree of power than six or seven. But it does not follow, that six or
seven hundred would be proportionably a better depositary. And if we carry on
this opposition to six or seven thousand, the whole reasoning ought to be
reversed. The truth is, that in all cases a certain number at least seems to be
necessary to secure the benefits of free consultation and discussion, and to guard
against too easy a combination for improper purposes: As on the other hand, the
number ought at most to be kept within a certain limit, in order to avoid the
confusion and intemperance of a multitude. In all very numerous assemblies, of
whatever characters composed, passion never fails to wrest the scepter from
reason. Had every Athenian citizen been a Socrates; every Athenian assembly
would still have been a mob.

So this consultation and discussion are meant to take place in an orderly
environment where the voice of reason can be heard, and the more we
enlarge it the more difficult we make it for reason. If for no other reason,
because reason tends to be less reason when it has to shout than when it can
speak softly. It's very hard to maintain not merely the appearance but even
the substance of reflection when one is speaking at the top of one's lungs.
Had every Athenian citizen been a Socrates, every Athenian assembly
would still have been a mob and therefore this criticism on Publius's part
has nothing to do with the difference between so-called natural aristocrats
and natural democrats. Were every legislator a Socrates we'd still have to
keep them small enough in number that they could carry on true discussion,
true deliberation. All of them could be Socrateses and it could still become
an unruly mob.

We must emphasize that what is in Publius we do not find in the
Antifederalist. Publius depends on what he calls deliberation, or "consultation and discussion." Deliberation makes a substantive contribution to the
development of policy. The Antifederalist perspective is one which would
dispose us to imagine that policy is formed more through negotiation than
through deliberation. Negotiation is coming together and saying, "this is
what I want and this is what you want, how much of each can we get?"
Publius is talking about an entirely different approach in which people raise
honestly the question of what ought to be done. They consult, they discuss.
Publius has told us already that they learn. They meet with others among

learn. They meet with others among whom they share insights about the order of society, the necessities of society and they arrive at informed opinions as to what they ought to do. This is an entirely different way of approaching the question than through the model of negotiations.

Publius says we want to raise the number to a certain level so as "to secure the benefits of free consultation and discussion, and to guard against too easy a combination for improper purposes." Now, that argument tells us one of the most important things about the praiseworthy characteristics of our representatives, namely, they are capable of participating in reasoned discourse. They're capable of deliberation. They're capable of weighing alternatives and selecting the better rather than merely resorting to negotiation in order to establish policy. So that one will presume that as people are to be chosen for the offices they will be chosen in part because they already show the inclination so to conduct themselves. As we've said before, there are societies in which people praise foremost military prowess. This is like unto that, then, but Publius wishes to see the people in this society praise foremost deliberation or genuine thoughtfulness about the good of the society.

No. 10

This is an important question. Many people think that once Publius advocates in *Federalist* ten the creation of a society in which the open pursuit of self-interest, of gain, is established, what follows is indifference to virtue. They seem to think we can either be the one or the other but not both. Publius, however, says, these are the natural offspring of free government. He believes that we can both recognize the reality of interests and organize them. We can provide that government requires to regulate them and still, according to Publius, ask that representatives do so in such a way as to aim beyond mere interests, beyond mere negotiation.

No. 51

This is a foremost consideration in the context of the House of Representatives because that is where, as it turns out, the interest will be most directly expressed. The people will come to their representatives first to pursue their interests. What did we say in *Federalist* fifty-one? We said this government has an ignition. That ignition is the clamant interests of the society. It's the demands that people will make that will begin policy making. That will take place first and foremost at the House of Representatives. The House of Representatives is where the greatest danger of corruption ought to exist under this government by its very structure, for it is being exposed to interests. That exposure is part and parcel of making it work. But the House of Representatives is also where, according to Publius, one expects the representative to rise above the corruption.

This is difficult because a representative is in for only two years and comes back very quickly to the people to have the lease on the office renewed. That means he has to satisfy the leaseholder. The leaseholder may not be satisfied by a detached, disinterested, and objective policy, and therefore, it's a very tricky road, a very high-wire act that the representative has to perform. But this is precisely what Publius is calling for, and in the process praising the kind of characteristics which make it possible to perform that high-wire dance that will be the true occupation of the member of the House of Representatives.

So, Publius says the number is not too small. We should say something about the way in which the convention arrived at this number. The original number, sixty-five, of course, is the product of negotiations in the Convention. But, it was meant to be temporary. It was to last only a couple of years until the first census was to be taken in 1790. Then in 1790 we have the beginning of what would become a decennial process and would recast the numbers in terms of representation to fit a ratio. But the arithmetic ratio was stated in the language of not more than one for every thirty thousand rather than an absolute.

That number was decided upon on the last day of the convention. Up until that time, the ratio had been one for forty thousand. There had been a number of ratios proposed but one for forty thousand was finally approved and they had come through several months in the convention in considering this. Once, earlier in the convention in August, they tried to lower it from forty to thirty thousand without success. On the last day of the convention, September 17, when the Constitution had been fully engrossed, ready to be signed, Mr. Gorham made a motion to change the rule of representation from one to forty thousand to one to thirty thousand, which of course would produce more representatives. He was seconded. There was some debate which is not recorded in Madison's notes, or anywhere else, except that very shortly afterwards George Washington rose and addressed the Convention. And he apologized for doing what he had not done throughout the entire Convention. He said to them that he thought this was sufficiently important that he wanted to take the opportunity to invite them to make the change recommended. He wanted to make the recommended change because he thought it would be a more democratic change, and a more democratic spirit would then inform the document that they were sending out to the country. To enlarge the representation would speak to the genius of the people. Then the Convention acted unanimously to approve the recommendation. They acted unanimously where until that point they were divided throughout the Convention in rejecting that very same recommendation.

The point of that story is essentially to show Washington's influence, but in this context, much more significantly, to show that a conscious effort was made to democratize the House of Representatives. The rule they came out with was far more generous than they were inclined at first to approve, twenty-five percent more generous than they were at first inclined to approve. Thus the Antifederalist charge that the representation is anti-democratic is especially ironic, in the face of that kind of endeavor. But Publius's response to the charge is not to say we settled on one for thirty thousand because we thought it was more democratic. He never defends it by saying, "it's more democratic." He defends the size of the House on the grounds of the function of the House; he defends what will enable it to work efficiently.

He does allow that over time the size will grow to reflect the growth of the country, but he thinks it's got to top out somewhere around five, six, or seven hundred, otherwise it would become impossible. Five hundred seems to be the most that he can entertain as a reasonable body in which to carry on the kind of work that he wants to see done. So that means for Publius (what is most important here) that we establish or enfranchise the right, the authority, of the representative to act independently. The emphasis on democracy conveys too much of the image of the representative on a tether; the representative held closely at hand by the constituents.

No. 55   Publius has defined dependence and responsibility for us. But in that context, he still wants to give the impression of the representative who can act freely and who will act therefore beyond the narrow limits that would otherwise be imposed by a negotiating environment. Look at the very end of the fifty-fifth essay, where we see that Publius makes clear why we take this approach. In the ninth paragraph, he says, there are dangers, but we guard against them by doing certain kinds of things. We say that they cannot occupy offices that they create or for which they raise the salary. I might point out parenthetically that's one that we have a lot of trouble sticking too today. It's clear why it was written into the Constitution, but today we find members of the House and Senate routinely aspiring to Cabinet offices and Supreme Court positions even if they have just voted to raise salaries for those offices or to create those offices. They are very sloppy in paying attention to that Constitutional language, but it had a role and its role was to still, to calm the fears of people like the Antifederalists at the outset.

At the end of the ninth paragraph he gives his general response to the overall concern:

> As there is a degree of depravity in mankind which requires a certain degree of circumspection and distrust: So there are other qualities in human nature, which justify a certain portion of esteem and confidence. Republican government presupposes the existence of these qualities in a higher degree than any other form. Were the pictures which have been drawn by the political jealously of some among us faithful likenesses of the human character, the inference would be that there is not sufficient virtue among men for self-government; and that nothing less than the chains of despotism can restrain them from destroying and devouring one another.

The ability to rise above the corruption justifies a certain portion of esteem and confidence. They are presupposed by republican government.

Now this, of course, balances the earlier statement of Publius when he said, "if men were angels, no government would be necessary." Government is itself a reflection on human nature. Yes, men need restraints. But, yes, we turn to men to restrain men. There are also the characteristics in human nature which enable us to entrust institutions, to entrust laws, and to entrust certain kinds of character to restrain human beings. So it is not a bleak picture of human nature that drives the *Federalist Papers*. I am anxious to beat down that old argument that somehow the *Federalist* had a narrow, cramped, crabbed view of human nature as something evil, and that government had to be designed to hold the evil in check. Everyone knows that human beings do evil and stupid things. But everyone also ought to know, and this is Publius teaching it seems to me, that human beings can both avoid and prevent stupid and evil things and at the same time that they alone are capable of providing the means for curing the ills that are produced thereby, whether technological or otherwise.

Through the specific powers that will be exercised by the government we further justify the existence of the House of Representatives. These people will come with a certain kind of knowledge that will allow the power to tax to be safely exercised. They are not going to abuse their own fellow citizens. One of the reasons they are not going to abuse them, according to Publius, is because they themselves have to live this life. They have to go back home. They have to account for themselves, but they also have to live under the laws that they pass. And Publius actually relies upon this concern far more than any other to establish the safety of the representatives. In the fifty-seventh and fifty-eighth essays we see this argument honed finely and sharply by Publius.

At the beginning of the fifty-seventh essay he remarks, "The aim of every political constitution is, or ought to be, first to obtain for rulers men **No. 57** who possess most wisdom to discern, and most virtue to pursue, the common good of the society." And this is what we've emphasized in the form of deliberation; that's what Publius wants. But he doesn't settle merely on the expectation of wisdom and virtue in order to defend the society against corruption or tyranny.

In the fifth paragraph he talks about the electors. Who will choose these federal representatives?

Not the rich more than the poor; not the learned more than the ignorant; not the haughty heirs of distinguished names, more than the humble sons of obscure and unpropitious fortune. The electors are to be the great body of the people of the United States. They are to be the same who exercise the right in every State of electing the corresponding branch of the Legislature of the State.

confidence of his country." The emphasis is on every citizen whose merit may recommend him. Publius does not wish to choose representatives by lot. Choosing them merely by their interests is akin to choosing them by lot. He wants to choose them by standards of merit, of judgment, and of excellence.

There are many motives we may depend upon to tie the representative to his constituents and to the country at large. In the fourteenth paragraph, he speaks of those ties which bind the representatives as being connected with ambition. So his pride and vanity attach him to a form of government which favors his pretensions. It's an interesting observation to make that it is largely the love of honor, which people often disparage, that is often the source of the greatest security they can have. By extending the opportunity to acquire honor to those who merit it, one enlists them in one's own service. That's what Publius is saying. The society is organized to make use of these natural human propensities for the common good rather than to stigmatize them.

We know of the situation that once prevailed in ancient Athens, where if an individual developed a reputation so extraordinarily beyond the ordinary that it gave rise to fears in the community, that individual would be ostracized. If he seemed greatly superior in some way, then they would conspire to get him out of the city. They were afraid that anyone that had that degree of excellence would become a threat to their liberties. Well, Publius suggests, rather than using ostracism, that one construct the regime so as to enlist excellence on behalf of liberty. He writes in the tenth paragraph:

Whatever hopes or projects might be entertained by a few aspiring characters, it must generally happen that a great proportion of the men deriving their advancement from their influence with the people, would have more to hope from a preservation of the favor, than from innovations in the government subversive of the authority of the people.

So all of these principles conspire to work together and have added to them the ultimate twist that is acknowledged in the twelfth paragraph, "that they can make no law which will not have its full operation on themselves and their friends, as well as on the great mass of the society."

That's an important principle, because it's possible to design a government in which the laws apply to everybody else but the person making them. Law that applies to everyone is new. In fact, some people would say that if we've lost anything in our Constitution today it's precisely that characteristic since in the twentieth Century we often found our Congress making laws that do not apply to Congress.

That was the very thing that Publius depended upon to defend the Constitution. Look at the thirteenth paragraph. He tells us how much he depended upon it: "If this spirit [which actuates the people of America] shall ever be so far debased as to tolerate a law not obligatory on the Legislature, as well as on the people, the people will be prepared to tolerate anything but liberty." It's an extraordinary statement.

What then are the characteristics of the representative and his relationship with the people? The fourteenth paragraph of the fifty-seventh essay lists those.

Duty, gratitude, interest, and ambition itself, are the chords by which they will be bound to fidelity and sympathy with the great mass of the people. It is possible that these may all be insufficient to controul the caprice and wickedness of man. But are they not all that government will admit, and that human prudence can devise? Are they not the genuine and the characteristic means by which Republican Government provides for the liberty and happiness of the people?

Duty, gratitude, interest, and ambition—these are the praiseworthy characteristics. When we can identify people by their words and deeds in which these elements take a preponderating influence, then we want to elevate them to the highest offices, at least the House of Representatives, according to Publius.

This argument again is an argument about the general thrust of the government and also the operation. We can reflect on what it says about the operation along the following lines. If the House of Representatives, the legislative body, will be characterized by people in whom duty, gratitude, interest, and ambition is foremost, however likely to negotiate with one another, what is it in their interaction that will establish the course or the pattern? Naturally, the simple things will be taken care of that will operate on the basis of majority rule. I say that perhaps more easily than it ought to be said, because as we know the Constitution leaves to each branch of the legislature to establish its own rules. So, the rules are not written in, but from the very outlook we see that the majority will rule.

One of the things that we noticed in essay fifty-one is that we have so structured the branches of government as to make the daily and essential operations of each branch part and parcel of the process of checks and balances. This includes the freedom they have to write their own rules. The rules were to be written in such a way as to bring all the participants into the activity of the House of Representatives. Otherwise, what would be the result? Take the representative who goes to Washington, who finds himself excluded by the rules? What would happen to his constituents? Not only is the representative left out of the process, but the constituents are left out of the process. What happens then in terms of their fidelity to the Constitution or their identification of the government as concerned with their own interests? The reason we include "interest" in that list of duty, gratitude, interest, and ambition is because interest is the most certain tool for

No. 51

guaranteeing that we keep a constant eye on the process, though it may be in some respects not the most encompassing motive to which to appeal. If we exclude altogether some players, then we create a constitutional crisis. How do we avoid that? We open the door to bring them in; but bringing them in gives them the chance to affect the interests of others.

The representative, who has to be brought into this all-encompassing process will take on certain characteristics. The best way for me to show what this means is to contrast the American system with most of the systems of the world, that is, parliamentary systems. They operate in a radically different way from the United States. There are parliaments almost everywhere else and they are very strictly organized by party, to begin with. And in a manner of speaking, the minority party is excluded. They are not excluded from the House, but they are excluded from meaningful participation in the formulation of policy. They usually exist as a shadow cabinet or a shadow government. So they come to the House and their role in the debates is strictly negative and critical. All policy is set by the party in control. And we don't change that except consequent to a new election or vote of confidence when one party is thrown out and another party comes in.

What happens in the American context? No doubt about it. Parties organize the Congress and select the Speaker of the House. The Speaker is always the spokesman of the major party in the House. But the fact of the matter is, we integrate all the participants throughout all the operations of the House of Representatives. Everyone takes part in all of the committees, the shaping of policy, and the introduction of legislation. They play a role not simply as criticizing but actually leading and formulating the policies themselves. This integrative aspect of the House of Representatives, which has been consistent throughout United States history, is part and parcel of what Publius aims for, because it's in that process of integrating all of those who come into the operations of the institution that that knowledge he depends upon is spread among all the participants.

Many people have criticized American government, and particularly the House of Representatives. They criticize it for not being parliamentary. They have asked for a change in the Constitution so as to make the system a more parliamentary system. They think it would be more efficient and that it would allow us to formulate policy strictly in accord with majoritarian sentiment. They maintain that in the United States we experience certain delays, deadlocks, irrationalities, and irregularities because of the open-endedness and inclusiveness of the process. For example, if we had a parliamentary system and we had a party position, and there was a member of the legislature of our party who does not follow the party position, we could expel the member. We could enforce party discipline, and they would have to line up with us.

Why is it so hard to enforce party discipline in the United States? For the very reasons, it seems to me, that have been set forth here. It's hard to enforce because the representative is not simply oriented towards the party; he doesn't owe his position to the party. It is rarely the case that someone goes into the Congress of the United States feeling gratitude to the party. This gratitude that Publius talks about is gratitude to his constituents, who play a fundamental role, not as members of a party but as members of that community, in sustaining him in office. So, he is independent of his party even though identifying with it and its aims. There is no party discipline accordingly.

The Constitution leaves much unstated. Nowhere in the Constitution is it written or required that the United States organize its House of Representatives on a non-parliamentary basis or the whole Congress for that matter. We could say any given party that succeeds in acquiring a majority in the House of Representatives elects a Speaker of the House, and the Speaker would set policy. The President doesn't have to send legislation into Congress. It's not required in the Constitution. The Constitution requires the President to make occasional recommendations as it occurs to him that these things are desirable. He is called upon to report on the state of the Union. But it doesn't say that the President shall submit a budget. And it doesn't say that if he submits the budget that the Congress has to look at it. So the Congress could organize itself in such a way that its Speaker would become a prime minister. And he would have the responsibility to generate a budget, he would have all the staff organized to do this, and they can exclude the minority party from that process.

Why does it not work that way? Because the process has been designed to place so strong an influence against the tendency to exclude and in favor of the tendency to include that there is in fact no opportunity for it. The break-out opportunities, to speak in the language of contemporary economics, for party members are so plentiful in the Congress of the United States, the independence of the representatives is so marked, the appeal to their ambition so strong, that they do not have to ascend by way of the approval of the party members, but can in fact climb quite independently of the party. This is so powerful that there is no way in that dynamic context that they're going to operate in the mold of European parliamentary systems.

According to Publius, producing these consequences is part and parcel of making the representation safe. Why? Because we have people who will take bold ventures, who will be independent enough to launch lines of inquiry not previously sanctioned. At the same time the representatives will remain sufficiently close to the public, to their constituents, to guarantee that the voice of public opinion will always play a role and will not be shut out by the process itself but would rather become a part of the process.

That should lead us to a final discussion of the question of the House of Representatives in terms of the House as the keystone of the arch with respect to public opinion. It seems that the best way to bring that question up is first to turn to the question of the role of the Senate under the Constitution; and when we compare the Senate and the House, we can recapture the central thrust of the question of where public opinion enters.

To discuss the Senate let's return to the discussion of the House of Representatives in *Federalist* fifty-seven momentarily. There is a passage in which we see a ground for comparing the design of the House and the design of the Senate in terms of the choices of their members. In the fifteenth paragraph of essay fifty-seven we read the following:

No. 57

Were the objection to be read by one who had not seen the mode prescribed by the Constitution for the choice of representatives, he could suppose nothing less than that some unreasonable qualification of property was annexed to the right of suffrage; or that the right of eligibility was limited to persons of particular families or fortunes; or at least that the mode prescribed by the State Constitutions was in some respect or other, very grossly departed from. We have seen how far such a supposition would err as to the first two points. Nor would it in fact be less erroneous as to the last. The only difference discoverable between the two cases, is, that each representative of the United States will be elected by five or six thousand citizens; whilst in the individual States the election of a representative is left to about as many hundreds. Will it be pretended that this difference is sufficient to justify an attachment to the State Government and an abhorrence to the Fœderal Government? If this be the point on which the objection turns, it deserves to be examined.

As we go through the following passages in that essay, we not only contrast ultimately the House and Senate, but contrast them with the British House of Commons and even Ireland. Notice the easy matter-of-fact manner in which Publius dismisses the fact that we have no property qualifications with the suffrage, that we don't determine eligibility by selecting families of fortune or impose any such qualifications upon our representatives. Of course we also see the same for the Senate and wonder why that can be so easily affirmed by him. Isn't it rather crazy not to have sensible qualifications on family and substance for admission into such high offices, insofar as the United States certainly aims to be a significant nation in the world? The more odd thing is not to have such qualifications rather than to have them. Yet he writes as if this is the most normal thing in the world. Well if it's odd in general, it surpasses odd in a body called the Senate.

No. 62

We remember of course that we derive *senate* from the Latin word, *senex,* that means elders. The word, *senate*, in politics is equivalent to the Greek word, *presbyteros*. In religion, the Presbyterian Church means a church with its government based on elders. It chooses the elders to rule.

And the Senate is, of course, historically just such an institution, not only elders but of course those who are distinguished in the ordinary ways. It separates the well-born from the ill-born in the ordinary society. When we turn to the sixty-second *Federalist Paper,* in order to find out what the qualifications of senators are, we then may be surprised, as we would be reading the Constitution itself, to see that it amounts to little more than an age limit, which is certainly well below elderly, of thirty years of age and a citizen of the United States for nine years.

The question is, why are the qualifications for the Senate of the United States so low? Why are we ready to admit anyone? Shouldn't this body be, in contrast to the House of Representatives, the kind of body where property, wisdom, and years should be represented? Why not just have one house, the House of Representatives, if we're going to have no greater difference in the two bodies than the fact that in one we have to be twenty-five and the other thirty, and in one we must be seven years a citizen and the other nine years a citizen? And there are no greater differences than that. If we aren't going to distinguish the characters of the persons in these two bodies by their status in life, why do we need separate bodies?

Historically, we have used separate bodies because they reflected either separate classes or separate characters. When Rome had differing assemblies of the plebeians and the patricians, in effect they reflected that distinction in their status. The plebeians were mainly the poor and the patricians were the aristocrats. They were represented in the government according to these distinctions. Recall in the fourteenth essay that Publius declares that America has made the extended republic and the principle of representation the foundation for an unmixed republic. But of course, what we notice in the fourteenth essay was that no one would ever consider it sensible to design an unmixed republic. The picture is still more complicated when we add to it to what looks like the institutions of a mixed republic.

The reason for a senate originally was to have a mixed republic which represents the different classes and so needs different bodies. Well, we have already read the argument in the fifty-first *Federalist Papers,* which shows us that we want a very complicated series of differentiations in branches and levels of government or a series of vertical and horizontal separations of checks and balances. And presumably, the senate has come into being as one in the series. We want to divide the legislature so as to retard tyrannical developments, for example, because we find it the most powerful branch. This is a different justification for a senate than anyone had ever made before. In Britain no one justified the House of Lords on the grounds that they needed to divide the legislative power. The House of Lords is the aristocratic body. It emerged historically to represent the aristocratic interests. They are "lords." It is not really a house but a house of "lords" and a people of substance.

No. 51

Here, we don't have a house of lords and one of the most vexing questions in dealing with our Constitution is the answer to the question, "what did the framers intend?" Did they borrow these old forms, because they intended old results? And so often people analyzing the Constitution of the United States make the mistake of trying to create an infinitely regressive evolutionary pattern saying, "well if we have a senate, it must be because Rome had a senate or it must be because in England there was a House of Lords." That is a very large mistake. The similarities between American republicanism and old republicanism are largely superficial. And the key is to ask, how do we justify the institutions of American republicanism? What we discover persistently and most shockingly here in the senate is that justifications are always democratic. They're always based on an appeal to the broad influence of the public at large. It is never based on an appeal to specific limitations or specific classes.

Historians have said that the founders were trying to defend their own class. I've yet to find the historian who has been able to answer the intuitive question, if they were trying to defend their own class, why didn't they say so? Why didn't they do it? Why didn't they design an institution that said, "we shall hold the power"? Why did they design it in such a way as to say anyone can enter office? It doesn't seem to be a very sensible way of defending one's own class.

We have reasons to take very seriously the founders' own insistence that this is a popular constitution. They have instituted these different branches, not on the old justifications, but on the new justification that it is a way to give scope to the operation of public opinion, such that it remains safe. The problem has been from the beginning, not whether to have a popular government, but how we can do so safely. How do we enable the people to rule and at the same time establish, what we notice

No. 49   from the forty-ninth *Federalist Paper,* the probability that their reason will rule and not their passions?

It is old-fashioned to speak this way about public opinion. Nobody thinks in the late twentieth century about people being carried away whimsically and establishing policies thoughtlessly with caprice, because, probably, people have lived too comfortably with Publius's Constitution. The things that are for Publius great questions are no longer questions and partly because, it seems to me, Publius resolved them.

We'll see this very clearly by looking at the Senate. Let's look at the

No. 62   second paragraph of the sixty-second essay where he begins the discussion of the qualifications. There it is much as I have elaborated, but then he goes on to say this:

The propriety of these distinctions is explained by the nature of the senatorial trust; which requiring greater extent of information and stability of character, requires at the same time that the senator should have reached a period of life most likely to supply these advantages; and which participating immediately in transactions with foreign nations, ought to be exercised by none who are not thoroughly weaned from the prepossessions and habits incident to foreign birth and education.

The question of trust is the reason we have five more years of age and two more years of citizenship. He wants senators with a greater extent of information and stability of character than representatives. That is, he wants senators to be educated and well-adjusted.

What is "greater extent of information and stability of character"? He doesn't say anything about the money we have, what family we were born into, what our estate was like, or anything. He doesn't even say whether we held office before, though we might think "stability of character" would entail, in some respect, having had the occasion to demonstrate our capacity in a lesser office before rising to the Senate of the United States. Then he goes on to "require at the same time that the senator should have reached a period of life most likely to supply these advantages." We can judge "greater extent of information and stability of character" by age, if nothing else.

Of course, senators were not chosen by the people; they were chosen by the state legislatures originally. The state legislators look at people of a certain age with the assumption that that will be easier than to focus on those who have the requisite characteristics. The reference to foreign influence we can get rid of very quickly. Because it's a new nation, it's still filled with new people and so that part is an ordinary precaution. Well, that's interesting, because if the citizenship distinction ceases to be a question beyond the first generation for practical purposes, then that collapses the requirement simply to the requirement of age. For all practical purposes there is only one requirement for membership in the Senate and in the House. And that's age.

In the next paragraph, Publius talks about the method of appointing them and ultimately that connects with the question of their qualifications.

It is equally unnecessary to dilate on the appointment of senators by the state legislatures. Among the various modes which might have been devised for constituting this branch of the government, that which has been proposed by the convention is probably the most congenial with the public opinion.

To be sure, people like James Wilson, James Madison, and Alexander Hamilton in the Constitutional Convention would rather have them elected than appointed by the state legislatures. Especially James Wilson wanted the people to elect everybody to all the branches. He was the only one that went quite that far. But, all of these nationalists would have thought that the states' involvement were something of an obstacle to the progress that they hoped to make.

"It is recommended," he goes on, "by the double advantage of favouring a select appointment, and of giving to the State governments such an agency in the formation of the federal government as must secure the authority of the former; and may form a convenient link between the two systems." So, we make a virtue out of necessity. The states were involved because we have a political battle that could not be settled other than by having them involved. We use it as a way to interest the states in the future of the nation to maintain their continued participation. Well, that only leads to another question. If the qualifications are collapsed only to the requirement of thirty years of age, and the states are going to choose these "young whipper snappers" based on their "extensive information and stability of character," then the next question is, of course, if we can choose from almost anyone, what numbers do we get to choose?

Aren't we reflecting very nearly the House of Representatives in the initial design of this body? And if that's true, shouldn't it be established on the same foundation as the House of Representatives; that is to say, the broad body of the people? Well, no. The Senate has, in the first place, the equality of representation, not proportionate representation. So, that large states and small states will all share an equal voice in this body. But what do we say about that? In the fourth paragraph, we begin the defense, but again I mention that the people who are uttering the defense are people who don't believe it. They would rather have proportionate representation in the Senate, not equality of representation. They thought this was a vicious principle. That's admitted if we go back and look at the discussion of this in the forty-second essay by Publius. He admits that there was a vicious principle which we had to accept. But, we turn it to our advantage as well as we can, and this is how he tries to turn it to his advantage in the fourth paragraph:

No. 42

The equality of representation in the senate is another point, which, being evidently the result of compromise between the opposite pretensions of the large and the small states, does not call for much discussion. If indeed it be right that among the people thoroughly incorporated into one nation, every district ought to have a *proportional* share in the government; and that among independent and sovereign states, bound together by a simple league, the parties however unequal in size, ought to have an *equal* share in the common councils, it does not appear to be without some reason, that in a compound republic partaking both of the national and federal character, the government ought to be founded on a mixture of the principles of proportional and equal representation.

He acknowledges it's a compromise, and allows that to become a mode of persuading people that the government is at the same time national and federal.

We reviewed this argument at some length in the thirty-ninth *Federalist Paper*. Publius went through a series of distinctions, some federal and some national, and at the end of the essay proved the government partly federal and partly national. It's a compound republic and not a simple consolidated republic. Here, however, it has an additional twist, speaking of the Senate more particularly than he did in the thirty-ninth essay. — No. 39

Publius goes on to say in the sixty-second essay:

But it is superfluous to try by the standards of theory, a part of the constitution, which is allowed on all hands to be the result, not of theory, but "of a spirit of amity, and that mutual deference and concession which the peculiarity of our political situation rendered indispensable." A common government with powers equal to its objects, is called for by the voice, and still more loudly by the political situation of America. — **No. 62**

Publius distinguished the voice of the political situation in America from the theory. Publius is one who hears the voice but insists no less clearly that he knows the theory. And all these tensions, whether in the convention or here in the *Federalist Papers*, reflect Publius's objective assessments of the political situation in the country. Publius has concluded that nationhood is needed and nationhood must be of a certain character independent of the voice of America. Happily, the voice of America largely concurs, as we saw in *Federalist Paper* two, in support for the Union. Publius aims to bring the voices of Americans together with political theory. To take a superior understanding and to make it part and parcel of the ordinary expression of public opinion is what the founding is about.

We often make the mistake, if I might just digress, of thinking of founders in the mode of Moses descending from the mountain with tablets of stone or of a Minos who went to visit with Zeus and brought back laws that are never to be questioned. Therefore, we assume that the founders are detached, superior persons who can do what ordinary humans cannot do—the founder-legislator. Well, what we're seeing in the *Federalist Papers*, is a differing way of regarding the question of founding and legislating in which it becomes very clear that the legislator-founder, no less than the ordinary politician, has to take into account public opinion and has to mold and shape, not only the laws, but the very souls of the people themselves. And Publius must do so while the people give their participation willingly. And that's the key. How do we get willing participation in the name of what's "right" and "good"? In any society, that's always the question, of course. But is it above all the question for a founder? For a founder's stance is the peculiar position of one knowing what needs to be done but requiring to find a way to do it. And sometimes it can't be found. It is not an automatic thing.

Though one knows what needs to be done, it is not automatic to accomplish it, and the conditions through which the Union is achieved are precisely what Publius identifies here as "the voice of America," and elsewhere as "the genius of the people," and "the spirit of the people." That deference to the voice of America is the most significant condition that is required for the successful accomplishment of a founding activity. Publius goes on then, having indicated that he is aware of this.

A government founded on principles more consonant to the wishes of the larger states, is not likely to be obtained from the smaller states. The only option then for the former lies between the proposed government and a government still more objectionable. Under this alternative the advice of prudence must be, to embrace the lesser evil; and instead of indulging a fruitless anticipation of the possible mischiefs which may ensue, to contemplate rather the advantageous consequences which may qualify the sacrifice.

So, Publius says, "I'm a practical chap. I know that I can't get everything I want, but I can at least get enough of what I want to create the expectation of constant motion in the direction of what is advisable." So, that is Publius's characterization of the founding, the achievement of as much as one can in principle and then everything one can achieve additionally so as to foster eventual progress towards the fulfillment of the principle itself.

With respect to the argument for the Senate then, concessions emerge most truly in the context of the equality of representation that Publius does not like but now accepts. The compromise recognizes the constitutional existence of the states and therefore an element of sovereignty remaining in the states, and it serves to help preserve that sovereignty. To that extent the equality is no less acceptable to the large than to the small states.

In the sixth paragraph, Publius suggests that the equality begins to play a role of its own.

Another advantage accruing from this ingredient in the constitution of the senate, is the additional impediment it must impose against improper acts of legislation. No law or resolution can now be passed without the concurrence first of a majority of the people, and then of a majority of the states.

No. 51

Why, would an equal vote be an impediment against improper acts of resolution? Now, we know where the majority of the people comes from? That's the House of Representatives. Second is the majority of the states. So what we see invoked here is the design of *Federalist* fifty-one, finding differing ways to count the voices. We want to find ways to slow the process down. We want to make it deliberative. And one of the ways to do this is to count not just once, but two times, three times, four times, before we decide. Each time we count again, we introduce new opportunities for further reflection, for further deliberation and, of course, for a change of course. This is what Publius means.

He continues:

It must be acknowledged that this complicated check on legislation may in some instances be injurious as well as beneficial; and that the peculiar defence which it involves in favour of the smaller states would be more rational, if any interests common to them, and distinct from those of other states, would otherwise be exposed to peculiar danger. But as the larger states will always be able, by their power over the supplies, to defeat unreasonable exertions of this prerogative of the lesser states; and as the facility and excess of lawmaking seem to be the diseases to which our governments are most liable, it is not impossible that this part of the constitution may be more convenient in practice than it appears to many in contemplation.

That is, the "complicated check" might prevent doing a good thing in a timely fashion. That's the risk we run; it may be injurious. Nevertheless, he is now able to see that in practice, this may not be such a bad thing. In practice it may mean that we eventually achieve something that would have happened a little more swiftly, but it may also mean that we may prevent an excess of lawmaking.

To say that we don't want to foster too much lawmaking in our legislature is a very curious statement to make. We haven't brought this out as clearly as is ultimately required. We saw in the forty-fifth *Federalist Paper* that Publius lamented the constant and unstable legislation in the No. 45 states. One of the objectives of the new Constitution is not to sponsor endless lawmaking, but as we said before, to sponsor deliberation. So, one does not want a lot of lawmaking. One wants a lot of pondering and a lot of reflection. That's why we wanted "extensive information and stability of character." We want to foster in office those people who have the ability to withhold their hands, to lean back and reflect, rather than always instinctively to act. Are we genuflectively to vote? If this becomes one of the devices that permits us to obtain a larger objective, eliminating the temptation to resort to laws to accomplish every social good, then it becomes a good thing. That is Publius's argument. He wants to minimize rather than maximize lawmaking in society at large. For this it's critical to understand the character of society Publius hopes to superintend.

Publius intends a society in which many of the activities that would otherwise be eligible for lawmaking would in fact transpire independent of lawmaking. These activities would have to take place through the mutual interactions and accommodations of persons and groups, rather than through the direct guidance of the political process itself.

What is the Senate's job and what reason accounts for their presence in this Constitution? What "inconveniences" might a republic suffer were the Senate not a part of the Constitution?

No. 62

First. It is a misfortune incident to republican government, though in a lesser degree than to other governments, that those who administer it may forget their obligations to their constituents, and prove unfaithful to their important trust. In this point of view, a senate, as a second branch of the legislative assembly, distinct from, and dividing the power with, a first, must be in all cases a salutary check on the government. It doubles the security to the people, by requiring the concurrence of two distinct bodies in schemes of usurpation or perfidy, where the ambition or corruption of one, would otherwise be sufficient. This is a precaution founded on such clear principles . . . that it would be more than superfluous to enlarge on it. I will barely remark that as the improbability of sinister combinations will be in proportion to the dissimilarity in the genius of the two bodies; it must be politic to distinguish them from each other by every circumstance which will consist with a due harmony in all proper measures, and with the genuine principles of republican government.

Publius says, do not put people into office for too long. They tend to forget. This is an odd way to begin a defense of the Senate, because its members have six-year terms. To think about the Senate as an independent legislature, however, is to misconstrue the role of the Senate. Its role is to be understood exclusively in the relationship to the other branch. And it is in their mutual interaction that one discovers the particular function of the body called the Senate, itself. The Senate will check the other body. The members of the other body are not in office for a very long time. They should not tend to forget the obligations to their constituents, because effort has been made to keep them dependent. The shorter term in office for the House means everything is decided with an eye to the need for re-election. All of that, Publius says, is not sufficient; the role of the Senate is to check them.

We asked before, why doesn't the Senate look different? And this is the answer. It ought not to look different from the other body. It ought to have a different kind of people in it to the extent consistent with the "republican government" and "a due harmony in all proper measures." Those are two different statements that are closely related.

"A due harmony in all proper measures" means we want the two branches to work together on proper measures. Proper measures will be themselves of a republican and democratic tendency. So, the Senate cannot be made so very different from the House that we don't have the opportunity to gain due harmony in proper measures. Further, it can be made no more different than is consistent with the genuine principles of republican government. The first and most fundamental principle of republican government is the fundamental equality of all human beings. Our Senate is not like those in other regimes, because it begins on the basis of the affirmation of a principle that none of the prior systems ever affirmed.

Publius then says, "The necessity of a senate is not less indicated by the propensity of all single and numerous assemblies to yield to the impulse of sudden and violent passions." That is, bicameralism takes passion, subdues it, quiets those within the body who are most likely to foster passion, and provides further occasion for deliberation. In the third area he says, "Another defect to be supplied by a senate lies in a want of due acquaintance with the objects and principles of legislation." Publius has said our representatives will be knowledgeable people, because they will gain knowledge by being brought into office. He says now that they will become knowledgeable, but in two years they can't possibly become sufficiently knowledgeable to provide all that's needed in the way of detached information. Therefore, we need senators who are in office for a longer period of time and who will gain knowledge of a more permanent character than what will ordinarily characterize a representative.

We begin to see how to distinguish representatives and senators. They are not distinguished by accident or birth, but by the functions of office. Senators will be people who show the greatest "stability of character" and "greater information," because the office is designed to foster that no less surely than the office of representative is designed to foster knowledge of federal or more enlarged questions over parochial questions. Still it will be the case, the representative must struggle under the constant influence of parochial interests and parochial questions; whereas the senator will become much more capable of reaching beyond the local interest and, therefore, appealing to the essential national interest.

The argument about the Senate boils down to the argument in the eleventh paragraph about "good government."

A good government implies two things; first, fidelity to the object of government, which is the happiness of the people; secondly, a knowledge of the means by which that object can be best attained. Some governments are deficient in both these qualities: Most governments are deficient in the first. I scruple not to assert that in American governments, too little attention has been paid to the last. The federal constitution avoids this error; and what merits particular notice, it provides for the last in a mode which increases the security for the first.

So, the Senate provides for the means of obtaining the people's happiness in a way that increases the security of that happiness. That is what Publius is saying. Remember, he always affirms the happiness of the people. In our times, when people say, "I'm concerned with the object of government," they usually leave unstated what it is, because they think nobody can state it, or if anyone does, people disagree and, of course, there's no standard to decide. Publius doesn't believe that. He thinks the object of government is rationally determinable, that it can be demonstrated, and that it is the happiness of the people.

The object of government requires eliminating unstable legislation, mutability he calls it, in public councils. We do that further by enabling the Senate to act in such a way as not to be under the continuing pressure of special interests.

At this point a question must arise. The Senate represents states. We say we take the vote by a majority of states, not by a majority of the people. States are local interests. Senators are appointed by state legislators. They seem to be appointed by smaller numbers of people than are representatives. The representatives we're told are elected by five or seven thousand. Senators will seldom be chosen by no more than the fifty or sixty people who constitute the state legislature. Why do we expect senators to be independent, since they are chosen in such a way as makes them directly accessible to the people who chose them and commits them very directly to the interests of those who chose them?

Two things make senators independent. The first, of course, is the length of term. Second after that, and which is the greatest source of concern to Antifederalists, is the fact that once they are chosen by the state legislatures, the state legislatures are impotent in that regard for six years. They cannot be recalled. The state legislatures have put them in office, but once in office, the senators are independent of those who put them there. Publius's argument has an additional dimension or characteristic, which is perhaps as well developed here as elsewhere.

The Senate is said to vote by a majority of the states, and that is not technically correct. We saw, even in the thirty-ninth *Federalist Paper,* that that might not be correct. And it turns out to be the case that votes in the Senate are cast individually rather than by states. When one consults the parliamentary process one discovers an interesting thing. If we vote per capita, which Publius now acknowledges to be the case in the Senate, it turns out that we may produce decisions sometimes by a majority of senators, that will not reflect a majority of the states, because of the way in which the vote has been counted. Votes are not only aye and nay, but also abstentions and absences. In a system in which a state vote is counted, if a delegation of two representatives were divided where one votes aye and the other votes nay, it will lose its voice. It abstains. Whereas if we count by individuals, each of those votes gets counted on the side on which it is voted. Because of that very subtle distinction, we foster the likelihood that senators may divide. They don't vote the same way from the same state once we open the possibility of deciding certain questions without having a roll call of states to decide it.

The per capita vote was a decisive accomplishment in the Constitutional Convention. While having to agree to the compromise that we would have an equality of votes in the Senate, the nationalists insisted upon per

No. 39

capita voting, so as to weaken the influence of that state equality. Thus, Publius's defense of the Senate's contribution to eliminating unstable, mutable legislation, its ability to check the House of Representatives, and its giving expression to state sovereignty are all qualified by recognition of the fact that we do not take votes in the Senate by states as in the Confederation Congress. So, we need to get a step beyond this in order to ask whether in fact the Senate makes a distinctive contribution rather than being just a second House of Representatives that's poorly populated in terms of representing the people of the country. And we will do that by looking next at the sixty-third essay and those following.

The Senate is a part of the bicameral legislature, but more importantly than that it plays an independent role in the government designed by the Constitution. The first justification of the Senate ties it strictly to the House of Representatives. The Senate occupies a space in the legislature of a democracy where its assigned function is to introduce a pattern of deliberation; it is to check what would otherwise be the excess of democracy. The best place to examine that first half of the argument, I submit, is in the context of the claim in *Federalist Paper* ten that we cure the ills of republicanism with more republicanism. There, of course, we are dealing with the question of faction, which in its own way has to do with the instability of legislative councils and with the need for a checking operation to take place.

No. 10

Some would question whether a senate is a republican means to cure those ills. Is this an additional provision over and above the extended republic that is discussed in *Federalist Paper* ten and over and above the question of representation? Or is this a specific form of representation which may still be regarded as republican? In the sixty-second essay Publius said this special form of representation must be consistent with genuine republicanism to be part of this constitution. But that doesn't answer the final question, which is, given the differences between the Senate and the House, is there a justification for the Senate which doesn't rely solely on the question of how to provide a retarding influence relative to the democratic tendencies of the popular House of Representatives? Well, the sixty-third essay and those following essentially undertake the task of showing this broader role for the Senate and how it fits in our overall vision of how institutions are expected to work and what they're expected to accomplish.

At the very outset of the sixty-third essay, we are told that the Senate fulfills a very pressing need; namely, it supplies "the want of a due sense of national character." Now this is one of those ineffable terms that Publius so often uses. One has to stop and say, "I don't want to assume the meaning of this." What is "a due sense of national character" and who's supposed to have it in the first place? Does he mean that the Senate is

No. 63

somehow a symbol of the nation, perhaps like a flag? Or does he mean
something that is more concrete in terms of the operations of government?
 The immediate elaboration is the following:

Without a select and stable member of the government, the esteem of foreign
powers will not only be forfeited by an unenlightened and variable policy,
proceeding from the causes already mentioned; but the national councils will not
possess that sensibility to the opinion of the world, which is perhaps not less
necessary in order to merit, than it is to obtain, its respect and confidence.

 This due sense of national character is at least specified. It's not
necessary in our own eyes that we have a due sense of national character.
It's in the eyes of those with whom the nation has to deal. They must see
that it is properly a nation. And that means, I would submit, a nation that's
able to do something; it can act in the world. So, others must take it into
account when consulting their own interest. That's what it means to have
"a due sense of national character."
 We convey national character by conveying an ability to act on
information, to make decisions, and to make good on the decisions that we
make. If our councils are mutable or changeable, we convey the impression
that we're not able to act consistently. We may act, but there is no way to
predict what we will do. And we may tomorrow undo what we did
yesterday. Therefore, we don't have a due sense of national character. A
due sense of national character, therefore, conveys with it an essentially
conservative thrust. It is conservative in the sense that policies are
established and maintained for a period of time long enough to convey to
others the impression that we mean business. That seems to be what
Publius means by a due sense of national character.
 In the second paragraph he goes on:

An attention to the judgment of other nations is important to every government
for two reasons: The one is, that independently of the merits of any particular
plan or measure, it is desirable on various accounts, that it should appear to other
nations as the offspring of a wise and honorable policy: The second is that in
doubtful cases, particularly where the national councils may be warped by some
strong passion, or momentary interest, the presumed or known opinion of the
impartial world, may be the best guide that can be followed.

First, we would like to be praised by others for our wisdom and our sense
of honor. The second point is extremely important. There may be times
within our own country when opinion is sufficiently confused by passion
or interest that it is important to be able to follow the known opinion of
what he called the impartial world. But to have access to the known
opinion of the impartial world, we must be sufficiently established as a
nation to carry on ordinary intercourse with the rest of the world. For only

in the context of a sustained intercourse is such known and established opinion accessible to us.

This language is familiar to late-twentieth-century Americans, because we often hear world opinion invoked in our politics. We hear policies arraigned because they are disliked by world opinion, or recommended to us because they are recommended by world opinion. We have seen events transpire in China that have been very much discussed in terms of the reaction of world opinion. And, of course, that always raises the question, what should any government care about world opinion when it's trying to take care of its own problem? How does that enter into the calculation of whether it is right or wrong to deal harshly or gently with one's own citizens? And yet that's the very kind of thing that is being invoked by Publius at this stage. It's safe to add that it is not mere world opinion. It is not any opinion. It's the opinion of what he calls an impartial world. This standard of the impartial world must consist at a minimum of those civilizations that carry on this discourse and that establish themselves as capable of relating to others outside their own borders. That is to say, we can carry on the human discourse in terms that identify the commonality that human beings have despite their differences within national borders. That's much like the language of the Declaration of Independence that appeals to a candid world. The candid world is the world that can carry on the discourse to which the Declaration appeals, which is the discourse of natural laws and of rights and of common humanity. This discourse recognizes those things that separate us; it also recognizes the way in which we are the same.

This impartial world will establish the best guide that can be known in times of turmoil or difficulty according to Publius.

What has not America lost by her want of character with foreign nations? And how many errors and follies would she not have avoided, if the justice and propriety of her measures had in every instance been previously tried by the light in which they would probably appear to the unbiassed part of mankind?

This is an argument which has its own history. It turns up again in the farewell address of George Washington in 1796. A major contributor to it is, of course, Alexander Hamilton, whom Washington corresponded with over several months in the elaboration of the farewell.

Washington argues in that farewell address that the United States is different from other nations. Other nations are able to pursue their interests in the world by adopting what we should call Machiavellian policies. These other nations are princely nations where one person may dispose of the full power and authority of the state. There it is entirely possible to act even whimsically, so long as to act whimsically serves one's interests. One can pledge one's faith today and violate it tomorrow, because one is in a position to act deceptively to defend one's position in the world. But a nation that is moved by public opinion is unable to act so deceptively, because public opinion cannot change so swiftly. It's set in its course much like rivers. Rivers, of course, change their course but only over a long succession of time. Therefore, according to Washington, it was necessary to pursue a constant policy of justice to make consistency and predictability one's chief asset where one couldn't have recourse to Machiavellian flexibility. Well, that's the same argument that's being made here. National character includes the ability to project to those who are conversant with the terms of human equality the consistent pursuit of a just and honorable policy. That's part and parcel of what this new government must do according to Publius.

In the third paragraph of this essay, therefore, he's able to continue:

> Yet however requisite a sense of national character may be, it is evident that it can never be sufficiently possessed by a numerous and changeable body. It can only be found in a number so small, that a sensible degree of the praise and blame of public measures may be the portion of each individual; or in an assembly so durably invested with public trust, that the pride and consequence of its members may be sensibly incorporated with the reputation and prosperity of the community.

One of the things we accomplish with our Senate is to heighten their responsibility for the decisions that they make by, in effect, making the body small enough for them to be identified and to be held accountable for their decisions. We want to be able to praise and blame them for their contributions to public measures and to use that praise and blame itself as a device for fostering excellence in the pursuit of such measures. We want to identify them with the community.

Publius is trying to do, in part, what people have often thought they wished to do with the executive. The Senate is to take the role of a monarch in that the monarch expressed in his person the personhood, so to speak, of the entire country. The interest and the identity of the nation was the monarch. One of the reasons monarchs could be trusted in the British Constitution, for example, was that the monarch could not betray his country without betraying himself. So, we didn't expect the monarch to sell the country. What would he do, where would he go? That is the kind of character that is now being ascribed to the Senate. It will have to do certain things in order to merit such a character. If it were going to be on the order of a monarchy for example, then it would have to take a role independently in governing the nation. It has a continuing role in the foreign policy of the nation. Its ability to ratify treaties, its advise and consent role with the executive, and its appointment authority all would become independent powers and authorities exercised by the Senate as if it were a fourth branch of government and not simply an expression of the bicameral legislature. So, those elements of the Senate which separate the Senate from the House of Representatives, according to Publius's argument, establish an organ in the government which can in some respects come to symbolize the nation as a whole.

Publius adds in the fourth paragraph a further reflection on a defect in the government prior to the Constitution which is of some significance. The defect is "the want, in some important cases, of a due responsibility in the government to the people, arising from the frequency of elections which in other cases produces this responsibility." Publius loves paradoxes. Recall that responsibility was very much dependent upon frequency of elections. Dependence and responsibility go together. Now we hear, "frequency of elections will undermine responsibility" somehow and, he says, this appears paradoxical but it is important.

No. 63

He explains in the fifth paragraph.

Responsibility in order to be reasonable must be limited to objects within the power of the responsible party; and in order to be effectual, must relate to operations of that power, of which a ready and proper judgment can be formed by the constituents. The objects of government may be divided into two general classes; the one depending on measures which have singly an immediate and sensible operation; the other depending on a succession of well-chosen and well-connected measures, which have a gradual and perhaps unobserved operation.

There is a distinction that makes a difference. To be responsible for what everyone can perceive immediately may, it appears, be consistent with the responsibility that is intended by the frequency of elections.

Who should answer for policies that require to be matured slowly, to express long range views, and to pursue remote objectives in the interest of the community? How, with frequent elections, can we provide for such necessities? Are they not needed? This is the kind of necessity that Franklin Roosevelt, in the period leading up to World War II, complained about when he wished to intervene on the side of the allies. He could foresee the interest of the United States being affected in a material way well beyond anything that the ordinary course of elections would allow for and permit the people to ratify. What is one supposed to do in that case? Well, some people would say about the executive, "that's easy. He takes a chance. If he thinks he sees it, he acts on the basis of what he sees and he tells the people. If he persuades them, good, and if he fails, not so good."

Publius suggests that there are some cases in which we cannot simply permit the public's failure to understand the necessity to settle the case, because indeed the issue could determine the very survival of the country.

And yet it is evident, that an assembly elected for so short a term as to be unable to provide more than one or two links in a chain of measures, on which the general welfare may essentially depend, ought not to be answerable for the final result, anymore than a steward or tenant, engaged for one year, could be justly made to answer for places or improvements, which could not be accomplished in less than half a dozen years. Nor is it possible for the people to estimate the *share* of influence which their annual assemblies may respectively have on events resulting from the mixed transactions of several years.

Notice, when the public appraises the work of their representatives, they will do it with respect to their specific accomplishments and policies that have been developed on behalf of the public good. Because we cannot provide for long term objectives with an assembly that meets annually or bi-annually, we need a second body. This is a different argument for bicameralism than we've looked at before, although it is part and parcel of the defense of bicameralism.

The question of national character is not connected with the question of the legislature's power. Character is not about trying to retard that power which is otherwise awesome and terrifying. The question is how to provide the essential needs of the society. We need a legislature which can look beyond the short term. If we had a unicameral legislature according to this argument, it would have to be in office for a long time to provide this ability. We would not only have to grant it great power, but keep it in office to exercise that power long enough for people who could foresee the remote necessities affecting their society to be able to act on the basis of their insight. So we need bicameralism in order to avoid conveying all power into the hands of those who will take on this role.

In the seventh paragraph Publius says, "Thus far I have considered the circumstances which point out the necessity of a well-constructed Senate only as they relate to the representatives of the people." That's only partially true. He then goes on in the seventh paragraph:

No. 63

To a people as little blinded by prejudice, or corrupted by flattery, as those whom I address, I shall not scruple to add, that such an institution may be sometimes necessary, as a defense to the people against their own temporary errors and delusions. As the cool and the deliberate sense of the community ought in all governments, and actually will in all free governments, ultimately prevail over the views of its rulers; so there are particular moments in public affairs, when the people stimulated by some irregular passion, or some illicit advantage, or misled by the artful misrepresentations of interested men, may call for measures which they themselves will afterward be the most ready to lament and condemn. In these critical moments, how salutary will be the interference of some temperate and respectable body of citizens, in order to check the misguided career, and to suspend the blow meditated by the people against themselves, until reason, justice, and truth, can regain their authority over the public mind?

So the Senate not only obstructs the House, which expresses the peoples' will, but the people themselves. We asked at the outset, how does public opinion manifest itself in this government? It's clear that it manifests itself through the House of Representatives most forcefully. What will it do with respect to the Senate? Well, apparently the Senate exists in part to resist that opinion, or at least what he calls its "temporary errors and delusions."

Some, perhaps many, would say that it is never appropriate for the will of the majority to be resisted by anyone whatever, and the will of the people ought always to prevail. That is not the perspective of the founding. That, however, is not even the perspective of Thomas Jefferson, who in his first inaugural made the express statement echoing these words, that the will of the majority is always to prevail but, to be rightful, the will of the majority must be reasonable. Jefferson understood standards by which one would resist the will of the majority.

The Senate must give voice to the cool and deliberate sense of the community. What is the cool and deliberate sense of the community? Well, we must connect this with the thought that it will always prevail. That is, if the people demand something, which it is reasonable and right for them to demand, and demand it for a long enough time, they will get it from their representatives. Presumably, these demands will take voice first through the House of Representatives and then ultimately it will also move the Senate, which has been around long enough to see that this is a settled will and not just a passing fancy. The point, of course, is that now the deliberation, which we see that Publius meant to foster, is not merely the deliberation of the representatives. It is the deliberation of the entire community that is being fostered by these institutions.

Publius ends the seventh paragraph by asking, "What bitter anguish would not the people of Athens have often escaped, if their government had contained so provident a safeguard against the tyranny of their own passions?" We ask, how do we establish the reason of the community to prevail over the passions of the community? So the political task is to make choices among things desired as to those which conduce to the ultimate interest of the community and those which are inconsistent with it.

Publius knows there is a mammoth problem with the argument. In *Federalist Paper* ten, Publius said we were going to cure the ills of No. 10 democracy with more democracy. We're going to cure the ills of faction; we're going to cure the ills of majority tyranny with more democracy. This doesn't sound like more democracy. So, we ask at this stage, did the extended republic fail? Is that why we need to have this check in order for the cool and deliberate sense of the community to prevail? Weren't we assured that in fact there would be no unjust majorities because the whole process had been structured in the extended republic through the multiplicity of interests which works to avoid an unjust majority ever coming to the fore? So why do we need to put anything in the way of the operation of majority will in this government? The next couple of paragraphs make this clear.

Let's skip to the end of the ninth paragraph to make sure that we understand what happens in between.

> The people can never wilfully betray their own interests: But they may possibly be betrayed by the representatives of the people; and the danger will be evidently greater where the whole legislative trust is lodged in the hands of one body of men, than where the concurrence of separate and dissimilar bodies is required in every public act.

At the end, Publius rescues the people. He says they won't really be the ones who make the mistakes. The problem is that the people will have compliant representatives, who will hear some passing fancy of the people and think it's a strongly felt desire and try to realize it. The Senate serves to check representatives who disserve the people so they will not in fact betray the people.

Prior to that he had said this beginning in the eighth paragraph, "It may be suggested that a people spread over an extensive region, cannot like the crowded inhabitants of a small district, be subject to the infection of violent passions; or to the danger of combining in pursuit of unjust measures." What does he mean "it may be suggested"? It has been suggested! And we know who suggested it. He suggested it in *Federalist* ten! He goes on:

No. 10

> I am far from denying that this is a distinction of peculiar importance. I have on the contrary endeavoured in a former paper to shew that it is one of the principal recommendations of a confederated republic. At the same time this advantage ought not to be considered as superseding the use of auxiliary precautions. It may even be remarked that the same extended situation which will exempt the people of America from some of the dangers incident to lesser republics, will expose them to the inconveniency of remaining for a longer time under the influence of those misrepresentations which the combined industry of interested men may succeed in distributing among them.

No. 51

We've seen this expression, "auxiliary precautions," before in *Federalist* fifty-one. There we were outlining the operation of the institutions of separation of powers and federalism to show that these "inventions of prudence" or these "auxiliary precautions" would in fact add additional safety.

Let me put that last part in a different context. Someone once inquired whether technology hadn't altered the picture in such a way as to make the emergence of interested majorities in our own time more likely, because there's more communication and people can discover their common interests. Well, in a way Publius is answering that question, yes. And he is not waiting for the invention of the computer. He's answering the question in 1787. Let me read that last sentence again:

It may even be remarked that the same expedient, the same extended situation which will exempt the people of America from some of the dangers of lesser republics, will expose them to the inconveniency of remaining for a longer time under the influences of those misrepresentations which the combined industry of interested men may succeed in distributing among them.

It is to avert this danger—beyond the provisions of *Federalist* ten—that Publius at length concedes that he exaggerated the claim of novelty in adopting the scheme of representation (as claimed in *Federalist* fourteen). Rather, he now asserts that even the ancients—not merely modern Europeans—knew the principle of representation. The true novelty—and improvement—in the United States is the move totally to exclude the people in their collective capacity from any direct share in governing. The Senate as institution makes this possible, for it is the vessel that carries the powers and functions that would not be safely entrusted to a more popular body. Nor will it corruptly abase those powers, both because hemmed in by enormous checks and balances and because itself shaped to the mission to defend popular liberty. I described the mechanism involved in the conception of "representative liberty" in discussing *Federalist* thirty-five above. The Senate, acting without dependence on popular will, provides the final bulwark against majority faction.

Nos. 10, 14

No. 35

Publius recognizes that people think that this is a dangerous thing to do. They think the Senate may be corrupt; it may be aristocratic. They fear that when it works with the President it may become like the monarch and his counsel in Great Britain. It may develop systems of influence as a means of developing policy rather than preserving republican openness. In the twelfth paragraph, Publius urges that we can only carry jealousy so far. There comes a point at which the jealousy itself becomes what he calls a bile that turns the eye of the body politic yellow. And so we must stop short of that point where the anti-toxin itself becomes a toxin. Power must at some point be conceded and once one has arranged it to make it as safe as human possibilities afford, one then has to place one's confidence in it.

Among the things that give one confidence are those human principles that Publius educes in the final paragraph of the sixty-fourth essay.

Every consideration that can influence the human mind, such as honor, oaths, reputations, conscience, the love of country, and family affections and attachments, afford security for their fidelity. In short, as the constitution has taken the utmost care that they shall be men of talents and integrity, we have reason to be persuaded that the treaties they make will be as advantageous as all circumstances considered could be made; and so far as the fear of punishment and disgrace can

No. 64

operate, that motive to good behavior is amply afforded by the article on the subject of impeachments.

We will see that Publius believes punishment is a restraint and one must make use of it. And we will discuss this in relation to the executive presently. But there's a more powerful restraint called censure.

It is censure that he invokes when he refers to these considerations that influence the human mind, "honor, oaths, reputations, conscience, the love of country, and family affections and attachments." One is motivated, moved, through appeals to these as much as by the fear of censure and the fear of loss and indeed more so than by fear of any particular punishment in one's own person or property. It is important to remember that these fundamental elements that lead to our understanding the very existence of a community are also principles of motivation consciously to be relied upon in seeking to establish the safety of a given system. We tend to forget that in the contemporary world. We tend to think that, unless we have clearly written rules that prescribe exactly what can and can't be done with punishments attached, we can express no confidence whatever in human judgment.

Not to be able to express confidence in human judgment presupposes that we have no knowledge of what the things are that human beings in general care most about. And Publius does not take that approach. Publius says we know people love their families. People pursue honor. People are bound by their oaths. They have a sense of conscience. They do enjoy reputation.

We may say that was an eighteenth century world in which these old mores were generally accepted and, therefore, eighteenth century founders could expect them and rely upon them, but they no longer apply to us. But if we make that argument, we then incur an enormous burden to suggest what has replaced those ordinary affections and principles of motivation in the human soul. For if people are not attached to their families, if they are not bound by their oaths, if they do not love reputation and do not have a conscience, then the question must of course arise, is there any ground for community at all? Is community nothing other than coercion? Do we have no more confidence in our fellow man than what we can impose through direct physical threat? And if, of course, we arrive at the conclusion that there is no more confidence than what can be imposed by direct physical threat, do we then accept the proposition that republican government is sensible? These are the kinds of questions that we would have to answer and deal with if we rejected Publius's perspective.

The most essential elements of a civilization are always founded rather on implicit principles than express principles. We don't have written into the Constitution express recognition of the family, and I don't believe, apart from the development of the principle of propinquity, it is discussed in the *Federalist Papers,*. Why would they overlook the family in the founding? What is more important? What is more central to organized society than the family? The principle of social organization begins with families. If we didn't have families, we would question the very need for society at all. So how could they avoid to speak about that, and does that mean the family is not protected? Is there not a right to have a family? Is that something that the government can do whatever it will with? Well, of course, the answer to those questions is no. One absolutely does have a right and it is more than a right; it is an absolute necessity that one be freed to form families, and that there be certain obligations that are encountered in the process of forming families.

It is not necessary to mention families if one only makes a single concession, that, in fact, all that is done is done on the basis of and departing from the necessity of families. If we try to account for everything retrospectively, then we fall into a pattern of infinite regress and at every point it is necessary to ask, where did that come from. This is a story that is related very effectively by Aristotle. A man from Larissa is making the argument vis-à-vis someone else that his city is better. They are better citizens; they're more virtuous people. Questioned how he came to be that way, he answered, because I'm a Larissan. That is to say, my city made me that way. But then the retort is, well who made Larissans? Well, the people who made Larissans are, of course, Larissan makers. Those who came before those we are now talking about. But sooner or later we reach the end of that chain. Who makes the Larissan maker? It has to start somewhere.

The point of the story, of course, is to point out that the search for a rational point of departure is bound to be frustrated with respect to the question of human community. One starts with human nature. One does not explain human nature in the sense that one can create it or originate it. One may understand it; one may explain it demonstratively; one may explain it as an axiom as we saw in the thirty-first *Federalist Paper,* or as we see in the Declaration of Independence; but one does not explain it in the sense of an original work. It is not an original work. It is inherent. It is what makes human beings what they are. And with that human nature come certain concomitants. Concomitant to human nature is, of course, life in families. Human beings are creatures that have life in families. Families, then, are the point of departure for the organization of communities, cities, or countries. This is the perspective of Publius.

No. 31

Of course, the family is protected. How could it not be when everything else is for the purpose of family? The whole idea of nature encompasses the idea of human family. The whole distinction of gender encompasses the idea of family and relationship. That perspective has to be part and parcel of our understanding of how these institutions are unfolded and what it is they're expected to defend and protect. They're not abstract institutions; they're not there to defend whatever it is we happen to like today, which is subject to infinite or arbitrary change. The institutions are there to defend something permanent; hence we should be no less conversant with those permanent things than those who originated the original defense. The balance of the essays on the Senate make this attitude very clear to us.

No. 70   Let's discuss the executive power or the powers of the executive as those are developed in essays seventy through seventy-seven. We start with the assertion by Publius, "There is an idea, which is not without its advocates, that a vigorous executive is inconsistent with the genius of republican government."

Remember that the arguments throughout the *Federalist Papers* have taken on this character of presenting the counter-intuitive view rather than simply what is expected or assumed. We say Publius's argument is counter-intuitive at the very outset with the specific defense of Union and of republican safety in the context of aiming for political prosperity. We say that in dealing with the question of domestic violence, or faction. We have seen it in dealing with the question of the separation of powers and with the House of Representatives and the Senate. Now we see it also in dealing with the executive: what we see is not what we get.

People have thought democracy meant holding officers of government on a tight leash and enhancing the immediate authority of the people over the government. No, according to Publius. That does not produce republican safety. That produces tyranny. Republican safety is brought about in quite a different way. The seventieth essay introduces us to this rather exotic world which Publius summarizes in a single sentence, although we must cover a full eight essays to understand what it means. The sentence is in the second paragraph: "A feeble executive implies a feeble execution of the government. A feeble execution is but another phrase for a bad execution: And a government ill executed, whatever it may be in theory, must be in practice a bad government."

We might take that to be the summary definition of what Publius means by the expression, *high-toned* government; it's government that emphasizes good execution. In that sense, it's not unlike other activities in life in which an accent on grace and address goes a long way to convey why we have appreciation for people who are skillful and who do things apparently with ease that strike us as being otherwise so very difficult. We want a government that will accomplish with ease things that appear very difficult. But we don't want to purchase ease at the price of liberty. That is the fundamental relationship from Publius's perspective.

Accordingly, we enumerate four conditions for this energy or vigor in the executive. We want to accomplish vigor in the executive through unity, through duration, through the adequate provisions for its support, and through competent powers; and we want to assure safety by emphasizing responsibility and dependence. That outlines a discussion. As it turns out, however, it is not the exact outline of the discussion. We may look at essay seventy-seven, the eleventh paragraph, in order to see that the outline doesn't quite follow what is suggested:

We have now completed a survey of the structure and powers of the executive No. 77
department, which I have endeavoured to show, combines, as far as republican
principles will admit, all the requisites to energy. The remaining inquiry is: does
it also combine the requisites to safety in the republican sense—a due dependence on the people—a due responsibility? The answer to this question has been
anticipated in the investigation of its other characteristics, and is satisfactorily
deducible from these circumstances, the election of the President once in four
years by persons immediately chosen by the people for that purpose; and his
being at all times liable to impeachment, trial, dismission from office, incapacity
to serve in any other; and to the forfeiture of life and estate by subsequent
prosecution in the common course of law.

Publius means that we have somehow discovered dependence and responsibility by talking about unity and duration.

As it turns out, dependence and responsibility are the same terms as unity and duration for Publius. He started out by suggesting that first we want to enhance energy, and second we want to assure safety. It turns out in the course of the discussion that those elements that assure safety are identical to the elements which enhance energy in the executive, and they are, of course, unity and duration.

Unity is simply one executive, not two, three, or more. Why do we choose unity over plurality? We choose unity in order to accomplish, not **No. 70** merely energy, but decision, activity, secrecy, and dispatch. These are the terms that he uses in the seventh paragraph of essay seventy. These things characterize the conduct of one man more than the conduct of any number of men associated in a common enterprise: unity, decision, activity, secrecy, and dispatch. What is the essential component of those four terms? What is it that brings those four things together to characterize executive conduct? Clearly, this is the image of an executive who is not simply carrying out the orders of a legislature. There may be the need to make decisions about how to implement the laws and there may be an activity associated with the laws, and perhaps in some cases requiring secrecy and dispatch, but our executive is not just some county sheriff. Why do we focus on this one man possessing the characteristics of decision, activity, secrecy, and dispatch, unless there are areas of state interest and concern which we expect to be the exclusive concern of the executive? This is the point that Publius addresses. There will be areas in which policy will be developed. The nation will be committed to policies wholly apart from areas that will form a legislative agenda. This, of course, is most evident in dealing with foreign relations.

In the lessons from history we will find in this and succeeding essays, Publius says much about foreign relations, but there are no fewer internal concerns that will demand the same kind of address on the part of an executive. Publius does not, however, hinge his argument on historical example. In the tenth paragraph he says: "By quitting the dim light of historical research, and attaching ourselves purely to the dictates of reason and good sense, we shall discover much greater cause to reject than to approve the idea of plurality in the executive, under any modification whatever."

When we set up competitors for the chief office in a society, we organize thereby faction in the community. There will be those who will ally themselves with one party or the other, and these will become respective parties, opponents, and enemies, as their tensions increase. To avoid organizing a society into factions by the very form of the Constitution, we emphasize unity. Unity meaning one has this curious analog to it in which unity means all. The unity in the executive, which reflects the choice of one man over several to exercise the executive power, nevertheless serves the point of the expressing in the first three words of the Constitution, "We the people," where unity means all. To avoid dividing the community, we give the community a single point of focus with respect to the executive power.

One of the further reasons for building unity is illustrated in the twelfth paragraph in the seventieth essay. We will set up an internal logic that is incompatible with the public interest if we divide the executive power. People will, in fact, begin to seek to hide their own responsibility for decisions in proportion as the decisions retrospectively seem to be ill made. Further, we appeal to competition, to jealousies, and to envies, in ways that are harmful to the overall objective of advancing public policy. "Men often oppose a thing merely because they have had no agency in planning it," he says. These are considerations that are dictated, according the Publius, by good reason and good sense. These are not to be deduced from historical example; but, rather we're to consult those principles of the human soul by which we know men to be moved. We're to consult their passions and their interests, as well as their *connections,* to use the broadest possible term. We consult the things that motivate them in order to assess how the government will be conducted if it's established one way or the other.

Then in the thirteenth paragraph, he argues, "Upon the principles of a free government, inconveniences from the source just mentioned must necessarily be submitted to in the formation of the legislature." That is, all of the divisions and dangers that are created by associating a number of people in a common enterprise are inconveniences. They are not advantages. Some people have said by looking at *Federalist* ten that Publius argues that divisions by interest are good and advantageous to a society. That is not Publius's argument; Publius argues that we can't avoid them. They are, as he says here, necessary inconveniences, and therefore it is intelligent so to organize a society as to turn them to the best account. He

No. 10

does not think it's good to have people's obstinacy, vanity, and conceit constitute the very language of discourse in a policy making environment. But in a legislature, that's unavoidable for what we attempt to accomplish in a legislature can not be entrusted to the hands of one person.

The executive office is different. "In the legislature, promptitude of decision is oftener an evil than a benefit." So, the inverse is true, of course; we want promptitude of decision in an executive. We want someone who will not spend forever arriving at a conclusion about what is required. "The differences of opinion, and the jarrings of parties in that department of the government, [the legislative,] though they may sometimes obstruct salutary plans, yet often promote deliberation and circumspection, and serve to check excesses in the majority." So these things are turned to account. They are not good in themselves, but they may produce good results when properly organized. The executive raises a different question. We want to distinguish the kinds of circumstances in the executive department that enhance its serviceability from those in the legislative department which enhance the legislative departments serviceability. In the executive department, the disadvantages of dissension, he says at the end of the thirteenth paragraph, "serve to embarrass and weaken the execution" of plans or measures. "They constantly counteract those qualities in the executive, which are the most necessary ingredients in its composition, vigour and expedition, and this without any counterballancing good."

And then, of course, we always take the ultimate example, the conduct of war. Generally no one ever denies that we need to have precisely this kind of energy and vigor to conduct a war. That there are decisions that have to be made on the spot, somebody has to be in command, and that the minute we introduce any division of command, any doubt about who's in charge, we count, in fact, on the likelihood of defeat. And so people, recognizing how important victory in war is, never have any difficulty assigning these responsibilities to someone who will decide in a clear cut fashion. As we abstract, or remove from war, into other forms of policy making, we become somewhat less convicted of this necessity. So, Publius's task is indeed, to show us that it is true elsewhere besides in war. The problem with the plural executive, again brought out in the thirteenth paragraph, is that it leads to an obscuring of responsibility. Publius makes this express in the fourteenth paragraph and he adds something there that I think is important.

He says that plurality "tends to conceal faults, and destroy responsibility. Responsibility is of two kinds, to censure and to punishment. The first is the more important of the two; especially in an elective office." Now, that's rather an important statement. Remember, we're discussing unity in the executive. We said unity and responsibility become, in fact, the same thing, which makes it odd to say that one allows the executive to do what it's supposed to do and at the same time makes it safe that it should do so.

No. 70

Ultimately, we will conclude that what Publius really believes constitutes republican safety in the executive is the ability to do the job. That's what makes the executive safest of all.

Now this argument that, of the two kinds of responsibility, censure is the most important emphasizes this point. Why is censure more important than punishment? It could only be that if the objects of censure are more valued than the objects threatened by punishment. What is it that censure aims at? Censure aims foremost of course, at reputation. He says:

Man, in public trust, will much oftener act in such a manner as to render him unworthy of being any longer trusted, than in such a manner as to make him obnoxious to legal punishments. But the multiplication of the executive adds to the difficulty of detection in either case. It often becomes impossible, amidst mutual accusations, to determine on whom the blame or the punishment of a pernicious measure, or series of pernicious measures ought really to fall.

The mention of blame or punishment always suggests the inverse, praise or reward. Censure is most important because that which moves human beings most of all is the love of praise, or reward, and love of praise is higher even than the love of reward. That is to say praise is the highest reward which makes censure therefore the surest means of assuring responsibility.

In the seventeenth paragraph, he tells us censure is the surest means of assuring responsibility:

It is evident from these considerations, that the plurality of the executive tends to deprive the people of the two greatest securities they can have for the faithful exercise of any delegated power; first, the restraints of public opinion, which lose their efficacy as well on account of the division of the censure attended on bad measures among a number, as on account of the uncertainty on whom it ought to fall; and secondly, the opportunity of discovering with facility and clearness the misconduct of the persons they trust, in order either to their removal from office, or to their actual punishment, in cases which admit of it.

So, plurality deprives the people of two securities: first, the restraint of public opinion. The restraint of public opinion operates through censure; it operates by injuring reputation. Publius wants a regime in which the opportunity to acquire reputation is sufficiently secure so that the punishment of destroying reputation is an instrument of safety.

The only way that we can make the opportunity to acquire reputation sufficiently secure, is to afford power to persons who, through the exercise of that power, would win their own fame and make their reputation. Again, the argument is that unity and responsibility are one thing, not two things. What is the greatest responsibility? It is responsibility to do a job. And if we have and attract those persons to do the job who are moved by the desire to be known for doing the job well, we will then create the surest circumstances of republican safety, according to Publius's argument. This is a different argument, as he said at the outset. It is inconsistent with what people take to be the genius of republican liberty. People think ordinarily we simply cannot trust human beings, because they will be moved by venial instincts—they will be subject to corruption; we must hold them on a tight leash. Leave aside reputation. Punishment is the means of safety from that perspective. Publius, however, seems to imagine himself to have delved into regions of the human soul which are not characteristically relied upon in fashioning institutions and designing laws.

Publius is aware that what he says about the executive goes beyond what one might ordinarily say about the republican officeholder. He acknowledges in the twentieth paragraph that "every magistrate ought to be personally responsible for his behavior in office," but there are circumstances in which that is qualified. One wants to know how far to qualify it under this Constitution. Should we have an executive council for example? In the twentieth paragraph he says:

The idea of a council to the executive, which has so generally obtained in the state constitutions has been derived from that maxim of republican jealousy, which considers power as safer in the hands of a number of men than of a single man. If the maxim should be admitted to be applicable to the case, I should contend that the advantage on that side would not counterballance the numerous disadvantages on the opposite side. But I do not think the rule at all applicable to the executive power.

Publius has to persuade people of this because, after all, it is not an intuitive argument. So we look at the twenty-first and twenty-second paragraphs to see in what the persuasion will consist. Now we've had the appeal to the love of reputation. It's a powerful argument, but it's not enough. It's a dangerous argument, because people are frightened by reliance on ambitious politicians. After all, everyone knows what it means to have a Bonaparte appear. One thinks that if we appeal to the love of reputation, we will feed the egomaniacs or what in the eighteenth century were called the monomaniacs. How do we protect ourselves against them? We need a further argument and that is adduced in the twenty-first paragraph:

When power therefore is placed in the hands of so small a number of men, as to admit of their interests and views being easily combined in a common enterprise, **No. 70** by an artful leader, it becomes more liable to abuse, and more dangerous when abused, than if it be lodged in the hands of one man.

This takes the counter-intuitive argument to the summit, doesn't it? Take a small number, give them great power, and that power is more liable to abuse than the same great power put in the hands of one. How could it be? Well, the balance of that paragraph and the following paragraph make that clear. One man "from the very circumstance of his being alone, will be more narrowly watched and more readily suspected, and who cannot unite so great a mass of influence as when he is associated with others." Publius then uses the example of the decemvirs of Rome, the Ten Rulers whose oppressions were much worse than if the oppressions had been carried out by one man. He concludes the paragraph:

The extreme of these numbers is not too great for an easy combination; and from such a combination America would have more to fear, than from the ambition of any single individual. A council to a magistrate, who is himself responsible for what he does, are generally nothing better than a clog upon his good intentions; are often the instruments and accomplices of his bad, and are almost always a cloak to his faults.

He goes on to make very clear that what he is saying is that combinations are more to be dreaded than ambition. Because when people are able to organize in a combination, in a conspiracy, in which they mutually cover one another, and therefore lose any sense of personal restraint in proportion as they do not have to own up to personal responsibility, they act worse than otherwise. Combinations, factions on a small scale, are more to be dreaded than ambitions.

Conspiracies are more to be dreaded than ambitious individuals because sooner or later, ambition has to declare itself. Ambition can't be satisfied without going public and declaring itself, whereas combination thrives in secrecy and obscurity. Publius settles on unity, because unity gives both vigor and responsibility.

No. 71 Duration operates in much the same way, and that is developed in the seventy-first essay. There we find duration and dependence are one, just as unity and responsibility are one. Duration means length of term, and he says this is the second requirement for energy in the executive. He says duration "has relation to two objects: To the personal firmness of the Executive Magistrate in the employment of his constitutional powers; and to the stability of the system of administration which may have been adopted under his auspices." The trait praised here is personal firmness. Always notice the emphasis on the things that move individual souls for Publius. How will the executive be personally firm? Publius says that if we reinforce those elements of character that sustain personal strength "a man will be interested in whatever he possesses, in proportion to the firmness or precariousness of the tenure, by which he holds it." So, let him have it long enough to become valuable to him.

Publius then says, "The inference from it is, that a man acting in the capacity of Chief Magistrate under a consciousness that in a very short time, he *must* lay down his office, will be apt to feel himself too little interested in it, to hazard any material censure or perplexity, from the independent exertion of his powers, or from encountering the ill-humors, however transient, which may happen to prevail" in society or the legislature. What does he mean? He says an officeholder won't try to do anything without some reasonable assurance of time to accomplish what he tries to do. The only reason he's going to try to accomplish something is the desire to make an impression on someone. If he doesn't have time to make an impression, then he's not going to care about making an impression. If he doesn't care about making an impression, he's not going to use the powers, he's not going to exert himself, and the country will be the loser as a consequence. This very important argument is reflected in the seventy-second essay, where he talks about re-eligibility of the President.

Re-eligibility is a sub-category of duration. Duration is length of term, once we set the term we ask the question, can I renew it? So it involves duration in a sub-category. It's important because it comes out of order. No. 72 Recall the list we were given in the seventieth essay, paragraph four; we were to talk about unity, duration, adequate support, and competent power. We discussed unity and duration, but we don't discuss adequate support; instead we discuss re-eligibility. Well, it seems to me that the reason that this is out of order, so to speak, is because, for Publius, re-eligibility is a component of duration.

Essay seventy-two deals with the very question of how to appeal to particular interest in the conduct of the office, by introducing the question of re-eligibility. With re-eligibility, we introduce the possibility of indefinite tenure and the pursuit of truly great objects. We will have someone whose mind will then be shaped by an ambition suited to activities that can in fact be compatible with the public interest, if, as **No. 71** Publius assumes, the public interest requires great and detached foresight of the necessities of the public. This is why in the seventy-first essay, again, he returns to the discussion of the deliberate sense of the community No. 63 which we invoked when we previously discussed the Senate.

We saw that the Senate operates so as to give scope to the deliberate expression of the good sense of the community; so, too, does the executive if the executive is in office long enough to formulate grand projects. But that's the burden of this argument in the second paragraph of the seventy-first essay. What that means practically, when he speaks about the instances in which an executive could stand against temporary delusions of the people, is that he's in office long enough to think about winning a reputation.

Pericles is a very good example of a leader with foresight acting for his city's benefit. One is always reminded of Pericles having virtually to berate the citizens of Athens for acting in a whimsical manner rather than following the cool and deliberate advice he had given them. Pericles had established sufficient personal command through the force of his character that he could get away with that in Athens. But as soon as Pericles was gone, Athens was then on the horn of the constant dilemma of an assembly changing its mind from day to day. Within twenty-four hours, Athens voted to execute all the citizens of Mitylene, who had revolted against Athenian rule, and then voted to rescind the sentence to execute them all. The assembly would oscillate with great swings of opinion, depending on whom it listened to on any given day. This is what Publius says can be avoided. Publius believes that people in office no longer than the pleasure of the mob endures, are not free to reach beyond the pleasure of the mob.

Do we want an executive to form projects? That's one of the questions of the *Federalist Papers*. The Antifederalists say, no, we don't want an executive forming projects. We want safety. We don't need projects. But Publius says there's no such thing as a great state where statesmen do not aim to accomplish some project or where they are not, in fact, shaped by some vision or ambition. If we want to afford ambition opportunity, then we must afford a long enough tenure in office to foster it. An executive, he says in the third paragraph, "should be in a situation to dare to act his own opinion with vigor and decision." This, remember, is dependence. Moreover, how could it be that being free to act one's own opinion constitutes dependence?

We will come to dependence, but let us look at what happens by the way in the fourth paragraph, where we begin to speak of the *independence* of the departments of government.

No. 71   The tendency of the legislative authority to absorb every other, has been fully displayed and illustrated by examples, in some preceding numbers. In government purely republican, this tendency is almost irresistible. The representatives of the people, in a popular assembly, seem sometimes to fancy that they are the people themselves; and betray strong symptoms of impatience and disgust at the least sign of opposition from any other quarter; as if the exercise of its rights by either the executive or judiciary, were a breach of their privilege and an outrage to their dignity.

The executive has a weighty task: to resist this impulse of a legislative assembly which thinks it is the people themselves and therefore brooks no interference with its powers. How will that develop an expressed dependence in the executive? It seems that the executive's desire to fulfill the projects we have discussed, connected with the subject of re-eligibility, in the essay following, will be sufficient to persuade the executive to resist the legislature, when the legislature is under these false delusions.

What will foster in the executive the willingness to resist a "Bonaparte legislature?" It is the hope thereby of being approved by the people. When the executive serves to demonstrate to the legislature that it is not the people, it will be the people's gratitude which will express the executive's dependence. The executive will aim to acquire that respect and attachment from his fellow citizens. That is how he expresses his dependence upon them. It is a dependence upon their judgment and opinion.

Paragraph seven of this essay develops this idea of the executive's dependence on public opinion. Publius says:

there would always be a considerable interval, in which the prospect of annihilation would be sufficiently remote not to have an improper effect upon the conduct of a man endowed with a tolerable portion of fortitude; and in which he might reasonably promise himself, that there would be time enough, before it arrived to make the community sensible of the propriety of the measures he might incline to pursue.

The day that his term ends is so far away that he will feel a little bit free. We're going to foster discussion, conversation. He is not simply going to act; he's not simply going to form projects, but he's going to carry these projects to the people. This is what the executive is expected to do.

Publius, skipping several sentences, then says, "He might, then, hazard with safety, in proportion to the proofs he had given of his wisdom and integrity, and to the title he acquired to the respect and attachment of his fellow-citizens."

Now, I want to be emphatic. This carrying his projects to the people is not meant here in the sense that we speak today of Presidents who carry their messages to the people over the heads of Congress. It sounds the same; procedurally it may even be the same. But we talk about a very different thing today. We talk about Presidents who are frustrated and who hope by appealing to the people to persuade the Congress to adopt a course of action. That is not what Publius has in mind. Publius has in mind not frustrated executives, but active, vigorous executives pursuing a course which they expect ultimately to be justified in the court of public opinion. Our contemporary Presidents are weak, not strong, and we can discern their weakness by the very necessity they're under not to form extended projects, but to appeal from moment to moment to the people to try to get anything at all done. How we've come to be in that state is a long story which we could properly discuss in a different forum, but it is well worth noting that Presidents who are strong, do not in fact have to preach so much as our Presidents have to do today. They are Presidents who, in the original model of Washington, said very little directly to the people because they could get very much done. Those who have to say so much to the people are doing so because they can get so very little done.

In the seventy-second essay, we then continue this discussion of **No. 72** duration, in the form of talking about the re-eligibility of the executive, and we go fairly quickly to the heart of the matter in the fourth paragraph. "One ill effect of the exclusion [of an executive from re-eligibility] would be a diminution of the inducements to good behavior." Here is the dependence coming out in full blossom as it is expressed in the sixth paragraph:

An ambitious man too, when he found himself seated on the summit of his country's honors, looking forward to the time at which he must descend from the exalted eminence forever; and reflected that no exertion of merit on his part could save him from the unwelcome reverse: Such a man in such a situation, would be much more violently tempted to embrace a favorable conjuncture for attempting the prolongation of his power.

That's how Publius expresses the fear of Bonapartism. But what is it that restrains us from expecting that to happen under the Constitution?

We return to the fourth paragraph: "There are few men who would not feel much less zeal in the discharge of a duty when they were conscious that the advantages of the station with which it was connected must be relinquished at a determinate period, than when they were permitted to entertain a hope of *obtaining,* by *meriting,* a continuance of them." Remember the appeal to merit is always an appeal to reputation. Merit, to be merit, must be recognized. There is such a thing as merit in itself, abstract, unrecognized, but in a political context, when one aims to merit something, one aims to have others recognize one's merit. That is a love of reputation, about which Publius is quite frank in the fourth paragraph:

This position will not be disputed, so long as it is admitted that the desire of reward is one of the strongest incentives of human conduct, or that the best security for the fidelity of mankind is to make their interest coincide with their duty. Even the love of fame, the ruling passion of the noblest minds, which would prompt a man to plan and undertake extensive and arduous enterprises for the public benefit, requiring considerable time to mature and perfect them, if he could flatter himself with the prospect of being allowed to finish what he had begun, would on the contrary deter him from the undertaking, when he foresaw that he must quit the scene, before he could accomplish the work.

There is a summation of the whole argument. Giving the executive the chance to do something worth doing is what we're required to do to make him dependable, to make his efforts worthwhile.

"The love of fame" is "the ruling passion of the noblest minds." Publius is clear that those whom he expects to attract into the executive office, and indeed into the offices of government in general, ought to be the noblest minds. How will they be the noblest minds? Only if we are willing to give space for the operation of their love of fame.

We should put this in perspective. Alexander Hamilton in a different place has expressed a parallel notion, in which he says the love of liberty is the noblest passion of the human soul. The love of fame is not the highest love; the love of liberty is the highest love. But the love of fame is the ruling passion of the noblest minds. And what one seeks to accomplish in a republican system is to take those who are motivated by the love of fame, and subordinate that love of fame to the advance of the highest and noblest passion, which is the love of liberty. That's what the design of the executive hopes to accomplish, and we may question, subsequently, how far we expect it to succeed in that regard, as we consider the actual business of the executive: politics.

A familiar but misleading conception of American politics holds that it consists primarily in the familiar horse-trading of competing interests in society. The theory is that the interests compete so as to gain control over the instrumentalities of the state and then to use those great powers specifically to feather the interests' own nests. I think I've wrung metaphors enough from this brief description, without exhausting the possibilities, which should make clear that I speak about the view of politics sometimes called log-rolling or pork barrel, and which President Eisenhower had in mind when he warned of the "military-industrial complex."

In short, this view holds that most, if not all political conflict is but an elaborate preface to the serious work of splitting up the booty once one or another interest has prevailed.

This view accounts for the further common opinion that politicians—practitioners of the art of politics—are uniformly dishonest. For it is generally reasoned that they subordinate every consideration—including integrity—to the goal of acquisition.

Something like this is the understanding the Riverside, California barber had in mind, when he wrote to H. L. Mencken to complain of the satire in which Mencken likened politicians to barbers and bartenders for their lying. The Riverside barber retorted, "I know *some* honest barbers."

This interest theory of politics is not merely a common view. Sophisticated and highly elaborate academic and philosophical arguments have been produced to demonstrate it. Marxism is only the most obvious of these. But I will stick to the American context for now.

Further, these arguments—with which we are all familiar—insist that the deliberative process—the process whereby binding rules or laws are produced—is precisely the arena in which the interests fight it out, and thus the heart of our political life. I believe that the view of politics as consisting of interested competitions is entirely incorrect and in fact inverts the understanding of the framers, at least as expressed in the *Federalist Papers*.

The description of the deliberative process offered in the eighth paragraph of *Federalist* seventy-three makes clear the distance between Publius and latter day historians:

No. 73 The oftener a measure is brought under examination, the greater the diversity in the situations of those who are to examine it, the less must be the danger of those errors which flow from want of due deliberation, or of those missteps which proceed from contagion of some common passion or interest.

Nos.
49, 63,
71, 73
This process, that is called deadlock by some, is defended by Publius in essay forty-nine as allowing the reason—the deliberate sense (essays sixty-three and seventy-one)—and not the passions of the public to prevail. Or, as he went on to add in the seventy-third essay, "the power of preventing bad laws includes that of preventing good ones. . . . The injury which may possibly be done by defeating a few good laws [deadlock!] will be amply compensated by the advantage of preventing a number of bad ones."

Of greatest interest, no doubt, is the fact that the process for "preventing bad laws" by no means relies exclusively on the filtered deliberative process and, more importantly, the prospect for generating good laws, certainly does not. The key to understanding this is found in those essays in which Publius defends primarily the constitution of the executive, but also those touching upon the Senate. Indeed, the much defended and valued unity of the executive acquires a characterization, in the fifth paragraph of *Federalist* seventy-six, that shows it to be quite the opposite of the legislative chambers:

No. 76 A single well directed man by a single understanding, cannot be distracted and warped by that diversity of views, feelings and interests, which frequently distract and warp the resolutions of a collective body.[*] . . . Hence, in every exercise of the power of appointing to offices by an assembly of men, we must expect to see a full display of all the private and party likings and dislikes, partialities and antipathies, attachments and animosities, which are felt by those who compose the assembly. [*In Cooke ed.; omitted in Rossiter ed.]

The framers, of course, never designed for the Congress any substantial appointing power, but rather relied upon the "sole and undivided responsibility of one man." Thus, the deliberative process ought not to be understood as determining the characteristic exercise of this power. There are other powers of like nature, reminding us of the need to distinguish those powers subject to the deliberative process from those that are not, in order to judge properly whether the system is designed for deadlock or, alternatively, efficient politics.

In the third paragraph of essay seventy-six Publius makes clear that the extended republic, whatever problems it brings, does not in itself create the problem of party, because it is virtually impossible for the people to receive "that systematic spirit of cabal and intrigue" needed to regulate their movements in such a case. That phenomenon applies more specifically to an assembly or body of men, not to the people generally. Thus, in pursuing the questions of the unity, duration, and powers of the executive, Publius is at pains to distinguish that office from the legislative function. The distinction he developed, at length, was one that leads us to conclude that politics, properly speaking, is largely concentrated in the hands of the executive.

In essay seventy-one Publius insisted that an executive must be independent of the legislature, even if he were complaisant before the people. The separation of powers exists more specifically to accomplish this independence than for any other reason. For the "republican principle demands, that the deliberate sense of the community should govern the conduct" of representatives. The executive, no less than members of the Senate (essay sixty-three), is expected to realize this deliberate sense by providing opportunity for "cool and sedate reflection." Still, it is not merely the qualified veto, and the executive's participation in legislation, that distinguish him. In those he contributes to deliberation not much differently than does the Senate. In essay seventy-one, paragraphs two and three, what truly distinguishes the president from those officers is that he has been provided means to "serve [the people] at the peril of their displeasure," like Pericles leading the Athenians sometimes against their inclinations. The executive, unlike the Senate, is "in a situation to dare to act his own opinion with vigor and decision." The consequence of this design is that, in America, politics is the drama of executive energy and agency, advancing a settled view about the conditions of political prosperity and happiness, and on a human scale at that. No. 71 No. 63

To see why these consequences flow from the design of the executive office, as well as to discover why the design demonstrates a view of politics as independent of interested competition, one needs to pay patient attention to Publius's discussion of the executive as an agent. One aspect of that discussion is Publius's emphasis on the "administration" of the government, which shall fall to the executive. It is far from accident that Americans speak characteristically about their respective administrations, such as the "Reagan Administration," while peoples elsewhere speak more characteristically about their "cabinets," "regimes," "governments," "secretariats," etc. Nowhere else is the term "administration" so characteristically used as here in the United States, and no other term is given so precise and extended emphasis in the pages of the *Federalist*.

In defending the union of the Senate with the President in the forming of treaties, Publius, in *Federalist* sixty-four, introduced in justification a conception other than the expected safety (which he addresses in essay seventy-five). Going beyond the exceptional qualifications of the men who would make such decisions (which he had already introduced in essay two), he referred in the fifth paragraph to the importance "in national affairs" of "system in the conduct of any business." The aim, he reasoned, was to allow for the "attainment of those great objects which require to be steadily contemplated in all their relations and circumstances. . . ." Nos. 2, 64, 75

Accordingly, the national purpose demanded not only "able and honest men" but also those "perfectly acquainted with our national concerns" and able "to form and introduce a system for the management of them."[4]

System, then, is the key, every bit as much as the "energy, secrecy, and dispatch" that otherwise characterize defenses of the Senate in essay sixty-four, and the executive in essay seventy-five. Indeed, by the conclusion of the defense in essay seventy-five, Publius acknowledged for the first time throughout these essays that he was aware of the effect of *per capita* voting in the Senate, which attenuates the federal aspect of the constitution of the Senate. The system that is urged, therefore, will be less a consequence of the relative interests of the different regions or different interests than the emergence of a "national character" in such a way that "the good of the whole [will] be more and more an object of attention." A system of management aiming at the public good—that is the key to understanding the term "administration" in the *Federalist Papers*.

Nos.
64, 75

In the eighth paragraph of essay sixty-eight, which properly begins the defense of the constitution of the executive, Publius praises the electoral device that minimized the intrusion of interest and influence in the selection of a "magistrate who was to have so important an agency in the administration of the government . . ." And respecting that administration, he added this:

No. 68

And this will be thought no inconsiderable recommendation of the constitution, by those, who are able to estimate the share, which the executive in every government must necessarily have in its good or ill administration. Though we cannot acquiesce in the political heresy of the poet who says:

"For forms of government let fools contest—
That which is best administered is best,"—

yet we may safely pronounce, that *the true test of a good government is its aptitude and tendency to produce a good administration.* [emphasis added]

As among the forms, democracy, monarchy, oligarchy, it remains the conviction that democracy is superior. But Publius has added the caveat—which was already spelled out in *Federalist* ten—that even good forms of government depend upon good administration for their success. How important is this reflection?

No. 10

As if to avert misconstruction, Publius took the extraordinary step of quoting himself in the second paragraph of *Federalist* seventy-six, where the conclusion of the argument from essay sixty-eight is repeated, in quotation marks:

No. 76

It has been observed in a former paper, "that the true test of a good government is its aptitude and tendency to produce a good administration."

At no other time throughout the eighty-five essays is Publius thus particular. While he constantly references other essays, and frequently paraphrases previous statements (most famously in essay forty-nine's "legitimate fountain of power" reference to essay twenty-two's "fountain of all legitimate authority," which recurs in fifty-one's "same fountain of authority"), he does not otherwise quote himself. Accordingly, we are justly minded to pay due heed to the present expression. This quotation in essay seventy-six occurs in the context, then, of the argument we have already noted, namely, that unity in the executive supports the idea of a single man, above party, moved by a single understanding. It bears further remark that Publius goes on in essay seventy-six to say in the fifth paragraph that one expects from the President a "livelier sense of duty and a more exact regard to reputation."[5]

Nos. 22, 49, 51

It is, then, chiefly these latter virtues which were in fact developed in the essays intervening between sixty-eight and seventy-six. In essay sixty-nine it is observed that the absence of due responsibility in the government of Britain produced an executive of great power but one who had to rely upon "substituting influence to authority" in order to govern effectively. Ultimately, of course, the pursuit of this option led to the complete cannibalization of the executive by the legislative body in England, absorbing administration into the deliberative process. The comparison between the monarch and the president produces the nominal conclusion of a weaker executive in the president. In reality, however, it is rather the monarch who in the end loses by the comparison, for he loses the opportunity to form a system of administration within his single hands.

Nos. 68–76

To strengthen this conclusion, Publius opened essay seventy by refuting the presumption that "a vigorous executive is inconsistent with the genius of republican government." Indeed, he insisted, "energy in the executive" defines "good government." What is relevant at this point is that the executive's strength is defended for its contribution to the community, and not for its relative role in the balance of forces between or among the branches of government. There is an independent and intrinsic value to be achieved from a "vigorous executive."

No. 70

It is essential to the protection of the community against foreign attacks: It is not less essential to the steady administration of the laws, to the protection of property against those irregular and high handed combinations, which sometimes interrupt the ordinary course of justice, to the security of liberty against the enterprises and assaults of ambition, of faction and of anarchy.

Accordingly, over and above the multiplicity of interests in the extended republic, and in addition to the auxiliary balances and checks provided in company with the separation of powers, the executive must provide additional guarantees for the attainment of the public good. In the second paragraph he says, "A feeble executive implies a feeble execution of the government. A feeble execution is but another phrase for a bad execution: And a government ill executed, whatever it may be in theory, must be in practice a bad government."

No. 70

We see in this formulation the negative statement of the highlighted quotation above. This negative statement is the prelude to a detailed examination of the leading elements of executive power, energy, and safety, analyzed in terms of their components, unity, duration, adequate support, and competent powers, on the one hand, and dependence and responsibility on the other. In the course of the analysis, we distinguish in the fifth paragraph the executive, who has energy, from the legislature, that is "best adapted to deliberation and wisdom." Now, unity in the executive is favored for several reasons, but above all for avoiding what he calls in the tenth paragraph the "danger of difference of opinion." Such developments are expected of legislatures, where, besides, "promptitude of decision is oftener an evil than a benefit."

A further consequence of unity in the executive is absolute and unambiguous responsibility, respecting the administration of the government. Thus, a President's responsibility is exactly opposite to that of a legislator, being heightened in proportion as his term is lengthened because his authority is unique. The executive's performance will be the object of general appraisal and the subject of continued reflection.

Unlike the British monarch, who is unaccountable in his administration ("the king can do no wrong"), such an executive will then, through his very own and very personal perils, constitute the focus of politics properly so-called—i.e., a systematic pursuit of a common good. For this reason, in opening essay seventy-one Publius urges "personal firmness" in the executive and "the stability of the system of administration" adopted at his command.

No. 71

a man acting in the capacity of Chief Magistrate, under a consciousness, that in a very short time he *must* lay down his office, will be apt to feel himself too little interested in it, to hazard any material censure or perplexity, from the independent exertion of his powers, or from encountering the ill-humors, however transient, which may happen to prevail either in a considerable part of the society itself, or even in a predominant faction in the legislative body.

It is to avoid a "feeble execution" of the laws that Publius urges an executive eligible for re-election and constituted so as to set the agenda for the society. That characteristic results not from evolution, but from the settled design at the founding. Nor does the executive set the agenda in the merely abstract sense that, it being set, then politics begins in the effort to tear it apart, or, as it was said recently of a certain President's budget proposals to Congress, they were "dead on arrival" in the face of interest politics. We see in the next paragraph that Publius rather designed to make the political discussion properly turn on systematic directions imparted by the executive, which themselves would address the

. . . purposes for which government was instituted, . . . the true means by which the public happiness may be promoted. The republican principle demands, that the deliberate sense of the community should govern the conduct of those to whom they entrust the management of their affairs; but it does not require an unqualified complaisance to every sudden breeze of passion, or to every transient impulse which the people may receive from the arts of men, who flatter their prejudices to betray their interests. It is a just observation, that the people commonly *intend* the PUBLIC GOOD. This often applies to their very errors. But their good sense would despise the adulator, who should pretend that they always *reason right* about the *means* of promoting it.

It would be a mistake to conclude from this analysis that the chief focus of Publius's concern is an executive acting so as to save the people from themselves. He aims rather at the systematic pursuit of the public good, and contemplates resisting the people only insofar as their inclinations depart from the public good. The "administration" question, then, is primarily a question about the systematic pursuit of the public good.

The seventy-second essay opens with a broad declaration:

The ADMINISTRATION of government, in its largest sense, comprehends all the operations of the body politic, whether legislative, executive or judiciary, but in its most usual and perhaps in its most precise signification, it is limited to executive details, and falls peculiarly within the province of the executive department.

No. 72

In this essay Publius develops a complete view of the conception of the Administration, covering all of its activities from the most mundane to the most elevated. Here, also, in the fourth paragraph Publius introduces the chief inducement to good behavior in the executive, namely, the love of fame, "the ruling passion of the noblest minds." The correct estimate of the operation of these principles and passions is one that inclines the office-holder to seek "the positive merit of doing good." The "settled administration" that results places the "system" or project of the executive in the central position vis-à-vis the politics of this regime.

That central position is identified in essay seventy-three, while defending the qualified veto in the sixth paragraph, as guarding "the community against the effects of faction." In the eighth paragraph Publius says the propriety of the veto "does not turn upon the supposition of superior wisdom or virtue in the executive." After acknowledging the primary reason that he needs to be able to defend himself, "the secondary one is to increase the chances in favor of the community. . . ." Now, we

No. 73

Nos.
71, 73

saw in essays seventy-one and seventy-three the tendency towards faction in the legislature is, in some measure, closely connected with the legislative tendency to absorb all the powers of the government. It is not possible to protect against the evil of faction in the legislature without at the same time mitigating the evil of legislative aggrandizement. Nor is it possible to mitigate the evil of legislative absorption of all powers without at the same time displacing from the legislature to elsewhere the power to define the public good. The combination of frequent change in the legislature, plus the effect of interest, operates precisely to undermine any serious defining of the public good through the legislature[6]. That same effect operates most powerfully to secure to an independent and energetic executive all the opportunity he requires to define the public good, which is, in any regime and not just in the American, the heart of all politics.

Turning from the splendor of the executive, we must finally discuss it as a coordinate branch of government. The Constitution itself says pitifully little about the powers of the President. It says expressly that the President will make appointments to offices; it instructs the President to report from time to time on the State of the Union, and to recommend such courses of action as he thinks appropriate to the Congress; and it of course assigns the President a veto power. Beyond those few simply outlined expressions of power, there are very few things at all that can be regarded as deliberately defining the power of the President in the Constitution.

One consequence of that is the need to recognize that there is more to an understanding of the executive power (and Publius is trying to make this clear) than simply the schematic outline of those powers in the Constitution. At the end of the first paragraph in the seventy-fourth essay, Publius makes the observation that "the power of directing and employing the common strength [of a nation] forms a usual and essential part in the definition of the executive authority." So we were justified to look at principles of executive authority to help explain the executive over and above the express enumeration of the powers of the executive. Yet, this expectation of a broad construction of executive power is not meant to be an open-ended grant of power but to be the expression of a natural consequence of political organization itself. Publius, therefore, still needed to distinguish the executive from the legislature.

The fourth paragraph of essay seventy-four is rather a long discussion of the power of pardoning and its relationship to treason and how an executive might use this power. He then makes the following observation:

The dilatory process of convening the Legislature, or one of its branches, for the purpose of obtaining its sanction to the measure, would frequently be the occasion of letting slip the golden opportunity. The loss of a week, a day, an hour, may sometimes be fatal. If it should be observed that a discretionary power with a view to such contingencies might be occasionally conferred upon the

No. 74

President; it may be answered in the first place, that it is questionable; whether, in a limited constitution, that power could be delegated by law.

This means that Congress doesn't have the power to assign powers to the President or anyone else. If all the powers assigned under the Constitution are expressly assigned already, Congress can't create new powers by acts of Congress. Powers are assigned by the Constitution. What it means to have a limited Constitution is to say that the government can exercise no power other than those granted, and that not even the legislature under that government can create new powers. But there is nevertheless an understanding of power associated with the powers actually granted and requiring to be exercised, and that covers most of the executive power. That explains why Publius thinks the pardoning power, even if it had not been expressly given, would nevertheless be a necessary adjunct to executive power.

This view of limited government further explains why it is Publius makes the argument that he made in the twenty-third *Federalist Paper* about the unlimited quality of the powers that are granted. We convey the power in an unlimited fashion because there's no way in advance to shape the quantum of power needed for the purpose aimed at by granting the power in the first place. That unlimited quantum of power not only entails what Congress may do, but all of those executive actions that are needed to make good on the specific powers that have been assigned under a limited Constitution.

No. 23

In the list of the elements of executive energy, we had in the third place the question of an adequate provision for its support with which Publius opened the seventy-third *Federalist*. It is interesting to observe that that means nothing more than that Congress shall provide at the outset of an administration compensation for the executive and shall not increase nor diminish it during the period for which he was elected. This seems so ordinary, so routine for us; but of course, one of the expectations in 1787, would have been that if we want to control an executive, we control the purse strings. If he gets out of line, we cut his money off; and it works as a motivation, as an incentive. Publius has rejected these attempts at safety, preferring to rely instead on what we previously discussed as the love of reputation as the first line of defense and, of course, punishment as a second line of defense. Publius rejects the forms of control which have the direct effect of interfering with the operation of government itself.

No. 73

Of the ordinary powers the most significant is the veto, or the qualified negative on acts of legislation. Publius mentions this in the sixth paragraph saying: "It establishes a salutary check upon the legislative body calculated to guard the community against the effects of faction, precipitancy, or of any impulse unfriendly to the public good, which may happen to influence a majority of that body." He recurs to this in the thirteenth paragraph when he argues, "But the convention have pursued a mean in this business; which will both facilitate the exercise of power vested in this respect in the executive magistrate, and make its efficacy to depend on the sense of a considerable part of the legislative body." And in the passages that then follow, we get an elaborate discussion of how a veto is announced and the opportunity will be afforded the legislature to override the veto through the vote of at least two-thirds of both houses of the legislative body.

The executive is in this respect a part of the legislature. We may calculate how the process works, exactly what part of it he is. He is effectively one-sixth of the whole legislature; for what it takes to override his veto is one-sixth of each of the possible decision making entities in the process. A bill can be passed by fifty percent, or three-sixths, plus one of each house. With a veto, it takes four-sixths. The difference of one-sixth then equals and exceeds the weight of his veto. As an exercise of the legislative power, this is only indirectly an expression of the executive power, particularly the executive power understood as "directing and employing the common strength" of the nation.

Publius did not try to isolate the different branches of the government but to mix them up in order to make them work together. Many people have questioned the existence of the negative in the hands of the executive alone, thinking it too great a power. Some suggested associating the judges with it to give the advantage of broad legal education and constitutional principle to the executive's decision. Publius resists this just as he resisted earlier a council for the executive. He argues that we shouldn't associate the judges in the veto process, because they will then become implicated in that decision prior to doing their own job, which is to expound the laws. Here, then, strict separation works. I emphasize that, because we have seen Publius consistently argue how far to bring the branches together to make them work rather than to be sure they remain separate. But we are somewhat more reluctant to mix them, when we are talking about associating the judges with the legislature or with the executive.

There are additional presidential powers that associate the President with the Senate. One of the reasons that we could never complete a discussion of the Senate on its own terms is because the Senate requires to be understood in its relationship to the executive. The veto relates the executive to the whole legislature, the House and the Senate, which is why we count the President as one-sixth of that unity, or field of action. The appointment power and treaty making power associate the President exclusively with the Senate and therefore raise questions about the character of that presidential or executive authority in that context.

The fourth paragraph of the seventy-fifth essay, develops the relationship between the President and the Senate with respect to the power of shaping treaties. Publius says:

No. 75

To have entrusted the power of making treaties to the senate alone, would have been to relinquish the benefits of the constitutional agency of the president, in the conduct of foreign negotiations. It is true, that the senate would in that case have the option of employing him in this capacity; but they would also have the option of letting it alone; and pique or cabal might induce the latter rather than the former. Besides this, this ministerial servant of the senate could not be expected to enjoy the confidence and respect of foreign powers in the same degree with the constitutional representative of the nation; and of course would not be able to act with an equal degree of weight or efficacy.

What's at stake in the association of the President and the Senate in the treaty-making power, and to a lesser degree in the appointing power, is the question of whether the President represents the nation as a constitutional officer or as a servant of the Senate. Publius chose not to make the President a servant of the Senate; therefore, it became necessary to separate them in the conduct of this shared power. They nevertheless had to have constitutionally distinct and separate roles in the exercise of this power, which accounts for requiring the President to present a treaty for ratification and not for requiring the Senate to negotiate a treaty.

It's also the case that the members of the Senate do not vote by States, whether in treaty-making, or appointments, or otherwise; they vote as individuals. And this turns out to be one of the more important aspects of the Constitution. This is brought out in the seventh paragraph of the seventy-fifth essay where he says they vote as individuals. The language in the Constitution itself is artful, but deliberate. It says: "Each Senator shall have one vote." That's how they expressed what was called in the constitutional convention the per capita vote rule. Interestingly, this was not mentioned in the essays that discussed the Senate itself. It is brought out in the essay which discusses the power of the executive; it was not mentioned in the thirty-ninth essay which raised the federal versus national question. The per capita voting was not mentioned in the context of the federal versus national question because it makes the Senate a less federal and more national body; it also makes the Senate more amenable to executive persuasion. Where Senators vote as individuals they may be listening to the voices of their states, but they may listen to other voices as well. In particular, as the dignity of the office of President is increased, the President's ability to persuade individual senators to pursue what he regards as the public interest, is correlatively increased. *No. 39*

In the seventy-sixth essay, similar observations in the case of appointments bring out the distinctions regarding the general character of republicanism, particularly in the extended republic. Within the legislative body parties will form quite naturally. One of the tasks of an executive will be so to manage parties in the executive branch as to make the results of legislation consistent with the objectives of an executive agenda. There- *No. 76*

fore, when we look at the appointment process, part of what we're seeing
is how far the executive and the Senate can coordinate their objectives.
How far can the politics of the process be made a part of the project of
pursuing the public interest? Publius is optimistic on that score, and of
course we observe that it does tend to be the case that in these kinds of
decisions it is next to impossible for a President merely to follow whims
and personal connections and equally impossible for the Senate merely to
pursue parochial interests. So the consequence of associating the two in the
act of appointing to offices is to force all to introduce standards of merit in
the process, as mutual checks upon one another.

    The general discussion of the power of the President in appointments
led Publius to make projections about how the power will be exercised, and
what the future is. In one of these projections Publius makes what is,

No. 74   retrospectively, a mistake. It's a mistake in terms of the history of the
Constitution that subsequently evolved but it is a highly informative
mistake that introduces us to the final question in this series of discussions,
namely, the question of constitutional construction. We saw a preliminary
glimpse of this problem at the end of the seventy-fourth essay when we
talked about the inability of Congress to assign or create new powers under
a limited Constitution. That suggests how the Constitution ought to be
construed. If we turn to the seventy-seventh essay, at the very beginning,
we see something similar and very relevant for our purposes.

No. 77   The association of the executive and the Senate in appointing officers
will produce what Publius calls stability in the administration of the
government. Remember, we've emphasized the term *administration*. One
of the reasons we talk of "the administration" traces itself back to this
emphasis on the administration of the government as having a certain tone
or character, which distinguishes itself in terms of its ultimate projects.
Because we want stability in the administration, we associate the Senate
with the executive in making appointments.

    The question of stability leads Publius to a conclusion, namely, that the
consent of the Senate would be as necessary to displace as to appoint.
Publius expected that the advise and consent role in appointing to the
Senate would also establish that someone couldn't be removed from office
without the advice and consent of the Senate. Now we know that is not the
way the system evolved. In fact, the question was raised immediately in
1789 in the first Congress, when the cabinet offices were being created.
James Madison led a discussion which affirmed that it was the President's
exclusive discretion to remove officers from government, and not the right
of the Senate, certainly not singly, nor the right of the legislature acting
together. Look at what Publius says about it in the first paragraph of the
seventy-seventh essay:

A change of the chief magistrate therefore would not occasion so violent or so general a revolution in the officers of the government, as might be expected if he were the sole disposer of offices. Where a man in any station had given satisfactory evidence of his fitness for it, a new president would be restrained from attempting a change, in favour of a person more agreeable to him by the apprehension that a discountenance of the senate might frustrate the attempt, and bring some degree of discredit upon himself.

Thus one President goes out of office, not the administration. That's the first thing we observe. All kinds of people, including cabinet officers, are still there, and may be subsequently replaced upon the nomination of new officers but will require the advice and consent of the Senate before they are out of office. We have built in a pattern of continuity or stability, as he puts it, that otherwise might not exist. Publius foresaw a government organized under the Constitution with a built-in form of Civil Service that could have been accomplished by construction.

The idea of construction of the Constitution takes us back to the fifty-first *Federalist Paper* and those which preceded it. Construction involves the same question of discussing dependence and responsibility by discussing the powers of the presidency, by discussing the things which make the presidency vigorous and energetic. We said earlier in essays forty-seven and fifty-one that we have constructed a system in which the real battle will be over who gets to do what, more than what gets to be done. We want the differing office holders, and the differing branches, when they have constitutional struggles, to struggle over the interpretation of their office, of the space they have been afforded to move in. That's what we want them to fight about. We want the Senate and the executive to compete over who gets to do what in the appointment process; we want the House and the Senate to compete over who gets to do what in the legislative process; we want the executive and whole Congress to compete over who gets to do what in the legislative process; and through these competitions over the ambit of their authority, we will over time breathe life into the constitutional arrangement.

No. 51

To have these kinds of constitutional checks, which operate in this dynamic fashion to insure public security, we must have some way to resolve constitutional difficulties. The questions are going to arise because they are being designed to arise. Reconsider the argument of the congressional inability to create new powers, because this is a limited Constitution. We could think, for example, about this in the context of the important case *McCulloch v. Maryland*, where the Court decided on the legitimacy of the second Bank of the United States. The Court relied upon the 1791 essay by Alexander Hamilton defending the first Bank of the United States. The "necessary and proper" clause was interpreted to extend to the federal government the power to incorporate a bank. If it's true, as Publius says, that new powers cannot be created, then the construction in *McCulloch v. Maryland* says not that there is a power we didn't know existed, a discretionary power, but rather that this power is indeed necessary. One of the conditions of interpretations must be first, to discover necessary powers, and then, second, to discover who has title to exercise those powers. The real constitutional questions in that light ought to be battles over who has title to exercise the power, more than what the power is.

Now permit me to digress momentarily to say that I am speaking in an antiquarian fashion by speaking about the Constitution as it was designed, and as it might have been. But the Constitution with the Bill of Rights and the post-war amendments, the thirteenth, fourteenth, and fifteenth, added to it, changes very much of that, such that our constitutional battles at least in the twentieth century have had very little to do with who has title to do what, and very much to do with what personal guarantees there are in the Constitution. That was not Publius's objective. And one of the criticisms that one might make of developments since the drafting of the original constitution is that we deflected the Constitution from its intended mission. Today the chief subject of debate is the very questions on which, from Publius's perspective, we ought to have had a consensus that structured our approach to the battles over who has title to do what. Instead the consensus itself became an open question, by raising the question of up and down votes on the things that are most fundamental in our common life.

In any case, constitutional construction is at the heart of Publius's project. It may not be the construction we know today, but it was absolutely necessary. Therefore we cannot escape discussing the judiciary, and discussing the role it must play in the project of constitutional construction. I emphasize this because many people argue that *judicial review* is the entirety of constitutional construction in the decisive sense, and that judicial review was not a part of the Constitution but was an invention of judicial statesmanship at the hands of John Marshall, who, in effect, came to the rescue of the radically defective Constitution because the Constitution was without judicial review.

Publius says that we do not wish to associate the executive with the judges in the exercising of the veto power because they have to be "interpreters of the law" already. By "interpreters of the law" he means those who expound the Constitution. We also find numerous references in the Constitutional Convention to the expectation that the power of judicial review will be exercised. The most emphatic reference we find in the historical context occurs in a 1787 letter by James Madison. In the letter, Madison responds to Thomas Jefferson's draft of a constitution for the state of Virginia, and he characterizes the various provisions of that draft in terms of what he expects the consequences to be. Regarding Jefferson's provisions for constitutional review through periodic resort to conventions, for provisions to guide the judiciary and confine the judiciary to laws, and for settling conflicts between branches of government or conflicts over the meanings of the constitution through additional devices, Madison says that they were all very cumbersome and unnecessary. It would be much more elegant, he said, to adopt the expedient which we have just adopted in the federal constitution, creating an independent judiciary that will have the responsibility to review the constitutionality of laws. That is the clearest statement and expression we have that the Constitution was understood to entail judicial review by those who played prominent roles in its construction.

We find judicial review also in the Brutus essays. Brutus fears it and thinks it not a very good idea. We also find judicial review in *Federalist* seventy-eight, in the essay on the judicial powers and the responsibilities of the judicial branch. In that seventy-eighth essay, Publius introduces the discussion of the judiciary as particularly applicable to the category on his outline which deals with the question of the defects of the existing confederation. One of its chief defects was the lack of a federal judiciary adequate to the task of enforcing federal laws. But that could lead us to think of enforcing federal laws in the ordinary sense, namely, seeing to it that taxes are properly collected, and that people are properly processed when they fail to pay their taxes, seeing to it that crimes are prosecuted, etc. It is not a necessity of a judicial institution to practice judicial review.

No. 78

The assertion in seventeenth-century England by Sir Edward Coke of something that looks like judicial review is in fact an extremely qualified and limited version of what we ultimately develop. Coke recognized himself that his asserted right to review the constitutionality of either orders of the Monarch or laws of Parliament was subject to revision, ultimately by the Parliament itself. This makes it, of course, not judicial review in the full and proper sense, namely that the court on its own, and not subject to being overridden by any other branch of the government, can refuse to enforce acts which it deems to be inconsistent with the superior law of the Constitution. The discussion in the seventy-eighth essay provides the reasons whereby we arrive at that kind of decision.

The judiciary, like the House, the Senate, and the Executive, is presented to us with a first focus on the most important question in any constitution. We know by now what that question is; it's the question of the suffrage and the object of choice. Who can choose and who can be chosen. In every constitution, those are the most important questions. Just as we opened the other articles by focusing on that, we open this article by focusing on it. We know that those who are to do the choosing are the executive in association with the Senate, and we know that those who are to be chosen are not specified in the Constitution. But we will see, in fact, that for Publius, there is an expectation even where there is not a specification. Let's open in the sixth paragraph:

According to the plan of the convention, all judges who may be appointed by the United States are to hold their offices *during good behavior,* which is conformable to the most approved of the State constitutions; and among the rest, to that of this state [New York]. Its propriety having been drawn into question by the adversaries of that plan, is no light symptom of the rage for objection which disorders their imaginations and judgments. The standard of good behaviour for the continuance in office of the judicial magistracy is certainly one of the most valuable of the modern improvements in the practice of government. In a monarchy it is an excellent barrier to the despotism of the prince: In a republic it is a no less excellent barrier to the encroachments and oppressions of the representative body. And it is the best expedient which can be devised in any government, to secure a steady, upright and impartial administration of the laws.

Publius said earlier that one of our great problems is to prevent the legislature from thinking of itself as the people, and we will use the executive to check them in that regard. Now we see that we also use the Court for that purpose. Publius writes in the seventh paragraph:

Whoever attentively considers the different departments of power must perceive, that in a government in which they are separated from each other, the judiciary, from the nature of its functions, will always be the least dangerous to the political rights of the constitution; because it will be least in a capacity to annoy or injure them.

So we have a problem of construction. We have set up trials or competitions of judicial construction. We will use the courts to approach this problem. We begin to use the Court partly because it is somehow least in the capacity to annoy or injure the rights of the community. That is, the judicial branch of government which will use this power of construction is least harmful to the rights of the community. This also reveals that they have a specific function to perform and it turns out in this essay that we can't find out who they are going to be in terms of their character until we know something more about their function.

The judiciary is contrasted here immediately with the executive and the legislative branches:

The executive not only dispenses the honors, but holds the sword of the community. The legislature not only commands the purse, but prescribes the rules by which the duties and rights of every citizen are to be regulated. The judiciary on the contrary has no influence over either the sword or the purse, no direction of either the strength or of the wealth of the society, and can take no active resolution whatever. It may truly be said to have neither FORCE nor WILL, but merely judgment; and must ultimately depend upon the aid of the executive arm even for the efficacy of its judgments.

So the judiciary has a very special characteristic. It is not able to initiate anything. It cannot therefore pose an immediate threat to any rights. It is passive, according to this account. It lacks force and will.

Force and will are two interesting words. If the judiciary lacks force and will, who possesses force and will? Well, will is a distinctive characteristic of the legislature; force is a distinctive characteristic of the executive. We are going to have three things because we have in addition a judiciary. I think it is obvious at this point that the third characteristic is judgment. The government has force, will, and judgment. These are the terms that characterize the constitutional relations; these are the ways in which we want to understand the functions and operations of the office holders in the respective branches.

Taking judgment as that which will characterize the judiciary, we wish, then, to inquire, who are the people who are best qualified to exercise judgment and why was this decision made in this way?

Let's look more closely at the argument of Brutus on the judiciary[7]. This argument is important because it is the best statement on the Antifederalist side of what the probable characteristics of the judiciary would be. It's also one of the most accurate statements in the entire founding on either side of the argument. Brutus sets forth a probable view of the operation of Article III of the Constitution. In the end it describes the court to us as we've come to know it and the practice of judicial review. With a few exceptions it is an accurate rendering. Note that his rendering is for the sake of pointing out the danger of the judiciary. He points out the danger of this interpreting body becoming the last authority on the law. By being the arbiter of every difference it will then become, in his view of the matter, a despotic authority under the Constitution. The reasons that lead to the conclusion that the court must interpret the Constitution are solid. We see them repeated in *Federalist* seventy-eight. We see Publius also defend them. So here's a case where the Federalist and Antifederalist agree in the general appraisal, but disagree as to the consequences.

Let's examine the significance of that appraisal. Publius maintains that this is a necessary thing and it doesn't produce despotic authority because indeed, the court remains subject to the ultimate ruler which is neither the court, the Congress, or the President, but, in fact, the people. In accomplishing this argument he does a very interesting thing. He refers to the judiciary as the weakest branch of government. He says they lack the source of will; they only have judgment. Nothing they do is of any consequence unless they have the aid of the executive department, at least, and perhaps also the legislature. Therefore, these are seen by Publius as checks. Theoretically speaking this is correct, though in terms of political practice we may doubt this.

To support his argument that the judiciary is the weakest branch of government, Publius cites the authority of Montesquieu. Montesquieu says, in fact, "of the three powers above mentioned, the judiciary is next to nothing." The argument needs to be carefully examined because of the way Publius recreates the context of Montesquieu's discussion. In Book 11, Chapter 6 of the *Spirit of the Laws* Montesquieu sets off the separation of authorities and he names them legislative, executive, and judiciary. He describes the action of the judiciary as essentially being called into existence for each particular case, giving the judgment of the law as applies to the case and then disappearing. That comes very close to what we know about the American judicial process. At one level we know the court only exists insofar as there exists a controversy. The court can't simply go out and say it wants to study something or make a ruling on something; someone has to come to the court and present a case of controversy to the court. That's a limitation on the power of the court, because its rulings then are structured only by the struggles that are taking place already in society. That's part of what Montesquieu means. Montesquieu also means that the court assembles to hear the problem. So the court in Montesquieu's account is not a sitting institution.

In fact, if we read the argument very carefully, we'll see that the word Montesquieu uses, *juges*, in French means not judges, which is also a translation of it, but what we call jurors. Montesquieu means juries as judges when he's talking about judiciary power in the *Spirit of the Laws*. We can see how jurors fit the description; they are called into being for a particular case and then disappear. They have no existence after that. This is a very elaborate argument to demonstrate that this is the essential condition for preserving the liberty of the citizen. Note that he distinguishes liberty of the citizen from political liberty in the *Spirit of the Laws*. That doesn't have an exact parallel in our accounts but is nevertheless important for us along the lines we have previously discussed. Political liberty, Montesquieu said, was liberty as it is expressed in the Constitution. This is essentially what I have been describing. To provide a free Constitution, that's political liberty. But it takes something more to assure the liberty of the citizen. Political liberty only assures that the processes of government are conformable to the liberty of the citizen. But to actually preserve the liberty of the citizen we must preserve a sense of security against arbitrary judgments, dispositions, inaccuracy. One of the ways to do this is to design a judiciary, according to him, in such a way that the judge does not have complete authority over the lives of the citizens. The way to do this is to make the judiciary a model of temporary juries.

Montesquieu goes on to say prior to that point, that the most fearful of all the powers is the power of the judge. That's why we have to go through this process to weaken it because the judge sits there with the ability to dispose completely of all one's property and indeed, one's person. Everything is uncertain in the face of the judge. Something has to be done to eliminate that so the citizens can be safe. It's a complicated process that leads to the statement of Montesquieu that the judiciary is the weakest. It's the weakest in a properly constructed constitution.

Publius's argument is the opposite. He suggests that we don't have to worry too much about the judiciary because it in itself is weak. He, moreover, is not talking about juries, he's talking about a court that sits permanently. So that theoretically, if he follows Montesquieu, he would have to make the argument that Brutus is right to be concerned about this judiciary. For they have constructed precisely the kind of judiciary which Montesquieu thought to be among the most dangerous. How then does Publius get out of this beside sleight of hand or quoting Montesquieu out of context? How then does he prove that the judiciary is safe for the Constitution? He uses one argument which we've seen earlier, namely, that the judiciary does not have control of the Constitution.

No. 78

The judiciary is safe for the Constitution because the separation of powers limits the judiciary. Remember in essay forty-seven, we noted that to separate them absolutely would make them ineffective. Complete separation of power would in fact produce a complete deadlock in government; nothing would be done. We have to intermix the powers somewhat. It turns out the governing principle of intermixture is less the particular connections among the three branches, than it is a subordination of all to a constitution. And the expectation of the overriding constitution will control their judgments. It is in this sense that he then gives us the definition of a limited constitution which, because it's limited, calls for an interpretation by the court. Also because it's limited, there is a residual of ultimate and plenary authority that doesn't fall within the sphere of the Constitution and that remains in the society. It's the expectation then that the branches of government, including the judiciary, acting together, will indeed be kept in due subordination to the society by the reliance ultimately upon the right of revolution, if it comes to that.

There may be some state short of that where we can imagine the people reclaiming the authority of the Constitution, or correcting interpretations through some kind of popular input, that changes the character of the operation of the branches of government. But ultimately he has to rely on the right of revolution in order to accomplish that result and that's why we see him quoting the Declaration of Independence. Leading up to this he says in the eighteenth paragraph, we will "guard the constitution and the rights of individuals from the effects of those ill humours which the arts of designing men, or the influence of particular conjunctures, sometimes disseminate among the people themselves." So this is yet one more check on the will of the majority. But is it a will independent of the community? In essay fifty-one, we said this was not permissible; there is no way we could accept that. No, he argues, it is not a will independent of the community. This really only retards the expression of the will of the community while they are given time for "more deliberate reflection." Just

No. 51

as in the case of the executive, we want the "cool and deliberate sense of the community" to prevail. Here again everything is subordinated to the purpose of enhancing the "deliberate reflection" of the community rather than giving an open door or green light to momentary impressions. If there are serious oppressions, then that's another question. Publius goes on to say, however, "I trust the friends of the proposed constitution will never concur with its enemies in questioning that fundamental principle of republican government which admits the right of the people to alter or abolish the established Constitution whenever they find it inconsistent with their happiness."

That then is the fundamental argument that he relies upon if the judiciary will not be like Montesquieu's judiciary. The simple fact is, with Montesquieu, there was no right of revolution. There was not this overriding authority of the people over the constitution. It's revolution that permits a permanent judiciary to be described as the weakest of the three branches of government, quite in contradistinction to what Montesquieu had intended.

The operation of our courts will be judged from two points of view. First is the necessity of a national judiciary in order to give fullest efficacy to the nation-building enterprise itself. As Washington said, "we have a national character to establish." So, if we take seriously this project of establishing a national character, the argument goes, then we must have a federal judiciary and we can't depend on the states. Second is the other side of the argument, we need this to complete the circle of protection of rights and it's safe to do so because we don't give everything into their hands. We're not creating a will independent of the society.

NOTES

1. Federal Farmer, Letters II, III, and XII *Country Journal* (Poughkeepsie) 9 and 10 October 1787, 12 January 1788 in *Essential Antifederalist*, 194.

2. Federal Farmer, Letter II, in *Essential Antifederalist,* 177.

3. Federal Farmer, Letter II in *Essential Antifederalist,* 182.

4. It is difficult to resist adding the reflection that this offers no less the key to understanding Hamilton's administration of the Treasury Department and his role in the Washington Administration in the 1790s. This relation has only partially been set forth by scholars, and a full explanation is badly needed, knitting together the 1780s and 1790s.

5. This addresses, let us not forget, the "magistrate possessing only a common share of firmness. There are men, who under any circumstances will have the courage to do their duty at every hazard," no doubt including the hazard of reputation. In proportion as the statesman of common firmness can take his story to the people in "a very plain case," he need not fear their misconstruction. And in every other case, the more daring statesman may be comforted by the knowledge that he or she cannot otherwise save his reputation. See the twelfth paragraph of essay seventy-three.   No. 73

6. Some would doubtless challenge this analysis on the basis of the six-year term for senators. I would remind readers, however, that the senate experiences a turn-over of one-third every two years, and that the *possibility* of a complete renewal of one-third of the membership of a deliberative body signifies no insignificant change in its direction.

7. Brutus, Essays IV, XI, XII, and XV, *New York Journal*, 29 November 1787, 31 January 1788, 7 and 14 February 1788 in *Essential Antifederalist,* 207.

Epilogue

History's dodo germinates future failures in the euphoric celebration of recent triumphs. Thus did Athens squander in Syracuse what she won in Greece. Thus did Rome despoil at home what she had gained in Carthage and Europe. Thus did American statesmen welcome the greatest military victory in human history—the victory of the United States over the Soviet Union—with the invocation of a New World Order predicated upon economic determinism: free markets make free men. The special insouciance of this blind reliance upon capitalism is its notable failure to recognize the opportunity to convert a merely military victory into a moral triumph. The world, therefore, joined the United States in easy assumption that the fall of Soviet-directed communism and parties of the left in Europe, Africa, and Latin America had disproved rather than merely disapproved of socialism. No one paused to inquire whether the soul of socialism had crept so nearly into the core of western liberal democracies, including the United States, that only the parasite's host had fallen, while the parasite had successfully migrated to fatter kine.

We reason correctly, when we argue that the most significant practical challenge to liberal democracy was socialist-sponsored totalitarianism. Before we close the door on the history of radical challenges to liberal democracy, however, we ought to take stock of the foundations on which those challenges emerged, the merits of their positions, and the reasons they at length failed. Such a project would exceed by a considerable space the occasion afforded me to launch this inquiry here. I can, however, frame the question suitably to later investigation. In the process, I will show why a return to the *Federalist Papers* with a careful analysis remains relevant to the challenges people face today. To that end I recapture the origins of radical challenges to liberal democracy, as reflected in Tocqueville and Marx, in order to demonstrate that we no less than the founders need to respond to the weightiest doubts regarding the moral sufficiency of this form of life.

Among radical challenges to liberal democracy I distinguish three that are separate and distinct: the moral, the political, and the intellectual. I would wish to demonstrate—but here can only suggest—that there are just these three and no more. To put the matter most succinctly: Liberal democracy fails insofar as, morally, it diminishes the weight and authority of moral principle in the lives of ordinary people; insofar as, politically, it entrusts the safety and prosperity of society to the hands of the foolish rather than the prudent; and insofar as, intellectually, it destroys the habit of deference to reason in regulating practical conduct.

The argument in favor of liberal democracy must be strong indeed to command the assent of respectable intelligences in the face of such an arraignment. While I focus on the long-perceived weaknesses of liberal democracy (in order to a better understanding of perceived cultural defects in the contemporary era), I also point out that liberal democracy emerged in its best form against a back-drop of similar reflections.

Remember that constitutionalism anciently won acclaim as a good, while democracy anciently won scorn as an ill. At the advent of the modern era, the two terms converged such that democracy became the only substantive content for the process called constitutionalism. This altered perspective did not merely evolve but was rather ushered forth through serious argument and long reflection on the part of thinkers and statesmen who eventually abandoned the ancient distinctions and came to view democracy as necessary at minimum and potentially even good. What we now call liberal democracy results from this process as much as any other, boasting modern architects schooled in the ideas of classical political philosophy right up through Machiavelli. Simultaneously and correlatively, with altered moral and political perspectives, the process engendered diverging conceptions of the nature of political and social study—political science. In these divergences we can locate the radical challenges to liberal democracy at the same time as we discover how constitutionalism and democracy came effectively to be synonymous. Indeed, it were far rather to be wished that United States policy, in the aftermath of the fifty-year war with the Soviet Union, had trumpeted constitutionalism and democracy rather than capitalism and democracy. It trumpeted capitalism and democracy, however, because radical challenges to liberal democracy still live.

We begin by taking John Locke seriously, rather than dismissing him simply because we are the children of Rousseau. We grapple with the same problem Locke grappled with, the same problem Montesquieu grappled with. The problem is to know how to generate liberalism, which is that form of society in which the individuals count for themselves as well as for their relationships. Political power there is exercised within limits that must respect that individualism, that individual liberty. Moreover, that liberty must be compatible with efforts towards acquisition of material goods. Thus, liberalism grew from an argument that holds that everyone has a right to defend his life, his liberty, and his property.

To be sure, equality was not less implicated in the founding of liberalism. However, the very fact that Rousseau diverged from the individualism of Locke and others demonstrates that equality was a contested and often misunderstood component of liberalism. This divergence, indeed, ultimately became the foundation for the radical challenges to liberalism which emerged in full throat in the nineteenth century, and which Tocqueville and Marx make clear not only for that century but for all time since. Because it was pre-nineteenth century liberalism that eventuated in the liberal democracy of the United States, that is the background we need in order to assess the implications and the propriety of the subsequent challenges.

E. S. Corwin wrote earlier last century of The "Higher Law" Background of American Constitutional Law and thereby situated the founding in the context of debates that still prevailed in the eighteenth century[1]. Those debates preserved an awareness of various forms of law beyond positive law, including divine, natural, and customary. Moreover, the idea of various forms of law descending from the Latin *lex* and *jus* entails an inherent distinction between the mere command of law (*lex*) and right inhering in law (*jus*). At its origins, then, liberalism enjoyed a vocabulary that has largely been lost to us now.

The question for Locke was the same as it had been for others. He speaks of law in the sixth paragraph of his Second Treatise, where he defines the law of nature, as reason[2]. The various forms of law depict the means by which human beings have sought to set limits on their engagements in the world or the terms of their organized pursuits. Law posits a quest for order against the threat of the arbitrary or chaos. Locke started humankind in the state of nature and introduced war right there in the state of nature. But raising the notion of law right there and at the same time suggests an inherent if not realized order in human life. When Locke identified reason as that law, he specified it rather as potential than enjoyed. Nature in some fashion prescribes to human beings certain ordered relationships in order to the attainment of certain specified ends. Those ends, though, are pitifully few, mainly turning around self-preservation. All of the terms Locke derived from this observation refer to things that exist in the way that they exist because of an order pre-existing or inhering in the constitution of humanity.

Locke then began with laws by definition distinguished from laws that human beings impose upon themselves—positive laws. Whether his definitions differ from customary law, and perhaps divine law, raises a separate but not trivial question. The more we entertain such quandaries, the more we veer away from the goal we imagined. Beginning with what appear to be necessary relations, we quickly meet with an assertion that a particular command is, say, divine law. Then the question becomes what is one's relationship to the law based on its source. That is a fundamental question—the human being's relationship to the law relative to the source of the law. Does one have more or less an option regarding laws depending on the source of the law? Is the law that derives from nature more exiguous than a law that derives from another human being or less exiguous than one coming from God? Is a law of greater import when written? Is it of greater import when evolved, as in the common law? Corwin places these questions in a perspective that serves as a form of shorthand to situate our conversations about liberalism in the entire flow of political philosophy in the western world.

We read in the first book of Montesquieu's *Esprit des Lois*, which is entitled, "About Laws in General," that "the laws in the broadest meaning are the necessary relationships that derive from the nature of things. In this sense, all beings have their laws; the divinity has its laws; the material world has its laws; intelligences superior to man have their laws; the beasts have their laws; man has his laws."[3] That statement and the following argument produce more problems than clarity, since the notion that everything that is has a law fails to rise above the banal. Without some distance between the way things are and the laws that are appropriate to things, or that govern the conduct or the behavior of things, no leverage over human action can be obtained.

Consider the implications of the difference between the terms, "behavior" and "conduct." These words do not refer to the same things, even if parents will occasionally speak loosely to children when admonishing or praising them. Characteristically, we speak of the behavior of inanimate matter—a passive recipient of forces existing in a Newtonian universe of equal and opposite actions and reactions. On the other hand, the word "conduct" invokes the notion that the being moves as if it conducts itself. It might move this way or that way upon election, upon choice. Hence, when we speak of humans our tendency, if we want to blame them for what they have done, is to speak of their conduct—their bad conduct. If we want to praise them as noble, we also speak of conduct. If we speak of their behavior, we do one of two things. We address ourselves to children, whom we conceive not to know what they are doing, or we adopt the modes of social scientists, who have reduced human things to things that are subhuman, as if we were only inanimate matter or at best beasts.

Montesquieu's opening sentence forces us to ask whether we must make a distinction between things passive and active when speaking of laws. Is all the world constructed of things passive, of equal and opposite actions and reactions? Or, is there some part of the world that is not passive, but active, and therefore sets motion in being rather than merely receiving motion from others?

Montesquieu opens with a fairly Newtonian view of the world, but he quickly goes through his first book to show a more complicated picture. He wrote of "intelligent beings," in particular. He means primarily human beings and he realizes the implication of the title of the work, the "spirit" of the laws [which we may take to mean the mind or intelligence of the laws], by focusing on the laws of human community. He affirmed that "individual intelligent beings" have laws that they have made and laws that they have not made, meaning that they are subject to both kinds of law—subject to being acted upon and capable of acting. It is important to discern, therefore, which spheres rely upon which of the varying kinds of law.

Montesquieu followed this introduction by making the claim that "relationships of equity" exist prior to positive law. This very special term derives from our law books—especially Anglo-American law books. Equity is the principle by which a judge may look at a particular case and decide it on the basis of what is right for the case rather than the literal terms of the law. This occurs for the reason that laws themselves are always general, and general language does not always address specific facts in the manner that lawmakers would wish. Judgment in equity may say of a case in which the law requires "x" that the facts of the case make "y" more appropriate. In order to have a judgment in equity based on fairness or what is right in the case, the one thing needful is manifestly a standard of right. Reason may disclose such a standard; something else may do so; but there must by all means be one.

Thus emerges the question of the relationship of human beings to the principle behind the law. That is also the relevance of Corwin's discussion of the "higher law background" of American law. The claim is that there exists beyond lawmakers, beyond constitutions, and beyond organized society a principle that animates all human law. Moreover, human beings have access to that principle even when they do not enjoy consensus around that principle. It has become in our time a hotly contested issue whether natural law—or any higher law principle—ought ever to enter the minds of the judges and others involved in the judicial process. On the other side, the point is urged that it is difficult to discern the source of law's authority absent some principle of right that establishes it. Advocates of civil disobedience, in the absence of an appeal to higher principle, stand nakedly on an insistence upon their own interest. Critics who arraign unjust law point to an emptiness where there exists no justice apart from the law's command. No one may judge the law apart from the law itself when positive law is the highest thing to which human beings can appeal.

The significance of this debate is what it reveals about our opinions regarding the current character of our political regime—what we think the Constitution is and what we think are our claims under that Constitution. Related to this problematic is the word most prominent, ultimately, in Locke's political philosophy, the word that anchors the claim that every man has a "right to life, liberty, and property." Locke introduced "right" in a different context than has characterized our discussion of the right behind the law. This right does not derive from a standard of justice, per se. For justice is invoked necessarily in judging differences between individuals.

Locke's "right," by contrast, is applied to an individual without respect to any other particular individual.[4]

Take the right to life. In Locke's argument it is a "right" to life because it is a course of action required of the being and from which the individual cannot desist. One cannot fail to act on the basis of this principle of self-preservation. It is inherent in one's being. What one does, and what makes one what he is is precisely to preserve one's life. Thus it becomes a right to life. The corollary is the "right" to liberty, because the action that preserves one's life presupposes the liberty to act for the purpose of preserving one's life. The "right" to property similarly becomes a right because property constitutes those things that one obtains with the end in view of preserving one's life. In the end it all comes back to the imperious necessity that we feed, shelter, and defend ourselves. Hence it is a right that no one can take from one, and it is a right that one cannot give away. Naturally, Locke is aware of suicide and self-sacrifice. He maintains, however, that in such cases people suffer from some disorder. For they cannot and have no right to take their lives. Thus, far from requiring judgment in the cases of conflict between individuals, a right is turned squarely on the individual himself.

Thinking through Locke's argument, we can discern the problem he aimed to resolve. That problem is not merely how to generate human society. That is the ultimate goal—what we may call state building. But the problem is to know the foundations, to know why it is that men do not simply live idly in what he called the state of nature. The principal reason he gave is that, in the state of nature they would be constantly in a state of war. It would be dangerous and insecure. Men would not be happy, and they would not live long. They leave the state of nature to preserve their lives.

But Locke is also mindful of locating the motivation of human action. He seeks a comprehensive, universal, scientific explanation. He seeks to eliminate external influences in order to identify the sameness that underlies the apparent differences in beings. He seeks that source of motivation, that source of human conduct, that is the same everywhere. At the first level he identified that as self-preservation, and at the next level he observed that this motive drives man straight into society. In that society they create governments, governments subject to certain rules, certain limitations on power. This results from the initial impulse, driving men into government, which defines the limits of governmental power. No one would join this club if it meant sacrificing the right to life. Thus the government must be such that it cannot arbitrarily deprive one of life, liberty, or property. This fosters a relationship between contracting citizens and a government limited by the contract.

Of course this argument suffers the defect of jumping from the initial impulse to society (self-preservation) to the consummation of individual desires (happiness) without so much as pausing amidst the disorderly facts of human relationships and mutual dependencies. The Declaration of Independence's "pursuit of happiness" is perfectly Lockeian—and more succinctly so in that regard. Human life lives itself out, and conduct is more determinative, not where ultimate motivations or enjoyments prevail, however. Rather, the messy state of classes and orders, ranks and positions, families and priests sets the measures that both inspire one's motives and set the limits to one's enjoyments. Hence, it matters to know whether a theory of individualism can provide prudent guidance through messiness.

To turn to our chroniclers, I want to focus ultimately on Tocqueville's personal reminiscences of revolutionary France in 1848, paving the way by revisiting his work on the revolution of 1789 (which he wrote in the same atmosphere in which he wrote his reminiscences). Afterwards I introduce reactions to the same events and from a slight distance by Karl Marx (who lived in London at the time of the troubles in France). It will be important to recall that the ferment in 1848 was not exclusive to France. Much if not all of Europe experienced radical ferment—Italy and Hungary prominently. Monarchy had been under pressure since the time of the first revolution in France, and democracy would undergo continual pressure after the revolutions of 1848. Tocqueville, then, provides a starting point for thinking about the issues involved in nineteenth-century radicalism.

We know Tocqueville as the author of *Democracy in America*, a great critic-analyst of democracy.[5] He was philosophically learned and some-thing of a historian to boot. Moreover he was a politician, one whom in 1848 we meet as a participant observer in the various assemblies and struggles of political parties as France underwent popular rebellion and reaction time after time. Tocqueville ended a minister in government under Louis Napoleon: that great non-democratic "voice of the people" of mid-nineteenth-century France.

Bearing in mind this history of Tocqueville, we can more readily comprehend his commentary on the original revolution, and there is no better place to begin our search than with the passage in his *Recollections* in which he discusses an episode with his man-servant, Eugène.[6] Tocque-ville retired to his room, exhausted from ongoing battles and deliberations in the city of Paris. He tried to fall asleep, when he heard a knock at his door. It was Eugène, who had looked in "to see if I had returned, and if I did not require his services." Eugène had left the bivouac that he had joined wearing a national guard uniform and carrying a good musket borrowed from Tocqueville.

This man was no socialist, either by temperament or in theory. He was not even touched to a slight degree by that most usual sickness of the times, a restless mind, and one should have had trouble to find even in any other era than ours, one more quiet in his station and without any regrets whatsoever. Always very pleased with himself and tolerably pleased with others, he ordinarily desired only what was within his reach, and he pretty nearly got, believed he had gotten, everything he desired. In this manner all by himself he followed the precepts philosophers teach but seldom observe, and he enjoyed as a gift of nature that happy balance between powers and wants that alone brings the happiness promised by philosophy. "Well, Eugène," I asked him, when he came in that morning, "how are things going?" "Very well, sir, perfectly well." "How do you mean very well, when I can still hear gunfire?" "Yes, they are still fighting. But everyone is saying that it will end very well." As he said that, he took off his uniform, cleaned my boots and brushed my clothes, and then, putting on his uniform again, said, "If you do not need anything else, sir, with your permission, I will go back to the battle."[7]

This is a particularly touching exchange between man—the aristocrat (Tocqueville was born an aristocrat, though in the politics of the day he was a republican)—and man—the servant. Both were then wrapped up in the great democratic turmoil of the insurgency of the people against their rulers and the bourgeoisie in May and June of 1848. The book opened in February amidst the first great overthrow, when the monarchy was overthrown directly by popular revolt. Tocqueville described this as the first time the people had actually rebelled and overthrown a government, as opposed to being led in that kind of activity by intellectuals or aristocrats or someone from the bourgeoisie.

To understand the significance of what happened in 1848, it is important to recapture a sense of what happened originally in France. The very first words in the first chapter of Tocqueville's book on the "old regime" are the words:

Nothing more fitly reminds philosophers and statesmen to be modest than the history of our Revolution. For never were so great events, carried so far and better prepared, and so little foreseen.[8]

This presents what for Tocqueville constitutes the paradox of the French Revolution: that it was not in every decisive respect save one an innovation. All that had happened was in fact laid out in a chain of cause and effect stretching back several centuries. It was really the story of the undoing of the French monarchy or feudal monarchy (since it happened all over Europe save England). The undoing of the feudal monarchy was at the hands of feudal monarchs.

The *Old Regime* tells the story of how the monarchs set about to destroy for purposes of political order what, in a Burkean sense, is best called the social order. There had existed a society of balanced classes—peasants, lords, noblemen, kings, councilors—with everything in its place, the clergy naturally playing a major role. Over time, through internecine struggles at the level of the ruling class, they discovered the art of playing the people

off against one another. And through the course of time they completely
undid that balanced constitution for the sake of expediency.

That is the story of the old regime. Tocqueville is French, though, and
he did not write about France in the manner that he wrote about America.
He visited America in the early 1830s, and many describe the writings that
resulted as more about France than America. The year 1832 marked the
beginning of the French monarchy that was overthrown in 1848. In 1832
the French enjoyed a breathing space, having undergone since 1789 several
revolutions—a constitutional revolution replaced by a radical state,
replaced by Robespierre and a Directory, replaced by Bonaparte, replaced
by a constitutional monarchy, replaced by another constitutional monarchy,
replaced by another despotism, and finally replaced by the constitutional
monarchy of 1832. The aristocrat in America provided a natural connection
between the two events. Thus, he traveled to the United States to inquire
why they had not undergone the same turmoil the French had undergone.
What in the way of France's enjoying democracy distinguishes it?

Tocqueville's writing about the events of 1848 and 1789 not only
described what happened in France but from the point of view of someone
seeking a useful perspective on those events. Nonetheless the details of the
stories he told focus largely on speculation, the part speculation plays in
driving political events. He identified the role of eighteenth-century
enlightenment in shaping all the political events which occurred at the end
of that century, meaning the American and French revolutions, and which
proceeded to reshape the human moral and political landscape. We may
throw in the economic landscape as well, for we see very shortly thereafter
that notions derived from economists—particularly those of the Scottish
philosophers—became completely wound up in the broader notions of
enlightenment and liberal democracy.

We may divide enlightenment philosophy into two lines of thought.
Tocqueville observed that:

We rightly judge eighteenth-century philosophy as one of the main causes of the
Revolution, and it is moreover true that that philosophy is profoundly irreligious.
But one should pay careful attention to two parts of it, which are at once distinct
and separable.

   In one gathered all the new or renovated opinions concerning the condition
of societies and the principles of civil and political law—such, for example, as
the natural equality of men, the abolition of all privileges of caste, class, and of
professions that are a consequence of it—i.e., the sovereignty of the people, the
omnipotence of the social power, the uniformity of rules. . . . All these doctrines
are not only the cause of the French Revolution, but constitute thus its substance,
so to speak. They are what is most fundamental, most lasting, and most true
throughout time in the work of the Revolution.

   In the second part of their doctrines eighteenth-century philosophers attacked
the church with a kind of fury. They attacked its clergy, its hierarchy, its

institutions, and its dogmas; and in order to be able to overthrow them, they sought to tear out even the fundamentals of Christianity.[9]

The two lines of development are clearly stated. One is the general argument about humanity and the rights of man (and it is important here to use the French Revolution language—"rights of man"—as opposed to the language which still echoes the classical world, "natural rights"—because a transformation has taken place. There is no longer from this vantage point natural law or natural rights. The single, most important dimension of human relations becomes power. Further, the principle used to organize and guide power is the principle of the rights of man as enunciated in the French *Declaration of the Rights of Man* in 1789.

The 1789 Declaration is a different tool than the Declaration of Independence in the United States; where it remains possible to speak of natural law; where it is still possible to speak of God as somehow the Creator of human rights; and where God is somehow the Creator of principles of association that are discerned to be inalienable as they apply to human beings. There is a gulf between that kind of reasoning and the claims that prevailed through the French Revolution. The gulf forms along the line that what one is concerned about is the question, what are the activities human beings can ordinarily pursue and from which they cannot reasonably desist.

The profoundest implication of this change is that efforts directed towards self-preservation come to be seen in another light. Men derived certain notions from this proposition that came increasingly to focus on the more material aspects of humanity, those things having to do with the immediate care and succor of our bodies. That came to be addressed as the rights of man, where the rights defined a certain kind of power. This led ultimately to a view that the failures of human beings to do the things they try to do constitute deprivations rather than failures relating to any intrinsic talents or abilities. The language of Rousseau rose to the fore: "Man is born free, but everywhere we see him in chains."[10] All inequalities began to be seen, not as the consequences of any individual conduct but as relationships of oppression. The assumption is that, if a human being cannot fail to act to acquire what is good for himself, to secure such material substance as will render him comfortable in this world, then the failure cannot lie to his account but must be attributed to some intrusion, some obstruction. It is a social disorder parallel to the individual disorder in the case of suicide. On these grounds men began to speak of poverty in a different way than they would when informed by previous conceptions.

Tocqueville claimed that this transition was part and parcel of an enlightenment philosophy that not only generated a general picture of humanity but also a ferocious attack on religion rooted in an older language. The notion of the higher law, which we know to play a role in the American constitutional tradition, was completely cut off from this new line of analysis that gave birth to the French Revolution and rendered an entirely different kind of revolution than that in the United States. How do they differ? In the first place the French Revolution was a revolution against society far more fundamentally than it was a revolution against government. The *Old Regime* explained that, when the revolution was accomplished, the French returned to the old powers of government. They tossed the social order upside down; they beheaded queens and princes, and they putatively enthroned the people. But they still had an all powerful, centralized state. The real objective was to overturn social relationships, the orders of society, insofar as men perceived in those orders the immediate cause of social disparity. Social disparity became the most direct evidence of denial of rights, with rights now interpreted as the power to acquire comfort in this world.

Tocqueville described politics as well as philosophy in the *Old Regime*. In fact, he argued that the philosophers (or the literary men, as he called them), who generated the ideas for the revolution (so much so that the revolution was carried out more in the language of literature than that of politics), had no political experience and little political judgment. The politicians, on the other hand, were totally oblivious to the consequences of their own choices and their own judgments. The kings themselves adopted the language of the rights of man. The power holders themselves insinuated the very ideas that would flower in the outburst of the revolution. He maintained that we witnessed rulers that:

strive within their realms to destroy immunities and abolish privileges. They confuse the orders of society, equalize social conditions, and replace the aristocracy with a bureaucracy, local regimes with centralized or uniform regulations, and the multiplicity of diverse powers with a unity of government. They undertake this revolutionary work with constant industry; and if they encounter some obstacle they adopt the procedures and maxims of the Revolution. They frequently adopt the expedient of playing poor against rich, commoner against nobleman, peasant against lord.[11]

By contrast, *Federalist* number ten identified the most constant source of faction as the "various and unequal distribution of property," but as a prelude to an argument about managing rather than eradicating the difference.[12] James Madison's argument held that this was essential in political life, and that the point of political thinking is to generate arrangements to deal with rather than eradicate a phenomenon intrinsic to our humanity. Thus, when projects begin that seek to eradicate the causes of inequality, one of the consequences is to watch bold and frightening initiatives that have no capacity to improve human life but extraordinary potential to destroy the order of society. Tocqueville, by discovering that

No. 10

it was not the philosophers or revolutionaries but the rulers themselves who made the crucial contribution by adopting the defective mode of reasoning, describes an intersection of politics and philosophy that returns in 1848 with devastating clarity.

The *Old Regime* constitutes a model of historical sleuthing. In it Tocqueville returned to all the old documents from the regional governments and municipalities in order to demonstrate systematically how a society of aristocrats and peasants used to have an organic connection. They were co-dependent and could each call upon the other for support, in much the manner of the interaction of Tocqueville and Eugène. This order was disestablished because monarchs, starting with Louis XIV, had decided that they needed to increase their power over the aristocrats. The aristocrats were like independent power centers in this era of the birth of the nation-state. They needed to be reduced, and one means of accomplishing that was to detach them from the peasants. By the time the monarchs consummated the work, however, what France had were millions of isolated peasants who had no one to turn to. Aristocrats and peasants became natural enemies to each other rather than people organically connected in a single society.

The philosophy of the era, then, holds that there are no justifications for the distinctions that we see in the social order. Parallel to the philosophy we find a politics in the era, in which those who are charged with preserving the social order sacrifice it for their own immediate political advantage. A third factor enters in the third chapter, and that is the observation that the French Revolution was "worldwide." The revolution was not carried out in the name of this tribe, the French, but in the name of humanity. The revolution in the United States, by contrast, had an impact that was worldwide (and, as Lincoln correctly observed, the example of the United States continues to do so), principally by structuring peoples' expectations of political decency. Although the *Declaration of Independence* appeals to the "candid" judgment of the world, and the first *Federalist*

No. 1   holds that the American founding settles a question for mankind and not just for the United States, this revolution was not directed outside the immediate political sphere of the United States. Americans required to justify themselves to the world, because the standard of reason was their standard, which in turn was attached to natural law. Thus, they created a particular society, although no longer determined by blood, in the context of a general conception of humanity. The French revolution lacked such modesty; it was projected to declare illegitimate every foundation of social order in political society but those mirroring the events that transpired in France and the principles that underlay those events.

This produced a harmful consequence. Where one refuses to identify the French nation as having a peculiar title to these revolutionary claims, and where one would, besides, urge the imminent necessity of all humans acting accordingly, one ends by separating human beings rather than uniting them. The reason is that on these terms a Frenchman is no longer a Frenchman, strictly speaking. A Frenchman is merely a human being, who has no greater reason to find intimacy with someone next door than with someone a thousand leagues away. There is no intrinsic principle by which one can argue that neighbors ought to sustain an immediate relationship, apart from going through the task of establishing a social contract and constitution and committing themselves to a specific political (not social) order, whose laws are binding with all the strength that Rousseau's "general will" called for. That also means an exaggeration of homogeneity among men. The existing social order that came under attack was not merely illegitimate, but all those who hold places within it become illegitimate—deserving punishment. Hence, attacks upon the church and churchmen followed in France.

Tocqueville's argument means that the political dynamic of the revolution in France is largely a question of political ideas without political judgment creating a movement that gets out of control. That creates in turn a situation in which the only control that can be established is despotic. This became the story of France for the sixty years between 1789 and 1848. He described a process that eventuated in a situation in which there was no longer an authority to which ordinary citizens would subordinate themselves, their urges, their desires, their inclinations—their rights. It had ceased to be a question of bringing the people into a common framework. A common framework can barely contain their appetites. In the *Recollections,* Tocqueville focused earliest and most powerfully on envy and resentment. These are the feelings that come to the fore in the aftermath of destructive revolution.

Arguably, there is no more powerful argument against liberal democracy than that it invariably leads to France—namely, it sets in motion leveling influences that destroy the respect human beings have for particular excellences. Thus it leaves human beings with nothing more to motivate their conduct than their own self-concern, which expresses itself most powerfully in envy and resentment at all superior endowments. It is a flattening of social distinction simultaneously with a heightening of "every the least difference" among men[13]. We learn in this form of society to hate those who are unlike ourselves, which affection paradoxically subtended most if not all of the conversation regarding diversity, racism, and multiculturalism in the late twentieth century. Nor does this imitate the ancient world, in which people saw themselves as belonging to an ethnos—a tribe, a family, a nation—and therefore unlike any outside. Those differences were important precisely because they were not individual differences. The differences that led some to call themselves civilized and others barbarians were differences those men ascribed to themselves in a corporate posture, as part of a collectivity. It was a question of belonging and cultivation. That is not the soul of the conversation in the modern world, where, instead, the true spirit is that every the least difference rankles. It becomes for us something that we cannot tolerate in proportion as we are imbued with the democratic ethos, in proportion as we believe that nothing apart from equality is acceptable and insofar as we can make no distinction between moral inequality and other forms of inequality. Tocqueville has shown us how these ideas came to be rooted in the mind of the modern west (from which they have spread largely throughout the world), and the process notably precedes the intrusion of organized socialism. These ideas reduce to an accentuated regard for equality coupled with a heightened intolerance for apparent difference (materially and morally).

Why did this happen? In the third book of *The Old Regime,* Tocqueville returned to the philosophers, to show how they introduced such chaos:

They ceaselessly busied themselves with thoughts concerning government; basically, that was their vocation. Folk daily listened to them discoursing on the origins of societies and on their primitive forms, on the primordial rights of citizens and those in authority, on the natural and artificial relations among men, the error or legitimacy of custom, and even on the fundamental principles of the laws. Thus prying apart each day the very foundations of the constitution of their day, they examined its structure with curiosity and critiqued its overall design.[14]

We may assume that earlier thinkers were led to raise these questions for the same reasons that we raise them so naturally and that they are intrinsic to our idea of progress.

In fact, however, contemporary man acquired a taste for such inquiry. So far is ancient man from identifying an evolutionary necessity with regard to change in human nature or human conduct, that he required first, and before raising a moral question about conduct or the origins of fundamental principles, to observe that such questions presuppose that he does not know already the answers. Human beings, however, do not commence empty and then fill themselves up bit by bit. They improve on the efficiency of mechanisms to pursue instrumental means, to make axes, hatchets, and slingshots; they do not become progressively certain of convictions that they should defend their lives, defend their families, raise their children, and live at peace with their neighbors. The latter are not, I would say, natural questions for man. Rather, one must be taught to ask such questions. Else he never would, for it is unnatural to look for the roots of conduct.

To assume otherwise is to presuppose that human beings evolve morally. Tocqueville, however, asked precisely why one would take apart the foundations of society. For to do so implies that one already expects to be able to do something to improve it. The precondition of such a question is already an inclination towards change. To ask what is the foundation of a given social order is to think that it might, or perhaps ought to, be different. That is the perspective that Tocqueville argues to be unnatural. The natural instinct is to defend what is one's own, to defend what one has and what is. One must learn to desire to be different from what one is; one must acquire a belief in evolution or progress.

Typically, human beings in the ancient world believed that what was old, what was accomplished, was better. In some distant golden age the forefathers were near-gods and the contemporary descendants but pale shadows of the distant gods. All that descendants do undermines their forefathers' greatness, and the most they can do is try very hard not to undermine it too much by securing themselves faithfully within piety to their fathers' memory.

Human society characteristically organized itself thus, but a different form of organization in the modem world has inverted the order. Now we say that everything old is inferior. We must evolve, for we will never be good enough unless we become better than they were. We prefer change to stability, for change is always for the better—never the worse. That is the modern attitude, and it is sponsored by the disposition that entered the French Revolution. There we do not find talk about the higher law, or a nice concern to separate natural law from positive law, customary law, or constitutional law. Everything reduces to positive law—the expression of contemporary will.

Since man drives the process of change, the single most important element is the contemporary expression of his will[15]. That becomes law, and all attempts to organize society are attempts to organize that expression of will—to make it as clear and resounding as possible. Viewing political debates from this perspective makes clear that the principal point of dispute is how one acts to bring people together in such a way as to silence discord and produce as near as possible a clear and coherent expression of will. Governments are deemed better as they approximate that and worse in proportion as they do not. For that reason, twentieth-century social scientists have frequently rejected as a system of "deadlock," in the words of James MacGregor Bums, the elaborate mechanism described by Publius[16]. The system is not designed to surface a single voice; its multiple interests and voices, variously checking and balancing, produce confusion. It does not satisfy the ambition to change man.

Whether and how we should change ourselves is a subject that generates a good many differences of view. The first thing that derives from the habit described by Tocqueville is the invention of political systems of all kinds—each now predicated on obtaining a certain goal, which is to turn the new political systems first identified as liberal democracies into the coherent expression of public will. But every new turn on that system becomes more and more eccentric, as if it were some wild trial and error experimentation. Moreover, frustration increases upon each iteration of the process, the inventors become more and more inventive and less intuitive. Their systems speak less directly to moral principles in a language that we would easily recognize and that we could easily adopt.

Tocqueville believed that what was wanted was to replace the complex of traditional customs governing the social order of the day by simple, elementary rules deriving from the exercise of human reason and the natural law. That was the starting point that, over time, became infinitely more complex. Looking closely into it, Tocqueville observed:

> . . . one sees that what may be called the political philosophy of the eighteenth century properly speaking consists in this single notion. Such a thought was not new: it ebbed and flowed ceaselessly through three thousand years without being able solidly to establish itself in human imagination. How on this occasion did it succeed in conquering the intelligences of every writer? Why, instead of expiring as it had so often done before in the brain of this or that philosopher, did it drop all the way to the mob and there acquire the consistency and heat of a political passion—so greatly that one might observe general and abstract theories on the nature of society becoming the topic of daily intercourse for the idle and even firing the imaginations of women and peasants?[17]

The argument is quite straightforward. Ordinary people today talk as though they were philosophers. They use abstractions and handle terms like "rights" as if they knew what they meant. They do not speak in terms of intimate relationship and the easy identifications and distinctions that one makes through mere familiarity. That was a change in the world, according to Tocqueville.

Now, does the fact that everyone speaks like a philosopher make everyone a philosopher—including so-called professors of philosophy? Is that what enlightenment comes to, to invent new vocabulary that, as it is used more widely, structures our experience and brings everyone to live like philosophers? We do tend to say today that everyone has a philosophy, do we not? Is it sufficient to use the language of philosophy to be able to philosophize?

In the political context, the question—Tocqueville's question—is how these abstract theories and generalizations regarding the nature of government were able to produce confidence in ordinary citizens. Consider religion in contrast. If we observed that ordinary citizens came to believe and use the language of the synoptic gospels, would it be appropriate to consider them divines? We need to inquire why we do not grant the same kind of authority to the common language of Christianity and religion in general that we grant to philosophy. Interestingly, we can trace the progress of religious language. We find people learning from missionaries and proselytizers, learning in Sunday schools regularly and tirelessly, repeating and memorizing the language. That is how we get this language worked into the soul of the believers, and not merely speaking and writing some books. It was a long and serious enterprise that took considerable effort and a long time to work its way even into the illiterate classes.

The revolution in France was different. Without having special schools set up for the purpose, the language of rights and abstract generalization, the language of humanity in place of nationality, became pervasive. Ordinary people came to use this language in the same way they used to quote gospel verses. How could it have happened?

Tocqueville does not answer the question phrased in that way. But he does suggest an answer. After noting that the literary people became bolder and bolder and contemptuous of the wisdom of the ages, he argued, "It was the [writers'] very ignorance [about politics] that won the ear and the heart of the mob,"[18] People, he meant, had been isolated from one another, so that the discourse of community was no longer clearly structured. There remained the underlying discourse of religion, but there was no conscious and open discourse of community that defined their circumstances. They were vulnerable to the first argument that came along.

The first argument to come along was a powerful appeal to their emotion. To identify the emotion, Tocqueville pointed out that in the twenty years prior to 1789 France enjoyed enormous prosperity. Louis XVI had presided over a recovery from the great depression that characterized the reign of Louis XV. In the attitude and atmosphere of great prosperity much of the imprudent language of class division was used. The emotion that was appealed to was greed, and in a circumstance in which people had no particular reason to be ashamed of being greedy. The social bonds that otherwise would have restrained had already been dissolved. They were left ripe for the picking. Tocqueville called this the debacle of freedom. In it the one freedom which overshadowed all others was "philosophizing without limit on the origins of societies, the essential nature of government, and the primordial rights of humankind . . . and the writers, assuming control of public opinion, also assumed momentarily the place that party leaders ordinarily occupy in free countries."[19]

France was not free but there was free discussion among people isolated from one another. They were alienated—not in the sense modern sociology employs but in a kind of political disarticulation. Tocqueville contrasts the American Revolution with the French Revolution:

[The American Revolution] effectively had great influence on the French Revolution, but owed it less to what was done at the time in the United States than to what folk were thinking at the same time in France. While for the rest of Europe the American Revolution was still nothing but a singular and novel fact, in France it reinforced more strikingly and palpably what folk already knew. Elsewhere it was surprising; in France it was convincing proof. The Americans seemed only to perform what our writers had conceived; they gave the reality of substance to things we were dreaming about.[20]

Thus, French thinkers were bolstered first by getting ordinary people to adopt their opinions, and then they were bolstered by the view that history was on their side. Things were moving their way.

Again, the problem is to know what it takes to make people want to change a political system. The key is to believe that making a change does not expose one to much peril or what is the same, not believing that it is better to remain the same than to risk a change. People gain that confidence, it seems, especially from resentment, deep resentment. In place of the hope of something better one can install a powerful hatred of what is. That plays a large role in modern revolutions. Tocqueville noted that, in America, there was a resistance to such a development, in the form of its religion.

Every American I meet, whether in his country or elsewhere, I ask whether he believes religion is useful for the stability of the laws and the good order of society. Without hesitating he responds that a civilized society, and above all a free society, cannot survive without religion. Respect for religion, in his eyes, is the greatest guarantee of the state's stability and the safety of individuals. The person least instructed in the science of government knows that much. Yet, there is in the world no country where the boldest political doctrines of eighteenth-century philosophers could be more rigorously instituted than America. Their anti-religious doctrines exclusively have never been able to see the light of day in America, even on behalf of the unlimited liberty of the press.[21]

The statement is extraordinary. Tocqueville described the origins of liberal democracy and how it operates in different arenas. Liberal democracy comes from the boldest theories of eighteenth-century philosophers, effectively put into practice in the United States, but with a condition attached. The condition is the expression of confidence in religion in addition to those theories to produce stability. But the philosophers attacked religion ferociously. Thus, Tocqueville means that the Americans adopted these theories up to a point but stopped, whereas the French did not stop.

While religion is the topic here, the underlying subject is the need for principles of relationship independent of politics in order to make a liberal democracy work. It is a conversation about the reason one requires social principles beyond political principles in order to make liberal democracy work. The idea is that if one tries to make politics the totality of the human experience and organizes politics on the grounds of liberal democracy, one will produce moral chaos. One will leave people who require social and moral guidance without any restraint or guidance. They will see politics as the only instrument suited to the pursuit of desire or ambition. They will turn all of their relationships and their differences into moments of political contest and struggle. Every political judgment will become a judgment of persons, positions, and status. Therefore, unless one can give people beyond politics all of those elements of person, position, and status, and at the same time preserve some moral leverage over them, one cannot prevent the harmful effects of the regime of equality, which is liberal democracy, from destroying the society.

Tocqueville observed in his *Recollections* that he had "sometimes thought that, though the mores of different societies varied, the morality of the politicians in charge of affairs was the same everywhere." He added in this context that "I often glide between good and evil with a soft indulgence that borders on weakness, and my quickness to forget grievances seems more like a lack of spirit, an inability to suffer the memory of an affront rather than any virtuous effort to efface such an impression." These statements show Tocqueville's struggle with the spirit of revolution in France. The real question in all of his writing—one that he addresses directly only in *Democracy in America,* so far as I know—is to know why we cannot have in the modern times someone who can exert an authority like the authority of founders in the ancient times. Why cannot we have a Moses or a Lycurgus? That question contains the further question whether there is any way out of chaos, once the march of liberal democracy has begun and has spun into the disorder manifested in 1848. The answer seems to be no. Although he commends ways in which men may mitigate the disorders with which they live, he does not seem to believe that it is possible to turn back modern principles. In that Tocqueville the critic poses the most powerful intellectual challenge to liberal democracy. He sees no way that it can be made safe for human beings, which is a far more important question than whether the world can be made safe for it.

The principle threat to liberal democracy, and for human beings, is its consistent tendency to surrender to radical challengers, the most potent political example of which has been socialism. Tocqueville correctly identified that as the underlying question of 1848 (as did Marx, though with different affection), and for more than a hundred years thereafter it grew in significance to become the overriding question. Little wonder, then, that as the world seemed finally to defeat socialism, many imagined that it had defeated the arguments against liberal democracy. When we look more closely at 1848 through the eyes of Tocqueville and Marx, however, we discover reasons to doubt the wisdom of the prevailing view.

Tocqueville (in the *Recollections*) and Marx (in the *Eighteenth Brumaire*) discuss the same issues. First, does society originate in justice or injustice? Second, do the institutions of society operate in such a way as to improve human life? Third, is there any prospect to realize the ambition referred to as universal suffrage when we talk only in institutional terms but which, morally and culturally, means something richer than just voting?

The proposition of universal suffrage must be based on the idea that human beings can come to be altogether capable of reasoning together about the things of human life and the common good. Human beings altogether (or to so wide an extent that the omissions are trivial) must come to be capable of moderation, self-government, and moral sense in order to justify confidence in universal suffrage.

Anyone who thought that people only acted out of callous self-interest should have trouble defending universal suffrage. This, then, was the question of revolution in France—the oscillation between centralized power and revolts of the people. After February 1848, and the great popular rebellion in the name of universal suffrage, one finds in 1849 universal suffrage itself taken away by the republican government, under the fear that the people will abuse the power.

Is it true that the people will abuse power in general; ought power to be reserved only to those who have moral strength and understanding sufficient to exercise it? Or is there yet another basis for political life? One wants more to know how Tocqueville stands on this question than on the mere question of political affections.

Tocqueville is no simple democrat. He is skeptical about democracy. He does regard it as the irresistible wave of the future, but he does not think it a very good idea. For it delivers power to people who do not know what to do with it—people who will act out of envy rather than wisdom, who will be more concerned to level from their passion for equality than concerned to establish their particular city or country safely. Such a people will override a range of questions that statesmen need to handle, driven by their relative status vis-à-vis others in the community. The first volume of *Democracy in America* had already signaled this.[22] Tocqueville described the disappearance of aristocracy in the United States, where even natural aristocrats go into hiding:

Nowadays, one may say that the wealthy social classes in the United States are almost entirely outside the political arena. Moreover, wealth—far from being a right—there is a real cause of disfavor and an obstacle to reaching power. . . .

The rich surrender to this state of affairs as an irremediable evil, while he avoids with exquisite care showing how hurt he is. . . . One hears him boast publicly of the benefits of republican government and the advantages of democratic forms. After all, what is more natural in men, after hating their enemies, than to flatter them?[23]

He suggests that real human distinction is an obstacle to gaining power in a democracy. The death of aristocracy tells us something about the character of liberal democracy. We ask, "How can we originate the society without a principle of sociality, and how can we expect it to function if people are motivated solely by self-interest?" The answer usually presented as a responding miracle is the supposed discovery that we do not need moral principles, and we can make society work by orchestrating the interactions of self-interest so as to create a social equilibrium from everyone pursuing his own goals and not caring about anyone else's.

Critics have denied the miracle. The Antifederalists, for example, favored some sense of community, some homogeneity, something social to hold things together sufficiently to foster mutual reliance in order to make democratic politics work. The argument from rights (understood as mere interest), however, says nothing about participation in politics and political responsibility. It ultimately assumes an almost utopian balance of forces in which all of the classical historical problems of human life have disappeared. Men have become consumed with pursuing their own interests and satiating their own passions.

Tocqueville urged that no such balance emerged in the revolution, for people were so bent on satiating their passions that they were almost resistless. One could not turn them back any time they had the idea that they could lay hands on someone else's goods. He described them:

Folk had assured these poor people that the property of the wealthy were somehow obtained by theft from them. Folk assured them that the inequality of fortunes was as contrary to morality and society as to nature. Many poor people believed it, assisted by needs and passions. That obscure and erroneous conception of right, which mated with brute force, imparted to this concept an energy, tenacity, and power that it never should have acquired singly.[24]

This is a portrait of the popular insurrection in June 1848. The "theories of socialism" held by the insurrectionists led them to believe they had a right to goods stolen from them on account of society's originating in injustice. They think the only way to recover their goods is to reach out and take them, because the inequalities they suffer are not only historically wrong but also a continuing moral injury to them.

The implication is that what began as an argument about individual rights veered off track, because it did not take into account the motivations of human beings. Men would see their own poverty, insofar as they experienced it, not as something momentary that they would overcome in due course as they enjoyed more and more of these rights, but as an injustice they had suffered. The only way to change those circumstances is to overthrow the regime and to take from others property wrongly owned. Tocqueville argues that a spirit of envy will undermine the supposed smooth operation of a system of entrepreneurial energy based on individual liberty.

Socialist theories in the shape of greedy, envious desires continued to spread among the people sowing the seeds of future revolutions, but the socialist party itself remained beaten and impotent. The Montagnards, who did not belong to that party, seemed to have been struck down beyond recall by the same blow that felled it. Even the moderate republicans were not slow to see that the victory that had saved them had left them on a slope sliding beyond a republic. They immediately made an effort to pull back but in vain.[25]

Naturally enough, Marx thinks very differently about these events than does Tocqueville. Nonetheless, in light of the foregoing Tocqueville passage, the following passage from Marx is instructive:

If the overthrow of the parliamentary republic contains within itself the germ of the triumph of the proletarian revolution, its immediate and palpable result was *the victory of Bonaparte over Parliament, of the executive power over the legislative power, of force without phrases over the force of phrases.*[26]

In other words, Marx describes Bonaparte's coming to be the representative of the people, after continuing internecine struggles among the various classes intermediate between the people and the dictator. Thus, the popular will was to become the law of the nation not through the people ruling directly but through the force of the dictator. Marx continued:

In Parliament the nation made its general will the law; that is, it made the law of the ruling class its general will. Before the executive power it renounces all will of its own and submits to the superior commands of an alien will—to authority. The executive power in contrast to the legislative power expresses the heteronomy[27] of a nation in contrast to its autonomy. France, therefore, seems to have escaped the despotism of a class only to fall back beneath the despotism of an individual.[28]

Now, Tocqueville agrees with Marx. He also sees the emergence of Napoleon Bonaparte as fulfilling the popular revolution rather than a reaction to the revolution. Nonetheless, what Marx is saying, and what is important about it, is that what Tocqueville calls the people's "envy" has driven this process less than the self-interested behavior of the various classes (as he has identified them). In an earlier passage he even questioned whether we can regard those who are called the petty peasants a class. They have lost the sense of class; they are no longer in contact with one another; they are no longer in community; and yet they are the people who drive the popular uprising and bring Bonaparte to power in an alliance with the urban proletariat.

Thus, these isolated individuals—whether inspired by envy or political submission—drive the nation relentlessly towards a concentration of power in the pursuit of their goal, which is to strike down the differences among themselves and the classes they see but do not acknowledge as their superiors. Both Tocqueville and Marx make this argument.

In context, we ask what the rhetoric of republicanism is all about? If liberal democracy is the rhetoric of republicanism, what is it all about? Why do not people simply talk politics, in the way they used to do in the old world. Why do not the French speak of the Italians, the Germans, and the Belgians in terms of their lack of civilization and the reason they ought to be destroyed? Why does politics become a language primarily about domestic concerns, which is true all over the earth today, including here in the United States? People who declaim that this is the greatest country in the world seem not to be talking politics but to be living in la-la land. Of course, though, politics classically and traditionally distinguished one people from another. While for us politics is what distinguishes one interest from another. In these writers, also, politics distinguishes one interest from another.

The question is: how did communities come to be disintegrated such that nothing important could be said about politics other than fellow citizens' mutual hatreds and struggles? Is it ever possible in terms of this discourse to refer to communities again? May we refer to the French as a community? If we read Marx's account of their struggles—struggles that always end in some degree of bloodshed—we find a people who kill over theories. They do not kill outsiders; they kill one another over theories.

Marx and Tocqueville wrote after the revolutionary struggles of 1848 to 1851 (and Tocqueville actually participated in them). In fact, though, many of those same conversations continue to resonate through the one hundred and forty years afterwards—first in many countries in Europe and then spreading to Latin America, Asia, and Africa. Ultimately it became a world conversation that came to be known as the "cold war," in which people debated perhaps the merits of their civilizations but always under the guise of debating the relative merits of socialism and liberal democracy.

Is socialism really an alternative to liberal democracy?[29] If so, what is its chief argument against liberal democracy? Far ahead of the development of explicit theories that fueled political revolutions, there was a notion that one had to do more than talk about the prospects of material progress or comfort. One also had to convert the discussion of material progress into a discussion of social cohesion. Socialists seem to have argued that liberal democracy does not permit social cohesion.

Marx provided the explanation for this conclusion, namely that liberal democracy is predicated on the conflict of classes. This is the form of life in which by definition they fight and kill one another by historical necessity—because of material conditions. Rousseau's discovery that society originates in the accidental discovery of property leads to Marx's discovery that the influence of the accident does not end with the social contract and a legislator, but sets in motion an historical train of events.

While Tocqueville has the concluding word, Marx has special relevance in this inquiry, because his methodological materialism lies at the foundation of much modern opinion regarding the relationship of economics and freedom. We have returned to the *Eighteenth Brumaire* because it is one of the first and clearest elaborations of the theory of historical materialism, and almost the only work in which Marx accomplishes a full illustration of the theory. Readers have previously underemphasized Marx's starting point as opposed to the end he envisioned, and in doing so they have obscured the implications of his teachings for all views of stratified, mediated, or complex communities.

Marx wrote clearly of the impossibility of community in general for all men who had lived until the time he wrote and for most if not all who would ever live. What makes community in general impossible is the view that what might be taken as the differentiated dynamics of a single community constitute in fact the inveterate antagonisms of true enemies and not potential friends. The theory runs thus:

Upon the different forms of property, upon the social conditions of existence, rises an entire superstructure of distinct and peculiarly formed sentiments, illusions, modes of thought and views of life. The entire class creates and forms them out of its material foundations and out of the corresponding social relations. The single individual, who derives them through tradition and upbringing, may imagine that they form the real motives and starting point of his activity.[30]

The beginning of the theory of Karl Marx—not the end, the utopianizing vision of a withering of the state—has the greatest relevance for continued theorizing about the state or society. That beginning is nothing less than a categorical refutation of the possibility of the *res publica*—that is, the reality of a true public and a common good in any of the arenas in which we traditionally observe politics.

The description of politics in Marx is a description of continuous warfare, where the terms "classes" or "social orders" replace the terms "armies" and "command and control." What this insight means for the present discussion is two-fold. First, the denial of the possibility of a public good for or within a liberal democracy is the most radical challenge to that regime (hence, Tocqueville was right). Second, all discussion of a restoration or renaissance of a sense of civic culture must succeed first—before it can have an impact on the contemporary stage—to reclaim from Marx's devastating attack a legitimate role for differential cultural actors—individually and in groups.

Every modestly informed observer will forgive my not eliciting a list of examples to illustrate the ways in which contemporary commentary echoes Marx in assumptions of interested behavior and inveterate oppositions of interests among social strata as the basis of society. Besides, it would be far simpler to enumerate the rare cases in which the socialist presumption does not contribute the starting point of inquiry.

If it is true, however, and as I maintain, that the socialist presumption (that is, there is no common good under forms of the political organization of society) thoroughly reigns as orthodoxy across the spectrum of contemporary political opinions, then it must surely follow that socialism has rather been disapproved in practice than disproved in theory. What would follow from that is recognition of the need to respond to the radical challenges to liberal democracy as a precondition for undertaking the cultural strengthening of liberal democracy.

Here, too, we may lean on Marx:

Men make their own history, but they do not make it just as they please; they do not make it under circumstances chosen by themselves, but under circumstances directly encountered, given and transmitted from the past. The traditions of all the dead generations weigh like a nightmare on the brain of the living.[31]

The pervasive circumstances constraining the makers of a new history today is the pervasive, deadly influence of socialism inherited from the past. Tocqueville recognized this process as it was just beginning. He saw in the revolutions of 1848 not just a reordering but a dissolution or fragmentation of society—one meant to be permanent.

This time, it was not merely a matter of the triumph of one party; people aspired to launch a social science, a philosophy, I could almost say a single religion that they could teach to all men and cause them to follow. That was the truly great departure from the old picture.[32]

Tocqueville stood among those who resisted the reduction of all human society to an abstract order. Indeed, they initially succeeded in branding socialism a sclerosis.

Marx foresaw that growing influence would follow the early defeats. But it was Tocqueville who explained why. Initially he explained how "socialist theories" penetrated the minds of the people "in the form of greedy and envious passions," planting "seeds of future revolutions" despite the impotence of the socialist party[33]. More profoundly, though, he asked:

Will socialism remain buried in the scorn that so justly covered the socialists of 1848? I raise the question without answering it. I am certain that the fundamental laws of our modern society might be sharply modified in the fullness of time; they have already been so altered in several of their main parts. But shall it ever occur that folk will destroy and install others in their place? That seems impracticable to me. That's all I can say, for to the extent that I study the ancient condition of the world more closely, and also see up close our own world today; whenever I weigh the immense diversity that one encounters between them, not only within the laws but within the principles of the laws and the different forms that the right to landholding have taken and retain, to this very day, no matter what folk say, I am tempted to believe that what folk call necessary institutions are often nothing but the institutions folk are used to. Regarding a social constitution the realm of possibility is so much vaster than the people living in any one society might imagine.[34]

In returning to the *Federalist Papers*, then, we returned to that "realm of possibility" that serves to enlarge our political imaginations. That is the realm, and the manner, in which what happened more than two hundred years ago, remains relevant to the challenges people face today.

Of course, in order to benefit from a reading of the *Federalist Papers*, people must first be able to read *and* understand them. This commentary demonstrates that possibility by example. Nevertheless, it remains appropriate to respond to the old canard that the *Federalist Papers* were not written to the level of understanding of the general public.

I believe it is fair to say that they were written without distinguishing those who could read them from those who could not. It would certainly be folly for us, even at this date, to pretend that these essays could be read by any and everybody. It's probably even true that these essays are, in one sense, less accessible today than they were to most Americans in 1787 and 1788, for the simple reason that very few people today are educated on the staples that would make these essays much more approachable; the staples are the King James Version of the Bible, Shakespeare, *Bunyan's Pilgrim's Progress*, and some of the more prominent philosophical works of the 18th century. Now the philosophical works were usually read by university people, but nearly everyone read such things as Bunyan, Shakespeare perhaps, and certainly the King James Version of the Bible. And people whose educations are framed from those elements are people whom I would expect to have no difficulty reading these essays.

They are people like Abraham Lincoln, and we know of course the character of his education. Much must be given to native intellect to be sure, but I think it's also fair to say that much more must be given to Lincoln's reading in those same common elements that would have been present in the eighteenth century, both for producing his wonderful power of oratory and rhetoric and also for his ability to understand these things. Never forget that in Lincoln's campaigns and his fight against slavery particularly, most of the time what he debated were questions centering on the origins—the historical origins—of the United States from the time of the Declaration of Independence through the Constitution—which meant that he was reading all these documents.

Now Lincoln had certainly a spare education, to say the least. His reading in law school was the closest thing to a genuinely formal education he had. I say "law school"—that's a mistake, it's reading in the law office. And I don't think that that is uncharacteristic of people in the late eighteenth century. So I say, "yes," the essays were written and published generally for general consumption. They appeared first in newspapers in New York; they were quickly picked up, as all such things in the colonies were, and published throughout the other states. They didn't worry about copyrights and therefore they were widely circulated.

It is a more interesting question, by the way, to extend this, to ask what role these essays played in the ratification of the Constitution. We know people *could* read them, but can we find out whether they had an influence? One of the things we do notice is that the first six states or so ratified the Constitution in advance of the publication of the bulk of these essays. States such as Delaware, Pennsylvania, and New Jersey had finished ratification before the end of 1787, when still fewer than half of the essays had been published. So we can say that they didn't contribute meaningfully to ratification in those states. They may have played a slight role in Massachusetts, which ratified the Constitution after the turn of the year, but there is no way to assess how far they played a role. The state in which we would have expected them to play the greatest role would, of course, have been New York. That's where they were aimed in the first place. That's where Hamilton initiated the project, and of course he was in the New York Convention. New York finally ratified in late June, and by one vote. By one vote! It was a close contest all the way. And the one vote was provided in the end by a clear Antifederalist who wrote essays against the Constitution during this debate, but who at that point, finally seeing that New Hampshire had ratified, that Virginia ratified, that the Union was going into effect, decided for prudential reasons that New York also should ratify. So we might say that, if they had an influence in New York, it was not necessarily of the direct variety, and if they had an influence, say, in a state like Virginia, it would be very hard for us to identify it. They may have contributed very much in South Carolina, to take another example, where there was closer communication with New York, and much greater reliance upon the work of people like Hamilton. So, trying to turn it into that kind of practical understanding of where the votes come from, we have a much more difficult time.

But we do know that they were read widely. We know that Thomas Jefferson received them in France where he was the American Minister to the French Court, and praised them highly. We know that Washington, when he saw them, praised them highly, as most people did, and that they were published widely. So they were a part of that larger constitution, the constitution that's represented in the on-going debate, in the conversation, even if they didn't determine the outcome in any particular state. We don't know that they did not influence the result, even when we can't verify that they did.

NOTES

1. E. S. Corwin, *The "Higher Law" Background of American Constitutional Law* (Ithaca, NY: Cornell University Press, 1965, c1929).

2. John Locke, *Second Treatise on Civil Government,* para. 6.

3. Charles de Montesquieu, *De l'esprit des lois,* Bk. I, ch. 1.

4. Locke, para. 6.

5. Alexis de Tocqueville, *Democracy in America* (New York: Modern Library, 1981).

6. Alexis de Tocqueville, *Souvenirs* (Paris: Gallimard, 1964), ed. J. P. Mayer and B. M. Wicks Boisson, Pt. II, Ch. 10, pp. 156f. [Translation by author. Hereinafter, *Recollections,* 156f.]

7. *Recollections,* 240f.

8. Alexis de Tocqueville, *L'ancien régime et la révolution* (Paris: Gallimard, 1967), ed. J. P. Mayer, Ch. 1, p. 57.

9. Tocqueville, *L'ancien régime,* 63.

10. Jean-Jacques Rousseau, *Contrat social; ou principes du droit politique* (Geneva: Chez Marc-Michel Bosquet, 1766), I, i.

11. Tocqueville, *L'ancien régime,* 66f.

12. *Federalist* ten, paragraph seven.

13. Locke, para. 21.

14. Tocqueville, *L'ancien régime,* Liv. III, ch. 1, p. 230.

15. "The earth belongs to the living," Thomas Jefferson exclaimed in a 1789 letter to James Madison. See *The Portable Thomas Jefferson,* ed. Merrill D. Peterson (New York: Viking Press, 1975).

16. James MacGregor Burns, *The Deadlock of Democracy; four party politics in America* (Engelwood Cliffs, NJ: Prentice Hall, 1963).

17. Tocqueville, *L'ancien régime,* Liv. III, ch. 1, p. 231.

18. Tocqueville, *L'ancien régime,* Liv. III, ch. 1, p. 233.

19. Tocqueville, *L'ancien régime,* Liv. III, ch. 1, p. 233f.

20. Tocqueville, *L'ancien régime,* Liv. III, ch. 1, p. 234.

21. Tocqueville, *L'ancien régime,* Liv. III, ch. 1, p. 248.

22. Tocqueville, *Democracy in America,* I. 178.

23. Tocqueville, *Democracy in America,* I, 262.

24. Tocqueville, *Souvenirs,* II, ix, 213.

25. Tocqueville, *Souvenirs,* II, x, 252f.

26. Karl Marx, *The Eighteenth Brumaire of Louis Bonaparte* (New York: International Publishers, 1963), 120. Italics in translation.

27. Today, this is called multiculturalism or diversity, and it contrasts with autonomy.

28. Marx, 121.

29. There were many early nineteenth century examples of state socialism, including within the United States. One of the more dramatic, however, occurred during the succession of constitutional struggles in Paraguay between 1816 and 1840.

30. Marx, 47.

31. Marx, 15.

32. Tocqueville, *Recollections,* 125.
33. Tocqueville, *Recollections,* 252.
34. Tocqueville, *Recollections,* 131.

APPENDIX

REFERENCES TO *THE FEDERALIST* IN SUPREME COURT CASES

Federalist 1
  Luther *v.* Borden, 48 U.S. 1; 1849 U.S. Lexis 337; 12 L. Ed. 581

Federalist 2
  Luther *v.* Borden, 48 U.S. 1; 1849 U.S. Lexis 337; 12 L. Ed. 581
  Communist Party of the United States *v.* Subversive Activities Control Bd., 367 U.S. 1;
    81 S. Ct. 1357; 1961 U.S. Lexis 1934; 6 L. Ed. 2d 625
  U.S. Term Limits, Inc., *et al. v.* Thornton *et al.*, 514 U.S. 779; 115 S. Ct. 1842; 1995
    U.S. Lexis 3487; 131 L. Ed. 2d 881

Federalist 3
  Hines *v.* Davidowitz, 312 U.S. 52; 61 S. Ct. 399; 1941 U.S. Lexis 1103; 85 L. Ed. 581
  Communist Party of the United States *v.* Subversive Activities Control Bd., 367 U.S. 1;
    81 S. Ct. 1357; 1961 U.S. Lexis 1934; 6 L. Ed. 2d 625
  Banco Nacional de Cuba *v.* Sabbatino, 376 U.S. 398; 84 S. Ct. 923; 1964 U.S. Lexis
    2252; 11 L. Ed. 2d 804
  Boos *v.* Barry, 485 U.S. 312; 108 S. Ct. 1157; 1988 U.S. Lexis 1445; 99 L. Ed. 2d 333

Federalist 4
  Hines *v.* Davidowitz, 312 U.S. 52; 61 S. Ct. 399; 1941 U.S. Lexis 1103; 85 L. Ed. 581
  Communist Party of the United States *v.* Subversive Activities Control Bd., 367 U.S. 1;
    81 S. Ct. 1357; 1961 U.S. Lexis 1934; 6 L. Ed. 2d 625
  Selective Serv. Sys. *v.* Minnesota Pub. Interest Research Group, 468 U.S. 841; 104 S. Ct.
    3348; 1984 U.S. Lexis 151; 82 L. Ed. 2d 632
  Wayte *v.* United States, 470 U.S. 598; 105 S. Ct. 1524; 1985 U.S. Lexis 71; 84 L. Ed. 2d
    547
  United States *v.* Lopez, 514 U.S. 549; 115 S. Ct. 1624; 1995 U.S. Lexis 3039; 131 L. Ed.
    2d 626

Federalist 5
  Hines *v.* Davidowitz, 312 U.S. 52; 61 S. Ct. 399; 1941 U.S. Lexis 1103; 85 L. Ed. 581
  Communist Party of the United States *v.* Subversive Activities Control Bd., 367 U.S. 1;
    81 S. Ct. 1357; 1961 U.S. Lexis 1934; 6 L. Ed. 2d 625

Federalist 6
   Ex parte Milligan, 71 U.S. 2; 1866 U.S. Lexis 861; 18 L. Ed. 281
   City of Chicago *v.* Morales, 527 U. S. 41; 119 S. Ct. 1849; 1999 U.S. Lexis 4005; 144
      L. Ed. 2d 67

Federalist 7
   Luther *v.* Borden, 48 U.S. 1; 1849 U.S. Lexis 337; 12 L. Ed. 581
   Veazie *v.* Moor, 55 U.S. 568; 1852 U.S. Lexis 469; 14 L. Ed. 545
   Case of the State Freight Tax, 82 U.S. 232; 1872 U.S. Lexis 1252; 21 L. Ed. 146
   Edwards *v.* Kearzey, 96 U.S. 595; 1877 U.S. Lexis 1704; 24 L. Ed. 793
   Farmers Loan & Trust Co. *v.* Minnesota, 280 U.S. 204; 50 S. Ct. 98; 1930 U.S. Lexis
      750; 74 L. Ed. 371
   Burnet *v.* Brooks, 288 U.S. 378; 53 S. Ct. 457; 1933 U.S. Lexis 42; 77 L. Ed. 844
   Home Bldg. & Loan Assn. *v.* Blaisdell, 290 U.S. 398; 54 S. Ct. 231; 1934 U.S. Lexis
      958; 78 L. Ed. 413
   Joseph *v.* Carter & Weekes Stevedoring Co., 330 U.S. 422; 67 S. Ct. 815; 1947 U.S.
      Lexis 2872; 91 L. Ed. 993
   Washington Stevedoring Cos., 435 U.S. 734; 98 S. Ct. 1388; 1978 U. S. Lexis 24; 55 L.
      Ed. 2d 682
   Exxon Corp. *v.* Governor of Maryland, 437 U.S. 117; 98 S. Ct. 2207; 1978 U.S. Lexis
      2; 57 L. Ed. 2d 91
   Garcia *v.* San Antonio Metro. Transit Auth., 469 U.S. 528; 105 S. Ct. 1005; 1985 U.S.
      Lexis 48; 83 L. Ed. 2d 1016
   Northeast Bancorp *v.* Board of Governors of the Fed. Reserve Sys., 472 U.S. 159; 105
      S. Ct. 2545; 1985 U.S. Lexis 126; 86 L. Ed. 2d 112
   Tyler Pipe Indus. *v.* Washington State Dept. of Revenue, 483 U.S. 232; 107 S. Ct. 2810;
      1987 U.S. Lexis 2872; 97 L. Ed. 2d 199
   Dennis *v.* Higgins, 498 U.S. 439; 111 S. Ct. 865; 1991 U.S. Lexis 1142; 112 L. Ed. 2d
      969
   Quill Corp. *v.* North Dakota, 504 U.S. 298; 112 S. Ct 1904; 1992 U. S. Lexis 3123; 119
      L. Ed. 2d 91
   Oklahoma Tax Commission *v.* Jefferson Lines, Inc., 514 U.S. 175; 115 S. Ct. 1331; 1995
      U.S. Lexis 2418; 131 L. Ed. 2d 261

Federalist 9
   Heath *v.* Alabama, 474 U.S. 82; 106 S. Ct. 433; 1985 U.S. Lexis 143; 88 L. Ed. 2d 387

Federalist 10
   Pacific States Tel. & Tel. Co. *v.* Oregon, 223 U.S. 118; 32 S. Ct. 224; 1912 U.S. Lexis
      2220; 56 L. Ed. 377
   Storer *v.* Brown, 415 U.S. 724; 94 S. Ct. 1274; 1974 U.S. Lexis 118; 39 L. Ed. 2d 714
   Brown *v.* Hartlage, 456 U.S. 45; 102 S. Ct. 1523; 1982 U.S. Lexis 92; 71 L. Ed. 2d 732
   Anderson *v.* Celebrezze, 460 U.S. 780; 103 S. Ct. 1564; 1983 U.S. Lexis 145; 75 L. Ed.
      2d 547
   Minnesota State Bd. for Community Colleges *v.* Knight, 465 U.S. 271; 104 S. Ct. 1058;
      1984 U.S. Lexis 28; 79 L. Ed. 2d 299

Lyng *v.* Northwest Indian Cemetery Protective Assn., 485 U.S. 439; 108 S. Ct. 1319; 1988 U.S. Lexis 1871; 99 L. Ed. 2d 534

City of Richmond *v.* J. A. Croson Co., 488 U.S. 469; 109 S. Ct. 706; 1989 U.S. Lexis 579; 102 L. Ed. 2d 854

Austin *v.* Michigan State Chamber of Commerce, 494 U.S. 652; 110 S. Ct. 1391; 1990 U.S. Lexis 1665; 108 L. Ed. 2d 652

Columbia *v.* Omni Outdoor Advertising, 499 U.S. 365; 111 S. Ct. 1344; 1991 U.S. Lexis 1858; 113 L. Ed. 2d 382

Norman *v.* Reed, 502 U.S. 279; 112 S. Ct. 698; 1992 U.S. Lexis 370; 116 L. Ed. 2d 711

Lucas *v.* South Carolina Coastal Council, 505 U.S. 1003; 112 S. Ct. 2886; 1992 U.S. Lexis 4537; 120 L. Ed. 2d 798

Adarand Constructors, Inc. *v.* Pena, Secretary of Transportation, *et al.*, 515 U.S. 200; 115 S. Ct. 2097; 1995 U.S. Lexis 4037; 132 L. Ed. 2d 158

Gutierrez de Martinez *et al. v.* Lamagno *et al.*, 515 U.S. 417; 115 S. Ct. 2227; 1995 U.S. Lexis 4043; 132 L. Ed. 2d 375

Timmons *v.* Twin Cities Area New Party, 117 S. Ct. 1364; 1997 U.S. Lexis 2796; 137 L. Ed. 2d 589

Federalist 11

Brown *v.* Maryland, 25 U.S. 419; 1827 U.S. Lexis 398; 6 L. Ed. 678

Veazie *v.* Moor, 55 U.S. 568; 1852 U.S. Lexis 469; 14 L. Ed. 545

Carter *v.* Carter Coal Co., 298 U.S. 238; 56 S. Ct. 855; 1936 U.S. Lexis 950; 80 L. Ed. 1160

Michelin Tire Corp. *v.* Wages, 423 U.S. 276; 96 S. Ct. 535; 1976 U. S. Lexis 120; 46 L. Ed. 2d 495

Washington Stevedoring Cos., 435 U.S. 734; 98 S. Ct. 1388; 1978 U. S. Lexis 24; 55 L. Ed. 2d 682

Exxon Corp. *v.* Governor of Maryland, 437 U.S. 117; 98 S. Ct. 2207; 1978 U.S. Lexis 2; 57 L. Ed. 2d 91

Reeves, Inc. *v.* Stake, 447 U.S. 429; 100 S. Ct. 2271; 1980 U.S. Lexis 40; 65 L. Ed. 2d 244

Garcia *v.* San Antonio Metro. Transit Auth., 469 U.S. 528; 105 S. Ct. 1005; 1985 U.S. Lexis 48; 83 L. Ed. 2d 1016

Dennis *v.* Higgins, 498 U.S. 439; 111 S. Ct. 865; 1991 U.S. Lexis 1142; 112 L. Ed. 2d 969

Quill Corp. *v.* North Dakota, 504 U.S. 298; 112 S. Ct 1904; 1992 U. S. Lexis 3123; 119 L. Ed. 2d 91

Oklahoma Tax Commission *v.* Jefferson Lines, Inc., 514 U.S. 175; 115 S. Ct. 1331; 1995 U.S. Lexis 2418; 131 L. Ed. 2d 261

City of Chicago *v.* Morales, 527 U. S. 41; 119 S. Ct. 1849; 1999 U.S. Lexis 4005; 144 L. Ed. 2d 67

Federalist 12

Brown *v.* Maryland, 25 U.S. 419; 1827 U.S. Lexis 398; 6 L. Ed. 678

Thurlow *v.* Massachusetts, 46 U.S. 504; 1847 U.S. Lexis 322; 12 L. Ed. 256

Youngstown Sheet & Tube Co. *v.* Bowers, 358 U.S. 534; 79 S. Ct. 383; 1959 U.S. Lexis 1489; 3 L. Ed. 2d 490

Michelin Tire Corp. *v.* Wages, 423 U.S. 276; 96 S. Ct. 535; 1976 U. S. Lexis 120; 46 L. Ed. 2d 495

Exxon Corp. *v.* Governor of Maryland, 437 U.S. 117; 98 S. Ct. 2207; 1978 U.S. Lexis 2; 57 L. Ed. 2d 91

United States *v.* Lopez, 514 U.S. 549; 115 S. Ct. 1624; 1995 U.S. Lexis 3039; 131 L. Ed. 2d 626

Camps Newfound/Owatonna, Inc. *v.* Town of Harrison, 117 S. Ct. 1590; 1997 U.S. Lexis 3227; 137 L. Ed. 2d 852

Federalist 14

Luther *v.* Borden, 48 U.S. 1; 1849 U.S. Lexis 337; 12 L. Ed. 581

Pacific States Tel. & Tel. Co. *v.* Oregon, 223 U.S. 118; 32 S. Ct. 224; 1912 U.S. Lexis 2220; 56 L. Ed. 377

Federalist 15

Penhallow *v.* Doane's Admrs., 3 U.S. 54; 1795 U.S. Lexis 329; 1 L. Ed. 507

National Prohibition Cases, 253 U.S. 350; 40 S. Ct. 486; 1920 U.S. Lexis 1371; 64 L. Ed. 946

Adickes *v.* S. H. Kress & Co., 398 U.S. 144; 90 S. Ct. 1598; 1970 U. S. Lexis 31; 26 L. Ed. 2d 142

FERC *v.* Mississippi, 456 U.S. 742; 102 S. Ct. 2126; 1982 U.S. Lexis 38; 72 L. Ed. 2d 532

New York *v.* United States *et al.*, 505 U.S. 144; 112 S. Ct. 2408; 1992 U.S. Lexis 3693; 120 L. Ed. 2d 120

U.S. Term Limits, Inc., *et al. v.* Thornton *et al.*, 514 U.S. 779; 115 S. Ct. 1842; 1995 U.S. Lexis 3487; 131 L. Ed. 2d 881

Printz *v.* United States, 117 S. Ct. 2365; 1997 U.S. Lexis 4044; 138 L. Ed. 2d 914

Alden *v.* Maine, 119 S. Ct. 2240; 1999 U.S. Lexis 4374; 144 L. Ed. 2d 636

Federalist 16

FERC *v.* Mississippi, 456 U.S. 742; 102 S. Ct. 2126; 1982 U.S. Lexis 38; 72 L. Ed. 2d 532

Federalist 17

Garcia *v.* San Antonio Metro. Transit Auth., 469 U.S. 528; 105 S. Ct. 1005; 1985 U.S. Lexis 48; 83 L. Ed. 2d 1016

Atascadero State Hosp. *v.* Scanlon, 473 U.S. 234; 105 S. Ct. 3142; 1985 U.S. Lexis 89; 87 L. Ed. 2d 171

United States *v.* Lopez, 514 U.S. 549; 115 S. Ct. 1624; 1995 U.S. Lexis 3039; 131 L. Ed. 2d 626

Federalist 18

Groves *v.* Slaughter, 40 U.S. 449; 1841 U.S. Lexis 278; 10 L. Ed. 800

Printz *v.* United States, 117 S. Ct. 2365; 1997 U.S. Lexis 4044; 138 L. Ed. 2d 914

Federalist 19

Printz *v.* United States, 117 S. Ct. 2365; 1997 U.S. Lexis 4044; 138 L. Ed. 2d 914

Federalist 20

Printz *v.* United States, 117 S. Ct. 2365; 1997 U.S. Lexis 4044; 138 L. Ed. 2d 914

Alden *v.* Maine, 119 S. Ct. 2240; 1999 U.S. Lexis 4374; 144 L. Ed. 2d 636

Federalist 21

Luther *v.* Borden, 48 U.S. 1; 1849 U.S. Lexis 337; 12 L. Ed. 581

Springer *v.* United States, 102 U.S. 586; 1880 U.S. Lexis 2066; 26 L. Ed. 253

Helvering *v.* Davis, 301 U.S. 619; 57 S. Ct. 904; 1937 U.S. Lexis 1200; 81 L. Ed. 1307

United States *v.* Lopez, 514 U.S. 549; 115 S. Ct. 1624; 1995 U.S. Lexis 3039; 131 L. Ed. 2d 626

Federalist 22

Luther *v.* Borden, 48 U.S. 1; 1849 U.S. Lexis 337; 12 L. Ed. 581

Dodge *v.* Woolsey, 59 U.S. 331; 1855 U.S. Lexis 704; 15 L. Ed. 401

United States *v.* Jin Fuey Moy, 241 U.S. 394; 36 S. Ct. 658; 1916 U.S. Lexis 1719; 60 L. Ed. 1061

Selective Draft Law Cases *v.* United States, 245 U.S. 366; 38 S. Ct. 159; 1918 U.S. Lexis 2138; 62 L. Ed. 349

National Prohibition Cases, 253 U.S. 350; 40 S. Ct. 486; 1920 U.S. Lexis 1371; 64 L. Ed. 946

United States *v.* South-Eastern Underwriters Assn., 322 U.S. 533; 64 S. Ct. 1162; 1944 U.S. Lexis 1199; 88 L. Ed. 1440

Joseph *v.* Carter & Weekes Stevedoring Co., 330 U.S. 422; 67 S. Ct. 815; 1947 U.S. Lexis 2872; 91 L. Ed. 993

Glidden Co. *v.* Zdanok, 370 U.S. 530; 82 S. Ct. 1459; 1962 U.S. Lexis 2139; 8 L. Ed. 2d 671

Washington Stevedoring Cos., 435 U.S. 734; 98 S. Ct. 1388; 1978 U.S. Lexis 24; 55 L. Ed. 2d 682

Exxon Corp. *v.* Governor of Maryland, 437 U.S. 117; 98 S. Ct. 2207; 1978 U.S. Lexis 2; 57 L. Ed. 2d 91

INS *v.* Chadha, 462 U.S. 919; 103 S. Ct. 2764; 1983 U.S. Lexis 80; 77 L. Ed. 2d 317

Garcia *v.* San Antonio Metro. Transit Auth., 469 U.S. 528; 105 S. Ct. 1005; 1985 U.S. Lexis 48; 83 L. Ed. 2d 1016

Northeast Bancorp *v.* Board of Governors of the Fed. Reserve Sys., 472 U.S. 159; 105 S. Ct. 2545; 1985 U.S. Lexis 126; 86 L. Ed. 2d 112

C & A Carbone, Inc. *v.* Town of Clarkstown, New York, 511 U.S. 383; 114 S. Ct. 1677; 1994 U.S. Lexis 3477; 128 L. Ed. 2d 399

American Dredging Co. *v.* Miller, 510 U.S. 443; 114 S. Ct. 981; 1994 U.S. Lexis 1870; 127 L. Ed. 2d 285

Seminole Tribe of Florida *v.* Florida, 517 U.S. 44; 116 S. Ct. 1114; 1996 U.S. Lexis 2165; 134 L. Ed. 2d 252

Federalist 23

United States *v.* Adams, 74 U.S. 463; 1868 U.S. Lexis 1022; 19 L. Ed. 249

Selective Draft Law Cases *v.* United States, 245 U.S. 366; 38 S. Ct. 159; 1918 U.S. Lexis 2138; 62 L. Ed. 349

United States *v.* South-Eastern Underwriters Assn., 322 U.S. 533; 64 S. Ct. 1162; 1944 U.S. Lexis 1199; 88 L. Ed. 1440

Lichter *v.* United States, 334 U.S. 742; 68 S. Ct. 1294; 1948 U.S. Lexis 2705; 92 L. Ed. 1694

Reid *v.* Covert, 354 U.S. 1; 77 S. Ct. 1222; 1957 U.S. Lexis 729; 1 L. Ed. 2d 1148

Kinsella *v.* United States *ex rel.* Singleton, 361 U.S. 234; 80 S. Ct. 297; 1960 U.S. Lexis 1742; 4 L. Ed. 2d 268

O'Callahan *v.* Parker, 395 U.S. 258; 89 S. Ct. 1683; 1969 U.S. Lexis 1436; 23 L. Ed. 2d 291

Solorio *v.* United States, 483 U.S. 435; 107 S. Ct. 2924; 1987 U.S. Lexis 2892; 97 L. Ed. 2d 364

Perpich *v.* DoD, 496 U.S. 334; 110 S. Ct. 2418; 1990 U.S. Lexis 3012; 110 L. Ed. 2d 312

Loving *v.* United States, 517 U.S. 748; 116 S. Ct. 1737; 1996 U.S. Lexis 3593; 135 L. Ed. 2d 36

Federalist 24

Reid *v.* Covert, 354 U.S. 1; 77 S. Ct. 1222; 1957 U.S. Lexis 729; 1 L. Ed. 2d 1148

Selective Serv. Sys. *v.* Minnesota Pub. Interest Research Group, 468 U.S. 841; 104 S. Ct. 3348; 1984 U.S. Lexis 151; 82 L. Ed. 2d 632

Wayte *v.* United States, 470 U.S. 598; 105 S. Ct. 1524; 1985 U.S. Lexis 71; 84 L. Ed. 2d 547

Harmelin *v.* Michigan, 501 U.S. 957; 111 S. Ct. 2680; 1991 U.S. Lexis 3816; 115 L. Ed. 2d 836

United States *v.* Lopez, 514 U.S. 549; 115 S. Ct. 1624; 1995 U.S. Lexis 3039; 131 L. Ed. 2d 626

Federalist 25

Reid *v.* United States, 211 U.S. 529; 29 S. Ct. 171; 1909 U.S. Lexis 1784; 53 L. Ed. 313

Selective Serv. Sys. *v.* Minnesota Pub. Interest Research Group, 468 U.S. 841; 104 S. Ct. 3348; 1984 U.S. Lexis 151; 82 L. Ed. 2d 632

Wayte *v.* United States, 470 U.S. 598; 105 S. Ct. 1524; 1985 U.S. Lexis 71; 84 L. Ed. 2d 547

Perpich *v.* DoD, 496 U.S. 334; 110 S. Ct. 2418; 1990 U.S. Lexis 3012; 110 L. Ed. 2d 312

Federalist 26

Ex parte Milligan, 71 U.S. 2; 1866 U.S. Lexis 861; 18 L. Ed. 281

Reid *v.* Covert, 354 U.S. 1; 77 S. Ct. 1222; 1957 U.S. Lexis 729; 1 L. Ed. 2d 1148

Federalist 27

Houston *v.* Moore, 18 U.S. 1; 1820 U.S. Lexis 244; 5 L. Ed. 19

Reid *v.* Covert, 354 U.S. 1; 77 S. Ct. 1222; 1957 U.S. Lexis 729; 1 L. Ed. 2d 1148

Printz *v.* United States, 117 S. Ct. 2365; 1997 U.S. Lexis 4044; 138 L. Ed. 2d 914

Federalist 28

Reid *v.* Covert, 354 U.S. 1; 77 S. Ct. 1222; 1957 U.S. Lexis 729; 1 L. Ed. 2d 1148

Gregory *v.* Ashcroft, 501 U.S. 452; 111 S. Ct. 2395; 1991 U.S. Lexis 3626; 115 L. Ed. 2d 410

Printz *v.* United States, 117 S. Ct. 2365; 1997 U.S. Lexis 4044; 138 L. Ed. 2d 914

Federalist 29
Martin *v.* Mott, 25 U.S. 19; 1827 U.S. Lexis 378; 6 L. Ed. 537
Luther *v.* Borden, 48 U.S. 1; 1849 U.S. Lexis 337; 12 L. Ed. 581

Federalist 30
Piqua Branch of the State Bank of Ohio *v.* Knoop, 57 U.S. 369; 1850 U.S. Lexis 1558; 14 L. Ed. 977
New York ex rel. Bank of Commer. *v.* Commissioners of Taxes for New York, 67 U.S. 620; 1862 U.S. Lexis 281; 17 L. Ed. 451
Pollock *v.* Farmers Loan & Trust Co., 158 U.S. 601; 15 S. Ct. 912; 1895 U.S. Lexis 2280; 39 L. Ed. 1108
United States *v.* South-Eastern Underwriters Assn., 322 U.S. 533; 64 S. Ct. 1162; 1944 U.S. Lexis 1199; 88 L. Ed. 1440
New York *v.* United States, 326 U.S. 572; 66 S. Ct. 310; 1946 U.S. Lexis 3140; 90 L. Ed. 326
Michelin Tire Corp. *v.* Wages, 423 U.S. 276; 96 S. Ct. 535; 1976 U. S. Lexis 120; 46 L. Ed. 2d 495
EEOC *v.* Wyoming, 460 U.S. 226; 103 S. Ct. 1054; 1983 U.S. Lexis 134; 75 L. Ed. 2d 18

Federalist 31
McCulloch *v.* Maryland, 17 U.S. 316; 1819 U.S. Lexis 320; 4 L. Ed. 579
Hall *v.* DeCuir, 95 U.S. 485; 1877 U.S. Lexis 2197; 24 L. Ed. 547
In re Neagle, 135 U.S. 1; 10 S. Ct. 658; 1890 U.S. Lexis 2006; 34 L. Ed. 55 [cited as *Federalist* 30]
Childers *v.* Beaver, 270 U.S. 555; 46 S. Ct. 387; 1926 U.S. Lexis 431; 70 L. Ed. 730
United States *v.* Sprague, 282 U.S. 716; 51 S. Ct. 220; 1931 U.S. Lexis 39; 75 L. Ed. 640
New York *v.* United States, 326 U.S. 572; 66 S. Ct. 310; 1946 U.S. Lexis 3140; 90 L. Ed. 326
National League of Cities *v.* Usery, 426 U.S. 833; 96 S. Ct. 2465; 1976 U.S. Lexis 158; 49 L. Ed. 2d 245

Federalist 32
McCulloch *v.* Maryland, 17 U.S. 316; 1819 U.S. Lexis 320; 4 L. Ed. 579
Houston *v.* Moore, 18 U.S. 1; 1820 U.S. Lexis 244; 5 L. Ed. 19
Gibbons *v.* Ogden, 22 U.S. 1; 1824 U.S. Lexis 370; 6 L. Ed. 23
Brown *v.* Maryland, 25 U.S. 419; 1827 U.S. Lexis 398; 6 L. Ed. 678
Weston *v.* City Council of Charleston, 27 U.S. 449; 1829 U.S. Lexis 414; 7 L. Ed. 481
Wheaton *v.* Peters, 33 U.S. 591; 1834 U.S. Lexis 619; 8 L. Ed. 1055 [cited as Federalist 34]
Mayor, Aldermen, & Commonalty of New York *v.* Miln, 36 U.S. 102; 1837 U.S. Lexis 169; 9 L. Ed. 648
Groves *v.* Slaughter, 40 U.S. 449; 1841 U.S. Lexis 278; 10 L. Ed. 800
Dobbins *v.* Commissioners of Erie Cty., 41 U.S. 435; 1842 U.S. Lexis 379; 10 L. Ed. 1022

Prigg v. Pennsylvania, 41 U.S. 539; 1842 U.S. Lexis 387; 10 L. Ed. 1060

Fox v. Ohio, 46 U.S.410; 1847 U.S. Lexis 320; 12 L. Ed. 213

Thurlow v. Massachusetts, 46 U.S. 504; 1847 U.S. Lexis 322; 12 L. Ed. 256

Smith v. Turner, 48 U.S. 283; 1849 U.S. Lexis 351; 12 L. Ed. 702

Nathan v. Louisiana, 49 U.S. 73; 1850 U.S. Lexis 1658; 12 L. Ed. 992

Cooley v. Board of Wardens of the Port of Philadelphia *ex rel.* Society for the Relief of Distressed Pilots, 53 U.S. 299; 1851 U.S. Lexis 658; 13 L. Ed. 996

Piqua Branch of the State Bank of Ohio v. Knoop, 57 U.S. 369; 1850 U.S. Lexis 1558; 14 L. Ed. 977

Gilman v. Philadelphia, 70 U.S. 713; 1865 U.S. Lexis 752; 18 L. Ed. 96

Woodruff v. Parham, 75 U.S. 123; 1868 U.S. Lexis 1088; 19 L. Ed. 382

Transportation Co. v. Wheeling, 99 U.S. 273; 1878 U.S. Lexis 1540; 25 L. Ed. 412

Leisy v. Hardin, 135 U.S. 100; 10 S. Ct. 681; 1890 U.S. Lexis 2007; 34 L. Ed. 128

Covington & Cincinnati Bridge Co. v. Kentucky, 154 U.S. 204; 14 S. Ct. 1087; 1894 U.S. Lexis 2229; 38 L. Ed. 962

Dooley v. United States, 183 U.S. 151; 22 S. Ct. 62; 1901 U.S. Lexis 1263; 46 L. Ed. 128

South Dakota v. North Carolina, 192 U.S. 286; 24 S. Ct. 269; 1904 U.S. Lexis 995; 48 L. Ed. 448

Utah Power & Light Co. v. United States, 243 U.S. 389; 37 S. Ct. 387; 1917 U.S. Lexis 2046; 61 L. Ed. 791

National Prohibition Cases, 253 U.S. 350; 40 S. Ct. 486; 1920 U.S. Lexis 1371; 64 L. Ed. 946

Hines v. Davidowitz, 312 U.S. 52; 61 S. Ct. 399; 1941 U.S. Lexis 1103; 85 L. Ed. 581

New York v. United States, 326 U.S. 572; 66 S. Ct. 310; 1946 U.S. Lexis 3140; 90 L. Ed. 326

Pennsylvania v. Nelson, 350 U.S. 497; 76 S. Ct. 477; 1956 U.S. Lexis 1730; 100 L. Ed. 640

Youngstown Sheet & Tube Co. v. Bowers, 358 U.S. 534; 79 S. Ct. 383; 1959 U.S. Lexis 1489; 3 L. Ed. 2d 490

Farmers Educ. & Coop. Union, North Dakota Div. v. WDAY, Inc., 360 U.S. 525; 79 S. Ct. 1302; 1959 U.S. Lexis 660; 3 L. Ed. 2d 1407

Goldstein v. California, 412 U.S. 546; 93 S. Ct. 2303; 1973 U.S. Lexis 15; 37 L. Ed. 2d 163

Michelin Tire Corp. v. Wages, 423 U.S. 276; 96 S. Ct. 535; 1976 U. S. Lexis 120; 46 L. Ed. 2d 495

Jones v. Rath Packing Co., 430 U.S. 519; 97 S. Ct. 1305; 1977 U.S. Lexis 68; 51 L. Ed. 2d 604

Southland Corp. v. Keating, 465 U.S. 1; 104 S. Ct. 852; 1984 U.S. Lexis 2; 79 L. Ed. 2d 1

Atascadero State Hosp. v. Scanlon, 473 U.S. 234; 105 S. Ct. 3142; 1985 U.S. Lexis 89; 87 L. Ed. 2d 171

U.S. Term Limits, Inc., *et al.* v. Thornton *et al.*, 514 U.S. 779; 115 S. Ct. 1842; 1995 U.S. Lexis 3487; 131 L. Ed. 2d 881

Seminole Tribe of Florida v. Florida, 517 U.S. 44; 116 S. Ct. 1114; 1996 U.S. Lexis 2165; 134 L. Ed. 2d 252

Camps Newfound/Owatonna, Inc. v. Town of Harrison, 117 S. Ct. 1590; 1997 U.S. Lexis 3227; 137 L. Ed. 2d 852

Federalist 33

McCulloch *v.* Maryland, 17 U.S. 316; 1819 U.S. Lexis 320; 4 L. Ed. 579
Brown *v.* Maryland, 25 U.S. 419; 1827 U.S. Lexis 398; 6 L. Ed. 678
Smith *v.* Turner, 48 U.S. 283; 1849 U.S. Lexis 351; 12 L. Ed. 702
New York *ex rel.* Bank of Commer. *v.* Commissioners of Taxes for New York, 67 U.S. 620; 1862 U.S. Lexis 281; 17 L. Ed. 451
Pacific States Tel. & Tel. Co. *v.* Oregon, 223 U.S. 118; 32 S. Ct. 224; 1912 U.S. Lexis 2220; 56 L. Ed. 377
Missouri *v.* Holland, 252 U.S. 416; 40 S. Ct. 382; 1920 U.S. Lexis 1520; 64 L. Ed. 641
National Prohibition Cases, 253 U.S. 350; 40 S. Ct. 486; 1920 U.S. Lexis 1371; 64 L. Ed. 946
Steward Mach. Co. *v.* Davis, 301 U.S. 548; 57 S. Ct. 883; 1937 U.S. Lexis 1199; 81 L. Ed. 1279
New York *v.* United States, 326 U.S. 572; 66 S. Ct. 310; 1946 U.S. Lexis 3140; 90 L. Ed. 326
United States *v.* Lopez, 514 U.S. 549; 115 S. Ct. 1624; 1995 U.S. Lexis 3039; 131 L. Ed. 2d 626
Printz *v.* United States, 117 S. Ct. 2365; 1997 U.S. Lexis 4044; 138 L. Ed. 2d 914
Alden *v.* Maine, 119 S. Ct. 2240; 1999 U.S. Lexis 4374; 144 L. Ed. 2d 636

Federalist 34

McCulloch *v.* Maryland, 17 U.S. 316; 1819 U.S. Lexis 320; 4 L. Ed. 579
Wheaton *v.* Peters, 33 U.S. 591; 1834 U.S. Lexis 619; 8 L. Ed. 1055
Smith *v.* Turner, 48 U.S. 283; 1849 U.S. Lexis 351; 12 L. Ed. 702
Pacific Ins. Co. *v.* Soule, 74 U.S. 433; 1868 U.S. Lexis 1019; 19 L. Ed. 95
New York *v.* United States, 326 U.S. 572; 66 S. Ct. 310; 1946 U.S. Lexis 3140; 90 L. Ed. 326
United States *v.* Lopez, 514 U.S. 549; 115 S. Ct. 1624; 1995 U.S. Lexis 3039; 131 L. Ed. 2d 626

Federalist 35

McCulloch *v.* Maryland, 17 U.S. 316; 1819 U.S. Lexis 320; 4 L. Ed. 579
New York *v.* United States, 326 U.S. 572; 66 S. Ct. 310; 1946 U.S. Lexis 3140; 90 L. Ed. 326
Michelin Tire Corp. *v.* Wages, 423 U.S. 276; 96 S. Ct. 535; 1976 U.S. Lexis 120; 46 L. Ed. 2d 495
United States *v.* Lopez, 514 U.S. 549; 115 S. Ct. 1624; 1995 U.S. Lexis 3039; 131 L. Ed. 2d 626

Federalist 36

McCulloch *v.* Maryland, 17 U.S. 316; 1819 U.S. Lexis 320; 4 L. Ed. 579
Smith *v.* Turner, 48 U.S. 283; 1849 U.S. Lexis 351; 12 L. Ed. 702
Scholey *v.* Rew, 90 U.S. 331; 1874 U.S. Lexis 1313; 23 L. Ed. 99
Pollock *v.* Farmers Loan & Trust Co., 157 U.S. 429; 15 S. Ct. 673; 1895 U.S. Lexis 2215; 39 L. Ed. 759
Pollock *v.* Farmers Loan & Trust Co., 158 U.S. 601; 15 S. Ct. 912; 1895 U.S. Lexis 2280; 39 L. Ed. 1108

Steward Mach. Co. *v.* Davis, 301 U.S. 548; 57 S. Ct. 883; 1937 U.S. Lexis 1199; 81 L. Ed. 1279

United States *v.* South-Eastern Underwriters Assn., 322 U.S. 533; 64 S. Ct. 1162; 1944 U.S. Lexis 1199; 88 L. Ed. 1440

New York *v.* United States, 326 U.S. 572; 66 S. Ct. 310; 1946 U.S. Lexis 3140; 90 L. Ed. 326

Michelin Tire Corp. *v.* Wages, 423 U.S. 276; 96 S. Ct. 535; 1976 U.S. Lexis 120; 46 L. Ed. 2d 495

United States *v.* Lopez, 514 U.S. 549; 115 S. Ct. 1624; 1995 U.S. Lexis 3039; 131 L. Ed. 2d 626

U.S. Term Limits, Inc., *et al. v.* Thornton *et al.*, 514 U.S. 779; 115 S. Ct. 1842; 1995 U.S. Lexis 3487; 131 L. Ed. 2d 881

Printz *v.* United States, 117 S. Ct. 2365; 1997 U.S. Lexis 4044; 138 L. Ed. 2d 914

Federalist 37

Griswold *v.* Connecticut, 381 U.S. 479; 85 S. Ct. 1678; 1965 U.S. Lexis 2282; 14 L. Ed. 2d 510

Sullivan *v.* Everhart, 494 U.S. 83; 110 S. Ct. 960; 1990 U.S. Lexis 1054; 108 L. Ed. 2d 72

Federalist 38

Scott *v.* Sandford, 60 U.S. 393; 1856 U.S. Lexis 472; 15 L. Ed. 691

De Lima *v.* Bidwell, 182 U.S. 1; 21 S. Ct. 743; 1901 U.S. Lexis 1225; 45 L. Ed. 1041

Federalist 39

Luther *v.* Borden, 48 U.S. 1; 1849 U.S. Lexis 337; 12 L. Ed. 581

Kiernan *v.* Portland, 223 U.S. 151; 32 S. Ct. 231; 1912 U.S. Lexis 2221; 56 L. Ed. 386

Pacific States Tel. & Tel. Co. *v.* Oregon, 223 U.S. 118; 32 S. Ct. 224; 1912 U.S. Lexis 2220; 56 L. Ed. 377

Utah Power & Light Co. *v.* United States, 243 U.S. 389; 37 S. Ct. 387; 1917 U.S. Lexis 2046; 61 L. Ed. 791

National Prohibition Cases, 253 U.S. 350; 40 S. Ct. 486; 1920 U.S. Lexis 1371; 64 L. Ed. 946

United States *v.* Sprague, 282 U.S. 716; 51 S. Ct. 220; 1931 U.S. Lexis 39; 75 L. Ed. 640

City of Eastlake *v.* Forest City Enterprises, 426 U.S. 668; 96 S. Ct. 2358; 1976 U.S. Lexis 186; 49 L. Ed. 2d 132

Garcia *v.* San Antonio Metro. Transit Auth., 469 U.S. 528; 105 S. Ct. 1005; 1985 U.S. Lexis 48; 83 L. Ed. 2d 1016

Atascadero State Hosp. *v.* Scanlon, 473 U.S. 234; 105 S. Ct. 3142; 1985 U.S. Lexis 89; 87 L. Ed. 2d 171

New York *v.* United States *et al.*, 505 U.S. 144; 112 S. Ct. 2408; 1992 U.S. Lexis 3693; 120 L. Ed. 2d 120

U.S. Term Limits, Inc., *et al. v.* Thornton *et al.*, 514 U.S. 779; 115 S. Ct. 1842; 1995 U.S. Lexis 3487; 131 L. Ed. 2d 881

Printz *v.* United States, 117 S. Ct. 2365; 1997 U.S. Lexis 4044; 138 L. Ed. 2d 914

Alden *v.* Maine, 119 S. Ct. 2240; 1999 U.S. Lexis 4374; 144 L. Ed. 2d 636

Federalist 40

Luther *v.* Borden, 48 U.S. 1; 1849 U.S. Lexis 337; 12 L. Ed. 581

United States *v.* South-Eastern Underwriters Assn., 322 U.S. 533; 64 S. Ct. 1162; 1944 U.S. Lexis 1199; 88 L. Ed. 1440

Federalist 41

Prigg *v.* Pennsylvania, 41 U.S. 539; 1842 U.S. Lexis 387; 10 L. Ed. 1060

Smith *v.* Turner, 48 U.S. 283; 1849 U.S. Lexis 351; 12 L. Ed. 702

Ex parte Milligan, 71 U.S. 2; 1866 U.S. Lexis 861; 18 L. Ed. 281

De Lima *v.* Bidwell, 182 U.S. 1; 21 S. Ct. 743; 1901 U.S. Lexis 1225; 45 L. Ed. 1041

Massachusetts *v.* Mellon, 262 U.S. 447; 43 S. Ct. 597; 1923 U.S. Lexis 2662; 67 L. Ed. 1078

Perry *v.* United States, 294 U.S. 330; 55 S. Ct. 432; 1935 U.S. Lexis 258; 79 L. Ed. 912

United States *v.* South-Eastern Underwriters Assn., 322 U.S. 533; 64 S. Ct. 1162; 1944 U.S. Lexis 1199; 88 L. Ed. 1440

Lichter *v.* United States, 334 U.S. 742; 68 S. Ct. 1294; 1948 U.S. Lexis 2705; 92 L. Ed. 1694

Dennis *v.* United States, 341 U.S. 494; 71 S. Ct. 857; 1951 U.S. Lexis 2407; 95 L. Ed. 1137

Reid *v.* Covert, 354 U.S. 1; 77 S. Ct. 1222; 1957 U.S. Lexis 729; 1 L. Ed. 2d 1148

Kinsella *v.* United States *ex rel.* Singleton, 361 U.S. 234; 80 S. Ct. 297; 1960 U.S. Lexis 1742; 4 L. Ed. 2d 268

Communist Party of the United States *v.* Subversive Activities Control Bd., 367 U.S. 1; 81 S. Ct. 1357; 1961 U.S. Lexis 1934; 6 L. Ed. 2d 625

United States *v.* Robel, 389 U.S. 258; 88 S. Ct. 419; 1967 U.S. Lexis 2741; 19 L. Ed. 2d 508

Laird *v.* Tatum, 408 U.S. 1; 92 S. Ct. 2318; 1972 U.S. Lexis 25; 33 L. Ed. 2d 154

EEOC *v.* Wyoming, 460 U.S. 226; 103 S. Ct. 1054; 1983 U.S. Lexis 134; 75 L. Ed. 2d 18

Federalist 42

United States *v.* Smith, 18 U.S. 153; 1820 U.S. Lexis 250; 5 L. Ed. 57

Gibbons *v.* Ogden, 22 U.S. 1; 1824 U.S. Lexis 370; 6 L. Ed. 23

Ogden *v.* Saunders, 25 U.S. 213; 1827 U.S. Lexis 394; 6 L. Ed. 606

Cherokee Nation *v.* Georgia, 30 U.S. 1;1831 U.S. Lexis 337;8 L. Ed. 25

Worcester *v.* Georgia, 31 U.S. 515; 1832 U.S. Lexis 489; 8 L. Ed. 483

Prigg *v.* Pennsylvania, 41 U.S. 539; 1842 U.S. Lexis 387; 10 L. Ed. 1060

Cook *v.* Moffat, 46 U.S. 295; 1847 U.S. Lexis 316; 12 L. Ed. 159

Thurlow *v.* Massachusetts, 46 U.S. 504; 1847 U.S. Lexis 322; 12 L. Ed. 256

Smith *v.* Turner, 48 U.S. 283; 1849 U.S. Lexis 351; 12 L. Ed. 702

United States *v.* Marigold, 50 U.S. 560; 1850 U.S. Lexis 1443; 13 L. Ed. 257

Cross *v.* Harrison, 57 U.S. 164; 1850 U.S. Lexis 1548; 14 L. Ed. 889

Scott *v.* Sandford, 60 U.S. 393; 1856 U.S. Lexis 472; 15 L. Ed. 691

Woodruff *v.* Parham, 75 U.S. 123; 1868 U.S. Lexis 1088; 19 L. Ed. 382

Legal Tender Cases, 79 U.S. 457; 1870 U.S. Lexis 1220; 20 L. Ed. 287

Ex parte Clarke, 100 U.S. 399; 1879 U.S. Lexis 1834; 25 L. Ed. 715

Hanover Natl. Bank *v.* Moyses, 186 U.S. 181; 22 S. Ct. 857; 1902 U.S. Lexis 885; 46 L. Ed. 1113

Employer's Liab. Cases, 207 U.S. 463; 28 S. Ct. 141; 1908 U.S. Lexis 1412; 52 L. Ed. 297

Marshall *v.* Gordon, 243 U.S. 521; 37 S. Ct. 448; 1917 U.S. Lexis 1970; 61 L. Ed. 881

Baldwin *v.* G. A. F. Seelig, Inc., 294 U.S. 511; 55 S. Ct. 497; 1935 U.S. Lexis 54; 79 L. Ed. 1032

South Carolina State Hwy. Dept. *v.* Barnwell Bros., 303 U.S. 177; 58 S. Ct. 510; 1938 U.S. Lexis 360; 82 L. Ed. 734

Hines *v.* Davidowitz, 312 U.S. 52; 61 S. Ct. 399; 1941 U.S. Lexis 1103; 85 L. Ed. 581

Richfield Oil Corp. *v.* State Bd. of Equalization, 329 U.S. 69; 67 S. Ct. 156; 1946 U.S. Lexis 3005; 91 L. Ed. 80

Joseph *v.* Carter & Weekes Stevedoring Co., 330 U.S. 422; 67 S. Ct. 815; 1947 U.S. Lexis 2872; 91 L. Ed. 993

Polar Ice Cream & Creamery Co. *v.* Andrews, 375 U.S. 361; 84 S. Ct. 378; 1964 U.S. Lexis 2157; 11 L. Ed. 2d 389

Banco Nacional de Cuba *v.* Sabbatino, 376 U.S. 398; 84 S. Ct. 923; 1964 U.S. Lexis 2252; 11 L. Ed. 2d 804

Goldstein *v.* California, 412 U.S. 546; 93 S. Ct. 2303; 1973 U.S. Lexis 15; 37 L. Ed. 2d 163

Michelin Tire Corp. *v.* Wages, 423 U.S. 276; 96 S. Ct. 535; 1976 U.S. Lexis 120; 46 L. Ed. 2d 495

Washington Stevedoring Cos., 435 U.S. 734; 98 S. Ct. 1388; 1978 U.S. Lexis 24; 55 L. Ed. 2d 682

Exxon Corp. *v.* Governor of Maryland, 437 U.S. 117; 98 S. Ct. 2207; 1978 U.S. Lexis 2; 57 L. Ed. 2d 91

Japan Line, Ltd. *v.* County of Los Angeles, 441 U.S. 434; 99 S. Ct. 1813; 1979 U.S. Lexis 20; 60 L. Ed. 2d 336

Reeves, Inc. *v.* Stake, 447 U.S. 429; 100 S. Ct. 2271; 1980 U.S. Lexis 40; 65 L. Ed. 2d 244

Railway Labor Executives' Assn. *v.* Gibbons, 455 U.S. 457; 102 S. Ct. 1169; 1982 U.S. Lexis 53; 71 L. Ed. 2d 335

Garcia *v.* San Antonio Metro. Transit Auth., 469 U.S. 528; 105 S. Ct. 1005; 1985 U.S. Lexis 48; 83 L. Ed. 2d 1016

County of Oneida *v.* Oneida Indian Nation of New York State, 470 U.S. 226; 105 S. Ct. 1245; 1985 U.S. Lexis 58; 84 L. Ed. 2d 169

Hoffman *v.* Connecticut Dept. of Income Maintenance, 492 U.S. 96; 109 S. Ct. 2818; 1989 U.S. Lexis 3138; 106 L. Ed. 2d 76

New York *v.* United States *et al.*, 505 U.S. 144; 112 S. Ct. 2408; 1992 U.S. Lexis 3693; 120 L. Ed. 2d 120

Oregon Waste Systems *v.* Environmental Dept., 511 U.S. 93; 114 S. Ct. 1345; 1994 U.S. Lexis 2659; 128 L. Ed. 2d 13

Oklahoma Tax Commission *v.* Jefferson Lines, Inc., 514 U.S. 175; 115 S. Ct. 1331; 1995 U.S. Lexis 2418; 131 L. Ed. 2d 261

United States *v.* Lopez, 514 U.S. 549; 115 S. Ct. 1624; 1995 U.S. Lexis 3039; 131 L. Ed. 2d 626

Federalist 43

Gibbons *v.* Ogden, 22 U.S. 1; 1824 U.S. Lexis 370; 6 L. Ed. 23

Wheaton *v.* Peters, 33 U.S. 591; 1834 U.S. Lexis 619; 8 L. Ed. 1055

Prigg *v.* Pennsylvania, 41 U.S. 539; 1842 U.S. Lexis 387; 10 L. Ed. 1060

Luther *v.* Borden, 48 U.S. 1; 1849 U.S. Lexis 337; 12 L. Ed. 581

Dodge *v.* Woolsey, 59 U.S. 331; 1855 U.S. Lexis 704; 15 L. Ed. 401

Scott *v.* Sandford, 60 U.S. 393; 1856 U.S. Lexis 472; 15 L. Ed. 691

Legal Tender Cases, 79 U.S. 457; 1870 U.S. Lexis 1220; 20 L. Ed. 287

Fort Leavenworth R. R. Co. *v.* Lowe, 114 U.S. 525; 5 S. Ct. 995; 1885 U.S. Lexis 1790; 29 L. Ed. 264

De Lima *v.* Bidwell, 182 U.S. 1; 21 S. Ct. 743; 1901 U.S. Lexis 1225; 45 L. Ed. 1041

Downes *v.* Bidwell, 182 U.S. 244; 21 S. Ct. 770; 1901 U.S. Lexis 286; 45 L. Ed. 1088

United States *v.* Keitel, 211 U.S. 370; 29 S. Ct. 123; 1908 U.S. Lexis 1549; 53 L. Ed. 230

Pacific States Tel. & Tel. Co. *v.* Oregon, 223 U.S. 118; 32 S. Ct. 224; 1912 U.S. Lexis 2220; 56 L. Ed. 377

Kiernan *v.* Portland, 223 U.S. 151; 32 S. Ct. 231; 1912 U.S. Lexis 2221; 56 L. Ed. 386

Marshall *v.* Dye, 231 U.S. 250; 34 S. Ct. 92; 1913 U.S. Lexis 2564; 58 L. Ed. 206

National Prohibition Cases, 253 U.S. 350; 40 S. Ct. 486; 1920 U.S. Lexis 1371; 64 L. Ed. 946

Heald *v.* District of Columbia, 259 U.S. 114; 42 S. Ct. 434; 1922 U.S. Lexis 2465; 66 L. Ed. 852

United States *v.* Sprague, 282 U.S. 716; 51 S. Ct. 220; 1931 U.S. Lexis 39; 75 L. Ed. 640

United States *v.* South-Eastern Underwriters Assn., 322 U.S. 533; 64 S. Ct. 1162; 1944 U.S. Lexis 1199; 88 L. Ed. 1440

Cramer *v.* United States, 325 U.S. 1; 65 S. Ct. 918; 1945 U.S. Lexis 2157; 89 L. Ed. 1441

Joint Anti-Fascist Refugee Comm. *v.* McGrath, 341 U.S. 123; 71 S. Ct. 624; 1951 U.S. Lexis 2349; 95 L. Ed. 817 [cited as 42]

District of Columbia *v.* John R. Thompson Co., 346 U.S. 100; 73 S. Ct. 1007; 1953 U.S. Lexis 2001; 97 L. Ed. 1480

Sears, Roebuck & Co. *v.* Stiffel Co., 376 U.S. 225; 84 S. Ct. 784; 1964 U.S. Lexis 2365; 11 L. Ed. 2d 661

Lee *v.* Runge, 404 U.S. 887; 92 S. Ct. 197; 1971 U. S. Lexis 3756; 30 L. Ed. 2d 169

Goldstein *v.* California, 412 U.S. 546; 93 S. Ct. 2303; 1973 U.S. Lexis 15; 37 L. Ed. 2d 163

Garcia *v.* San Antonio Metro. Transit Auth., 469 U.S. 528; 105 S. Ct. 1005; 1985 U.S. Lexis 48; 83 L. Ed. 2d 1016

Bonito Boats, Inc. *v.* Thunder Craft Boats, Inc, 489 U.S. 141; 109 S. Ct. 971; 1989 U.S. Lexis 629; 103 L. Ed. 2d 118

Florida Prepaid Postsecondary E. Expense Bd *v.* College Savings Bank, 119 S. Ct. 2199; 1999 U.S. Lexis 4376; 144 L. Ed. 2d 575

Federalist 44

Fletcher *v.* Peck, 10 U.S. 87; 1810 U.S. Lexis 322; 3 L. Ed. 162

Trustees of Dartmouth College *v.* Woodward, 17 U.S. 518; 1819 U.S. Lexis 330; 4 L. Ed. 629

Ogden v. Saunders, 25 U.S. 213; 1827 U.S. Lexis 394; 6 L. Ed. 606

Craig v. Missouri, 29 U.S. 410; 1830 U.S. Lexis 486; 7 L. Ed. 903

Lessee of Livingston v. Moore, 32 U.S. 469; 1833 U.S. Lexis 359; 8 L. Ed. 751

Briscoe v. President & Dirs. Of the Bank of Kentucky, 36 U.S.257; 1837 U.S. Lexis 178; 9 L. Ed. 709

Cook v. Moffat, 46 U.S. 295; 1847 U.S. Lexis 316; 12 L. Ed. 159

Thurlow v. Massachusetts, 46 U.S. 504; 1847 U.S. Lexis 322; 12 L. Ed. 256

Planters' Bank of Mississippi v. Sharp 47 U.S. 301; 1848 U.S. Lexis 318; 12 L. Ed. 447

Luther v. Borden, 48 U.S. 1; 1849 U.S. Lexis 337; 12 L. Ed. 581

Cummings v. Missouri, 71 U.S. 277; 1866 U.S. Lexis 885; 18 L. Ed. 356

Ex parte Garland, 71 U.S. 333; 1866 U.S. Lexis 886; 18 L. Ed. 366

Legal Tender Cases, 79 U.S. 457; 1870 U.S. Lexis 1220; 20 L. Ed. 287

Edwards v. Kearzey, 96 U.S. 595; 1877 U.S. Lexis 1704; 24 L. Ed. 793

Legal Tender Case, 110 U.S. 421; 4 S. Ct. 122; 1884 U.S. Lexis 1712; 28 L. Ed. 204

Home Bldg. & Loan Assn. v. Blaisdell, 290 U.S. 398; 54 S. Ct. 231; 1934 U.S. Lexis 958; 78 L. Ed. 413

Norman v. Baltimore & Ohio R.R. Co., 294 U.S. 240; 55 S. Ct. 407; 1935 U.S. Lexis 257; 79 L. Ed. 885

Bute v. Illinois, 333 U.S. 640; 68 S. Ct. 763; 1948 U.S. Lexis 2290; 92 L. Ed. 986

Youngstown Sheet & Tube Co. v. Bowers, 358 U.S. 534; 79 S. Ct. 383; 1959 U.S. Lexis 1489; 3 L. Ed. 2d 490

City of El Paso v. Simmons, 379 U.S. 497; 85 S. Ct. 577; 1965 U.S. Lexis 2230; 13 L. Ed. 2d 446

United States v. Brown, 381 U.S. 437; 85 S. Ct. 1707; 1965 U.S. Lexis 2206; 14 L. Ed. 2d 484

Michelin Tire Corp. v. Wages, 423 U.S. 276; 96 S. Ct. 535; 1976 U.S. Lexis 120; 46 L. Ed. 2d 495

United States Steel Corp. v. Multistate Tax Commn., 434 U.S. 452; 98 S. Ct. 799; 1978 U.S. Lexis 58; 54 L. Ed. 2d 682

Weaver v. Graham, 450 U.S. 24; 101 S. Ct. 960; 1981 U.S. Lexis 67; 67 L. Ed. 2d 17

Collins v. Youngblood 497 U.S. 37; 110 S. Ct. 2715; 1990 U.S. Lexis 3294; 111 L. Ed. 2d 30.

Coleman v. Thompson, 501 U.S. 722; 111 S. Ct. 2546; 1991 U.S. Lexis 3640; 115 L. Ed. 2d 640

Landgraf v. USI Film Products et al., 511 U.S. 244; 114 S. Ct. 1483; 1994 U.S. Lexis 3292; 128 L. Ed. 2d 229

California Department of Corrections et al. v. Morales, 514 U.S. 499; 115 S. Ct. 1597; 1995 U.S. Lexis 3037; 131 L. Ed. 2d 588

United States v. Lopez, 514 U.S. 549; 115 S. Ct. 1624; 1995 U.S. Lexis 3039; 131 L. Ed. 2d 626

Printz v. United States, 117 S. Ct. 2365; 1997 U.S. Lexis 4044; 138 L. Ed. 2d 914

Federalist 45

Mayor, Aldermen, & Commonalty of New York v. Miln, 36 U.S. 102; 1837 U.S. Lexis 169; 9 L. Ed. 648

Moore v. Illinois, 55 U.S. 13; 1852 U.S. Lexis 420; 14 L. Ed. 306

Cummings v. Missouri, 71 U.S. 277; 1866 U.S. Lexis 885; 18 L. Ed. 356

Steamboat Co. *v.* Chase, 83 U.S. 522; 1872 U.S. Lexis 1180; 21 L. Ed. 369

Utah Power & Light Co. *v.* United States, 243 U.S. 389, 37 S. Ct. 387; 1917 U.S. Lexis 2046; 61 L. Ed. 791

Myers *v.* United States, 272 U.S. 52; 47 S. Ct. 21; 1926 U.S. Lexis 36; 71 L. Ed. 160 [cited as 44]

Missouri *v.* Holland, 252 U.S. 416; 40 S. Ct. 382; 1920 U.S. Lexis 1520; 64 L. Ed. 641

Newberry *v.* United States, 256 U.S. 232; 41 S. Ct. 469; 1921 U.S. Lexis 1632; 65 L. Ed. 913

Massachusetts *v.* Mellon, 262 U.S. 447; 43 S. Ct. 597; 1923 U.S. Lexis 2662; 67 L. Ed. 1078

Steward Mach. Co. *v.* Davis, 301 U.S. 548; 57 S. Ct. 883; 1937 U.S. Lexis 1199; 81 L. Ed. 1279

Bute *v.* Illinois, 333 U.S. 640; 68 S. Ct. 763; 1948 U.S. Lexis 2290; 92 L. Ed. 986

National League of Cities *v.* Usery, 426 U.S. 833; 96 S. Ct. 2465; 1976 U.S. Lexis 158; 49 L. Ed. 2d 245

FERC *v.* Mississippi, 456 U.S. 742; 102 S. Ct. 2126; 1982 U.S. Lexis 38; 72 L. Ed. 2d 532

EEOC *v.* Wyoming, 460 U.S. 226; 103 S. Ct. 1054; 1983 U.S. Lexis 134; 75 L. Ed. 2d 18

Garcia *v.* San Antonio Metro. Transit Auth., 469 U.S. 528; 105 S. Ct. 1005; 1985 U.S. Lexis 48; 83 L. Ed. 2d 1016

Atascadero State Hosp. *v.* Scanlon, 473 U.S. 234; 105 S. Ct. 3142; 1985 U.S. Lexis 89; 87 L. Ed. 2d 171

Tyler Pipe Indus. *v.* Washington State Dept. of Revenue, 483 U.S. 232; 107 S. Ct. 2810; 1987 U.S. Lexis 2872; 97 L. Ed. 2d 199

Gregory *v.* Ashcroft, 501 U.S. 452; 111 S. Ct. 2395; 1991 U.S. Lexis 3626; 115 L. Ed. 2d 410

United States *v.* Lopez, 514 U.S. 549; 115 S. Ct. 1624; 1995 U.S. Lexis 3039; 131 L. Ed. 2d 626

Printz *v.* United States, 117 S. Ct. 2365; 1997 U.S. Lexis 4044; 138 L. Ed. 2d 914

City of Boerne *v.* Flores, 117 S. Ct. 2157; 1997 U.S. Lexis 4035; 138 L. Ed. 2d 624

Federalist 46

Luther *v.* Borden, 48 U.S. 1; 1849 U.S. Lexis 337; 12 L. Ed. 581

Lane County *v.* Oregon, 74 U.S. 71; 1868 U.S. Lexis 979; 19 L. Ed.101

Pollock *v.* Farmers Loan & Trust Co., 157 U.S. 429; 15 S. Ct. 673; 1895 U.S. Lexis 2215; 39 L. Ed. 759

United States *ex rel.* Turner *v.* Williams, 194 U.S. 279; 24 S. Ct. 719; 1904 U.S. Lexis 822; 48 L. Ed. 979

Bute *v.* Illinois, 333 U.S. 640; 68 S. Ct. 763; 1948 U.S. Lexis 2290; 92 L. Ed. 986

National League of Cities *v.* Usery, 426 U.S. 833; 96 S. Ct. 2465; 1976 U.S. Lexis 158; 49 L. Ed. 2d 245

Garcia *v.* San Antonio Metro. Transit Auth., 469 U.S. 528; 105 S. Ct. 1005; 1985 U.S. Lexis 48; 83 L. Ed. 2d 1016

Atascadero State Hosp. *v.* Scanlon, 473 U.S. 234; 105 S. Ct. 3142; 1985 U.S. Lexis 89; 87 L. Ed. 2d 171

CFTC *v.* Schor, 478 U.S. 833; 106 S. Ct. 3245; 1986 U.S. Lexis 144; 92 L. Ed. 2d 675

United States *v.* Lopez, 514 U.S. 549; 115 S. Ct. 1624; 1995 U.S. Lexis 3039; 131 L. Ed. 2d 626

Seminole Tribe of Florida *v.* Florida, 517 U.S. 44; 116 S. Ct. 1114; 1996 U.S. Lexis 2165; 134 L. Ed. 2d 252

Federalist 47

Bugajewitz *v.* Adams, 228 U.S. 585; 33 S. Ct. 607; 1913 U.S. Lexis 2400; 57 L. Ed. 978

Myers *v.* United States, 272 U.S. 52; 47 S. Ct. 21; 1926 U.S. Lexis 36; 71 L. Ed. 160 [cited as 46]

United States *v.* Brown, 381 U.S. 437; 85 S. Ct. 1707; 1965 U.S. Lexis 2206; 14 L. Ed. 2d 484

United States *v.* Nixon, 418 U.S. 683; 94 S. Ct. 3090; 1974 U.S. Lexis 93; 41 L. Ed. 2d 1039

Schick *v.* Reed, 419 U.S. 256; 95 S. Ct. 379; 1974 U.S. Lexis 159; 42 L. Ed. 2d 430

Buckley *v.* Valeo, 424 U.S. 1; 96 S. Ct. 612; 1976 U.S. Lexis 16; 46 L. Ed. 2d 659

Nixon *v.* Administrator of Gen. Servs., 433 U.S. 425; 97 S. Ct. 2777; 1977 U.S. Lexis 24; 53 L. Ed. 2d 867

Northern Pipeline Constr. Co. *v.* Marathon Pipe Line Co., 458 U.S. 50; 102 S. Ct. 2858; 1982 U.S. Lexis 143; 73 L. Ed. 2d 598

INS *v.* Chadha, 462 U.S. 919; 103 S. Ct. 2764; 1983 U.S. Lexis 80; 77 L. Ed. 2d 317

Thomas *v.* Union Carbide Agric. Prods. Co., 473 U.S. 568; 105 S. Ct. 3325; 1985 U.S. Lexis 121; 87 L. Ed. 2d 409

Bowsher *v.* Synar, 478 U.S. 714; 106 S. Ct. 3181; 1986 U.S. Lexis 141; 92 L. Ed. 2d 583

Morrison *v.* Olson, 487 U.S. 654; 108 S. Ct. 2597; 1988 U.S. Lexis 3034; 101 L. Ed. 2d 569

Mistretta *v.* United States, 488 U.S. 361; 109 S. Ct. 647; 1989 U.S. Lexis 434; 102 L. Ed. 2d 714

Public Citizen *v.* United States DoJ, 491 U.S. 440; 109 S. Ct. 2558; 1989 U.S. Lexis 3119; 105 L. Ed. 2d 377

Freytag *v.* Commissioner, 501 U.S. 868; 111 S. Ct. 2631; 1991 U.S. Lexis 3818; 115 L. Ed. 2d 764

Harmelin *v.* Michigan, 501 U.S. 957; 111 S. Ct. 2680; 1991 U.S. Lexis 3816; 115 L. Ed. 2d 836

Plaut *et al. v.* Spendthrift Farm, Inc., *et al.*, 514 U.S. 211; 115 S. Ct 1447; 1995 U.S. Lexis 2843; 131 L. Ed. 2d 328

Loving *v.* United States, 517 U.S. 748; 116 S. Ct. 1737; 1996 U.S. Lexis 3593; 135 L. Ed. 2d 36

Clinton *v.* Jones, 117 S. Ct. 1636; 1997 U.S. Lexis 3254; 137 L. Ed. 2d 945

Clinton *v.* City of New York, No. 97-1374; 1998 U.S. LEXIS 4215; 141 L. Ed. 2d 393

Federalist 48

Burton *v.* United States, 202 U.S. 344; 26 S. Ct. 688; 1906 U.S. Lexis 1541; 50 L. Ed. 1057

Pacific States Tel. & Tel. Co. *v.* Oregon, 223 U.S. 118; 32 S. Ct. 224; 1912 U.S. Lexis 2220; 56 L. Ed. 377

Blackmer *v.* United States, 284 U.S. 421; 52 S. Ct. 252; 1932 U.S. Lexis 882; 76 L. Ed. 375

O'Donoghue *v.* United States, 289 U.S. 516; 53 S. Ct. 740; 1933 U.S. Lexis 933; 77 L. Ed. 1356

Humphrey's Extr. *v.* United States, 295 U.S. 602; 55 S. Ct. 869; 1935 U.S. Lexis 1089; 79 L. Ed. 1611

Tenney *v.* Brandhove, 341 U.S. 367; 71 S. Ct. 783; 1951 U.S. Lexis 1836; 95 L. Ed. 1019

Youngstown Sheet & Tube Co. *v.* Sawyer, 343 U.S. 579; 72 S. Ct. 863; 1952 U.S. Lexis 2625; 96 L. Ed. 1153

Trop *v.* Dulles, 356 U.S. 86; 78 S. Ct. 590; 1958 U.S. Lexis 1284; 2 L. Ed. 2d 630

United States *v.* Brown, 381 U.S. 437; 85 S. Ct. 1707; 1965 U.S. Lexis 2206; 14 L. Ed. 2d 484

United States *v.* Johnson, 383 U.S. 169; 86 S. Ct. 749; 1966 U.S. Lexis 2213; 15 L. Ed. 2d 681

United States *v.* Brewster, 408 U.S. 501; 92 S. Ct. 2531; 1972 U.S. Lexis 109; 33 L. Ed. 2d 507

Buckley *v.* Valeo, 424 U.S. 1; 96 S. Ct. 612; 1976 U.S. Lexis 16; 46 L. Ed. 2d 659

Nixon *v.* Administrator of Gen. Servs., 433 U.S. 425; 97 S. Ct. 2777; 1977 U.S. Lexis 24; 53 L. Ed. 2d 867

Industrial Union Dept. *v.* API, 448 U.S. 607; 100 S. Ct. 2844; 1980 U. S. Lexis 55; 65 L. Ed. 2d 1010

INS *v.* Chadha, 462 U.S. 919; 103 S. Ct. 2764; 1983 U.S. Lexis 80; 77 L. Ed. 2d 317

Mistretta *v.* United States, 488 U.S. 361; 109 S. Ct. 647; 1989 U.S. Lexis 434; 102 L. Ed. 2d 714

Public Citizen *v.* United States DoJ, 491 U.S. 440; 109 S. Ct. 2558; 1989 U.S. Lexis 3119; 105 L. Ed. 2d 377

Missouri *v.* Jenkins, 495 U.S. 33; 110 S. Ct. 1651; 1990 U.S. Lexis 2033; 109 L. Ed. 2d 31

Wash. Airports *v.* Noise Abatement Citizens, 501 U.S. 252; 111 S. Ct. 2298; 1991 U.S. Lexis 3491; 115 L. Ed. 2d 236

Freytag *v.* Commissioner, 501 U.S. 868; 111 S. Ct. 2631; 1991 U.S. Lexis 3818; 115 L. Ed. 2d 764

Manuel Lujan, Jr., Secretary of the Interior, Petitioner *v.* Defenders of Wildlife, *et al.*, 504 U.S. 555; 112 S. Ct. 2130; 1992 U.S. Lexis 3543; 119 L. Ed. 2d 351

Weiss *v.* United States, 510 U.S. 163; 114 S. Ct. 752; 1994 U.S. Lexis 1137; 127 L . Ed. 2d 1

Plaut *et al. v.* Spendthrift Farm, Inc., *et al.*, 514 U.S. 211; 115 S. Ct 1447; 1995 U.S. Lexis 2843; 131 L. Ed. 2d 328

Federalist 49

Myers *v.* United States, 272 U.S. 52; 47 S. Ct. 21; 1926 U.S. Lexis 36; 71 L. Ed. 160

United States *v.* Sprague, 282 U.S. 716; 51 S. Ct. 220; 1931 U.S. Lexis 39; 75 L. Ed. 640

United States *v.* Brown, 381 U.S. 437; 85 S. Ct. 1707; 1965 U.S. Lexis 2206; 14 L. Ed. 2d 484

Morrison *v.* Olson, 487 U.S. 654; 108 S. Ct. 2597; 1988 U.S. Lexis 3034; 101 L. Ed. 2d 569

Public Citizen *v.* United States DoJ, 491 U.S. 440; 109 S. Ct. 2558; 1989 U.S. Lexis 3119; 105 L. Ed. 2d 377

Freytag *v.* Commissioner, 501 U.S. 868; 111 S. Ct. 2631; 1991 U.S. Lexis 3818; 115 L. Ed. 2d 764

Crawford-El *v.* Britton, No. 96-827, 1998 U.S. LEXIS 2966; 140 L. Ed. 2d 759

Federalist 50

INS *v.* Chadha, 462 U.S. 919; 103 S. Ct. 2764; 1983 U.S. Lexis 80; 77 L. Ed. 2d 317

Public Citizen *v.* United States DoJ, 491 U.S. 440; 109 S. Ct. 2558; 1989 U.S. Lexis 3119; 105 L. Ed. 2d 377

Federalist 51

Kendall *v.* United States *ex rel.* Stokes, 37 U.S. 524; 1838 U.S. Lexis 379; 9 L. Ed. 1181

Pacific States Tel. & Tel. Co. *v.* Oregon, 223 U.S. 118; 32 S. Ct. 224; 1912 U.S. Lexis 2220; 56 L. Ed. 377

Myers *v.* United States, 272 U.S. 52; 47 S. Ct. 21; 1926 U.S. Lexis 35; 71 L. Ed. 160 [cited as "XLVI, XVII"]

Gibson *v.* Florida Legislative Investigation Comm., 372 U.S. 539; 83 S. Ct 889; 1963 U.S. Lexis 2503; 9 L. Ed. 2d 929

School Dist. of Abington Twp. *v.* Schempp, 374 U.S. 203; 83 S. Ct. 1560; 1963 U.S. Lexis 2611; 10 L. Ed. 2d 844

United States *v.* Brown, 381 U.S. 437; 85 S. Ct. 1707; 1965 U.S. Lexis 2206; 14 L. Ed. 2d 484

Duncan *v.* Louisiana, 391 U.S. 145; 88 S. Ct. 1444; 1968 U.S. Lexis 1631; 20 L. Ed. 2d 491

Furman *v.* Georgia, 408 U.S. 238; 92 S. Ct. 2726; 1972 U.S. Lexis 169; 33 L. Ed. 2d 346

Buckley *v.* Valeo, 424 U.S. 1; 96 S. Ct. 612; 1976 U.S. Lexis 16; 46 L. Ed. 2d 659

Coleman *v.* Balkcom, 451 U.S. 949; 101 S. Ct. 2031; 1981 U.S. Lexis 1896; 68 L. Ed. 2d 334

Schad *v.* Borough of Mt. Ephraim, 452 U.S. 61; 101 S. Ct. 2176; 1981 U.S. Lexis 108; 68 L. Ed. 2d 671

Brown *v.* Hartlage, 456 U.S. 45; 102 S. Ct. 1523; 1982 U.S. Lexis 92; 71 L. Ed. 2d 732

Larson *v.* Valente, 456 U.S. 228; 102 S. Ct. 1673; 1982 U.S. Lexis 98; 72 L. Ed. 2d 33

INS *v.* Chadha, 462 U.S. 919; 103 S. Ct. 2764; 1983 U.S. Lexis 80; 77 L. Ed. 2d 317

Garcia *v.* San Antonio Metro. Transit Auth., 469 U.S. 528; 105 S. Ct. 1005; 1985 U.S. Lexis 48; 83 L. Ed. 2d 1016

Morrison *v.* Olson, 487 U.S. 654; 108 S. Ct. 2597; 1988 U.S. Lexis 3034; 101 L. Ed. 2d 569

Mistretta *v.* United States, 488 U.S. 361; 109 S. Ct. 647; 1989 U.S. Lexis 434; 102 L. Ed. 2d 714

Public Citizen *v.* United States DoJ, 491 U.S. 440; 109 S. Ct. 2558; 1989 U.S. Lexis 3119; 105 L. Ed. 2d 377

Missouri *v.* Jenkins, 495 U.S. 33; 110 S. Ct. 1651; 1990 U.S. Lexis 2033; 109 L. Ed. 2d 31

Wash. Airports *v.* Noise Abatement Citizens, 501 U.S. 252; 111 S. Ct. 2298; 1991 U.S. Lexis 3491; 115 L. Ed. 2d 236

Gregory *v.* Ashcroft, 501 U.S. 452; 111 S. Ct. 2395; 1991 U.S. Lexis 3626; 115 L. Ed. 2d 410

Coleman *v.* Thompson, 501 U.S. 722; 111 S. Ct. 2546; 1991 U.S. Lexis 3640; 115 L. Ed. 2d 640

Freytag *v.* Commissioner, 501 U.S. 868; 111 S. Ct. 2631; 1991 U.S. Lexis 3818; 115 L. Ed. 2d 764

New York *v.* United States *et al.*, 505 U.S. 144; 112 S. Ct. 2408; 1992 U.S. Lexis 3693; 120 L. Ed. 2d 120

United States *v.* Lopez, 514 U.S. 549; 115 S. Ct. 1624; 1995 U.S. Lexis 3039; 131 L. Ed. 2d 626

Clinton *v.* Jones, 117 S. Ct. 1636; 1997 U.S. Lexis 3254; 137 L. Ed. 2d 945

Printz *v.* United States, 117 S. Ct. 2365; 1997 U.S. Lexis 4044; 138 L. Ed. 2d 914

Clinton *v.* City of New York, No. 97-1374; 1998 U.S. LEXIS 4215; 141 L. Ed. 2d 393

Federalist 52

Newberry *v.* United States, 256 U.S. 232; 41 S. Ct. 469; 1921 U.S. Lexis 1632; 65 L. Ed. 913

Powell *v.* McCormak, 395 U.S. 486; 89 S. Ct. 1944; 1969 U.S. Lexis 3103; 23 L. Ed. 2d 491

Oregon *v.* Mitchell, 400 U.S. 112; 91 S. Ct. 260; 1970 U.S. Lexis 1; 27 L. Ed. 2d 272

Tashjian *v.* Republican Party of Connecticut, 479 U.S. 208; 107 C. Ct. 544; 1986 U.S. Lexis 25; 93 L. Ed. 2d 514

U.S. Term Limits, Inc., *et al. v.* Thornton *et al.*, 514 U.S. 779; 115 S. Ct. 1842; 1995 U.S. Lexis 3487; 131 L. Ed. 2d 881

Federalist 54

Groves *v.* Slaughter, 40 U.S. 449; 1841 U.S. Lexis 278; 10 L. Ed. 800

Pollock *v.* Farmers Loan & Trust Co., 157 U.S. 429; 15 S. Ct. 673; 1895 U.S. Lexis 2215; 39 L. Ed. 759

Baker *v.* Carr, 369 U.S. 186; 82 S. Ct. 691; 1962 U.S. Lexis 1567; 7 L. Ed. 2d 663

Wesberry *v.* Sanders, 376 U.S. 1; 84 S. Ct. 526; 1964 U.S. Lexis 1773; 11 L. Ed. 2d 481

Federalist 56

Baker *v.* Carr, 369 U.S. 186; 82 S. Ct. 691; 1962 U,S. Lexis 1567; 7 L. Ed. 2d 663

U.S. Term Limits, Inc., *et al. v.* Thornton *et al.*, 514 U.S. 779; 115 S. Ct. 1842; 1995 U.S. Lexis 3487; 131 L. Ed. 2d 881

Federalist 57

Wesberry *v.* Sanders, 376 U.S. 1; 84 S. Ct. 526; 1964 U.S. Lexis 1773; 11 L. Ed. 2d 481

U.S. Term Limits, Inc., *et al. v.* Thornton *et al.*, 514 U.S. 779; 115 S. Ct. 1842; 1995 U.S. Lexis 3487; 131 L. Ed. 2d 881

Federalist 58

Newberry *v.* United States, 256 U.S. 232; 41 S. Ct. 469; 1921 U.S. Lexis 1632; 65 L. Ed. 913

United States *v.* Munoz-Flores, 495 U.S. 385; 110 S. Ct. 1964; 1990 U.S. Lexis 2675; 109 L. Ed. 2d 384

Federalist 59

In re Neagle, 135 U.S. 1; 10 S. Ct. 658; 1890 U.S. Lexi 2006; 34 L. Ed. 55 [cited as *Federalist* 58]

United States *v.* Gradwell, 243 U.S. 476; 37 S. Ct. 407; 1917 U.S. Lexis 2015; 61 L. Ed. 857

Blair *v.* United States, 250 U.S. 273; 39 S. Ct. 468; 1919 U.S. Lexis 1744; 63 L. Ed. 979

Newberry *v.* United States, 256 U.S. 232; 41 S. Ct. 469; 1921 U.S. Lexis 1632; 65 L. Ed. 913

Leser *v.* Garnett, 258 U.S. 130; 42 S. Ct. 217; 1922 U.S. Lexis 2250; 66 L. Ed. 505

Wesberry *v.* Sanders, 376 U.S. 1; 84 S. Ct. 526; 1964 U.S. Lexis 1773; 11 L. Ed. 2d 481

U.S. Term Limits, Inc., *et al. v.* Thornton *et al.*, 514 U.S. 779; 115 S. Ct. 1842; 1995 U.S. Lexis 3487; 131 L. Ed. 2d 881

Federalist 60

Newberry *v.* United States, 256 U.S. 232; 41 S. Ct. 469; 1921 U.S. Lexis 1632; 65 L. Ed. 913

United States *v.* Classic, 313 U.S. 299; 61 S. Ct. 1031; 1941 U.S. Lexis 601; 85 L. Ed. 1368

Bond *v.* Floyd, 385 U.S. 116; 87 S. Ct. 339; 1966 U.S. Lexis 75; L. Ed. 2d 235

Powell *v.* McCormak, 395 U.S. 486; 89 S. Ct. 1944; 1969 U.S. Lexis 3103; 23 L. Ed. 2d 491

Oregon *v.* Mitchell, 400 U.S. 112; 91 S. Ct. 260; 1970 U.S. Lexis 1; 27 L. Ed. 2d 272

Nixon *v.* United States, 506 U.S. 224; 113 S. Ct. 732; 1993 U.S. Lexis 834; 122 L . Ed. 2d 1

U.S. Term Limits, Inc., *et al. v.* Thornton *et al.*, 514 U.S. 779; 115 S. Ct. 1842; 1995 U.S. Lexis 3487; 131 L. Ed. 2d 881

Federalist 61

Pope *v.* Williams, 193 U.S. 621; 24 S. Ct. 573; 1904 U.S. Lexis 903; 48 L. Ed. 817

Federalist 62

Howard *v.* Fleming, 191 U.S. 126; 24 S. Ct. 49; 1903 U.S. Lexis 1470; 48 L. Ed. 121

MacDougall *v.* Green, 335 U.S. 281; 69 S. Ct. 1; 1948 U.S. Lexis 1668; 93 L. Ed. 3

Baker *v.* Carr, 369 U.S. 186; 82 S. Ct. 691; 1962 U.S. Lexis 1567; 7 L. Ed. 2d 663

INS *v.* Chadha, 462 U.S. 919; 103 S. Ct. 2764; 1983 U.S. Lexis 80; 77 L. Ed. 2d 317

Garcia *v.* San Antonio Metro. Transit Auth., 469 U.S. 528; 105 S. Ct. 1005; 1985 U.S. Lexis 48; 83 L. Ed. 2d 1016

Johnson *v.* Transportation Agency, 480 U.S. 616; 107 S. Ct. 1442; 1987 U.S. Lexis 1387; 94 L. Ed. 2d 615

Raines *v.* Byrd, 117 S. Ct. 2312; 1997 U.S. Lexis 4040; 138 L. Ed. 2d 849

Federalist 63

Luther *v.* Borden, 48 U.S. 1; 1849 U.S. Lexis 337; 12 L. Ed. 581

United States *v.* Munoz-Flores, 495 U.S. 385; 110 S. Ct. 1964; 1990 U.S. Lexis 2675; 109 L. Ed. 2d 384

Federalist 64

United States *v.* Pink, 315 U.S. 203; 62 S. Ct. 552; 1942 U.S. Lexis 1060; 86 L. Ed. 796

United States *v.* Nixon, 418 U.S. 683; 94 S. Ct. 3090; 1974 U.S. Lexis 93; 41 L. Ed. 2d 1039

Haig *v.* Agee, 453 U.S. 280; 101 S. Ct. 2766; 1981 U.S. Lexis 39; 69 L. Ed. 2d 640

INS *v.* Chadha, 462 U.S. 919; 103 S. Ct. 2764; 1983 U.S. Lexis 80; 77 L. Ed. 2d 317

TWA *v.* Franklin Mint Corp., 466 U.S. 243; 104 S. Ct. 1776; 1984 U.S. Lexis 58; 80 L. Ed. 2d 273

United States *v.* Munoz-Flores, 495 U.S. 385; 110 S. Ct. 1964; 1990 U.S. Lexis 2675; 109 L. Ed. 2d 384

Federalist 65

Nixon *v.* Fitzgerald, 457 U.S. 731; 102 S. Ct. 2690; 1982 U.S. Lexis 42; 73 L. Ed. 2d 349

Nixon *v.* United States, 506 U.S. 224; 113 S. Ct. 732; 1993 U.S. Lexis 834; 122 L . Ed. 2d 1

Federalist 66

INS *v.* Chadha, 462 U.S. 919; 103 S. Ct. 2764; 1983 U.S. Lexis 80; 77 L. Ed. 2d 317

Public Citizen *v.* United States DoJ, 491 U.S. 440; 109 S. Ct. 2558; 1989 U.S. Lexis 3119; 105 L. Ed. 2d 377

Nixon *v.* United States, 506 U.S. 224; 113 S. Ct. 732; 1993 U.S. Lexis 834; 122 L . Ed. 2d 1

Federalist 67

Reid *v.* United States, 211 U.S. 529; 29 S. Ct. 171; 1909 U.S. Lexis 1784; 53 L. Ed. 313

Federalist 68

McPherson *v.* Blacker, 146 U.S. 1; 13 S. Ct. 3; 1892 U.S. Lexis 2171; 36 L. Ed. 869

Ray *v.* Blair, 343 U.S. 214; 72 S. Ct. 654; 1952 U.S. Lexis 2246; 96 L. Ed. 894

Gray *v.* Sanders, 372 U.S. 368; 83 S. Ct. 801; 1963 U.S. Lexis 1944; 9 L. Ed. 2d 821

Williams *v.* Rhodes, 393 U.S. 23; 89 S. Ct. 5; 1968 U.S. Lexis 2959; 21 L. Ed. 2d 24

Federalist 69

Kendall *v.* United States *ex rel.* Stokes, 37 U.S. 524; 1838 U.S. Lexis 379; 9 L. Ed. 1181

Reid *v.* United States, 211 U.S. 529; 29 S. Ct. 171; 1909 U.S. Lexis 1784; 53 L. Ed. 313

Mora *v.* McNamara, 389 U.S. 934; 88 S. Ct. 282; 1967 U.S. Lexis 389; 19 L. Ed. 2d 287

Schick *v.* Reed, 419 U.S. 256; 95 S. Ct. 379; 1974 U.S. Lexis 159; 42 L. Ed. 2d 430

Holder, Individually and in his Official Capacity as County Commissioner for Bleckley County, Georgia, *et al. v.* Hall *et al.*, 512 U.S. 874; 114 S. Ct 2581; 1994 U.S. Lexis 5083; 129 L. Ed. 2d 687

Federalist 70

Kendall *v.* United States *ex rel.* Stokes, 37 U.S. 524; 1838 U.S. Lexis 379; 9 L. Ed. 1181

Youngstown Sheet & Tube Co. *v.* Sawyer, 343 U.S. 579; 72 S. Ct. 863; 1952 U.S. Lexis 2625; 96 L. Ed. 1153

Morrison *v.* Olson, 487 U.S. 654; 108 S. Ct. 2597; 1988 U.S. Lexis 3034; 101 L. Ed. 2d 569

Clinton *v.* Jones, 117 S. Ct. 1636; 1997 U.S. Lexis 3254; 137 L. Ed. 2d 945

Printz *v.* United States, 117 S. Ct. 2365; 1997 U.S. Lexis 4044; 138 L. Ed. 2d 914

Federalist 71

Kendall *v.* United States *ex rel.* Stokes, 37 U.S. 524; 1838 U.S. Lexis 379; 9 L. Ed. 1181
Clinton *v.* Jones, 117 S. Ct. 1636; 1997 U.S. Lexis 3254; 137 L. Ed. 2d 945

Federalist 73

Pocket Veto Case, 279 U.S. 655; 49 S. Ct. 463; 1929 U.S. Lexis 364; 73 L. Ed. 894
United States *v.* Brewster, 408 U.S. 501; 92 S. Ct. 2531; 1972 U.S. Lexis 109; 33 L. Ed. 2d 507
Buckley *v.* Valeo, 424 U.S. 1; 96 S. Ct. 612; 1976 U.S. Lexis 16; 46 L. Ed. 2d 659
INS *v.* Chadha, 462 U.S. 919; 103 S. Ct. 2764; 1983 U.S. Lexis 80; 77 L. Ed. 2d 317
Morrison *v.* Olson, 487 U.S. 654; 108 S. Ct. 2597; 1988 U.S. Lexis 3034; 101 L. Ed. 2d 569
Wash. Airports *v.* Noise Abatement Citizens, 501 U.S. 252; 111 S. Ct. 2298; 1991 U.S. Lexis 3491; 115 L. Ed. 2d 236
Freytag *v.* Commissioner, 501 U.S. 868; 111 S. Ct. 2631; 1991 U.S. Lexis 3818; 115 L. Ed. 2d 764

Federalist 74

Reid *v.* United States, 211 U.S. 529; 29 S. Ct. 171; 1909 U.S. Lexis 1784; 53 L. Ed. 313
Ruppert *v.* Caffey, 251 U.S. 264; 40 S. Ct. 141; 1920 U.S. Lexis 1735; 64 L. Ed. 260
Ex parte Grossman, 267 U.S. 87; 45 S. Ct. 332; 1925 U.S. Lexis 359; 69 L. Ed. 527
Schick *v.* Reed, 419 U.S. 256; 95 S. Ct. 379; 1974 U.S. Lexis 159; 42 L. Ed. 2d 430
Herrera *v.* Collins, 506 U.S. 390; 113 S. Ct. 853; 1993 U.S. Lexis 1017; 122 L. Ed. 2d 203

Federalist 75

Pacific States Tel. & Tel. Co. *v.* Oregon, 223 U.S. 118; 32 S. Ct. 224; 1912 U.S. Lexis 2220; 56 L. Ed. 377
Myers *v.* United States, 272 U.S. 52; 47 S. Ct. 21; 1926 U.S. Lexis 36; 71 L. Ed. 160 [cited as 74]
INS *v.* Chadha, 462 U.S. 919; 103 S. Ct. 2764; 1983 U.S. Lexis 80; 77 L. Ed. 2d 317

Federalist 76

Schlesinger *v.* Reservists Comm. to Stop, 418 U.S. 208; 94 S. Ct. 2925; 1974 U.S. Lexis 17; 41 L. Ed. 2d 706
Public Citizen *v.* United States DoJ, 491 U.S. 440; 109 S. Ct. 2558; 1989 U.S. Lexis 3119; 105 L. Ed. 2d 377
Freytag *v.* Commissioner, 501 U.S. 868; 111 S. Ct. 2631; 1991 U.S. Lexis 3818; 115 L. Ed. 2d 764
Weiss *v.* United States, 510 U.S. 163; 114 S. Ct. 752; 1994 U.S. Lexis 1137; 127 L . Ed. 2d 1
Edmond *v.* United States, 117 S. Ct. 1573; 1997 U.S. Lexis 3076; 137 L. Ed. 2d 917

Federalist 77

> Kendall *v.* United States *ex rel.* Stokes, 37 U.S. 524; 1838 U.S. Lexis 379, 9 L. Ed. 1181
>
> Luther *v.* Borden, 48 U.S. 1; 1849 U.S. Lexis 337; 12 L. Ed. 581
>
> United States *ex rel.* Goodrich *v.* Guthrie, 58 U.S. 284; 1854 U.S. Lexis 518; 15 L. Ed. 102
>
> Myers *v.* United States, 272 U.S. 52; 47 S. Ct. 21; 1926 U.S. Lexis 35; 71 L. Ed. 160 [also referenced as 76]
>
> Nixon *v.* Fitzgerald, 457 U.S. 731; 102 S. Ct. 2690; 1982 U.S. Lexis 42; 73 L. Ed. 2d 349
>
> Weiss *v.* United States, 510 U.S. 163; 114 S. Ct. 752; 1994 U.S. Lexis 1137; 127 L . Ed. 2d 1

Federalist 78

> Marbury *v.* Madison, 5 U.S. 137; 1803 U.S. Lexis 352; 2 L. Ed. 60
>
> Stuart *v.* Laird, 5 U.S. 299; 1803 U.S. Lexis 362; 2 L. Ed. 115
>
> *Ex parte* Garland, 71 U.S. 333; 1866 U.S. Lexis 886; 18 L. Ed. 366
>
> Legal Tender Cases, 79 U.S. 457; 1870 U.S. Lexis 1220; 20 L. Ed. 287
>
> United States *v.* Jones, 131 U.S. 1; 9 S. Ct. 669; 1889 U.S. Lexis 1793; 33 L. Ed. 90
>
> McCray *v.* United States, 195 U.S. 27; 24 S. Ct. 769; 1904 U.S. Lexis 818; 49 L. Ed. 78
>
> Utah Power & Light Co. *v.* United States, 243 U.S. 389; 37 S. Ct. 387; 1917 U.S. Lexis 2046; 61 L. Ed. 791
>
> McAllister *v.* United States, 141 U.S. 174; 11 S. Ct. 949; 1891 U.S. Lexis 2508; 35 L. Ed. 693
>
> Evans *v.* Gore, 253 U.S. 245; 40 S. Ct. 550; 1920 U.S. Lexis 1419; 64 L. Ed. 887
>
> Sunderland *v.* United States, 266 U.S. 226; 45 S. Ct. 64; 1924 U.S. Lexis 2919; 69 L. Ed. 259
>
> O'Donoghue *v.* United States, 289 U.S. 516; 53 S. Ct. 740; 1933 U.S. Lexis 933; 77 L. Ed. 1356
>
> O'Malley *v.* Woodrough, 307 U.S. 277; 59 S. Ct. 838; 1939 U.S. Lexis 993; 83 L. Ed. 1289
>
> United States *v.* Lovett, 328 U.S. 303; 66 S. Ct. 1073; 1946 U.S. Lexis 2280; 90 L. Ed. 1252
>
> Dennis *v.* United States, 339 U.S. 162; 70 S. Ct. 519; 1950 U.S. Lexis 2178; 94 L. Ed. 734
>
> Reid *v.* Covert, 354 U.S. 1; 77 S. Ct. 1222; 1957 U.S. Lexis 729; 1 L. Ed. 2d 1148
>
> United States *v.* Brown, 381 U.S. 437; 85 S. Ct. 1707; 1965 U.S. Lexis 2206; 14 L. Ed. 2d 484
>
> Furman *v.* Georgia, 408 U.S. 238; 92 S. Ct. 2726; 1972 U.S. Lexis 169; 33 L. Ed. 2d 346
>
> United States *v.* Richardson, 418 U.S. 166; 94 S. Ct. 2940; 1974 U.S. Lexis 3; 41 L. Ed. 2d 678
>
> United States *v.* Raddatz, 447 U.S. 667; 100 S. Ct. 2406; 1980 U.S. Lexis 49; 65 L. Ed. 2d 424
>
> Northern Pipeline Constr. Co. *v.* Marathon Pipe Line Co., 458 U.S. 50; 102 S. Ct. 2858; 1982 U.S. Lexis 143; 73 L. Ed. 2d 598
>
> Garcia *v.* San Antonio Metro. Transit Auth., 469 U.S. 528; 105 S. Ct. 1005; 1985 U.S. Lexis 48; 83 L. Ed. 2d 1016
>
> CFTC *v.* Schor, 478 U.S. 833; 106 S. Ct. 3245; 1986 U.S. Lexis 144; 92 L. Ed. 2d 675

Young *v.* United States *ex rel.* Vuitton et Fils S. A., 481 U.S. 787; 107 S. Ct. 2124; 1987 U.S. Lexis 2261; 95 L. Ed. 2d 740

Morrison *v.* Olson, 487 U.S. 654; 108 S. Ct. 2597; 1988 U.S. Lexis 3034; 101 L. Ed. 2d 569

Patterson *v.* McLean Credit Union, 491 U.S. 164; 109 S. Ct. 2363; 1989 U.S. Lexis 2976; 105 L. Ed. 2d 132

Public Citizen *v.* United States DoJ, 491 U.S. 440; 109 S. Ct. 2558; 1989 U.S. Lexis 3119; 105 L. Ed. 2d 377

Missouri *v.* Jenkins, 495 U.S. 33; 110 S. Ct. 1651; 1990 U.S. Lexis 2033; 109 L. Ed. 2d 31

Freytag *v.* Commissioner, 501 U.S. 868; 111 S. Ct. 2631; 1991 U.S. Lexis 3818; 115 L. Ed. 2d 764

Payne *v.* Tennessee, 501 U.S. 808; 111 S. Ct. 2597; 1991 U.S. Lexis 3821; 115 L. Ed. 2d 720

Planned Parenthood of SE PA *v.* Casey, 505 U.S. 833; 112 S. Ct. 2791; 1992 U.S. Lexis 4751; 120 L. Ed. 2d 674

Nixon *v.* United States, 506 U.S. 224; 113 S. Ct. 732; 1993 U.S. Lexis 834; 122 L . Ed. 2d 1

Plaut *et al. v.* Spendthrift Farm, Inc., *et al.*, 514 U.S. 211; 115 S. Ct 1447; 1995 U.S. Lexis 2843; 131 L. Ed. 2d 328

United States *v.* Lopez, 514 U.S. 549; 115 S. Ct. 1624; 1995 U.S. Lexis 3039; 131 L. Ed. 2d 626

Hubbard *v.* United States, 514 U.S. 695; 115 S. Ct. 1754; 1995 U.S. Lexis 3184; 131 L. Ed. 2d 779

Missouri *et al. v.* Jenkins *et al.*, 515 U.S. 70; 115 S. Ct. 2038; 1995; U.S. Lexis 4041; 132 L. Ed. 2d 63

Lonchar *v.* Thomas, 517 U.S. 314; 116 S. Ct. 1293; 1996 U.S. Lexis 2167; 134 L. Ed. 2d 440

Kansas *v.* Hendricks, 117 S. Ct. 2072; 1997 U.S. Lexis 3999; 138 L. Ed. 2d 501

Schenck *v.* Pro-Choice Network of Western New York, 117 S. Ct. 855; 1997 U.S. Lexis 1270; 137 L. Ed. 2d 1

Federalist 79

Marbury *v.* Madison, 5 U.S. 137; 1803 U.S. Lexis 352; 2 L. Ed. 60

Evans *v.* Gore, 253 U.S. 245; 40 S. Ct. 550; 1920 U.S. Lexis 1419; 64 L. Ed. 887

O'Donoghue *v.* United States, 289 U.S. 516; 53 S. Ct. 740; 1933 U.S. Lexis 933; 77 L. Ed. 1356

Booth *v.* United States, 291 U.S. 339; 54 S. Ct. 379; 1934 U.S. Lexis 961; 78 L. Ed. 836

O'Malley *v.* Woodrough, 307 U.S. 277; 59 S. Ct. 838; 1939 U.S. Lexis 993; 83 L. Ed. 1289

Glidden Co. *v.* Zdanok, 370 U.S. 530; 82 S. Ct. 1459; 1962 U.S. Lexis 2139; 8 L. Ed. 2d 671

Palmore *v.* United States, 411 U.S. 389; 93 S. Ct. 1670; 1973 U.S. Lexis 78; 36 L. Ed. 2d 342

United States *v.* Raddatz, 447 U.S. 667; 100 S. Ct. 2406; 1980 U.S. Lexis 49; 65 L. Ed. 2d 424

United States *v.* Will, 449 U.S. 200; 101 S. Ct. 471; 1980 U.S. Lexis 160; 66 L. Ed. 2d 392

Northern Pipeline Constr. Co. *v.* Marathon Pipe Line Co., 458 U.S. 50; 102 S. Ct. 2858; 1982 U.S. Lexis 143; 73 L. Ed. 2d 598

Thomas *v.* Union Carbide Agric. Prods. Co., 473 U.S. 568; 105 S. Ct. 3325; 1985 U.S. Lexis 121; 87 L. Ed. 2d 409

Nixon *v.* United States, 506 U.S. 224; 113 S. Ct. 732; 1993 U.S. Lexis 834; 122 L. Ed. 2d 1

Federalist 80

Osborn *v.* President, Dirs., & Co. Of the Bank of the United States, 22 U.S. 738; 1824 U.S. Lexis 409; 6 L. Ed. 204

Cook *v.* Moffat, 46 U.S. 295; 1847 U.S. Lexis 316; 12 L. Ed. 159

Waring *v.* Clarke, 46 U.S. 441; 1847 U.S. Lexis 321; 12 L. Ed. 226

Teal *v.* Felton, 53 U.S. 284; 1851 U.S. Lexis 656; 13 L. Ed. 990

Pennsylvania *v.* Wheeling & Belmont Bridge Co., 54 U.S. 518; 1851 U.S. Lexis 876; 14 L. Ed. 249

Marshall *v.* Baltimore & Ohio R. R. Co., 57 U.S. 314; 1850 U.S. Lexis 1556; 14 L. Ed. 953

Den *ex dem.* Murray *v.* Hoboken Land & Improvement Co., 59 U.S. 272; 1855 U.S. Lexis; 15 L. Ed. 372

Jackson *v.* The Steamboat Magnolia, 61 U.S. 296; 1857 U.S. Lexis 461; 15 L. Ed. 909

Insurance Co. *v.* Dunham, 78 U.S. 1; 1870 U.S. Lexis 1455; 20 L. Ed. 90

Case of the Sewing Machine Cos., 85 U.S. 553; 1873 U.S. Lexis 1330; 21 L. Ed. 914

Wisconsin *v.* Pelican Ins. Co., 127 U.S. 265; 8 S. Ct. 1370; 1888 U.S. Lexis 1989; 32 L. Ed. 239

South Dakota *v.* North Carolina, 192 U.S. 286; 24 S. Ct. 269; 1904 U.S. Lexis 995; 48 L. Ed. 448

Georgia *v.* Tennessee Copper Co., 206 U.S. 230; 27 S. Ct. 618; 1907 U.S. Lexis 1158; 51 L. Ed. 1038

Southern Pac. Co. *v.* Jensen, 244 U.S. 205; 37 S. Ct. 524; 1917 U.S. Lexis 1628; 61 L. Ed. 1086

Massachusetts *v.* Mellon, 262 U.S. 447; 43 S. Ct. 597; 1923 U.S. Lexis 2662; 67 L. Ed. 1078

Ex parte Gruber, 269 U.S. 302; 46 S. Ct. 112; 1925 U.S. Lexis 30; 70 L. Ed. 280

Principality of Monaco *v.* Mississippi, 292 U.S. 313; 54 S. Ct. 745; 1934 U.S. Lexis 711; 78 L. Ed. 1282

Hines *v.* Davidowitz, 312 U.S. 52; 61 S. Ct. 399; 1941 U.S. Lexis 1103; 85 L. Ed. 581

National Mut. Ins. Co. *v.* Tidewater Transfer Co., 337 U.S. 582; 69 S. Ct. 1173; 1949 U.S. Lexis 2924; 93 L. Ed. 1556

Romero *v.* International Terminal Operating Co., 358 U.S. 354; 79 S. Ct. 468; 1959 U.S. Lexis 1747; 3 L. Ed. 2d 368

Glidden Co. *v.* Zdanok, 370 U.S. 530; 82 S. Ct. 1459; 1962 U.S. Lexis 2139; 8 L. Ed. 2d 671

Banco Nacional de Cuba *v.* Sabbatino, 376 U.S. 398; 84 S. Ct. 923; 1964 U.S. Lexis 2252; 11 L. Ed. 2d 804

Flast *v.* Cohen, 392 U.S. 83; 88 S. Ct. 1942; 1968 U.S. Lexis 1347; 20 L. Ed. 2d 947

Illinois *v.* City of Milwaukee, 406 U.S. 91; 92 S. Ct. 1385; 1972 U.S. Lexis 107; 31 L. Ed. 2d 712

Northern Pipeline Constr. Co. *v.* Marathon Pipe Line Co., 458 U.S. 50; 102 S. Ct. 2858; 1982 U.S. Lexis 143; 73 L. Ed. 2d 598

United Bldg. & Constr. Trades Council of Camden Cty. & Vicinity *v.* Mayor & Council of Camden, 465 U.S. 208; 104 S. Ct. 1020; 1984 U.S. Lexis 26; 79 L. Ed. 2d 249

Atascadero State Hosp. *v.* Scanlon, 473 U.S. 234; 105 S. Ct. 3142; 1985 U.S. Lexis 89; 87 L. Ed. 2d 171

Welch *v.* Texas Dept. of Hwys. & Pub. Transp., 483 U.S. 468; 107 S. Ct. 2941; 1987 U.S. Lexis 2893; 97 L. Ed. 2d 389

Freytag *v.* Commissioner, 501 U.S. 868; 111 S. Ct. 2631; 1991 U.S. Lexis 3818; 115 L. Ed. 2d 764

Grubart, Inc. *v.* Great Lakes Dredge & Dock, 513 U.S. 527; 115 S. Ct. 1043; 1995 U.S. Lexis 1622; 130 L. Ed. 2d 1024

American Dredging Co. *v.* Miller, 510 U.S. 443; 114 S. Ct. 981; 1994 U.S. Lexis 1870; 127 L. Ed. 2d 285

Seminole Tribe of Florida *v.* Florida, 517 U.S. 44; 116 S. Ct. 1114; 1996 U.S. Lexis 2165; 134 L. Ed. 2d 252

Idaho *et al. v.* Coeur D'Alene Tribe of Idaho *et al.*, 117 S. Ct. 2028; 1997 U.S. Lexis 4030; 138 L. Ed. 2d 438

Missouri *et al. v.* Jenkins *et al.*, 515 U.S. 70; 115 S. Ct. 2038; 1995; U.S. Lexis 4041; 132 L. Ed. 2d 63

Federalist 81

Respublica *v.* Cobbet, 3 U.S. 467; 1798 U.S. Lexis 150; 1 L. Ed. 683

Marbury *v.* Madison, 5 U.S. 137; 1803 U.S. Lexis 352; 2 L. Ed. 60

Waring *v.* Clarke, 46 U.S. 441; 1847 U.S. Lexis 321; 12 L. Ed. 226

Florida *v.* Georgia, 58 U.S. 478; 1854 U.S. Lexis 538; 15 L. Ed. 181

The Moses Taylor, 71 U.S. 411; 1866 U.S. Lexis 891; 18 L. Ed. 397

Justices *v.* Murray, 76 U.S. 274; 1869 U.S. Lexis 964; 19 L. Ed. 658

New Hampshire *v.* Louisiana; 108 U.S. 76; 2 S. Ct. 176; 1883 U.S. Lexis 1008; 27 L. Ed. 656

In re Ayers, 123 U.S. 443; 8 S. Ct. 164; 1887 U.S. Lexis 2187; 31 L. Ed. 216

Hans *v.* Louisiana, 134 U.S. 1; 10 S. Ct. 504; 1890 U.S. Lexis 1943; 33 L. Ed. 842

Capital Traction Co. *v.* Hof, 174 U.S. 1; 19 S. Ct. 580; 1899 U.S. Lexis 1480; 43 L. Ed. 873

South Dakota *v.* North Carolina, 192 U.S. 286; 24 S. Ct. 269; 1904 U. S. Lexis 995; 48 L. Ed. 448

Southern Pac. Co. *v.* Jensen, 244 U.S. 205; 37 S. Ct. 524; 1917 U.S. Lexis 1628; 61 L. Ed. 1086

Virginia *v.* West Virginia, 246 U.S. 565; 38 S. Ct. 400; 1918 U.S. Lexis 1579; 62 L. Ed. 883

Berizzi Bros. Co. *v.* Steamship Pesaro, 271 U.S. 562; 46 S. Ct. 611; 1926 U.S. Lexis 878; 70 L. Ed. 1088

Principality of Monaco *v.* Mississippi, 292 U.S. 313; 54 S. Ct. 745; 1934 U.S. Lexis 711; 78 L. Ed. 1282

Lynch *v.* United States, 292 U.S. 571; 54 S. Ct. 840; 1934 U.S. Lexis 969; 78 L. Ed. 1434

Galloway *v.* United States, 319 U.S. 372; 63 S. Ct. 1077; 1943 U.S. Lexis 1118; 87 L. Ed. 1458

National Mut. Ins. Co. *v.* Tidewater Transfer Co., 337 U.S. 582; 69 S. Ct. 1173; 1949 U.S. Lexis 2924; 93 L. Ed. 1556

Glidden Co. *v.* Zdanok, 370 U.S. 530; 82 S. Ct. 1459; 1962 U.S. Lexis 2139; 8 L. Ed. 2d 671

Parden *v.* Terminal Ry. of the Alabama State Docks Dept., 377 U.S. 184; 84 S. Ct. 1207; 1964 U.S. Lexis 2161; 12 L. Ed. 2d 233

Employees of the Dept. of Pub. Health & Welfare of Missouri *v.* Department of Pub. Health & Welfare of Missouri, 411 U.S. 279; 93 S. Ct. 1614; 1973 U.S. Lexis 156; 36 L. Ed. 2d 251

Edelman *v.* Jordan, 415 U.S. 651; 94 S. Ct. 1347; 1974 U.S. Lexis 115; 39 L. Ed. 2d 662

California *v.* Arizona, 440 U.S. 59; 99 S. Ct. 919; 1979 U.S. Lexis 2; 59 L. Ed. 2d 144

Nevada *v.* Hall, 440 U.S. 410; 99 S. Ct. 1182; 1979 U.S. Lexis 69; 59 L. Ed. 2d 416

Northern Pipeline Constr. Co. *v.* Marathon Pipe Line Co., 458 U.S. 50; 102 S. Ct. 2858; 1982 U.S. Lexis 143; 73 L. Ed. 2d 598

South Carolina *v.* Regan, 465 U.S. 367; 104 S. Ct. 1107; 1984 S. Ct. 32; 79 L. Ed. 2d 372

Patsy *v.* Board of Regents of Florida, 457 U.S. 496; 102 S. Ct. 2557; 1982 U.S. Lexis 133; 73 L. Ed. 2d 172

Atascadero State Hosp. *v.* Scanlon, 473 U.S. 234; 105 S. Ct. 3142; 1985 U.S. Lexis 89; 87 L. Ed. 2d 171

Welch *v.* Texas Dept. of Hwys. & Pub. Transp., 483 U.S. 468; 107 S. Ct. 2941; 1987 U.S. Lexis 2893; 97 L. Ed. 2d 389

Morrison *v.* Olson, 487 U.S. 654; 108 S. Ct. 2597; 1988 U.S. Lexis 3034; 101 L. Ed. 2d 569

Pennsylvania *v.* Union Gas Co., 491 U.S. 1; 109 S. Ct. 2273; 1989 U.S. Lexis 2970; 105 L. Ed. 2d 1

Port Auth. Trans-Hudson Corp. *v.* Feeney, 495 U.S. 299; 110 S. Ct. 1868; 1990 U.S. Lexis 2294; 109 L. Ed. 2d 264

Blatchford *v.* Native Village of Noatak and Circle Village, 501 U.S. 775; 111 S. Ct. 2578; 1991 U.S. Lexis 3637; 115 L. Ed. 2d 686

Nixon *v.* United States, 506 U.S. 224; 113 S. Ct. 732; 1993 U.S. Lexis 834; 122 L. Ed. 2d 1

Plaut *et al. v.* Spendthrift Farm, Inc., *et al.*, 514 U.S. 211; 115 S. Ct 1447; 1995 U.S. Lexis 2843; 131 L. Ed. 2d 328

Seminole Tribe of Florida *v.* Florida, 517 U.S. 44; 116 S. Ct. 1114; 1996 U.S. Lexis 2165; 134 L. Ed. 2d 252

Idaho *et al. v.* Coeur D'Alene Tribe of Idaho *et al.*, 117 S. Ct. 2028; 1997 U.S. Lexis 4030; 138 L. Ed. 2d 438

Alden *v.* Maine, 119 S. Ct. 2240; 1999 U.S. Lexis 4374; 144 L. Ed. 2d 636

College Savings Bank *v.* Florida Prepaid Postsecondary Ed. Expense Bd., 119 S. Ct. 2219; 1999 U.S. Lexis 4375; 144 L. Ed. 2d 605

Florida Prepaid Postsecondary E. Expense Bd *v.* College Savings Bank, 119 S. Ct. 2199; 1999 U.S. Lexis 4376; 144 L. Ed. 2d 575

Federalist 82

Respublica *v.* Cobbet, 3 U.S. 467; 1798 U.S. Lexis 150; 1 L. Ed. 683

Commonwealth *v.* Schaffer, Mayor's Court, 4 U.S. 26; 1797 U.S. Lexis 225

Houston *v.* Moore, 18 U.S. 1; 1820 U.S. Lexis 244; 5 L. Ed. 19

Cohens *v.* Virginia, 19 U.S. 264; 1821 U.S. Lexis 362; 5 L. Ed. 257

Gibbons *v.* Ogden, 22 U.S. 1; 1824 U.S. Lexis 370; 6 L. Ed. 23

United States *v.* Bailey, 34 U.S. 238; 1835 U.S. Lexis 348; 9 L. Ed. 113

Kendall *v.* United States ex rel. Stokes, 37 U.S. 524; 1838 U.S. Lexis 379; 9 L. Ed. 1181

Bank of Augusta *v.* Earle, 38 U.S. 519; 1839 U.S. Lexis 455; 10 L. Ed. 274

Suydam *v.* Broadnax, 39 U.S. 67; 1840 U.S. Lexis 355; 10 L. Ed. 357

Smith *v.* Turner, 48 U.S. 283; 1849 U.S. Lexis 351; 12 L. Ed. 702

Propeller Genesee Chief *v.* Fitzhugh, 53 U.S. 443; 1851 U.S. Lexis 674; 13 L. Ed. 1058

Cummings *v.* Missouri, 71 U.S. 277; 1866 U.S. Lexis 885; 18 L. Ed. 356

The Moses Taylor, 71 U.S. 411; 1866 U.S. Lexis 891; 18 L. Ed. 397

Justices *v.* Murray, 76 U.S. 274; 1869 U.S. Lexis 964; 19 L. Ed. 658

Claflin *v.* Houseman, 93 U.S. 130; 1876 U.S. Lexis 1361; 23 L. Ed. 833

Dennick *v.* Railroad Co., 103 U.S. 11; 1880 U.S. Lexis 2084; 26 L. Ed. 439

Plaquemines Tropical Fruit Co. *v.* Henderson, 170 U.S. 511; 18 S. Ct. 685; 1898 U.S. Lexis 1560; 42 L. Ed. 1126

Illinois Cent. R.R. Co. *v.* Henderson Elevator Co., 226 U.S. 441; 33 S. Ct. 176; 1913 U.S. Lexis 2246

Southern Pac. Co. *v.* Jensen, 244 U.S. 205; 37 S. Ct. 524; 1917 U.S. Lexis 1628; 61 L. Ed. 1086

Miles *v.* Illinois Cent. R.R. Co., 315 U.S. 698; 62 S. Ct. 827; 1942 U. S. Lexis 785; 86 L. Ed. 1129

National Mut. Ins. Co. *v.* Tidewater Transfer Co., 337 U.S. 582; 69 S. Ct. 1173; 1949 U.S. Lexis 2924; 93 L. Ed. 1556

Brown *v.* Allen, 344 U.S. 443; 73 S. Ct. 397; 1953 U.S. Lexis 2391; 97 L. Ed. 469

Charles Dowd Box Co. *v.* Courtney, 368 U.S. 502; 82 S. Ct. 519; 1962 U.S. Lexis 2144; 7 L. Ed. 2d 483

Banco Nacional de Cuba *v.* Sabbatino, 376 U.S. 398; 84 S. Ct. 923; 1964 U.S. Lexis 2252; 11 L. Ed. 2d 804

Gulf Offshore Co. *v.* Mobil Oil Corp., 453 U.S. 473; 101 S. Ct. 2870; 1981 U.S. Lexis 41; 69 L. Ed. 2d 784

Northern Pipeline Constr. Co. *v.* Marathon Pipe Line Co., 458 U.S. 50; 102 S. Ct. 2858; 1982 U.S. Lexis 143; 73 L. Ed. 2d 598

Tafflin *v.* Levitt, 493 U.S. 455; 110 S. Ct. 792; 1990 U.S. Lexis 568; 107 L. Ed. 2d 887

McKesson Corp. *v.* Division of Alcoholic Beverages & Tobacco, 496 U.S. 18; 110 S. Ct. 2238; 1990 U.S. Lexis 2826; 110 L. Ed. 2d 17

Howlett *v.* Rose, 496 U.S. 356; 110 S. Ct. 2430; 1990 U.S. Lexis 3077; 110 L. Ed. 2d 332

New York *v.* United States *et al.*, 505 U.S. 144; 112 S. Ct. 2408; 1992 U.S. Lexis 3693; 120 L. Ed. 2d 120

Seminole Tribe of Florida *v.* Florida, 517 U.S. 44; 116 S. Ct. 1114; 1996 U.S. Lexis 2165; 134 L. Ed. 2d 252

Federalist 83

Waring *v.* Clarke, 46 U.S. 441; 1847 U.S. Lexis 321; 12 L. Ed. 226

Propeller Genesee Chief *v.* Fitzhugh, 53 U.S. 443; 1851 U.S. Lexis 674; 13 L. Ed. 1058

Ex parte Milligan, 71 U.S. 2; 1866 U.S. Lexis 861; 18 L. Ed. 281

Capital Traction Co. *v.* Hof, 174 U.S. 1; 19 S. Ct. 580; 1899 U.S. Lexis 1480; 43 L. Ed. 873

Southern Pac. Co. *v.* Jensen, 244 U.S. 205; 37 S. Ct. 524; 1917 U.S. Lexis 1628; 61 L. Ed. 1086

Galloway *v.* United States, 319 U.S. 372; 63 S. Ct. 1077; 1943 U.S. Lexis 1118; 87 L. Ed. 1458

Duncan *v.* Kahanamoku, 327 U.S. 304; 66 S. Ct. 606; 1946 U.S. Lexis 3016; 90 L. Ed. 688

Reid *v.* Covert, 354 U.S. 1; 77 S. Ct. 1222; 1957 U.S. Lexis 729; 1 L. Ed. 2d 1148

Green *v.* United States, 356 U.S. 165; 78 S. Ct. 632; 1958 U.S. Lexis 1756; 2 L. Ed. 2d 672

Banco Nacional de Cuba *v.* Sabbatino, 376 U.S. 398; 84 S. Ct. 923; 1964 U.S. Lexis 2252; 11 L. Ed. 2d 804

Singer *v.* United States, 380 U.S. 24; 85 S. Ct. 783; 1965 U.S. Lexis 1730; 13 L. Ed. 2d 630

Parklane Hosiery Co. *v.* Shore, 439 U.S. 322; 99 S. Ct. 645; 1979 U. S. Lexis 50; 58 L. Ed. 2d 552

McCleskey *v.* Kemp, 481 U.S. 279; 107 S. Ct. 1756; 1987 U.S. Lexis 1817; 95 L. Ed. 2d 262

Missouri *et al.* *v.* Jenkins *et al.*, 515 U.S. 70; 115 S. Ct. 2038; 1995; U.S. Lexis 4041; 132 L. Ed. 2d 63

Neder *v.* United Stats, 527 U.S. 1; 119 S. Ct. 1827; 1999 U.S. Lexis 4007; 144 L. Ed. 2d 35

Federalist 84

Legal Tender Cases, 79 U.S. 457; 1870 U.S. Lexis 1220; 20 L. Ed. 287

United States *v.* Union Pac. R. R. Co., 98 U.S. 569; 1878 U.S. Lexis 1420; 25 L. Ed. 143

Sinking-Fund Cases, 99 U.S. 700; 1878 U.S. Lexis 1595; 25 L. Ed. 496

Kring *v.* Missouri, 107 U.S. 221; 2 S. Ct. 443; 1882 U.S. Lexis 1218; 27 L. Ed. 506

Pollock *v.* Farmers Loan & Trust Co., 157 U.S. 429; 15 S. Ct. 673; 1895 U.S. Lexis 2215; 39 L. Ed. 759

Reid *v.* United States, 211 U.S. 529; 29 S. Ct. 171; 1909 U.S. Lexis 1784; 53 L. Ed. 313

Chicago, Burlington & Quincy Ry. Co. *v.* United States, 220 U.S. 559; 31 S. Ct. 612; 1911 U.S. Lexis 1701; 55 L. Ed. 582.

Pacific States Tel. & Tel. Co. *v.* Oregon, 223 U.S. 118; 32 S. Ct. 224; 1912 U.S. Lexis 2220; 56 L. Ed. 377

United States *v.* Sprague, 282 U.S. 716; 51 S. Ct. 220; 1931 U.S. Lexis 39; 75 L. Ed. 640

Grosjean *v.* American Press Co., 297 U.S. 233; 56 S. Ct. 444; 1936 U. S. Lexis 524; 80 L. Ed. 660.

Draper *v.* United States, 358 U.S. 307; 79 S. Ct. 329; 1959 U.S. Lexis 1607; 3 L. Ed. 2d 327

Griswold *v.* Connecticut, 381 U.S. 479; 85 S. Ct. 1678; 1965 U.S. Lexis 2282; 14 L. Ed. 2d 510

Osborn *v.* United States, 385 U.S. 323; 87 S. Ct. 429; 1966 U.S. Lexis 2940; 17 L. Ed. 2d 394

Duncan *v.* Louisiana, 391 U.S. 145; 88 S. Ct. 1444; 1968 U.S. Lexis 1631; 20 L. Ed. 2d 491

Richmond Newspapers, Inc. *v.* Virginia, 448 U.S. 555; 100 S. Ct. 2814; 1980 U.S. Lexis 18; 65 L. Ed. 2d 973

Weaver *v.* Graham, 450 U.S. 24; 101 S. Ct. 960; 1981 U.S. Lexis 67; 67 L. Ed. 2d 17

EEOC *v.* Wyoming, 460 U.S. 226; 103 S. Ct. 1054; 1983 U.S. Lexis 134; 75 L. Ed. 2d 18

Minneapolis Star & Tribune Co. *v.* Minnesota Commr. of Revenue, 460 U.S. 575; 103 S. Ct. 1365; 1983 U.S. Lexis 6; 75 L. Ed. 2d 295

Massachusetts *v.* Upton, 466 U.S. 727; 104 S. Ct. 2085; 1984 U.S. Lexis 81; 80 L. Ed. 2d 721

United States *v.* Verdugo-Urquidez, 494 U.S. 259; 110 S. Ct. 1056; 1990 U.S. Lexis 1175; 108 L. Ed. 2d 222

California Department of Corrections *et al. v.* Morales, 514 U.S. 499; 115 S. Ct. 1597; 1995 U.S. Lexis 3037; 131 L. Ed. 2d 588

City of Boerne *v.* Flores, 117 S. Ct. 2157; 1997 U.S. Lexis 4035; 138 L. Ed. 2d 624

Clinton *v.* City of New York, No. 97-1374; 1998 U.S. LEXIS 4215; 141 L. Ed. 2d 393

Federalist 85

National Prohibition Cases, 253 U.S. 350; 40 S. Ct. 486; 1920 U.S. Lexis 1371; 64 L. Ed. 946

United States *v.* Sprague, 282 U.S. 716; 51 S. Ct. 220; 1931 U.S. Lexis 39; 75 L. Ed. 640

General References to the *Federalist Papers*

Calder *v.* Bull, 3 U.S. 386; 1798 U.S. Lexis 148; 1 L. Ed. 648

Cohens *v.* Virginia, 19 U.S. 264; 1821 U.S. Lexis 362; 5 L. Ed. 257

Brown *v.* Maryland, 25 U.S. 419; 1827 U.S. Lexis 398; 6 L. Ed. 678

Weston *v.* City Council of Charleston, 27 U.S. 449; 1829 U.S. Lexis 414; 7 L. Ed. 481

Kendall *v.* United States ex rel. Stokes, 37 U.S. 524; 1838 U.S. Lexis 379; 9 L. Ed. 1181

Scott *v.* Sandford, 60 U.S. 393; 1856 U.S. Lexis 472; 15 L. Ed. 691

Mississippi *v.* Johnson, 71 U.S. 475; 1866 U.S. Lexis 897; 18 L. Ed. 437 [general context is *Federalist* 78, but see also *Federalist* 16]

Legal Tender Cases, 79 U.S. 457; 1870 U.S. Lexis 1220; 20 L. Ed. 287

Edwards *v.* Kearzey, 96 U.S. 595; 1877 U.S. Lexis 1704; 24 L. Ed. 793

Ex parte Clarke, 100 U.S. 399; 1879 U.S. Lexis 1834; 25 L. Ed. 715

Pollock *v.* Farmers Loan & Trust Co., 157 U.S. 429; 15 S. Ct. 673; 1895 U.S. Lexis 2215; 39 L. Ed. 759

Pollock *v.* Farmers Loan & Trust Co., 158 U.S. 601; 15 S. Ct. 912; 1895 U.S. Lexis 2280; 39 L. Ed. 1108

Fairbank *v.* United States, 181 U.S. 283; 21 S. Ct. 648; 1901 U.S. Lexis 1367; 45 L. Ed. 862

Pacific States Tel. & Tel. Co. *v.* Oregon, 223 U.S. 118; 32 S. Ct. 224; 1912 U.S. Lexis 2220; 56 L. Ed. 377

Evans *v.* Gore, 253 U.S. 245; 40 S. Ct. 550; 1920 U.S. Lexis 1419; 64 L. Ed. 887

National Prohibition Cases, 253 U.S. 350; 40 S. Ct. 486; 1920 U.S. Lexis 1371; 64 L. Ed. 946

Newberry *v*. United States, 256 U.S. 232; 41 S. Ct. 469; 1921 U.S. Lexis 1632; 65 L. Ed. 913

United States *v*. Wood, 299 U.S. 123; 57 S. Ct. 177; 1936 U.S. Lexis 952; 81 L. Ed. 78

Talley *v*. California, 362 U.S. 60; 80 S. Ct. 536; 1960 U.S. Lexis 1948; 4 L. Ed. 2d 559

Furman *v*. Georgia, 408 U.S. 238; 92 S. Ct. 2726; 1972 U.S. Lexis 169; 33 L. Ed. 2d 346

Branzburg *v*. Hayes, 408 U.S. 665; 92 S. Ct. 2646; 1972 U.S. Lexis 132; 33 L. Ed. 2d 626

Buckley *v*. Valeo, 424 U.S. 1; 96 S. Ct. 612; 1976 U.S. Lexis 16; 46 L. Ed. 2d 659

Hynes *v*. Mayor & Council of Oradell, 425 U.S. 610; 96 S. Ct. 1755; 1976 U.S. Lexis 149; 48 L. Ed. 2d 243

Nixon *v*. Administrator of Gen. Servs., 433 U.S. 425; 97 S. Ct. 2777; 1977 U.S. Lexis 24; 53 L. Ed. 2d 867

Dames & Moore *v*. Regan, 453 U.S. 654; 101 S. Ct. 2972; 1981 U.S. Lexis 44; 69 L. Ed. 2d 918

Citizens Against Rent Control/Coalition for Fair Hous. *v*. City of Berkeley, 454 U.S. 290; 102 S. Ct. 434; 1981 U.S. Lexis 135; 70 L. Ed. 2d 492

Garcia *v*. San Antonio Metro. Transit Auth., 469 U.S. 528; 105 S. Ct. 1005; 1985 U.S. Lexis 48; 83 L. Ed. 2d 1016

Atascadero State Hosp. *v*. Scanlon, 473 U.S. 234; 105 S. Ct. 3142; 1985 U.S. Lexis 89; 87 L. Ed. 2d 171

Bowsher *v*. Synar, 478 U.S. 714; 106 S. Ct. 3181; 1986 U.S. Lexis 141; 92 L. Ed. 2d 583

Rutan *v*. Republican Party of Illinois, 497 U.S. 62; 110 S. Ct. 2729; 1990 U.S. Lexis 3298; 111 L. Ed. 2d 52.

New York *v*. United States *et al*., 505 U.S. 144; 112 S. Ct. 2408; 1992 U.S. Lexis 3693; 120 L. Ed. 2d 120

Weiss *v*. United States, 510 U.S. 163; 114 S. Ct. 752; 1994 U.S. Lexis 1137; 127 L . Ed. 2d 1

McIntyre, Executor of Estate of McIntyre, deceased, *v*. Ohio Elections Commission, 514 U.S. 334; 115 S. Ct. 1511; 1995 U.S. Lexis 2847; 131 L. Ed. 2d 426

U.S. Term Limits, Inc., *et al. v*. Thornton *et al.*, 514 U.S. 779; 115 S. Ct. 1842; 1995 U.S. Lexis 3487; 131 L. Ed. 2d 881

Seminole Tribe of Florida *v*. Florida, 517 U.S. 44; 116 S. Ct. 1114; 1996 U.S. Lexis 2165; 134 L. Ed. 2d 252

Loving *v*. United States, 517 U.S. 748; 116 S. Ct. 1737; 1996 U.S. Lexis 3593; 135 L. Ed. 2d 36

Printz *v*. United States, 117 S. Ct. 2365; 1997 U.S. Lexis 4044; 138 L. Ed. 2d 914

Masterworks in the Western Tradition

Nicholas Capaldi, *General Editor*
Stuart D. Warner, *Associate Editor*

This series is intended to exhibit for the intelligent reader why certain authors, texts, and ideas are the key to understanding ourselves and our relation to the world as well as each other. The series answers the question: What is the core of western civilization? While there are many series on major thinkers, no such series is designed to respond to this theme of the core of Western Civilization and to do so in a uniform format with some consideration of how individual authors relate to other authors.

For additional information about this series or for the submission of manuscripts, please contact:

Acquisitions Department
Peter Lang Publishing
275 Seventh Avenue, 28th floor
New York, New York 10001

To order other books in this series, please contact our Customer Service Department:

(800) 770-LANG (within the U.S.)
(212) 647-7706 (outside the U.S.)
(212) 647-7707 FAX

Or browse online by series:

www.peterlang.com